Cisco CCNA

Routing and Switching
ICND2 200-101
Official Cert Guide

WENDELL ODOM, CCIE No. 1624

Cisco Press
800 East 96th Street
Indianapolis, IN 46240

Cisco CCNA Routing and Switching
ICND2 200-101 Official Cert Guide

Wendell Odom, CCIE No. 1624

Copyright© 2013 Pearson Education, Inc.

Published by:
Cisco Press
800 East 96th Street
Indianapolis, IN 46240 USA

Printed in the United States of America

Fifth Printing: March 2014

Library of Congress Cataloging-in-Publication data is on file.

ISBN-13: 978-1-58714-373-1

ISBN-10: 1-58714-373-9

Warning and Disclaimer

This book provides information about the Cisco 200-101 ICND2 and 200-120 CCNA exams. Every effort has been made to make this book as complete and as accurate as possible, but no warranty or fitness is implied.

The information is provided on an "as is" basis. The authors, Cisco Press, and Cisco Systems, Inc. shall have neither liability nor responsibility to any person or entity with respect to any loss or damages arising from the information contained in this book or from the use of the discs or programs that may accompany it.

The opinions expressed in this book belong to the author and are not necessarily those of Cisco Systems, Inc.

Trademark Acknowledgments

All terms mentioned in this book that are known to be trademarks or service marks have been appropriately capitalized. Cisco Press or Cisco Systems, Inc., cannot attest to the accuracy of this information. Use of a term in this book should not be regarded as affecting the validity of any trademark or service mark.

Corporate and Government Sales

The publisher offers excellent discounts on this book when ordered in quantity for bulk purchases or special sales, which may include electronic versions and/or custom covers and content particular to your business, training goals, marketing focus, and branding interests.

For more information, please contact:
U.S. Corporate and Government Sales
1-800-382-3419
corpsales@pearsontechgroup.com

For sales outside the United States, please contact:
International Sales
international@pearsoned.com

Feedback Information

At Cisco Press, our goal is to create in-depth technical books of the highest quality and value. Each book is crafted with care and precision, undergoing rigorous development that involves the unique expertise of members from the professional technical community.

Readers' feedback is a natural continuation of this process. If you have any comments regarding how we could improve the quality of this book, or otherwise alter it to better suit your needs, you can contact us through email at feedback@ciscopress.com. Please make sure to include the book title and ISBN in your message.

We greatly appreciate your assistance.

Publisher: Paul Boger	**Copy Editor:** Keith Cline
Associate Publisher: Dave Dusthimer	**Technical Editor:** Elan Beer
Business Operation Manager, Cisco Press: Jan Cornelssen	**Editorial Assistant:** Vanessa Evans
Executive Editor: Brett Bartow	**Cover Designer:** Mark Shirar
Managing Editor: Sandra Schroeder	**Illustrator:** Michael Tanamachi
Development Editor: Andrew Cupp	**Composition:** Bronkella Publishing
Senior Project Editor: Tonya Simpson	**Indexer:** Erika Millen
	Proofreader: Sarah Kearns

Americas Headquarters
Cisco Systems, Inc.
San Jose, CA

Asia Pacific Headquarters
Cisco Systems (USA) Pte. Ltd.
Singapore

Europe Headquarters
Cisco Systems International BV
Amsterdam, The Netherlands

Cisco has more than 200 offices worldwide. Addresses, phone numbers, and fax numbers are listed on the Cisco Website at www.cisco.com/go/offices.

About the Author

Wendell Odom, CCIE No. 1624, has been in the networking industry since 1981. He has worked as a network engineer, consultant, systems engineer, instructor, and course developer; he currently works writing and creating certification tools. He is the author of all the previous books in the Cisco Press *CCNA Official Certification Guide* series, as well as author of the *CCNP ROUTE 642-902 Official Certification Guide*, the *QoS 642-642 Exam Certification Guide*, and co-author of the *CCIE Routing and Switch Official Certification Guide* and several other titles. He is also a consultant for the *CCNA 640-802 Network Simulator* from Pearson and for a forthcoming replacement version of that product. He maintains study tools, links to his blogs, and other resources at http://www.certskills.com.

About the Contributing Author

Anthony Sequeira, CCIE No. 15626, is a Cisco Certified Systems Instructor (CCSI) and author regarding all levels and tracks of Cisco certification. Anthony formally began his career in the information technology industry in 1994 with IBM in Tampa, Florida. He quickly formed his own computer consultancy, Computer Solutions, and then discovered his true passion: teaching and writing about Microsoft and Cisco technologies. Anthony joined Mastering Computers in 1996 and lectured to massive audiences around the world about the latest in computer technologies. Mastering Computers became the revolutionary online training company KnowledgeNet, and Anthony trained there for many years. Anthony is currently pursuing his second CCIE in the area of Security and is a full-time instructor for the next generation of KnowledgeNet, StormWind Live. Anthony is also a VMware Certified Professional.

About the Technical Reviewer

Elan Beer, CCIE No. 1837, is a senior consultant and Cisco instructor specializing in data center architecture and multiprotocol network design. For the past 25 years, Elan has designed networks and trained thousands of industry experts in data center architecture, routing, and switching. Elan has been instrumental in large-scale professional service efforts designing and troubleshooting internetworks, performing Data center and network audits, and assisting clients with their short- and long-term design objectives. Elan has a global perspective of network architectures via his international clientele. Elan has used his expertise to design and troubleshoot data centers and internetworks in Malaysia, North America, Europe, Australia, Africa, China, and the Middle East. Most recently, Elan has been focused on data center design, configuration, and troubleshooting as well as service provider technologies. In 1993, Elan was among the first to obtain Cisco's Certified System Instructor (CCSI) certification, and in 1996, he was among the first to attain Cisco System's highest technical certification, the Cisco Certified Internetworking Expert. Since then, Elan has been involved in numerous large-scale data center and telecommunications networking projects worldwide.

Dedication

In memory of Carcel Lanier (C.L.) Odom: Dad's Pop, Poppa, wearing khakis, quiet, tearing down the old house (one board at a time), tagging along at the cow sales barn, walking the property, and napping during the Sunday morning sermon.

Acknowledgments

Although published as a first edition for various reasons, this book (and the companion *Cisco CCENT/CCNA ICND1 100-101 Exam Cert Guide*) represents the seventh book in a long line of Cisco Press books focused on helping people pass the CCENT and CCNA R/S certifications. Given the long history, many people have worked on these books from their inception back in 1998. To those many people who have touched these books over these past 15 years—technical edits, development, copy edits, project editing, proofing, indexing, managing the production process, interior design, cover design, marketing, and all the other details that happen to get these books out the door—thanks so much for playing a role in this CCENT/CCNA franchise.

Many of the contributors to the previous editions returned to work on creating these new editions, including Development Editor Drew Cupp. Drew kept all the details straight, with my frequent changes to the outlines and titles, keeping the sequencing on track, while still doing his primary job: keeping the text and features clear and consistent throughout the book. Thanks, Drew, for walking me through the development.

Contributing author Anthony Sequeira did a nice job stepping in on the network management part of the book. Anthony was a perfect fit, given his interest in management protocols and tools, and his writing experience and his great teaching skills (with enthusiasm!). Thanks for helping make this book complete and doing such a great job.

As for technical editors, Elan Beer did his normal job. That is, he did his usual amazing job of doing every part of the technical edit job well, from finding the tiny little cross-reference errors that lie pages apart, to anticipating how readers might misunderstand certain phrasing, to being all over the details of every technical feature. Fantastic job as usual; thanks, Elan.

Brett Bartow again served as executive editor of the book, as he has almost since the beginning of these titles. When my family has asked me over the years about Brett's role with these books, the best single word definition is *teammate*. Brett may be employed at Pearson Education, but he is always working with me and for me, watching out for the business end of the books and finding ways to make the publisher/author relationship work seamlessly. Thanks for another great ride through these books, Brett!

Word docs go in, and out come these beautiful finished products. Thanks to Sandra Schroeder, Tonya Simpson, and all the production team for working through the magic that takes those Word docs and makes the beautiful finished product. From fixing all my grammar, crummy word choices, passive-voice sentences, and then pulling the design and layout together, they do it all. Thanks for putting it all together and making it look easy. And Tonya, managing the details through several process steps for roughly 100 elements between the pair of CCNA books in a short timeframe: Wow, thanks for the amazing juggling act! And thanks especially for the attention to detail.

The figures for these books go through a little different process than they do for other books. Together we invested a large amount of labor in updating the figures for these books, both for the design, the number of figures, and for the color versions of the figures for the electronic versions of the books. A special thanks goes out to Laura Robbins for working with me on the color and design standards early in the process. Also, thanks to Mike Tanamachi for drawing all the figures so well (and then redrawing them every time I changed my mind about something).

Thanks to Chris Burns of CertSkills for all the work on the mind maps, both those used in the final product and those used to build the book, as well as for being a bit of a test case for some of the chapters.

A special thank you to you readers who write in with suggestions, possible errors, and especially those of you who post online at the Cisco Learning Network. Without question, the comments I receive directly and overhear by participating at CLN made this edition a better book.

Thanks to my wife, Kris. Book schedules have a bigger impact than I would like, but you always make it work. Thanks to my daughter, Hannah, for all the great study/work breaks on some of these busy schooldays. And thanks to Jesus Christ, for this opportunity to write.

Contents at a Glance

Contents

Icons Used in This Book

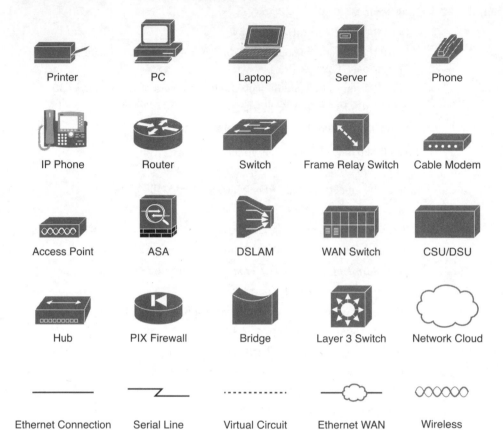

Command Syntax Conventions

The conventions used to present command syntax in this book are the same conventions used in the IOS Command Reference. The Command Reference describes these conventions as follows:

- **Boldface** indicates commands and keywords that are entered literally as shown. In actual configuration examples and output (not general command syntax), boldface indicates commands that are manually input by the user (such as a **show** command).

- *Italic* indicates arguments for which you supply actual values.

- Vertical bars (|) separate alternative, mutually exclusive elements.

- Square brackets ([ ]) indicate an optional element.

- Braces ({ }) indicate a required choice.

- Braces within brackets ([{ }]) indicate a required choice within an optional element.

Introduction

About the Exams

Congratulations! If you're reading far enough to look at this book's Introduction, you've probably already decided to go for your Cisco certification. If you want to succeed as a technical person in the networking industry at all, you need to know Cisco. Cisco has a ridiculously high market share in the router and switch marketplace, with more than 80 percent market share in some markets. In many geographies and markets around the world, networking equals Cisco. If you want to be taken seriously as a network engineer, Cisco certification makes perfect sense.

The Exams That Help You Achieve CCENT and CCNA

Cisco announced changes to the CCENT and CCNA Routing and Switching certifications, and the related 100-101 ICND1, 200-101 ICND2, and 200-120 CCNA exams, early in the year 2013. For those of you who understand how the old Cisco ICND1, ICND2, and CCNA exams worked, the structure remains the same. For those of you new to Cisco certifications, this introduction begins by introducing the basics.

Most everyone new to Cisco certifications begins with either CCENT or CCNA Routing and Switching. CCENT certification requires knowledge and skills on about half as much material as does CCNA Routing and Switching, so CCENT is the easier first step.

The CCENT certification requires a single step: pass the ICND1 exam. Simple enough.

The CCNA Routing and Switching certification gives you two options, as shown in Figure I-1: pass both the ICND1 and ICND2 exams, or just pass the CCNA exam. (Note that there is no separate certification for passing the ICND2 exam.)

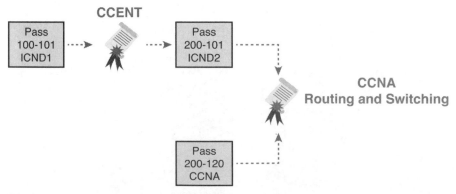

Figure I-1 *Cisco Entry-Level Certifications and Exams*

As you can see, although you can obtain the CCENT certification by taking the ICND1 exam, you do not have to be CCENT certified before you get your CCNA Routing and Switching certification. You can choose to take the CCNA exam and bypass the CCENT certification.

As for the topics themselves, the ICND1 and ICND2 exams cover different topics (but with some overlap required). For example, ICND1 covers the basics of the Open Shortest Path First (OSPF) routing protocol. ICND2 covers more detail about OSPF, but to discuss those additional details, ICND2 must rely on the parts of OSPF included in ICND1. Many topics in ICND2 build on topics in ICND1, causing some overlap.

The CCNA exam covers all the topics in both ICND1 and ICND2, no more, no less.

Types of Questions on the Exams

The ICND1, ICND2, and CCNA exams all follow the same general format. At the testing center, you sit in a quiet room with a PC. Before the exam timer begins, you have a chance to do a few other tasks on the PC; for instance, you can take a sample quiz just to get accustomed to the PC and the testing engine. Anyone who has user-level skills in getting around a PC should have no problems with the testing environment.

Once the exam starts, the screen shows you question after question. The questions usually fall into one of the following categories:

- Multiple choice, single answer
- Multiple choice, multiple answer
- Testlet
- Drag-and-drop
- Simulated lab (sim)
- Simlet

The first three items in the list are all multiple choice questions. The multiple choice format simply requires that you point and click a circle beside the correct answer(s). Cisco traditionally tells you how many answers you need to choose, and the testing software prevents you from choosing too many answers. The testlet style gives you one larger scenario statement, with multiple different multiple choice questions about that one scenario.

Drag-and-drop questions require you to move some items around on the GUI. You left-click and hold, move a button or icon to another area, and release the clicker to place the object somewhere else—usually into a list. So, for some questions, to answer the question correctly, you might need to put a list of five things in the proper order.

The last two types both use a network simulator to ask questions. Interestingly, the two types actually allow Cisco to assess two very different skills. First, sim questions generally describe a problem, and your task is to configure one or more routers and switches to fix the problem. The exam then grades the question based on the configuration you changed or added.

The simlet questions may well be the most difficult style of question on the exams. Simlet questions also use a network simulator, but instead of you answering the question by changing the configuration, the question includes one or more multiple choice questions. The questions require that you use the simulator to examine the current behavior of a network, interpreting the output of any **show** commands that you can remember to answer the question. Whereas sim questions require you to troubleshoot problems related to a configuration, simlets require you to both analyze both working and broken networks, correlating **show** command output with your knowledge of networking theory and configuration commands.

You can watch and even experiment with these command types using the Cisco Exam Tutorial. To find the Cisco Certification Exam Tutorial, go to http://www.cisco.com and search for "exam tutorial."

What's on the CCNA Exams?

Ever since I was in grade school, whenever the teacher announced that we were having a test soon, someone would always ask, "What's on the test?" Even in college, people would try to get more information about what would be on the exams. At heart, the goal is to know what to study hard, what to study a little, and what to not study at all.

Cisco tells the world the topics on each of their exams. Cisco wants the public to know both the variety of topics, and an idea about the kinds of knowledge and skills required for each topic, for every Cisco certification exam. To that end, Cisco publishes a set of exam topics for each exam.

Many Cisco exam topics list both a networking topic plus an important verb. The verb tells us to what degree the topic must be understood and what skills are required. The topic also implies the kinds of skills required for that topic. For example, one topic might start with "Describe…," another with "Configure…," another with "Verify…," and another might begin with "Troubleshoot…." That last topic has the highest required skill level, because to troubleshoot you must understand the topic, be able to configure it (to see what's wrong with the configuration), and verify it (to find the root cause of the problem). By listing the topics and skill level, Cisco helps us all prepare for its exams. Although the exam topics are helpful, keep in mind that Cisco adds a disclaimer that the posted exam topics for all of its certification exams are *guidelines*. Cisco makes the effort to keep the exam questions within the confines of the stated exam topics, and I know from talking to those involved that every question is analyzed for whether it fits within the stated exam topics.

ICND1 Exam Topics

Tables I-1 through I-7 lists the exam topics for the ICND1 exam. Following those tables, Tables I-8 through I-12 list the exam topics for ICND2. These tables note the book chapters in which each exam topic is covered.

Note that the tables follow Cisco's organization of topics, by both grouping similar topics and listing sub-topics. The subtopics simply give more specific terms and concepts to provide more detail about some exam topics. The tables show the main topics in bold and the subtopics as indented text inside the tables.

Table I-1   ICND1 Exam Topics: Operation of IP Data Networks

Chapter	Operation of IP Data Networks
1–4, 6, 15	Recognize the purpose and functions of various network devices such as Routers, Switches, Bridges and Hubs.
1–4, 6, 15	Select the components required to meet a given network specification.
5	Identify common applications and their impact on the network
1	Describe the purpose and basic operation of the protocols in the OSI and TCP/IP models.
2–5, 6, 9, 16, 24, 25	Predict the data flow between two hosts across a network.
2, 6, 15	Identify the appropriate media, cables, ports, and connectors to connect Cisco network devices to other network devices and hosts in a LAN

Table I-2   ICND1 Exam Topics: LAN Switching Technologies

Chapter	LAN Switching Technologies
2, 6	Determine the technology and media access control method for Ethernet networks
6, 8, 9	Identify basic switching concepts and the operation of Cisco switches.
6, 8	Collision Domains
6, 9	Broadcast Domains
6	Types of switching
6, 8, 9	CAM Table
7	Configure and verify initial switch configuration including remote access management.
7	Cisco IOS commands to perform basic switch setup
7, 18, 28	Verify network status and switch operation using basic utilities such as ping, telnet and ssh.
9	Describe how VLANs create logically separate networks and the need for routing between them.
9	Explain network segmentation and basic traffic management concepts
9	Configure and verify VLANs
9, 10	Configure and verify trunking on Cisco switches
9, 10	DTP
10	Auto negotiation

Table I-3   ICND1 Exam Topics: IP Addressing (IPv4/IPv6)

Chapter	IP Addressing (IPv4/IPv6)
11	Describe the operation and necessity of using private and public IP addresses for IPv4 addressing
25, 26	Identify the appropriate IPv6 addressing scheme to satisfy addressing requirements in a LAN/WAN environment.
11, 19, 20, 21	Identify the appropriate IPv4 addressing scheme using VLSM and summarization to satisfy addressing requirements in a LAN/WAN environment.
27, 28, 29	Describe the technological requirements for running IPv6 in conjunction with IPv4 such as dual stack
25–28	Describe IPv6 addresses
25, 26	Global unicast
27	Multicast
27	Link local
26	Unique local
27	eui 64
28	autoconfiguration

Table I-4   ICND1 Exam Topics: IP Routing Technologies

Chapter	IP Routing Technologies
16	Describe basic routing concepts
16	CEF
16	Packet forwarding
16	Router lookup process
15–18, 27	Configure and verify utilizing the CLI to set basic Router configuration
16–18, 27	Cisco IOS commands to perform basic router setup
16, 27	Configure and verify operation status of an ethernet interface
16–18, 27–29	Verify router configuration and network connectivity
16–18, 27, 29	Cisco IOS commands to review basic router information and network connectivity
16, 29	Configure and verify routing configuration for a static or default route given specific routing requirements
4, 16, 17, 25, 29	Differentiate methods of routing and routing protocols
4, 17, 29	Static vs. Dynamic
17	Link state vs. Distance Vector

Chapter	IP Routing Technologies
16, 25	next hop
16, 25	ip routing table
17, 29	Passive interfaces
17, 29	**Configure and verify OSPF (single area)**
17, 29	Benefit of single area
17	Configure OSPF v2
29	Configure OSPF v3
17, 29	Router ID
17, 29	Passive interface
16	**Configure and verify interVLAN routing (Router on a stick)**
16	sub interfaces
16	upstream routing
16	encapsulation
8, 16	**Configure SVI interfaces**

Table I-5 ICND1 Exam Topics: IP Services

Chapter	IP Services
18, 28	**Configure and verify DHCP (IOS Router)**
18, 28	configuring router interfaces to use DHCP
18	DHCP options
18	excluded addresses
18	lease time
22, 23	**Describe the types, features, and applications of ACLs**
22	Standard
23	Sequence numbers
23	Editing
23	Extended
23	Named
22, 23	Numbered
22	Log option
22, 23	**Configure and verify ACLs in a network environment**
23	Named

Chapter	IP Services
22, 23	Numbered
22	Log option
24	**Identify the basic operation of NAT**
24	Purpose
24	Pool
24	Static
24	1 to 1
24	Overloading
24	Source addressing
24	One way NAT
24	**Configure and verify NAT for given network requirements**
23	**Configure and verify NTP as a client**

Table I-6   ICND1 Exam Topics: Network Device Security

Chapter	Network Device Security
8, 15	**Configure and verify network device security features such as**
8, 15	Device password security
8, 15	Enable secret vs enable
23	Transport
23	Disable telnet
8	SSH
8	VTYs
23	Physical security
8	Service password
8	Describe external authentication methods
8, 10	**Configure and verify Switch Port Security features such as**
8	Sticky MAC
8	MAC address limitation
8, 10	Static / dynamic
8, 10	Violation modes
8, 10	Err disable
8, 10	Shutdown

Chapter	Network Device Security
8, 10	Protect restrict
8	Shutdown unused ports
8	Err disable recovery
8	Assign unused ports to an unused VLAN
23	Setting native VLAN to other than VLAN 1
22, 23	**Configure and verify ACLs to filter network traffic**
23	**Configure and verify an ACLs to limit telnet and SSH access to the router**

Table I-7 ICND1 Exam Topics: Troubleshooting

Chapter	Troubleshooting
12–15, 18–21, 25–28	**Troubleshoot and correct common problems associated with IP addressing and host configurations.**
9, 10	**Troubleshoot and Resolve VLAN problems**
9, 10	identify that VLANs are configured
9, 10	port membership correct
9, 10	IP address configured
9, 10	**Troubleshoot and Resolve trunking problems on Cisco switches**
9, 10	correct trunk states
9, 10	correct encapsulation configured
9, 10	correct vlans allowed
22, 23	**Troubleshoot and Resolve ACL issues**
22, 23	Statistics
22, 23	Permitted networks
22, 23	Direction
22, 23	Interface
10	**Troubleshoot and Resolve Layer 1 problems**
10	Framing
10	CRC
10	Runts
10	Giants
10	Dropped packets
10	Late collision
10	Input / Output errors

ICND2 Exam Topics

Tables I-8 through I-12 list the exam topics for ICND2. These tables note the book chapters in which each exam topic is covered. Note that each table covers a main exam topic. Cisco released further information about each topic to several sublevels of hierarchy. In this table, those sublevels are indented to indicate the topic above them they are related to.

Table I-8   ICND2 Exam Topics: LAN Switching Technologies

Chapters	LAN Switching Technologies
1	**Identify enhanced switching technologies**
1	RSTP
1	PVSTP
1	Etherchannels
1, 2	**Configure and verify PVSTP operation**
1, 2	describe root bridge election
2	spanning tree mode

Table I-9   ICND2 Exam Topics, IP Routing Technologies

Chapters	IP Routing Technologies
20	**Describe the boot process of Cisco IOS routers**
20	POST
20	Router bootup process
12	**Configure and verify operation status of a Serial interface.**
20, 21	**Manage Cisco IOS Files**
20	Boot preferences
20	Cisco IOS image(s)
21	Licensing
21	Show license
21	Change license
8–11, 16–18	**Differentiate methods of routing and routing protocols**
8	Administrative distance
9	split horizon
8, 9, 17, 18	metric
8, 9, 17, 18	next hop
8, 17	**Configure and verify OSPF (single area)**

Chapters	IP Routing Technologies
8, 11, 17	neighbor adjacencies
8, 11, 17	OSPF states
8, 17	Discuss Multi area
8	Configure OSPF v2
17	Configure OSPF v3
8, 17	Router ID
8, 17	LSA types
9, 10, 18	**Configure and verify EIGRP (single AS)**
9, 10, 18	Feasible Distance / Feasible Successors /Administrative distance
9, 18	Feasibility condition
9, 18	Metric composition
9, 10, 18	Router ID
9, 10	Auto summary
9, 10, 18	Path selection
9, 10, 18	Load balancing
9, 10, 18	Equal
9, 10, 18	Unequal
9, 10, 18	Passive interface

Table I-10   ICND2 Exam Topics, IP Services

Chapters	IP Services
6	**Recognize High availability (FHRP)**
6	VRRP
6	HSRP
6	GLBP
19	**Configure and verify Syslog**
19	Utilize Syslog Output
19	**Describe SNMP v2 & v3**

Table I-11   ICND2 Exam Topics, Troubleshooting

Chapters	Troubleshooting
3–5, 16	**Identify and correct common network problems**
19	**Utilize netflow data**
2	**Troubleshoot and Resolve Spanning Tree operation issues**
2	root switch
2	priority
2	mode is correct
2	port states
4, 5, 16	**Troubleshoot and Resolve routing issues**
4, 5, 16	routing is enabled
4, 5, 16	routing table is correct
4, 5, 16	corrcct path selection
11, 17	**Troubleshoot and Resolve OSPF problems**
11, 17	neighbor adjacencies
11, 17	Hello and Dead timers
11, 17	OSPF area
11, 17	Interface MTU
11, 17	Network types
11, 17	Neighbor states
11, 17	OSPF topology database
11, 18	**Troubleshoot and Resolve EIGRP problems**
11, 18	neighbor adjacencies
11, 18	AS number
11, 18	Load balancing
11, 18	Split horizon
3, 5	**Troubleshoot and Resolve interVLAN routing problems**
5	Connectivity
5	Encapsulation
5	Subnet
3, 5	Native VLAN
3, 5	Port mode trunk status
12, 14	**Troubleshoot and Resolve WAN implementation issues**

Chapters	Troubleshooting
12	Serial interfaces
12	PPP
14	Frame relay
19	**Monitor NetFlow statistics**
2	**Troubleshoot etherchannel problems**

Table I-12 ICND2 Exam Topics: WAN Technologies

Chapters	WAN Technologies
7, 13, 15	**Identify different WAN Technologies**
15	Metro Ethernet
15	VSAT
15	Cellular 3G / 4G
15	MPLS
12, 15	T1 / E1
15	ISDN
15	DSL
13	Frame relay
15	Cable
7	VPN
12	**Configure and verify a basic WAN serial connection**
12	**Configure and verify a PPP connection between Cisco routers**
14	**Configure and verify Frame Relay on Cisco routers**
15	**Implement and troubleshoot PPPoE**

CCNA Exam Topics

The 200-120 CCNA exam actually covers everything from both the ICND1 and ICND2 exams, at least based on the published exam topics. As of publication, the CCNA exam topics include all topics in Tables I-1 through I-12. In short, CCNA = ICND1 + ICND2.

NOTE   Because it is possible that the exam topics may change over time, it might be worth the time to double-check the exam topics as listed on the Cisco website (http://www.cisco.com/go/ccent and http://www.cisco.com/go/ccna). If Cisco does happen to add exam topics at a later date, note that Appendix B, "ICND2 Exam Updates," describes how to go to http://www.ciscopress.com and download additional information about those newly added topics.

About the Book

This book discusses the content and skills needed to pass the 200-101 ICND2 exam. That content also serves as basically the second half of the CCNA content, with this book's companion title, the *Cisco CCENT/CCNA ICND1 100-101 Official Cert Guide*, discussing the first half of the content.

Each of these books uses the same kinds of book features, so if you are reading both this book and the ICND1 book, you do not need to read the Introduction to the other book. Also, for those of you using both books to prepare for the 200-120 CCNA exam (rather than taking the two-exam option), the end of this Introduction lists a suggested reading plan.

Book Features

The most important and somewhat obvious objective of this book is to help you pass the ICND2 exam or the CCNA exam. In fact, if the primary objective of this book were different, the book's title would be misleading! However, the methods used in this book to help you pass the exams are also designed to make you much more knowledgeable about how to do your job.

This book uses several tools to help you discover your weak topic areas, to help you improve your knowledge and skills with those topics, and to prove that you have retained your knowledge of those topics. So, this book does not try to help you pass the exams only by memorization, but by truly learning and understanding the topics. The CCNA certification is the foundation for many of the Cisco professional certifications, and it would be a disservice to you if this book did not help you truly learn the material. Therefore, this book helps you pass the CCNA exam by using the following methods:

- Helping you discover which exam topics you have not mastered
- Providing explanations and information to fill in your knowledge gaps
- Supplying exercises that enhance your ability to recall and deduce the answers to test questions
- Providing practice exercises on the topics and the testing process via test questions on the DVD

Chapter Features

To help you customize your study time using these books, the core chapters have several features that help you make the best use of your time:

■ **"Do I Know This Already?" quizzes:** Each chapter begins with a quiz that helps you determine the amount of time you need to spend studying that chapter.

■ **Foundation Topics:** These are the core sections of each chapter. They explain the protocols, concepts, and configuration for the topics in that chapter.

■ **Exam Preparation Tasks:** At the end of the "Foundation Topics" section of each chapter, the "Exam Preparation Tasks" section lists a series of study activities that should be done at the end of the chapter. Each chapter includes the activities that make the most sense for studying the topics in that chapter. The activities include the following:

  ■ **Review Key Topics:** The Key Topic icon appears next to the most important items in the "Foundation Topics" section of the chapter. The Key Topics Review activity lists the key topics from the chapter and their corresponding page numbers. Although the contents of the entire chapter could be on the exam, you should definitely know the information listed in each key topic.

  ■ **Complete Tables and Lists from Memory:** To help you exercise your memory and memorize some lists of facts, many of the more important lists and tables from the chapter are included in a document on the DVD. This document lists only partial information, allowing you to complete the table or list.

  ■ **Define Key Terms:** Although the exams may be unlikely to ask a question like "Define this term," the CCNA exams require that you learn and know a lot of networking terminology. This section lists the most important terms from the chapter, asking you to write a short definition and compare your answer to the Glossary at the end of this book.

  ■ **Command Reference Tables:** Some book chapters cover a large amount of configuration and EXEC commands. These tables list the commands introduced in the chapter, along with an explanation. For exam preparation, use it for reference, but also read the table once when performing the Exam Preparation Tasks to make sure that you remember what all the commands do.

Part Review

The Part Review tasks help you prepare to apply all the concepts in each respective part of the book. (Each book part contains a number of related chapters.) The Part Review includes sample test questions, which require you to apply the concepts from multiple chapters in that part, uncovering what you truly understood and what you did not quite yet understand. The Part Review also uses mind map exercises that help you mentally connect concepts, configuration, and verification, so that no matter what perspective a single exam question takes, you can analyze and answer the question.

The Part Reviews list tasks, along with checklists, so you can track your progress. The following list explains the most common tasks you will see in the Part Review; note that not all Part Reviews use every type of task.

- **Review DIKTA Questions:** Although you have already seen the DIKTA questions from the chapters in a part, re-answering those questions can prove a useful way to review facts. The Part Review suggests that you repeat the DIKTA questions, but using the Pearson IT Certification Practice Test (PCPT) exam software that comes with the book, for extra practice in answering multiple choice questions on a computer.

- **Answer Part Review Questions:** The PCPT exam software includes several exam databases. One exam database holds Part Review questions, written specifically for Part Review. These questions purposefully include multiple concepts in each question, sometimes from multiple chapters, to help build the skills needed for the more challenging analysis questions on the exams.

- **Review Key Topics:** Yes, again! They are indeed the most important topics in each chapter.

- **Create Configuration Mind Maps:** Mind maps are graphical organizing tools that many people find useful when learning and processing how concepts fit together. The process of creating mind maps helps you build mental connections between concepts and configuration commands, as well as develop your recall of the individual commands. For this task, you may create the mind map on paper or using any mind mapping or graphic organizer software. (For more information about mind maps, see the section "About Mind Maps and Graphic Visualization" in the Introduction of this book.)

- **Create Verification Mind Maps:** These mind mapping exercises focus on helping you connect router and switch **show** commands to either networking concepts or to configuration commands. Simply create the mind maps on paper or using any mind mapping or graphic organizer software.

- **Repeat Chapter Review Tasks** (Optional): Browse through the Chapter Review tasks and repeat any that you think might help your review at this point.

Final Prep Tasks

Chapter 22, at the end of this book, lists a series of preparation tasks that you can best use for your final preparation before taking the exam.

Other Features

In addition to the features in each of the core chapters, this book, as a whole, has additional study resources, including the following:

- **DVD-based practice exam:** The companion DVD contains the powerful Pearson IT Certification Practice Test exam engine. You can take simulated ICND2 exams, as well as simulated CCNA exams, with the DVD and activation code included in this book. (You can take simulated ICND1 and CCNA exams with the DVD in the *Cisco CCENT/CCNA ICND1 Official Cert Guide*.)

- **CCNA ICND2 Simulator Lite:** This lite version of the best-selling CCNA Network Simulator from Pearson provides you with a means, right now, to experience the Cisco command-line interface (CLI). No need to go buy real gear or buy a full simulator to start learning the CLI. Just install it from the DVD in the back of this book.

- **eBook:** If you are interested in obtaining an eBook version of this title, we have included a special offer on a coupon card inserted in the DVD sleeve in the back of the book. This offer allows you to purchase the *Cisco CCNA Routing and Switching ICND2 200-101 Official Cert Guide Premium Edition eBook and Practice Test* at a 70 percent discount off the list price. In addition to three versions of the eBook, PDF (for reading on your computer), EPUB (for reading on your tablet, mobile device, or Nook or other eReader), and Mobi (the native Kindle version), you also receive additional practice test questions and enhanced practice test features.

- **Mentoring videos:** The DVD included with this book includes four other instructional videos, about the following topics: OSPF, EIGRP, EIGRP Metrics, plus PPP and CHAP.

- **Companion website:** The website http://www.ciscopress.com/title/1587143739 posts up-to-the-minute materials that further clarify complex exam topics. Check this site regularly for new and updated postings written by the author that provide further insight into the more troublesome topics on the exam.

- **PearsonITCertification.com:** The website http://www.pearsonitcertification.com is a great resource for all things IT-certification related. Check out the great CCNA articles, videos, blogs, and other certification preparation tools from the industry's best authors and trainers.

- **CCNA Simulator:** If you are looking for more hands-on practice, you might want to consider purchasing the CCNA Network Simulator. You can purchase a copy of this software from Pearson at http://pearsonitcertification.com/networksimulator or other retail outlets. To help you with your studies, I have created a mapping guide that maps each of the labs in the simulator to the specific sections in these CCNA cert guides. You can get this mapping guide for free on the Extras tab of the companion website.

- **Author's website and blogs:** The author maintains a website that hosts tools and links useful when studying for CCENT and CCNA. The site lists information to help you build your own lab, study pages that correspond to each chapter of this book and the ICND1 book, and links to the author's CCENT Skills blog and CCNA Skills blog. Start at http://www.certskills.com; check the tabs for study and blogs in particular.

Book Organization, Chapters, and Appendices

This book contains 21 core chapters, Chapters 1 through 21, with Chapter 22 including some suggestions for how to approach the actual exams. Each core chapter covers a subset of the topics on the ICND2 exam. The core chapters are organized into sections. The core chapters cover the following topics:

Part I: LAN Switching

- **Chapter 1, "Spanning Tree Protocol Concepts,"** discusses the concepts behind IEEE Spanning Tree Protocol (STP) and how it makes some switch interfaces block frames to prevent frames from looping continuously around a redundant switched LAN.

- **Chapter 2, "Spanning Tree Protocol Implementation,"** shows how to configure, verify, and troubleshoot STP implementation on Cisco switches.

- **Chapter 3, "Troubleshooting LAN Switching,"** reviews LAN switching topics from the ICND1 book, while moving toward a deeper understanding of those topics. In particular, this chapter examines the most common LAN switching issues and how to discover those issues when troubleshooting a network.

Part II: IP Version 4 Routing

- **Chapter 4, "Troubleshooting IPv4 Routing Part I,"** reviews IPv4 routing, and then focuses on how to use two key troubleshooting tools to find routing problems: the **ping** and **traceroute** commands.

- **Chapter 5, "Troubleshooting IPv4 Routing Part II,"** looks at the most common IPv4 problems and how to find the root causes of those problems when troubleshooting.

- **Chapter 6, "Creating Redundant First-Hop Routers,"** discusses the need for a First Hop Redundancy Protocol (FHRP), how the protocols make multiple routers act like a single default router, and the configuration and verification details of both Hot Standby Router Protocol (HSRP) and Gateway Load Balancing Protocol (GLBP).

- **Chapter 7, "Virtual Private Networks,"** discusses the need for VPN technology when sending private network data over public networks like the Internet. It also discusses basic tunneling configuration using generic routing encapsulation (GRE) tunnels on Cisco routers.

Part III: IP Version 4 Routing Protocols

- **Chapter 8, "Implementing OSPF for IPv4,"** reviews the ICND1 book's coverage of OSPF Version 2 (OSPFv2). It also takes the concepts deeper, with more discussion of the OSPF processes and database and with additional configuration options.

- **Chapter 9, "Understanding EIGRP Concepts,"** introduces the fundamental operation of the Enhanced Interior Gateway Routing Protocol (EIGRP) for IPv4 (EIGRPv4), focusing on EIGRP neighbor relationships, how it calculates metrics, and how it quickly converges to alternate feasible successor routes.

- **Chapter 10, "Implementing EIGRP for IPv4,"** takes the concepts discussed in the previous chapter and shows how to configure and verify those same features.

- **Chapter 11, "Troubleshooting IPv4 Routing Protocols,"** walks through the most common problems with IPv4 routing protocols, while alternating between OSPF examples and EIGRP examples.

Part IV: Wide-Area Networks

- **Chapter 12, "Implementing** Point-to-Point WANs," explains the core concepts of how to build a leased-line WAN and the basics of the two common data link protocols on these links: HDLC and PPP.

- **Chapter 13, "Understanding Frame Relay Concepts,"** explains how to build a Frame Relay WAN between routers, focusing on the protocols and concepts rather than the configuration.

- **Chapter 14, "Implementing Frame Relay,"** takes the concepts discussed in Chapter 13 and shows how to configure, verify, and troubleshoot those same features.

- **Chapter 15, "Identifying Other Types of WANs,"** gives a broad description of many other types of WAN technology, including Ethernet WANs, Multiprotocol Label Switching (MPLS), and digital subscriber line (DSL).

Part V: IP Version 6

- **Chapter 16, "Troubleshooting IPv6 Routing,"** reviews IPv6 routing as discussed in the ICND1 book. It then shows some of the most common problems with IPv6 routing and discusses how to troubleshoot these problems to discover the root cause.

- **Chapter 17, "Implementing OSPF for IPv6,"** reviews the ICND1 book's coverage of OSPF Version 3 (OSPFv3). It then compares some deeper OSPFv3 concepts and configuration with these same concepts for OSPFv2, as discussed earlier in Chapter 8.

- **Chapter 18, "Implementing EIGRP for IPv6,"** takes the EIGRP concepts discussed for IPv4 in Chapter 9 and shows how those same concepts apply to EIGRP for IPv6 (EIGRPv6). It then shows how to configure and verify EIGRPv6 as well.

Part VI: Network Management

- **Chapter 19, "Managing Network Devices,"** discusses the concepts and configuration of three common network management tools: Simple Network Management Protocol (SNMP), syslog, and NetFlow.

- **Chapter 20, "Managing IOS Files,"** explains some necessary details about router internals and IOS. In particular, it discusses the boot process on a router, how a router choosing which IOS image to use, and the different locations where a router can store its IOS images.

- **Chapter 21, "Managing IOS Licensing,"** discusses Cisco's current methods of granting a particular router the right to use a particular IOS image and feature set through the use of IOS licenses.

Part VII: Final Review

- **Chapter 22, "Final Review,"** suggests a plan for final preparation once you have finished the core parts of the book, in particular explaining the many study options available in the book.

Part VIII: Appendixes (In Print)

- **Appendix A, "Numeric Reference Tables,"** lists several tables of numeric information, including a binary-to-decimal conversion table and a list of powers of 2.

- **Appendix B, "ICND2 Exam Updates,"** covers a variety of short topics that either clarify or expand on topics covered earlier in the book. This appendix is updated from time to time and posted at http://www.ciscopress.com/title/1587143739, with the most recent version available at the time of printing included here as Appendix B. (The first page of the appendix includes instructions on how to check to see if a later version of Appendix B is available online.)

- The **Glossary** contains definitions for all of the terms listed in the "Definitions of Key Terms" section at the conclusion of Chapters 1 through 21.

Appendixes (on the DVD)

The following appendixes are available in digital format on the DVD that accompanies this book:

- **Appendix C, "Answers to the 'Do I Know This Already?' Quizzes"** includes the explanations to all the questions from Chapters 1 through 21.

- **Appendix D, "Memory Tables,"** holds the key tables and lists from each chapter, with some of the content removed. You can print this appendix and, as a memory exercise, complete the tables and lists. The goal is to help you memorize facts that can be useful on the exams.

- **Appendix E, "Memory Tables Answer Key,"** contains the answer key for the exercises in Appendix D.

- **Appendix F, "Mind Map Solutions,"** shows an image of sample answers for all the part-ending mind map exercises.

- **Appendix G, "Study Planner,"** is a spreadsheet with major study milestones, where you can track your progress through your study.

Reference Information

This short section contains a few topics available for reference elsewhere in the book. You may read these when you first use the book, but you may also skip these topics and refer back to them later. In particular, make sure to note the final page of this introduction, which lists several contact details, including how to get in touch with Cisco Press.

Install the Pearson IT Certification Practice Test Engine and Questions

The DVD in the book includes the Pearson IT Certification Practice Test (PCPT) engine—software that displays and grades a set of exam-realistic multiple choice, drag-and-drop, fill-in-the-blank, and testlet questions. Using the PCPT engine, you can either study by going through the questions in study mode or take a simulated ICND2 or CCNA exam that mimics real exam conditions.

The installation process requires two major steps. The DVD in the back of this book has a recent copy of the PCPT engine. The practice exam—the database of ICND2 and CCNA exam questions—is not on the DVD. After you install the software, the PCPT software downloads the latest versions of both the software and the question databases for this book using your Internet connection.

NOTE   The cardboard DVD case in the back of this book includes both the DVD and a piece of thick paper. The paper lists the activation code for the practice exam associated with this book. *Do not lose the activation code.*

NOTE   Also on this same piece of paper, on the opposite side from the exam activation code, you will find a one-time-use coupon code that gives you 70 percent off the purchase of the *Cisco CCNA Routing and Switching ICND2 200-101 Official Cert Guide, Premium Edition eBook and Practice Test.*

Install the Software from the DVD

The software installation process is pretty routine as compared with other software installation processes. If you have already installed the Pearson IT Certification Practice Test software from another Pearson product, you do not need to reinstall the software. Instead, just launch the software on your desktop and proceed to activate the practice exam from this book by using the activation code included in the DVD sleeve. The following steps outline the installation process:

Step 1.   Insert the DVD into your PC.

Step 2.   The software that automatically runs is the Cisco Press software to access and use all DVD-based features, including the exam engine and the DVD-only appendixes. From the main menu, click the **Install the Exam Engine** option.

Step 3.   Respond to windows prompts as with any typical software installation process.

The installation process gives you the option to activate your exam with the activation code supplied on the paper in the DVD sleeve. This process requires that you establish a Pearson website login. You need this login to activate the exam, so please do register when prompted. If you already have a Pearson website login, you do not need to register again. Just use your existing login.

Activate and Download the Practice Exam

When the exam engine is installed, you should then activate the exam associated with this book (if you did not do so during the installation process) as follows:

Step 1.   Start the PCPT software from the Windows Start menu or from your desktop shortcut icon.

Step 2.   To activate and download the exam associated with this book, from the My Products or Tools tab, click the **Activate** button.

Step 3.   At the next screen, enter the activation key from paper inside the cardboard DVD holder in the back of the book. When it is entered, click the **Activate** button.

Step 4.   The activation process downloads the practice exam. Click **Next**, and then click **Finish**.

After the activation process is completed, the My Products tab should list your new exam. If you do not see the exam, make sure you have selected the My Products tab on the menu. At this point, the software and practice exam are ready to use. Simply select the exam and click the **Open Exam** button.

To update a particular product's exams that you have already activated and downloaded, simply select the **Tools** tab and click the **Update Products** button. Updating your exams ensures that you have the latest changes and updates to the exam data.

If you want to check for updates to the PCPT software, simply select the **Tools** tab and click the **Update Application** button. This will ensure that you are running the latest version of the software engine.

Activating Other Products

The exam software installation process and the registration process have to happen only once. Then for each new product, you have to complete just a few steps. For instance, if you buy another new Cisco Press Official Cert Guide or Pearson IT Certification Cert Guide, extract the activation code from the DVD sleeve in the back of that book; you don't even need the DVD at this point. From there, all you have to do is start PCPT (if not still up and running), and perform steps 2 through 4 from the previous list.

PCPT Exam Databases with This Book

This book includes an activation code that allows you to load a set of practice questions. The questions come in different exams or exam databases. When you install the PCPT software and type in the activation code, the PCPT software downloads the latest version of all these exam databases. And with the ICND2 book alone, you get six different "exams," or six different sets of questions, as listed in Figure I-2.

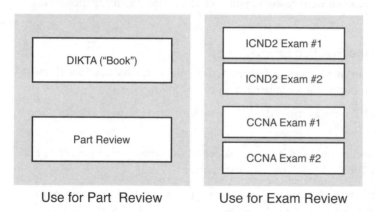

Figure I-2   *PCPT Exams/Exam Databases and When to Use Them*

You can choose to use any of these exam databases at any time, both in study mode and practice exam mode. However, many people find it best to save some of the exams until exam review time, after you have finished reading the entire book. Figure I-2 begins to suggest a plan, spelled out here:

- During Part Review, use PCPT to review the DIKTA questions for that part, using study mode.

- During Part Review, use the questions built specifically for Part Review (the Part Review questions) for that part of the book, using study mode.

- Save the remaining exams to use with Chapter 22, "Final Review," using practice exam mode, as discussed in that chapter.

The two modes inside PCPT give you better options for study versus practicing a timed exam event. In study mode, you can see the answers immediately, so you can study the topics more easily. Also, you can choose a subset of the questions in an exam database; for instance, you can view questions from only the chapters in one part of the book.

Practice exam mode creates an event somewhat like the actual exam. It gives you a preset number of questions, from all chapters, with a timed event. Practice exam mode also gives you a score for that timed event.

How to View Only DIKTA Questions by Part

Each Part Review asks you to repeat the DIKTA quiz questions from the chapters in that part. You can simply scan the book pages to review these questions, but it is slightly better to review these questions from inside the PCPT software, just to get a little more practice in how to read questions from the testing software. But you can just read them in the book, as well.

To view these DIKTA (book) questions inside the PCPT software, you need to select **Book Questions**, and the chapters in this part, using the PCPT menus. To do so, follow these steps:

Step 1. Start the PCPT software.

Step 2. From the main (home) menu, select the item for this product, with a name like Cisco CCNA Routing and Switching ICND2 200-101 Official Cert Guide, and click **Open Exam**.

Step 3. The top of the next window that appears should list some exams; check the **ICND2 Book Questions** box, and uncheck the other boxes. This selects the "book" questions (that is, the DIKTA questions from the beginning of each chapter).

Step 4. On this same window, click at the bottom of the screen to deselect all objectives (chapters). Then select the box beside each chapter in the part of the book you are reviewing.

Step 5. Select any other options on the right side of the window.

Step 6. Click **Start** to start reviewing the questions.

How to View Part Review Questions by Part Only

The exam databases you get with this book include a database of questions created solely for study during the Part Review process. DIKTA questions focus more on facts, with basic application. The Part Review questions instead focus more on application and look more like real exam questions.

To view these questions, follow the same process as you did with DIKTA/book questions, but select the Part Review database rather than the book database. Specifically, follow these steps:

Step 1. Start the PCPT software.

Step 2. From the main (home) menu, select the item for this product, with a name like Cisco CCNA Routing and Switching ICND2 200-101 Official Cert Guide, and click **Open Exam**.

Step 3. The top of the next window should list some exams; check the **Part Review Questions** box, and uncheck the other boxes. This selects the questions intended for part-ending review.

Step 4. On this same window, click at the bottom of the screen to deselect all objectives, and then select (check) the box beside the book part you want to review. This tells the PCPT software to give you Part Review questions from the selected part.

Step 5. Select any other options on the right side of the window.

Step 6. Click **Start** to start reviewing the questions.

About Mind Maps

Mind maps are a type of visual organization tool that you can use for many purposes. For instance, you can use mind maps as an alternative way to take notes.

You can also use mind maps to improve how your brain organizes concepts. Mind maps stress the connections and relationships between ideas. When you spend time thinking about an area of study, and organize your ideas into a mind map, you strengthen existing mental connections, create new connections, all into your own frame of reference.

In short, mind maps help you internalize what you learn.

Mind Map Mechanics

Each mind map begins with a blank piece of paper or blank window in an application. You then add a large central idea, with branches that move out in any direction. The branches contain smaller concepts, ideas, commands, pictures, whatever idea needs to be represented. Any concepts that can be grouped should be put near each other. As need be, you can create deeper and deeper branches, although for this book's purposes, most mind maps will not go beyond a couple of levels.

NOTE Many books have been written about mind maps, but Tony Buzan often gets credit for formalizing and popularizing mind maps. You can learn more about mind maps at his website, http://www.thinkbuzan.com.

For example, Figure I-3 shows a sample mind map that begins to output some of the IPv6 content from Part VII of the ICND1 book. The central concept of the mind map is IPv6 addressing, and the Part Review activity asks you to think of all facts you learned about IPv6 addressing, and organize them with a mind map. The mind map allows for a more visual representation of the concepts as compared with just written notes.

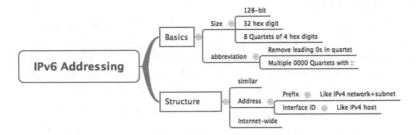

Figure I-3 *Sample Mind Map*

About Mind Maps Used During Part Review

This book suggests mind mapping exercises during Part Review. This short topic lists some details about the Part Review mind mapping exercises, listed in one place for reference.

Part Review uses two main types of mind mapping exercises:

Configuration exercises ask you to recall the related configuration commands and group them. For instance, in a configuration exercise, related commands that happen to be interface subcommands should be grouped, but as shown as being inside interface configuration mode.

Verification exercises ask you to think about the output of **show** commands and link the output to either the configuration commands that cause that output or the concepts that explain the meaning of some of that output.

Create these configuration mind maps on paper, using any mind mapping software, or even any drawing application. Many mind mapping apps exist as well. Regardless of how you draw them, follow these rules:

■ If you have only a little time for this exercise, spend your time making your own mind map, instead of looking at suggested answers. The learning happens when thinking through the problem of making your own mind map.

■ Set aside the book and all your notes, and do not look at them, when first creating these maps, and do as much as you can without looking at the book or your notes (or Google, or anything else).

■ Try all the mind maps listed in a Part Review before looking at your notes.

■ Finally, look at your notes to complete all the mind maps.

■ Make a note of where you put your final results so that you can find them later during final exam review.

Finally, when learning to use these tools, take two other important suggestions as well. First, use as few words as possible for each node in your mind map. The point is for you to remember the idea and its connections, rather than explain the concept to someone else. Just write enough to remind yourself of the concept. Second, if the mind map process is just not working for you, discard the tool. Instead, take freeform notes on a blank piece of paper. Try to do the important part of the exercise—the thinking about what concepts go together—without letting the tool get in the way.

About Building Hands-On Skills

You need skills in using Cisco routers and switches, specifically the Cisco command-line interface (CLI). The Cisco CLI is a text-based command-and-response user interface; you type a command, and the device (a router or switch) displays messages in response. To answer sim and simlet questions on the exams, you need to know a lot of commands, and you need to be able to navigate to the right place in the CLI to use those commands.

The best way to master these commands is to use them. Sometime during your initial reading of the first part of this book, you need to decide how you personally plan to build your CLI skills. This next topic discusses your options for getting the tools you need to build CLI skills.

Overview of Lab Options

To effectively build your hands-on CLI skills, you either need real routers and switches, or at least something that acts like routers and switches. People who are new to Cisco technology often choose from a few options to get those skills.

First, you can use real Cisco routers and switches. You can buy them, new or used, or borrow them at work. You can rent them for a fee. You can even rent virtual Cisco router and switch lab pods from Cisco, in an offering called Cisco Learning Labs.

Simulators provide another option. Router and switch simulators are software products that mimic the behavior of the Cisco CLI, generally for the purpose of allowing people to learn. These products have an added advantage when learning: They usually have lab exercises as well.

Simulators come in many shapes and sizes, but the publisher sells simulators that are designed to help you with CCENT and CCNA study—plus they match this book! The Pearson CCENT Network Simulator and the Pearson CCNA Network Simulator both provide an excellent environment to practice the commands, as well as hundreds of focused labs to help you learn what you need to know for the exams. Both products have the same software code base; the CCNA product simply has labs for both ICND1 and ICND2, whereas the CCENT product has only the ICND1 labs.

This book does not tell you what option to use, but you should plan on getting some hands-on practice somehow. The important thing to know is that most people need to practice using the Cisco CLI to be ready to pass these exams.

I (Wendell) have collected some information and opinions about this decision on my website, at http://certskills.com/labgear. Those pages link to sites for Dynamips and for the Pearson simulator. Also, because the information never seemed to exist in any one place, this website includes many details about how to build a CCNA lab using used real Cisco routers and switches.

A Quick Start with Pearson Network Simulator Lite

The decision of how to get hands-on skills can be a little scary at first. The good news: You have a free and simple first step. Install the Pearson NetSim Lite that comes with this book.

This lite version of the best-selling CCNA Network Simulator from Pearson provides you with a means, right now, to experience the Cisco CLI. No need to go buy real gear or buy a full simulator to start learning the CLI. Just install it from the DVD in the back of this book.

Of course, one reason that NetSim Lite comes on the DVD is that the publisher hopes you will buy the full product. However, even if you do not use the full product, you can still learn from the labs that come with NetSim Lite while deciding about what options to pursue.

NOTE   The ICND1 and ICND2 books each contain a different version of the Sim Lite product, each with labs that match the book content. If you bought both books, make sure you install both Sim Lite products.

For More Information

If you have any comments about the book, submit them via http://www.ciscopress.com. Just go to the website, select **Contact Us**, and type your message.

Cisco might make changes that affect the CCNA certification from time to time. You should always check http://www.cisco.com/go/ccna and http://www.cisco.com/go/ccent for the latest details.

The *Cisco CCNA Routing and Switching ICND2 200-101 Official Cert Guide* helps you attain CCNA Routing and Switching certification. This is the CCNA ICND2 certification book from the only Cisco-authorized publisher. We at Cisco Press believe that this book certainly can help you achieve CCNA certification, but the real work is up to you! I trust that your time will be well spent.

Getting Started

You just got this book. You have probably already read (or quickly skimmed) the Introduction. And you are wondering, is this where I really start reading or can I skip ahead to Chapter 1, "Spanning Tree Protocol Concepts"?

Stop to read this "Getting Started" section to think about how you will study for this exam. Your study will go much better if you take time (maybe 15 minutes) to think about a few key points about how to study before starting on this journey that will take you many hours, over many weeks. That is what this "Getting Started" section will help you do.

A Brief Perspective on Cisco Certification Exams

Cisco sets the bar pretty high for passing the ICND1, ICND2, and CCNA exams. Most anyone can study and pass these exams, but it takes more than just a quick read through the book and the cash to pay for the exam.

The challenge of these exams comes from many angles. Each of these exams covers a lot of concepts and many commands specific to Cisco devices. Beyond knowledge, these Cisco exams also require deep skills. You must be able to analyze and predict what really happens in a network. You must be able to configure Cisco devices to work correctly in those networks. And you must be ready to troubleshoot problems when the network does not work correctly.

The more challenging questions on these exams work a lot like a jigsaw puzzle, but with four out of every five puzzle pieces not even in the room. To solve the puzzle, you have to mentally re-create the missing pieces. To do that, you must know each networking concept and remember how the concepts work together. You also have to match the concepts with what happens on the devices with the configuration commands that tell the devices what to do. You also have to connect the concepts and the configuration with the meaning of the output of various troubleshooting commands to analyze how the network is working and why it is not working right now.

For instance, the ICND2 exam includes many troubleshooting topics. A simple question might ask you why a router that uses Open Shortest Path Version 2 (OSPFv2) might fail to form a neighbor relationship with another neighboring router. But a more exam-realistic question would make you think about why a router is missing a route, whether the root cause is related to OSPF, and, if OSPF, whether the root cause is related to OSPF neighbors.

The questions supply some of the information, like some pieces of the jigsaw puzzle, as represented with the white pieces in Figure 1. You have to apply your knowledge of IP routing and OSPF theory to the facts to come up with some of the other pieces of the puzzle. For a given question, some pieces of the puzzle may remain a mystery, but with enough of the puzzle filled in, you should be able to answer the question. And some pieces will just remain unknown for a given question.

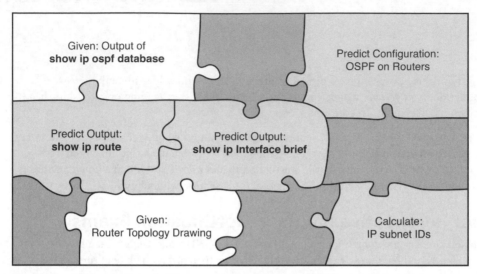

Figure 1   *Filling in Puzzle Pieces with Your Analysis Skills*

These skills require that you prepare by doing more than just reading and memorizing what you read. Of course, you need to read many pages in this book to learn many individual facts and how these facts relate to each other. But a big part of this book lists exercises beyond reading, exercises that help you build the skills to solve these networking puzzles.

Suggestions for How to Approach Your Study with This Book

These exams are challenging, but many people pass them every day. So, what do you need to do to be ready to pass, beyond reading and remembering all the facts? You need to develop skills. You need to mentally link each idea with other related ideas. Doing that requires additional work. To help you along the way, the next few pages give you five key perspectives about how to use this book to build those skills and make those connections, before you dive into this exciting but challenging world of learning networking on Cisco gear.

Not One Book: 21 Short Read-and-Review Sessions

First, look at your study as a series of read-and-review tasks, each on a relatively small set of related topics.

Each of the core chapters of this book (1 through 21) have around 23 pages of content on average. If you glance around any of those chapters, you will find a heading called "Foundation Topics" on about the fifth page of each chapter. From there, to the "Exam Preparation Tasks" at the end of the chapter, the chapters average about 23 pages.

So, do not approach this book as one big book. Treat the task of your first read of a chapter as a separate task. Anyone can read 23 pages. Having a tough day? Each chapter has two or three major sections, so read just one of them. Or, do some related labs, or review something you have already read. The book organizes the content into topics of a more manageable size to give you something more digestible to manage your study time throughout the book.

For Each Chapter, Do Not Neglect Practice

Next, plan to use the practice tasks at the end of each chapter.

Each chapter ends with practice and study tasks under a heading "Exam Preparation Tasks." Doing these tasks, and doing them at the end of the chapter, really does help you get ready. Do not put off using these tasks until later! The chapter-ending exam preparation tasks help you with the first phase of deepening your knowledge and skills of the key topics, remembering terms, and linking the concepts together in your brain so that you can remember how it all fits together.

The following list describes most of the activities you will find in the "Exam Preparation Tasks" sections:

- Review key topics
- Complete memory tables
- Define key terms
- Review command summary tables
- Review feature configuration checklists
- Do subnetting exercises

Approach each chapter with the same plan. You can choose to read the entire core ("Foundation Topics") section of each chapter, or you can choose to skim some chapters based on your score on the "Do I Know This Already?" (DIKTA) quiz, a pre-chapter self-assessment quiz at the beginning of most chapters. However, regardless of whether you skim or read thoroughly, do the study tasks in the "Exam Preparation Tasks" section at the end of the chapter. Figure 2 shows the overall flow.

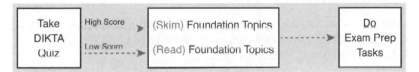

Figure 2   *Suggested Approach to Each Chapter*

Use Book Parts for Major Milestones

Third, view the book as having six major milestones, one for each major topic.

Beyond the more obvious organization into chapters, this book also organizes the chapters into six major topic areas called book parts. Completing each part means you have completed a major area of study. At the end of each part, take a little extra time. Do the Part Review tasks at the end of each part. Ask yourself where you are weak and where you are strong. And give yourself some reward for making it to a major milestone. Figure 3 lists the six parts in this book.

Six Major Milestones: Book Parts

LAN Switching	Part Prep Tasks
IP Version 4 Routing	Part Prep Tasks
IP Version 4 Routing Protocols	Part Prep Tasks
Wide Area Networks	Part Prep Tasks
IP Version 6	Part Prep Tasks
Network Management	Part Prep Tasks

Figure 3   *Parts as Major Milestones*

The tasks in the Part Reviews focus on helping you apply concepts (from that book part) to new scenarios for the exam. Some tasks use sample test questions so that you can think through and analyze a problem. This process helps you refine what you know and to realize what you did not quite yet understand. Some tasks use mind map exercises that help you mentally connect the theoretical concepts with the configuration and verification commands. These Part Review activities help build these skills.

Note that the Part Review directs you to use the Pearson IT Certification Practice Test (PCPT) software to access the practice questions. Each Part Review tells you to repeat the DIKTA questions, but using the PCPT software. Each Part Review also directs you how to access a specific set of questions reserved for reviewing concepts at part review. Note that the PCPT software and exam databases with this book give you the rights to additional questions, as well; Chapter 22, "Final Review," gives some recommendations on how to best use those questions for your final exam preparation.

Also, consider setting a goal date for finishing each part of the book (and a reward, as well). Plan a break, some family time, some time out exercising, eating some good food, whatever helps you get refreshed and motivated for the next part.

Use the Final Review Chapter to Refine Skills

Fourth, do the tasks outlined in the final preparation chapter (Chapter 22) at the end of this book.

The "Final Review" chapter has two major goals. First, it helps you further develop the analysis skills you need to answer the more complicated questions on the exam. Many questions require that you connect ideas about concepts, configuration, verification, and troubleshooting. More reading on your part does not develop all these skills; this chapter's tasks give you activities to further develop these skills.

The tasks in the "Final Review" chapter also help you find your weak areas. This final element gives you repetition with high-challenge exam questions, uncovering any gaps in your knowledge. Many of the questions are purposefully designed to test your knowledge of the most common mistakes and misconceptions, helping you avoid some of the common pitfalls people experience with the actual exam.

Set Goals and Track Your Progress

Finally, before you start reading the book and doing the rest of these study tasks, take the time to make a plan, set some goals, and be ready to track your progress.

While making lists of tasks may or may not appeal to you, depending on your personality, goal setting can help everyone studying for these exams. And to do the goal setting, you need to know what tasks you plan to do.

As for the list of tasks to do when studying, you do not have to use a detailed task list. (You could list every single task in every chapter-ending "Exam Preparation Tasks" section, every task in the Part Reviews, and every task in the "Final Preparation" chapter.) However, listing the major tasks can be enough.

You should track at least two tasks for each typical chapter: reading the "Foundation Topics" section and doing the "Exam Preparation Tasks" at the end of the chapter. And of course, do not forget to list tasks for Part Reviews and Final Review. Table 1 shows a sample for Part I of this book.

Table 1   Sample Excerpt from a Planning Tabl

Element	Task	Goal Date	First Date Completed	Second Date Completed (Optional)
Chapter 1	Read Foundation Topics			
Chapter 1	Do Exam Prep Tasks			
Chapter 2	Read Foundation Topics			
Chapter 2	Do Exam Prep Tasks			
Chapter 3	Read Foundation Topics			
Chapter 3	Do Exam Prep Tasks			
Part I Review	Do Part Review Activities			

NOTE   Appendix G, "Study Planner," on the DVD that comes with this book, contains a complete planning checklist like Table 1 for the tasks in this book. This spreadsheet allows you to update and save the file to note your goal dates and the tasks you have completed.

Use your goal dates as a way to manage your study, and not as a way to get discouraged if you miss a date. Pick reasonable dates that you can meet. When setting your goals, think about how fast you read and the length of each chapter's "Foundation Topics" section, as listed in the table of contents. Then, when you finish a task sooner than planned, move up the next few goal dates.

If you miss a few dates, do *not* start skipping the tasks listed at the ends of the chapters! Instead, think about what is impacting your schedule—real life, commitment, and so on— and either adjust your goals or work a little harder on your study.

Two Options When Studying for the 200-120 CCNA Exam

To get a CCNA Routing and Switching certification, you choose either a one-exam or two-exam path.

When using the two-exam path, use each book separately, and take the matching Cisco exam. In other words, use the *Cisco CCENT/CCNA ICND1 100-101 Official Cert Guide*, and then pass the 100-101 ICND1 exam, and then do the same with the *Cisco CCNA Routing and Switching ICND2 200-101 Official Cert Guide* and the 200-101 ICND2 exam.

The one-exam path gives you a couple of study options. The 200-120 CCNA exam covers the topics in the combined ICND1 and ICND2 books. The only question is when to read each part of the two books. You have two reasonable options when going with the one-exam option:

■ Complete all the ICND1 book, then move on to the ICND2 book

■ Move back and forth between the ICND1 and ICND2 books, by part, based on topics

The first option is pretty obvious, but the second one is less obvious. So, Figure 4 shows a study plan when you are using the one-exam option and want to move back and forth between the two books. Why move back and forth? To read about similar topics all at once, as shown in Figure 4.

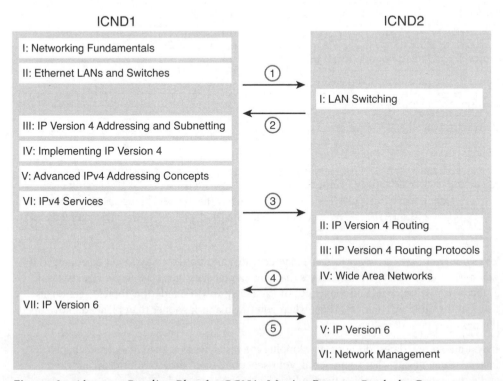

Figure 4   *Alternate Reading Plan for CCNA: Moving Between Books by Part*

Note that you should wait to use the "Final Review" chapter of either book until you complete both books. However, do the Part Review activities at the end of each part.

Other Small Tasks Before Getting Started

You need to do a few overhead tasks to install software, find some PDFs, and so on. You can do these tasks now or do them in your spare moments when you need a study break during the first few chapters of the book. But do these early. That way, if you do stumble upon an installation problem, you have time to work through it before you need a particular tool.

Register (for free) at the Cisco Learning Network (CLN, http://learningnetwork.cisco.com) and join the CCENT and CCNA study groups. These mailing lists allow you to lurk and participate in discussions about topics related to CCENT (ICND1) and CCNA (ICND1 + ICND2). Register, join the groups, and set up an email filter to redirect the messages to a separate folder. Even if you do not spend time reading all the posts yet, later, when you have time to read, you can browse through the posts to find interesting topics (or just search the posts from the CLN website).

Find and print a copy of Appendix D, "Memory Tables." Many of the "Chapter Review" sections use this tool, in which you take the incomplete tables from the appendix and complete the table to help you remember some key facts.

If you bought an ebook version of this book, find and download the media files (videos and Sim Lite software) per the instructions supplied on the last page of the ebook file under a "Where Are the Companion Files" heading.

Install the PCPT exam software and activate the exams. For more details on how to load the software, refer back to the Introduction, in the section "Install the Pearson Certification Practice Test Engine and Questions."

Finally, install the Sim Lite software (unless you bought the full simulator product already). The Sim Lite that comes with this book contains a subset of the lab exercises in the full Pearson Network Simulator product.

Getting Started: Now

Now dive in to your first of many short, manageable tasks: reading the relatively short introductory Chapter 1. Enjoy!

Part I of the book focuses on Ethernet LAN topics. In practice, many fundamental Ethernet LAN topics are pre-requisites for this book. The CCENT certification, and the matching *Cisco CCENT/CCNA ICND1 100-101 Official Cert Guide*, contains a fairly deep discussion about Ethernet LANs; roughly 20% of the *Cisco CCENT/CCNA ICND1 100-101 Official Cert Guide* is devoted to LAN topics. Part I of this ICND2 book picks up the Ethernet story assuming you already know Ethernet LAN basics.

Part I of this book completes the Ethernet LAN topics for the CCNA exam by adding to what is included in CCENT. In particular, this part discusses the concepts, configuration, and verification of the Spanning Tree Protocol (STP, Chapters 1 and 2). In addition, this part reviews most of the Ethernet LAN topics from CCENT—first to help you remember some of the details, but also to prepare everyone for learning about how to troubleshoot Ethernet LANs (Chapter 3).

Part I

LAN Switching

This chapter covers the following exam topics:

LAN Switching Technologies

Identify advanced switching technologies

RSTP

PVSTP

EtherChannels

Configure and verify PVSTP operation

Describe root bridge election

CHAPTER 1

Spanning Tree Protocol Concepts

Spanning Tree Protocol (STP) allows Ethernet LANs to have the added benefits of installing redundant links in a LAN, while overcoming the known problems that occur when adding those extra links. Using redundant links in a LAN design allows the LAN to keep working even when some links fail or even when some entire switches fail. Proper LAN design should add enough redundancy so that no single point of failure crashes the LAN; STP allows the design to use redundancy without causing some other problems.

This chapter discusses the concepts behind STP. In particular, it discusses why LANs need STP, what STP does to solve certain problems in LANs with redundant links, and how STP does its work. This chapter breaks the STP discussions into two major sections: the first about the core functions of STP, and the second about some optional STP features.

However, before moving on to STP, the first section of this chapter reviews LAN switching topics. For some of you reading this book, you easily remember about LAN switching, forwarding frames, MAC address tables, and everything to do with Ethernet LANs. Maybe you recently got your CCENT certification by passing the ICND1 exam, or maybe you just finished reading the ICND1 Official Cert Guide. However, some of you might not remember these details. So, the first section of the chapter provides a brief review of some important Ethernet topics from ICND1, so that when you read about STP, the Ethernet details will be fresh in your mind.

"Do I Know This Already?" Quiz

Use the "Do I Know This Already?" quiz to help decide whether you might want to skim this chapter, or a major section, moving more quickly to the "Exam Preparation Tasks" section near the end of the chapter. You can find the answers at the bottom of the page following the quiz. For thorough explanations, see DVD Appendix C, "Answers to the 'Do I Know This Already?' Quizzes."

Table 1-1 "Do I Know This Already?" Foundation Topics Section-to-Question Mapping

Foundation Topics Section	Questions
LAN Switching Review	1–2
Spanning Tree Protocol (IEEE 802.1D)	3–6
Optional STP Features	7

1. An Ethernet frame arrives at switch SW1, entering on port F0/1. F0/1 does not trunk. SW1 forwards the frame out F0/2. Which of the following statements is true about the logic SW1 uses when forwarding the frame?

    a. Forward based on MAC table entries for the F0/1's access VLAN

    b. Forward based on MAC table entries for the F0/2's access VLAN

    c. Forward based on MAC table entries for the F0/1's native VLAN

    d. Forward based on MAC table entries in all VLANs

2. Consider the following command output:

    ```
    SW1# show interfaces f0/11 status

    Port       Name            Status     Vlan      Duplex Speed Type
    Fa0/11                     connected  3         a-full   100 10/100BaseTX
    ```

    A frame arrives on this same switch's port F0/1, an access port in VLAN 3. The frame is destined to MAC address FFFF.FFFF.FFFF. Which of the following statements is true, based on the information about F0/11 in the **show** command output, about whether SW1 will forward the frame out port F0/11?

    a. The output confirms that SW1 will definitely forward the frame out F0/11.

    b. The output confirms that SW1 will definitely not forward the frame out F0/11.

    c. The output confirms that it is possible for SW1 to forward the frame out F0/11, but not definitely.

3. Which of the following IEEE 802.1D port states are stable states used when STP has completed convergence? (Choose two answers.)

    a. Blocking

    b. Forwarding

    c. Listening

    d. Learning

    e. Discarding

4. Which of the following are transitory IEEE 802.1D port states used only during the process of STP convergence? (Choose two answers.)

    a. Blocking

    b. Forwarding

    c. Listening

    d. Learning

    e. Discarding

5. Which of the following bridge IDs win election as root, assuming that the switches with these bridge IDs are in the same network?

   a. 32769:0200.1111.1111

   b. 32769:0200.2222.2222

   c. 4097:0200.1111.1111

   d. 4097:0200.2222.2222

   e. 40961:0200.1111.1111

6. Which of the following facts determines how often a nonroot bridge or switch sends an 802.1D STP hello BPDU message?

   a. The hello timer as configured on that switch.

   b. The hello timer as configured on the root switch.

   c. It is always every 2 seconds.

   d. The switch reacts to BPDUs received from the root switch by sending another BPDU 2 seconds after receiving the root BPDU.

7. What STP feature causes an interface to be placed in the forwarding state as soon as the interface is physically active?

   a. STP

   b. EtherChannel

   c. Root Guard

   d. PortFast

Foundation Topics

LAN Switching Review

> **NOTE**   This section reviews Ethernet LAN switching topics from the ICND1 exam and CCENT certification. Feel free to skim or skip forward to the next major heading, "Spanning Tree Protocol," if you remember Ethernet LAN topics well.

Modern LANs create a network of both wired and wireless connections to a variety of devices. Those connections give any device the fundamental means to send and receive data to and from other devices in a network. Combined with WAN connections and the Internet, these LAN-connected devices can communicate with other devices in other parts of an Enterprise network and across the world.

The wired parts of modern LANs use Ethernet standards and LAN switches. The Ethernet standards define the cabling details, as well as the data link layer rules, including framing and addresses. Physically, an Ethernet LAN may be small or large, but it has three basic components:

■ Devices with an Ethernet network interface card (NIC)

■ Ethernet LAN switches

■ Cables that connect devices (NICs to switch ports, switch ports to each other, and so on)

Figure 1-1 shows an example with six PCs connected to a single LAN switch.

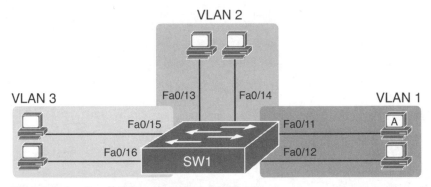

Figure 1-1   *Small Ethernet LAN with VLANs*

LAN Switch Forwarding Logic

STP limits where a switch chooses to forward frames, for the purpose of preventing problems with loops. These problems happen because, in some cases, the core LAN switch logic

---

Answers to the "Do I Know This Already?" quiz:

1 A   **2** C   **3** A and B   **4** C and D   **5** C   **6** B   **7** D

would literally forward a frame around the LAN forever without some external method like STP to prevent it. So, to understand STP, you need a good recall of the core logic of a LAN switch, particularly the switch forwarding logic. Then you can understand why frames would loop without STP, and then how STP prevents the loop.

The following list details all the steps in how a LAN switch forwards a frame, while ignoring the role of STP.

Step 1. Determine the VLAN in which the frame should be forwarded, as follows:

   A. If the frame arrives on an access interface, use the interface's access VLAN.

   B. If the frame arrives on a trunk interface, use the VLAN listed in the frame's trunking header.

Step 2. Add the source MAC address to the MAC address table, with incoming interface and VLAN ID.

Step 3. Look for the destination MAC address of the frame in the MAC address table, but only for entries in the VLAN identified at Step 1. Follow one of the next steps depending on whether the destination MAC is found:

   A. **Found:** Forward the frame out the only interface listed in the matched address table entry.

   B. **Not found:** Flood the frame out all other access ports in that same VLAN and out all trunk ports that list this VLAN as fully supported (active, in the allowed list, not pruned, STP forwarding).

For example, in Figure 1-1, consider a frame sent by PC A. The figure implies that switch port F0/11 is in VLAN 1, so at Step 1 in the process, the switch determines the frame is in VLAN 1. The switch would not forward the frame out the ports in VLAN 2 (F0/13 and F0/14) or VLAN 3 (F0/15 and F0/16). Then, the switch would look for the destination MAC address in the MAC address table, but only for entries in VLAN 1.

Later, this chapter discusses how STP adds to this logic, limiting the interfaces that a switch uses when both receiving frames and forwarding frames, thereby preventing loops.

Switch Verification

LAN switch logic really does reduce to a pretty short description, and it should, because switches need to forward potentially millions of frames per second (fps). Receive the frame, determine the VLAN, match the destination MAC to the MAC table, choose the outgoing interfaces, and forward the frame. However, making sense of the **show** commands can be a little more challenging, particularly if you do not get to use them in real networks every day. This section reviews a couple of key **show** commands that will prove useful when thinking about STP.

Viewing the MAC Address Table

The first example lists the MAC address table on two switches, SW1 and SW2, as shown in Figure 1-2. The figure shows the concept behind these MAC address tables, with the two PCs and one router being in VLAN 10. Example 1-1 that follows shows the output of the

show mac address-table dynamic command, which lists all dynamically learned MAC table entries on a switch, for all VLANs.

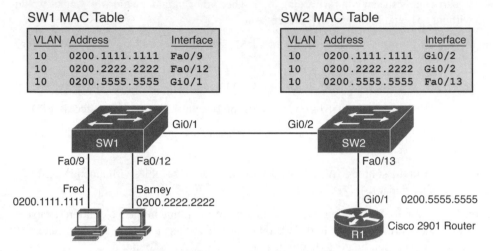

Figure 1-2   *Sample LAN with Pseudo MAC Address Tables*

Example 1-1   *Examining SW1 and SW2 Dynamic MAC Address Table Entries*

```
SW1# show mac address-table dynamic
          Mac Address Table
-------------------------------------------


Vlan    Mac Address      Type      Ports
----    -----------      --------  -----
  10    0200.1111.1111   DYNAMIC   Fa0/9
  10    0200.2222.2222   DYNAMIC   Fa0/12
  10    0200.5555.5555   DYNAMIC   Gi0/1
```
```
SW2# show mac address-table dynamic
          Mac Address Table
-------------------------------------------


Vlan    Mac Address      Type      Ports
----    -----------      --------  -----
  10    0200.1111.1111   DYNAMIC   Gi0/2
  10    0200.2222.2222   DYNAMIC   Gi0/2
  10    0200.5555.5555   DYNAMIC   Fa0/13
```

Note that each command, on each switch, basically repeats the same MAC table information shown in Figure 1-2. Both have learned all three MAC addresses, so each of the three devices must have sent frames that reached both switches. However, note that each switch has different forwarding (port) information. For instance, Fred's MAC address of 0200.1111.1111 is listed off SW1's Fa0/9 port, but SW2's MAC address table lists SW2's Gi0/2 port. So, the forwarding details in the table tell the local switch out which of its local ports to forward the frame.

STP does not leave any specific tracks or notes in the output of this command. However, STP will impact the set of ports on which a switch can learn MAC addresses, so STP indirectly changes what output shows up in the output of the **show mac address-table** command. As will be discussed later in the chapter, STP will cause a port to block, meaning that the switch ignores frames entering the interface. As a result, the switch will not learn MAC addresses from those frames, which affects the entries listed in the **show mac address-table** command.

Determining the VLAN of a Frame

The forwarding process of a Layer 2 switch forwards the frame in the context of a single VLAN. That is, the frame enters a switch, and the switch must determine the VLAN in which the frame arrived. Then, the Layer 2 switch forwards the frame out ports in that same VLAN only, or out trunk ports that support that VLAN.

Cisco switch ports operate either as an access port or a trunk port, and the type of port determines how the switch determines the incoming frame's VLAN. As an access port, the switch associates a single VLAN with the interface. Frames that arrive on an access port are assumed to be part of the access VLAN, which you configure using the **switchport access vlan** *vlan-id* interface subcommand. For trunk ports, the frame arrives with a VLAN tag as part of the trunking header; that tag identifies the VLAN ID.

Example 1-2 lists a couple of **show** commands that list switch interfaces and related VLAN information. The **show interfaces status** command lists all switch interfaces and their current status. It also lists either the interface's VLAN, if operating as an access port, or it lists the fact that the port is working as a trunk.

Example 1-2 *Displaying Interfaces and VLANs*

```
SW1# show interfaces status

Port       Name              Status       Vlan   Duplex  Speed Type
Fa0/1                        notconnect   1        auto    auto 10/100BaseTX
Fa0/2                        notconnect   1        auto    auto 10/100BaseTX
Fa0/3                        notconnect   1        auto    auto 10/100BaseTX
Fa0/4                        connected    1      a-full   a-100 10/100BaseTX
Fa0/5                        connected    1      a-full   a-100 10/100BaseTX
Fa0/6                        notconnect   1        auto    auto 10/100BaseTX
Fa0/7                        notconnect   1        auto    auto 10/100BaseTX
Fa0/8                        notconnect   1        auto    auto 10/100BaseTX
Fa0/9                        connected    10       auto    auto 10/100BaseTX
Fa0/10                       notconnect   1        auto    auto 10/100BaseTX
Fa0/11                       connected    1      a-full      10 10/100BaseTX
Fa0/12                       connected    10       half     100 10/100BaseTX
Fa0/13                       connected    1      a-full   a-100 10/100BaseTX
Fa0/14                       disabled     1        auto    auto 10/100BaseTX
```

```
Fa0/15                         connected    3          auto  auto 10/100BaseTX
Fa0/16                         connected    3        a-full   100 10/100BaseTX
Fa0/17                         connected    1        a-full a-100 10/100BaseTX
Fa0/18                         notconnect   1          auto  auto 10/100BaseTX
Fa0/19                         notconnect   1          auto  auto 10/100BaseTX
Fa0/20                         notconnect   1          auto  auto 10/100BaseTX
Fa0/21                         notconnect   1          auto  auto 10/100BaseTX
Fa0/22                         notconnect   1          auto  auto 10/100BaseTX
Fa0/23                         notconnect   1          auto  auto 10/100BaseTX
Fa0/24                         notconnect   1          auto  auto 10/100BaseTX
Gi0/1                          connected    trunk       full  1000 10/100/1000BaseTX
Gi0/2                          notconnect   1          auto  auto 10/100/1000BaseTX


SW1# show vlan brief

VLAN Name                         Status    Ports
---- ------------------------------ --------- -------------------------------
1    default                        active    Fa0/1, Fa0/2, Fa0/3, Fa0/4
                                              Fa0/5, Fa0/6, Fa0/7, Fa0/8
                                              Fa0/10, Fa0/11, Fa0/13, Fa0/14
                                              Fa0/17, Fa0/18, Fa0/19, Fa0/20
                                              Fa0/21, Fa0/22, Fa0/23, Fa0/24
                                              Gi0/2
3    VLAN0003                       active    Fa0/15, Fa0/16
10   WO-example                     active    Fa0/9, Fa0/12
1002 fddi-default                   act/unsup
1003 token-ring-default             act/unsup
1004 fddinet-default                act/unsup
1005 trnet-default                  act/unsup
```

The bottom of the example lists output from the **show vlan brief** command, which lists all VLANs, with a matching list of all access ports assigned to each VLAN. (Note that these commands match Figure 1-2, shown earlier.)

Taking a moment to think about STP's job again. STP has no impact on either of the commands in Example 1-2, either. For instance, with **show interfaces status**, STP does not change the VLAN assignments, change the trunking status, or change an interface's status from "connected" to something else. STP requires the use of commands that begin with **show spanning-tree**, with that information applied to all the usual information about interfaces, whether they are access or trunk links, and the VLANs they support.

Verifying Trunks

The final review topic lists the output of the one LAN switching command from the earlier discussions that does happen to show some direct evidence of STP: the **show interfaces trunk** command.

A Cisco switch interface will operate in VLAN trunking mode if configured correctly on both ends of the trunk. That trunk can support all VLANs known to the local switch. However, the trunk can choose to not forward frames for some VLANs, due to various switch features; one of those features is STP.

The **show interfaces trunk** command identifies a couple of important ideas. First, it lists only currently operational trunks; it does not list trunks that might negotiate trunking at some future time. It also lists the VLANs for which the switch currently forwards frames, in the last line of output for each port. Example 1-3 shows an example.

Example 1-3   **show interfaces trunk** *with Focus on the Last List of VLANs*

```
SW1# show interfaces trunk

Port       Mode         Encapsulation  Status       Native vlan
Gi0/1      desirable    802.1q         trunking     1


Port       Vlans allowed on trunk
Gi0/1      1-4094


Port       Vlans allowed and active in management domain
Gi0/1      1, 3, 10


Port       Vlans in spanning tree forwarding state and not pruned
Gi0/1      1, 3, 10
```

The output of this command lists four groups of messages. The first summarizes the list of operational trunks and their settings. The next three list the VLANs supported on each trunk, in progressively more restrictive lists. Any VLANs listed in the final list (highlighted) can be forwarded and received by that port. In this case, SW1's port Gi0/1 will forward frames for VLANs 1, 3, and 10, but for no others.

This command is important to STP because it lists some information directly impacted by STP. STP uses port states called forwarding and blocking, per VLAN. If STP blocks a port in a particular VLAN, that VLAN will not be in the final list at the bottom of the **show interfaces trunk** command. (Chapter 2, "Spanning Tree Protocol Implementation," which discusses STP configuration and verification, shows examples of STP blocking and the effects on this command.)

Spanning Tree Protocol (IEEE 802.1D)

Without Spanning Tree Protocol (STP), a LAN with redundant links would cause Ethernet frames to loop for an indefinite period of time. With STP enabled, some switches block ports so that these ports do not forward frames. STP intelligently chooses which ports block, with two goals in mind:

■ All devices in a VLAN can send frames to all other devices. In other words, STP does not block too many ports, cutting off some parts of the LAN from other parts.

■ Frames have a short life and do not loop around the network indefinitely.

STP strikes a balance, allowing frames to be delivered to each device, without causing the problems that occur when frames loop through the network over and over again.

STP prevents looping frames by adding an additional check on each interface before a switch uses it to send or receive user traffic. That check: If the port is in STP forwarding state in that VLAN, use it as normal; if it is in STP blocking state, however, block all user traffic and do not send or receive user traffic on that interface in that VLAN.

Note that these STP states do not change the other information you already know about switch interfaces. The interface's state of connected/notconnect does not change. The interface's operational state as either an access or trunk port does not change. STP adds this additional STP state, with the blocking state basically disabling the interface.

In many ways, those last two paragraphs sum up what STP does. However, the details of how STP does its work can take a fair amount of study and practice. This second major section of the chapter begins by explaining the need for STP and the basic ideas of what STP does to solve the problem of looping frames. The majority of this section then looks at how STP goes about choosing which switch ports to block to accomplish STP's goals.

The Need for Spanning Tree

STP prevents three common problems in Ethernet LANs that would occur if the LAN were to have redundant links and STP were not used. All three problems are actually side effects of the fact that without STP, some Ethernet frames would loop around the network for a long time (hours, days, literally forever if the LAN devices and links never failed).

Just one frame that loops around a network causes what is called a broadcast storm. Broadcast storms happen when broadcast frames, multicast frames, or unknown-destination unicast frames loop around a LAN indefinitely. Broadcast storms can saturate all the links with copies of that one single frame, crowding out good frames, as well as significantly impacting end-user PC performance by making the PCs process too many broadcast frames.

To help you understand how this occurs, Figure 1-3 shows a sample network in which Bob sends a broadcast frame. The dashed lines show how the switches forward the frame when STP does not exist.

NOTE   Bob's original broadcast would also be forwarded around the other direction as well, with SW3 sending a copy of the original frame out its Gi0/1 port. The figure does not show that frame just to reduce the clutter.

Remember that LAN switch logic that was reviewed earlier in the chapter? That logic tells switches to flood broadcasts out all interfaces in the same VLAN except the interface in which the frame arrived. In the figure, that means SW3 forwards Bob's frame to SW2, SW2 forwards the frame to SW1, SW1 forwards the frame back to SW3, and SW3 forwards it back to SW2 again.

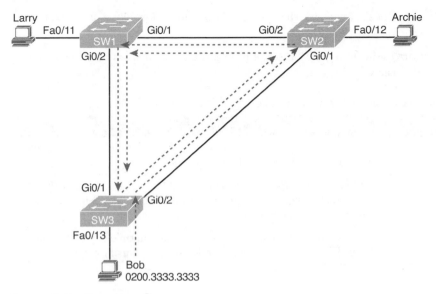

Figure 1-3 *Broadcast Storm*

When broadcast storms happen, frames like the one in Figure 1-3 keep looping until something changes—someone shuts down an interface, reloads a switch, or does something else to break the loop. Also note that the same event happens in the opposite direction. When Bob sends the original frame, SW3 also forwards a copy to SW1, SW1 forwards it to SW2, and so on.

Looping frames also cause a MAC table instability problem. MAC table instability means that the switches' MAC address tables keep changing the information listed for the source MAC address of the looping frame. For example, SW3 begins Figure 1-3 with a MAC table entry for Bob, at the bottom of the figure, as follows:

   0200.3333.3333   Fa0/13   VLAN 1

However, now think about the switch-learning process that occurs when the looping frame goes to SW2, then SW1, and then back into SW3's Gi0/1 interface. SW3 thinks, "Hmm… the source MAC address is 0200.3333.3333, and it came in my Gi0/1 interface. Update my MAC table!" resulting in the following entry on SW3:

   0200.3333.3333   Gi0/1   VLAN 1

At this point, SW3 itself cannot correctly deliver frames to Bob's MAC address. At that instant, if a frame arrives at SW3 destined for Bob—a different frame than the looping frame that causes the problems—SW3 incorrectly forwards the frame out Gi0/1 to SW1.

The looping frames also cause a third problem: multiple copies of the frame arrive at the destination. Consider a case in which Bob sends a frame to Larry but none of the switches know Larry's MAC address. Switches flood frames sent to unknown destination unicast MAC addresses. When Bob sends the frame destined for Larry's MAC address, SW3 sends a copy to both SW1 and SW2. SW1 and SW2 also flood the frame, causing copies of the frame to loop. SW1 also sends a copy of each frame out Fa0/11 to Larry. As a result, Larry gets multiple copies of the frame, which may result in an application failure, if not more pervasive networking problems.

Table 1-2 summarizes the main three classes of problems that occur when STP is not used in a LAN with redundancy.

Table 1-2   Three Classes of Problems Caused by Not Using STP in Redundant LANs

Problem	Description
Broadcast storms	The forwarding of a frame repeatedly on the same links, consuming significant parts of the links' capacities
MAC table instability	The continual updating of a switch's MAC address table with incorrect entries, in reaction to looping frames, resulting in frames being sent to the wrong locations
Multiple frame transmission	A side effect of looping frames in which multiple copies of one frame are delivered to the intended host, confusing the host

What IEEE 802.1D Spanning Tree Does

STP prevents loops by placing each switch port in either a forwarding state or a blocking state. Interfaces in the forwarding state act as normal, forwarding and receiving frames. However, interfaces in a blocking state do not process any frames except STP messages (and some other overhead messages). Interfaces that block do not forward user frames, do not learn MAC addresses of received frames, and do not process received user frames.

Figure 1-4 shows a simple STP tree that solves the problem shown in Figure 1-3 by placing one port on SW3 in the blocking state.

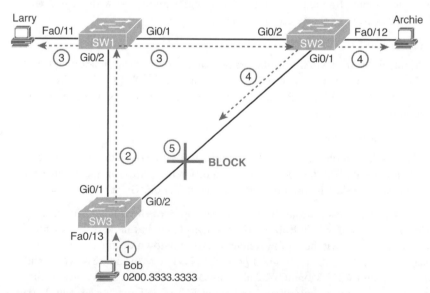

Figure 1-4   *What STP Does: Blocks a Port to Break the Loop*

Now when Bob sends a broadcast frame, the frame does not loop. As shown in the steps in the figure:

Step 1.   Bob sends the frame to SW3.

Step 2.   SW3 forwards the frame only to SW1, but not out Gi0/2 to SW2, because SW3's Gi0/2 interface is in a blocking state.

Step 3.   SW1 floods the frame out both Fa0/11 and Gi0/1.

Step 4.   SW2 floods the frame out Fa0/12 and Gi0/1.

Step 5.   SW3 physically receives the frame, but it ignores the frame received from SW2 because SW3's Gi0/2 interface is in a blocking state.

With the STP topology in Figure 1-4, the switches simply do not use the link between SW2 and SW3 for traffic in this VLAN, which is the minor negative side effect of STP. However, if either of the other two links fails, STP converges so that SW3 forwards instead of blocks on its Gi0/2 interface.

NOTE   The term *STP convergence* refers to the process by which the switches collectively realize that something has changed in the LAN topology and so the switches might need to change which ports block and which ports forward.

That completes the description of what STP does, placing each port into either a forwarding or blocking state. The more interesting question, and the one that takes a lot more work to understand, is the question of how and why STP makes its choices. How does STP manage to make switches block or forward on each interface? And how does it converge to change state from blocking to forwarding to take advantage of redundant links in response to network outages? The following sections answer these questions.

How Spanning Tree Works

The STP algorithm creates a spanning tree of interfaces that forward frames. The tree structure of forwarding interfaces creates a single path to and from each Ethernet link, just like you can trace a single path in a living, growing tree from the base of the tree to each leaf.

NOTE   STP was created before LAN switches even existed. In those days, Ethernet bridges used STP. Today, switches play the same role as bridges, implementing STP. However, many STP terms still refer to bridge. For the purposes of STP and this chapter, consider the terms *bridge* and *switch* synonymous.

The process used by STP, sometimes called the *spanning-tree algorithm* (STA), chooses the interfaces that should be placed into a forwarding state. For any interfaces not chosen to be in a forwarding state, STP places the interfaces in blocking state. In other words, STP simply picks which interfaces should forward, and any interfaces left over go to a blocking state.

STP uses three criteria to choose whether to put an interface in forwarding state:

■ STP elects a root switch. STP puts all working interfaces on the root switch in forwarding state.

■ Each nonroot switch considers one of its ports to have the least administrative cost between itself and the root switch. The cost is called that switch's *root cost*. STP places its port that is part of the least root cost path, called that switch's *root port* (RP), in forwarding state.

■ Many switches can attach to the same Ethernet segment, but in modern networks, normally two switches connect to each link. The switch with the lowest root cost, as compared with the other switches attached to the same link, is placed in forwarding state. That switch is the designated switch, and that switch's interface, attached to that segment, is called the *designated port* (DP).

NOTE   The real reason the root switches places all working interfaces in a forwarding state is that all its interfaces will become DPs, but it is easier to just remember that all the root switches' working interfaces will forward frames.

All other interfaces are placed in blocking state. Table 1-3 summarizes the reasons STP places a port in forwarding or blocking state.

Table 1-3   STP: Reasons for Forwarding or Blocking

Characterization of Port	STP State	Description
All the root switch's ports	Forwarding	The root switch is always the designated switch on all connected segments.
Each nonroot switch's root port	Forwarding	The port through which the switch has the least cost to reach the root switch (lowest root cost).
Each LAN's designated port	Forwarding	The switch forwarding the hello on to the segment, with the lowest root cost, is the designated switch for that segment.
All other working ports	Blocking	The port is not used for forwarding user frames, nor are any frames received on these interfaces considered for forwarding.

NOTE   STP only considers working interfaces (those in a connected state). Failed interfaces (for example, interfaces with no cable installed) or administratively shutdown interfaces are instead placed into an STP disabled state. So, this section uses the term *working ports* to refer to interfaces that could forward frames if STP placed the interface into a forwarding state.

The STP Bridge ID and Hello BPDU

The STA begins with an election of one switch to be the root switch. To better understand this election process, you need to understand the STP messages sent between switches as well as the concept and format of the identifier used to uniquely identify each switch.

The STP bridge ID (BID) is an 8-byte value unique to each switch. The bridge ID consists of a 2-byte priority field and a 6-byte system ID, with the system ID being based on a universal (burned-in) MAC address in each switch. Using a burned-in MAC address ensures that each switch's bridge ID will be unique.

STP defines messages called *bridge protocol data units* (BPDU), which switches use to exchange information with each other. The most common BPDU, called a hello BPDU, lists many details, including the sending switch's BID. By listing its own unique BID, switches can tell which switch sent which hello BPDU. Table 1-4 lists some of the key information in the hello BPDU.

Table 1-4   Fields in the STP Hello BPDU

Field	Description
Root bridge ID	The bridge ID of the switch the sender of this hello currently believes to be the root switch
Sender's bridge ID	The bridge ID of the switch sending this hello BPDU
Sender's root cost	The STP cost between this switch and the current root
Timer values on the root switch	Includes the hello timer, MaxAge timer, and forward delay timer

For the time being, just keep the first three items from Table 1-4 in mind as the following sections work through the three steps in how STP chooses the interfaces to place into a forwarding state. Next, the text examines the three main steps in the STP process.

Electing the Root Switch

Switches elect a root switch based on the BIDs in the BPDUs. The root switch is the switch with the lowest numeric value for the BID. Because the two-part BID starts with the priority value, essentially the switch with the lowest priority becomes the root. For example, if one switch has priority 4096, and another switch has priority 8192, the switch with priority 4096 wins, regardless of what MAC address was used to create the BID for each switch.

If a tie occurs based on the priority portion of the BID, the switch with the lowest MAC address portion of the BID is the root. No other tiebreaker should be needed because switches use one of their own universal (burned-in) MAC addresses as the second part of their BIDs. So if the priorities tie, and one switch uses a MAC address of 0200.0000.0000 as part of the BID and the other uses 0911.1111.1111, the first switch (MAC 0200.0000.0000) becomes the root switch.

STP elects a root switch in a manner not unlike a political election. The process begins with all switches claiming to be the root by sending hello BPDUs listing their own BID as the root BID. If a switch hears a hello that lists a better (lower) BID, that switch stops advertising itself as root and starts forwarding the superior hello. The hello sent by the better switch lists the better switch's BID as the root. It works like a political race in which a less-popular candidate gives up and leaves the race, throwing his support behind the more popular candidate. Eventually, everyone agrees which switch has the best (lowest) BID, and everyone supports the elected switch—which is where the political race analogy falls apart.

> **NOTE**   A better hello, meaning that the listed root's BID is better (numerically lower), is called a *superior hello*; a worse hello, meaning that the listed root's BID is not as good (numerically higher), is called an *inferior hello*.

Figure 1-5 shows the beginning of the root election process. In this case, SW1 has advertised itself as root, as have SW2 and SW3. However, SW2 now believes that SW1 is a better root, so SW2 is now forwarding the hello originating at SW1. So, at this point, the figure shows SW1 is saying hello, claiming to be root; SW2 agrees, and is forwarding SW1's hello that lists SW1 as root; but, SW3 is still claiming to be best, sending his own hello BPDUs, listing SW3's BID as the root.

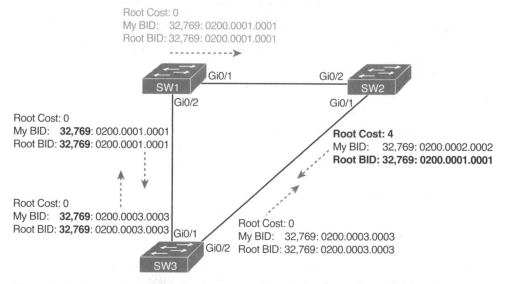

Figure 1-5   *Beginnings of the Root Election Process*

Two candidates still exist in Figure 1-5: SW1 and SW3. So who wins? Well, from the BID, the lower-priority switch wins; if a tie occurs, the lower MAC address wins. As shown in the figure, SW1 has a lower BID (32769:0200.0000.0001) than SW3 (32769:0200.0003.0003), so SW1 wins, and SW3 now also believes that SW1 is the better switch. Figure 1-6 shows the resulting hello messages sent by the switches.

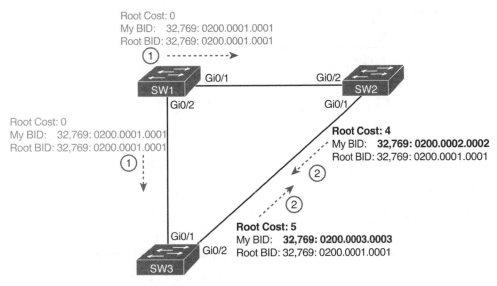

Figure 1-6 *SW1 Wins the Election*

After the election is complete, only the root switch continues to originate STP hello BPDU messages. The other switches receive the hellos, update the sender's BID field (and root cost field), and forward the hellos out other interfaces. The figure reflects this fact, with SW1 sending hellos at Step 1, and SW2 and SW3 independently forwarding the hello out their other interfaces at Step 2.

Summarizing, the root election happens through each switch claiming to be root, with the best switch being elected based on the numerically lowest BID. Breaking down the BID into its components, the comparisons can be made as

- The lowest bridge ID
- If that ties, the lowest switch MAC address

Choosing Each Switch's Root Port

The second part of the STP process occurs when each nonroot switch chooses its one and only *root port*. A switch's RP is its interface through which it has the least STP cost to reach the root switch (least root cost).

The idea of a switch's cost to reach the root switch can be easily seen for humans. Just look at a network diagram that shows the root switch, lists the STP cost associated with each switch port, and the nonroot switch in question. Switches use a different process than looking at a network diagram, of course, but using a diagram can make it easier to learn the idea.

Figure 1-7 shows just such a figure, with the same three switches shown in the last several figures. SW1 has already won the election as root, and the figure considers the cost from SW3's perspective.

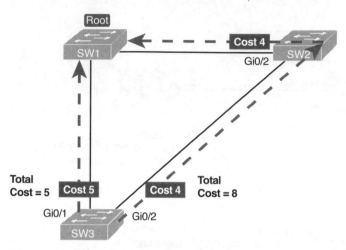

Figure 1-7 *How a Human Might Calculate STP Cost from SW3 to the Root (SW1)*

SW3 has two possible physical paths to send frames to the root switch: the direct path to the left, and the indirect path to the right through switch SW2. The cost is the sum of the costs of all the *switch ports the frame would exit* if it flowed over that path. (The calculation ignores the inbound ports.) As you can see, the cost over the direct path out SW3's G0/1 port has a total cost of 5, and the other path has a total cost of 8. SW3 picks its G0/1 port as root port because it is the port that is part of the least-cost path to send frames to the root switch.

Switches come to the same conclusion, but using a different process. Instead, they add their local interface STP cost to the root cost listed in each received hello BPDU. The STP port cost is simply an integer value assigned to each interface, per VLAN, for the purpose of providing an objective measurement that allows STP to choose which interfaces to add to the STP topology. The switches also look at their neighbor's root cost, as announced in hello BPDUs received from each neighbor.

Figure 1-8 shows an example of how switches calculate their best root cost and then choose their root port, using the same topology and STP costs as shown in Figure 1-7. STP on SW3 calculates its cost to reach the root over the two possible paths by adding the advertised cost (in hello messages) to the interface costs listed in the figure.

Focus on the process for a moment. The root switch sends hellos, with a listed root cost of 0. The idea is that the root's cost to reach itself is 0.

Next, look on the left of the figure. SW3 takes the received cost (0) from the hello sent by SW1, adds the interface cost (5) of the interface on which that hello was received. SW3 calculates that the cost to reach the root switch, out that port (G0/1), is 5.

On the right side, SW2 has realized its best cost to reach the root is cost 4. So, when SW2 forwards the hello toward SW3, SW2 lists a root cost 4. SW3's STP port cost on port G0/2 is 4, so SW3 determines a total cost to reach root out its G0/2 port of 8.

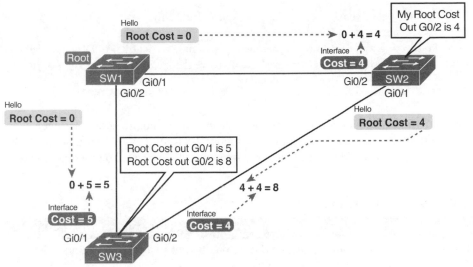

Figure 1-8 *How STP Actually Calculates the Cost from SW3 to the Root*

As a result of the process depicted in Figure 1-8, SW3 chooses Gi0/1 as its RP, because the cost to reach the root switch through that port (5) is lower than the other alternative (Gi0/2, cost 8). Similarly, SW2 chooses Gi0/2 as its RP, with a cost of 4 (SW1's advertised cost of 0 plus SW2's Gi0/2 interface cost of 4). Each switch places its root port into a forwarding state.

In more complex topologies, the choice of root port will not be so obvious. The section "STP Troubleshooting" in Chapter 2 discusses these more complex examples, including the tiebreakers to use if the root costs tie.

Choosing the Designated Port on Each LAN Segment

STP's final step to choose the STP topology is to choose the designated port on each LAN segment. The designated port (DP) on each LAN segment is the switch port that advertises the lowest-cost hello onto a LAN segment. When a nonroot switch forwards a hello, the nonroot switch sets the root cost field in the hello to that switch's cost to reach the root. In effect, the switch with the lower cost to reach the root, among all switches connected to a segment, becomes the DP on that segment.

For example, earlier Figure 1-6 shows in bold text the parts of the hello messages from both SW2 and SW3 that determine the choice of DP on that segment. Note that both SW2 and SW3 list their respective cost to reach the root switch (cost 4 on SW2 and cost 5 on SW3). SW2 lists the lower cost, so SW2's Gi0/1 port is the designated port on that LAN segment.

All DPs are placed into a forwarding state; so in this case, SW2's Gi0/1 interface will be in a forwarding state.

If the advertised costs tie, the switches break the tie by choosing the switch with the lower BID. In this case, SW2 would also have won, with a BID of 32769:0200.0002.0002 versus SW3's 32769:0200.0003.0003.

NOTE   Two additional tiebreakers are needed in some cases, although these would be unlikely today. A single switch can connect two or more interfaces to the same collision domain by connecting to a hub. In that case, the one switch hears its own BPDUs. So, if a switch ties with itself, two additional tiebreakers are used: the lowest interface STP priority and, if that ties, the lowest internal interface number.

The only interface that does not have a reason to be in a forwarding state on the three switches in the examples shown in Figures 1-5 through 1-8 is SW3's Gi0/2 port. So, the STP process is now complete. Table 1-5 outlines the state of each port and shows why it is in that state.

Table 1-5   State of Each Interface

Switch Interface	State	Reason Why the Interface Is in Forwarding State
SW1, Gi0/1	Forwarding	The interface is on the root switch, so it becomes the DP on that link.
SW1, Gi0/2	Forwarding	The interface is on the root switch, so it becomes the DP on that link.
SW2, Gi0/2	Forwarding	The root port of SW2.
SW2, Gi0/1	Forwarding	The designated port on the LAN segment to SW3.
SW3, Gi0/1	Forwarding	The root port of SW3.
SW3, Gi0/2	Blocking	Not the root port and not the designated port.

Influencing and Changing the STP Topology

Switches do not just use STP once and never again. The switches continually watch for changes. Those changes can be because a link or switch fails or it can be a new link that can now be used. The configuration can change in a way that changes the STP topology. This section briefly discusses the kinds of things that change the STP topology, either through configuration or through changes in the status of devices and links in the LAN.

Making Configuration Changes to Influence the STP Topology

The network engineers can choose to change the STP settings to then change the choices STP makes in a given LAN. Two main tools available to the engineer are to configure the bridge ID and to change STP port costs.

Switches have a way to create a default BID, by taking a default priority value, and adding a universal MAC address that comes with the switch hardware. However, engineers typically want to choose which switch becomes the root. Chapter 2 shows how to configure a Cisco switch to override its default BID setting to make a switch become root.

Port costs also have default values, per port, per VLAN. You can configure these port costs, or you can use the default values. Table 1-6 lists the default port costs defined by IEEE; Cisco uses these same defaults.

Table 1-6   Default Port Costs According to IEEE

Ethernet Speed	IEEE Cost
10 Mbps	100
100 Mbps	19
1 Gbps	4
10 Gbps	2

With STP enabled, all working switch interfaces will settle into an STP forwarding or block-ing state, even access ports. For switch interfaces connected to hosts or routers, which do not use STP, the switch still forwards hellos on to those interfaces. By virtue of being the only device sending a hello onto that LAN segment, the switch is sending the least-cost hello on to that LAN segment, making the switch become the designated port on that LAN seg-ment. So, STP puts working access interfaces into a forwarding state as a result of the desig-nated port part of the STP process.

Reacting to State Changes That Affect the STP Topology

Once the engineer has finished all STP configuration, the STP topology should settle into a stable state and not change, at least until the network topology changes. This section exam-ines the ongoing operation of STP while the network is stable, and then it covers how STP converges to a new topology when something changes.

The root switch sends a new hello BPDU every 2 seconds by default. Each nonroot switch forwards the hello on all DPs, but only after changing items listed in the hello. The switch sets the root cost to that local switch's calculated root cost. The switch also sets the "send-er's bridge ID" field to its own bridge ID. (The root's bridge ID field is not changed.)

By forwarding the received (and changed) hellos out all DPs, all switches continue to receive hellos every 2 seconds. The following steps summarize the steady-state operation when noth-ing is currently changing in the STP topology:

Step 1.   The root creates and sends a hello BPDU, with a root cost of 0, out all its work-ing interfaces (those in a forwarding state).

Step 2.   The nonroot switches receive the hello on their root ports. After changing the hello to list their own BID as the sender's BID, and listing that switch's root cost, the switch forwards the hello out all designated ports.

Step 3.   Steps 1 and 2 repeat until something changes.

Each switch relies on these periodic received hellos from the root as a way to know that its path to the root is still working. When a switch ceases to receive the hellos, or receives a hello that lists different details, something has failed, so the switch reacts and starts the pro-cess of changing the spanning-tree topology.

How Switches React to Changes with STP

For various reasons, the convergence process requires the use of three timers. Note that all switches use the timers as dictated by the root switch, which the root lists in its periodic hello BPDU messages. Table 1-7 describes the timers.

Table 1-7   STP Timers

Timer	Description	Default Value
Hello	The time period between hellos created by the root.	2 seconds
MaxAge	How long any switch should wait, after ceasing to hear hellos, before trying to change the STP topology.	10 times hello
Forward delay	Delay that affects the process that occurs when an interface changes from blocking state to forwarding state. A port stays in an interim listening state, and then an interim learning state, for the number of seconds defined by the forward delay timer.	15 seconds

If a switch does not get an expected hello BPDU within the hello time, the switch continues as normal. However, if the hellos do not show up again within MaxAge time, the switch reacts by taking steps to change the STP topology. With default settings, MaxAge is 20 seconds (10 times the default hello timer of 2 seconds). So, a switch would go 20 seconds without hearing a hello before reacting.

After MaxAge expires, the switch essentially makes all its STP choices again, based on any hellos it receives from other switches. It reevaluates which switch should be the root switch. If the local switch is not the root, it chooses its RP. And it determines whether it is DP on each of its other links. The best way to describe STP convergence is to show an example using the same familiar topology. Figure 1-9 shows the same familiar figure, with SW3's Gi0/2 in a blocking state, but SW1's Gi0/2 interface has just failed.

SW3 reacts to the change because SW3 fails to receive its expected hellos on its Gi0/1 interface. However, SW2 does not need to react because SW2 continues to receive its periodic hellos in its Gi0/2 interface. In this case, SW3 reacts either when MaxAge time passes without hearing the hellos, or as soon as SW3 notices that interface Gi0/1 has failed. (If the interface fails, the switch can assume that the hellos will not be arriving in that interface anymore.)

Now that SW3 can act, it begins by reevaluating the choice of root switch. SW3 still receives the hellos from SW2, as forwarded from the root (SW1). SW1 still has a lower BID than SW3; otherwise, SW1 would not have already been the root. So, SW3 decides that SW1 is still the best switch and that SW3 is not the root.

Next, SW3 reevaluates its choice of RP. At this point, SW3 is receiving hellos on only one interface: Gi0/2. Whatever the calculated root cost, Gi0/2 becomes SW3's new RP. (The cost would be 8, assuming the STP costs had no changes since Figures 1-7 and 1-8.)

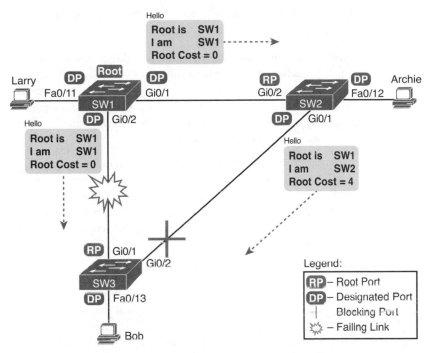

Figure 1-9 *Initial STP State Before SW1-SW3 Link Fails*

SW3 then reevaluates its role as DP on any other interfaces. In this example, no real work needs to be done. SW3 was already DP on interface Fa0/13, and it continues to be the DP because no other switches connect to that port.

Changing Interface States with STP

STP uses the idea of roles and states. Roles, like root port and designated port, relate to how STP analyzes the LAN topology. States, like forwarding and blocking, tell a switch whether to send or receive frames. When STP converges, a switch chooses new port roles, and the port roles determine the state (forwarding or blocking).

Switches can simply move immediately from forwarding to blocking state, but they must take extra time to transition from blocking state to forwarding state. For instance, when a switch formerly used port G0/1 as its RP (a role), that port was in a forwarding state. After convergence, G0/1 might be neither an RP nor DP; the switch can immediately move that port to a blocking state.

When a port that formerly blocked needs to transition to forwarding, the switch first puts the port through two intermediate interface states. These temporary states help prevent temporary loops:

- **Listening:** Like the blocking state, the interface does not forward frames. The switch removes old stale (unused) MAC table entries for which no frames are received from each MAC address during this period. These stale MAC table entries could be the cause of the temporary loops.

■ **Learning:** Interfaces in this state still do not forward frames, but the switch begins to learn the MAC addresses of frames received on the interface.

STP moves an interface from blocking to listening, then to learning, and then to forwarding state. STP leaves the interface in each interim state for a time equal to the forward delay timer, which defaults to 15 seconds. As a result, a convergence event that causes an interface to change from blocking to forwarding requires 30 seconds to transition from blocking to forwarding. In addition, a switch might have to wait MaxAge seconds before even choosing to move an interface from blocking to forwarding state.

For example, follow what happens with an initial STP topology as shown in Figures 1-5 through 1-8, with the SW1-to-SW3 link failing as shown in Figure 1-9. If SW1 simply quit sending hello messages to SW3, but the link between the two did not fail, SW3 would wait MaxAge seconds before reacting (20 seconds is the default). SW3 would actually quickly choose its ports' STP roles, but then wait 15 seconds each in listening and learning states on interface Gi0/2, resulting in a 50-second convergence delay.

Table 1-8 summarizes spanning tree's various interface states for easier review.

Table 1-8   IEEE 802.1D Spanning-Tree States

State	Forwards Data Frames?	Learns MACs Based on Received Frames?	Transitory or Stable State?
Blocking	No	No	Stable
Listening	No	No	Transitory
Learning	No	Yes	Transitory
Forwarding	Yes	Yes	Stable
Disabled	No	No	Stable

Optional STP Features

STP has been around for more than 30 years, first being used even before the IEEE took over the development of Ethernet standards from Xerox and other vendors. The IEEE first standardized STP as IEEE 802.1D back in the 1980s. Cisco switches today still use STP. And other than changes to the default cost values, the description of STP in this chapter so far works like the original STP as created all those years ago.

Even with such an amazingly long life, STP has gone through several changes over these decades, some small, some large. For instance, Cisco added proprietary features to make improvements to STP. In some cases, the IEEE added these same improvements, or something like them, to later IEEE standards, whether as a revision of the 802.1D standard or as an additional standard. And STP has gone through one major revision that improves convergence, called the *Rapid Spanning Tree Protocol* (RSTP), as originally defined in IEEE 802.1w.

This final of three major sections of this chapter briefly discusses the basics of several of these optional features that go beyond the base 802.1D STP concepts, including EtherChannel, PortFast, and BPDU Guard.

EtherChannel

One of the best ways to lower STP's convergence time is to avoid convergence altogether. EtherChannel provides a way to prevent STP convergence from being needed when only a single port or cable failure occurs.

EtherChannel combines multiple parallel segments of equal speed (up to eight) between the same pair of switches, bundled into an EtherChannel. The switches treat the EtherChannel as a single interface with regard to STP. As a result, if one of the links fails, but at least one of the links is up, STP convergence does not have to occur. For example, Figure 1-10 shows the familiar three-switch network, but now with two Gigabit Ethernet connections between each pair of switches.

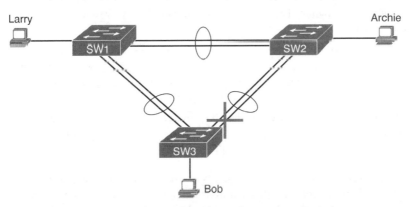

Figure 1-10   *Two-Segment EtherChannels Between Switches*

With each pair of Ethernet links configured as an EtherChannel, STP treats each EtherChannel as a single link. In other words, both links to the same switch must fail for a switch to need to cause STP convergence. Without EtherChannel, if you have multiple parallel links between two switches, STP blocks all the links except one. With EtherChannel, all the parallel links can be up and working at the same time, while reducing the number of times STP must converge, which in turn makes the network more available.

When a switch makes a forwarding decision to send a frame out an EtherChannel, the switch then has to take an extra step in logic: Out which physical interface does it send the frame? The switches have load-balancing logic that let it pick an interface for each frame, with a goal of spreading the traffic load across all active links in the channel. As a result, a LAN design that uses EtherChannels makes much better use of the available bandwidth between switches, while also reducing the number of times that STP must converge.

PortFast

PortFast allows a switch to immediately transition from blocking to forwarding, bypassing listening and learning states. However, the only ports on which you can safely enable

PortFast are ports on which you know that no bridges, switches, or other STP-speaking devices are connected. Otherwise, using PortFast risks creating loops, the very thing that the listening and learning states are intended to avoid.

PortFast is most appropriate for connections to end-user devices. If you turn on PortFast on ports connected to end-user devices, when an end-user PC boots, the switch port can move to an STP forwarding state and forward traffic as soon as the PC NIC is active. Without PortFast, each port must wait while the switch confirms that the port is a DP, and then wait while the interface sits in the temporary listening and learning states before settling into the forwarding state.

BPDU Guard

STP opens up the LAN to several different types of possible security exposures. For example:

- An attacker could connect a switch to one of these ports, one with a low STP priority value, and become the root switch. The new STP topology could have worse performance than the desired topology.
- The attacker could plug into multiple ports, into multiple switches, become root, and actually forward much of the traffic in the LAN. Without the networking staff realizing it, the attacker could use a LAN analyzer to copy large numbers of data frames sent through the LAN.
- Users could innocently harm the LAN when they buy and connect an inexpensive consumer LAN switch (one that does not use STP). Such a switch, without any STP function, would not choose to block any ports and would likely cause a loop.

The Cisco BPDU Guard feature helps defeat these kinds of problems by disabling a port if any BPDUs are received on the port. So, this feature is particularly useful on ports that should be used only as an access port and never connected to another switch.

In addition, the BPDU Guard feature helps prevent problems with PortFast. PortFast should be enabled only on access ports that connect to user devices, not to other LAN switches. Using BPDU Guard on these same ports makes sense because if another switch connects to such a port, the local switch can disable the port before a loop is created.

Rapid STP (IEEE 802.1w)

As mentioned earlier in this chapter, the IEEE defines STP in the 802.1D IEEE standard. The IEEE has improved the 802.1D protocol with the definition of Rapid Spanning Tree Protocol (RSTP), as defined in standard 802.1w.

RSTP (802.1w) works just like STP (802.1D) in several ways:

- It elects the root switch using the same parameters and tiebreakers.
- It elects the root port on nonroot switches with the same rules.
- It elects designated ports on each LAN segment with the same rules.
- It places each port in either forwarding or blocking state, although RSTP calls the blocking state the discarding state.

RSTP can be deployed alongside traditional 802.1D STP switches, with RSTP features working in switches that support it, and traditional 802.1D STP features working in the switches that support only STP.

With all these similarities, you might be wondering why the IEEE bothered to create RSTP in the first place. The overriding reason is convergence. STP takes a relatively long time to converge (50 seconds with the default settings). RSTP improves network convergence when topology changes occur, usually converging within a few seconds, or in poor conditions, in about 10 seconds.

In real life, most enterprise LANs use designs that require STP, and most of those prefer to use RSTP because of the better convergence. However, with the current exams, Cisco defers the deeper discussion of RSTP until the CCNP Switch exam and the CCNP certification. For those of you working with LAN switching for work, make sure to look further at 802.1w/RSTP and how to implement it in your switches.

Exam Preparation Tasks

Review All the Key Topics

Review the most important topics from this chapter, noted with the Key Topic icon. Table 1-9 lists these key topics and where each is discussed.

Table 1-9   Key Topics for Chapter 1

Key Topic Element	Description	Page Number
List	Summary of LAN switch's forwarding logic	17
Table 1-2	Lists the three main problems that occur when not using STP in a LAN with redundant links	24
Table 1-3	Lists the reasons why a switch chooses to place an interface into forwarding or blocking state	26
Table 1-4	Lists the most important fields in hello BPDU messages	27
List	Logic for the root switch election	29
Figure 1-8	Shows how switches calculate their root cost	31
Table 1-6	Lists the original and current default STP port costs for various interface speeds	33
Step list	A summary description of steady-state STP operations	33
Table 1-7	STP timers	34
List	Definitions of what occurs in the listening and learning states	35
Table 1-8	Summary of 802.1D states	36

Complete the Tables and Lists from Memory

Print a copy of DVD Appendix D, "Memory Tables," or at least the section for this chapter, and complete the tables and lists from memory. DVD Appendix E, "Memory Tables Answer Key," includes completed tables and lists to check your work.

Definitions of Key Terms

After your first reading of the chapter, try to define these key terms, but do not be concerned about getting them all correct at that time. Chapter 22, "Final Review," directs you in how to use these terms for late-stage preparation for the exam.

blocking state, BPDU Guard, bridge ID, bridge protocol data unit (BPDU), designated port, EtherChannel, forward delay, forwarding state, hello BPDU, IEEE 802.1D, learning state, listening state, MaxAge, PortFast, root port, root switch, root cost, Spanning Tree Protocol (STP)

This chapter covers the following exam topics:

LAN Switching Technologies

Configure and verify PVSTP operation

Describe root bridge election

Spanning-tree mode

Troubleshooting

Troubleshoot and resolve spanning-tree operation issues

Root switch

Priority

Mode is correct

Port states

Troubleshoot EtherChannel problems

CHAPTER 2

Spanning Tree Protocol Implementation

Cisco LAN switches enable Spanning Tree Protocol (STP) by default on all interfaces in every VLAN. However, network engineers who work with medium-size to large-size Ethernet LANs usually want to configure at least some STP settings, with the goal of influencing the choices made by STP. For instance, a network engineer configures so that, when all switches and links work, the engineer knows which switch is the root and which ports block. The configuration can also be set so that when links or switches fail, the engineer can predict the STP topology in those cases, as well.

This chapter discusses the configuration options for STP, assuming the switches use 802.1D STP. The first major section weaves a story of how to change different settings, per VLAN, with the **show** commands that reveal the current STP status affected by each configuration command. The second major section of this chapter looks at how to troubleshoot STP, which includes a deeper examination of the STP rules discussed in Chapter 1, "Spanning Tree Protocol Concepts," plus more discussion of various switch **show** commands.

"Do I Know This Already?" Quiz

Use the "Do I Know This Already?" quiz to help decide whether you might want to skim this chapter, or a major section, moving more quickly to the "Exam Preparation Tasks" section near the end of the chapter. You can find the answers at the bottom of the page following the quiz. For thorough explanations, see DVD Appendix C, "Answers to the 'Do I Know This Already?' Quizzes."

Table 2-1   "Do I Know This Already?" Foundation Topics Section-to-Question Mapping

Foundation Topics Section	Questions
STP Configuration and Verification	1–4
STP Troubleshooting	5–6

1. On a 2960 switch, which of the following commands change the value of the bridge ID? (Choose two answers.)

   a. **spanning-tree bridge-id** *value*

   b. **spanning-tree vlan** *vlan-number* **root {primary | secondary}**

   c. **spanning-tree vlan** *vlan-number* **priority** *value*

   d. **set spanning-tree priority** *value*

2. Examine the following extract from the **show spanning-tree** command on a Cisco switch:

   ```
   Bridge ID  Priority    32771  (priority 32768 sys-id-ext 3)
              Address     0019.e86a.6f80
   ```

   Which of the following answers is true about the switch on which this command output was gathered?

   a. The information is about the STP instance for VLAN 1.

   b. The information is about the STP instance for VLAN 3.

   c. The command output confirms that this switch cannot possibly be the root switch.

   d. The command output confirms that this switch is currently the root switch.

3. A switch's G0/1 interface, a trunk that supports VLANs 1-10, has autonegotiated a speed of 100 Mbps. The switch currently has all default settings for STP. Which of the following actions results in the switch using a STP cost of 19 for that interface in VLAN 3? (Choose two answers.)

   a. **spanning-tree cost 19**

   b. **spanning-tree port-cost 19**

   c. **spanning-tree vlan 3 port-cost 19**

   d. Adding no configuration

4. An engineer configures a switch to put interfaces G0/1 and G0/2 into the same EtherChannel. Which of the following terms is used in the configuration commands?

   a. EtherChannel

   b. PortChannel

   c. Ethernet-Channel

   d. Channel-group

5. Switch SW3 is receiving only two hello BPDUs, both of which identify the same root switch, received on the two interfaces listed as follows:

```
SW3# show interfaces status
Port        Name     Status       Vlan     Duplex     Speed     Type
Fa0/13               connected    1        a-half     a-100     10/100BaseTX
Gi0/1                connected    1        a-full     a-1000    1000BaseTX
```

SW3 has no STP-related configuration commands. The hello received on Fa0/13 lists root cost 10, and the hello received on Gi0/1 lists root cost 20. Which of the following is true about STP on SW3?

a. SW3 will choose Fa0/13 as its root port.

b. SW3 will choose Gi0/1 as its root port.

c. SW3's Fa0/13 will become a designated port.

d. SW3's Gi0/1 will become a designated port.

6. Which of the following commands lists a nonroot switch's root cost? (Choose two answers.)

a. show spanning-tree root

b. show spanning-tree root-cost

c. show spanning-tree bridge

d. show spanning-tree

Foundation Topics

STP Configuration and Verification

Cisco switches usually use STP (IEEE 802.1D) by default. You can buy some Cisco switches and connect them with Ethernet cables in a redundant topology, and STP will ensure that frames do not loop. And you never even have to think about changing any settings!

Although STP works without any configuration, most medium-size to large-size campus LANs benefit from some STP configuration. With all defaults, the switches choose the root based on the lowest burned-in MAC address on the switches because they all default to use the same STP priority. As a better option, configure the switches so that the root is predictable.

For instance, Figure 2-1 shows a typical LAN design model, with two distribution layer switches (D1 and D2). The design may have dozens of access layer switches that connect to end users; the figure shows just three access switches (A1, A2, and A3). For a variety of reasons, most network engineers make the distribution layer switches be the root. For instance, the configuration could make D1 be the root by having a lower priority, with D2 configured with the next lower priority, so it becomes root if D1 fails.

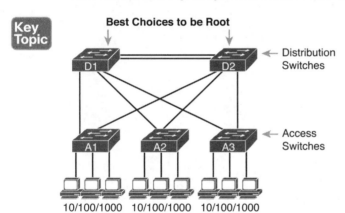

Figure 2-1 *Typical Configuration Choice: Making Distribution Switch Be Root*

This first section of the chapter examines a variety of topics that somehow relate to STP configuration. It begins with a look at STP configuration options, as a way to link the concepts of Chapter 1 to the configuration choices in this chapter. Following that, this section introduces some **show** commands for the purpose of verifying the default STP settings before changing any configuration. At that point, this section shows examples of how to configure core STP features and some of the optional STP features.

Answers to the "Do I Know This Already?" quiz:
1 B and C   **2** B   **3** A and D   **4** D   **5** B   **6** A and D

Setting the STP Mode

Chapter 1 described how 802.1D STP works in one VLAN. Now that this chapter turns our attention to STP configuration in Cisco switches, one of the first questions is this: Which kind of STP do you intend to use in a LAN? And to answer that question, you need to know a little more background.

The IEEE first standardized STP as the IEEE 802.1D standard, first published back in 1990. To put some perspective on that date, Cisco sold no LAN switches at the time, and virtual LANs did not exist yet. As a result, the STP protocol has gone through several significant changes with the introduction of switches, VLANs, and other improvements in LAN technology.

Today, Cisco LAN switches allow you to use one of three STP modes that reflect that history. For instance, the one mode discussed in this chapter, Per-VLAN Spanning Tree Plus (PVST+, or sometimes PVSTP), is a Cisco-proprietary improvement of 802.1D STP. The *per-VLAN* part of the name gives away the main feature: PVST+ creates a different STP topology per VLAN, whereas 802.1D actually did not. PVST+ also introduced PortFast.

Over time, the IEEE improved STP beyond the 802.1D standard with the Rapid STP (802.1w) protocol. Then Cisco took that standard and made another proprietary improvement, creating another mode in Cisco switches: Rapid PVST+, or simply RPVST+. It has all the improvements of the newer IEEE standard per-VLAN.

This book focuses on one mode only: PVST+. Cisco switches generally default to using PVST+, but to set a switch to use this mode, use the **spanning-tree mode pvst** global command. Alternatively, switches allow RPVST+ with the **spanning-tree mode rapid-pvst** command, and Multiple Spanning Tree (MST) with the **spanning-tree mode mst** command.

All the examples in this chapter use 2960 switches, with PVST+ as the default STP mode.

Connecting STP Concepts to STP Configuration Options

If you think back to the details of STP operation in Chapter 1, STP uses two types of numbers for most of its decisions: the BID and STP port costs. Focusing on those two types of numbers, consider this summary of what STP does behind the scenes:

- Use the BID to elect the root switch, electing the switch with the numerically lowest BID.
- Use the total STP cost in each path to the root, when each nonroot switch chooses its own root port (RP).
- Use each switch's root cost, which is in turn based on STP port costs, when switches decide which switch port becomes the designated port (DP) on each LAN segment.

Unsurprisingly, Cisco switches let you configure part of a switch's BID and the STP port cost, which in turn influences the choices each switch makes with STP.

Per-VLAN Configuration Settings

Beyond supporting the configuration of the BID and STP port costs, Cisco switches support configuring both settings per VLAN. By default, Cisco switches use IEEE 802.1D, not RSTP (802.1w), with a Cisco-proprietary feature called Per-VLAN Spanning Tree Plus (PVST+).

PVST+ (often abbreviated as simply PVST today) creates a different instance of STP for each VLAN. So, before looking at the tunable STP parameters, you need to have a basic understanding of PVST+, because the configuration settings can differ for each instance of STP.

PVST+ gives engineers a load-balancing tool with STP. By changing some STP configuration parameters differently for different VLANs, the engineer could cause switches to pick different RPs and DPs in different VLANs. As a result, some traffic in some VLANs can be forwarded over one trunk, and traffic for other VLANs can be forwarded over a different trunk.

Figure 2-2 shows the basic idea, with SW3 forwarding odd-numbered VLAN traffic over the left trunk (Gi0/1) and even-numbered VLANs over the right trunk (Gi0/2).

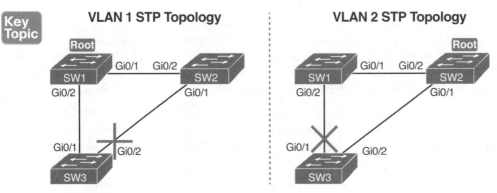

Figure 2-2   *Load Balancing with PVST+*

The next few pages look specifically at how to change the BID and STP port cost settings, per VLAN, when using the default PVST+ mode.

The Bridge ID and System ID Extension

Originally, a switch's BID was formed by combining the switch's 2-byte priority and its 6-byte MAC address. Later, the IEEE changed the rules, splitting the original priority field into two separate fields, as shown in Figure 2-3: a 4-bit priority field and a 12-bit subfield called the *system ID extension* (which represents the VLAN ID).

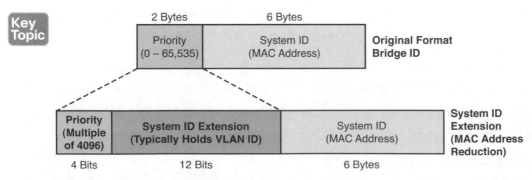

Figure 2-3   *STP System ID Extension*

Cisco switches let you configure the BID, but only the priority part. The switch fills in its universal (burned-in) MAC address as the system ID. It also plugs in the VLAN ID of a VLAN in the 12-bit system ID extension field. The only part configurable by the network engineer is the 4-bit priority field.

Configuring the number to put in the priority field, however, is one of the strangest things to configure on a Cisco router or switch. As shown at the top of Figure 2-3, the priority field was originally a 16-bit number, which represented a decimal number from 0 to 65,535. Because of that history, the current configuration command (**spanning-tree vlan** *vlan-id* **priority** *x*) requires a decimal number between 0 and 65,535. And not just any number in that range, either: It must be a multiple of 4096: 0, 4096, 8192, 12288, and so on, up through 61,440.

The switch still sets the first 4 bits of the BID based on the configured value. As it turns out, of the 16 allowed multiples of 4096, from 0 through 61,440, each has a different binary value in their first 4 bits: 0000, 0001, 0010, and so on, up through 1111. The switch sets the true 4-bit priority based on the first 4 bits of the configured value.

Although the history and configuration might make the BID priority idea seem a bit convoluted, having an extra 12-bit field in the BID works well in practice because it can be used to identify the VLAN ID. VLAN IDs range from 1 to 4094, requiring 12 bits. Cisco switches place the VLAN ID into the System ID Extension field, so each switch has a unique BID per VLAN.

For example, a switch configured with VLANs 1 through 4, with a default base priority of 32,768, has a default STP priority of 32,769 in VLAN 1, 32,770 in VLAN 2, 32,771 in VLAN 3, and so on. So, you can view the 16-bit priority as a base priority (as configured on the **spanning-tree vlan** *vlan-id* **priority** *x* command) plus the VLAN ID.

Per-VLAN Port Costs

Each switch interface defaults its per-VLAN STP cost based on the IEEE recommendations listed in Table 1-6 in Chapter 1. On interfaces that support multiple speeds, Cisco switches base the cost on the current actual speed. So, if an interface negotiates to use a lower speed, the default STP cost reflects that lower speed. If the interface negotiates to use a different speed, the switch dynamically changes the STP port cost as well.

Alternatively, you can configure a switch's STP port cost with the **spanning-tree [vlan** *vlan-id*] **cost** *cost* interface subcommand. You see this command most often on trunks because setting the cost on trunks has an impact on the switch's root cost, whereas setting STP costs on access ports does not.

For the command itself, it can include the VLAN ID, or not. The command only needs a **vlan** parameter on trunk ports to set the cost per VLAN. On a trunk, if the command omits the VLAN parameter, it sets the STP cost for all VLANs whose cost is not set by a **spanning-tree vlan** *x* **cost** command for that VLAN.

STP Configuration Option Summary

Table 2-2 summarizes the default settings for both the BID and the port costs and lists the optional configuration commands covered in this chapter.

Table 2-2   STP Defaults and Configuration Options

Setting	Default	Command(s) to Change Default
BID priority	Base: 32,768	**spanning-tree vlan** *vlan-id* **root** {**primary**	**secondary**} **spanning-tree vlan** *vlan-id* **priority** *priority*
Interface cost	100 for 10 Mbps 19 for 100 Mbps 4 for 1 Gbps 2 for 10 Gbps	**spanning-tree vlan** *vlan-id* **cost** *cost*
PortFast	Not enabled	**spanning-tree portfast**
BPDU Guard	Not enabled	**spanning-tree bpduguard enable**

Next, the configuration section shows how to examine the operation of STP in a simple network, along with how to change these optional settings.

Verifying STP Operation

Before taking a look at how to change the configuration, first consider a few STP verification commands. Looking at these commands first will help reinforce the default STP settings. In particular, the examples in this section use the network shown in Figure 2-4.

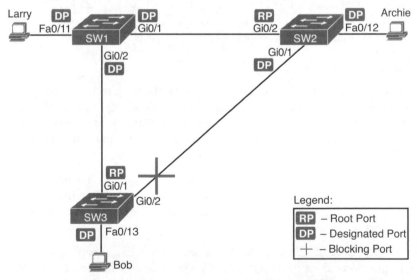

Figure 2-4 *Sample LAN for STP Configuration and Verification Examples*

Example 2-1 begins the discussion with a useful command for STP: the **show spanning-tree vlan 10** command. This command identifies the root switch and lists settings on the local switch. Example 2-1 lists the output of this command on both SW1 and SW2, as explained following the example.

Example 2-1   *STP Status with Default STP Parameters on SW1 and SW2*

```
SW1# show spanning-tree vlan 10


VLAN0010
  Spanning tree enabled protocol ieee
  Root ID    Priority    32778
             Address     1833.9d7b.0e80
             This bridge is the root
             Hello Time   2 sec  Max Age 20 sec  Forward Delay 15 sec

  Bridge ID  Priority    32778  (priority 32768 sys-id-ext 10)
             Address     1833.9d7b.0e80
             Hello Time   2 sec  Max Age 20 sec  Forward Delay 15 sec
             Aging Time  300 sec


Interface           Role Sts Cost      Prio.Nbr Type
------------------- ---- --- --------- -------- --------------------------------
Fa0/11              Desg FWD 19        128.11   P2p Edge
Gi0/1               Desg FWD 4         128.25   P2p
Gi0/2               Desg FWD 4         128.26   P2p
```

```
SW2# show spanning-tree vlan 10


VLAN0010
  Spanning tree enabled protocol ieee
  Root ID    Priority    32778
             Address     1833.9d7b.0e80
             Cost        4
             Port        26 (GigabitEthernet0/2)
             Hello Time   2 sec  Max Age 20 sec  Forward Delay 15 sec

  Bridge ID  Priority    32778  (priority 32768 sys-id-ext 10)
             Address     1833.9d7b.1380
             Hello Time   2 sec  Max Age 20 sec  Forward Delay 15 sec
             Aging Time  300 sec


Interface           Role Sts Cost      Prio.Nbr Type
------------------- ---- --- --------- -------- --------------------------------
Fa0/12              Desg FWD 19        128.12   P2p
Gi0/1               Desg FWD 4         128.25   P2p
Gi0/2               Root FWD 4         128.26   P2p
```

Example 2-1 begins with the output of the **show spanning-tree vlan 10** command on SW1. This command first lists three major groups of messages: one group of messages about the root switch, followed by another group about the local switch, and ending with interface role and status information. In this case, SW1 lists its own BID as the root, with even a specific statement that "This bridge is the root," confirming that SW1 is now the root of the VLAN 10 STP topology.

Next, compare the highlighted lines of the same command on SW2 in the lower half of the example. SW2 lists SW1's BID details as the root; in other words, SW2 agrees that SW1 has won the root election. SW2 does not list the phrase "This bridge is the root." SW1 then lists its own (different) BID details in the lines after the details about the root's BID.

The output also confirms a few default values. First, each switch lists the priority part of the BID as a separate number: 32778. This value comes from the default priority of 32768, plus VLAN 10, for a total of 32778. The output also shows the interface cost for some Fast Ethernet and Gigabit Ethernet interfaces, defaulting to 19 and 4, respectively.

Finally, the bottom of the output from the **show spanning-tree** command lists each interface in the VLAN, including trunks, with the STP port role and port state listed. For instance, on switch SW1, the output lists three interfaces, with a role of Desg for designated port (DP) and a state of FWD for forwarding. SW2 lists three interfaces, two DPs, and one root port, so all three are in an FWD or forwarding state.

Example 2-1 shows a lot of good STP information, but two other commands, shown in Example 2-2, work better for listing BID information in a shorter form. The first, **show spanning-tree root**, lists the root's BID for each VLAN. This command also lists other details, like the local switch's root cost and root port. The other command, **show spanning-tree vlan 10 bridge**, breaks out the BID into its component parts. In this example, it shows SW2's priority as the default of 32768, the VLAN ID of 10, and the MAC address.

Example 2-2 *Listing Root Switch and Local Switch BIDs on Switch SW2*

```
SW2# show spanning-tree root

                                 Root    Hello Max Fwd
Vlan                   Root ID   Cost    Time  Age Dly  Root Port
---------------- -------------------- --------- ----- --- ---  ------------

VLAN0001        32769 1833.9d5d.c900      23     2    20  15  Gi0/1
VLAN0010        32778 1833.9d7b.0e80       4     2    20  15  Gi0/2
VLAN0020        32788 1833.9d7b.0e80       4     2    20  15  Gi0/2
VLAN0030        32798 1833.9d7b.0e80       4     2    20  15  Gi0/2
VLAN0040        32808 1833.9d7b.0e80       4     2    20  15  Gi0/2


SW2# show spanning-tree vlan 10 bridge

                                               Hello  Max  Fwd
Vlan                       Bridge ID           Time   Age  Dly  Protocol
---------------- ----------------------------------- ----- --- ---  --------
VLAN0010        32778 (32768,  10) 1833.9d7b.1380     2     20  15  ieee
```

Note that both the commands in Example 2-2 have a VLAN option: **show spanning-tree [vlan x] root** and **show spanning-tree [vlan x] bridge**. Without the VLAN listed, each command lists one line per VLAN; with the VLAN, the output lists the same information, but just for that one VLAN.

Configuring STP Port Costs

Changing the STP port costs requires a simple interface subcommand: **spanning-tree [vlan *x*] cost *x*.** To show how it works, consider the following example, which changes what happens in the network shown in Figure 2-4.

Back in Figure 2-4, with default settings, SW1 became root, and SW3 blocked on its G0/2 interface. A brief scan of the figure, based on the default STP cost of 4 for Gigabit interfaces, shows that SW3 should have found a cost 4 path and a cost 8 path to reach the root, as shown in Figure 2-5.

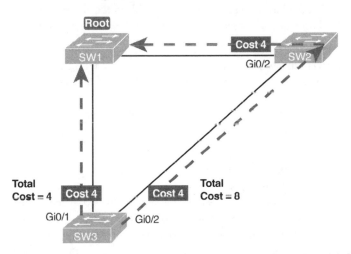

Figure 2-5 *Analysis of SW3's Current Root Cost of 4 with Defaults*

To show the effects of changing the port cost, the next example shows a change to SW3's configuration, setting its G0/1 port cost higher so that the better path to the root goes out SW3's G0/2 port instead. Example 2-3 also shows several other interesting effects.

Example 2-3 *Manipulating STP Port Cost and Watching the Transition to Forwarding State*

```
SW3# debug spanning-tree events
Spanning Tree event debugging is on
SW3# configure terminal
Enter configuration commands, one per line.  End with CNTL/Z.
SW3(config)# interface gigabitethernet0/1
SW3(config-if)# spanning-tree vlan 10 cost 30
SW3(config-if)# ^Z
SW3#
*Mar 11 06:28:00.860: STP: VLAN0010 new root port Gi0/2, cost 8
*Mar 11 06:28:00.860: STP: VLAN0010 Gi0/2 -> listening
*Mar 11 06:28:00.860: STP: VLAN0010 sent Topology Change Notice on Gi0/2
```

```
*Mar 11 06:28:00.860: STP[10]: Generating TC trap for port GigabitEthernet0/1
*Mar 11 06:28:00.860: STP: VLAN0010 Gi0/1 -> blocking
*Mar 11 06:28:15.867: STP: VLAN0010 Gi0/2 -> learning
*Mar 11 06:28:30.874: STP[10]: Generating TC trap for port GigabitEthernet0/2
*Mar 11 06:28:30.874: STP: VLAN0010 sent Topology Change Notice on Gi0/2
*Mar 11 06:28:30.874: STP: VLAN0010 Gi0/2 -> forwarding
```

This example starts with the **debug spanning-tree events** command on SW3. This command tells the switch to issue debug log messages whenever STP performs changes to an interface's role or state. These messages show up in the example as a result of the configuration.

Next, the example shows the configuration to change SW3's port cost, in VLAN 10, to 30, with the **spanning-tree vlan 10 cost 30** interface subcommand. Based on the figure, the root cost through SW3's G0/1 will now be 30 instead of 4. As a result, SW3's best cost to reach the root is cost 8, with SW3's G0/2 as its root port.

The debug messages tell us what STP on SW3 is thinking behind the scenes, with time-stamps. Note that the first five debug messages, displayed immediately after the user exited configuration mode in this case, all happen at the same time (down to the same millisecond). Notably, G0/1, which had been forwarding, immediately moves to a blocking state. Interface G0/2, which had been blocking, does not go to a forwarding state, instead moving to a listening state (at least, according to this message).

Now look for the debug message that lists G0/2 transitioning to learning state, and then the next one that shows it finally reaching forwarding state. How long between the messages? In each case, the message's timestamps show that 15 seconds passed. In this experiment, the switches used a default setting of forward delay (15 seconds). So, these debug messages confirm the steps that STP takes to transition an interface from blocking to forwarding state.

If you did not happen to enable a debug when configuring the cost, using **show** commands later can confirm the same choice by SW3, to now use its G0/2 port as its RP. Example 2-4 shows the new STP port cost setting on SW3, along with the new root port and root cost, using the **show spanning-tree vlan 10** command. Note that G0/2 is now listed as the root port. The top of the output lists SW3's root cost as 8, matching the analysis shown in Figure 2-5.

Example 2-4   *New STP Status and Settings on SW3*

```
SW3# show spanning-tree vlan 10

VLAN0010
  Spanning tree enabled protocol ieee
  Root ID    Priority    32778
             Address     1833.9d7b.0e80
             Cost        8
             Port        26 (GigabitEthernet0/2)
             Hello Time   2 sec  Max Age 20 sec  Forward Delay 15 sec

  Bridge ID  Priority    32778   (priority 32768 sys-id-ext 10)
```

```
                  Address      f47f.35cb.d780
                  Hello Time    2 sec  Max Age 20 sec  Forward Delay 15 sec
                  Aging Time   300 sec


Interface            Role Sts Cost      Prio.Nbr Type
------------------   ---- --- --------   -------- -------------------------------
Fa0/23               Desg FWD 19         128.23   P2p
Gi0/1                Altn BLK 30         128.25   P2p
Gi0/2                Root FWD 4          128.26   P2p
```

Configuring Priority to Influence the Root Election

The other big STP configuration option is to influence the root election by changing the priority of a switch. The priority can be set explicitly with the **spanning-tree vlan** *vlan-id* **priority** *value* global configuration command, which sets the base priority of the switch. (This is the command that requires a parameter of a multiple of 4096.)

However, Cisco gives us a better configuration option than configuring a specific priority value. In most designs, the network engineers pick two switches to be root: one to be root if all switches are up, and another to take over if the first switch fails. Switch IOS supports this idea with the **spanning-tree vlan** *vlan-id* **root primary** and **spanning-tree vlan** *vlan-id* **root secondary** commands

The **spanning-tree vlan** *vlan-id* **root primary** command tells the switch to set its priority low enough to become root right now. The switch looks at the current root in that VLAN, and at the root's priority. Then the local switch chooses a priority value that causes the local switch to take over as root.

Remembering that Cisco switches use a default base priority of 32,768, this command chooses the base priority as follows:

- If the current root has a base priority higher than 24,576, *the local switch uses a base priority of 24,576.*

- If the current root's base priority is 24,576 or lower, the local switch sets its base priority to the highest multiple of 4096 that still results in the local switch becoming root.

For the switch intended to take over as the root if the first switch fails, use the **spanning-tree vlan** *vlan-id* **root secondary** command. This command is much like the **spanning-tree vlan** *vlan-id* **root primary** command, but with a priority value worse than the primary switch but better than all the other switches. This command sets the switch's base priority to 28,672 regardless of the current root's current priority value.

For example, in Figures 2-4 and 2-5, SW1 was the root switch, and as shown in various commands, all three switches defaulted to use a base priority of 32,768. Example 2-5 shows a configuration that makes SW2 the primary root, and SW1 the secondary, just to show the role move from one to the other. These commands result in SW2 having a base priority of 24,576, and SW1 having a base priority of 28,672.

Example 2-5   *Making SW2 Become Root Primary, and SW1 Root Secondary*

```
! First, on SW2:
SW2# configure terminal
Enter configuration commands, one per line.  End with CNTL/Z.
SW2(config)# spanning-tree vlan 10 root primary
SW2(config)# ^Z
```

```
! Next, SW1 is configured to back-up SW1
SW1# configure terminal
Enter configuration commands, one per line.  End with CNTL/Z.
SW1(config)# spanning-tree vlan 10 root secondary
SW1(config)# ^Z
SW1#


! The next command shows the local switch's BID (SW1)
SW1# show spanning-tree vlan 10 bridge


                                              Hello  Max  Fwd
Vlan                       Bridge ID          Time   Age  Dly  Protocol
----------------  -----------------------------------  -----  ---  ---  --------
VLAN0010          28682 (28672,  10) 1833.9d7b.0e80    2     20   15   ieee

! The next command shows the root's BID (SW2)
SW1# show spanning-tree vlan 10 root


                                    Root   Hello Max Fwd
Vlan                   Root ID      Cost   Time  Age Dly  Root Port
----------------  --------------------  ---------  -----  ---  ---  ------------
VLAN0010          24586 1833.9d7b.1380     4     2    20   15   Gi0/1
```

The two **show** commands in the output clearly point out the resulting priority values on each switch. First, the **show spanning-tree bridge** command lists the local switch's BID information, while the **show spanning-tree root** command lists the root's BID, plus the local switch's root cost and root port (assuming it is not the root switch). So, SW1 lists its own BID, with priority 28,682 (base 28,672, with VLAN 10) with the **show spanning-tree bridge** command. Still on SW1, the output lists the root's priority as 24,586 in VLAN 10, implied as base 24,576 plus 10 for VLAN 10, with the **show spanning-tree root** command.

Note that alternatively you could have configured the priority settings specifically. SW1 could have used the **spanning-tree vlan 10 priority 28672** command, with SW2 using the **spanning-tree vlan 10 priority 24576** command. In this particular case, both options would result in the same STP operation.

Configuring PortFast and BPDU Guard

You can easily configure the PortFast and BPDU Guard features on any interface, but with two different configuration options. One option works best when you only want to enable these features on a few ports, and the other works best when you want to enable these features on most every access port.

First, to enable the features on just one port at a time, use the **spanning-tree portfast** and the **spanning-tree bpduguard enable** interface subcommands. Example 2-6 shows an example of the process, with SW3's F0/4 interface enabling both features. (Also, note the long warning message IOS lists when enabling PortFast; using portfast on a port connected to other switches can indeed cause serious problems.)

Example 2-6 *Enabling PortFast and BPDU Guard on One Interface*

```
SW3# configure terminal
Enter configuration commands, one per line.  End with CNTL/Z.
SW3(config)# interface fastEthernet 0/4
SW3(config-if)# spanning-tree portfast
%Warning: portfast should only be enabled on ports connected to a single
 host. Connecting hubs, concentrators, switches, bridges, etc... to this
 interface  when portfast is enabled, can cause temporary bridging loops.
 Use with CAUTION

%Portfast has been configured on FastEthernet0/4 but will only
 have effect when the interface is in a non-trunking mode.

SW3(config-if)# spanning-tree bpduguard ?
  disable  Disable BPDU guard for this interface
  enable   Enable BPDU guard for this interface

SW3(config-if)# spanning-tree bpduguard enable
SW3(config-if)# ^Z
SW3#
*Mar  1 07:53:47.808: %SYS-5-CONFIG_I: Configured from console by console
SW3# show running-config interface f0/4
Building configuration...

Current configuration : 138 bytes
!
interface FastEthernet0/4
 switchport access vlan 104
 spanning-tree portfast
 spanning-tree bpduguard enable
end

SW3# show spanning-tree interface fastethernet0/4 portfast
VLAN0104             enabled
```

The second half of the example confirms the configuration on the interface and the PortFast status. The **show running-config** command simply confirms that the switch recorded the two configuration commands. The **show spanning-tree interface fastethernet0/4 portfast** command lists the PortFast status of the interface; note that the status only shows up as enabled if PortFast is configured and the interface is up.

The alternative configuration works better when most of a switch's ports need PortFast and BPDU Guard. By default, switches disable both features on each interface. The alternative configuration lets you reverse the default, making the default for PortFast and BPDU Guard to be enabled on each interface. Then you have the option to disable the features of a port-by-port basis.

To change the defaults, use these two global commands:

- **spanning-tree portfast default**
- **spanning-tree portfast bpduguard default**

Then, to override the defaults, to disable the features, use these interface subcommands:

- **spanning-tree portfast disable**
- **spanning-tree bpduguard disable**

Configuring EtherChannel

As introduced back in Chapter 1, two neighboring switches can treat multiple parallel links between each other as a single logical link called an *EtherChannel*. STP operates on the EtherChannel, instead of the individual physical links, so that STP either forwards or blocks on the entire logical EtherChannel for a given VLAN. As a result, a switch in a forwarding state can then load balance traffic over all the physical links in the EtherChannel. Without EtherChannel, only one of the parallel links between two switches would be allowed to forward traffic, with the rest of the links blocked by STP.

EtherChannel may be one of the most challenging switch features to make work. First, the configuration has several options, so you have to remember the details of which options work together. Second, the switches also require a variety of other interface settings to match among all the links in the channel, so you have to know those settings as well.

This section focuses on the correct EtherChannel configuration. The later section titled "Troubleshooting EtherChannel" looks at many of the potential problems with EtherChannel, including all those other configuration settings that a switch checks before allowing the EtherChannel to work.

Configuring a Manual EtherChannel

The simplest way to configure an EtherChannel is to add the correct **channel-group** configuration command to each physical interface, on each switch, all with the **on** keyword. The **on** keyword tells the switches to place a physical interface into an EtherChannel.

Before getting into the configuration and verification, however, you need to start using three terms as synonyms: *EtherChannel*, *PortChannel*, and *Channel-group*. Oddly, IOS uses the **channel-group** configuration command, but then to display its status, IOS uses the **show etherchannel** command. Then, the output of this **show** command refers to neither an

"EtherChannel" nor a "Channel-group," instead using the term "PortChannel." So, pay close attention to these three terms in the example.

To configure an EtherChannel manually, follow these steps:

Step 1.   Add the **channel-group** *number* **mode on** interface subcommand under each physical interface that should be in the channel.

Step 2.   Use the same number for all commands on the same switch, but the channel-group number on the neighboring switch can differ.

Example 2-7 shows a simple example, with two links between switches SW1 and SW2, as shown in Figure 2-6. The configuration shows SW1's two interfaces placed into channel-group 1, with two **show** commands to follow.

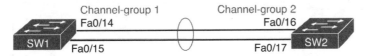

Figure 2-6   *Sample LAN Used in EtherChannel Example*

Example 2-7   *Configuring and Monitoring EtherChannel*

```
SW1# configure terminal
Enter configuration commands, one per line.  End with CNTL/Z.
SW1(config)# interface fa 0/14
SW1(config-if)# channel-group 1 mode on
SW1(config)# interface fa 0/15
SW1(config-if)# channel-group 1 mode on
SW1(config-if)# ^Z

SW1# show spanning-tree vlan 3

VLAN0003
  Spanning tree enabled protocol ieee
  Root ID    Priority    28675
             Address     0019.e859.5380
             Cost        12
             Port        72 (Port-channel1)
             Hello Time   2 sec  Max Age 20 sec  Forward Delay 15 sec

  Bridge ID  Priority    28675  (priority 28672 sys-id-ext 3)
             Address     0019.e86a.6f80
             Hello Time   2 sec  Max Age 20 sec  Forward Delay 15 sec
             Aging Time 300
```

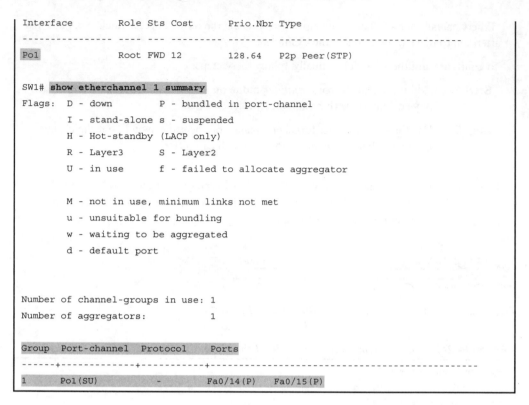

```
Interface          Role Sts Cost      Prio.Nbr Type
---------------- ---- --- --------- -------- --------------------------------
Po1                Root FWD 12        128.64   P2p Peer(STP)

SW1# show etherchannel 1 summary
Flags:  D - down        P - bundled in port-channel
        I - stand-alone s - suspended
        H - Hot-standby (LACP only)
        R - Layer3      S - Layer2
        U - in use      f - failed to allocate aggregator

        M - not in use, minimum links not met
        u - unsuitable for bundling
        w - waiting to be aggregated
        d - default port


Number of channel-groups in use: 1
Number of aggregators:           1


Group  Port-channel  Protocol     Ports
------+-------------+-----------+-------------------------------------------
1      Po1(SU)         -          Fa0/14(P)   Fa0/15(P)
```

Take a few moments to look at the output in the two **show** commands in the example, as well. First, the **show spanning-tree** command lists Po1, short for PortChannel1, as an interface. This interface exists because of the **channel-group** commands using the **1** parameter. STP no longer operates on physical interfaces F0/14 and F0/15, instead operating on the PortChannel1 interface, so only that interface is listed in the output.

Next, note the output of the **show etherchannel 1 summary** command. It lists as a heading "Port-channel," with Po1 below it. It also lists both F0/14 and F0/15 in the list of ports, with a (P) beside each. Per the legend, the *P* means that the ports are bundled in the port channel, which is a code that means these ports have passed all the configuration checks and are valid to be included in the channel.

Configuring Dynamic EtherChannels

Cisco switches support two different protocols that allow the switches to negotiate whether a particular link becomes part of an EtherChannel or not. Basically, the configuration enables the protocol for a particular channel-group number. At that point, the switch can use the protocol to send messages to/from the neighboring switch and discover whether their configuration settings pass all checks. If a given physical link passes, the link is added to the EtherChannel and used; if not, it is placed in a down state, and not used, until the configuration inconsistency can be resolved.

For now, this section focuses on how to make it work, with the later "Troubleshooting EtherChannel" section focusing on these specific settings that can make it fail.

Cisco switches support the Cisco proprietary Port Aggregation Protocol (PAgP) and the IEEE standard Link Aggregation Control Protocol (LACP), based on IEEE standard 802.3ad. Although differences exist between the two, to the depth discussed here, they both accomplish the same task: negotiate so that only links that pass the configuration checks are actually used in an EtherChannel.

To configure either protocol, a switch uses the **channel-group** configuration commands on each switch, but with a keyword that either means "use this protocol and begin negotiations" or "use this protocol and wait for the other switch to begin negotiations." As shown in Figure 2-7, the **desirable** and **auto** keywords enable PAgP, and the **active** and **passive** keywords enable LACP. With these options, at least one side has to begin the negotiations. In other words, with PAgP, at least one of the two sides must use **desirable**, and with LACP, at least one of the two sides must use **active**.

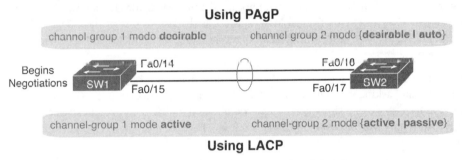

Figure 2-7 *Correct EtherChannel Configuration Combinations*

> **NOTE** Do not use the **on** parameter on one end, and either **auto** or **desirable** (or for LACP, **active** or **passive**) on the neighboring switch. The **on** option uses neither PAgP nor LACP, so a configuration that uses **on**, with PAgP or LACP options on the other end, would prevent the EtherChannel from working.

For instance, you could replace the configuration in Example 2-7 with **channel-group 1 mode desirable** for both interfaces, with SW2 using **channel-group 2 mode auto**.

STP Troubleshooting

The final section of this chapter focuses on how to apply the information covered in Chapter 1 and in the first half of this chapter. Although this section helps you prepare to troubleshoot STP problems in real networks, the main goal for this section is to prepare you to answer STP questions on the CCNA exams.

STP questions tend to intimidate many test takers. STP uses many rules, with tiebreakers in case one rule ends with a tie. Without much experience with STP, people tend to distrust their own answers. Also, even those of us with networking jobs already probably do not troubleshoot STP very often, because STP runs by default and works well using default configuration settings in medium to small networks, so engineers seldom need to troubleshoot STP problems. So, STP begs for a good troubleshooting strategy before examining a complex STP question.

This section reviews the rules for STP, while emphasizing some important troubleshooting points. In particular, this section takes a closer look at the tiebreakers that STP uses to make decisions. It also makes some practical suggestions about how to go about answering exam questions such as "which switch is the root switch."

Determining the Root Switch

Determining the STP root switch is easy if you know all the switches' BIDs: Just pick the lowest value. If the question lists the priority and MAC address separately, as is common in some **show** command output, pick the switch with the lowest priority, or in the case of a tie, pick the lower MAC address value.

And just to be extra clear, STP does not have nor need a tiebreaker for electing the root switch. The BID uses a switch universal MAC address as the last 48 bits of the BID. These MAC addresses are unique in the universe, so there should never be identical BIDs, with no need for a tiebreaker.

For the exam, a question that asks about the root switch might not be so simple as listing a bunch of BIDs and asking you which one is "best." A more likely question is a sim question in which you have to do any **show** commands you like or a multiple choice question that lists the output from only one or two commands. Then you have to apply the STP algorithm to figure out the rest.

When faced with an exam question using a simulator, or just the output in an exhibit, use a simple strategy of ruling out switches, as follows:

Step 1.   Begin with a list or diagram of switches, and consider all as possible root switches.

Step 2.   Rule out any switches that have an RP (**show spanning-tree, show spanning-tree root**), because root switches do not have a RP.

Step 3.   Always try **show spanning-tree**, because it identifies the local switch as root directly: "This switch is the root" on the fifth line of output.

Step 4.   Always try **show spanning-tree root**, because it identifies the local switch as root indirectly: The RP column is empty if the local switch is the root.

Step 5.   When using a sim, rather than try switches randomly, chase the RPs. For example, if starting with SW1, and SW1's G0/1 is an RP, next try the switch on the other end of SW1's G0/1 port.

Step 6.   When using a Sim, using **show spanning-tree vlan** x on a few switches, and recording the root switch, RP, and DP ports can quickly show you most STP facts. Use that strategy if available.

The one step in this list that most people ignore is the idea of ruling out switches that have an RP. Root switches do not have an RP, so any switch with an RP can be ruled out as not being the root switch for that VLAN. Example 2-8 shows two commands on switch SW2 in some LAN that confirms that SW2 has an RP and is therefore not the root switch.

Example 2-8   *Ruling Out Switches as Root Based on Having a Root Port*

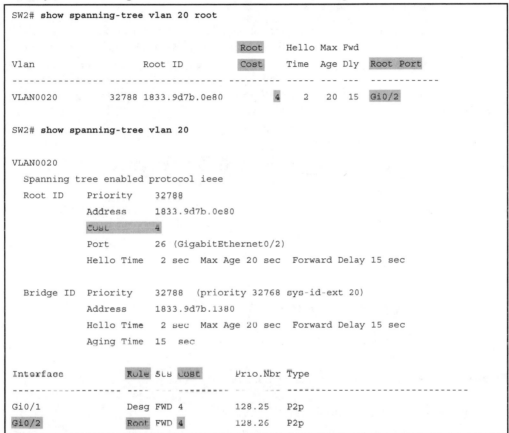

```
SW2# show spanning-tree vlan 20 root

                                  Root    Hello Max Fwd
Vlan                  Root ID     Cost    Time  Age Dly  Root Port
----------------  --------------------  ----------  -----  ---  ---  ------------

VLAN0020          32788 1833.9d7b.0e80      4       2    20   15   Gi0/2

SW2# show spanning-tree vlan 20

VLAN0020
  Spanning tree enabled protocol ieee
  Root ID    Priority    32788
             Address     1833.9d7b.0e80
             Cost        4
             Port        26 (GigabitEthernet0/2)
             Hello Time   2 sec  Max Age 20 sec  Forward Delay 15 sec

  Bridge ID  Priority    32788  (priority 32768 sys-id-ext 20)
             Address     1833.9d7b.1380
             Hello Time   2 sec  Max Age 20 sec  Forward Delay 15 sec
             Aging Time  15  sec


Interface          Role  Sts  Cost       Prio.Nbr Type
-----------------  ----  ---  ---------  --------  ------------------------------
Gi0/1              Desg  FWD  4          128.25    P2p
Gi0/2              Root  FWD  4          128.26    P2p
```

Both commands identify SW2's G0/2 port as its RP, so if you follow the suggestions, the next switch to try in a sim question would be the switch on the other end of SW2's G0/2 interface.

Determining the Root Port on Nonroot Switches

Determining the RP of a switch when **show** command output is available is relatively easy. As shown recently in Example 2-8, both **show spanning-tree** and **show spanning-tree root** list the root port of the local switch, assuming it is not the root switch. The challenge comes more when an exam question makes you think through how the switches choose the RP based on the root cost of each path to the root switch with some tiebreakers as necessary.

As a review, each nonroot switch has one, and only one, RP for a VLAN. To choose its RP, a switch listens for incoming hello bridge protocol data units (BPDU). For each received hello, the switch adds the cost listed in the hello BPDU to the cost of the incoming interface (the interface on which the hello was received). That total is the root cost over that path. The lowest root cost wins, and the local switch uses its local port that is part of the least root cost path as its root port.

Although that description has a lot of twists and turns in the words, it is the same concept described for Chapter 1's Figure 1-8.

For the exam, if the question has a diagram of the LAN, most humans work better with a slightly different way to look at the problem. Instead of thinking about hello messages and so on, approach the question as this: the sum of all outgoing port costs between the nonroot switch and the root. Repeating a familiar example, with a twist, Figure 2-8 shows the calculation of the root cost. Note that SW3's Gi0/1 port has yet again had its cost configured to a different value.

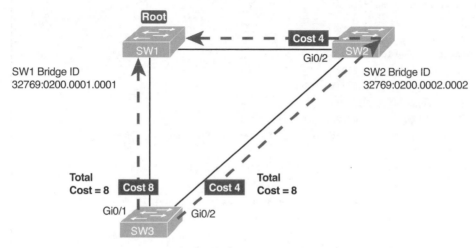

Figure 2-8 *SW3's Root Cost Calculation Ends in a Tie*

STP Tiebreakers When Choosing the Root Port

The figure shows the easier process of adding the STP costs of the outgoing interfaces over each from SW3, a nonroot, to SW1, the root. It also shows a tie (on purpose), to talk about the tiebreakers.

When a switch chooses its root port, the first choice is to choose the local port that is part of the least root cost path. When those costs tie, the switch picks the port connected to the neighbor with the lowest BID. This tiebreaker usually breaks the tie, but not always. So, for completeness, the three tiebreakers are, in the order a switch uses them, as follows:

1. Choose based on the lowest neighbor bridge ID.
2. Choose based on the lowest neighbor port priority.
3. Choose based on the lowest neighbor internal port number.

(Note that the switch only considers the root paths that tie when thinking about these tiebreakers.)

For example, Figure 2-8 shows that SW3 is not root and that its two paths to reach the root tie with their root costs of 8. The first tiebreaker is the lowest neighbor's BID. SW1's BID value is lower than SW2's, so SW3 chooses its G0/1 interface as its RP in this case.

The last two RP tiebreakers come into play only when two switches connect to each other with multiple links, as shown in Figure 2-9. In that case, a switch receives hellos on more than one port from the same neighboring switch, so the BIDs tie.

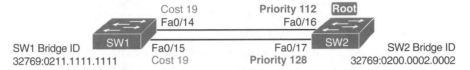

Figure 2-9   *Topology Required for the Last Two Tiebreakers for Root Port*

In this particular example, SW2 becomes root, and SW1 needs to choose its RP. SW1's port costs tie, at 19 each, so SW1's root cost over each path will tie at 19. SW2 sends hellos over each link to SW1, so SW1 cannot break the tie based on SW1's neighbor BID because both list SW2's BID. So, SW1 has to turn to the other two tiebreakers.

> **NOTE**   In real life, most engineers would put these two links into an EtherChannel.

The next tiebreaker is a configurable option: the neighboring switch's port priority on each neighboring switch interface. Cisco switch ports default to a setting of 128, with a range of values from 0 through 255, with lower being better (as usual). In this example, the network engineer has set SW2's F0/16 interface with the **spanning-tree vlan 10 port-priority 112** command. SW1 learns that the neighbor has a port priority of 112 on the top link and 128 on the bottom, so SW1 uses its top (F0/14) interface as the root port.

If the port priority ties, which it often does due to the default values, STP relies on an internal port numbering on the neighbor. Cisco switches assign an internal integer to identify each interface on the switch. The nonroot looks for the neighbor's lowest internal port number (as listed in the hello messages) and chooses its RP based on the lower number.

Cisco switches use an obvious numbering, with Fa0/1 having the lowest number, then Fa0/2, then Fa0/3, and so on. So, in Figure SW2, SW2's Fa0/16 would have a lower internal port number than Fa0/17; SW1 would learn those numbers in the hello; and SW1 would use its Fa0/14 port as its RP.

Suggestions for Attacking Root Port Problems on the Exam

Exam questions that make you think about the RP can be easy if you know where to look and the output of a few key commands are available. However, the more conceptual the question, the more you have to calculate the root cost over each path, correlate that to different **show** commands, and put the ideas together. The following list makes a few suggestions about how to approach STP problems on the exam:

1. If available, look at the **show spanning-tree** and **show spanning-tree root** commands. Both commands list the root port and the root cost (see Example 2-8).

2. The **show spanning-tree** command list cost in two places: the root cost at the top, in the section about the root switch; and the interface cost, at the bottom, in the per-interface section. Be careful, though; the cost at the bottom is the interface cost, not the root cost!

3. For problems where you have to calculate a switch's root cost:

   a. Memorize the default cost values: 100 for 10 Mbps, 19 for 100 Mbps, 4 for 1 Gbps, and 2 for 10 Gbps.

   b. Look for any evidence of the **spanning-tree cost** configuration command on an interface, because it overrides the default cost. Do not assume default costs are used.

   c. When you know a default cost is used, if you can, check the current actual speed as well. Cisco switches choose STP cost defaults based on the current speed, not the maximum speed.

Determining the Designated Port on Each LAN Segment

Each LAN segment has a single switch that acts as the designated port (DP) on that segment. On segments that connect a switch to a device that does not even use STP—for example, segments connecting a switch to a PC or a router—the switch always wins, because it is the only device sending a hello onto the link. However, links with two switches require a little more work to discover which should be the DP. By definition:

Step 1. For switches connected to the same LAN segment, the switch with the lowest cost to reach the root, as advertised in the hello they send onto the link, becomes the DP on that link.

Step 2. In case of a tie, among the switches that tied on cost, the switch with the lowest BID becomes the DP.

For example, consider Figure 2-10. This figure notes the root, RPs, and DPs and each switch's least cost to reach the root over its respective RP.

Focus on the segments that connect the nonroot switches for a moment.

SW2–SW4 segment: SW4 wins because of its root cost of 19, compared to SW2's root cost of 20.

SW2-SW3 segment: SW3 wins because of its root cost of 19, compared to SW2's root cost of 20.

SW3-SW4 segment: SW3 and SW4 tie on root cost, both with root cost 19. SW3 wins due to its better (lower) BID value.

Interestingly, SW2 loses and does not become DP on the links to SW3 and SW4 even though SW2 has the better (lower) BID value. The DP tiebreaker does use the lowest BID, but the first DP criteria is the lowest root cost, and SW2's root cost happens to be higher than SW3's and SW4's.

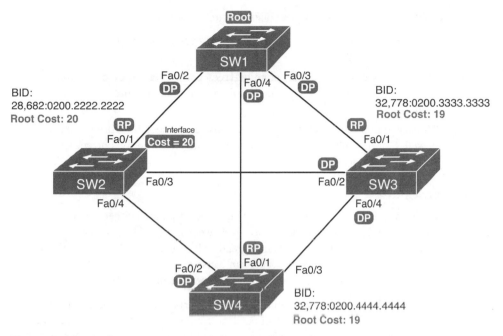

Figure 2-10   *Picking the DPs*

> **NOTE**   A single switch can connect two or more interfaces to the same collision domain, and compete to become DP, if hubs are used. In such cases, two different switch ports on the same switch tie, the DP choice uses the same two final tiebreakers as used with the RP selection: the lowest interface STP priority, and if that ties, the lowest internal interface number.

Suggestions for Attacking Designated Port Problems on the Exam

As with exam questions asking about the RP, exam questions that make you think about the DP can be easy if you know where to look and the output of a few key commands are available. However, the more conceptual the question, the more you have to think about the criteria for choosing the DP: first the root cost of the competing switches, and then the better BID if they tie based on root cost.

The following list gives some tips to keep in mind when digging into a given DP issue. Some of this list repeats the suggestions for finding the RP, but to be complete, this list includes each idea as well.

1.   If available, look at the **show spanning-tree** commands, at the list of interfaces at the end of the output. Then, look for the Role column, and look for Desg, to identify any DPs.

2.   Identify the root cost of a switch directly by using the **show spanning-tree** command. But be careful! This command lists the cost in two places, and only the mention at the top, in the section about the root, lists the root cost.

3. For problems where you have to calculate a switch's root cost, do the following:

   a. Memorize the default cost values: 100 for 10 Mbps, 19 for 100 Mbps, 4 for 1 Gbps, and 2 for 10 Gbps.

   b. Look for any evidence of the **spanning-tree cost** configuration command on an interface, because it overrides the default cost. Do not assume default costs are used.

   c. When you know a default cost is used, if you can, check the current actual speed as well. Cisco switches choose STP cost defaults based on the current speed, not the maximum speed.

STP Convergence

STP puts each RP and DP into a forwarding state, and ports that are neither RP nor DP into a blocking state. Those states may remain as is for days, weeks, or months. But at some point, some switch or link will fail, a link may change speeds (changing the STP cost), or the STP configuration may change. Any of these events can cause switches to repeat their STP algorithm, which may in turn change their own RP and any ports that are DPs.

When STP converges based on some change, not all the ports have to change their state. For instance, a port that was forwarding, if it still needs to forward, just keeps on forwarding. Ports that were blocking that still need to block keep on blocking. But when a port needs to change state, something has to happen, based on the following rules:

■ For interfaces that stay in the same STP state, nothing needs to change.

■ For interfaces that need to move from a forwarding state to a blocking state, the switch immediately changes the state to blocking.

■ For interfaces that need to move from a blocking state to a forwarding state, the switch first moves the interface to listening state, then learning state, each for the time specified by the forward delay timer (default 15 seconds). Only then is the interface placed into forwarding state.

Because the transition from blocking to forwarding does require some extra steps, you should be ready to respond to conceptual questions about the transition. To be ready, review the section "Reacting to Changes in the Network," in Chapter 1.

Troubleshooting EtherChannel

EtherChannels can prove particularly challenging to troubleshoot for a couple of reasons. First, you have to be careful to match the correct configuration, and there are many more incorrect configuration combinations than there are correct combinations. Second, many interface settings must match on the physical links, both on the local switch and on the neighboring switch, before a switch will add the physical link to the channel. This last topic in the chapter works through both sets of issues.

Incorrect Options on the channel-group Command

Earlier, the section titled "Configuring EtherChannel" listed the small set of working configuration options on the **channel-group** command. Those rules can be summarized as follows, for a single EtherChannel:

1. On the local switch, all the **channel-group** commands for all the physical interfaces must use the same channel-group number.

2. The **channel-group** number can be different on the neighboring switches.

3. If using the **on** keyword, you must use it on the corresponding interfaces of both switches.

4. If you use the **desirable** keyword on one switch, the switch uses PAgP; the other switch must use either **desirable** or **auto**.

5. If you use the **active** keyword on one switch, the switch uses LACP; the other switch must use either **active** or **passive**.

These rules summarize the correct configuration options, but the options actually leave many more incorrect choices. The following list shows some incorrect configurations that the switches allow, even though they would result in the EtherChannel not working. The list compares the configuration on one switch to another based on the physical interface configuration. Each lists the reasons why the configuration is incorrect:

■ Configuring the **on** keyword on one switch, and **desirable**, **auto**, **active**, or **passive** on the other switch. The **on** keyword does not enable PAgP, and does not enable LACP, and the other options rely on PAgP or LACP.

■ Configuring the **auto** keyword on both switches. Both use PAgP, but both wait on the other switch to begin negotiations.

■ Configuring the **passive** keyword on both switches. Both use LACP, but both wait on the other switch to begin negotiations.

■ Configuring the **active** keyword on one switch and either **desirable** or **auto** on the other switch. The **active** keyword uses LACP, whereas the other keywords use PAgP.

■ Configuring the **desirable** keyword on one switch and either **active** or **passive** on the other switch. The **desirable** keyword uses PAgP, whereas the other keywords use LACP.

Example 2-9 shows an example that matches the last item in the list. In this case, SW1's two ports (F0/14 and F0/15) have been configured with the **desirable** keyword, and SW2's matching F0/16 and F0/17 have been configured with the **active** keyword. The example lists some telling status information about the failure, with notes following the example.

Example 2-9 *Ruling Out Switches as Root Based on Having a Root Port*

```
SW1# show etherchannel summary
Flags:  D - down        P - bundled in port-channel
        I - stand-alone s - suspended
        H - Hot-standby (LACP only)
        R - Layer3       S - Layer2
        U - in use       f - failed to allocate aggregator

        M - not in use, minimum links not met
        u - unsuitable for bundling
        w - waiting to be aggregated
```

```
            d - default port


Number of channel-groups in use: 1
Number of aggregators:           1


Group  Port-channel  Protocol    Ports
------+-------------+-----------+----------------------------------------------
1      Po1(SD)         PAgP        Fa0/14(I)   Fa0/15(I)


SW1# show interfaces status | include Po|14|15
Port      Name              Status       Vlan       Duplex  Speed Type
Fa0/14                      connected    301        a-full  a-100 10/100BaseTX
Fa0/15                      connected    301        a-full  a-100 10/100BaseTX
Po1                         notconnect   unassigned auto    auto
```

Start at the top, in the legend of the **show etherchannel summary** command. The *D* code letter means that the channel itself is down, with *S* meaning that the channel is a Layer 2 EtherChannel. Code *I* means that the physical interface is working independently from the PortChannel (described as "stand-alone"). Then, the bottom of that command's output highlights Portchannel (Po1) as Layer 2 EtherChannel in a down state (SD), with F0/14 and F0/15 as stand-alone interfaces (I).

Interestingly, because the problem is a configuration mistake, the two physical interfaces still operate independently, as if the port channel did not exist. The last command in the example shows that while the Portchannel 1 interface is down, the two physical interfaces are in a connected state.

> **NOTE**   As a suggestion for attacking EtherChannel problems on the exam, rather than memorizing all the incorrect configuration options, concentrate on the list of correct configuration options. Then look for any differences between a given question's configuration as compared to the known correct configurations and work from there.

Configuration Checks Before Adding Interfaces to EtherChannels

Even when the **channel-group** commands have all been configured correctly, other configuration settings can cause problems as well. This last topic examines those configuration settings and their impact.

First, a local switch checks each new physical interface that is configured to be part of an EtherChannel, comparing each new link to the existing links. That new physical interface's settings must be the same as the existing links; otherwise, the switch does not add the new link to the list of approved and working interfaces in the channel. That is, the physical interface remains configured as part of the port channel, but it is not used as part of the channel, often being placed into some nonworking state.

The list of items the switch checks includes the following:

- Speed
- Duplex
- Operational access or trunking state (all must be access, or all must be trunks)
- If an access port, the access VLAN
- If a trunk port, the allowed VLAN list (per the **switchport trunk allowed** command)
- If a trunk port, the native VLAN
- STP interface settings

In addition, switches check the settings on the neighboring switch. To do so, the switches either use PAgP or LACP (if already in use), or Cisco Discovery Protocol (CDP) if using manual configuration. The neighbor must match on all parameters in this list except the STP settings.

As an example, SW1 and SW2 again use two links in one EtherChannel. Before configuring the EtherChannel, SW1's F0/15 was given a different STP port cost than F0/14. Example 2-10 picks up the story just after configuring the correct **channel-group** commands, when the switch is deciding whether to use F0/14 and F0/15 in this EtherChannel.

Example 2-10 *Local Interfaces Fail in EtherChannel Because of Mismatched STP Cost*

```
*Mar  1 23:18:56.132: %PM-4-ERR_DISABLE: channel-misconfig (STP) error detected on
Po1, putting Fa0/14 in err-disable state
*Mar  1 23:18:56.132: %PM-4-ERR_DISABLE: channel-misconfig (STP) error detected on
Po1, putting Fa0/15 in err-disable state
*Mar  1 23:18:56.132: %PM-4-ERR_DISABLE: channel-misconfig (STP) error detected on
Po1, putting Po1 in err-disable state
*Mar  1 23:18:58.136: %LINK-3-UPDOWN: Interface FastEthernet0/14, changed state to
down
*Mar  1 23:18:58.137: %LINK-3-UPDOWN: Interface Port-channel1, changed state to down
*Mar  1 23:18:58.137: %LINK-3-UPDOWN: Interface FastEthernet0/15, changed state to
down


SW1# show etherchannel summary
Flags:  D - down        P - bundled in port-channel
        I - stand-alone s - suspended
        H - Hot-standby (LACP only)
        R - Layer3       S - Layer2
        U - in use       f - failed to allocate aggregator

        M - not in use, minimum links not met
        u - unsuitable for bundling
        w - waiting to be aggregated
        d - default port


Number of channel-groups in use: 1
```

```
Number of aggregators:              1

Group  Port-channel  Protocol     Ports
------+-------------+-----------+-------------------------------------------------
1       Po1(SD)          -         Fa0/14(D)    Fa0/15(D)
```

The messages at the top of the example specifically state what the switch does when think-ing about whether the interface settings match. In this case, SW1 detects the different STP costs. SW1 does not use F0/14, does not use F0/15, and even places them into an err-disabled state. The switch also puts the PortChannel into err-disabled state. As a result, the Port Channel is not operational, and the physical interfaces are also not operational.

To solve this problem, you must reconfigure the physical interfaces to use the same STP settings. In addition, the portchannel and physical interfaces must be **shutdown**, and then **no shutdown**, to recover from the err-disabled state. (Note that when a switch applies the **shutdown** and **no shutdown** commands to a port channel, it applies those same commands to the physical interfaces, as well; so, just do the **shutdown/no shutdown** on the portchannel interface.)

Exam Preparation Tasks

Review All the Key Topics

Review the most important topics from this chapter, noted with the Key Topic icon. Table 2-3 lists these key topics and where each is discussed.

Table 2-3   Key Topics for Chapter 2

Key Topic Element	Description	Page Number
Figure 2-1	Typical design choice for which switches should be made to be root	46
Figure 2-2	Conceptual view of load-balancing benefits of PVST+	48
Figure 2-3	Shows the format of the system ID extension of the STP priority field	48
Table 2-2	Lists default settings for STP optional configuration settings and related configuration commands	50
List	Two branches of logic in how the **spanning-tree root primary** command picks a new base STP priority	55
List	Steps to manually configure an EtherChannel	59
List	Strategy for finding the root switch for exam questions	62
List	Strategy for finding the root port on nonroot switches for exam questions	66
List	Strategy for finding the designated port for exam questions	66
List	Suggestions when examining questions as a designated port	67
List	Summary of STP convergence actions	68
List	Interface settings that must match with other interfaces on the same switch for an interface to be included in an EtherChannel	69

Definitions of Key Terms

After your first reading of the chapter, try to define these key terms, but do not be concerned about getting them all correct at that time. Chapter 22 directs you in how to use these terms for late-stage preparation for the exam.

Rapid PVST+, PVST+, system ID extension, PAgP, LACP, PortChannel, Channel Group

Command Reference to Check Your Memory

Although you should not necessarily memorize the information in the tables in this section, this section does include a reference for the configuration and EXEC commands covered in this chapter. Practically speaking, you should memorize the commands as a side effect of reading the chapter and doing all the activities in this exam preparation section. To check to see how well you have memorized the commands as a side effect of your other studies, cover the left side of the table with a piece of paper, read the descriptions on the right side, and see whether you remember the command.

Table 2-4 Chapter 2 Configuration Command Reference

Command	Description
spanning-tree mode { pvst	rapid-pvst	mst }	Global configuration command to set the STP mode.
spanning-tree vlan *vlan-number* root primary	Global configuration command that changes this switch to the root switch. The switch's priority is changed to the lower of either 24,576 or 4096 less than the priority of the current root bridge when the command was issued.
spanning-tree vlan *vlan-number* root secondary	Global configuration command that sets this switch's STP base priority to 28,672.
spanning-tree [vlan *vlan-id*] {priority *priority*}	Global configuration command that changes the bridge priority of this switch for the specified VLAN.
spanning-tree [vlan *vlan-number*] cost *cost*	Interface subcommand that changes the STP cost to the configured value.
spanning-tree [vlan *vlan-number*] port-priority *priority*	Interface subcommand that changes the STP port priority in that VLAN (0 to 240, in increments of 16).
channel-group *channel-group-number* mode {auto	desirable	active	passive	on}	Interface subcommand that enables EtherChannel on the interface.
spanning-tree portfast	Interface subcommand that enables PortFast on the interface.
spanning-tree bpduguard enable	Interface subcommand to enable BPDU Guard on an interface
spanning-tree portfast default	Global command that changes the switch default for PortFast on access interfaces from disabled to enabled.
spanning-tree portfast bpduguard default	Global command that changes the switch default for BPDU Guard on access interfaces from disabled to enabled.
spanning-tree portfast disable	Interface subcommand that disables PortFast on the interface.
spanning-tree bpduguard disable	Interface subcommand to disable BPDU Guard on an interface

Table 2-5   Chapter 2 EXEC Command Reference

Command	Description
show spanning-tree	Lists details about the state of STP on the switch, including the state of each port
show spanning-tree *interface interface-id*	Lists STP information only for the specified port
show spanning-tree vlan *vlan-id*	Lists STP information for the specified VLAN
show spanning-tree [vlan *vlan-id*] root	Lists information about each VLAN's root or for just the specified VLAN
show spanning-tree [vlan *vlan-id*] bridge	Lists STP information about the local switch for each VLAN or for just the specified VLAN
debug spanning-tree events	Causes the switch to provide informational messages about changes in the STP topology
show spanning-tree interface *type number* portfast	Lists a one-line status message about PortFast on the listed interface
show etherchannel [*channel-group-number*] {brief | detail | port | port-channel | summary}	Lists information about the state of EtherChannels on this switch

This chapter covers the following exam topics:

Troubleshooting

Identify and correct common network problems

Troubleshoot and resolve interVLAN routing problems

Native VLAN

Port mode trunk status

CHAPTER 3

Troubleshooting LAN Switching

This troubleshooting chapter, along with several other entire chapters and other sections of chapters, has an important job: to help you develop the troubleshooting skills required to quickly and confidently answer certain types of questions on the exams. At the same time, this chapter should make you better prepared to solve real networking problems.

The troubleshooting chapters and sections in this book do not have the same primary goal as the other materials. Simply put, the nontroubleshooting topics focus on individual features and facts about an area of technology. Troubleshooting topics pull a much broader set of concepts together. These troubleshooting chapters take a broader look at the networking world, focusing on how the parts work together, assuming that you already know about the individual components.

This chapter has one obvious goal and one not-so-obvious goal. First, it discusses how to troubleshoot LANs. Not so obvious is that this chapter also reviews many of the pre-requisite Ethernet LAN topics for this book. Chapter 1, "Spanning Tree Protocol Concepts," reviewed some of the topics, and this chapter reviews many others, while also showing how to use both old and new topics to troubleshoot Ethernet LAN topics.

This long chapter breaks the materials into three sections, as follows:

- "Generalized Troubleshooting Methodologies"
- "Troubleshooting the LAN Switching Data Plane"
- "Troubleshooting Examples and Exercises"

Given the length, consider breaking each of the three major sections into a separate reading session; they are approximately 10, 20, and 20 pages in length, respectively. All three sections are related, so they are in the same chapter, but the middle section contains the core LAN switch troubleshooting topics. The first section defines some troubleshooting terms before diving into the first entire chapter on network troubleshooting. And the final section is essentially two long examples, with plenty of **show** commands. These long examples should help you build some skills at thinking through what the **show** commands mean on Cisco switches.

"Do I Know This Already?" Quiz

Because the troubleshooting chapters of this book pull in concepts from many other chapters, including some chapters in *Cisco CCENT/CCNA ICND1 100-101 Official Cert Guide*, and show how to approach some of the more challenging questions on the CCNA exams, you should read these chapters regardless of your current knowledge level. For these reasons, the troubleshooting chapters do not include a "Do I Know This Already?" quiz. However, if you feel particularly confident about troubleshooting LAN switching features covered in this book and *Cisco CCENT/CCNA ICND1 100-101 Official Cert Guide*, feel free to move to the "Exam Preparation Tasks" section, near the end of this chapter, to bypass the majority of the chapter.

Foundation Topics

Generalized Troubleshooting Methodologies

NOTE   The generic troubleshooting strategies and methods described here are a means to an end. You do not need to study these processes or memorize them for the purposes of the exam. Instead, these processes can help you think through problems on the exam so that you can answer the questions a little more quickly and with a little more confidence.

When faced with a need to solve a networking problem, everyone uses some troubleshooting methodology, whether informal or formal. Some people like to start by checking the physical cabling or by checking the interface status of all the physical links that could affect the problem. Some people like to start by pinging everything that could tell you more about the problem and then drilling deeper into the details. Some people might even just try whatever comes to mind until they intuitively know the general problem. None of these methods is inherently bad or good; I've tried all these methods, and others, and had some success with each approach.

Most people develop troubleshooting habits and styles that work well based on their own experiences and strengths. However, when learning about troubleshooting, or learning about how to troubleshoot a particular area of expertise, a more systematic troubleshooting methodology can help anyone learn to troubleshoot problems with better success. The following sections describe one such systematic troubleshooting methodology for the purpose of helping you prepare for the CCNA exams.

This troubleshooting methodology has three major branches, which generally occur in the order shown here:

- **Analyzing/predicting normal operation:** This step answers this question: What should happen in this network? This step results in a description and prediction of the details of what should happen if the network is working correctly, based on documentation, configuration, and **show** and **debug** command output.

- **Problem isolation:** This step keeps answering the same question: What specifically is not working? When some problem might be occurring, find the components that do not work correctly as compared to the predicted behavior. Then find out what might be causing that problem and so on. The answers are again based on documentation, configuration, and **show** and **debug** command output.

- **Root cause analysis:** This step answers this question: What can we fix that solves the problem? This step identifies the underlying causes of the problems identified in the previous step, specifically the causes that have a specific action with which the problem can be fixed.

Following these three steps should result in the engineer knowing how to fix the problem, not just the problem symptoms. Next, the text explains some thoughts about how to approach each step of the troubleshooting process.

Analyzing and Predicting Normal Network Operation

Any network's job is to deliver data from one end-user device to another. To analyze a network, an engineer needs to understand the logic used by each successive device as it forwards the data to the next device. By thinking about what should happen at each device, the engineer can describe the entire flow of data.

The term *data plane* refers to actions devices take to forward data. To forward each frame or packet, a device applies its data plane logic and processes to the frame or packet. For example, when a LAN switch receives a frame in an interface in VLAN 3, the switch makes a forwarding decision based on the VLAN 3 entries in the MAC address table, and forwards the packet. All this logic focuses on forwarding the user's data, so it is part of a switch's data plane processing.

The term *control plane* refers to the overhead processes that control the work done by the network device, but does not directly impact the forwarding of individual frames or packets. For example, Spanning Tree Protocol (STP) and any IP routing protocol are examples of control plane processes.

Also, some control plane processes do not even indirectly change how the device forwards data. For example, Cisco Discovery Protocol (CDP) can be useful for confirming the accuracy of network documentation, but CDP can be disabled with no effect on the data plane forwarding processes. CDP would also be a control plane process.

To predict the expected operation of a network or to explain the details of how a correctly functioning network is currently working, the person troubleshooting the problem can start with either the control plane or data plane. This text shows the data plane first, but in real life, you can pick one or the other in part based on the known symptoms of the problem.

Data Plane Analysis

Data plane troubleshooting examines, in order, each device in the expected forwarding path for the data. The analysis begins with the host creating the original data. That host sends the data to some other device, which then sends the data to another device, and so on, until the data reaches the endpoint host.

The data plane troubleshooting process should look at both directions of data flowing between two devices. When one device sends data, the receiving host usually sends some sort of reply. So, a problem like "I cannot talk to Server1" may be caused by a problem with packets flowing from the user toward Server1. However, the problem might instead be because of problems with the packets flowing from Server1 back to the user. So, to fully understand how useful communications happen, you also need to analyze the reverse process.

Unless a particular problem's symptoms already suggest a specific problem, data plane troubleshooting should begin with an analysis of the Layer 3 data plane. If you start with Layer 3, you can see the major steps in sending and receiving data between two hosts. You can then examine each individual Layer 3 forwarding step more closely, looking at the underlying Layer 1 and 2 details. For example, Figure 3-1 shows the six major IP forwarding (data plane) steps in a small network.

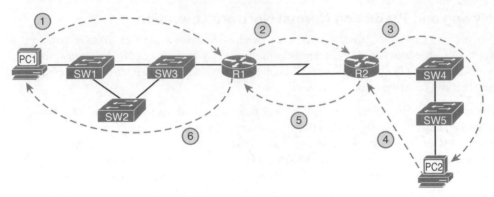

Figure 3-1   *Major Steps in an IP Forwarding Example*

When trying to understand the expected behavior of Layer 3 in this case, you would need to consider how the packet flows from left to right, and then how the reply flows from right to left. Using the six steps in the figure, the following analysis could be done:

Step 1.   Think about PC1's IP address and mask, the IP address and mask of PC2, and PC1's logic to realize that PC2 is in another subnet. This causes PC1 to choose to send the packet to its default gateway (R1).

Step 2.   Consider R1's forwarding logic for matching the packet's destination IP address with R1's routing table, with the expectation that R1 chooses to send the packet to R2 next.

Step 3.   On R2, consider the same routing table matching logic as used on R1 in the previous step, using R2's routing table. The matching entry should be a connected route on R2.

Step 4.   This step relates to PC2's reply packet, which uses the same basic logic as Step 1. Compare PC2's IP address/mask with PC1's IP address, noting that they are in different subnets. As a result, PC2 should send the packet to its default gateway, R2.

Step 5.   Consider R2's forwarding logic for packets destined to PC1's IP address, with the expectation that the matching route would cause R2 to send these packets to R1 next.

Step 6.   The final routing step, on R1, should show that a packet destined to PC1's IP address matches a connected route on R1, which causes R1 to send the packet directly to PC1's MAC address.

After you have a good grasp of the expected behaviors of each step at Layer 3, you could then more closely examine Layer 2. Following the same ordering again, you could take a closer look at the first Layer 3 routing step in Figure 3-1 (PC1 sending a packet to R1), examining the Layer 1 and 2 details of how the frame is sent by PC1 to be delivered to R1, as shown in Figure 3-2.

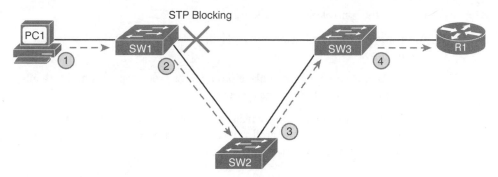

Figure 3-2 *Major Steps in a LAN Switching Forwarding Example*

For this analysis, you again begin with PC1, this time considering the Ethernet header and trailer, particularly the source and destination MAC addresses. Then, at Step 2, you consider SW1's forwarding logic, which compares the frame's destination MAC address to SW1's MAC address table, telling SW1 to forward the frame to SW2. Steps 3 and 4 repeat Step 2's logic from SW2 and SW3, respectively.

Control Plane Analysis

Many control plane processes directly affect the data plane process. For example, the data plane process of IP routing cannot work without appropriate IP routes, so routers usually use a dynamic routing protocol—a control plane protocol—to learn the routes. Routing protocols are considered to be control plane protocols in part because the work done by a routing protocol does not play a direct role in forwarding a frame or packet.

Although the data plane processes lend themselves to a somewhat generic troubleshooting process of examining the forwarding logic at each device, control plane processes differ too much to allow such generalized troubleshooting. Each control plane process can be examined separately. For example, Chapter 2, "Spanning Tree Protocol Implementation," explains how to approach troubleshooting various types of STP problems.

Predicting Normal Operations: Summary of the Process

On the exams, some questions simply require that you analyze and predict the normal operation of a working network. In other cases, predicting the normal behavior is just a precursor to isolating and fixing a problem. Regardless, if the question gives you no specific clues about the part of the network on which to focus, the following list summarizes a suggested approach for finding the answers:

Step 1.   Examine the data plane as follows:

> **A.** Determine the major Layer 3 steps—including origin host to default router, each router to the next router, and last router to the destination host—in both directions.
>
> **B.** For each Layer 2 network between a host and router or between two routers, analyze the forwarding logic for each device.

Step 2.   Examine the control plane as follows:

A. Identify the control plane protocols that are used and vital to the forwarding process.

B. Examine each vital control plane protocol for proper operation; the details of this analysis differ for each protocol.

C. Defer any analysis of control plane protocols that do not affect the data plane's correct operation until you clearly see a need for the protocol to answer that question (for example, CDP).

Problem Isolation

Troubleshooting requires that you find the root cause of the problem and then fix it. The process to find the root cause begins with problem isolation. Problem isolation moves you from the general ideas about a problem, to a specific idea of what the problem is, as follows:

Before problem isolation: I have no idea, except for some general symptoms.

After problem isolation: I have an idea of what is not working, a comparison to how it should be working, and I know on which devices it should be working differently.

For example, consider Figure 3-1 again, which shows a packet being delivered from PC1 to PC2, and back, in six routing steps. In this case, however, you determine that R2 gets the packet that flows left to right in the figure, but the packet is never delivered to PC2. So, you take closer look at the third routing step in the figure, between R2 and PC2, to further isolate the problem. That process of narrowing down the reason for the problem is called *problem isolation.*

After you isolate the problem to one IP forwarding step (as shown in Figure 3-1), you should continue to further isolate the problem to as small a number of components as possible. For example, if R2 gets the packet, but PC2 does not, the problem might be in R2, SW4, SW5, PC2, the cabling, or possibly in devices left out of the network documentation.

The process to further isolate the problem typically requires thinking about functions at many layers of the OSI model and about both data plane and control plane functions. For instance, R2 needs to know PC2's MAC address as learned using Address Resolution Protocol (ARP). If you discover that R2 does not have an ARP entry to PC2, you might be tempted to think that some sort of IP-related problem exists. However, the root cause might be any of these:

■ The SW4–SW5 trunk might be shut down.

■ The SW5-PC2 cable might be bad.

■ The PC2 IPv4 configuration may not have set PC2's IP address.

■ The Dynamic Host Configuration Protocol (DHCP) server might be misconfigured, so PC2 did not learn a DHCP address.

Problem isolation refers to the process of starting with a general idea, and getting more and more specific. In the example, that problem was isolated to the point where it was clear that R2's ARP Request for PC2 failed, but as described, the specific reason why the ARP failed had not yet been determined.

If an exam question gives no hints as to where to start, the following process summarizes a good general systematic problem isolation strategy:

Step 1. Begin by examining the Layer 3 data plane (IP forwarding), comparing the results to the expected normal behavior until you identify the first major routing step that fails.

Step 2. Further isolate the problem to as few components as possible:

   A. Examine functions at all layers, but focusing on Layers 1, 2, and 3.

   B. Examine both data plane and control plane functions.

On the exams, remember that you get no style points for good troubleshooting methods, so just find the answer any way you can, even if that means you guessed a bit based on the context of the question. For example, the suggested process in Step 2A says to focus on Layers 1, 2, and 3; that suggestion is based on the fact that the CCNA exams focus mainly on these three layers. But you should look to shortcut this process as much as possible based on what the question says.

Root Cause Analysis

The final of the three steps, root cause analysis, strives to finish the troubleshooting process to identify the specific device and function that needs to be fixed. The root cause is a problem in the network, that once it is fixed, solves at least part of the original problem.

Finding the root cause is vitally important because the root cause can be fixed. For example, continuing the same problem with R2 not being able to forward packets to PC2, consider the list of problems identified through problem isolation:

■ R2 cannot forward packets to PC2.

■ R2 gets no ARP Reply from PC2.

■ SW4's interface for the trunk to SW5 is in a down/down state.

■ The cable used between SW4 and SW5 uses the wrong cabling pinouts.

All these statements might be true about a particular problem scenario, but only the last item has an obvious actionable solution (replace with a correctly wired cable). Although the other statements are valid, and are important facts to think about during problem isolation, they do not imply the specific action to take to solve the problem. As a result, the root cause analysis step reduces to two simple statements:

Step 1. Continue isolating the problem until you identify the true root cause, which in turn has an obvious solution.

Step 2. If you cannot reduce the problem to its true root cause, isolate the problem as much as possible and change something in the network, which may change the symptoms and help you identify the root cause.

Real World Versus the Exams

On the exam, look for clues as to the general topic for which you need to do some part of the troubleshooting process. For example, if the figure shows a network like the one in Figure 3-1, but all the multiple-choice answers refer to VLANs and STP, start by looking at the LAN environment. Note that you might still want to consider Layers 1 through 3, and both the data and control plane details, to help you find the answers.

> **NOTE**   This section applies generally to troubleshooting, but it is included only in this chapter because this is the first chapter in the book dedicated to troubleshooting.

The introduction to troubleshooting methods is now ended. Now on to some specifics of how to troubleshoot pretty much all of the LAN switching topics covered in the ICND1 exam.

Troubleshooting the LAN Switching Data Plane

> **NOTE**   Here are a few study tips to begin the second section of this chapter. Take a break, catch your breath, and get ready. This next major section is long, about as long as the average "Foundation Topics" part of most other chapters. If you need to stop reading before the end of this long section, try to end before beginning the next heading that starts with "Step 1," "Step 2," and so on.

The generic troubleshooting strategies explained so far in this chapter suggest beginning with the IP routing process at Layer 3. If the engineer identifies a problem at a particular step in the IP forwarding process, the next step should be to examine that routing step more closely, including looking at the underlying Layer 1 and 2 status. If that routing step happens to flow over a LAN, the details in this section can be used to isolate the problem and find the root cause.

This page begins the second of three major sections in this chapter, with a detailed look at the tools and processes used to troubleshoot the LAN data plane processes at Layers 1 and 2. The rest of this chapter assumes that the root cause is a LAN issue, and not a Layer 3 issue; Chapters 4, "Troubleshooting IPv4 Routing Part I," 5, "Troubleshooting IPv4 Routing Part II," and 11, "Troubleshooting IPv4 Routing Protocols," examine Layer 3 troubleshooting for IPv4. This chapter also makes some references to control plane protocols, specifically Spanning Tree Protocol (STP), but STP has already been well covered in the two previous chapters. So, these sections focus specifically on the LAN switching data plane.

As for organization, this major section has five main topics. The first is a review of the LAN switch forwarding processes, and an introduction to the four major steps in the LAN switching troubleshooting process as suggested in this chapter. The other four topics take each of the four troubleshooting steps and break them down, one step at a time.

An Overview of the Normal LAN Switch Forwarding Process

Chapter 1 of this book reviewed the logic a LAN switch uses when forwarding frames. However, that list described the logic without STP. The following process steps outline that logic, with added notes that focus on the impact of STP on the switch forwarding process:

Step 1.   Determine the VLAN in which the frame should be forwarded, as follows:

  A. If the frame arrives on an access interface, use the interface's access VLAN.

  B. If the frame arrives on a trunk interface, use the VLAN listed in the frame's trunking header.

Step 2.   If the incoming interface is in an STP learning or forwarding state in that VLAN, add the source MAC address to the MAC address table, with incoming interface and VLAN ID (if not already in the table).

Step 3.   If the incoming interface is not in an STP forwarding state in that VLAN, discard the frame.

Step 4.   Look for the destination MAC address of the frame in the MAC address table, but only for entries in the VLAN identified at Step 1. If the destination MAC is found or not found, follow these steps:

  A. **Found:** Forward the frame out the only interface listed in the matched address table entry.

  B. **Not found:** Flood the frame out all other access ports in that same VLAN that are in an STP forwarding state and out all trunk ports that list this VLAN as fully supported (active, in the allowed list, not pruned, STP forwarding).

To forward a frame, a switch must first determine in which VLAN the frame should be forwarded (Step 1), learn the source MAC addresses as needed (Step 2), and then choose where to forward the frame. Just to make sure that the process is clear, consider an example using Figure 3-3, in which PC1 sends a frame to its default gateway, R1, with the MAC addresses shown in the figure.

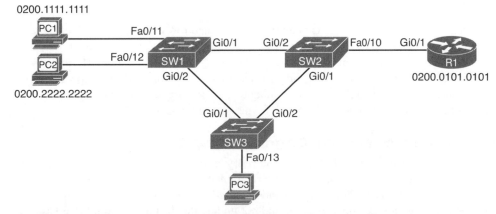

Figure 3-3   *Switched Network Used in Data Plane Analysis in Chapter 3*

In this case, consider the frame as sent from PC1 (source MAC 0200.1111.1111) to R1 (destination MAC 0200.0101.0101). The following list details the logic at each step of the summary of switching logic:

■ SW1, using Step 1, determines whether interface Fa0/11 is operating as an access interface or a trunk. In this case, it is an access interface assigned to VLAN 3.

■ For Step 2, SW1 adds an entry to its MAC address table, listing MAC address 0200.1111.1111, interface Fa0/11, and VLAN 3.

■ At Step 3, SW1 confirms that the incoming interface, Fa0/11, is in an STP forwarding state.

■ Finally, at Step 4, SW1 looks for an entry with MAC address 0200.0101.0101 in VLAN 3. If SW1 finds an entry that lists interface Gigabit 0/1, SW1 then forwards the frame only out Gi0/1. If the outgoing interface (Gi0/1) is a trunk interface, SW1 adds a VLAN trunking header that lists VLAN 3, the VLAN ID determined at Step 1.

For another slightly different example, consider a broadcast sent by PC1. Steps 1 through 3 occur as in this list, but at Step 4, SW1 floods the frame. However, SW1 only floods the frame out access ports in VLAN 3 and trunk ports that support VLAN 3, with the restriction that SW1 will not forward a copy of the frame out ports not in an STP forwarding state.

Although this forwarding logic is relatively simple, the troubleshooting process requires the application of most every LAN-related concept in both the ICND1 and ICND2 books, plus other topics as well. For example, knowing that PC1 first sends frames to SW1, it makes sense to check the interface's status, ensure that the interface is "up and up," and fix the problem with the interface if it is not. Dozens of individual items might need to be checked to troubleshoot a problem. So, this chapter suggests a LAN data plane troubleshooting process that organizes the actions into four main steps:

Step 1.   Confirm the network diagrams using CDP.

Step 2.   Isolate interface problems.

Step 3.   Isolate filtering and port security problems.

Step 4.   Isolate VLANs and trunking problems.

The next four sections review and explain the concepts and tools to perform each of these four steps. Although some facts and information are new, most of the specific underlying concepts have already been covered, either in *Cisco CCENT/CCNA ICND1 100-101 Official Cert Guide* or in Chapters 1 and 2 of this book. The main goal is to help you pull all the concepts together so that analyzing unique scenarios—as will be required on the exams—takes a little less time, with a much better chance for success.

Step 1: Confirm the Network Diagrams Using CDP

The Cisco Discovery Protocol (CDP) help you verify the information in the network diagram and to complete the rest of the necessary information about the devices and topology. In real life, the network diagrams can be old and outdated, and a problem might be caused because someone moved some cables and did not update the diagrams. I doubt that Cisco would write a question with purposefully inaccurate information in the figure, but the exam might easily include questions for which the network diagram does not list all the required information, and you need to use CDP to find the rest of the details. So, this section reviews CDP, and a good first LAN data plane troubleshooting step is as follows:

Step 1.   Verify the accuracy of and complete the information listed in the network diagram using CDP.

NOTE   This chapter shows a series of numbered troubleshooting steps for LAN switching, begun here with Step 1. The steps and their numbers are unimportant for the exam; the steps are just numbered in this chapter for easier reference.

Cisco routers, switches, and other devices use CDP for a variety of reasons, but routers and switches use it to announce basic information about themselves to their neighbors—information like the hostname, device type, IOS version, and interface numbers. Three commands in particular list the CDP information learned from neighbors, as listed in Table 3-1. In fact, in cases for which no diagram exists, an engineer could create a diagram of routers and switches using **show cdp** command output.

Table 3-1   show cdp Commands That List Information About Neighbors

Command	Description
show cdp neighbors [*type number*]	Lists one summary line of information about each neighbor or just the neighbor found on a specific interface if an interface was listed
show cdp neighbors detail	Lists one large set (approximately 15 lines) of information, one set for every neighbor
show cdp entry *name*	Lists the same information as the **show cdp neighbors detail** command, but only for the named neighbor

CDP output can be a little tricky because it may not be obvious whether a listed interface is on the local device, or on a neighbor. Reading left to right, the output usually lists the hostname of the neighboring device under the heading Device ID. However, the next heading of Local Intrfce, meaning local interface, is the local device's interface name/number. The neighboring device's interface name/number is on the right side of the command output under the heading Port ID.

Example 3-1 lists an example **show cdp neighbors** command from SW2 in Figure 3-3. Take the time to compare the shaded portions of the command output to the accurate details in Figure 3-3 to see which fields list interfaces for which devices.

Example 3-1 show cdp *Command Example*

```
SW2# show cdp neighbors
Capability Codes: R - Router, T - Trans Bridge, B - Source Route Bridge
                  S - Switch, H - Host, I - IGMP, r - Repeater, P - Phone,
                  D - Remote, C - CVTA, M - Two-port Mac Relay


Device ID        Local Intrfce     Holdtme    Capability  Platform  Port ID
SW1              Gig 0/2           154               S I  WS-C2960- Gig 0/1
SW3              Gig 0/1           170               S I  WS-C2960- Gig 0/2
R1               Fas 0/10          134             R S I  CISCO2901 Gig 0/1
```

CDP creates a security exposure when enabled. To avoid the exposure of allowing an attacker to learn details about each switch, you can easily disable CDP. Cisco recommends that CDP be disabled on all interfaces that do not have a specific need for it. The most likely interfaces that need to use CDP are interfaces connected to other Cisco routers and switches and interfaces connected to Cisco IP phones. Otherwise, CDP can be disabled per interface using the **no cdp enable** interface subcommand. (The **cdp enable** interface subcommand reenables CDP.) Alternatively, the **no cdp run** global command disables CDP for the entire switch, with the **cdp run** global command reenabling CDP globally.

Step 2: Isolate Interface Problems

A Cisco switch interface must be in a working state before the switch can process frames received on the interface or send frames out the interface. So, a somewhat obvious troubleshooting step should be to examine the state of each interface, specifically those expected to be used when forwarding frames, and verify that the interfaces are up and working.

This section examines the possible interface states on a Cisco IOS–based switch, lists root causes for the nonoperational states, and covers a popular problem that occurs even when the interface appears to be in a working state. The specific tasks for this step can be summarized with the following troubleshooting steps:

Step 2.   Check for interface problems as follows:

   A. Determine interface status code(s) for each required interface, and if not in a connected or up/up state, resolve the problems until the interface reaches the connected or up/up state.

   B. For interfaces in a connected (up/up) state, also check for two other problems: duplex mismatches and some variations of port security purposefully dropping frames.

Interface Status Codes and Reasons for Nonworking States

Cisco switches use two different sets of status codes: one set of two codes (words) that uses the same conventions as do router interface status codes, and another set with a single code (word). Both sets of status codes can determine whether an interface is working.

The switch **show interfaces** and **show interfaces description** commands list the two-code status just like routers. The two codes are named the *line status* and *protocol status*, with the codes generally referring to whether Layer 1 is working and whether Layer 2 is working, respectively. LAN switch interfaces typically show an interface with both codes as "up" or both codes as "down" because all switch interfaces use the same Ethernet data link layer protocols, so the data link layer protocol should never have a problem.

NOTE   This book refers to these two status codes in shorthand by just listing the two codes with a slash between them (for example, up/up).

The **show interfaces status** command lists a single interface status code. This single interface status code corresponds to different combinations of the traditional two-code interface status codes and can be easily correlated to those codes. For example, the **show interfaces status** command lists a "connected" state for working interfaces, which corresponds to the up/up state seen with the **show interfaces** and **show interfaces description** commands.

Any interface state other than connected and up/up means that the switch cannot forward or receive frames on the interface. Each nonworking interface state has a small set of root causes. Also, note that the exams could easily ask a question that only showed one or the other type of status code, so to be prepared for the exams, know the meanings of both sets of interface status codes. Table 3-2 lists the code combinations and some root causes that could have caused a particular interface status.

Table 3-2   LAN Switch Interface Status Codes

Line Status	Protocol Status	Interface Status	Typical Root Cause
admin. down	down	disabled	Interface is configured with the **shutdown** command.
down	down	notconnect	No cable, bad cable, wrong cable pinouts, speeds mismatched on the two connected devices, or device on the other end of the cable is either powered off or the other interface is shut down.
up	down	notconnect	Not expected on LAN switch interfaces.
down	down (err-disabled)	err-disabled	Port security has disabled the interface. EtherChannel uses this state for interfaces in the channel whose configuration does not match other interfaces in the channel.
up	up	connected	Interface is working.

The notconnect State and Cabling Pinouts

Table 3-2 lists several reasons why a switch interface can be in the notconnect state. Most of those reasons do not need much further explanation than the text in the table. For example, if an interface is connected to another switch, the local switch shows a notconnect state when the other switch's interface has been shut down. However, one of the reasons for a not-connect state—incorrect cable pinouts—deserves a little more attention because it is both a common mistake and is not otherwise covered in this book. (Ethernet cabling pinouts are covered in *Cisco CCENT/CCNA ICND1 100-101 Official Cert Guide* Chapter 2.)

Ethernet unshielded twisted-pair (UTP) cabling standards specify the pins to which each of the wires should connect on the RJ-45 connectors on the ends of the cable. The devices transmit using pairs of wires, with 10BASE-T and 100BASE-T using two pairs: one to transmit and one to receive data. When connecting two devices that use the same pair of pins to transmit, the cable—a crossover cable—must connect or cross the wires connected to each device's transmit pair over to the other device's expected receive pair. Conversely, devices that already use opposite pairs for transmitting data need a straight-through cable that does not cross the pairs. Figure 3-4 shows an example in a typical switched LAN, with the types of cabling pinouts shown.

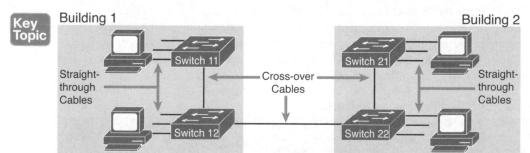

Figure 3-4 *Crossover and Straight-Through Cables in Use*

Effective troubleshooting requires knowledge of which devices transmit on which pairs. Table 3-3 lists the more common devices seen in the context of CCNA, along with the pairs used. Note that when you are connecting two types of devices from the same column, a crossover cable is required; when you are connecting two devices from different columns of the table, a straight-through cable is required.

Table 3-3   10BASE-T and 100BASE-T Pin Pairs Used

Devices That Transmit on 1,2 and Receive on 3,6	Devices That Transmit on 3,6 and Receive on 1,2
PC NICs	Hubs
Routers	Switches
Wireless access points (Ethernet interface)	—
Ethernet-connected network printers	—

Determining Switch Interface Speed and Duplex

Switch interfaces can find their speed and duplex settings in several ways. By default, interfaces that use copper wiring use the IEEE-standard autonegotiation process. Alternately, switch interfaces, routers, and most network interface cards (NIC) can also be configured to use a specific speed or duplex setting. On switches and routers, the **speed {10 | 100 | 1000}** interface subcommand with the **duplex {half | full}** interface subcommand sets these values.

The **show interfaces** and **show interfaces status** commands on LAN switches list both the speed and duplex settings on an interface, as shown in Example 3-2.

Example 3-2 *Displaying Speed and Duplex Settings on Switch Interfaces*

```
SW1# show interfaces f0/11 status


Port      Name          Status       Vlan    Duplex  Speed Type
Fa0/11    link to PC1   connected    3       a-full    100 10/100BaseTX


SW1# show interfaces f0/12 status


Port      Name          Status       Vlan    Duplex  Speed Type
Fa0/12    link to PC2   connected    3       a-full  a-100 10/100BaseTX


SW1# show interfaces fa0/12
FastEthernet0/12 is up, line protocol is up (connected)
  Hardware is Fast Ethernet, address is 1833.9d7b.0e8c (bia 1833.9d7b.0e8c)
  Description: link to PC2
  MTU 1500 bytes, BW 100000 Kbit/sec, DLY 100 usec,
     reliability 255/255, txload 1/255, rxload 1/255
  Encapsulation ARPA, loopback not set
  Keepalive set (10 sec)
  Full-duplex, 100Mb/s, media type is 10/100BaseTX
  input flow-control is off, output flow-control is unsupported
  ARP type: ARPA, ARP Timeout 04:00:00
  Last input never, output 00:00:01, output hang never
  Last clearing of "show interface" counters never
  Input queue: 0/75/0/0 (size/max/drops/flushes); Total output drops: 0
  Queueing strategy: fifo
  Output queue: 0/40 (size/max)
  5 minute input rate 0 bits/sec, 0 packets/sec
  5 minute output rate 0 bits/sec, 0 packets/sec
     1453 packets input, 138334 bytes, 0 no buffer
     Received 1418 broadcasts (325 multicasts)
     0 runts, 0 giants, 0 throttles
     0 input errors, 0 CRC, 0 frame, 0 overrun, 0 ignored
     0 watchdog, 325 multicast, 0 pause input
     0 input packets with dribble condition detected
     33640 packets output, 2651335 bytes, 0 underruns
```

3

```
    0 output errors, 0 collisions, 1 interface resets
    0 unknown protocol drops
    0 babbles, 0 late collision, 0 deferred
    0 lost carrier, 0 no carrier, 0 pause output
    0 output buffer failures, 0 output buffers swapped out
```

Although both commands can be useful, only the **show interfaces status** command implies how the switch determined the speed and duplex settings. The command output lists auto-negotiated settings with an a-. For example, a-full means full-duplex as autonegotiated, whereas full means full duplex but as manually configured. The example's shaded areas show the following evidence of the use of autonegotiation on F0/11 and F0/12:

F0/11: 100 Mbps due to configuration (100, without an a-), and full duplex due to auto-negotiation (a-full)

F0/12: Both values from autonegotiation (both a-100 and a-full with the a- prefix)

Note that the **show interfaces Fa0/12** command (without the **status** option) identifies the speed and duplex but does not state anything about how the switch learned or set the values.

Issues Related to Speed and Duplex

When troubleshooting, and looking at the speed and duplex, looking at the devices on both ends of the link can be helpful. The devices do not have to use the same speed or duplex settings, but with different results, as follows:

- **Speed mismatch:** If the endpoints on an Ethernet link use different speeds, both should show the interface status as notconnect or down/down.

- **Duplex mismatch:** If the endpoints use the same speed, but different duplex settings, the interfaces will come up, but other performance counters will show problems on the half-duplex end of the link.

Interestingly, Cisco switches actually make a speed mismatch difficult to achieve. Clearly, if both devices on the link use autonegotiation, they will choose to use the same speed. However, if the neighboring device disables autonegotiation, a Cisco switch, even without autonegotiation, still figures out the right speed and uses it—unless configured to run at a preset speed with the **speed** command. When configured with a **speed** command, like **speed 100**, the switch interface must attempt to use that speed.

NOTE Cisco switches do not have a single command to disable IEEE autonegotiation; however, configuring the speed and duplex commands to a specific speed and duplex has the side effect of disabling autonegotiation.

For example, in Figure 3-3, imagine that SW2's Gi0/2 interface were configured with the **speed 100** and **duplex half** commands (not recommended settings on a Gigabit-capable interface, by the way). SW2 would use those settings and disable the IEEE-standard autone-gotiation process because both the **speed** and **duplex** commands have been configured. If SW1's Gi0/1 (on the other end of the link) interface did not have a **speed** command config-ured, SW1 would still recognize the speed (100 Mbps)—even though SW2 would not use IEEE-standard negotiation—and SW1 would also use a speed of 100 Mbps. Example 3-3 shows the results of this specific case on SW1.

Example 3-3 *Displaying Speed and Duplex Settings on Switch Interfaces*

```
SW1# show interfaces gi0/1 status

Port      Name             Status        Vlan      Duplex  Speed Type
Gi0/1     Link to SW2      connected     trunk     a-half  a-100 10/100/1000BaseTX
```

The speed and duplex still show up with a prefix of a- in the example, implying autonego-tiation. The reason is that, in this case, the speed was found automatically, and the duplex setting was chosen because of the default values used by the IEEE autonegotiation process. The IEEE standards state that if autonegotiation fails for ports running at 100 Mbps, use a default half-duplex setting.

A speed mismatch can be created by simply configuring different speeds on the devices on both ends of the link. Assuming the link was enabled (**no shutdown**), the switch interface would settle to a disabled or down/down state.

Finding a duplex mismatch can be much more difficult than finding a speed mismatch because the switch interface will be in a connected (up/up) state. In this case, the interface works, but it might work poorly, with poor performance and with symptoms of intermittent problems.

A duplex mismatch on a link causes problems because one device (the half-duplex end) uses carrier sense multiple access with collision detection (CSMA/CD) logic, and the other does not. The half-duplex end waits to send if receiving a frame. The half-duplex end believes that when it is sending and another frame starts arriving that a collision has occurred, so the half-duplex end stops sending the frame. The full-duplex end sends frames at any time, causing the half-duplex end to incorrectly believe collisions happen. With enough traffic load, the interface could be in a connected state, but essentially useless for passing traffic, even caus-ing the loss of vital STP messages.

To identify duplex mismatch problems, try the following actions:

- Use commands like **show interfaces** on each end of the link to confirm the duplex setting on each end.
- Watch for increases to certain counters on half-duplex interfaces. The counters—runts, collisions, and late collisions—occur when the other device uses full duplex. (Note that these counters can also increment when legitimate collisions occur as well.)

Example 3-2 (earlier in this section) uses shading to indicate these counters in the output of the **show interfaces** command.

The root cause of duplex mismatches might be related to the defaults chosen by the IEEE autonegotiation process. When a device attempts autonegotiation and the other device does not respond, the first device chooses the default duplex setting based on the current speed. The default duplex settings, per the IEEE, are chosen as follows:

- If the speed is 10 Mbps or 100 Mbps, default to use half duplex.
- If the speed is 1000 Mbps, default to use full duplex.

NOTE   Ethernet interfaces using speeds faster than 1 Gbps always use full duplex.

Step 3: Isolate Filtering and Port Security Problems

Generally speaking, any analysis of the forwarding process should consider any security features that might discard some frames or packets. For example, both routers and switches can be configured with access control lists (ACL) that examine the packets and frames being sent or received on an interface, with the router or switch discarding those packets/frames.

The CCNA exams do not include coverage of switch ACLs, but the exams do cover a switch feature called port security. As covered in *Cisco CCENT/CCNA ICND1 100-101 Official Cert Guide*, Chapter 8, the port security feature can be used to cause the switch to discard some frames sent into and out of an interface. Port security has three basic features with which it determines which frames to filter:

- Limit which specific MAC addresses can send and receive frames on a switch interface, discarding frames to/from other MAC addresses
- Limit the number of MAC addresses using the interface, discarding frames to/from MAC addresses learned after the maximum limit is reached
- A combination of the previous two points

The first port security troubleshooting step should be to find which interfaces have port security enabled, followed by a determination as to whether any violations are currently occurring. The trickiest part relates to the differences in what the IOS does in reaction to violations based on the **switchport port-security violation** *violation-mode* interface subcommand, which tells the switch what to do when a violation occurs. The general process is as follows:

Step 3.   Check for port security problems as follows:

   A.   Identify all interfaces on which port security is enabled (**show running-config** or **show port-security**).

   B.   Determine whether a security violation is currently occurring based in part on the *violation mode* of the interface's port security configuration, as follows:

   i.   **shutdown:** The interface will be in an err-disabled state.

   ii.   **restrict:** The interface will be in a connected state, but the **show port-security interface** command will show an incrementing violations counter.

      iii. **protect:** The interface will be in a connected state, and the **show port-security interface** command will not show an incrementing violations counter.

    C. In all cases, compare the port security configuration to the diagram and to the Last Source Address field in the output of the **show port-security interface** command.

One of the difficulties when troubleshooting port security relates to the fact that some port security configurations discard only the offending frames but they do not disable the interface as a result, all based on the configured violation mode. All three violation modes discard the traffic as dictated by the configuration.

For example, if only one predefined MAC address of 0200.1111.1111 is allowed, the switch discards all traffic on that interface, other than traffic to or from 0200.1111.1111. However, "shutdown" mode causes all future traffic to be discarded—even legitimate traffic from address 0200.1111.1111—after a violation has occurred. Table 3-4 summarizes some of these key points for easier study.

Table 3-4   Actions When Port Security Violation Occurs, Based on Mode

Option on the switchport port-security violation Command	Protect	Restrict	Shut Down*
Discards offending traffic	Yes	Yes	Yes
Disables the interface, discarding all traffic	No	No	Yes
Increments violation counter for each violating frame	No	Yes	Yes

* Shut down is the default setting.

Troubleshooting Step 3b refers to the interface err disabled (error disabled) state. This state verifies that the interface has been configured to use port security, that a violation has occurred, and that no traffic is allowed on the interface at the present time. This interface state implies that the shutdown violation mode is used, because it is the only one of the three port security modes that causes the interface to be disabled.

To recover from an err-disabled state, the interface must be shut down with the **shutdown** command, and then enabled with the **no shutdown** command. Example 3-4 lists an example in which the interface is in an err-disabled state.

Example 3-4   *Using Port Security to Define Correct MAC Addresses of Particular Interfaces*

```
! The first command lists all interfaces on which port security has been enabled,
! and the violation mode, under the heading "Security Action".
SW1# show port-security
Secure Port  MaxSecureAddr  CurrentAddr  SecurityViolation  Security Action
             (Count)        (Count)      (Count)
-----------------------------------------------------------------------
    Fa0/13             1            1                  1        Shutdown
-----------------------------------------------------------------------
```

```
Total Addresses in System (excluding one mac per port)     : 0
Max Addresses limit in System (excluding one mac per port) : 8192

!
! The next command shows the err-disabled state, implying a security violation.
SW1# show interfaces Fa0/13 status

Port       Name          Status       Vlan      Duplex  Speed Type
Fa0/13                   err-disabled 1                  auto    auto 10/100BaseTX
!
! The next command's output has shading for several of the most important facts.
SW1# show port-security interface Fa0/13
Port Security              : Enabled
Port Status                : Secure-shutdown
Violation Mode             : Shutdown
Aging Time                 : 0 mins
Aging Type                 : Absolute
SecureStatic Address Aging : Disabled
Maximum MAC Addresses      : 1
Total MAC Addresses        : 1
Configured MAC Addresses   : 1
Sticky MAC Addresses       : 0
Last Source Address:Vlan   : 0200.3333.3333:2
Security Violation Count   : 1
```

The output of the **show port-security interface** command lists a couple of items helpful in the troubleshooting process. The port status of secure-shutdown means that the interface is disabled for all traffic as a result of a violation, and that the interface state should be err-disabled. The end of the command output lists a violations counter, incremented by 1 for each new violation. Interestingly, with a violation mode of shutdown, the counter increments by 1, the interface is placed into err-disabled state, and the counter cannot increment anymore until the engineer uses the **shutdown** and **no shutdown** commands on the interface, in succession.

Finally, note that the second-to-last line lists the source MAC address of the last frame received on the interface. This value can prove useful in identifying the MAC address of the device that caused the violation.

Moving on to another example, the restrict and protect violation modes still cause frame discards, but with much different behavior. With these violation modes, the interface remains in a connected (up/up) state while still discarding the inappropriate frames because of port security. So, avoid the pitfall of assuming that an interface in a connected, or up/up, state cannot have any other reasons for not passing traffic.

Example 3-5 shows a sample configuration and **show** command when using protect mode. In this case, a PC with MAC address 0200.3333.3333 sent frames into port Fa0/13, with the port configured to restrict Fa0/13 to only receive frames sent by 0200.1111.1111.

Example 3-5 *Port Security Using Protect Mode*

```
SW1# show running-config
! Lines omitted for brevity
interface FastEthernet0/13
 switchport mode access
 switchport port-security
 switchport port-security mac-address 0200.1111.1111
 switchport port-security violation protect
! Lines omitted for brevity


SW1# show port-security interface Fa0/13
Port Security              : Enabled
Port Status                : Secure-up
Violation Mode             : Protect
Aging Time                 : 0 mins
Aging Type                 : Absolute
SecureStatic Address Aging : Disabled
Maximum MAC Addresses      : 1
Total MAC Addresses        : 1
Configured MAC Addresses   : 1
Sticky MAC Addresses       : 0
Last Source Address:Vlan   : 0200.3333.3333:1
Security Violation Count   : 0
```

This **show** command output was gathered after many frames had been sent by a PC with MAC address 0200.3333.3333, with all the frames being discarded by the switch because of port security. The command output shows the disallowed PC's 0200.3333.3333 MAC address as the last source MAC address in a received frame. However, note that the port status is listed as secure-up and the violation count as 0—both indications that might make you think all is well. However, in protect mode, the **show port-security interface** command does not show any information confirming that an actual violation has occurred. The only indication is that end-user traffic does not make it to where it needs to go.

If this example had used violation mode restrict, the port status would have also stayed in a secure-up state, but the security violation counter would have incremented once for each violating frame.

For the exams, a port security violation might not be a problem; it might be the exact function intended. The question text might well explicitly state what port security should be doing. In these cases, it can be quicker to just immediately look at the port security configuration. Then, compare the configuration to the MAC addresses of the devices connected to the interface. The most likely problem on the exams is that the MAC addresses have been misconfigured or that the maximum number of MAC addresses has been set too low.

The following list summarizes the port security configuration steps, repeated from Chapter 8 of the ICND1 book, for reference:

Step 1. Make the switch interface either a static access or trunk interface, using the **switchport mode access** or the **switchport mode trunk** interface subcommands, respectively.

Step 2. Enable port security using the **switchport port-security** interface subcommand.

Step 3. (Optional) Override the default maximum number of allowed MAC addresses associated with the interface (1) by using the **switchport port-security maximum** *number* interface subcommand.

Step 4. (Optional) Override the default action to take upon a security violation (shutdown) using the **switchport port-security violation** {**protect** | **restrict** | **shutdown**} interface subcommand.

Step 5. (Optional) Predefine any allowed source MAC addresses for this interface using the **switchport port-security mac-address** *mac-address* command. Use the command multiple times to define more than one MAC address.

Step 6. (Optional) Tell the switch to "sticky learn" dynamically learned MAC addresses with the **switchport port-security mac-address sticky** interface subcommand.

Step 4: Isolate VLAN and Trunking Problems

A switch's forwarding process depends on both the definitions of access VLANs on access interfaces and on VLAN trunks that can pass traffic for many VLANs. In addition, before a switch can forward frames in a particular VLAN, the switch must know about a VLAN, either through configuration or VTP, and the VLAN must be active. The following sections examine some of the tools regarding all these VLAN-related issues. This configuration step includes the following steps:

Step 4. Check VLANs and VLAN trunks as follows:

    A. Identify all access interfaces and their assigned access VLANs, and reassign into the correct VLANs as needed.

    B. Determine whether the VLANs both exist (configured or learned with VTP) and are active on each switch. If not, configure and activate the VLANs to resolve problems as needed.

    C. Identify the operationally trunking interfaces on each switch and determine the VLANs that can be forwarded over each trunk.

The next three sections discuss Steps 4A, 4B, and 4C in succession.

Ensuring That the Right Access Interfaces Are in the Right VLANs

To ensure that each access interface has been assigned to the correct VLAN, engineers simply need to determine which switch interfaces are access interfaces instead of trunk interfaces, determine the assigned access VLANs on each interface, and compare the information to the documentation. The **show** commands listed in Table 3-5 can help you with this process.

Table 3-5   Commands That Can Find Access Ports and VLANs

EXEC Command	Description
show vlan	Lists each VLAN and all interfaces assigned to that VLAN but does not include trunks
show vlan brief	Lists a briefer version of the same information in the **show vlan** command
show vlan id *num*	Lists both access and trunk ports in the VLAN
show interfaces *type number* switchport	Identifies the interface's access VLAN, voice VLAN, plus the configured and operational mode (access or trunk)
show mac address-table dynamic	Lists MAC table entries: MAC addresses with associated interfaces and VLANs

If possible, start this step with the **show vlan** and **show vlan brief** commands , because they list all the known VLANs and the access interfaces assigned to each VLAN. Be aware, however, that the output of these commands includes many interfaces, but not all; specifically, these commands list the following:

- Interfaces that are not currently operating as trunks
- Interfaces in any current interface state, including those in a notconnect or err-disabled state

For example, these commands might include interface Gi0/2 in the list of interfaces in VLAN 1 when G0/2 is not trunking. However, as soon as Gi0/2 comes up, the interface might negotiate trunking—at which point the interface would no longer be an access interface and would no longer be listed in the output of the **show vlan brief** command.

If the **show vlan** and **show interface switchport** commands are not available in a particular test question, the **show mac address-table** command can also help identify the access VLAN. This command lists the MAC address table, with each entry including a MAC address, interface, and VLAN ID. If the test question implies that a switch interface connects to a single device PC, you should only see one MAC table entry that lists that particular access interface; the VLAN ID listed for that same entry identifies the access VLAN. (You cannot make such assumptions for trunking interfaces.)

After you determine the access interfaces and associated VLANs, if the interface is assigned to the wrong VLAN, use the **switchport access vlan** *vlan-id* interface subcommand to assign the correct VLAN ID.

Access VLANs Not Being Defined or Not Being Active

A switch will not forward a frame in VLAN x if the switch

- Has no definition for VLAN x (for example, with the **vlan** x command)
- VLAN x exists on the switch, but it is disabled (**shutdown**)

The next troubleshooting step, Step 4B, is a reminder to make sure each switch has a definition for the VLAN, and that it is not shut down.

Switches normally know of the existence of a VLAN by either learning about the VLAN using VTP or through direct configuration on the local switch. For the purposes of this book, assume that VTP has been disabled or set to use transparent mode. So, for this book, to support a VLAN number x, all switches must be directly configured with the **vlan** x command.

Both issues can be easily found from the output of the **show vlan** or **show vlan brief** commands. If the VLAN does not exist on the switch, these commands simply do not list the VLAN; in that case, add the VLAN to the configuration using the **vlan** *vlan-id* configuration command. If listed, the status will be listed as active or act/lshut. The second of these states means that the VLAN is shut down. To solve this problem, use the **no shutdown vlan** *vlan-id* global configuration command.

Identify Trunks and VLANs Forwarded on Those Trunks

At this step (4C), you can separate problems into two general categories as you begin to isolate the problem: problems with the details of how an operational trunk works and problems caused when an interface that should trunk does not trunk.

The first category in this step can be easily done using the **show interfaces trunk** command, which only lists information about currently operational trunks. The best place to begin with this command is the last section of output, which lists the VLANs whose traffic will be forwarded over the trunk. Any VLANs that make it to this final list of VLANs in the command output meet the following criteria:

- The VLAN exists and is active on the local switch (as covered in the previous section and seen in the **show vlan** command).
- The VLAN has not been removed from the allowed VLAN list on the trunk (as configured with the **switchport trunk allowed vlan** interface subcommand).
- The VLAN has not been VTP-pruned from the trunk. (This is a VTP feature, which this section will now otherwise ignore. It is only listed here because the **show** command output mentions it.)
- The trunk is in an STP forwarding state in that VLAN (as also seen in the **show spanning-tree vlan** *vlan-id* command).

Example 3-6 shows a sample of the command output from the **show interfaces trunk** command, with the final section of the command output shaded. In this case, the trunk only forwards traffic in VLANs 1 and 4.

Example 3-6   *Allowed VLAN List and List of Active VLANs*

```
SW1# show interfaces trunk

Port        Mode         Encapsulation  Status        Native vlan
Gi0/1       desirable    802.1q         trunking      1


Port        Vlans allowed on trunk
Gi0/1       1-2,4-4094


Port        Vlans allowed and active in management domain
Gi0/1       1,4


Port        Vlans in spanning tree forwarding state and not pruned
Gi0/1       1,4
```

The absence of a VLAN in this last part of the command's output does not necessarily mean that a problem has occurred. In fact, a VLAN might be legitimately excluded from a trunk for any of the reasons in the list just before Example 3-6. However, for a given exam question, it can be useful to know why traffic for a VLAN will not be forwarded over a trunk, and the details inside the output identify the specific reasons.

The output of the **show interfaces trunk** command creates three separate lists of VLANs, each under a separate heading. These three lists show a progression of reasons why a VLAN is not forwarded over a trunk. Table 3-6 summarizes the headings that precede each list and the reasons why a switch chooses to include or not include a VLAN in each list.

Table 3-6   VLAN Lists In the **show interfaces trunk** Command

List Position	Heading	Reasons
First	VLANs allowed	VLAN 1–4094, minus those removed by the **switchport trunk allowed** command
Second	VLANs allowed and active...	The first list, minus those either not defined to the local switch or those in shutdown mode
Third	VLANs in spanning tree...	The second list, minus STP blocking and VTP pruned interfaces

Moving on to another trunking topic, you should also check a trunk's native VLAN configuration at this step. The native VLAN ID can be manually set to different VLANs on either end of the trunk, using the **switchport trunk native vlan** *vlan-id* command. If the native VLANs differ, the switches will accidentally cause frames to leave one VLAN and enter another.

For example, if switch SW1 sends a frame using native VLAN 1 on an 802.1Q trunk, SW1 does not add a VLAN header, as is normal for the native VLAN. When switch SW2 receives the frame, noticing that no 802.1Q header exists, SW2 assumes that the frame is part of SW2's configured native VLAN. If SW2 has been configured to think VLAN 2 is the native VLAN on that trunk, SW2 will try to forward the received frame into VLAN 2.

Finally, check for links that should trunk but that are not trunking. The most likely cause of this problem is a misconfiguration of trunking on the opposite ends of the link. The **switchport mode** {access | trunk | dynamic {desirable | auto}} interface subcommand tells the interface whether to trunk and the rules with which to negotiate trunking. You can display any interface's administrative (configured) trunking mode, as set by this configuration command, using the **show interface switchport** command.

Make sure that you know the meaning of each of these configuration command's options. The particularly bad combination is to use **dynamic auto** on both ends, which happens to be the default setting on some Cisco switches. This setting on both ends means that both ends will negotiate trunking—if the other end starts the process. So, both ends wait, and never form a trunk. Table 3-7 lists the options on the **switchport trunk mode** command, and what trunking mode that should result.

Table 3-7   Expected Trunking Operational Mode Based on the Configured Administrative Modes

Administrative Mode	Access	Dynamic Auto	Trunk	Dynamic Desirable
access	Access	Access	Access	Access
dynamic auto	Access	Access	Trunk	Trunk
trunk	Access	Trunk	Trunk	Trunk
dynamic desirable	Access	Trunk	Trunk	Trunk

In some cases, an interface can fail to use trunking because of a misconfiguration of the type of trunking—in other words, whether to use Inter-Switch Link (ISL) or 802.1Q. For example, if two switches on opposite ends of a segment configured the **switchport trunk encapsulation isl** and **switchport trunk encapsulation dot1Q** commands, respectively, the trunk would not form, because the types of trunks (the encapsulation) do not match.

Troubleshooting Examples and Exercises

The rest of this chapter is basically practice. It's up to you to decide whether you want to learn by doing more reading, learn by trying to find the answers before reading, or decide that you know how to apply what you read in this chapter and move on to the next chapter.

The rest of this chapter shows two lengthy examples of how to apply troubleshooting concepts and processes to LANs. The first example shows a LAN and lots of **show** commands. The LAN has configuration problems. So, the text uses the four-step process, as described in this chapter, to do problem isolation and uncover the root causes of the problems.

The second example starts with the same LAN as the first problem, with all the problems fixed. In this example, this question is asked: Where do the frames flow in this LAN? This example then examines many **show** commands that prove where the frames will go.

Troubleshooting is a skill, and these examples help you build that skill. One specific skill is to look at a bunch of text in the output of a **show** command and apply what that means to a network diagram. These two examples have 34 **show** commands combined as of the last count. These examples are the last LAN-specific topics in your CCNA study and can help you pull many concepts together. The pieces have probably started to fall into place, and you now understand how much Ethernet LAN technology you have added to your skill set.

Troubleshooting Example 1: Find Existing LAN Data Plane Problems

The first example shows a network diagram, plus a series of examples with **show** command output. The example takes about 12 pages of space in the book. You may use this example in one of two ways:

- **Guided Tour:** Read just like you normally would.

- **Exercise:** Look at the figures and examples, try to find all problems, and develop a plan to fix them. Specifically, look at Figure 3-5. Read Examples 3-7 through 3-14. Ignore the text, and ignore Figure 3-6 at the end of this example. While reading the examples, find as many problems as you can by analyzing the output of the commands, as compared to the figure. Compare your list to the list at the end of the chapter (hidden there to avoid spoiling the answer). Then you can read the text surrounding the examples if you want to fill in the holes in your understanding.

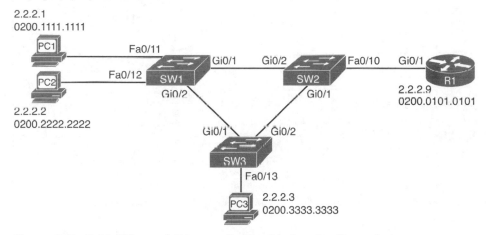

Figure 3-5   *Initial Network Diagram for Troubleshooting Example 1*

This example walks through an examination of the network shown in Figure 3-5, using the output of various **show** commands. The text follows the same four-step process discussed throughout the second major section of this chapter. The beginning of that section summarizes all the troubleshooting steps for reference; to see those steps, refer to the section "An Overview of the Normal LAN Switch Forwarding Process."

For those of you using this troubleshooting example as an exercise, start ignoring the text now and start reading the examples, looking for problems. For those of you using the walk-through method, keep reading.

Step 1: Verify the Accuracy of the Diagram Using CDP

Example 3-7 shows a variety of example output from the **show cdp neighbors** and **show cdp entry** commands on the three switches in Figure 3-5. A simple comparison confirms the names and interfaces in the figure, with the exception that SW2's Fa0/9 interface connects to Router R1, instead of SW2's Fa0/10 interface shown in Figure 3-5.

Example 3-7 *Verifying Figure 3-5 Using CDP*

```
SW1# show cdp neighbors
Capability Codes: R - Router, T - Trans Bridge, B - Source Route Bridge
                  S - Switch, H - Host, I - IGMP, r - Repeater, P - Phone,
                  D - Remote, C - CVTA, M - Two-port Mac Relay


Device ID          Local Intrfce     Holdtme    Capability  Platform  Port ID
SW2                Gig 0/1           170               S I  WS-C2960- Gig 0/2
SW3                Gig 0/2           167               S I  WS-C2960- Gig 0/1
```

```
! SW2 commands next
SW2# show cdp neighbors
Capability Codes: R - Router, T - Trans Bridge, B - Source Route Bridge
                  S - Switch, H - Host, I - IGMP, r - Repeater, P - Phone,
                  D - Remote, C - CVTA, M - Two-port Mac Relay


Device ID          Local Intrfce     Holdtme    Capability  Platform  Port ID
SW1                Gig 0/2           146               S I  WS-C2960- Gig 0/1
SW3                Gig 0/1           162               S I  WS-C2960- Gig 0/2
R1                 Fas 0/9           139             R S I  CISCO2901 Gig 0/1


SW2# show cdp entry R1
-------------------------
Device ID: R1
Entry address(es):
  IP address: 2.2.2.9
Platform: Cisco CISCO2901/K9,  Capabilities: Router Switch IGMP
Interface: FastEthernet0/9,  Port ID (outgoing port): GigabitEthernet0/1
Holdtime : 148 sec


Version :
Cisco IOS Software, C2900 Software (C2900-UNIVERSALK9-M), Version 15.2(4)M1, RELEASE
SOFTWARE (fc1)
Technical Support: http://www.cisco.com/techsupport
Copyright (c) 1986-2012 by Cisco Systems, Inc.
Compiled Thu 26-Jul-12 20:54 by prod_rel_team


advertisement version: 2
VTP Management Domain: ''
```

```
Duplex: full
Management address(es):
! SW3 command next
SW3# show cdp neighbors
Capability Codes: R - Router, T - Trans Bridge, B - Source Route Bridge
                  S - Switch, H - Host, I - IGMP, r - Repeater, P - Phone,
                  D - Remote, C - CVTA, M - Two-port Mac Relay


Device ID         Local Intrfce    Holdtme    Capability  Platform  Port ID
SW1               Gig 0/1          167            S I     WS-C2960- Gig 0/2
SW2               Gig 0/2          176            S I     WS-C2960- Gig 0/1
```

This mistake in documentation in Figure 3-5 (listing SW2 interface Fa0/10 instead of Fa0/9) may or may not affect the current network's operation. For instance, had trunking been required between SW2 and R1, SW2 interface Fa0/9—not Fa0/10—would have to have been explicitly configured to enable trunking, because routers cannot automatically negotiate to use trunking.

Note that CDP does not identify documentation problems with the interfaces that connect to the end-user PCs; for the purposes of this example, know that the rest of the interfaces shown in Figure 3-5 are the correct interfaces.

Step 2: Check for Interface Problems

The next step examines the interface status on each of the interfaces that should currently be used. Example 3-8 lists several **show interface status** commands on both SW1 and SW3. (For this chapter's purposes, assume that all interfaces on SW2 are working correctly.) Examine the output, identify any problems you see, and make a list of other interface related problems you might want to investigate further based on this output.

Example 3-8 *Interface Problems on SW1 and SW3*

```
SW1# show interfaces fa0/11 status
Port      Name            Status       Vlan      Duplex  Speed Type
Fa0/11                    connected    3         a-full  a-100 10/100BaseTX


SW1# show interfaces fa0/12 status
Port      Name            Status       Vlan      Duplex  Speed Type
Fa0/12                    notconnect   3          auto    auto 10/100BaseTX


SW1# show interfaces Gi0/1 status
Port      Name            Status       Vlan      Duplex  Speed Type
Gi0/1                     connected    trunk     a-full  a-1000 10/100/1000BaseTX
```

```
SW1# show interfaces Gi0/2 status
Port       Name             Status       Vlan       Duplex  Speed Type
Gi0/2                       connected    trunk       a-full a-1000 10/100/1000BaseTX
! Switching to SW3 next
SW3# show interfaces fa0/13 status
Port       Name             Status       Vlan       Duplex  Speed Type
Fa0/13                      connected    3           a-half a-100  10/100BaseTX

SW3# show interfaces Gi0/1 status
Port       Name             Status       Vlan       Duplex  Speed Type
Gi0/1                       connected    trunk       a-full a-1000 1000BaseTX

SW3# show interfaces Gi0/2 status
Port       Name             Status       Vlan       Duplex  Speed Type
Gi0/2                       connected    trunk       a-full a-1000 1000BaseTX
```

One obvious problem exists on SW1, with interface Fa0/12 in a notconnect state. Many reasons for this state exist, almost all relating to some cabling problem—anything from a cable that is not fully inserted into the switch port to difficult-to-find interference problems on the cable. (See Table 3-2 for suggested reasons.)

SW3's interfaces appear not to have any problems. However, all three interfaces have a duplex setting that is the same setting as what the switch would use if the autonegotiation process failed, with the use of half duplex on Fa0/13 being notable. That raises the possibility of a duplex mismatch.

You can determine that SW3's Gigabit 0/1 and 0/2 interfaces do not have a mismatch by simply using the **show interfaces status** command on SW1 and SW2 on the other end of those links, respectively. However, ports connected to a PC pose a troubleshooting problem in that you probably will not be near the PC, so you might have to guide the end user through some steps to verify the speed and duplex settings. However, it is helpful to look for the telltale signs of runts, collisions, and late collisions, as listed in the output of the **show interfaces** command in Example 3-9.

Example 3-9 *Signs of a Duplex Mismatch*

```
SW3# show interfaces fa0/13
FastEthernet0/13 is up, line protocol is up (connected)
  Hardware is Fast Ethernet, address is f47f.35cb.d78d (bia f47f.35cb.d78d)
  MTU 1500 bytes, BW 100000 Kbit/sec, DLY 100 usec,
     reliability 255/255, txload 1/255, rxload 1/255
  Encapsulation ARPA, loopback not set
  Keepalive set (10 sec)
  Half-duplex, 100Mb/s, media type is 10/100BaseTX
  input flow-control is off, output flow-control is unsupported
  ARP type: ARPA, ARP Timeout 04:00:00
  Last input never, output 00:00:01, output hang never
  Last clearing of "show interface" counters never
```

```
   Input queue: 0/75/0/0 (size/max/drops/flushes); Total output drops: 0
   Queueing strategy: fifo
   Output queue: 0/40 (size/max)
   5 minute input rate 0 bits/sec, 0 packets/sec
   5 minute output rate 0 bits/sec, 0 packets/sec
      14507 packets input, 1003344 bytes, 0 no buffer
      Received 14488 broadcasts (466 multicasts)
      54 runts, 0 giants, 0 throttles
      0 input errors, 0 CRC, 0 frame, 0 overrun, 0 ignored
      0 watchdog, 466 multicast, 0 pause input
      0 input packets with dribble condition detected
      43824 packets output, 3440304 bytes, 0 underruns
      0 output errors, 114 collisions, 2 interface resets
      0 unknown protocol drops
      0 babbles, 78 late collision, 0 deferred
      0 lost carrier, 0 no carrier, 0 pause output
      0 output buffer failures, 0 output buffers swapped out
```

In this case, a duplex mismatch does indeed exist, with the switch port using half duplex. However, note that these same counters do increment under normal half-duplex operations, so these counters do not definitively identify the problem as a duplex mismatch.

In this case, SW3's configuration needs to be changed from half duplex to full duplex on interface Fa0/13, matching the manual setting on PC3.

Step 3: Check for Port Security Problems

The next step examines the port security configuration and status on each switch. Starting with the **show port-security** command is particularly helpful because it lists the interfaces on which the feature has been enabled. Example 3-10 shows this command on SW1 and SW2, plus a few other commands. Note that both SW2 and SW3 do not have the port security feature enabled.

Examine the output in Example 3-10, and before reading beyond the end of the example, make a few notes about what next steps you would take to either rule out port security as a potential problem or what command you would use to further isolate a potential problem.

Example 3-10 *Port Security on SW1 and SW2*

```
SW1# show port-security
Secure Port  MaxSecureAddr  CurrentAddr  SecurityViolation  Security Action
             (Count)        (Count)      (Count)
---------------------------------------------------------------------------
   Fa0/11            1            1               97          Restrict
---------------------------------------------------------------------------
Total Addresses in System (excluding one mac per port)    : 0
Max Addresses limit in System (excluding one mac per port) : 4096
! On SW2 below, no interfaces have port security enabled.
```

```
SW2# show port-security
Secure Port  MaxSecureAddr  CurrentAddr  SecurityViolation  Security Action
             (Count)        (Count)      (Count)
--------------------------------------------------------------------------
--------------------------------------------------------------------------

Total Addresses in System (excluding one mac per port)     : 0
Max Addresses limit in System (excluding one mac per port) : 8192
```

The **show port-security** commands in the example list the interfaces on which port security has been enabled—specifically, SW1 interface Fa0/11 and no interfaces on SW2. On SW1, the notable items for troubleshooting are that the security action heading, which matches the violation mode setting, shows an action of restrict. With the restrict setting, SW1 interface Fa0/11 can be in the connected state (as seen in Example 3-8), but port security can be discarding traffic that violates the port security configuration. So, a closer examination of the port security configuration is in order, as shown in Example 3-11.

Example 3-11   *Port Security on SW1 and SW2*

```
SW1# show port-security interface fa0/11
Port Security               : Enabled
Port Status                 : Secure-up
Violation Mode              : Restrict
Aging Time                  : 0 mins
Aging Type                  : Absolute
SecureStatic Address Aging  : Disabled
Maximum MAC Addresses       : 1
Total MAC Addresses         : 1
Configured MAC Addresses    : 1
Sticky MAC Addresses        : 0
Last Source Address:Vlan    : 0200.1111.1111:3
Security Violation Count    : 97
!
! Next, the configuration shows that the configured MAC address does not
! match PC1's MAC address.
SW1# show running-config interface fa0/11

interface FastEthernet0/11
 switchport access vlan 3
 switchport mode access
 switchport port-security
 switchport port-security violation restrict
 switchport port-security mac-address 0200.3333.3333
!
! The following log message also points to a port security issue.
01:46:58: %PORT_SECURITY-2-PSECURE_VIOLATION: Security violation occurred, caused by
MAC address 0200.1111.1111 on port FastEthernet0/11.
```

The example begins by confirming the security mode and violation counter and showing the last MAC address (0200.1111.1111) to send a frame into interface Fa0/11. PC1's MAC address (0200.1111.1111) does not match the port security configuration as shown in the second part of the example, a configuration that defaults to a maximum of one MAC address with an explicitly configured MAC address of 0200.3333.3333.

A simple solution is to reconfigure port security to instead list PC1's MAC address. Note that the engineer would not need to use the **shutdown** and then the **no shutdown** commands on this interface to recover the interface, because the configuration uses violation mode restrict, which leaves the interface up while discarding the traffic to/from PC1.

Finally, the end of the example shows a log message generated by the switch for each violation when using restrict mode. This log message would be seen from the console, or from a Telnet or Secure Shell (SSH) connection to the switch, if the remote user had issued the **terminal monitor** EXEC command. It can also be collected at a syslog server, as described in Chapter 19, "Managing Network Devices."

Step 4: Check for VLAN and VLAN Trunk Problems

Step 4A begins by examining the access interfaces to ensure that the interfaces have been assigned to the correct VLANs. In this case, all interfaces connected to PCs and routers in Figure 3-5 should be assigned to VLAN 3. Example 3-12 provides some useful **show** command output. Take a few moments to read through the example and look for any VLAN assignment problems.

Example 3-12 *Checking Access Interface VLAN Assignments*

```
SW1# show interfaces fa0/11 status


Port       Name            Status       Vlan      Duplex Speed Type
Fa0/11                     connected    3         a-full a-100 10/100BaseTX
SW1# show interfaces fa0/12 status


Port       Name            Status       Vlan      Duplex Speed Type
Fa0/12                     notconnect   3          auto   auto 10/100BaseTX
! SW2 next
SW2# show interfaces status
! lines omitted for brevity
Fa0/9                      connected    1         a-full a-100 10/100BaseTX
Fa0/10                     notconnect   3          auto   auto 10/100BaseTX
! SW3 next
SW3# show interfaces fa0/13 status


Port       Name            Status       Vlan      Duplex Speed Type
Fa0/13                     connected    3          full  a-100 10/100BaseTX
```

The only problem in this case is the fact that while SW2's Fa0/10 interface was assigned to VLAN 3, per the drawing in Figure 3-5, SW2 connects to R1 using Fa0/9 (as shown with

CDP in Example 3-7). Interface Fa0/9 defaults to be in VLAN 1. To solve this particular problem, on SW2, configure the **switchport access vlan 3** interface subcommand on interface Fa0/9.

The next part of Step 4 (Step 4B) suggests to check the VLANs to ensure that they are active on each switch. This ongoing example only uses VLAN 3, so Example 3-13 shows that VLAN 3 indeed is known on each switch. When reading the example, look for any problems with VLAN 3.

Example 3-13 *Checking for Active VLANs*

```
SW1# show vlan id 3

VLAN Name                             Status    Ports
---- -------------------------------- --------- -------------------------------
3    book-vlan3                       active    Fa0/11, Fa0/12, Gi0/1, Gi0/2
! lines omitted for brevity

! SW2 next
SW2# show vlan brief

VLAN Name                             Status    Ports
---- -------------------------------- --------- -------------------------------
1    default                          active    Fa0/1, Fa0/2, Fa0/3, Fa0/4
                                                Fa0/5, Fa0/6, Fa0/7, Fa0/8
                                                Fa0/11, Fa0/12, Fa0/13, Fa0/14
                                                Fa0/15, Fa0/16, Fa0/17, Fa0/18
                                                Fa0/19, Fa0/20, Fa0/21, Fa0/22
                                                Fa0/23, Fa0/24
3    VLAN0003                         active    Fa0/9, Fa0/10
! lines omitted for brevity

! SW3 next
SW3# show vlan brief

VLAN Name                             Status    Ports
---- -------------------------------- --------- -------------------------------
1    default                          active    Fa0/1, Fa0/2, Fa0/3, Fa0/4
                                                Fa0/5, Fa0/6, Fa0/7, Fa0/8
                                                Fa0/9, Fa0/10, Fa0/11, Fa0/12
                                                Fa0/14, Fa0/15, Fa0/16, Fa0/17
                                                Fa0/18, Fa0/19, Fa0/20, Fa0/21
                                                Fa0/22, Fa0/23, Fa0/24
3    book-vlan3                       active    Fa0/13
! lines omitted for brevity
```

In this case, VLAN 3 exists and is active on all three switches. However, SW2 lists a different name than do the other two switches. The name is unimportant to the operation of the VLAN, so this difference does not matter.

Finally , the last part of troubleshooting Step 4 (Step 4C) suggests that you confirm the trunking status of all expected trunk interfaces. It is also helpful to determine on which trunks the VLANs will be forwarded. Example 3-14 lists output that helps supply the answers. Examine the output in the example, and before reading past the end of the example, list any trunks that do not currently forward traffic in VLAN 3 and make a list of possible reasons why VLAN 3 is omitted from the trunk.

Example 3-14   *Verifying Trunking and VLAN 3*

```
SW1# show interfaces trunk

Port        Mode            Encapsulation  Status       Native vlan
Gi0/1       desirable       802.1q         trunking     1
Gi0/2       desirable       802.1q         trunking     1


Port        Vlans allowed on trunk
Gi0/1       1-4094
Gi0/2       1-4094


Port        Vlans allowed and active in management domain
Gi0/1       1,3
Gi0/2       1,3


Port        Vlans in spanning tree forwarding state and not pruned
Gi0/1       3
Gi0/2       1,3
! SW2 next
SW2# show interfaces trunk

Port        Mode            Encapsulation  Status       Native vlan
Gi0/1       auto            802.1q         trunking     1
Gi0/2       auto            802.1q         trunking     1


Port        Vlans allowed on trunk
Gi0/1       1-4094
Gi0/2       1-4094


Port        Vlans allowed and active in management domain
Gi0/1       1,3
Gi0/2       1,3


Port        Vlans in spanning tree forwarding state and not pruned
Gi0/1       1,3
Gi0/2       1
! SW3 next
SW3# show interfaces trunk
```

```
Port        Mode        Encapsulation  Status       Native vlan
Gi0/1       auto        802.1q         trunking     1
Gi0/2       desirable   802.1q         trunking     1


Port        Vlans allowed on trunk
Gi0/1       1-4094
Gi0/2       1-4094


Port        Vlans allowed and active in management domain
Gi0/1       1,3
Gi0/2       1,3


Port        Vlans in spanning tree forwarding state and not pruned
Gi0/1       1,3
Gi0/2       1,3
```

First, look at the end of the output for all three commands in the example and focus on VLAN 3. Of the trunk ports on these switches, all list VLAN 3 in their last list of VLANs, with one exception: SW2's G0/2 port. Why? STP chose to block in VLAN 3 on that port.

Several different **show spanning-tree** commands could confirm that SW2's G0/2 port blocks in VLAN 3, but you can also deduce that SW2's G0/2 must be blocking from the output in the example. To do so, just rule out the other reasons as to why VLAN 3 would not be included in the lists in the output of the **show interfaces trunk** command, as follows:

■ VLAN 3 is listed in the first list of VLANs from SW2's **show interfaces trunk** command output, meaning that VLAN 3 must be in the allowed list for that trunk.

■ VLAN 3 is listed in the second list of VLANs from SW2's **show interfaces trunk** command output, meaning that VLAN 3 is active on SW2.

After finding and fixing all the problems in this ongoing example, PC1, PC3, and R1 can all ping each other. PC2, with an unspecified cabling problem, still does not work.

Troubleshooting Example 2: Predicting LAN Data Plane Behavior

This second example takes a much different approach than the first. Instead of starting with many problems, this example has a completely working LAN. Your job is to analyze the LAN to predict where the data plane will forward frames.

This example actually uses the same LAN as the previous example, but this time, all the errors have been fixed. In this case, the LAN works, and the example focuses on using show commands to predict exactly where frames flow in the LAN. In particular, this example focuses on two messages:

■ PC1 sends an ARP Request for Router R1 as a broadcast frame.

■ R1 sends an ARP Reply, which is a unicast frame, back to PC1.

Figure 3-6 correctly details the network. Figures 3-7 and 3-8, at the end of this section, show the flow of the ARP Request and Reply, respectively.

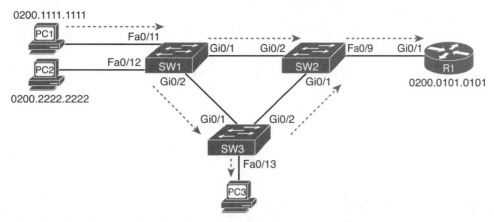

Figure 3-6 *Network for Troubleshooting Example 2*

> **NOTE**   The network for this example uses the same design as the previous example, but with the problems fixed. All access ports are in VLAN 3.

For those of you wanting to use this example as a practice exercise, use Figure 3-6; just read the examples and ignore the text between the examples. Make all the notes you can about where PC1's ARP broadcast will flow, and where R1's ARP Reply will flow. If you prefer, just keep reading for a walkthrough of what happens.

PC1 ARP Request (Broadcast)

When PC1 needs to send an IP packet to another subnet, PC1 will want to send the packet to PC1's default router. R1 serves as PC1's default router in this case. If PC1 does not list R1's MAC address in PC1's ARP cache, PC1 sends an ARP broadcast with an Ethernet destination address of FFFF.FFFF.FFFF.

To analyze the flow of the broadcast, see the generic forwarding process, as summarized in the section "An Overview of the Normal LAN Switching Forwarding Process," earlier in this chapter. Earlier examples confirmed that SW1 port Fa0/11 is assigned to VLAN 3 and that SW1's Fa0/11 interface is an access interface. Because the frame is a broadcast, SW1 will flood the frame. So now, Example 3-15 lists enough information to predict the interfaces out which SW1 will forward the broadcast frame sent by PC1 by listing the output of the **show spanning-tree vlan 3 active** command.

Example 3-15 *SW1's List of Forwarding Interfaces in VLAN 3*

```
SW1# show spanning-tree vlan 3 active

VLAN0003
  Spanning tree enabled protocol ieee
  Root ID    Priority    20483
             Address     f47f.35cb.d780
```

```
                   Cost         1
                   Port         26 (GigabitEthernet0/2)
                   Hello Time   2 sec  Max Age 20 sec  Forward Delay 15 sec


   Bridge ID  Priority    32771  (priority 32768 sys-id-ext 3)
              Address     1833.9d7b.0e80
              Hello Time   2 sec  Max Age 20 sec  Forward Delay 15 sec
              Aging Time  300 sec


Interface         Role Sts Cost      Prio.Nbr Type
----------------- ---- --- --------- -------- --------------------------------
Fa0/11            Desg FWD 19         128.11   P2p Edge
Fa0/12            Desg FWD 19         128.12   P2p
Gi0/1             Desg FWD 4          128.25   P2p
Gi0/2             Root FWD 1          128.26   P2p
```

Note that SW1 will not forward the frame back out Fa0/11, as the frame came in on Fa0/11. Also, SW1 will forward the frame out both trunk interfaces (Gi0/1 and Gi0/2), and out Fa0/12. Also, earlier in this chapter, Example 3-14 shows evidence that both SW1's trunks use 802.1Q, with native VLAN 1, so SW1 will add an 802.1Q header, with VLAN ID 3, to each copy of the broadcast frame sent over those two trunks.

SW1's actions mean that both SW2 and SW3 should receive a copy of the broadcast frame sent by PC1. In SW2's case, SW2 happens to discard its copy of PC1's broadcast frame received on SW2's Gi0/2 interface. SW2 discards the frame because of Step 3 of the generic forwarding process from earlier in this chapter, because SW2's incoming interface (Gi0/2) is in a blocking state in VLAN 3, as shown in Example 3-16.

Example 3-16   *SW2: Blocking on Gi0/2, Ignoring the Incoming Broadcast Frame*

```
SW2# show spanning-tree vlan 3


VLAN0003
  Spanning tree enabled protocol ieee
  Root ID    Priority    20483
             Address     f47f.35cb.d780
             Cost        4
             Port        25 (GigabitEthernet0/1)
             Hello Time   2 sec  Max Age 20 sec  Forward Delay 15 sec


   Bridge ID  Priority    32771  (priority 32768 sys-id-ext 3)
              Address     1833.9d7b.1380
              Hello Time   2 sec  Max Age 20 sec  Forward Delay 15 sec
              Aging Time  300 sec
```

```
Interface           Role Sts Cost      Prio.Nbr Type
------------------- ---- --- --------- -------- --------------------------------
Fa0/9               Desg FWD 19        128.9    P2p
Gi0/1               Root FWD 4         128.25   P2p
Gi0/2               Altn BLK 4         128.26   P2p
```

Note that SW2's blocking state did not prevent SW1 from sending the frame to SW2; instead, SW2 silently discards the received frame.

For the copy of PC1's broadcast frame received by SW3 on its Gi0/1 interface, SW3 floods the frame. SW3 determines the frame's VLAN based on the incoming 802.1Q header and finds the incoming interface in an STP forwarding state. Based on these facts, SW3 will forward the frame inside VLAN 3. Example 3-17 shows the information that's needed to know on which interfaces SW3 forwards the VLAN 3 broadcast.

Example 3-17   *SW3: Forwarding a Broadcast in VLAN 3*

```
SW3# show mac address-table dynamic vlan 3
          Mac Address Table
-------------------------------------------


Vlan    Mac Address        Type        Ports
----    -----------        --------    -----
   3    0200.0101.0101     DYNAMIC     Gi0/2
   3    0200.1111.1111     DYNAMIC     Gi0/1
   3    0200.2222.2222     DYNAMIC     Gi0/1
   3    0200.3333.3333     DYNAMIC     Fa0/13
Total Mac Addresses for this criterion: 4


SW3# show spanning-tree vlan 3 active
VLAN0003
  Spanning tree enabled protocol ieee
  Root ID    Priority    20483
             Address     f47f.35cb.d780
             This bridge is the root
             Hello Time    2 sec  Max Age 20 sec  Forward Delay 15 sec

  Bridge ID  Priority    20483  (priority 20480 sys-id-ext 3)
             Address     f47f.35cb.d780
             Hello Time    2 sec  Max Age 20 sec  Forward Delay 15 sec
             Aging Time  300 sec


Interface           Role Sts Cost      Prio.Nbr Type
------------------- ---- --- --------- -------- --------------------------------
Fa0/13              Desg FWD 19        128.13   P2p
Gi0/1               Desg FWD 4         128.25   P2p
Gi0/2               Desg FWD 4         128.26   P2p
```

As with SW1, SW3 does not forward the broadcast out the same interface in which the frame arrived (Gi0/1 in this case), but SW3 does flood the frame out all other interfaces in that VLAN and in an STP forwarding state, namely Fa0/13 and Gi0/2. Also, because SW3's Gi0/2 interface currently uses 802.1Q trunking, with native VLAN 1, SW3 adds an 802.1Q header with VLAN ID 3 listed.

Finally, when SW2 receives the copy of the broadcast in SW2's Gi0/1 interface, from SW3, SW2 follows the same generic process as the other switches. SW2 identifies the VLAN based on the incoming 802.1Q header, confirms that the incoming interface is in a forwarding state, and floods the broadcast out all its interfaces that are both in a forwarding state and in VLAN 3. In this case, SW2 forwards the frame only out interface Fa0/9, connected to Router R1. Example 3-18 shows the supporting command output.

Example 3-18   *SW2: Forwarding a Broadcast in VLAN 3 Received from SW3*

```
! First, note that the broadcast address FFFF.FFFF.FFFF is not
! in the VLAN 3 MAC table.
SW2# show mac address-table dynamic vlan 3
          Mac Address Table
-------------------------------------------

Vlan    Mac Address       Type        Ports
----    -----------       --------    -----
   3    0200.0101.0101    DYNAMIC     Fa0/9
   3    0200.1111.1111    DYNAMIC     Gi0/1
   3    0200.2222.2222    DYNAMIC     Gi0/1
   3    0200.3333.3333    DYNAMIC     Gi0/1
   3    f47f.35cb.d79a    DYNAMIC     Gi0/1
Total Mac Addresses for this criterion: 5


! Next, note that on Fa0/9 and Gi0/1 are in an STP forwarding state,
! and the broadcast came in Gi0/1 - so SW2 floods the frame only out Fa0/9.
SW2# show spanning-tree vlan 3 active
!lines omitted for brevity


Interface       Role Sts Cost      Prio.Nbr Type
--------------- ---- --- --------- -------- -----------------------------------
Fa0/9           Desg FWD 19        128.9    P2p
Gi0/1           Root FWD 4         128.25   P2p
Gi0/2           Altn BLK 4         128.26   P2p
```

SW2 does not forward the frame out Gi0/1 because the frame entered SW2's Gi0/1 interface.

R1 ARP Reply (Unicast)

The response from R1, an ARP Reply, flows as a unicast frame. The destination L2 MAC address of R1's ARP reply is PC1's MAC addresses. Figure 3-8 at the end of this topic shows the path, but the figure is shown there, instead of here, to avoid spoiling the answer for anyone using this example as an exercise.

The ARP Reply flows inside an Ethernet frame addressed to PC1's unicast Ethernet address: 0200.1111.1111. When SW2 receives this frame from R1, SW2 notes that the frame entered interface Fa0/9, an access interface in VLAN 3. The end of Example 3-18 previously showed Fa0/9 on SW2 in an STP forwarding state in VLAN 3, so SW2 will attempt to forward the frame in VLAN 3. As seen next in Example 3-19, SW2's MAC address table lists PC1's MAC address—0200.1111.1111—off interface Gi0/1 and in VLAN 3, so SW2 forwards the frame out Gi0/1 to SW3.

Example 3-19   *SW2's Logic When Forwarding a Known Unicast to PC1*

```
SW2# show mac address-table dynamic vlan 3
          Mac Address Table
-------------------------------------------

Vlan    Mac Address       Type        Ports
----    -----------       --------    -----
   3    0200.0101.0101    DYNAMIC     Fa0/9
   3    0200.1111.1111    DYNAMIC     Gi0/1
   3    0200.2222.2222    DYNAMIC     Gi0/1
   3    0200.3333.3333    DYNAMIC     Gi0/1
   3    f47f.35cb.d79a    DYNAMIC     Gi0/1
Total Mac Addresses for this criterion: 5
```

When SW3 receives the frame destined to PC1's MAC address, from SW2, SW3 first looks at the incoming interface. SW3 notes that the frame entered interface Gi0/2, a trunking interface, and that the trunking header listed VLAN ID 3. The end of Example 3-17 previously showed Gi0/2 in an STP forwarding state in VLAN 3 (forwarding Step 3), so SW3 will not discard the received frame because of STP. As seen next in Example 3-20, SW3's MAC address table lists PC1's MAC address—0200.1111.1111—off interface Gi0/1 and in VLAN 3, so SW3 forwards the frame out Gi0/1 to SW1.

Example 3-20   *SW3's Logic When Forwarding a Known Unicast to PC1*

```
SW3# show mac address-table dynamic vlan 3
          Mac Address Table
-------------------------------------------

Vlan    Mac Address       Type        Ports
----    -----------       --------    -----
   3    0200.0101.0101    DYNAMIC     Gi0/2
   3    0200.1111.1111    DYNAMIC     Gi0/1
   3    0200.2222.2222    DYNAMIC     Gi0/1
   3    0200.3333.3333    DYNAMIC     Fa0/13
Total Mac Addresses for this criterion: 4
```

When SW1 receives the frame from SW3, SW1 notes that the frame entered interface Gi0/2, a trunking interface, and that the trunking header listed VLAN ID 3. The end of Example 3-15 previously showed SW1's Gi0/2 in an STP forwarding state in VLAN 3, so SW1 will process the frame, and not ignore it, because that interface is not in an STP Blocking state in VLAN 3. As shown next in Example 3-21, SW1's MAC address table lists PC1's MAC address—0200.1111.1111—off interface Fa0/11, so SW1 forwards the frame out Fa0/11 to PC1. In this case, SW1 strips off the 802.1Q VLAN header, because interface Fa0/11 is an access interface.

Example 3-21 *SW1's Logic When Forwarding a Known Unicast to PC1*

```
SW1# show mac address-table dynamic vlan 3
          Mac Address Table
-------------------------------------------

Vlan    Mac Address       Type        Ports
----    -----------       --------    -----
   3    0200.2222.2222    DYNAMIC     Fa0/12
   3    0200.3333.3333    DYNAMIC     Gi0/2
   3    f47f.35cb.d799    DYNAMIC     Gi0/2
Total Mac Addresses for this criterion: 3


SW1# show mac address-table vlan 3
          Mac Address Table
-------------------------------------------

Vlan    Mac Address       Type        Ports
----    -----------       --------    -----
 All    0100.0ccc.cccc    STATIC      CPU
 All    0100.0ccc.cccd    STATIC      CPU
 All    0180.c200.0000    STATIC      CPU
 All    0180.c200.0001    STATIC      CPU
 All    0180.c200.0002    STATIC      CPU
 All    0180.c200.0003    STATIC      CPU
 All    0180.c200.0004    STATIC      CPU
 All    0180.c200.0005    STATIC      CPU
 All    0180.c200.0006    STATIC      CPU
 All    0180.c200.0007    STATIC      CPU
 All    0180.c200.0008    STATIC      CPU
 All    0180.c200.0009    STATIC      CPU
 All    0180.c200.000a    STATIC      CPU
 All    0180.c200.000b    STATIC      CPU
 All    0180.c200.000c    STATIC      CPU
 All    0180.c200.000d    STATIC      CPU
 All    0180.c200.000e    STATIC      CPU
 All    0180.c200.000f    STATIC      CPU
 All    0180.c200.0010    STATIC      CPU
```

```
 All     ffff.ffff.ffff    STATIC    CPU
  3      0200.1111.1111    STATIC    Fa0/11
  3      0200.2222.2222    DYNAMIC   Fa0/12
  3      0200.3333.3333    DYNAMIC   Gi0/2
  3      f47f.35cb.d799    DYNAMIC   Gi0/2
Total Mac Addresses for this criterion: 24
```

This last step points out an important fact about the MAC address table and port security. Note that the **show mac address-table dynamic** command on SW1 does not list PC1's MAC address of 0200.1111.1111, so you might have been tempted to think that SW1 will flood the frame because it is an unknown unicast frame. However, because SW1 has configured port security on Fa0/11, including the **switchport port-security mac-address 0200.1111.1111** interface subcommand, IOS considers this MAC address a static MAC address. So, by leaving off the **dynamic** keyword, the **show mac address-table vlan 3** command lists all MAC addresses known in the VLAN, including 0200.1111.1111. This command output confirms that SW1 will forward the unicast to 0200.1111.1111 only out interface Fa0/11.

Figure 3-7 shows the flow of the ARP Request (broadcast) through this LAN, and Figure 3-8 shows the flow of the unicast ARP Reply.

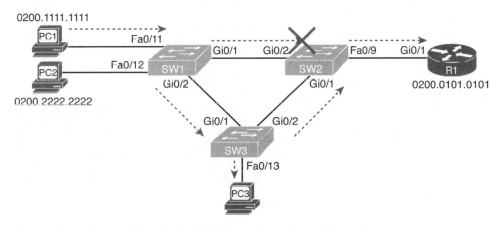

Figure 3-7   *Forwarding Path of ARP Broadcast, from PC1 to R1*

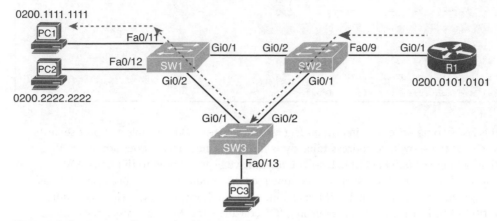

Figure 3-8 *Forwarding Path of ARP Reply, From R1 to PC1*

Exam Preparation Tasks

Review All the Key Topics

Review the most important topics from this chapter, noted with the Key Topic icon. Table 3-8 lists these key topics and where each is discussed.

Table 3-8   Key Topics for Chapter 3

Key Topic Element	Description	Page Number
Table 3-2	Lists both sets of interface status codes and typical root causes for each state	89
Figure 3-4	Typical uses of Ethernet straight-through and crossover cables	90
Table 3-3	Lists devices and the pins on which they transmit for 10BASE-T and 100BASE-Tx	90
List	Definitions of speed mismatch and duplex mismatch	92
List	Suggestions for noticing duplex mismatch problems	93
List	Default IEEE autonegotiation duplex choices based on current speed	94
Table 3-4	Port security violation modes with differences in behavior and **show** commands	95
List	Port security configuration steps	98
Table 3-5	Lists **show** commands useful for finding access interfaces and their assigned VLANs	99
Table 3-6	The four reasons a switch does not pass a VLAN's traffic over a particular trunk	101
Table 3-7	Combinations of the **switchport mode** command and the results of whether a link trunks	102

Complete the Tables and Lists from Memory

Print a copy of DVD Appendix D, "Memory Tables," or at least the section for this chapter, and complete the tables and lists from memory. DVD Appendix E, "Memory Tables Answer Key," includes completed tables and lists to check your work.

Answers to Troubleshooting Example 1

For those of you who used Troubleshooting Example 1 as an exercise, the following list summarizes the problems that could have been uncovered in that exercise:

- Figure 3-5 shows SW2 port Fa0/10 connected to Router R1, while CDP showed that, in reality, SW2's F0/9 port is used. The example fixed the problem by updating the network diagram to list Fa0/9.

- SW1's F0/12 port, presumably connected to PC2 per Figure 3-5, is in a notconnect state. The examples could not identify the specific reason for the notconnect state. (In reality, the cable was unplugged; the cable was plugged in, in preparation for the second example.)

- SW3's Fa0/13 port is possibly in a duplex mismatch state. It lists a speed/duplex setting of a-100/a-half, which can happen if the other device (PC13) disables autonegotiation and sets itself for 100/full and disables autonegotiation. The problem was fixed by manually configuring the switch to also use full duplex.

- Port security on SW1's F0/11 port is filtering traffic from the only device connected to that port (PC1, 0200.1111.1111), because of its incorrect configuration of MAC address 0200.3333.3333. The port security configuration was updated to list the correct 0200.1111.1111 MAC address.

- SW2, port F0/9, which is the port actually connected to R1, is assigned to VLAN 1, while port F0/10, the port that Figure 3-5 shows as connected to R1, is assigned to (correct) VLAN 3. Either the cable should be moved or F0/9 needs to be placed into VLAN 3. The book shows the reconfiguration of SW2's F0/9 port with the **switchport access vlan 3** command.

Part I Review

Keep track of your part review progress with the checklist in Table P1-1. Details about each task follow the table.

Table P1-1 Part I Part Review Checklist

Activity	First Date Completed	Second Date Completed
Repeat All DIKTA Questions		
Answer Part Review Questions		
Review Key Topics		
Create STP Concepts Mind Map		

Repeat All DIKTA Questions

For this task, answer the "Do I Know This Already?" questions again for the chapters in Part I of this book using the PCPT software. See the section "How to View Only DIKTA Questions by Part" in the Introduction to this book to learn how to make the PCPT software show you DIKTA questions for this part only.

Answer Part Review Questions

For this task, answer the Part Review questions for this part of the book using the PCPT software. See the section "How to View Only DIKTA Questions by Part" in the Introduction to this book to learn how to make the PCPT software show you DIKTA questions for this part only.

Review Key Topics

Browse back through the chapters and look for the Key Topic icons. If you do not remember some details, take the time to reread those topics.

Create STP Concepts Mind Map

Spanning Tree Protocol (STP) defines a lot of ideas that you might find hard to mentally organize. Create a mind map to help organize STP concepts into three areas, as follows:

- **Rules:** Rules include any of the rules a switch uses when making choices (for instance, the rules about how switches choose the root switch).
- **Roles:** STP defines both roles and states; an example of a role is the root port role.
- **States:** For example, forwarding.

Create a mind map with three branches (rules, roles, and states) and fill in as many ideas about each that you can recall.

NOTE   For more information about mind mapping, see the section "About Mind Maps" in the Introduction to this book.

Create the mind maps in Table P1-2 on paper using any mind mapping software (or even any drawing application). If you use an application, note for later reference the filename and location where you saved the file. Appendix F, "Mind Map Solutions," provides sample mind map answers.

Table P1-2   Configuration Mind Maps for Part I Review

Map	Description	Where You Saved It
1	STP Concepts Mind Map	

Finally, keep the following important points in mind when working on this project:

- Most of the learning with this exercise happens when you do it; jumping straight to the sample in Appendix F may be tempting but does not help you learn as much.

- Use as few words as possible for you to remember the thought. Do not attempt to write complete phrases or sentences.

- Do not look at the book or your notes at first. After you have completed the mind map as much as you can from memory, only then look back at your notes.

- Repeat this exercise from scratch, without notes, later in your study, as a way to strengthen your mental connectors and memory.

Part II of this book turns this book's attention away from the LAN topics in Part I, moving on to IPv4 routing. The ICND1 book (and exam) introduced many details of IPv4 routing—the concepts, all the subnetting math, and the implementation details on routers—and now Part II of this book goes further. This part reviews the IPv4 routing topics from ICND1, but now with an eye toward troubleshooting problems with IPv4 internetworks, with the entirety of Chapters 4 and 5 devoted to troubleshooting IPv4 routing.

The last two chapters in this part add new topics as compared with ICND1's coverage of IPv4, with two unrelated topics. Chapter 6 introduces the idea of having redundant default routers, and Chapter 7 discusses how to create a private network connection using IPv4 over the Internet.

Part II

IP Version 4 Routing

This chapter covers the following exam topics:

Troubleshooting

Identify and correct common network problems

Troubleshoot and resolve routing issues

routing is enabled

routing table is correct

correct path selection

CHAPTER 4

Troubleshooting IPv4 Routing Part I

IPv4 routing requires the cooperation of hosts and routers. Hosts first create IPv4 packets and send those packets to some nearby router (the host's default router, or default gateway). The router then makes a routing decision of where to forward the IPv4 packet next and sends the packet over the next physical link. Each router that receives the IPv4 packet repeats the process, until the packet finally arrives at the destination host.

This chapter focuses on how to troubleshoot problems with IPv4 routing. Specifically, this chapter focuses on packet forwarding (that is, the data plane of IPv4). For the most part, this chapter leaves most of the discussion of data link and physical layer problems to Part I (LANs) and Part IV (WANs), instead focusing on the network layer functions for IP routing. This chapter also leaves the discussion of IPv4 control plane issues, specifically IP routing protocols, to Part III (IP Version 4 Routing Protocols) of this book.

This chapter reviews IPv4 routing as a means to an end: to help you learn how to troubleshoot IPv4 routing issues. Cisco put most IPv4 routing concepts, configuration, and verification topics into the ICND1 exam's side of the scope of CCNA, but the troubleshooting of those same topics into the ICND2 side of CCNA. As a result, this book holds the IPv4 troubleshooting chapters; so to help make sense of the details, this book weaves IPv4 review topics throughout the chapter.

This chapter breaks the materials into three major sections, with all three presenting the information from the perspective of troubleshooting a network. The first section reviews IPv4 routing on hosts and routers; that knowledge can be used to predict normal operation when troubleshooting a network problem. The second section discusses the **ping** command, specifically how this command can isolate a problem to smaller and smaller parts of the network and fewer and fewer reasons—always driving toward finding the root cause. The final section focuses on traceroute, with the same goal as the ping section: looking for ways to isolate the problem.

"Do I Know This Already?" Quiz

The troubleshooting chapters of this book pull in concepts from many other chapters, including some chapters in *Cisco CCENT/CCNA ICND1 100-101 Official Cert Guide*. They also show you how to approach some of the more challenging questions on the CCNA exams. Therefore, it is useful to read these chapters regardless of your current knowledge level. For these reasons, the troubleshooting chapters do not include a "Do I Know This Already?" quiz. However, if you feel particularly confident about troubleshooting IP routing features covered in this book and *Cisco CCENT/CCNA ICND1 100-101 Official Cert Guide*, feel free to move to the "Exam Preparation Tasks" section near the end of this chapter to bypass the majority of the chapter.

Foundation Topics

Predicting Normal IPv4 Routing Behavior

Different people solve networking problems with different methods. No one method can lay claim as the best method in all conditions. However, as mentioned in Chapter 3, "Troubleshooting LAN Switching," when learning how to troubleshoot, it helps to take some systematic approach to troubleshooting. So, this chapter (as do the other troubleshooting topics in this book) approaches problems with the same general strategy, as follows:

1.   Predict how things should work normally.

2.   When a problem occurs, isolate the problem to as specific a reason as possible on as few devices as possible.

3.   Discover and fix the root cause of the problem.

This first major section of the chapter reviews IPv4 routing, for the purpose of the first step in this troubleshooting process: predicting what happens normally when an IPv4 packet flows from one host to another.

So, how does IPv4 routing work? When focusing on the network layer logic, any internetwork can be viewed as a series of routing steps. The first step begins with a host creating and sending the packet to its default router. After the packet arrives at a router, one or more routers forward (route) the packet until it arrives at the destination, as shown in the first three steps of the example in Figure 4-1.

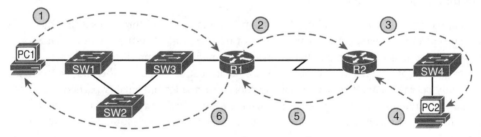

Figure 4-1   *Major Steps in an IP Forwarding Example*

The first three steps in the example of Figure 4-1 show how to route a packet over an internetwork. However, most applications require packet flow in both directions. So, when troubleshooting, any analysis of normal operations should also consider the packet that will be sent back to the first host (PC1 in this case), as shown in Steps 4, 5, and 6 in the figure.

To deliver an IPv4 packet end to end from one host to another and back, hosts and routers must cooperate. This section breaks down the logic based on the host logic first and then the router logic.

Host IPv4 Routing Logic

The IPv4 routing process starts with the host that creates the IP packet. After the host has created the IP packet, the host asks this question: Is the destination IP address of this new packet in my local subnet? The host uses its own IP address/mask to determine the range of addresses in the local subnet, compares that range to the destination IP address, and then chooses as follows:

1. If the destination is local, send directly:

   A. Find the destination host's MAC address. Use the already-known Address Resolution Protocol (ARP) table entry, or use ARP messages to learn the information.

   B. Encapsulate the IP packet in a data link frame with the destination data link address of the *destination host*.

2. If the destination is not local, send to the default router (default gateway):

   A. Find the default router's MAC address. Use the already known ARP table entry, or use ARP messages to learn the information.

   B. Encapsulate the IP packet in a data link frame with the destination data link address of the *default router*.

These detailed steps in the list do summarize host IPv4 routing logic, but Figure 4-2 summarizes the big decision on the left side of the figure. The figure shows host A sending a local packet directly to host D. However, for packets to host B—on the other side of a router and therefore in a different subnet—host A sends the packet to its default router (R1).

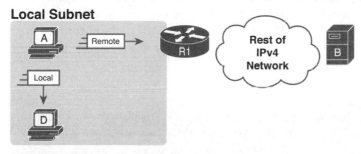

Figure 4-2   *Host Routing Logic Summary*

Routing Logic Used by IPv4 Routers

Routers act independently. That is, the process of routing a single packet requires a router to go through its own logic without help from any other router.

At the same time, routers act in concert with each other. One router after another forwards a packet so that, eventually, the packet reaches the correct destination host. Each router's independent action forwards the packet over one hop of an end-to-end route to the destination host.

This next topic discusses what routers do to route packets—first as an independent process on one router, and then as an overall effect.

IP Routing Logic on a Single Router

Compared to hosts, routers have a little more work to do to route IPv4 packets. While the host logic begins with an IP packet sitting in memory, a router has some work to do before getting to that point, at which point the router does the most important part: matching the IP routing table. The specific steps are as follows:

Step 1. For each received data link frame, choose whether to process the frame. Process it if:

   A. The frame has no errors (per the data link trailer frame check sequence or FCS field).

   B. The frame's destination data link address is the router's address (or an appropriate multicast or broadcast).

Step 2. If choosing to process the frame at Step 1, deencapsulate the packet from inside the data link frame.

Step 3. Make a routing decision. To do so, compare the packet's destination IP address to the routing table and find the route that matches the destination address. This route identifies the outgoing interface of the router and possibly the next-hop router.

Step 4. Encapsulate the packet into a data link frame appropriate for the outgoing interface. When forwarding out Ethernet LAN interfaces, this may require the use of ARP if the next device's MAC address is not in the ARP cache of the router.

Step 5. Transmit the frame out the outgoing interface, as listed in the matched IP route.

> **NOTE**   The step numbers in this list do not matter. The concepts inside each step matter a lot. So, know them! For the exams, though, you do not need to memorize which idea goes with a particular step number.

This detailed list is accurate, but sometimes it helps to think about routing in simpler terms, like in this one-sentence summary:

   The router receives a frame, removes the packet from inside the frame, decides which interface to forward the packet out of, puts the packet into another frame, and sends the frame (with packet inside it) out the correct router interface.

Although reading text about how routing works might be useful, sometimes it helps to see the process as a drawing. Figure 4-3 breaks down the same five-step routing process with a packet that enters a router from the left and exits on the right. A packet arrives from the left, entering a router Ethernet interface, with a destination IP address that is host B's address. Router R1 processes the frame and packet as shown with the numbers in the figure matching the five-step routing process described earlier. Eventually, the router forwards the packet, inside a new High-Level Data Link Control (HDLC) frame, out the serial link on the right.

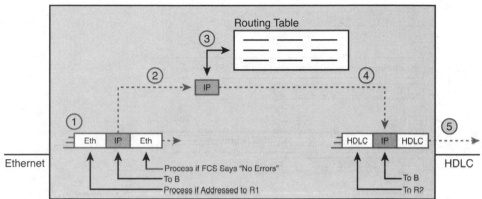

Figure 4-3 *Router Routing Logic Summary*

IP Routing from Host to Host

So far, this review of routing logic has focused on a single router, with three different views of the process: a long written process, a short written process, and a diagram of the same. But the logic on one router does not deliver the packet from end to end through the IP internetwork. End-to-end delivery requires every router to use the same logic, with IP routes that tell each router to forward the packet to the next router, and the next, and the next, to deliver the packet to the destination.

Figure 4-4 shows the end-to-end effects of routing a packet, focusing on the deencapsulation (Step 2) and encapsulation (Step 4) on each router. Each router discards the incoming frame's data link header and trailer, so each frame moves only from a host to a router or between routers. Each router adds a new data link header and trailer, creating a new frame, each time the router forwards a packet. And the data link header's address fields matter only on that local data link.

The figure shows PC1 sending a packet to PC2, with the various frames shown. At the top, PC1 sends an Ethernet frame to R1. R1 then deencapsulates the packet and reencapsulates it in an HDLC frame. R2 repeats the same process, this time encapsulating the packet inside a Frame Relay frame. R3 repeats the process, encapsulating the packet inside an Ethernet frame and sending the frame to PC2.

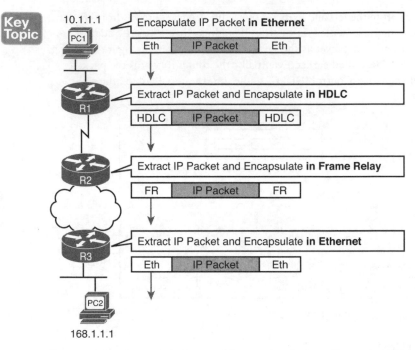

Figure 4-4 *Encapsulation and Deencapsulation of a Packet When Routed*

Building New Data Link Headers Using ARP Information

Another important part of the routing process relates to how a router chooses the data link addresses to use in a new data link header. Data link headers typically list an address, like the MAC addresses used in Ethernet data link headers. To encapsulate an IP packet and send it onto some types of data links, the router has to first know the data link address of the other device on the outgoing link. For instance, in Figure 4-4, router R3 has to know PC2's MAC address before it can build and send a unicast Ethernet frame to PC2 at the bottom of the figure.

To support the process of learning MAC addresses of other devices on LANs, IPv4 uses the Address Resolution Protocol (ARP). ARP defines two messages (ARP Request and ARP Reply). The sending host or router uses an ARP Request to make this request: If this is your IP address, tell me your MAC address. The second host sends back an ARP Reply, listing their IPv4 address and Ethernet MAC address. For instance, Figure 4-5 shows the ARP process that would have occurred in the same network as Figure 4-4, before R3 could have forwarded a packet (encapsulated within a frame) to PC2's MAC address.

The CCENT and CCNA topics include only one LAN data link protocol (Ethernet) and three WAN data link protocols (HDLC, PPP, and Frame Relay), at least to any depth. Ethernet uses ARP, as shown in Figure 4-5. HDLC and PPP, used on serial links in a point-to-point topology, do not need a function like ARP. Frame Relay uses a similar function called Inverse ARP, as discussed later in Chapter 13, "Understanding Frame Relay Concepts."

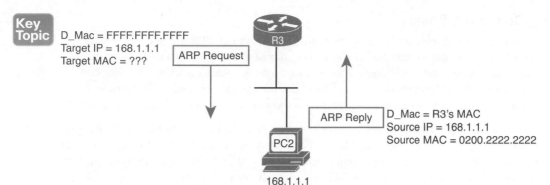

Figure 4-5 *Sample ARP Process*

In summary, hosts forward packets to their default routers when the packet's destination address is in another subnet. Each router deencapsulates the packet, chooses where to forward it, and encapsulates the packet in a new data link frame. Only the IP packet flows from source to destination host, while each data link header/trailer serves as a means to move the packet from host to router, router to router, or router to host.

Now that you understand how hosts and routers forward IPv4 packets, the next two topics look at how to isolate the root cause of a problem using the **ping** and **traceroute** commands. These commands let you rule out parts of the IPv4 routing process, because these commands confirm that parts of the process work.

Problem Isolation Using the ping Command

Someone sends you an email or text, or a phone message, asking you to look into a user's network problem. You Secure Shell (SSH) to a router and issue a **ping** command that works. What does that result rule out as a possible reason for the problem? What does it rule in as still being a possible root cause?

Then you issue another **ping** to another address, and this time the ping fails. Again, what does the failure of that **ping** command tell you? What parts of IPv4 routing may still be a problem, and what parts do you now know are not a problem?

The **ping** command gives us one of the most common network troubleshooting tools. When the **ping** command succeeds, it confirms many individual parts of how IP routing works, ruling out some possible causes of the current problem. When a **ping** command fails, it often helps narrow down where in the internetwork the root cause of the problem may be happening, further isolating the problem.

This section begins with a brief review of how ping works. It then moves on to some suggestions and analysis of how to use the **ping** command to isolate problems by removing some items from consideration.

Ping Command Basics

The **ping** command tests connectivity by sending packets to an IP address, expecting the device at that address to send packets back. The command sends packets that mean "if you receive this packet, and it is addressed to you, send a reply back." Each time the **ping** command sends one of these packets and receives back the message sent back by the other host, the **ping** command knows a packet made it from the source host to the destination and back.

More formally, the **ping** command uses the Internet Control Message Protocol (ICMP), specifically the ICMP Echo Request and ICMP Echo Reply messages. ICMP defines many other messages as well, but these two messages were made specifically for connectivity testing by commands like ping. As a protocol, ICMP does not rely on TCP or UDP, and it does not use any application layer protocol. It exists as a protocol used to assist IP by helping manage the IP network functions.

Figure 4-6 shows the ICMP messages, with IP headers, in an example. In this case, the user at host A opens a command prompt and issues the **ping 172.16.2.101** command, testing connectivity to host B. The command sends one Echo Request, and waits (Step 1); host B receives the messages, and sends back an Echo Reply (Step 2).

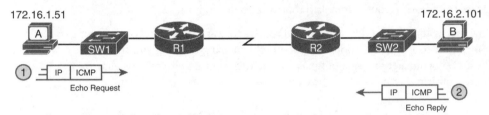

Figure 4-6   *Concept Behind* **ping 172.16.2.101** *on Host A*

The **ping** command is supported on many different devices and many common operating systems. The command has many options: the name or IP address of the destination, how many times the command should send an Echo Request, how long the command should wait (timeout) for an Echo Reply, how big to make the packets, and many other options. Example 4-1 shows a sample from host A, with the same command that matches the concept in Figure 4-6: a **ping 172.16.2.101** command on host A.

Example 4-1   *Sample Output from Host A's* **ping 172.16.2.101** *Command*

```
Wendell-Odoms-iMac:~ wendellodom$ ping 172.16.2.101
PING 172.16.2.101 (172.16.2.101): 56 data bytes
64 bytes from 172.16.2.101: icmp_seq=0 ttl=64 time=1.112 ms
64 bytes from 172.16.2.101: icmp_seq=1 ttl=64 time=0.673 ms
64 bytes from 172.16.2.101: icmp_seq=2 ttl=64 time=0.631 ms
64 bytes from 172.16.2.101: icmp_seq=3 ttl=64 time=0.674 ms
64 bytes from 172.16.2.101: icmp_seq=4 ttl=64 time=0.642 ms
64 bytes from 172.16.2.101: icmp_seq=5 ttl=64 time=0.656 ms
^C
--- 172.16.2.101 ping statistics ---
6 packets transmitted, 6 packets received, 0.0% packet loss
round-trip min/avg/max/stddev = 0.631/0.731/1.112/0.171 ms
```

Strategies and Results When Testing with the ping Command

Often, the person handling initial calls from users about problems (often called a customer support rep, or CSR) cannot issue **ping** commands from the user's device. In some cases, talking users through typing the right commands and making the right clicks on their machines can be a problem. Or, the user just might not be available. As an alternative, using different **ping** commands from different routers can help isolate the problem.

> **NOTE**   For the exam, it helps to practice pinging from the routers, as discussed in the next several pages.

The problem with using **ping** commands from routers, instead of from the host that has the problem, is that no single router **ping** command can exactly replicate a **ping** command done from the user's device. However, each different **ping** command can help isolate a problem further. The rest of this section of **ping** commands discusses troubleshooting IPv4 routing by using various **ping** commands from the command-line interface (CLI) of a router.

Testing Longer Routes from Near the Source of the Problem

Most problems begin with some idea like "host X cannot communicate with host Y." A great first troubleshooting step is to issue a **ping** command from X for host Y's IP address. However, assuming the engineer does not have access to host X, the next best test is to ping host X's IP address from the router nearest the host that has the problem.

For instance, in Figure 4-6, imagine that the user of host A had called IT support with a problem related to sending packets to host B. A **ping 172.16.2.101** command on host A would be a great first troubleshooting step, but the CSR cannot access host A or get in touch with the user of host A. So, the CSR telnets to router R1, and pings host B from there, as shown in Example 4-2.

Example 4-2   *Router R2 Pings Host B (Two Commands)*

```
R1# ping 172.16.2.101
Type escape sequence to abort.
Sending 5, 100-byte ICMP Echos to 172.16.2.101, timeout is 2 seconds:
.!!!!
Success rate is 80 percent (4/5), round-trip min/avg/max = 1/2/4 ms
R1# ping 172.16.2.101
Type escape sequence to abort.
Sending 5, 100-byte ICMP Echos to 172.16.2.101, timeout is 2 seconds:
!!!!!
Success rate is 100 percent (5/5), round-trip min/avg/max = 1/2/4 ms
```

First, take a moment to review the output of the first IOS **ping** command. By default, the Cisco IOS **ping** command sends five Echo messages, with a timeout of 2 seconds. If the command does not receive an Echo Reply within 2 seconds, the command considers that message to be a failure, and the command lists a period. If a successful reply is received within 2 seconds, the command displays an exclamation point. So, in this first command, the first Echo Reply timed out, whereas the other four received a matching Echo Reply within 2 seconds.

As a quick aside, the example shows a common and normal behavior with **ping** commands: the first **ping** command shows one failure to start, but then the rest of the messages work. This usually happens because some device in the end-to-end route is missing an ARP table entry.

Now think about troubleshooting and what a working **ping** command tells us about the current behavior of this internetwork. First, focus on the big picture for a moment:

■ R1 can send ICMP Echo Request messages to host B (172.16.2.101).

■ R1 sends these messages from its outgoing interface's IP address (by default), 172.16.4.1 in this case.

■ Host B can send ICMP Echo Reply messages to R1's 172.16.4.1 IP address (hosts send Echo Reply messages to the IP address from which the Echo Request was received).

Figure 4-7 shows the packet flow.

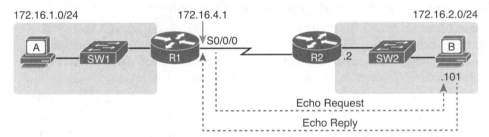

Figure 4-7   *Standard* **ping** *172.6.2.101 Command Using the Source Interface IP Address*

Next, think about IPv4 routing. In the forward direction, R1 must have a route that matches host B's address (172.16.2.101); this route will be either a static route or one learned with a routing protocol. R2 also needs a route for host B's address, in this case a connected route to B's subnet (172.16.2.0/24), as shown in the top arrow lines in Figure 4-8.

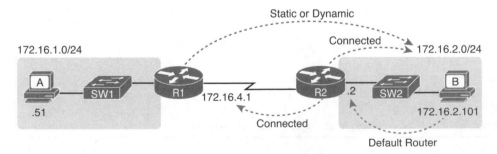

Figure 4-8   *Layer 3 Routes Needed for R1's Ping 172.16.2.101 to Work*

The arrow lines on the bottom of Figure 4-8 shows the routes needed to forward the ICMP Echo Reply message back to router R1's 172.16.4.1 address. First, host B must have a valid default router setting because 172.16.4.1 sits in a different subnet than host B. R2 must also have a route that matches destination 172.16.4.1 (in this case, likely to be a connected route).

The working **ping** commands in Example 4-2 also require the data link and physical layer details to be working. The serial link must be working: The router interfaces must be up/up, which typically indicates that the link can pass data. On the LAN, R2's LAN interface must be in an up/up state. In addition, everything discussed about Ethernet LANs must be working because the **ping** confirmed that the packets went all the way from R1 to host B and back. In particular

- The switch interfaces in use are in a connected (up/up) state.

- Port security does not filter frames sent by R2 or host B.

- STP has placed the right ports into a forwarding state.

> **NOTE**   While this figure shows a small LAN with one switch, if a larger LAN existed, with many switches, a working ping confirms that STP has indeed converged to a working topology.

The **ping 172.16.2.101** in Example 4-2 also confirms that IP access control lists (ACL) did not filter the ICMP messages. As a reminder, an ACL on a router does not filter packets created on that same router, so R1 would not have filtered its own ICMP Echo Request message. The rest of the ICMP messages could have been filtered entering or exiting the router interfaces. Figure 4-9 shows the locations where an IP ACL could have filtered the messages generated as a result of R1's **ping 172.16.2.101** command.

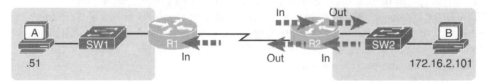

Figure 4-9   *Locations Where IP ACLs Could Have Filtered the Ping Messages*

Finally, the working **ping 172.16.2.101** command on R1 can also be used to reasonably predict that ARP worked on R2 and host B and that switch SW2 learned MAC addresses for its MAC address table. R2 and host B need to know each other's MAC addresses so that they can encapsulate the IP packet inside an Ethernet frame, which means both must have a matching ARP table entry. The switch learns the MAC address used by R2 and by host B when it sends the ARP messages or when it sends the frames that hold the IP packets. Figure 4-10 shows the type of information expected in those tables.

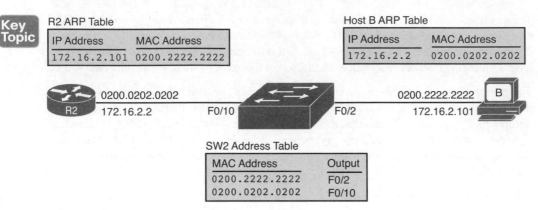

Figure 4-10 *ARP and MAC Address Tables*

As you can see from the last few pages, a strategy of using a **ping** command from near the source of the problem can rule out a lot of possible root causes of any problems between two hosts—assuming the **ping** command succeeds. However, this **ping** command does not act exactly like the same **ping** command on the actual host. To overcome some of what is missing in the **ping** command from a nearby router, the next several examples show some strategies for testing other parts of the path between the two hosts that may have a current problem.

Using Extended Ping to Test the Reverse Route

Pinging from the default router, as discussed in the past few pages, misses an opportunity to test IP routes more fully. In particular, it does not test the reverse route back toward the original host.

For instance, referring back to the internetwork in Figure 4-7 again, note that the reverse routes do not point to an address in host A's subnet. When R1 processes the **ping 172.16.2.101** command, R1 has to pick a source IP address to use for the Echo Request, and routers choose the *IP address of the outgoing interface*. The Echo Request from R1 to host B flows with source IP address 172.16.4.1 (R1's S0/0/0 IP address). The Echo Reply flows back to that same address (172.16.4.1).

The standard **ping 172.16.2.101** command on R1 does not test whether the routers can route back to subnet 172.16.1.0/24. A better ping test would test the route back to host A's subnet; an extended ping from R1 can cause that test to happen. Extended ping allows R1's **ping** command to use R1's LAN IP address from within subnet 172.16.1.0/24. Then, the Echo Reply messages would flow to host A's subnet, as shown in Figure 4-11.

For review, take a look at how the router extended **ping** command works at the CLI. It allows the user to choose from several additional parameters on the **ping** command as compared to the standard **ping** command. While the extended **ping** command does allow the user to type all the parameters on a potentially long command, it also allows users to simply issue the **ping** command, press Enter, with IOS then asking the user to answer questions to complete the command, as shown in Example 4-3. The example shows the **ping** command on R1 that matches the logic in Figure 4-11.

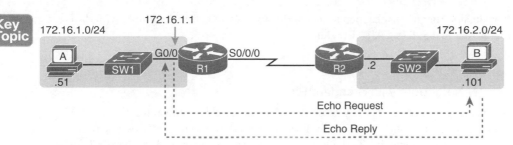

Figure 4-11   *Extended Ping Command Tests the Route to 172.16.1.51*

Example 4-3   *Testing the Reverse Route Using the Extended Ping*

```
R1# ping
Protocol [ip]:
Target IP address: 172.16.2.101
Repeat count [5]:
Datagram size [100]:
Timeout in seconds [2]:
Extended commands [n]: y
Source address or interface: 172.16.1.1
Type of service [0]:
Set DF bit in IP header? [no]:
Validate reply data? [no]:
Data pattern [0xABCD]:
Loose, Strict, Record, Timestamp, Verbose[none]:
Sweep range of sizes [n]:
Type escape sequence to abort.
Sending 5, 100-byte ICMP Echos to 172.16.2.101, timeout is 2 seconds:
Packet sent with a source address of 172.16.1.1
!!!!!
Success rate is 100 percent (5/5), round-trip min/avg/max = 1/2/4 ms
```

This particular extended **ping** command tests the same routes for the Echo Request going to the right, but it forces a better test of routes pointing back to the left for the ICMP Echo Reply. For that direction, R2 needs a route that matches address 172.16.1.1, which is likely to be a route for subnet 172.16.1.0/24—the same subnet in which host A resides.

From a troubleshooting perspective, using both standard and extended **ping** commands can be useful. However, neither can exactly mimic a **ping** command created on the host itself because the routers cannot send packets with the host's IP address. For instance, the extended **ping** in Example 4-3 uses source IP address 172.16.1.1, which is not host A's IP address. As a result, neither the standard or extended **ping** commands in these two examples so far in this chapter can test for some kinds of problems, such as the following:

■ ACLs that discard packets based on host A's IP address, while that same ACL permits packets matched on the router's IP address

■ LAN switch port security issues that filter A's packets (based on A's MAC address)

■ IP routes on routers that happen to match the host A's 172.16.1.51 address, with different routes that match R1's 172.16.1.1 address

■ Problems with host A's default router setting

Testing LAN Neighbors with Standard Ping

Testing using a **ping** of another device on the LAN can quickly confirm whether the LAN can pass packets and frames. Specifically, a working **ping** rules out many possible root causes of a problem, including all the Ethernet LAN features discussed in Chapter 3, "Troubleshooting LAN Switching." For instance, Figure 4-12 shows the ICMP messages that occur if from R1 the command **ping 172.16.1.51** is issued, pinging host A, which sits on the same VLAN as R1.

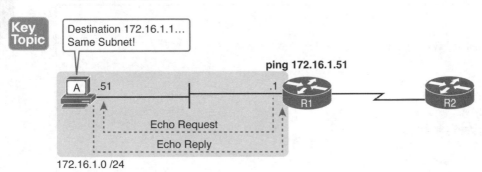

Figure 4-12 *Standard* **ping** *Command Confirms that the LAN Works*

If the ping works, it confirms the following, which rules out some potential issues:

■ The host with address 172.16.1.51 replied.

■ The LAN can pass unicast frames from R1 to host 172.16.1.51 and vice versa.

■ You can reasonably assume that the switches learned the MAC addresses of the router and the host, adding those to the MAC address tables.

■ Host A and router R1 completed the ARP process and list each other in their respective ARP tables.

If the **ping 172.16.1.51** on R1 fails, that result points to list of potential root causes, as well, including the following:

■ Host A could be statically configured with the wrong IP address.

■ If you are using Dynamic Host Configuration Protocol (DHCP), many problems could exist: Host A could be using a different IP address than 172.16.1.51, the DHCP configuration could be wrong, the routers may be missing the DHCP relay configuration and so host A never got its IPv4 address lease, and so on.

■ The router could be configured for 802.1Q trunking, when the switch is not (or vice versa).

■ Any LAN problem discussed in Part I of this book.

So, whether the ping works or fails, simply pinging a LAN host from a router can help further isolate the problem.

Testing LAN Neighbors with Extended Ping

A standard ping of a LAN host from a router does not test that host's default router setting. However, an extended ping can test the host's default router setting. Both tests can be useful, especially for problem isolation, because

- If a standard ping of a local LAN host works...
- But an extended ping of the same LAN host fails...
- The problem likely relates somehow to the host's default router setting.

First, to understand why the standard and extended ping results have different effects, consider first the standard **ping 172.16.1.51** command on R1, as shown previously in Figure 4-12. As a standard **ping** command, R1 used its LAN interface IP address (172.16.1.1) as the source of the ICMP Echo. So, when the host (A) sent back its ICMP Echo Reply, host A considered the destination of 172.16.1.1 as being on the same subnet. Host A's ICMP Echo Reply message, sent back to 172.16.1.1, would work even if host A did not have a default router setting at all!

In comparison, Figure 4-13 shows the difference when using an extended ping on router R1. An extended ping from local router R1, using R1's S0/0/0 IP address of 172.16.4.1 as the source of the ICMP Echo Request, means that host A's ICMP Echo Reply will flow to an address in another subnet, which makes host A use its default router setting.

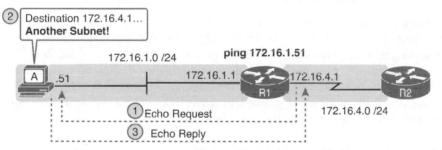

Figure 4-13   *Extended* **ping** *Command Does Test Host A's Default Router Setting*

The comparison between the previous two figures shows one of the most classic mistakes when troubleshooting networks. Sometimes, the temptation is to connect to a router and ping the host on the attached LAN, and it works. So, the engineer moves on, thinking that the network layer issues between the router and host work fine, when the problem still exists with the host's default router setting.

Testing WAN Neighbors with Standard Ping

As with a standard ping test across a LAN, a standard ping test between routers over a serial WAN link tests whether the link can pass IPv4 packets. With a properly designed IPv4 addressing plan, two routers on the same serial link should have IP addresses in the same subnet. A ping from one router to the serial IP address of the other router confirms that an

IP packet can be sent over the link and back, as shown in the **ping 172.16.4.2** command on R1 in Figure 4-14.

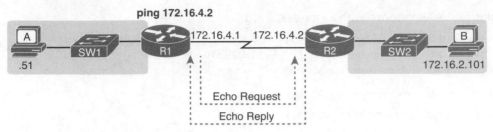

Figure 4-14   *Pinging Across a WAN Link*

If the ping works, it confirms some specific facts:

- Both router's serial interfaces are in an up/up state.
- The Layer 1 and 2 features of the link work.
- The routers believe that the neighboring router's IP address is in the same subnet.
- Inbound ACLs on both routers do not filter the incoming packets, respectively.
- The remote router is configured with the expected IP address (172.16.4.2 in this case).

If this ping test fails, use this same list to help find the root cause. For instance, connect to the routers' CLI and do a quick check of the routers' interface states and IP address/mask combinations. Then, for Layer 1 and 2 issues, use the details discussed in Chapter 12, "Implementing Point-to-Point WANs."

Testing by pinging the other neighboring router does not test many other features, though. For instance, pinging the neighboring router's serial IP address only tests one route on each router: the connected route to the subnet on the serial link. This ping does not test any routes for subnets on LANs. Also, neither the source or destination IP address matches the two hosts that have the original problem, so this test does not do much to help find issues with ACLs. However, although the test is limited in scope, it does let you rule out WAN links as having a Layer 1 or 2 problem, and it rules out some basic Layer 3 addressing problems.

Using Ping with Names and with IP Addresses

All the ping examples so far in this chapter show a ping of an IP address. However, the **ping** command can use hostnames, and pinging a hostname allows the network engineer to further test whether the Domain Name System (DNS) process works.

First, most every TCP/IP application today uses hostnames rather than IP addresses to identify the other device. No one opens a web browser and types in http://72.163.4.161/. Instead, they type in a web address, like http://www.cisco.com, which includes the hostname www.cisco.com. Then, before a host can send data to a specific IP address, the host must first ask a DNS server to resolve that hostname into the matching IP address.

For example, in the small internetwork used for several examples in this chapter, a **ping B** command on host A tests A's DNS settings, as shown in Figure 4-15. When host A sees the use of a hostname (B), it first looks in its local DNS name cache to find out whether it has already resolved the name B. If not, host A first asks the DNS to supply (resolve) the name into its matching IP address (Step 1 in the figure). Only then does host A send a packet to 172.16.2.101, host B's IP address (Step 2).

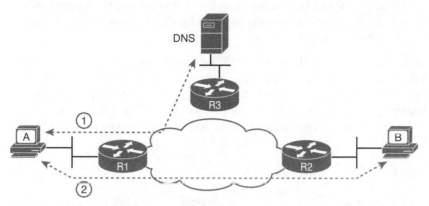

Figure 4-15 *DNS Name Resolution by Host A*

When troubleshooting, testing from the host by pinging using a hostname can be very helpful. The command, of course, tests the host's own DNS client settings. For instance, a classic comparison is to first ping the destination host using the hostname, which requires a DNS request. Then, repeat the same test, but use the destination host's IP address instead of its name, which does not require the DNS request. If the ping of the hostname fails but the ping of the IP address works, the problem usually has something to do with DNS.

Problem Isolation Using the traceroute Command

Like **ping**, the **traceroute** command helps network engineers isolate problems. Here is a comparison of the two:

- Both send messages in the network to test connectivity.
- Both rely on other devices to send back a reply.
- Both have wide support on many different operating systems.
- Both can use a hostname or an IP address to identify the destination.
- On routers, both have a standard and extended version, allowing better testing of the reverse route.

The biggest differences relate to the more detailed results in the output of the **traceroute** command and the extra time and effort it takes **traceroute** to build that output. This third of three major sections examines how traceroute works, plus some suggestions of how to use this more detailed information to more quickly isolate IP routing problems.

traceroute Basics

Imagine some network engineer or CSR starts to troubleshoot some problem. They **ping** from the user's host, **ping** from a nearby router, and after a few commands, convince themselves that the host can indeed send and receive IP packets. The problem might not be solved yet, but the problem does not appear to be a network problem.

Now imagine the next problem comes along, and this time the **ping** command fails. It appears that some problem does exist in the IP network. Where is the problem? Where should the engineer look more closely? Although **ping** can prove helpful in isolating the source of the problem, the **traceroute** command may be a better option. The **traceroute** command systematically helps pinpoint routing problems by showing how far a packet goes through an IP network before being discarded.

The **traceroute** command identifies the routers in the path from source host to destination host. Specifically, it lists the next-hop IP address of each router that would be in each of the individual routes. For instance, a **traceroute 172.16.2.101** command on host A in Figure 4-16 would identify an IP address on router R1, another on router R2, and then host B, as shown in the figure. Example 4-4 that follows lists the output of the command, taken from host A.

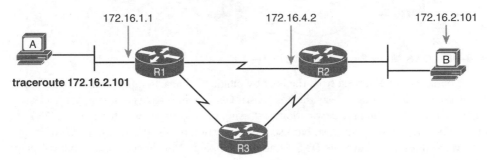

Figure 4-16   *IP Addresses Identified by a Successful* **traceroute 172.16.2.101** *Command on Host A*

Example 4-4   *Output from* **traceroute 172.16.2.101** *on Host A*

```
Wendell-Odoms-iMac:~ wendellodom$traceroute 172.16.2.101
traceroute to 172.16.2.101, 64 hops max, 52 byte packets
 1  172.16.1.1 (172.16.1.1)  0.870 ms  0.520 ms  0.496 ms
 2  172.16.4.2 (172.16.4.2) 8.263 ms  7.518 ms  9.319 ms
 3  172.16.2.101 (172.16.2.101) 16.770 ms  9.819 ms  9.830 ms
```

How the traceroute Command Works

The **traceroute** command gathers information by generating packets that trigger error messages from routers; these messages identify the routers, letting the **traceroute** command list the routers' IP addresses in the output of the command. That error message is the ICMP Time-to-Live Exceeded (TTL Exceeded) message, originally meant to notify hosts when a packet had been looping around a network.

IPv4 routers defeat routing loops in part by discarding looping IP packets. To do so, the IPv4 header holds a field called Time To Live (TTL). The original host that creates the packet sets an initial TTL value. Then, each router that forwards the packet decrements the TTL value by 1. When a router decrements the TTL to 0, the router perceives the packet is looping, and the router discards the packet. The router also notifies the host that sent the discarded packet by sending an ICMP TTL Exceeded message.

Now back to traceroute. Traceroute sends messages with low TTL values, to make the routers send back a TTL Exceeded message. Specifically, a **traceroute** command begins by sending several packets (usually three), each with the header TTL field equal to 1. When that packet arrives at the next router—host A's default router R1 in the example of Figure 4-17—the router decrements TTL to 0 and discards the packet. The router then sends host A the TTL Exceeded message, which identifies the router's IP address to the **traceroute** command.

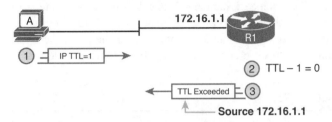

Figure 4-17 *How* traceroute *Identifies the First Router in the Route*

The **traceroute** command sends several TTL=1 packets, checking them to see whether the TTL Exceeded messages flow from the same router, based on the source IP address of the TTL Exceeded message. Assuming the messages come from the same router, the **traceroute** command lists that IP address as the next line of output on the command. Routers have a choice of IP addresses to use, but as you might guess at this point, routers use the IP address of the outgoing interface. In this case, R1's outgoing interface for the TTL Exceeded message is 172.16.1.1.

To find all the routers in the path, and finally confirm that packets flow all the way to the destination host, the **traceroute** command sends packet with TTL=1, TTL=2, then 3, 4, and so on, until the destination host replies. Figure 4-18 shows the packet from the second set with a TTL=2. In this case, one router (R1) actually forwards the packet, while another router (R2) happens to decrement the TTL to 0, causing a TTL Exceeded message being sent back to host A.

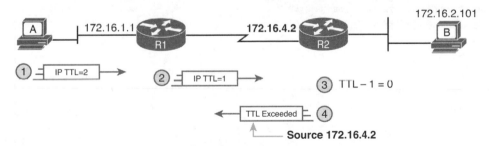

Figure 4-18 *TTL=2 Message Sent by* traceroute

The figure shows these four steps:

1. The **traceroute** command sends a packet from the second set with TTL=2.
2. Router R1 processes the packet and decrements TTL to 1. R1 forwards the packet.
3. Router R2 processes the packet and decrements TTL to 0. R2 discards the packet.

4. R2 notifies the sending host of the discarded packet by sending a TTL Exceeded ICMP message. The source IP address of that message is R2's outgoing interface for the message (in this case, 172.16.4.2).

Standard and Extended traceroute

The standard and extended options for the **traceroute** command give you many of the same options as the **ping** command. For instance, Example 4-5 lists the output of a standard **traceroute** commands on router R1. Like the standard **ping** command, a standard **traceroute** command chooses an IP address based on the outgoing interface for the packet sent by the command. So, in this example, the packets sent by R1 come from source IP address 172.16.4.1, R1's S0/0/0 IP address.

Example 4-5 *Standard* traceroute *on R1*

```
R1# traceroute 172.16.2.101
Type escape sequence to abort.
Tracing the route to 172.16.2.101
VRF info: (vrf in name/id, vrf out name/id)
  1 172.16.4.2 0 msec 0 msec 0 msec
  2 172.16.2.101 0 msec 0 msec *
```

The extended **traceroute** command, as shown in Example 4-6, follows the same basic command structure as the extended **ping** command. The user can type all the parameters on one command line, but it is much easier to just type **traceroute**, press Enter, and let IOS prompt for all the parameters, including the source IP address of the packets (172.16.1.1 in this example).

Example 4-6 *Extended* traceroute *on R1*

```
R1# traceroute
Protocol [ip]:
Target IP address: 172.16.2.101
Source address: 172.16.1.1
Numeric display [n]:
Timeout in seconds [3]:
Probe count [3]:
Minimum Time to Live [1]:
Maximum Time to Live [30]:
Port Number [33434]:
Loose, Strict, Record, Timestamp, Verbose[none]:
Type escape sequence to abort.
Tracing the route to 172.16.2.101
VRF info: (vrf in name/id, vrf out name/id)
  1 172.16.4.2 0 msec 0 msec 0 msec
  2 172.16.2.101 0 msec 0 msec *
```

Both the **ping** and **traceroute** commands exist on most operating systems, including Cisco IOS. However, some operating systems use a slightly different syntax for traceroute. For example, most Windows operating systems support **tracert** and **pathping**, and not **traceroute**. Linux and OS X support the **traceroute** command.

> **NOTE** Host OS **traceroute** commands usually create ICMP Echo Requests. The Cisco IOS **traceroute** command instead creates IP packets with a UDP header. This bit of information may seem trivial at this point. However, note that an ACL may actually filter the traffic from a host's **traceroute** messages but not the router **traceroute** command, or vice versa.

Using traceroute to Isolate the Problem to Two Routers

One of the best features of the **traceroute** command, as compared to ping, is that when it does not complete it gives an immediate clue as to where to look next. With ping, when the ping fails, the next step is usually to use more **ping** commands. With **traceroute**, it tells you what router to try and connect and look at the routes and in which direction.

> **NOTE** As a reminder, this term uses the term *forward route* for routes that send the packets sent by the **ping** or **traceroute** command, and *reverse route* for the packets sent back.

When a problem exists, a **traceroute** command results in a partial list of routers. Then the command either finishes with an incomplete list or it runs until the user must stop the command. In either case, the output does not list all routers in the end-to-end route, because of the underlying problem.

> **NOTE** In addition, the **traceroute** command may not finish even though the network has not problems. Routers and firewalls may filter the messages sent by the **traceroute** command, or the TTL Exceeded messages, which would prevent the display of portions or all or part of the path.

The last router listed in the output tells us where to look next, as follows:

- Connect to the CLI of the last router listed, to look at forward route issues.
- Connect to the CLI of the next router that should have been listed, to look for reverse route issues.

To see why, consider an example based on the internetwork in Figure 4-19. In this case, R1 uses an extended traceroute to host 5.5.5.5, with source IP address 1.1.1.1. This command's output lists router 2.2.2.2, then 3.3.3.3, and then the command cannot complete.

First, Figure 4-19 focuses on the first line of output: the line that lists first-hop router 2.2.2.2.

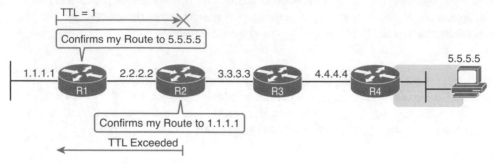

Figure 4-19   *Messages That Cause the* **traceroute** *Command to List 2.2.2.2*

The figure shows the TTL=1 message at the top and the TTL Exceeded message back on the bottom. This first pair of messages in the figure must have worked, because without them, the **traceroute** command on R1 cannot have learned about a router with address 2.2.2.2. The first (top) message required R1 to have a route for 5.5.5.5, which sent the packets to R2 next. The TTL Exceeded message required that R2 have a route that matched address 1.1.1.1, to send the packets back to R1's LAN IP address.

Next, Figure 4-20 focuses on the messages that allow the second line of output on R1's sample **traceroute** command: the line that correctly lists 3.3.3.3 as the next router in the route.

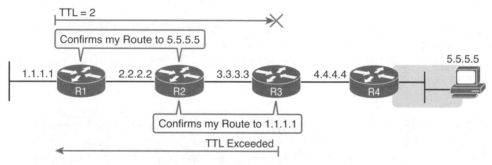

Figure 4-20   *Messages That Cause the* **traceroute** *Command to List 3.3.3.3*

Following the same logic, the **traceroute** output lists 3.3.3.3 because the messages in Figure 4-20 must have worked. For these messages to flow, the routes listed in Figure 4-19 must exist, plus new routes listed in Figure 4-20. Specifically, the TTL=2 packet at the top requires R2 to have a route for 5.5.5.5, which sends the packets to R3 next. The TTL Exceeded message requires that R3 have a route that matches address 1.1.1.1, to send the packets back toward R1's LAN IP address.

In this example, the **traceroute 5.5.5.5** command does not list any routers beyond 2.2.2.2 and 3.3.3.3 However, based on the figures, it is clear that 4.4.4.4 should be the next IP address listed. To help isolate the problem further, why might the next messages—the message with TTL=3 and the response—fail?

Figure 4-21 points out the routing issues that can cause this command to not be able to list 4.4.4.4 as the next router. First, R3 must have a forward route matching destination 5.5.5.5 and forwarding the packet to router R4. The return message requires a reverse route matching destination 1.1.1.1 and forwarding the packet back to router R3.

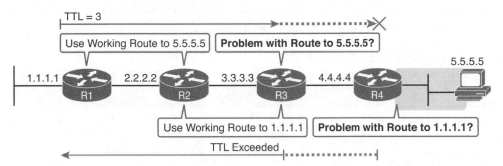

Figure 4-21   *Messages That Could Have Caused* traceroute *to List 4.4.4.4*

In conclusion, for this example, if a routing problem prevents the **traceroute** command from working, the problem exists in one of two places: the forward route to 5.5.5.5 on router R3, or the reverse route to 1.1.1.1 on R4.

Exam Preparation Tasks

Review All the Key Topics

Review the most important topics from this chapter, noted with the Key Topic icon. Table 4-1 lists these key topics and where each is discussed.

Table 4-1   Key Topics for Chapter 4

Key Topic Element	Description	Page Number
List	Host routing logic	133
List	Router routing logic	134
Figure 4-3	Router routing logic	135
Figure 4-4	Router deencapsulation and encapsulation end to end through an internetwork	136
Figure 4-5	ARP example and concept	137
Figure 4-10	ARP tables on Layer 3 hosts, with MAC address tables on Layer 2 switch	142
Figure 4-11	How extended ping in IOS performs a better test of the reverse route	143
List	Types of root causes of host connectivity problems that cannot be found by router **ping** commands	143
Figure 4-12	Why a standard ping over a LAN does not exercise a host's default router logic	144
List	Network layer problems that could cause a ping to fail between a router and host on the same LAN subnet	144
List	Testing a host's default router setting using extended ping	145
List	Items confirmed as working when pinging the router IP address on the other end of a serial link	146
List	Comparisons between the **ping** and **traceroute** commands	147
List	The two places to look for routing problems when a **traceroute** command does not complete	151

Definitions of Key Terms

After your first reading of the chapter, try to define these key terms, but do not be concerned about getting them all correct at that time. Chapter 22 directs you in how to use these terms for late-stage preparation for the exam.

encapsulation, deencapsulation, default router, ARP, ping, traceroute, ICMP Echo Request, ICMP Echo Reply, extended ping, forward route, reverse route, DNS

This chapter covers the following exam topics:

Troubleshooting

Identify and correct common network problems

Troubleshoot and resolve interVLAN routing problems

    Connectivity

    Encapsulation

    Subnet

    Native VLAN

    Port mode trunk status

Troubleshoot and resolve routing issues

    routing is enabled

    routing table is correct

    correct path selection

Troubleshooting IPv4 Routing Part II

Chapter 4, "Troubleshooting IPv4 Routing Part I," began the discussion of IPv4 troubleshooting, looking at the usual first steps when troubleshooting a problem. This chapter moves on to a later stage, when the problem has been isolated to a smaller part of the network, and to a smaller set of possible causes of the problem. The topics in this chapter get specific and look for those root causes: the causes of network problems that have specific solutions that, once a change is made, will solve the original problem.

This chapter breaks down the discussion based on the two major divisions in how packets are forwarded in an IPv4 internetwork. The first half of the chapter focuses on the root causes of problems between a host and its default router. The second half looks at the routers that forward the packet over the rest of a packet's journey, from the router acting as default router all the way to the destination host.

Note that in addition to Chapters 4 and 5, other chapters in this book discuss troubleshooting topics that help when troubleshooting IPv4 internetworks. In particular, Chapter 11, "Troubleshooting IPv4 Routing Protocols," discusses troubleshooting IPv4 routing protocols, namely Open Shortest Path First (OSPF) and Enhanced Interior Gateway Routing Protocol (EIGRP). Chapter 3, "Troubleshooting LAN Switching," discussed how to troubleshoot LAN issues. Some topics inside the chapters in Part IV explain how to troubleshoot WAN links. Finally, Chapter 16, "Troubleshooting IPv6 Routing," discusses how to apply these same IPv4 troubleshooting concepts to IPv6.

"Do I Know This Already?" Quiz

The troubleshooting chapters of this book pull in concepts from many other chapters, including some chapters in *Cisco CCENT/CCNA ICND1 100-101 Official Cert Guide*. They also show you how to approach some of the more challenging questions on the CCNA exams. Therefore, it is useful to read these chapters regardless of your current knowledge level. For these reasons, the troubleshooting chapters do not include a "Do I Know This Already?" quiz. However, if you feel particularly confident about troubleshooting IP routing features covered in this book and *Cisco CCENT/CCNA ICND1 100-101 Official Cert Guide*, feel free to move to the "Exam Preparation Tasks" section near the end of this chapter to bypass the majority of the chapter.

Foundation Topics

Problems Between the Host and the Default Router

Imagine that you work as a customer support rep (CSR) fielding calls from users about problems. A user left a message stating that he couldn't connect to a server. You could not reach him when you called back, so you did a series of pings from that host's default router, using some of the problem isolation strategies described in Chapter 4. And at the end of those pings, you think the problem exists somewhere between the user's device and the default router—for instance, between router R1 and host A, as shown in Figure 5-1.

Problem Domain

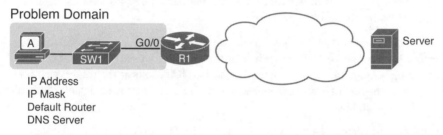

IP Address
IP Mask
Default Router
DNS Server

Figure 5-1 *Focus of the Discussions in This Section of the Chapter*

This first major section of the chapter focuses on problems that can occur on hosts, their default routers, and between the two. To begin, this section looks at the host itself, and its four IPv4 settings, as listed in the figure. Following that, the discussion moves to the default router, with focus on the LAN interface, and the settings that must work for the router to serve as a host's default router.

Root Causes Based on a Host's IPv4 Settings

A typical IPv4 host gets its four key IPv4 settings in one of two ways: either through static configuration or by using DHCP. In both cases, the settings can actually be incorrect. Clearly, any static settings can be set to a wrong number just through human error when typing the values. More surprising is the fact that the DHCP can set the wrong values: The DHCP process can work, but with incorrect values configured at the DHCP server, the host can actually learn some incorrect IPv4 settings.

This section first reviews the settings on the host, and what they should match, followed by a discussion of typical issues.

Ensure IPv4 Settings Correctly Match

Once an engineer thinks that a problem exists somewhere between a host and its default router, the engineer should review of the host's IPv4 settings versus the intended settings. That process begins by guiding the user through the GUI of the host operating system or by using command-line commands native to host operating systems, such as **ipconfig** and **ifconfig**. This process should uncover obvious issues, like completely missing parameters, or if using DHCP, the complete failure of DHCP to learn any of the IPv4 settings.

If the host has all its settings, the next step is to check the values to match them with the rest of the internetwork. The Domain Name System (DNS) server IP address—usually a list of at least two addresses—should match the DNS server addresses actually used in the internetwork. The rest of the settings should be compared to the correct LAN interface on the router that is used as this host's default router. Figure 5-2 collects all the pieces that should match, with some explanation to follow.

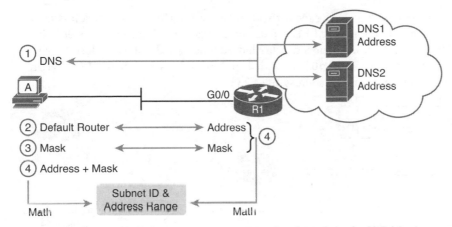

Figure 5-2 *Host IPv4 Settings Compared to What the Settings Should Match*

As numbered in the figure, these steps should be followed to check the host's IPv4 settings:

Step 1. Check the host's list of DNS server addresses against the actual addresses used by those servers.

Step 2. Check the host's default router setting against the router's LAN interface configuration, for the **ip address** command.

Step 3. Check the subnet mask used by the router and the host; if they use a different mask, the subnets will not exactly match, which will cause problems for some host addresses.

Step 4. The host and router should attach to the exact same subnet—same subnet ID and same range of IP addresses. So, use both the router's and host's IP address and mask, calculate the subnet ID and range of addresses, and confirm they are in the same subnet as the subnet implied by the address/mask of the router's **ip address** command.

If an IPv4 host configuration setting is missing, or simply wrong, checking these settings can quickly uncover the root cause. For instance, if you can log in to the router and do a **show interfaces G0/0** command, and then ask the user to issue an **ipconfig /all** (or similar) command and read the output to you, you can compare all the settings in Figure 5-2.

However, although checking the host settings is indeed very useful, some problems related to hosts are not so easy to spot. The next few topics walk through some example problems to show some symptoms that occur when some of these less obvious problems occur.

Mismatched Masks Impact Route to Reach Subnet

A host and its default router should agree about the range of addresses in the subnet. Sometimes, people are tempted to skip over this check, ignoring the mask either on the host or the router and assuming that the mask used on one device must be the same mask as on the other device. However, if the host and router have different subnet mask values, and therefore each calculates a different range of addresses in the subnet, problems happen.

To see one such example, consider the network in Figure 5-3. Host A has IP address/mask 10.1.1.9/24, with default router 10.1.1.150. Some quick math puts 10.1.1.150—the default router address—inside host A's subnet, right? Indeed it does, and it should. Host A's math for this subnet reveals subnet ID 10.1.1.0, with a range of addresses from 10.1.1.1 through 10.1.1.254, and subnet broadcast address 10.1.1.255.

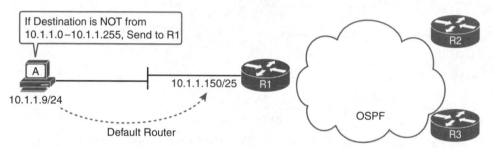

Figure 5-3 *Mismatched Subnet Calculations Appear Workable from Host Toward Network*

In this case, the host routing of packets, to destinations outside the subnet, works well. However, the reverse direction, from the rest of the network back toward the host, does not. A quick check of router R1's configuration reveals the IP address/mask as shown in Figure 5-3, which results in the connected route for subnet 10.1.1.128/25, as shown in Example 5-1.

Example 5-1 *R1's IP Address, Mask, Plus the Connected Subnet That Omits Host A's Address*

```
R1# show running-config interface g0/0
Building configuration...


Current configuration : 185 bytes
!
interface GigabitEthernet0/0
 description LAN at Site 1
 mac-address 0200.0101.0101
 ip address 10.1.1.150 255.255.255.128
 ip helper-address 10.1.2.130
 duplex auto
 speed auto
end
```

```
R1# show ip route connected
! Legend omitted for brevity


      10.0.0.0/8 is variably subnetted, 9 subnets, 4 masks
C        10.1.1.128/25 is directly connected, GigabitEthernet0/0
L        10.1.1.150/32 is directly connected, GigabitEthernet0/0
! Other routes omitted for brevity
```

Because of this particular mismatch, R1's view of the subnet puts host A (10.1.1.9) outside R1's view of the subnet (10.1.1.128/25, range 10.1.1.129 to 10.1.1.254). R1 adds a connected route for subnet 10.1.1.128/25 into R1's routing table, and even advertises this route (with OSPF in this case) to the other routers in the network, as seen in Figure 5-4. All the routers know how to route packets to subnet 10.1.1.128/25, but unfortunately, that route does not include host A's 10.1.1.9 IP address.

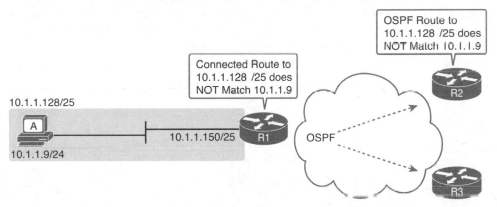

Figure 5-4 *Routers Have No Route That Matches Host A's 10.1.1.9 Address*

Hosts should use the same subnet mask as the default router, and the two devices should agree as to what subnet exists on their common LAN. Otherwise, problems may exist immediately, as in this example, or they might not exist until other hosts are added later.

Typical Root Causes of DNS Problems

When a host lists the wrong IP addresses for the DNS servers, the symptoms are somewhat obvious: Any user actions that require name resolution fail. Assuming that the only problem is the incorrect DNS setting, any network testing with commands like **ping** and **traceroute** fails when using names, but it works when using IP addresses instead of names.

When a ping of another host's hostname fails, but a ping of that same host's IP address works, some problem exists with DNS. For example, imagine a user calls the help desk complaining that he cannot connect to Server1. The CSR issues a **ping server1** command from the CSR's own PC, which both works and identifies the IP address of Server1 as 1.1.1.1. Then the CSR asks the user to try two commands from the user's PC: both a **ping Server1** command (which fails), and a **ping 1.1.1.1** command (which works). Clearly, the DNS name resolution process on the user's PC is having some sort of problem.

This book does not go into much detail about how DNS truly works behind the scenes, but the following two root causes of DNS problems do fit within the scope of the CCENT and CCNA:

- An incorrect DNS server setting
- An IP connectivity problem between the user's host and the DNS server

Although the first problem may be more obvious, note that it can happen both with static settings on the host and with DHCP. If a host lists the wrong DNS server IP address, and the setting is static, just change the setting. If the wrong DNS server address is learned with DHCP, you need to examine the DHCP server configuration. (If using the IOS DHCP server feature, you make this setting with the **dns-server** *server-address* command in DHCP pool mode.)

The second bullet point brings up an important issue for troubleshooting any real-world networking problem. Most every real user application uses names, not addresses, and most hosts use DNS to resolve names. So, every connection to a new application involves two sets of packets: packets that flow between the host and the DNS server, and packets that flow between the host and the real server, as shown in Figure 5-5.

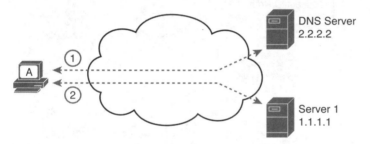

Figure 5-5   *DNS Name Resolution Packets Flow First; Then Packets to the Real Server*

Finally, before leaving the topic of name resolution, note that the router can be configured with the IP addresses of the DNS servers, so that router commands will attempt to resolve names. For instance, a user of the router command-line interface (CLI) could issue a command **ping server1** and rely on a DNS request to resolve server1 into its matching IP address. To configure a router to use a DNS for name resolution, the router needs the **ip name-server** *dns1-address dns2-address...* global command. It also needs the **ip domain-lookup** global command, which is enabled by default.

For troubleshooting, it can be helpful to set a router or switch DNS settings to match that of the local hosts. However, note that these settings have no impact on the user DNS requests.

NOTE   On a practical note, IOS defaults with the **ip domain-lookup** command, but with no DNS IP address known. Most network engineers either add the configuration to point to the DNS servers or disable DNS using the **no ip domain-lookup** command.

Wrong Default Router IP Address Setting

Clearly, having a host that lists the wrong IP address as its default router causes problems. Hosts rely on the default router when sending packets to other subnets, and if a host lists the wrong default router setting, the host may not be able to send packets to a different subnet.

Figure 5-6 shows just such an example. In this case, hosts A and B both misconfigure 10.1.3.4 as the default router due to the same piece of bad documentation. Router R3 uses IP address 10.1.3.3. (For the sake of discussion, assume that no other host or router in this subnet currently uses address 10.1.3.4.)

Figure 5-6   *Incorrect Default Router Setting on Hosts A and B*

In this case, several functions do work. For instance, hosts A and B can send packets to other hosts on the same LAN. The CSR at the router CLI can issue a **ping 10.1.3.9** and **ping 10.1.3.8** command, and both work. As a result of those two working pings, R3 would list the MAC address of the two PCs in the output of the **show arp** command. Similarly, the hosts would list R3's 10.1.3.3 IP address (and matching MAC address) in their ARP caches (usually displayed with the **arp –a** command). The one big problem in this case happens when the hosts try to send packets off-subnet. In that case, try to send the packets to IP address 10.1.3.4 next, which fails.

Root Causes Based on the Default Router's Configuration

While hosts must have correct IPv4 settings to work properly, having correct settings does not guarantee that a LAN-based host can successfully send a packet to the default router. The LAN between the host and the router must work. In addition, the router itself must be working correctly, based on the design of the internetwork.

This next topic looks at problems between hosts and their default router in which the root cause exists on the router. In particular, this topic looks at three main topics. The first topic looks at the trunking configuration required on a router to support multiple VLANs (known as router on a stick, or ROAS). Following that, the text examines typical DHCP issues. The final root cause discussed here is the status of the router interface and what causes that interface to fail.

Mismatched VLAN Trunking Configuration with Router on a Stick

Examples that teach configuration details often focus on one topic at a time. For instance, IPv4 configuration examples may show a host and its default router setting with the IP address configured on the router's LAN interface, as shown earlier in Example 5-1. However, the details of the LAN to which the host and router attach may be completely omitted, to focus on the IPv4 details.

Troubleshooting, both in real life and on the exams, requires that you put all the pieces together. This next example shows a great case of how the troubleshooting process suffers if you forget to think about both the router and switch part of the problem. This example shows a valid router configuration that, unfortunately, does not match the configuration on the neighboring LAN switch like it should.

The next example focuses on how to connect routers to the subnets on multiple VLANs in the same campus LAN. Today, most sites in an enterprise LAN use at least two VLANs. To make routing work today, one of two options is typically used:

■ **Router on a Stick (ROAS):** A router connects to the LAN, with one physical interface configured for VLAN trunking. The router has an IP address in each subnet, with one subnet per VLAN. The router configuration adds each matched subnet and associated VLAN to a subinterface.

■ **Layer 3 switch:** Also called a multilayer switch, a Layer 3 switch performs the same job as a router using ROAS, but the switch has routing functions built in. The switch configuration adds each matched subnet and associated VLAN to a VLAN interface.

This example happens to use ROAS, but many of the same kinds of mistakes shown here can be made with Layer 3 switch configurations as well.

First, the following list outlines the rules for configuring ROAS, using 802.1Q, on both the router and the neighboring switch:

Step 1.   On the router, for each VLAN that is not the native VLAN, do the following:

    A.   Create a unique subinterface for each VLAN that needs to be routed (**interface** *type number.subint*).

    B.   Enable 802.1Q, and associate one specific VLAN with the subinterface in subinterface config mode (**encapsulation dot1q** *vlan-id*).

    C.   Configure IP settings (address and mask) in subinterface config mode (**ip address** *address mask*).

Step 2.   On the router, for the native VLAN, if using it, use one of the two following options:

    A.   Configure just like for other VLANs, except add the **native** keyword to the encapsulation command (**encapsulation dot1q** *vlan-id* **native**).

    Or

    B.   Configure the IP address on the physical LAN interface, without a subinterface and without the **encapsulation dot1q** command.

Step 3.   On the switch, enable trunking (because the router will not negotiate to enable 802.1Q trunking):

    A.   Enable trunking with the **switchport mode trunk** interface subcommand.

    B.   Set the native VLAN to the same VLAN expected on the router, using the **switchport trunk native vlan** *vlan-id* interface subcommand.

Keeping that long list handy for reference, let's next walk through a brief example of the router configuration. First, imagine that previously a site used a single VLAN; so, the router configuration ignored VLAN trunking, with the IP address configured on the physical LAN interface on the router. All hosts sat in default VLAN 1. The router could ignore the VLAN details, not use trunking, and act as default router for all hosts in VLAN 1, as shown in Figure 5-7.

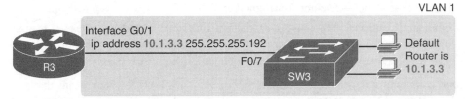

Figure 5-7   *Router IP Address Configuration, Without Trunking*

Then, management planned an expansion in which a second VLAN will be used. This particular company has one network engineer in charge of routers and the other in charge of switches. When planning the changes with the switch engineer, the two engineers did not listen to each other very well, and then the router engineer went off to plan the changes to the router. The router engineer planned to make the following changes to use ROAS:

- Use ROAS on interface G0/1 to support both users in old subnet 10.1.3.0/26, in VLAN 1, and users in new subnet 10.1.3.64/26, in VLAN 2.

- To support VLAN 1 users, leave 10.1.3.3/26 configured as is on the physical interface. This takes advantage of the option to configure the native VLAN IP address on the physical interface because VLAN 1 is the default native VLAN.

- Add a ROAS subinterface to the router configuration to support VLAN 2, using address 10.1.3.65/26 as the router IP address/mask in that subnet.

Figure 5-8 shows the concepts and configuration.

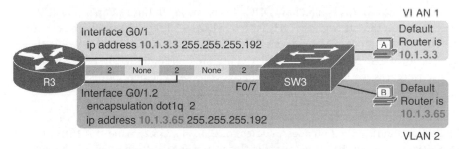

Figure 5-8   *Router IP Address Configuration, with ROAS, and Native VLAN 1*

This configuration could work perfectly well—as long as the switch has a matching correct VLAN trunking configuration. The router configuration implies a couple of things about VLAN trunking, as follows:

- With the IP address listed on physical interface G0/1, the configuration implies that the router intends to use the native VLAN, sending and receiving untagged frames.

- The router intends to use VLAN 2 as a normal VLAN, sending and receiving frames tagged as VLAN 2.

The switch (SW3) needs to configure VLAN trunking to match that logic. In this case, that means to enable trunking on that link, support VLANs 1 and 2, and make sure VLAN 1 is the native VLAN. Instead, in this case, the switch engineer actually added the trunk configuration to the wrong port, with the F0/7 port, connected to router R3, having these settings:

switchport mode access—The port does not trunk.

switchport access vlan 7—The port is assigned to VLAN 7.

The first command confirms, without a doubt, that the link from R3 to SW3 does not trunk. SW1 will not pass any VLAN 2 traffic over that link at all. A standard ping of host B's IP address from R3 fails; likewise, a **ping 10.1.3.65** command from host B fails.

The second command states that the access VLAN on F0/7 is VLAN 7, which means that SW1 will not forward VLAN 1's traffic over the link to R3, either. Again, pings between R3 and hosts in VLAN 1 will fail as well.

In summary, for ROAS configurations, take the time to verify the matching configuration on the neighboring switch. In particular

- Make sure the switch enables trunking (**switchport mode trunk**).

- Make sure the switch sets the correct VLAN as that trunk's native VLAN (**switchport trunk native vlan** *vlan-id*).

- Make sure the switch knows about all the VLANs the router has configured (**vlan** *vlan-id*).

DHCP Relay Issues

Hosts that use DHCP to lease an IP address (and learn other settings) rely on the network to pass the DHCP messages. In particular, if the internetwork uses a centralized DHCP server, with many remote LAN subnets using the DHCP server, the routers have to enable a feature called *DHCP Relay* to make DHCP work. Without DHCP Relay, DHCP requests from hosts never leave the local LAN subnet.

Figure 5-9 shows the big ideas behind how DHCP Relay works. In this example, a DHCP client (Host A) sits on the left, with the DHCP server (172.16.2.11) on the right. The client begins the DHCP lease process by sending a DHCP Discover message, one that would flow only across the local LAN without DHCP Relay configured on router R1. To be ready to forward the Discover message, R1 enables DHCP Relay with the **ip helper-address 172.16.2.11** command configured under its G0/0 interface.

The steps in the figure point out the need for DHCP Relay. At Step 1, host A sends a message, with destination IP and L2 broadcast address of 255.255.255.255 and ff:ff:ff:ff:ff:ff, respectively. Packets sent to this IP address, the "local subnet broadcast address," should never be forwarded past the router. All devices on the subnet receive and process the frame. Additionally, because the **ip helper-address** command configured on R1, router R1 will continue to deencapsulate the frame and packet to identify that it is a DHCP request and take action. Step 2 shows the results of DHCP Relay, where R1 changes both the source and destination IP address, with R1 routing the packet to the address listed in the command: 172.16.2.11.

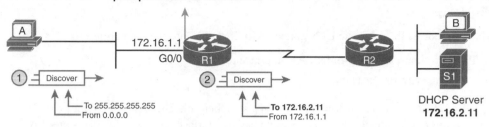

Figure 5-9 *IP Helper Address Effect*

Now, back to troubleshooting. Messages sent by a DHCP client can reach the DHCP server if the following are true:

- The server is in the same subnet as the client, with connectivity working between the two.
- The server is on another subnet, with the router on the same subnet as the client correctly implementing DHCP Relay, and with IP connectivity from that router to the DHCP server.

Two common mistakes can be made with DHCP Relay, both of which are fairly obvious. If the router omits the **ip helper-address** command on a LAN interface (or subinterface when using ROAS, or VLAN interface with a multilayer switching [MLS] configuration), DHCP fails for those clients. If the configuration includes the **ip helper-address** command but lists the wrong DHCP server IP address, again DHCP fails completely.

The symptom in both cases is that the client learns nothing with DHCP.

For instance, Example 5-2 shows an updated configuration for ROAS on router R3, based on the same scenario as in Figure 5-8. The router configuration works fine for supporting IPv4 and making the router reachable. However, only one subinterface happens to list an **ip helper-address** command.

Example 5-2 *Forgetting to Support DHCP Relay on a ROAS Subinterface*

```
interface GigabitEthernet0/1
 ip address 10.1.3.3 255.255.255.192
 ip helper-address 10.1.2.130
!
interface GigabitEthernet0/1.2
 encapsulation dot1q 2
 ip address 10.1.3.65 255.255.255.192
```

In this case, hosts in VLAN 1 that want to use DHCP can, assuming the host at address 10.1.2.130 is indeed the DHCP server. However, hosts in VLAN 2 will fail to learn settings with DHCP because of the lack of an **ip helper-address** command.

Router LAN Interface and LAN Issues

At some point, the problem isolation process may show that a host cannot ping its default router and vice versa. That is, neither device can send an IP packet to the other device on the same subnet. This basic test tells the engineer that the router, host, and LAN between them, for whatever reasons, cannot pass the packet encapsulated in an Ethernet frame between the two devices.

The root causes for this basic LAN connectivity issue fall into two categories:

■ Problems that cause the router LAN interface to fail

■ Problems with the LAN itself

A router's LAN interface must be in a working state before the router will attempt to send packets out that interface (or receive packets in that interface). Specifically, the router LAN interface must be in an up/up state; if in any other state, the router will not use the interface for packet forwarding. So, if a ping from the router to a LAN host fails (or vice versa), check the interface status, and if not up, find the root cause for the router interface to not be up.

Alternatively, the router interface can be in an up/up state, but problems can exist in the LAN itself. In this case, every topic related to Ethernet LANs may be a root cause. In particular, all the topics reviewed in Chapter 3, such as Ethernet cable pinouts, port security, and even Spanning Tree Protocol, may be root causes of LAN issues.

For instance, in Figure 5-10, router R3 connects to a LAN with four switches. R3's LAN interface (G0/1) can reach an up/up state if the link from R3 to SW1 works. However, many other problems could prevent R3 from successfully sending an IP packet, encapsulated in an Ethernet frame, to the hosts attached to switches SW3 and SW4.

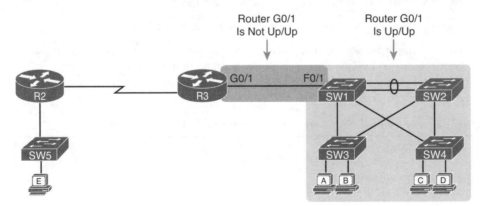

Figure 5-10   *Where to Look for Problems Based on Router LAN Interface Status*

NOTE   This book leaves the discussion of LAN issues, as shown on the right side of Figure 5-10, to Part I of this book.

Router LAN interfaces can fail to reach a working up/up state for several reasons. Table 5-1 lists the common reasons discussed within the scope of the CCNA exam.

Table 5-1 Common Reasons Why Router LAN Interfaces Are Not Up/Up

Reason	Description	Router Interface State
Speed mismatch	The router and switch can both use the **speed** interface subcommand to set the speed, but to different speeds.	down/down
Shutdown	The router interface has been configured with the **shutdown** interface subcommand.	Admin down/down
Err-disabled switch	The neighboring switch port uses port security, which has put the port in an err-disabled state.	down/down
No cable/bad cable	The router has no cable installed, or the cable pinouts are incorrect.*	down/down

* Cisco switches use a feature called auto-mdix, which automatically detects some incorrect cabling pinouts and internally changes the pin logic to allow the cable to be used. As a result, not all incorrect cable pinouts result in an interface failing.

Using the speed mismatch root cause as an example, you could configure Figure 5-10's R3's G0/1 with the **speed 1000** command and SW1's F0/1 interface with the **speed 100** command. The link simply cannot work at these different speeds, so the router and switch interfaces both fall to a down/down state. Example 5-3 shows the resulting state, this time with the **show interfaces description** command, which lists one line of output per interface.

Example 5-3 show interfaces description *Command with Speed Mismatch*

```
R3# show interfaces description
Interface              Status         Protocol Description
Gi0/0                  up             up
Gi0/1                  down           down       link to campus LAN
Se0/0/0                admin down     down
Se0/0/1                up             up
Se0/1/0                up             up
Se0/1/1                admin down     down
```

Problems with Routing Packets Between Routers

The first half of this chapter focused on the first hop that an IPv4 packet takes when passing over a network. This second major section now looks at issues related to how routers forward the packet from the default router to the final host.

In particular, this section begins by looking at the IP routing logic inside a single router. These topics review how to understand what a router currently does. Following that, the discussion expands to look at some common root causes of routing problems, causes that come from incorrect IP addressing, particularly when the addressing design uses variable-length subnet masks (VLSM).

The end of this section turns away from the core IP forwarding logic, looking at other issues that impact packet forwarding, including issues related to router interface status (which needs to be up/up) and how IPv4 access control lists (ACL) can filter IPv4 traffic.

IP Forwarding by Matching the Most Specific Route

Any router's IP routing process requires that the router compare the destination IP address of each packet with the existing contents of that router's IP routing table. Often, only one route matches a particular destination address. However, in some cases, a particular destination address matches more than one of the router's routes.

The following CCENT and CCNA features can create overlapping subnets:

- Autosummary (as discussed in Chapter 10, "Implementing EIGRP for IPv4")
- Manual route summarization
- Static routes
- Incorrectly designed subnetting plans that cause subnets overlap their address ranges

In some cases, overlapping routes cause a problem; in other cases, the overlapping routes are just a normal result of using some feature. This section focuses on how a router chooses which of the overlapping routes to use, for now ignoring whether the overlapping routes are a problem. The section "Routing Problems Caused by Incorrect Addressing Plans," later in this chapter, discusses some of the problem cases.

Now on to how a router matches the routing table, even with overlapping routes in its routing table. If only one route matches a given packet, the router uses that one route. However, when more than one route matches a packet's destination address, the router uses the "best" route, defined as follows:

When a particular destination IP address matches more than one route in a router's IPv4 routing table, the router uses the most specific route—in other words, the route with the longest prefix length mask.

Using **show ip route** and Subnet Math to Find the Best Route

We humans have a couple of ways to figure out what choice a router makes for choosing the best route. One way uses the **show ip route** command, plus some subnetting math, to decide the route the router will choose. To let you see how to use this option, Example 5-4 shows a series of overlapping routes.

Example 5-4   show ip route *Command with Overlapping Routes*

```
R1# show ip route ospf
Codes: L - local, C - connected, S - static, R - RIP, M - mobile, B - BGP
       D - EIGRP, EX - EIGRP external, O - OSPF, IA - OSPF inter area
       N1 - OSPF NSSA external type 1, N2 - OSPF NSSA external type 2
       E1 - OSPF external type 1, E2 - OSPF external type 2
       i - IS-IS, su - IS-IS summary, L1 - IS-IS level-1, L2 - IS-IS level-2
       ia - IS-IS inter area, * - candidate default, U - per-user static route
```

```
            o - ODR, P - periodic downloaded static route, H - NHRP, l - LISP
            + - replicated route, % - next hop override

Gateway of last resort is 172.16.25.129 to network 0.0.0.0


      172.16.0.0/16 is variably subnetted, 9 subnets, 5 masks
O        172.16.1.1/32 [110/50] via 172.16.25.2, 00:00:04, Serial0/1/1
O        172.16.1.0/24 [110/100] via 172.16.25.129, 00:00:09, Serial0/1/0
O        172.16.0.0/22 [110/65] via 172.16.25.2, 00:00:04, Serial0/1/1
O        172.16.0.0/16 [110/65] via 172.16.25.129, 00:00:09, Serial0/1/0
O        0.0.0.0/0 [110/129] via 172.16.25.129, 00:00:09, Serial0/1/0
!
```

NOTE   As an aside, the **show ip route ospf** command lists only OSPF-learned routes, but the statistics for numbers of subnets and masks (9 and 5 in the example, respectively) are for all routes, not just OSPF-learned routes.

To predict which of its routes a router will match, two pieces of information are required: the destination IP address of the packet and the contents of the router's routing table. The subnet ID and mask listed for a route defines the range of addresses matched by that route. With a little subnetting math, a network engineer can find the range of addresses matched by each route. For instance, Table 5-2 lists the five subnets listed in Example 5-4 and the address ranges implied by each.

Table 5-2   Analysis of Address Ranges for the Subnets in Example 5-4

Subnet / Prefix	Address Range
172.16.1.1/32	172.16.1.1 (just this one address)
172.16.1.0/24	172.16.1.0–172.16.1.255
172.16.0.0/22	172.16.0.0–172.16.3.255
172.16.0.0/16	172.16.0.0–172.16.255.255
0.0.0.0/0	0.0.0.0–255.255.255.255 (all addresses)

NOTE   The route listed as 0.0.0.0/0 is the default route.

As you can see from these ranges, several of the routes' address ranges overlap. When matching more than one route, the route with the longer prefix length is used. That is, a route with /16 is better than a route with /10; a route with a /25 prefix is better than a route with a /20 prefix; and so on.

For example, a packet sent to 172.16.1.1 actually matches all five routes listed in the routing table in Example 5-4. The various prefix lengths range from /0 to /32. The longest prefix (largest /P value, meaning the best and most specific route) is /32. So, a packet sent to 172.16.1.1 uses the route to 172.16.1.1/32, and not the other routes.

The following list gives some examples of destination IP addresses. For each address, the list describes the routes from Table 5-2 that the router would match, and which specific route the router would use.

- **172.16.1.1:** Matches all five routes; the longest prefix is /32, the route to 172.16.1.1/32.

- **172.16.1.2:** Matches last four routes; the longest prefix is /24, the route to 172.16.1.0/24.

- **172.16.2.3:** Matches last three routes; the longest prefix is /22, the route to 172.16.0.0/22.

- **172.16.4.3:** Matches the last two routes; the longest prefix is /16, the route to 172.16.0.0/16.

Using **show ip route** *address* to Find the Best Route

A second way to identify the route a router will use, one that does not require any subnetting math, is the **show ip route** *address* command. The last parameter on this command is the IP address of an assumed IP packet. The router replies by listing the route it would use to route a packet sent to that address.

For example, Example 5-5 lists the output of the **show ip route 172.16.4.3** command on the same router used in Example 5-4. The first line of (highlighted) output lists the matched route: the route to 172.16.0.0/16. The rest of the output lists the details of that particular route, like the outgoing interface of S0/1/0 and the next-hop router of 172.16.25.129.

Example 5-5 show ip route *Command with Overlapping Routes*

```
R1# show ip route 172.16.4.3
Routing entry for 172.16.0.0/16
  Known via "ospf 1", distance 110, metric 65, type intra area
  Last update from 10.2.2.5 on Serial0/1/0, 14:22:06 ago
  Routing Descriptor Blocks:
  * 172.16.25.129, from 172.16.25.129, 14:22:05 ago, via Serial0/1/0
      Route metric is 65, traffic share count is 1
```

Certainly, if you have an option, just using a command to check what the router actually chooses is a much quicker option than doing the subnetting math.

show ip route Reference

The **show ip route** command plays a huge role in troubleshooting IP routing and IP routing protocol problems. Many chapters in this book and in the ICND1 book mention various facts about this command. This section pulls the concepts together in one place for easier reference and study.

Figure 5-11 shows the output of a sample **show ip route** command. The figure numbers various parts of the command output for easier reference, with Table 5-3 describing the output noted by each number.

```
        (1)                              (2)        (3)
   10.0.0.0/8 is variably subnetted, 13 subnets, 5 masks
C     10.1.3.0/26 is directly connected, GigabitEthernet0/1
L     10.1.3.3/32 is directly connected, GigabitEthernet0/1
O     10.1.4.64/26 [110/65] via 10.2.2.10, 14:31:52, Serial0/1/0
O     10.2.2.0/30 [110/128] via 10.2.2.5, 14:31:52, Serial0/0/1
(4)      (5)  (6)(7)(8)          (9)       (10)        (11)
```

Figure 5-11   show ip route *Command Output Reference*

Table 5-3   Descriptions of the **show ip route** Command Output

Item	Idea	Value in the Figure	Description
1	Classful network	10.0.0.0/8	The routing table is organized by classful network. This line is the heading line for classful network 10.0.0.0; it lists the default mask for class A networks (/8).
2	Number of subnets	13 subnets	Lists the number of routes for subnets of the classful network known to this router, from all sources, including local routes—the /32 routes that match each router interface IP address.
3	Number of masks	5 masks	The number of different masks used in all routes known to this router inside this classful network.
4	Legend code	C, L, O	A short code that identifies the source of the routing information. *O* is for OSPF, *D* for EIGRP, *C* for Connected, *S* for Static, and *L* for Local. (See Example 5-4 for a sample of the legend.)
5	Subnet ID	10.2.2.0	The subnet number of this particular route.
6	Prefix length	/30	The prefix mask used with this subnet.
7	Administrative distance	110	If a router learns routes for the listed subnet from more than one source of routing information, the router uses the source with the lowest AD.
8	Metric	128	The metric for this route.
9	Next-hop router	10.2.2.5	For packets matching this route, the IP address of the next router to which the packet should be forwarded.
10	Timer	14:31:52	For OSPF and EIGRP routes, this is the time since the route was first learned.
11	Outgoing interface	Serial0/0/1	For packets matching this route, the interface out which the packet should be forwarded.

5

Routing Problems Caused by Incorrect Addressing Plans

The existence of overlapping routes in a router's routing table does not necessarily mean a problem exists. Both automatic and manual route summarization result in overlapping routes on some routers, with those overlaps not causing problems. However, some overlaps, particularly those related to addressing mistakes, can cause problems for user traffic. So, when troubleshooting, if overlapping routes exist, the engineer should also look for the specific reasons for overlaps that actually cause a problem.

Simple mistakes in either the IP addressing plan or the implementation of that plan can cause overlaps that also cause problems. In these cases, one router claims to be connected to a subnet with one address range, while another router claims to be connected to another subnet with an overlapping range, breaking IP addressing rules. The symptoms are that the routers sometimes forward the packets to the right host, but sometimes not.

This problem can occur whether or not VLSM is used. However, the problem is much harder to find when VLSM is used. This section reviews VLSM, shows examples of the problem both with and without VLSM, and discusses the configuration and verification commands related to these problems.

Recognizing When VLSM Is Used or Not

An internetwork is considered to be using VLSM when multiple subnet masks are used for different subnets of *a single classful network*. For example, if in one internetwork all subnets come from network 10.0.0.0, and masks /24, /26, and /30 are used, the internetwork uses VLSM.

Sometimes people fall into the trap of thinking that any internetwork that uses more than one mask must be using VLSM, but that is not always the case. For instance, if an internetwork uses subnets of network 10.0.0.0, all of which use mask 255.255.240.0, and subnets of network 172.16.0.0, all of which use a 255.255.255.0 mask, the design does not use VLSM. Two different masks are used, but only one mask is used in any single classful network. The design must use more than one mask for subnets of a single classful network to be using VLSM.

Only classless routing protocols can support VLSM. The current CCENT and CCNA Routing and Switching certifications cover only classless routing protocols (OSPF and EIGRP), so in all routing protocol discussions for this book, VLSM should be supported. However, for real life, note that RIPv2 (as a classless routing protocol) also supports VLSM, whereas classful routing protocols RIPv1 and Interior Gateway Routing Protocol (IGRP) cannot.

Overlaps When Not Using VLSM

Even when you are not using VLSM, addressing mistakes that create overlapping subnets can occur. For instance, Figure 5-12 shows a sample network with router LAN IP address/mask information. An overlap exists, but it might not be obvious at first glance.

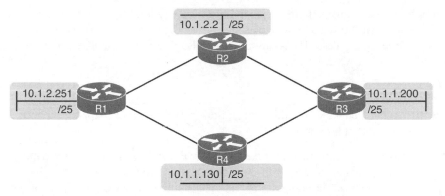

Figure 5-12 *IP Addresses on LAN Interfaces, with One Mask (/25) in Network 10.0.0.0*

If an overlap exists when all subnets use the same mask, the overlapping subnets have the exact same subnet ID, and the exact same range of IP addresses in the subnet. To find the overlap, all you have to do is calculate the subnet ID of each subnet and compare the numbers. For instance, Figure 5-13 shows an updated version of Figure 5-12, with subnet IDs shown and with identical subnet IDs for the LANs off R3 and R4.

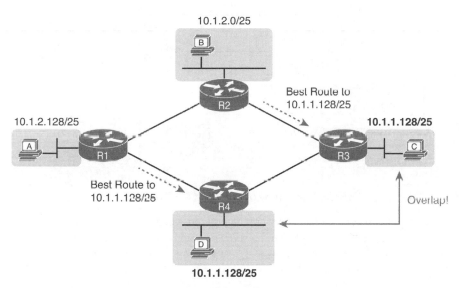

Figure 5-13 *Subnet IDs Calculated from Figure 5-12*

Using the same subnet in two different places (as is done in Figure 5-13) breaks the rules of IPv4 addressing because the routers get confused about where to send packets. In this case, for packets sent to subnet 10.1.1.128/25, some routers send packets so they arrive at R3, whereas others think the best route points toward R4. Assuming all routers use a routing protocol, such as OSPF, both R3 and R4 advertise a route for 10.1.1.128/25.

In this case, R1 and R2 will likely send packets to two different instances of subnet 10.1.1.128/25. With these routes, hosts near R1 will be able to communicate with 10.1.1.128/25 hosts off R4's LAN, but not those off R3's LAN, and vice versa.

Finally, although the symptoms point to some kind of routing issues, the root cause is an invalid IP addressing plan. No IP addressing plan should use the same subnet on two different LANs, as was done in this case. The solution: Change R3 or R4 to use a different, non-overlapping subnet on its LAN interface.

Overlaps When Using VLSM

When using VLSM, the same kinds of addressing mistakes can lead to overlapping subnets; they just may be more difficult to notice.

First, overlaps between subnets that have different masks will cause only a partial overlap. That is, two overlapping subnets will have different sizes and possibly different subnet IDs. The overlap occurs between all the addresses of the smaller subnet, but with only part of the larger subnet. Second, the problems between hosts only occur for some destinations (specifically the subset of addresses in the overlapped ranges), making it even tougher to characterize the problem.

For instance, Figure 5-14 shows an example with a VLSM overlap. The figure shows only the IP address/mask pairs of router and host interfaces. First, look at the example and try to find the overlap by looking at the IP addresses.

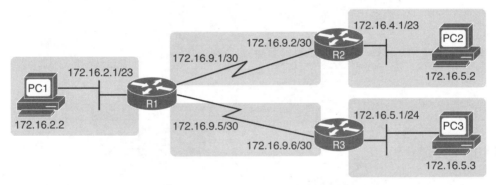

Figure 5-14   *VLSM IP Addressing Plan in Network 172.16.0.0*

To find the overlap, the person troubleshooting the problem needs to analyze each subnet, finding not only the subnet ID but also the subnet broadcast address and the range of addresses in the subnet. If the analysis stops with just looking at the subnet ID, the overlap may not be noticed (as is the case in this example).

Figure 5-15 shows the beginning analysis of each subnet, with only the subnet ID listed. Note that the two overlapping subnets have different subnet IDs, but the lower-right subnet (172.16.5.0/24) completely overlaps with part of the upper-right subnet (172.16.4.0/23). (Subnet 172.16.4.0/23 has a subnet broadcast address of 172.16.5.255, and subnet 172.16.5.0/24 has a subnet broadcast address of 172.16.5.255.)

To be clear, the design with actual subnets whose address ranges overlap is incorrect and should be changed. However, once implemented, the symptoms show up as routing problems, like the similar case without VLSM. **ping** commands fail, and **traceroute** commands do complete for only certain hosts (but not all).

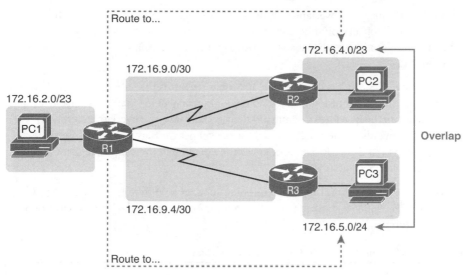

Figure 5-15   *A VLSM Overlap Example, But with Different Subnet IDs*

Configuring Overlapping VLSM Subnets

IP subnetting rules require that the address ranges in the subnets used in an internetwork should not overlap. IOS sometimes can recognize when a new **ip address** command creates an overlapping subnet, but sometimes not, as follows:

Key Topic

- **Preventing the overlap on a single router:** IOS detects the overlap when the **ip address** command implies an overlap with another **ip address** command *on the same router*.

- **Allowing the overlap on different routers:** IOS cannot detect an overlap when an **ip address** command overlaps with an **ip address** command on another router.

The router shown in Example 5-6 prevents the configuration of an overlapping VLSM subnet. The example shows router R3 configuring Fa0/0 with IP address 172.16.5.1/24 and attempting to configure Fa0/1 with 172.16.5.193/26. The ranges of addresses in each subnet are as follows:

>   **Subnet 172.16.5.0/24:** 172.16.5.1 – 172.16.5.254
>   **Subnet 172.16.5.192/26:** 172.16.5.193 – 172.16.5.254

Example 5-6   *Single Router Rejects Overlapped Subnets*

```
R3# configure terminal
R3(config)# interface Fa0/0
R3(config-if)# ip address 172.16.5.1 255.255.255.0
R3(config-if)# interface Fa0/1
R3(config-if)# ip address 172.16.5.193 255.255.255.192
% 172.16.5.192 overlaps with FastEthernet0/0
R3(config-if)#
```

IOS knows that it is illegal to overlap the ranges of addresses implied by a subnet. In this case, because both subnets would be connected subnets, this single router knows that these two subnets should not coexist because that would break subnetting rules, so IOS rejects the second command.

As an aside of how IOS handles these errors, IOS only performs the subnet overlap check for interfaces that are not in a shutdown state. When configuring an interface in shutdown state, IOS actually accepts the **ip address** command that would cause the overlap. Later, when the **no shutdown** command is issued, IOS checks for the subnet overlap and issues the same error message shown in Example 5-6. IOS leaves the interface in the shutdown state until the overlap condition has been resolved.

IOS cannot detect the configuration of overlapping subnets on different routers, as shown in Example 5-7. The example shows the configuration of the two overlapping subnets on R2 and R3 from Figure 5-15.

Example 5-7   *Two Routers Accept Overlapped Subnets*

```
! First, on router R2
R2# configure terminal
R2(config)# interface G0/0
R2(config-if)# ip address 172.16.4.1 255.255.254.0
! Next, on router R3
R3# configure terminal
R3(config)# interface G0/0
R3(config-if)# ip address 172.16.5.1 255.255.255.0
```

Router WAN Interface Status

One of the steps in the IP routing troubleshooting process described earlier, in the "Router LAN Interface and LAN Issues" section, says to check the interface status, ensuring that the required interface is working. For a router interface to be working, the two interface status codes must both be listed as up, with engineers usually saying the interface is "up and up."

So far, the ICND1 and ICND2 books have explored only basic information about how serial links work. For now, know that both routers must have working serial interfaces in an up/up state before they can send IPv4 packets to each other. The two routers should also have serial IP addresses in the same subnet.

Later, the chapters in Part IV further develop the details of WAN links, including what is required for routers to use these links to forward IP packets.

Filtering Packets with Access Lists

Access control lists (ACL) cause some of the biggest challenges when troubleshooting problems in real networking jobs. End-user packets sent by user applications do not look exactly like packets sent by testing tools such as ping and traceroute. The ACLs sometimes filter the ping and traceroute traffic, making the network engineer think some other kind of problems exists when no problems exist at all. Or, the problem with the end-user traffic really is caused by the ACL, but the ping and traceroute traffic works fine, because the ACL filters the user traffic but not the ping and traceroute traffic.

This section summarizes some tips for attacking ACL-related problems in real life and on the exams:

Step 1. Determine on which interfaces ACLs are enabled, and in which direction (**show running-config, show ip interfaces**).

Step 2. Determine which ACL statements are matched by test packets (**show access-lists, show ip access-lists**).

Step 3. Analyze the ACLs to predict which packets should match the ACL, focusing on the following points:

   A. Remember that the ACL uses first-match logic.

   B. Consider using the (possibly) faster math described in the ICND1 book, Chapter 22, "Basic IP Access Control Lists," to find the range of addresses matched by an ACL command: Add the address and wildcard mask to find the end of the numeric range.

   C. Note the direction of the packet in relation to the server (going to the server, coming from the server). Make sure that the packets have particular values as either the source IP address and port, or as the destination IP address and port, when processed by the ACL enabled for a particular direction (in or out).

   D. Remember that the **tcp** and **udp** keywords must be used if the command needs to check the port numbers.

   E. Note that ICMP packets do not use UDP or TCP. ICMP is considered to be another protocol matchable with the **icmp** keyword (instead of **tcp** or **udp**).

   F. Instead of using the implicit **deny any** at the end of each ACL, use an explicit configuration command to deny all traffic at the end of the ACL so that the **show** command counters increment when that action is taken.

If you suspect ACLs are causing a problem, the first problem-isolation step is to find the location and direction of the ACLs. The fastest way to do this is to look at the output of the **show running-config** command and to look for **ip access-group** commands under each interface. However, in some cases, enable mode access may not be allowed, and **show** commands are required. In that case, another way to find the interfaces and direction for any IP ACLs is the **show ip interfaces** command, as shown in Example 5-8.

Example 5-8 *Sample* **show ip interface** *Command*

```
R1>show ip interface s0/0/1
Serial0/0/1 is up, line protocol is up
  Internet address is 10.1.2.1/24
  Broadcast address is 255.255.255.255
  Address determined by setup command
  MTU is 1500 bytes
```

```
 Helper address is not set
 Directed broadcast forwarding is disabled
 Multicast reserved groups joined: 224.0.0.9
 Outgoing access list is not set
 Inbound  access list is 102
! roughly 26 more lines omitted for brevity
```

Note that the command output lists whether an ACL is enabled, in both directions, and which ACL it is. The example shows an abbreviated version of the **show ip interface S0/0/1** command, which lists messages for just this one interface. The **show ip interface** command would list the same messages for every interface in the router.

Step 2 then says that the contents of the ACL must be found. Again, the quickest way to look at the ACL is to use the **show running-config** command. If not available, the **show access-lists** and **show ip access-lists** commands list the same details shown in the configuration commands and a counter for the number of packets matching each line in the ACL. Example 5-9 shows an example.

Example 5-9   show ip access-lists *Command Example*

```
R1# show ip access-lists
Extended IP access list 102
    10 permit ip 10.1.2.0 0.0.0.255 10.1.4.0 0.0.1.255 (15 matches)
```

After the locations, directions, and configuration details of the various ACLs have been discovered in Steps 1 and 2, the hard part begins—interpreting what the ACL really does.

Of particular interest is the last item in the troubleshooting tips list, item 3F. In the ACL shown in Example 5-9, some packets (15 so far) have matched the single configured **access-list** statement in ACL 102. However, some packets have probably been denied because of the implied deny all packets logic at the end of an ACL. If you configure the **access-list 102 deny ip any any** command at the end of the ACL, which explicitly matches all packets and discards them, the **show ip access-lists** command would then show the number of packets being denied at the end of the ACL.

Finally, as a reminder about interpreting ACL commands, when you know the command comes from a router, it is easy to decide the range of addresses matched by an address and wildcard mask. The low end of the range is the address (the first number), and the high end of the range is the sum of the address and wildcard mask. For instance, with ACL 102 in Example 5-9, which is obviously configured in some router, the ranges are as follows:

Source 10.1.2.0, wildcard 0.0.0.255: Matches from 10.1.2.0 through 10.1.2.255

Destination 10.1.4.0, wildcard 0.0.1.255: Matches from 10.1.4.0 through 10.1.5.255

Exam Preparation Tasks

Review All the Key Topics

Review the most important topics from this chapter, noted with the Key Topic icon. Table 5-4 lists these key topics and where each is discussed.

Table 5-4   Key Topics for Chapter 5

Key Topic Element	Description	Page Number
List	Two root causes of DNS problems.	162
List	The rules for configuring ROAS.	164
List	Items to verify for switch trunking configuration to match a router's ROAS configuration.	166
List	Conditions that must be true for DHCP messages to be able to flow from a client to a DHCP server.	167
Table 5-1	Common reasons why router LAN interfaces are not up/up.	169
Definition	When more than one route matches a packet's destination address, the router uses the "best" (most specific) route.	170
List	Types of overlapping IP address configuration issues that IOS can and cannot recognize.	177

Complete the Tables and Lists from Memory

Print a copy of DVD Appendix D, "Memory Tables," or at least the section for this chapter, and complete the tables and lists from memory. DVD Appendix E, "Memory Tables Answer Key," includes completed tables and lists to check your work.

Definitions of Key Terms

After your first reading of the chapter, try to define these key terms, but do not be concerned about getting them all correct at that time. Chapter 22 directs you in how to use these terms for late-stage preparation for the exam.

This chapter covers the following exam topics:

IP Routing Technologies

Recognize high availability (FHRP)

VRRP

HSRP

GLBP

CHAPTER 6

Creating Redundant First-Hop Routers

Businesses rely on their networks to get their work done. Some businesses rely more on the network than others, with a direct connection between network outages and lost revenue. For instance, when the network is down, some companies lose customers, or lose sales, or they cannot ship their goods to market, affecting sales volume in the future. Companies can design their networks to use redundancy—extra devices and extra links—so that when a device fails, or a link fails, the network still works. The extra devices may cost more money, but the cost may be justified, given the cost of an outage.

Networks that have redundant devices and links sometimes require additional protocols to deal with changes to how the network functions with the added redundancy. This chapter discusses one such class of protocols, called First Hop Redundancy Protocol (FHRP).

FHRPs allow network engineers to install multiple routers in a subnet, which collectively act as a single default router. The FHRP makes the routers appear like a single default router to the hosts, letting the hosts be completely unaware of the redundant routers while receiving the benefits of that redundancy. The routers exchange messages to coordinate which router does the work and how to recognize a router problem and take over the function of the other router when needed.

This chapter breaks the content into two major sections. The first looks at the reasons for FHRP protocols, and introduces the three FHRP options: Hot Standby Routing Protocol (HSRP), Virtual Router Redundancy Protocol (VRRP), and Gateway Load Balancing Protocol (GLBP). The second half looks at the configuration and verification of HSRP and GLBP.

"Do I Know This Already?" Quiz

Use the "Do I Know This Already?" quiz to help decide whether you might want to skim this chapter, or a major section, moving more quickly to the "Exam Preparation Tasks" section near the end of the chapter. You can find the answers at the bottom of the page following the quiz. For thorough explanations, see DVD Appendix C, "Answers to the 'Do I Know This Already?' Quizzes."

Table 6-1 "Do I Know This Already?" Foundation Topics Section-to-Question Mapping

Foundation Topics Section	Questions
FHRP Concepts	1–4
FHRP Configuration and Verification	5–6

1. R1 and R2 attach to the same Ethernet VLAN, with subnet 10.1.19.0/25, with address-es 10.1.19.1 and 10.1.19.2, respectively, configured with the **ip address** interface sub-command. Host A refers to 10.1.19.1 as its default router, and host B refers to 10.1.19.2 as its default router. The routers do not use an FHRP. Which of the following are prob-lems for this LAN?

   a. The design breaks IPv4 addressing rules, because two routers cannot connect to the same LAN subnet.

   b. If one router fails, neither host can send packets off-subnet.

   c. If one router fails, both hosts will use the one remaining router as default router.

   d. If one router fails, the host that uses that router as a default router cannot send packets off-subnet.

2. R1 and R2 attach to the same Ethernet VLAN, with subnet 10.1.19.0/25, with address-es 10.1.19.1 and 10.1.19.2, respectively, configured with the **ip address** interface sub-command. The routers use an FHRP. Host A and host B attach to the same LAN and have correct default router settings per the FHRP configuration. Which of the follow-ing statements is true for this LAN?

   a. The design breaks IPv4 addressing rules, because two routers cannot connect to the same LAN subnet.

   b. If one router fails, neither host can send packets off-subnet.

   c. If one router fails, both hosts will use the one remaining router as default router.

   d. If one router fails, only one of the two hosts will still be able to send packets off-subnet.

3. Which of the following FHRP options uses an active/active approach (per subnet) to support first-hop (default router) traffic when implemented with two routers on the same LAN?

   a. GLBP

   b. HSRP

   c. BFD

   d. VRRP

4. R1 and R2 attach to the same Ethernet VLAN, with subnet 10.1.19.0/25, with addresses 10.1.19.1 and 10.1.19.2, respectively, configured with the **ip address** inter-face subcommand. The routers use HSRP. The network engineer prefers to have R1 be the default router when both R1 and R2 are up. Which of the following are the likely default router setting for hosts in this subnet?

   a. 10.1.19.1

   b. 10.1.19.2

   c. Another IP address in subnet 10.1.19.0/25 other than 10.1.19.1 and 10.1.19.2

   d. A hostname that the FHRP mini-DNS will initially point to 10.1.19.1

5. The following text lists output taken from router R3, which is using HSRP. Subnet 10.1.12.0 uses mask 255.255.255.0. Based on the output of this command, which of the following answers is true?

```
R3# show standby brief
Interface   Grp  Pri P State   Active   Standby     Virtual IP
Gi0/0        1   105   Active  local    10.1.12.1   10.1.12.2
```

    a. Hosts with a default router setting of 10.1.12.1 are sending their packets to router R3.

    b. Hosts with a default router setting of 10.1.12.2 are sending their packets to router R3.

    c. Router R3 has an **ip address 10.1.12.2 255.255.255.0** command configured on its G0/0 interface.

    d. Router R3 has an **ip address 10.1.12.1 255.255.255.0** command configured on its G0/0 interface.

6. The following text lists output taken from router R3, which is using GLBP. Subnet 10.1.12.0 uses mask 255.255.255.0. Based on the output of this command, which of the following answers is true?

```
R3# show glbp brief
Interface   Grp  Fwd Pri  State    Address         Active router  Standby router
Gi0/0        1    -   100  Standby  10.1.12.2       10.1.12.4      local
Gi0/0        1    1   -    Active   0007.b400.0101  local          -
Gi0/0        1    2   -    Listen   0007.b400.0102  10.1.12.4      -
```

    a. R3 is the active virtual gateway.

    b. The router with an interface IP address of 10.1.12.2, configured with the **ip address** command, is the active virtual gateway.

    c. The router with an interface IP address of 10.1.12.4, configured with the **ip address** command, is the active virtual gateway.

    d. The output does not identify the active virtual gateway, because the AVG concept is a VRRP concept, not GLBP.

Foundation Topics

FHRP Concepts

When networks use a design that includes redundant routers, switches, LAN links, and WAN links, in some cases other protocols are required to both take advantage of that redundancy and to prevent problems caused by it. For instance, imagine a WAN with many remote branch offices. If each remote branch has two WAN links connecting it to the rest of the network, those routers can use an IP routing protocol to pick the best routes. When one WAN link fails, the routing protocol can learn routes that all happen to use the one remaining WAN link, taking advantage of the redundant link.

As another example, consider a LAN with redundant links and switches, as discussed in Chapters 1, "Spanning Tree Protocol Concepts," and 2, "Spanning Tree Protocol Implementation," of this book. Those LANs have problems unless the switches use Spanning Tree Protocol (STP). STP prevents the problems created by frames that loop through those extra redundant paths in the LAN.

This chapter examines yet another type of protocol that helps when a network uses some redundancy, this time with redundant default routers. When two or more routers connect to the same LAN subnet, all those routers could be used as the default router for the hosts in the subnet. However, to make the best use of the redundant default routers, another protocol is needed. The term *First Hop Redundancy Protocol* (FHRP) refers to the category of protocols that can be used so that the hosts take advantage of redundant routers in a subnet.

The first of two major sections of the chapter discusses the major concepts behind how different FHRPs work. This section begins by discussing a network's need for redundancy in general and the need for redundant default routers. It then shows how the three available FHRP options can each solve the problems that occur when using redundant default routers.

The Need for Redundancy in Networks

Networks need redundant links to improve the availability of the network. Eventually, something in the network will fail. A router power supply might fail, or a cable might break, or a switch might lose power. And those WAN links, drawn as simple lines in most drawings in this book, are actually the most complicated physical parts of the network, with many individual parts that can fail as well.

Depending on the design of the network, the failure of a single component might mean an outage that affects at least some part of the user population. Network engineers refer to any one component that, if it fails, brings down that part of the network as a *single point of failure*. For instance, in Figure 6-1, the LANs appear to have some redundancy, whereas the WAN does not. If most of the traffic flows between sites, many single points of failure exist, as shown in the figure.

Answers to the "Do I Know This Already?" quiz:

1 D   **2** C   **3** A   **4** C   **5** B   **6** C

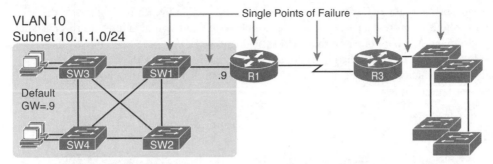

Figure 6-1 *R1 and the One WAN Link as Single Points of Failure*

The figure notes several components as a single point of failure. If any one of the noted parts of the network fail, packets cannot flow from the left side of the network to the right.

Generally speaking, to improve availability the network engineer first looks at a design and finds the single points of failure. Then, the engineer chooses where to add to the network, so that one (or more) single points of failure now have redundant options, increasing availability. In particular, the engineer:

■ Adds redundant devices and links

■ Implements any necessary functions that take advantage of the redundant device or link

For instance, of all the single points of failure in Figure 6-1, the most expensive over the long term would likely be the WAN link, because of the ongoing monthly charge. However, statistically, the WAN links are the most likely component to fail. So, a reasonable upgrade from the network in Figure 6-1 would be to add a WAN link and possibly even connect to another router on the right side of the network, as shown in Figure 6-2.

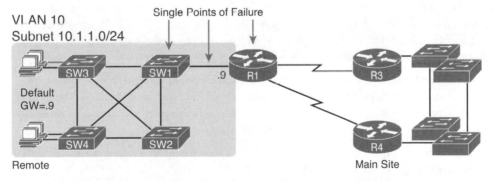

Figure 6-2 *Higher Availability, But with R1 Still as a Single Point of Failure*

Many real enterprise networks follow designs like Figure 6-2, with one router at each remote site, two WAN links connecting back to the main site, and with redundant routers at the main site (on the right side of the figure). Compared to Figure 6-1, the design in Figure 6-2 has fewer single points of failure. Of the remaining single points of failure, a risk remains, but it is a calculated risk. For many outages, a reload of the router solves the problem, and the outage is short. But the risk still exists that the switch or router hardware fails completely and requires time to deliver a replacement device on-site before that site can work again.

For enterprises that can justify more expense, the next step in higher availability for that remote site is to protect against those catastrophic router and switch failures. In this particular design, adding one router on the left side of the network in Figure 6-2 removes all the single points of failure that had been noted earlier. Figure 6-3 shows the design with a second router, which connects to a different LAN switch so that SW1 is also no longer a single point of failure.

VLAN 10
Subnet 10.1.1.0/24

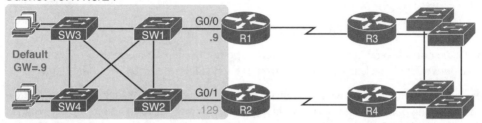

Figure 6-3 *Removing All Single Points of Failure from the Network Design*

> **NOTE** Medium to large enterprise networks work hard at striking a balance of high-availability features versus the available budget dollars. The Cisco website has many design documents that discuss tradeoffs in high-availability design. If interested in learning more, search cisco.com for "high availability campus network design."

The Need for a First Hop Redundancy Protocol

Now back to the topic of this chapter. Of the designs shown so far in this chapter, only Figure 6-3's design has two routers on the LAN of the left side of the figure, specifically the same VLAN and subnet. While having the redundant routers on the subnet helps, the network needs to use an FHRP when these redundant routers exist.

To see the need and benefit of using an FHRP, first think about how these redundant routers could be used as default routers by the hosts in VLAN 10/subnet 10.1.1.0/24. The host logic will remain unchanged, so each host has a single default router setting. So, some design options for default router settings include the following:

- All hosts in the subnet use R1 (10.1.1.9) as their default router, and they statically reconfigure their default router setting to R2's 10.1.1.129 if R1 fails.

- All hosts in the subnet use R2 (10.1.1.129) as their default router, and they statically reconfigure their default router setting to R1's 10.1.1.9 if R2 fails.

- Half the hosts use R1, and half use R2, as default router, and if either router fails, that half of the users statically reconfigure their default router setting.

To make sure the concept is clear, Figure 6-4 shows this third option, with half the hosts using R1, and the other half using R2. The figure removes all the LAN switches just to unclutter the figure. Hosts A and B use R1 as default router, and hosts C and D use R2 as default router.

VLAN10, Subnet 10.1.1.0/24

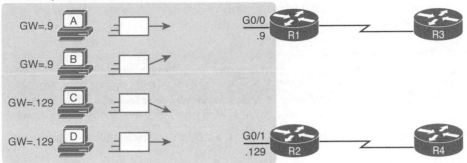

Figure 6-4 *Balancing Traffic by Assigning Different Default Routers to Different Clients*

All of these options have a problem: The users have to take action. They have to know an outage occurred. They have to know how to reconfigure their default router setting. And they have to know when to change it back to the original setting.

FHRPs make this design work better. The two routers appear to be a single default router. The users never have to do anything: Their default router setting remains the same, and their ARP table even remains the same.

To allow the hosts to remain unchanged, the routers have to do some more work, as defined by one of the FHRP protocols. Generically, each FHRP makes the following happen:

1. All hosts act like they always have, with one default router setting that never has to change.

2. The default routers share a virtual IP address in the subnet, defined by the FHRP.

3. Hosts use the FHRP virtual IP address as their default router address.

4. The routers exchange FHRP protocol messages, so that both agree as to which router does what work at any point in time.

5. When a router fails, or has some other problem, the routers use the FHRP to choose which router takes over responsibilities from the failed router.

The Three Solutions for First-Hop Redundancy

The term *First Hop Redundancy Protocol* does not name any one protocol. Instead, it names a family of protocols that fill the same role. For a given network, like the left side of Figure 6-4, the engineer would pick one of the protocols from the FHRP family.

> **NOTE** *First Hop* is a reference to the default router being the first router, or first router hop, through which a packet must pass.

Table 6-2 lists the three FHRP protocols in chronological order, based on when these were first used. Cisco first introduced the proprietary Hot Standby Router Protocol (HSRP), and it worked well for many of their customers. Later, the IETF developed an RFC for a very similar protocol, Virtual Router Redundancy Protocol (VRRP). Finally, Cisco developed a more robust option, Gateway Load Balancing Protocol (GLBP).

Table 6-2   Three FHRP Options

Acronym	Full Name	Origin	Redundancy Approach	Load Balancing
HSRP	Hot Standby Router Protocol	Cisco	Active/standby	Per subnet
VRRP	Virtual Router Redundancy Protocol	IETF (RFC 5798)	Active/standby	Per subnet
GLBP	Gateway Load Balancing Protocol	Cisco	Active/active	Per host

The next few pages walk through the concepts of how HSRP works, followed by GLBP. HSRP and VRRP have many similarities, at least to the depth discussed in this book, so this section uses HSRP rather than VRRP as an example. These upcoming topics explain the meaning of the different approaches to redundancy (active/standby and active/active) and the load balancing differences as well.

HSRP Concepts

HSRP operates with an active/standby model (also more generally called *active/passive*). HSRP allows two (or more) routers to cooperate, all being willing to act as the default router. However, at any one time, only one router actively supports the end-user traffic. The packets sent by hosts to their default router flow to that one active router. Then, the other routers, with an HSRP standby state, sit there patiently waiting to take over should the active HSRP router have a problem.

The HSRP active router implements a virtual IP address and matching virtual MAC address. This virtual IP address exists as part of the HSRP configuration, which is an additional configuration item compared to the usual **ip address** interface subcommand. This virtual IP address is in the same subnet as the interface IP address, but it is a different IP address. The router then automatically creates the virtual MAC address. All the cooperating HSRP routers know these virtual addresses, but only the HSRP active router uses these addresses at any one point in time.

Hosts refer to the virtual IP address as their default router address, instead of any one router's interface IP address. For instance, in Figure 6-5, R1 and R2 use HSRP. The HSRP virtual IP address is 10.1.1.1, with the virtual MAC address referenced as VMAC1 for simplicity's sake.

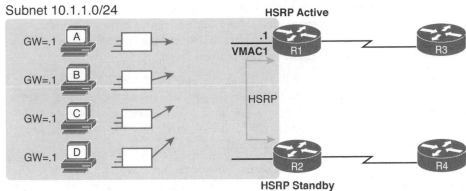

Host ARP Table

IP	MAC
10.1.1.1	**VMAC1**

Figure 6-5 *All Traffic Goes to .1 (R1, Which Is Active); R2 Is Standby*

HSRP Failover

HSRP on each router has some work to do to make the network function as shown in Figure 6-5. The two routers need HSRP configuration, including the virtual IP address. The two routers send HSRP messages to each other to negotiate and decide which router should currently be active, and which should be standby. Then, the two routers continue to send messages to each other so that the standby router knows when the active router fails so that it can take over as the new active router.

Figure 6-6 shows the result when the R1, the HSRP active router in Figure 6-5, fails. R1 quits using the virtual IP and MAC address, while R2, the new active router, starts using these addresses. The hosts do not need to change their default router settings at all, with traffic now flowing to R2 instead of R1.

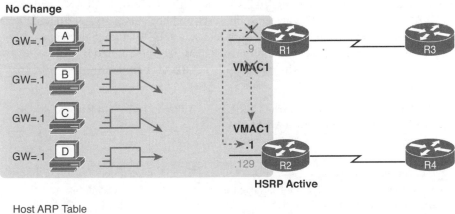

Host ARP Table

IP	MAC
10.1.1.1	**VMAC1**

← **No Change**

Figure 6-6 *Packets Sent Through R2 (New Active) Once It Takes Over for Failed R1*

When the failover happens, some changes do happen, but none of those changes happen on the hosts. The host keeps the same default router setting, set to the virtual IP address (10.1.1.1 in this case). The host's ARP table does not have to change either, with the HSRP virtual MAC being listed as the MAC address of the virtual router.

When the failover occurs, changes happen on both the routers and the LAN switches. Clearly, the new active router has to be ready to receive packets (encapsulated inside frames) using the virtual IP and MAC addresses. However, the LAN switches, hidden in the last few figures, formerly sent frames destined for VMAC1 to router R1. Now the switches must know to send the frames to the new active router, R2.

To make the switches change their MAC address table entries for VMAC1, R2 sends an Ethernet frame with VMAC1 as the source MAC address. The switches, as normal, learn the source MAC address (VMAC1), but with new ports that point toward R2. The frame is also a LAN broadcast, so all the switches learn a MAC table entry for VMAC1 that leads toward R2. (By the way, this Ethernet frame holds an ARP Reply message, called a gratuitous ARP, because the router sends it without first receiving an ARP Request.)

HSRP Load Balancing

The active/standby model of HSRP means that in one subnet all hosts send their off-subnet packets through only one router. In other words, the routers do not share the workload, with one router handling all the packets. For instance, back in Figure 6-5, R1 was the active router, so all hosts in the subnet sent their packets through R1, and none of the hosts in the subnet sent their packets through R2.

HSRP does support load balancing by preferring different routers to be the active router in different subnets. Most sites that require a second router for redundancy are also big enough to use several VLANs and subnets and the site. The two routers will likely connect to all the VLANs, acting as the default router in each VLAN. HSRP then can be configured to prefer one router as active in one VLAN, and another router as active in another VLAN, balancing the traffic.

For instance, Figure 6-7 shows a redesigned LAN, now with two hosts in VLAN 1 and two hosts in VLAN 2. Both R1 and R2 connect to the LAN, and both use a VLAN trunking and router-on-a-stick (ROAS) configuration. Both routers use HSRP in each of the two subnets, supporting each other. However, on purpose, R1 has been configured so that it wins the negotiation to become HSRP active in VLAN 1, and R2 has been configured to win in VLAN 2.

Note that by having each router act as the HSRP active router in some subnets, the design makes use of both routers and both WAN links.

> **NOTE** For designs that use Layer 3 switches, the Layer 3 switches act as the default router of the hosts. In that case, the HSRP configuration goes on the Layer 3 switch. Figure 6-7 shows the alternative, which is to use VLAN trunking on the routers with Layer 2 switches in the LAN.

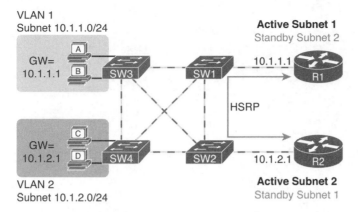

VLAN 1
Subnet 10.1.1.0/24

Active Subnet 1
Standby Subnet 2

GW=
10.1.1.1

SW3

SW1

10.1.1.1

R1

HSRP

GW=
10.1.2.1

SW4

SW2

10.1.2.1   R2

VLAN 2
Subnet 10.1.2.0/24

Active Subnet 2
Standby Subnet 1

Figure 6-7 *Load Balancing with HSRP by Using Different Active Routers per Subnet*

GLBP Concepts

HSRP and VRRP, which were introduced before Gateway Load Balancing Protocol (GLBP), balanced the packet load per subnet, as shown in Figure 6-7. However, because traffic loads vary unpredictably from subnet to subnet, Cisco wanted an FHRP option with better load-balancing options than just the per-subnet load balancing of HSRP and VRRP. To meet that need, Cisco introduced GLBP.

GLBP balances the packet load per host by using an active/active model in each subnet. Each GLBP router in a subnet receives off-subnet packets from some of the hosts in the subnet. Each host still remains unaware of the FHRP, allowing the hosts to configure the same default gateway/router setting and for the hosts to make no changes when a router fails.

GLBP creates a world that at first glance looks like HSRP, but with a few twists that let GLBP balance the traffic. Like HSRP, all the routers configure a virtual IP address, which is the IP address used by hosts as their default router. Like with HSRP, hosts use a default router setting that points to the virtual IP address, and that setting does not need to change. GLBP differs from HSRP with regard to the MAC addresses it uses and the ARP process, because GLBP actually uses ARP Reply messages to balance traffic from different hosts through different routers.

With GLBP, one router acts in a special role called the *active virtual gateway* (AVG). The AVG replies to all ARP requests for the virtual IP address. Each router has a unique virtual MAC address, so that the AVG can reply to some ARP Requests with one virtual MAC, and some with the other. As a result, some hosts in the subnet send frames to the Ethernet MAC address of one of the routers, with other hosts sending their frames to the MAC address of the second router.

As an example, Figure 6-8 shows the process by which a GLBP balances traffic for host A based on the Address Resolution Protocol (ARP) Reply sent by the AVG (R1). The figure uses the same IP addresses as earlier HSRP examples with Figures 6-5 and 6-6. The two routers support virtual IP address 10.1.1.1, with the hosts using that address as their default router setting.

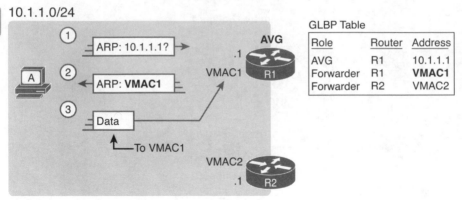

Figure 6-8   *GLBP Directs Host A by Sending Back ARP Reply with R1's MAC1*

The figure shows three messages, top to bottom, with the following action:

1. Host A has no ARP table entry for its default router, 10.1.1.1, so host A sends an ARP Request to learn 10.1.1.1's MAC address.

2. The GLBP AVG, R1 in this case, sends back an ARP Reply. The AVG chooses to include its own virtual MAC address in the ARP Reply, VMAC1.

3. Future IP packets sent by host A are encapsulated in Ethernet frames, destined to VMAC1, so that they arrive at R1.

From now on, host A sends off-subnet packets to R1 due to host A's ARP table entry for its default gateway (10.1.1.1). Host A's ARP table entry for 10.1.1.1 now refers to a MAC address on R1 (VMAC1), so packets host A sends off-subnet flow through R1.

To balance the load, the AVG answers each new ARP Request with the MAC addresses of alternating routers. Figure 6-9 continues the load-balancing effect with the ARP Request for 10.1.1.1 coming from host B. The router acting as AVG (R1) still sends the ARP Reply, but this time with R2's virtual MAC (VMAC2).

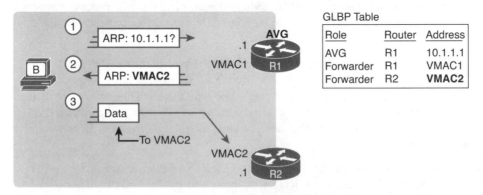

Figure 6-9   *GLBP Directs Host B by Sending Back ARP Reply with R2's VMAC2*

Here are the steps in the figure:

1. Host B sends an ARP Request to learn 10.1.1.1's MAC address.

2. The GLBP AVG (R1) sends back an ARP Reply, listing VMAC2, R2's virtual MAC address.

3. For future packets sent off-subnet, host B encapsulates the packets in Ethernet frames, destined to VMAC2, so that they arrive at R2.

The process shown in Figures 6-8 and 6-9 balances the traffic, per host, but the routers must also be ready to take over for the other router if it fails. GLBP refers to each router as a forwarder. When all is well, each router acts as forwarder for their own virtual MAC address, but it listens to GLBP messages to make sure the other forwarders are still working. If another forwarder fails, the still-working forwarder takes over the failed forwarder's virtual MAC address role and continues to forward traffic.

FHRP Configuration and Verification

This second major section of this chapter shows the configuration for basic functions of both HSRP and GLBP, with the matching **show** commands. The goal of this section is to show enough of the operation of each tool to reinforce the concepts discussed in the first section.

Configuring and Verifying HSRP

HSRP configuration requires only one command on the two (or more) routers that want to share default router responsibilities with HSRP: the **standby** *group* **ip** *virtual-ip* interface subcommand. The first value defines the HSRP group number, which must match on both routers. The group number lets one router support multiple HSRP groups at a time, and it allows the routers identify each other based on the group. The command also configures the virtual IP address shared by the routers in the same group.

Example 6-1 shows a configuration example, matching the HSRP examples related to Figures 6-5 and 6-6. Both routers use group 1, with virtual IP address 10.1.1.1, with the **standby 1 ip 10.1.1.1** interface subcommand.

Example 6-1 *HSRP Configuration on R1 and R2, Sharing IP Address 10.1.1.1*

```
R1# show running-config
! Lines omitted for brevity
interface GigabitEthernet0/0
 ip address 10.1.1.9 255.255.255.0
 standby version 2
 standby 1 ip 10.1.1.1
 standby 1 priority 110
 standby 1 name HSRP-group-for-book
! The following configuration, on R2, is identical except for the priority,
! the interface IP address, and the HSRP priority
R2# show running-config
! Lines omitted for brevity
```

```
interface GigabitEthernet0/0
 ip address 10.1.1.129 255.255.255.0
 standby version 2
 standby 1 ip 10.1.1.1
 standby 1 name HSRP-group-for-book
```

The configuration shows other optional parameters, as well. For instance, R1 has a priority of 110 in this group, and R2 defaults to 100. With HSRP, if the two routers are brought up at the same time, the router with the higher priority wins the election to become the active router. The configuration also shows a name that can be assigned to the group (when using **show** commands) and a choice to use HSRP Version 2.

Once configured, the two routers negotiate the HSRP settings and choose which router will currently be active and which will be standby. With the configuration as shown, R1 will win the election and become active because of its higher (better) priority. Both routers reach the same conclusion, as confirmed with the output of the **show standby brief** command on both R1 and R2 in Example 6-2.

Example 6-2   *HSRP Status on R1 and R2 with* **show standby brief**

```
! First, the group status as seen from R1
R1# show standby brief
                     P indicates configured to preempt.
                     |
Interface   Grp  Pri P State   Active       Standby       Virtual IP
Gi0/0       1    110   Active  local        10.1.1.129    10.1.1.1
! The output here on R2 shows that R2 agrees with R1.
R2# show standby brief
                     P indicates configured to preempt.
                     |
Interface   Grp  Pri P State   Active       Standby       Virtual IP
Gi0/0       1    100   Standby 10.1.1.9     local         10.1.1.1
```

First, look at the Grp column for each command. This lists the HSRP group number, so when looking at output from multiple routers, you need to look at the lines with the same group number to make sure the data relates to that one HSRP group. In this case, both routers have only one group number (1), so it is easy to find the information.

Each line of output lists the local router's view of the HSRP status for that group. In particular, based on the headings, the **show standby brief** command identifies the following:

Key Topic

Interface: The local router's interface on which the HSRP group is configured

Grp: The HSRP group number

Pri: The local router's HSRP priority

State: The local router's current HSRP state

Active: The interface IP address of the currently-active HSRP router (or "local" if the local router is HSRP active)

Standby: The interface IP address of the currently-standby HSRP router (or "local" if the local router is HSRP standby)

Virtual IP: The virtual IP address defined by this group

For instance, following the highlighted text in Example 6-2, R2 believes that its own current state is standby, that the router with interface address 10.1.1.9 is active, with a confirmation that the "local" router (R2, on which this command was issued) is the standby router.

As you can see, the **show standby brief** command actually packs a lot of detail in a single line of output. In comparison, the **show standby** command lists a more detailed description of the current state, while repeating many of the facts from the **show standby brief** command. Example 6-3 shows an example of the new information with the **show standby** command, listing several counters and timers about the HSRP protocol itself, plus the virtual MAC address 0000.0c9f.f001.

Example 6-3 *HSRP Status on R1 and R2 with* **show standby**

```
R1# show standby
GigabitEthernet0/0 - Group 1 (version 2)
  State is Active
    6 state changes, last state change 00:12:53
  Virtual IP address is 10.1.1.1
  Active virtual MAC address is 0000.0c9f.f001
    Local virtual MAC address is 0000.0c9f.f001 (v2 default)
  Hello time 3 sec, hold time 10 sec
    Next hello sent in 1.696 secs
  Preemption disabled
  Active router is local
  Standby router is 10.1.1.129, priority 100 (expires in 8.096 sec)
  Priority 110 (configured 110)
  Group name is "HSRP-group-for-book" (cfgd)
! The output here on R2 shows that R2 agrees with R1.
R2# show standby
GigabitEthernet0/0 - Group 1 (version 2)
  State is Standby
    4 state changes, last state change 00:12:05
  Virtual IP address is 10.1.1.1
  Active virtual MAC address is 0000.0c9f.f001
    Local virtual MAC address is 0000.0c9f.f001 (v2 default)
  Hello time 3 sec, hold time 10 sec
    Next hello sent in 0.352 secs
  Preemption disabled
  Active router is 10.1.1.9, priority 110 (expires in 9.136 sec)
    MAC address is 0200.0101.0101
  Standby router is local
  Priority 100 (default 100)
  Group name is "HSRP-group-for-book" (cfgd)
```

6

Configuring and Verifying GLBP

GLBP configuration mimics HSRP configuration to a great degree. In fact, if you took the configuration in Example 6-1, removed the **standby version 2** command (which applies only to HSRP), and replaced each **standby** with **glbp**, the result would be a completely valid GLBP configuration.

GLBP requires only a single interface subcommand on each router: the **glbp** *group* **ip** *virtual-ip* interface subcommand. The ideas behind this one command work just like HSRP as well: All routers use the same group number, and all routers configure the same virtual IP address.

Example 6-4 shows a GLBP configuration that would be typical if migrating from using HSRP, as shown in Example 6-1, to the equivalent GLBP configuration. Both routers use GLBP group 1, with virtual IP address 10.1.1.1, with the **glbp 1 ip 10.1.1.1** interface sub-command.

Example 6-4   *GLBP Configuration on R1 and R2, Sharing IP Address 10.1.1.1*

```
! First, the configuration on R1
R1# show running-config
! Lines omitted for brevity
interface GigabitEthernet0/0
 ip address 10.1.1.9 255.255.255.0
 glbp 1 ip 10.1.1.1
 glbp 1 priority 110
 glbp 1 name GLBP-group-for-book
! The following configuration, on R2, is identical except for
! the interface IP address, and the GLBP priority
R2# show running-config
! Lines omitted for brevity
interface GigabitEthernet0/0
 ip address 10.1.1.129 255.255.255.0
 glbp 1 ip 10.1.1.1
 glbp 1 name GLBP-group-for-book
```

Once configured, the two routers negotiate as to which will be the AVG. As with HSRP, if both come up at the same time, R1 will win, with a priority set to 110 with the **glbp 1 priority 110** command versus R2's default priority of 100. However, if either router comes up before the other, that router goes ahead and takes on the AVG role.

Sifting through the GLBP **show** command output takes a little more work with HSRP, in particular because of the added detail in how GLBP works. First, consider the **show glbp brief** command on router R1, as shown in Example 6-5. (Note that many **show glbp** commands have the same options as equivalent HSRP **show standby** commands.)

Example 6-5 *GLBP Status on R1 with* **show glbp brief**

```
R1# show glbp brief
Interface    Grp  Fwd  Pri  State    Address          Active router    Standby router
Gi0/0        1    -    110  Active   10.1.1.1         local            10.1.1.129
Gi0/0        1    1    -    Listen   0007.b400.0101   10.1.1.129       -
Gi0/0        1    2    -    Active   0007.b400.0102   local
```

Before looking at the right side of the output, first consider the context for a moment. This example lists a heading line and three rows of data. These data rows are identified by the Grp and Fwd headings, short for Group and Forwarder. With only one GLBP group configured, R1 lists lines only for group 1. More important, each row defines details about a different part of what GLBP does, as follows:

Fwd is -: This line refers to none of the forwarders, and instead describes the AVG.

Fwd is 1: This line describes GLBP forwarder (router) 1.

Fwd is 2: This line describes GLBP forwarder (router) 2.

The output usually lists the line about the AVG first, as noted with a dash in the Forwarder column. Now looking at the highlighted portions on the right of Example 6-5. This line will list the virtual IP address and identify the active AVG and the standby AVG. This particular command, from router R1, lists R1 itself ("local") as the active router. So, R1 is the current AVG.

Each of the next two lines lists status information about one of the forwarder roles; that is, a router that uses a virtual MAC address, receives frames sent to that address, and routes the packets encapsulated in those frames. To that end, the Address column lists MAC addresses, specifically the virtual MAC addresses used by GLBP, and not the interface MAC addresses.

Each forwarder row also identifies the router that currently uses the listed virtual MAC in the Active Router column. In Example 6-5, 0007.b400.0101 is used by the router with interface IP address 10.1.1.129 (which happens to be R2). 0007.b400.0102 is supported by the local router (the router on which the **show** command was issued), which is R1.

The brief output of the **show glbp brief** lists many details, but with some effort to learn how to sift through it all. For more perspective on the output, Example 6-6 lists this same **show glbp brief** command, this time on R2. Note that the Fwd column again identifies the first line of output as being about the AVG, with the next two lines about the two forwarders.

Example 6-6 *GLBP Status on R2 with* **show glbp brief**

```
R2# show glbp brief
Interface    Grp  Fwd  Pri  State    Address          Active router    Standby router
Gi0/0        1    -    100  Standby  10.1.1.1         10.1.1.9         local
Gi0/0        1    1    -    Active   0007.b400.0101   local            -
Gi0/0        1    2    -    Listen   0007.b400.0102   10.1.1.9         -
```

6

The State column in the output in Examples 6-5 and 6-6 can pull the GLBP concepts together. First, to define the meaning of the state values, the following short list defines the states expected for the first line of output, about the AVG, and then about each GLBP forwarder:

AVG: One router should be the active AVG, with the other acting as standby, ready to take over the AVG role if the AVG fails.

Each forwarder: One router should be active, while the other should be listening, ready to take over that virtual MAC address if that forwarder fails.

Table 6-3 collects the values of the State column from Example 6-5 and 6-6 for easier reference side by side. Note that, indeed, each line has either an active/standby pair (for the AVG) or an active/listen pair (for the forwarder function).

Table 6-3   Comparing Local State in **show glbp brief** Commands

Row Is About...	Fwd Column Value	R1 State	R2 State
AVG	-	Active	Standby
Forwarder 1	1	Listen	Active
Forwarder 2	2	Active	Listen

Finally, the **show glbp** command lists a more detailed view of the current GLBP status. Example 6-7 shows a sample from router R1. Note that the first half of the output has similar information compared to HSRP's **show standby** command, plus it lists the IP and MAC addresses of the routers in the GLBP group. Then, the end of the output lists a group of messages per GLBP forwarder.

Example 6-7   *GLBP Status on R1 with* show glbp

```
R1# show glbp
GigabitEthernet0/0 - Group 1
  State is Active
    2 state changes, last state change 00:20:59
  Virtual IP address is 10.1.1.1
  Hello time 3 sec, hold time 10 sec
    Next hello sent in 2.112 secs
  Redirect time 600 sec, forwarder timeout 14400 sec
  Preemption disabled
  Active is local
  Standby is 10.1.1.129, priority 100 (expires in 8.256 sec)
  Priority 110 (configured)
  Weighting 100 (default 100), thresholds: lower 1, upper 100
  Load balancing: round-robin
  IP redundancy name is "GLBP-group-for-book"
  Group members:
    0200.0101.0101 (10.1.1.9) local
```

```
 0200.0202.0202 (10.1.1.129)
There are 2 forwarders (1 active)
Forwarder 1
   State is Listen
     2 state changes, last state change 00:20:34
   MAC address is 0007.b400.0101 (learnt)
   Owner ID is 0200.0202.0202
   Redirection enabled, 598.272 sec remaining (maximum 600 sec)
   Time to live: 14398.272 sec (maximum 14400 sec)
   Preemption enabled, min delay 30 sec
   Active is 10.1.1.129 (primary), weighting 100 (expires in 8.352 sec)
   Client selection count: 1
Forwarder 2
   State is Active
     1 state change, last state change 00:24:25
   MAC address is 0007.b400.0102 (default)
   Owner ID is 0200.0101.0101
   Redirection enabled
   Preemption enabled, min delay 30 sec
   Active is local, weighting 100
   Client selection count: 1
```

Exam Preparation Tasks

Review All the Key Topics

Review the most important topics from this chapter, noted with the Key Topic icon. Table 6-4 lists these key topics and where each is discussed.

Table 6-4   Key Topics for Chapter 6

Key Topic Element	Description	Page Number
List	Common characteristics of all FHRPs	189
Table 6-2	List of FHRPs and their attributes	190
Figure 6-5	HSRP concepts	191
Figure 6-6	HSRP failover results	191
Figure 6-8	GLBP AVG concept	194
List	Interpretation of the output from the **show standby brief** command	196
List	Key to identifying the line for the AVG and the lines for forwarders in the output from the **show glbp brief** command	199
List	Summary of the different states expected for GLBP AVG and forwarders	200

Complete the Tables and Lists from Memory

Print a copy of DVD Appendix D, "Memory Tables," or at least the section for this chapter, and complete the tables and lists from memory. DVD Appendix E, "Memory Tables Answer Key," includes completed tables and lists to check your work.

Definitions of Key Terms

After your first reading of the chapter, try to define these key terms, but do not be concerned about getting them all correct at that time. Chapter 22 directs you in how to use these terms for late-stage preparation for the exam.

single point of failure, First Hop Redundancy Protocol (FHRP), Hot Standby Router Protocol (HSRP), Virtual Router Redundancy Protocol (VRRP), Gateway Load Balancing Protocol (GLBP), virtual IP address, virtual MAC address, HSRP active, HSRP standby, GLBP active, GLBP standby, GLBP Forwarder, active virtual gateway

Command Reference to Check Your Memory

Although you should not necessarily memorize the information in the tables in this section, this section does include a reference for the configuration and EXEC commands covered in this chapter. Practically speaking, you should memorize the commands as a side effect of reading the chapter and doing all the activities in this exam preparation section. To check to see how well you have memorized the commands as a side effect of your other studies, cover the left side of the table with a piece of paper, read the descriptions on the right side, and see whether you remember the command.

Table 6-5   Chapter 6 Configuration Command Reference

Command	Description
standby *group-number* ip *virtual-ip*	Interface subcommand that enables HSRP, defines a virtual IP address, and associates it with a particular HSRP group.
standby *group-number* priority *0...255*	Interface subcommand that configures a priority, influencing which router becomes the active HSRP router. The higher the number wins, with a default of 100. This command associates the setting with a particular HSRP group.
standby *group number* name *descriptive name*	Interface subcommand that defines a name and associates it with a particular GLBP group.
standby version 1 | 2	Interface subcommand that sets the HSRP version used for all groups on the interface.
glbp *group-number* ip *virtual-ip*	Interface subcommand that enables GLBP, defines a virtual IP address, and associates it with a particular GLBP group.
glbp *group-number* priority *0..255*	Interface subcommand that configures a priority, influencing which router becomes the active HSRP router. The higher the number wins, with a default of 100. This command associates the setting with a particular HSRP group.
glbp *group-number* name *descriptive-name*	Interface subcommand that defines a name and associates it with a particular HSRP group.

Table 6-6   Chapter 6 EXEC Command Reference

Command	Description
show standby	Lists details about HSRP status, including the virtual IP address, currently active and standby routers, virtual MAC addresses, and counters.
show standby brief	Lists a single line of status information for each HSRP group, with the currently active and standby routers and virtual IP address.
show glbp	Lists details about GLBP status, including the virtual IP address, the current AVG, each forwarder (router), and which routers currently support each virtual MAC address.
show glbp brief	For each GLBP group, it lists one initial line of status information about the AVG, with another line for each forwarder (router) in the GLBP group. The data identifies the AVG, the standby AVG, the virtual MAC addresses, and which routers are currently active and listening for each virtual MAC address.

This chapter covers the following exam topics:

WAN Technologies

Identify different WAN technologies

VPN

CHAPTER 7

Virtual Private Networks

A company with 1 main site and 10 remote sites could lease several different types of WAN services to connect the sites: leased lines, Frame Relay, or more likely today, Multiprotocol Label Switching (MPLS). However, another option for connecting remote sites is to simply connect each site to the Internet using some high-speed Internet access technology like cable or digital subscriber line (DSL). Then the sites can send IP packets to each other over the Internet, using the Internet as a WAN.

Unfortunately, the Internet is not nearly as secure as leased lines and other WAN options. For example, for an attacker to steal a copy of data frames passing over a leased line, the attacker would have to physically tap into the cable, often inside a secure building, under the street, or at the telco central office (CO); all of these actions can result in a jail sentence. With the Internet, an attacker can find less-intrusive ways to get copies of packets, without even having to leave his home computer, and with a much smaller risk of getting carted off to jail.

Virtual private networks (VPN) solve the security problems associated with using the public Internet as a private WAN service. This chapter explains the concepts and terminology related to VPNs.

This chapter has two main sections. The first section introduces the basic concept of a VPN and discusses some details of two main types: IP Security (IPsec) and Secure Sockets Layer (SSL). The second section looks at one of the fundamental building blocks of VPNs, the concept of a tunnel between two routers, as created by an IP network.

"Do I Know This Already?" Quiz

Use the "Do I Know This Already?" quiz to help decide whether you might want to skim this chapter, or a major section, moving more quickly to the "Exam Preparation Tasks" section near the end of the chapter. You can find the answers at the bottom of the page following the quiz. For thorough explanations, see DVD Appendix C, "Answers to the 'Do I Know This Already?' Quizzes."

Table 7-1 "Do I Know This Already?" Foundation Topics Section-to-Question Mapping

Foundation Topics Section	Questions
VPN Fundamentals	1–3
GRE Tunnels	4–5

1. Which of the following terms refers to a VPN that uses the Internet to connect the sites of a single company rather than using leased lines or Frame Relay?

    a. Intranet VPN

    b. Extranet VPN

    c. Remote-access VPN

    d. Enterprise VPN

2. Which of the following are not considered to be security functions provided by a site-to-site VPN?

    a. Message integrity checks

    b. Privacy (encryption)

    c. Antivirus

    d. Authentication

3. Which of the following is not a function of IPsec?

    a. Authentication

    b. Intrusion prevention

    c. Message integrity checks

    d. Anti-replay

4. Router A configures a tunnel using the **tunnel destination 5.5.5.5** command. Router B serves as the router on the other end of the tunnel. Which of the following answers is accurate about the configuration on router B?

    a. Router B will list 5.5.5.5 in an **ip address** subcommand under a tunnel interface.

    b. Router B will list 5.5.5.5 in an **ip address** subcommand under an interface other than a tunnel.

    c. Router A must use an IP address in the same subnet as 5.5.5.5 on its **tunnel source** command.

5. Routers A and B configure and use a GRE tunnel, using OSPFv2 to learn IPv4 routes over that tunnel. Router A has a LAN IP address/mask of 172.16.1.0/24 and a tunnel source of 8.8.8.8. Router B has a LAN IP address/mask of 172.16.2.0/24 and a tunnel source of 9.9.9.9. Which of the following routes will router A likely learn with OSPFv2 so that the route lists the tunnel interface as the outgoing interface?

    a. A route for 172.16.1.0/24

    b. A route for 172.16.2.0/24

    c. A route for 8.8.8.8

    d. A route for 9.9.9.9

Foundation Topics

VPN Fundamentals

Leased lines have some wonderful security features. The router on one end knows with confidence the identity of the device on the other end of the link. The receiving router also has good reason to believe that no attackers saw the data in transit, or even changed the data to cause some harm.

VPNs try to provide the same secure features as a leased line while sending data over a network that is open to other parties. In fact, the data often crosses the Internet. Even when sending data over public networks like the Internet, VPNs can provide the following:

- **Confidentiality (Privacy):** Preventing anyone in the middle of the Internet (man in the middle) from being able to read the data

- **Authentication:** Verifying that the sender of the VPN packet is a legitimate device and not a device used by an attacker

- **Data integrity:** Verifying that the packet was not changed as the packet transited the Internet

- **Anti-replay:** Preventing a man in the middle from copying and later replying the packets sent by a legitimate user, for the purpose of appearing to be a legitimate user

To accomplish these goals, two devices near the edge of the Internet create a VPN, sometimes called a *VPN tunnel*. These devices add headers to the original packet, with these headers including fields that allow the VPN devices to perform all the functions. The VPN devices also encrypt the original IP packet, meaning that the original packet's contents are undecipherable to anyone who happens to see a copy of the packet as it traverses the Internet.

Figure 7-1 shows the general idea of what typically occurs with a VPN tunnel. The figure shows a VPN created between a branch office router and a Cisco Adaptive Security Appliance (ASA). In this case, the VPN is called a *site-to-site VPN* because it connects two sites of a company. This VPN is also called a site-to-site *intranet* VPN because it connects sites that belong inside a single company.

The figure shows the following steps, which explain the overall flow in the figure:

1. Host PC1 (10.2.2.2) on the right sends a packet to the web server (10.1.1.1), just as it would without a VPN.

2. The router encrypts the packet, adds some VPN headers, adds another IP header (with public IP addresses), and forwards the packet.

3. A man in the middle copies the packet, but cannot change the packet without being noticed, and cannot read the contents of the original packet.

4. ASA-1 receives the packet, confirms the authenticity of the sender, confirms that the packet has not been changed, and then decrypts the original packet.

5. Server S1 receives the unencrypted packet.

Answers to the "Do I Know This Already?" quiz:

1 A   **2** C   **3** B   **4** B   **5** B

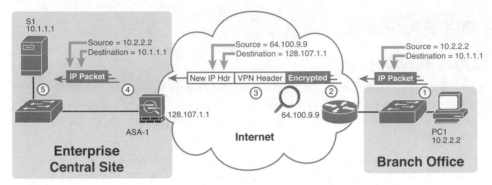

Figure 7-1 *VPN Tunnel Concepts for a Site-to-Site Intranet VPN*

The benefits of using an Internet-based VPN as shown in Figure 7-1 are many. The cost of a high-speed Internet connection is usually much less than that of many modern WAN options. The Internet is seemingly everywhere, making this kind of solution available worldwide. And by using VPN technology and protocols, the communications are secure.

> **NOTE**   The term *tunnel* generically refers to any protocol's packet that is sent by encapsulating the packet inside another packet. The term *VPN tunnel* implies that the encapsulated packet has been encrypted, whereas the term *tunnel* does not imply whether the packet has been encrypted.

VPNs can be built with a variety of devices and for a variety of purposes. Figure 7-2 shows an example of three of the primary reasons for building an Internet-based VPN today.

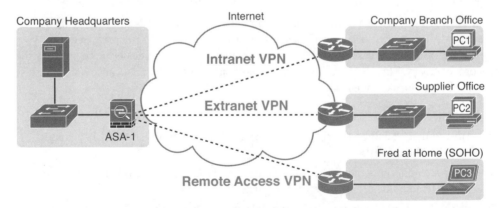

Figure 7-2 *Intranet, Extranet, and Access VPNs*

In the top part of the figure, the central site and a remote branch office of a fictitious company are connected with an *intranet VPN*. The middle of the figure shows the Company connecting to a supplier, making that VPN an *extranet VPN*. Finally, when Fred brings his laptop home at the end of the day and connects to the Internet, the secure VPN connection from the laptop back into the company network is called a *remote-access VPN*, or simply an *access VPN*. In this case, the laptop itself is the end of the VPN tunnel, rather than the Internet access router. Table 7-2 summarizes the key points about these three types of VPNs.

Table 7-2 Types of VPNs

Type	Typical Purpose
Intranet	A site-to-site VPN that connects all the computers at two sites of the same organization, usually using one VPN device at each site
Extranet	A site-to-site VPN that connects all the computers at two sites of different but partnering organizations, usually using one VPN device at each site
Remote Access	Connects individual Internet users to the enterprise network

To build a VPN, one device at each site needs to have hardware/software that understands a chosen set of VPN security standards and protocols. The devices include the following:

- **Routers:** In addition to packet forwarding, the router can provide VPN functions. The router can have specialized add-on cards that help the router perform the encryption more quickly.

- **Adaptive Security Appliances (ASA):** The Cisco leading security appliance that can be configured for many security functions, including acting as a VPN concentrator, supporting large numbers of VPN tunnels.

- **VPN client:** For remote-access VPNs, the PC might need to do the VPN functions; the laptop needs software to do those functions, with that software being called a *VPN client*.

Finally, when comparing VPNs to other WAN technologies, VPNs have several advantages. For instance, consider a company with 1000 small retail locations. The company could create a private WAN using leased lines, or Frame Relay, Ethernet WAN, Multiprotocol Label Switching (MPLS), and so on. However, each branch could instead have an Internet connection and use VPN technology, usually saving money over the other WAN options. Here are some of the benefits:

Cost: Internet VPN solutions can be cheaper than alternative private WAN options.

Security: Internet VPN solutions can be as secure as private WAN connections.

Scalability: Internet VPN solutions scale to many sites at a reasonable cost. Each site connects via any Internet connection, with most business locations having multiple competitive options to choose from for Internet access.

Next, the text examines the use of a set of protocols called *IPsec* to create VPNs, followed by a brief description of SSL VPNs.

IPsec VPNs

IPsec is an architecture or framework for security services for IP networks. The name itself is not an acronym, but rather a name derived from the title of the RFC that defines it (RFC 4301, *Security Architecture for the Internet Protocol*), more generally called IP Security, or IPsec.

7

IPsec defines how two devices, both connected to the Internet, can achieve the main goals of a VPN as listed at the beginning of this chapter: confidentiality, authentication, data integrity, and anti-replay. IPsec does not define just one way to implement a VPN, instead allowing several different protocol options for each VPN feature. One of IPsec's strengths is that its role as an architecture allows it to be added to and changed over time as improvements to individual security functions are made.

This chapter does not go through the details of each part of IPsec, but to give you some general idea of some of IPsec's work, this section shows how two IPsec endpoints encrypt data and add IPsec VPN headers to the encrypted data.

The idea of IPsec encryption might sound intimidating, but if you ignore the math—and thankfully, you can—IPsec encryption is not too difficult to understand. IPsec encryption uses a pair of encryption algorithms, which are essentially math formulas, to meet a couple of requirements. First, the two math formulas are a matched set:

- One to hide (encrypt) the data
- Another to re-create (decrypt) the original data based on the encrypted data

Besides those somewhat obvious functions, the two math formulas were chosen so that if you intercept the encrypted text but do not have the secret password (called an *encryption key*), decrypting that one packet would be difficult. In addition, the formulas are also chosen so that if an attacker did happen to decrypt one packet, that information would not give the attacker any advantages in decrypting the other packets.

The process for encrypting data for an IPsec VPN works generally as shown in Figure 7-3. Note that the *encryption key* is also known as the *session key*, *shared key*, or *shared session* key.

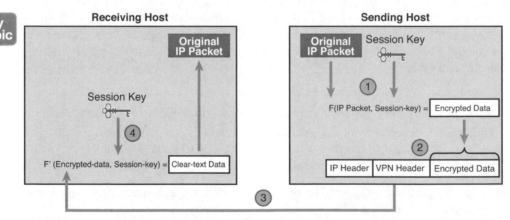

Figure 7-3 *Basic IPsec Encryption Process*

The four steps highlighted in the figure are as follows:

1. The sending VPN device (like the remote office router in Figure 7-1) feeds the orignal packet and the session key into the encryption formula, calculating the encrypted data.

2. The sending device encapsulates the encrypted data into a packet, which includes the new IP header and VPN header.

3. The sending device sends this new packet to the destination VPN device (ASA-1 back in Figure 7-1).

4. The receiving VPN device runs the corresponding decryption formula, using the encrypted data and session key—the same key value as was used on the sending VPN device—to decrypt the data.

Next, to give you some perspective about the flexibility of IPsec, IPsec has been changed over time to support newer and better encryption standards. For instance, newer standards have new algorithms, plus they often use longer keys. These changes make it more difficult for attackers to decrypt any data copied as it passes over the Internet. Table 7-3 summarizes several of these options and the lengths of the keys.

Table 7-3   Comparing VPN Encryption Algorithms

Encryption Algorithm	Key Length (Bits)	Comments
Data Encryption Standard (DES)	56	Older and less secure than the other options listed here
Triple DES (3DES)	56 x 3	Applies three different 56-bit DES keys in succession, improving the encryption strength versus DES
Advanced Encryption Standard (AES)	128 and 256	Considered the current best practice, with strong encryption and less computation than 3DES

SSL VPNs

The Secure Socket Layer (SSL) protocol serves as an alternative VPN technology to IPsec. In particular, today's web browsers support SSL as a way to dynamically create a secure connection from the web browser to a web server, supporting safe online access to financial transactions. This brief topic explains a few details about how you can use SSL to create remote-access VPNs.

Web browsers use HTTP as the protocol with which to connect to web servers. However, when the communications with the web server need to be secure, the browser switches to use SSL. SSL uses well-known port 443, encrypting data sent between the browser and the server and authenticating the user. Then, the HTTP messages flow over the SSL VPN connection.

The built-in SSL functions of a web browser create one secure web browsing session, but this same SSL technology can be used create a remote access VPN using a Cisco VPN client. The Cisco AnyConnect VPN client is software that sits on a user's PC and uses SSL to create one end of a VPN remote-access tunnel. As a result, all the packets sent to the other end of the tunnel are encrypted, not just those sent over a single HTTP connection in a web browser.

Finally, note that many types of devices can sit on the server side of an SSL connection as well. The web server can be the endpoint of an SSL connection from a web browser, but often, to improve server performance, the SSL tunnel on the server side terminates on specialized devices like the Cisco ASA.

Figure 7-4 combines all the SSL concepts into one example with two SSL tunnels. One SSL VPN tunnel connects a web browser at host A to the ASA on the right, supporting a single web browsing session. Host B uses the Cisco VPN client, so all packets from host B to the site on the right will be secured over the SSL connection.

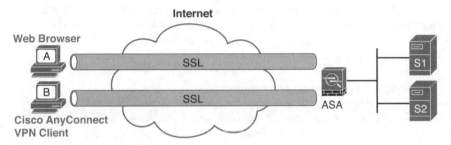

Figure 7-4   *SSL VPN Options*

Now that you have read about a couple of VPN options, the next section examines how to create a tunnel with configuration in a router.

GRE Tunnels

The device on the endpoint of a VPN takes a normal unencrypted packet and performs several functions before forwarding that packet. One of those functions is to encrypt the packet, and another is to encapsulate the packet in a new IP header. The new IP header uses addresses that allow the routers in the unsecured network between the two VPN tunnel endpoints to forward the VPN IP packet. The original IP packet, including the original IP header, is encrypted and unreadable.

This second major section of this chapter takes a little different approach to configuring a VPN tunnel, by looking at only the tunneling part of the work and ignoring the encryption function. Specifically, this section looks at the concepts and configuration of how routers create a tunnel, encapsulating the original IP packet inside another IP packet. The goal is to give you some general ideas about how tunneling works, while leaving the detailed security configuration to other certifications like CCNA Security.

GRE Tunnel Concepts

This chapter looks at one type of IP tunnel: generic routing encapsulation (GRE). GRE, defined in RFC 2784, defines an additional header, along with the new IP header, that encapsulates the original packet. Two routers work together, with matching configuration settings, to create a GRE IP tunnel. Then, IPsec configuration can be added to encrypt the traffic.

The discussion of GRE tunnels looks at the concepts from several perspectives. The first section shows how packets can be routed over a GRE tunnel, much like using a serial link inside a secured enterprise network. The rest of this topic then explains how GRE does its work.

Routing over GRE Tunnels

A GRE tunnel exists between two routers, with the tunnel working very much like a serial link with regard to packet forwarding. So, before discussing GRE tunnels, this section first reviews some familiar facts about routers and serial links, using Figure 7-5 as an example.

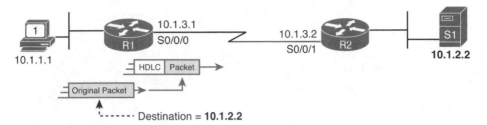

Figure 7-5   *Routing an IP Packet over a Serial Link*

The small network in Figure 7-5 looks like a part of many enterprise networks. It uses private IP addresses (network 10.0.0.0). It has an IP address on each router interface, including on each serial interface. The IP addresses on the serial interfaces (10.1.3.1 and 10.1.3.2, respectively) are in the same subnet. And when PC1 sends a packet to destination IP address 10.1.2.2, R1 will encapsulate the packet in the data link protocol used on the link, like the default High-Level Data Link Control (HDLC) encapsulation shown in the figure.

Also, note that all the parts of this small enterprise network exist in secure spaces. This network has no need to encrypt data using a VPN.

GRE creates a concept that works just like the serial link in Figure 7-5, at least with regard to IP routing. Instead of a serial link with serial interfaces, the routers use virtual interfaces called *tunnel interfaces*. The two routers have IP addresses on their tunnel interfaces in the same subnet. Figure 7-6 shows an example where the serial link has been replaced with these virtual tunnel interfaces.

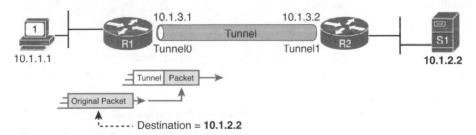

Figure 7-6   *Replacing the Serial Link with an IP Tunnel*

Sticking with the big ideas about IP routing for now, the tunnel looks like just another link in the secure part of the network. The tunnel IP addresses are from the secure enterprise network. The routers encapsulate the original packet inside a tunnel header, which takes the place of the serial link's HDLC header. And the routers will even have routes that list the tunnel interfaces (Tunnel0 and Tunnel1 in this case) as the outgoing interfaces.

To make use of the GRE tunnel, the routers treat it like any other link with a point-to-point topology. The routers have IPv4 addresses in the same subnet. The routers using a routing protocol become neighbors and exchange routes over the tunnel. And the routes learned over the tunnel list the tunnel interface as the outgoing interface, with the neighboring router's tunnel interface IP address as the next-hop router. Figure 7-7 shows an example, with the routes learned by each router listed at the bottom.

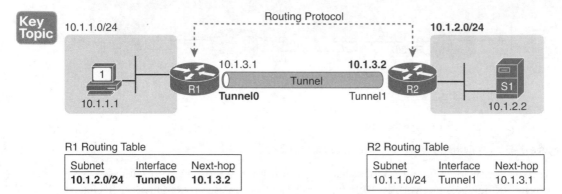

Figure 7-7 *Tunnel Routers Learning Private Routes over the IP Tunnel*

Take a moment and look closely at the route for subnet 10.1.2.0/24, on the right side of the figure. R2 will have a connected route to that subnet. R1 and R2 will use some routing protocol (for instance, OSPF) to exchange routing information. R1 will add a new route for subnet 10.1.2.0/24, and that route will list R1's own tunnel interface, Tunnel0, as the outgoing interface. That route lists R2's tunnel interface IP address, 10.1.3.2, as the next hop router, as shown in R1's IP routing table on the bottom-left part of the figure.

All these concepts show how the GRE tunnel acts like just one more link in the secure part of an internetwork. The next few pages look at how GRE tunnels forward these packets over an unsecure network between the two routers.

GRE Tunnels over the Unsecured Network

The last few figures may have a tunnel between two routers, one that looks like a pipe, but those diagrams do not tell us much about the physical network behind the tunnel. The tunnel can exist over any IP network. The tunnel is created using an IP network to forward the original packets, so any IP network between routers R1 and R2 would allow the tunnel to exist.

Often, site-to-site VPNs, like the one shown in Figure 7-6, use an unsecured network like the Internet as the IP network. The whole idea ties back to economics. The monthly cost of high-speed Internet access at each site is often less than paying for other WAN services. But no matter what type of Internet connection exists, the routers on the tunnel can use the Internet as a way to forward the packets between the two tunnel routers, as shown in Figure 7-8.

The routers on the ends of the GRE tunnel create the tunnel by agreeing to send each other packets over the unsecure network between the two. Figure 7-8 shows many of the details that the engineer needs to know about the two routers before configuring the GRE tunnel on both ends. The figure shows the interfaces R1 and R2 each use to connect to the Internet. And it shows the IP addresses each router uses on their Internet connections, in this case 1.1.1.1 and 2.2.2.2, just to use more memorable numbers.

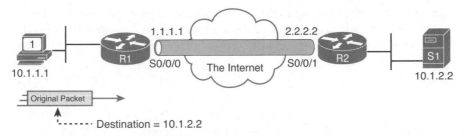

Figure 7-8 *Sending the Tunnel over the Internet*

The router configuration uses virtual interfaces called *tunnel interfaces*. These interfaces do not exist until the engineer creates the tunnel with the **interface tunnel** command. For instance, the command **interface tunnel 0** creates a tunnel interface numbered as 0. To create a tunnel, both routers create a tunnel interface and use IP addresses as if the tunnel were a point-to-point link.

Figure 7-9 shows a conceptual diagram of a packet coming into router R1 from PC1, one that needs to be forwarded over the GRE tunnel to server S1 (10.1.2.2). When the router uses its IP routing logic from the secured part of the network, as shown in Figure 7-6, R1 wants to send the packet over the tunnel. Figure 7-9 shows the encapsulation done by R1.

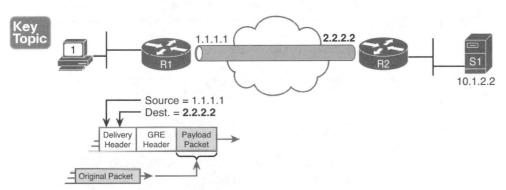

Figure 7-9 *Encapsulating the Original IP Packet in a GRE-Formatted Packet*

> **NOTE** If the two routers creating this tunnel also configured the IPsec encryption part of the tunnel, before encapsulating the original packet as shown in Figure 7-8, the sending router would first encrypt the packet.

GRE specifies the use of two headers to create the tunnel. GRE defines its own header, used to manage the tunnel itself. GRE also defines the use of a complete 20-byte IP header, called the *delivery header*. This header will use IP addresses from the unsecure network. In this case, the delivery IP header will list R1's 1.1.1.1 Internet IP address as the source and R2's 2.2.2.2 Internet IP address as the destination.

While this packet passes through the Internet, the routers in the Internet use this outer GRE delivery IP header to route the packet. The fact that this packet happens to hold another entire IP packet inside does not matter to the IP forwarding process in those routers; they just forward the IP packet based on the 2.2.2.2 destination IP address. Figure 7-10 shows the concept; note that this packet may be routed by many routers in the Internet before arriving at R2.

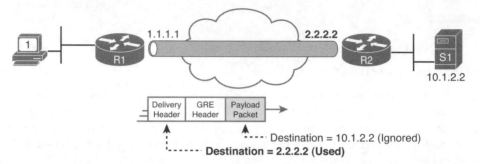

Figure 7-10 *Internet Routers Forwarding GRE IP Packet Based on Public IP Addresses*

When the GRE packet in Figure 7-10 finally arrives on the right side of the Internet, at R2, R2 needs to extract the original IP packet. With physical links, R2 would normally simply remove the old incoming data link header. With a GRE-encapsulated packet, the receiving router (R2) also needs to remove the delivery header and the GRE header, leaving the original packet, as shown in Figure 7-11.

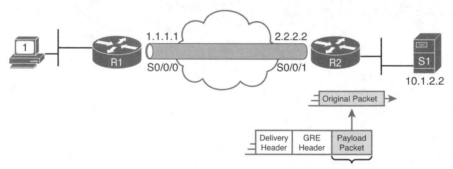

Figure 7-11 *Internet Routers Forwarding GRE IP Packet Based on Public IP Addresses*

> **NOTE** If the routers also configured the IPsec encryption part of the tunnel, just after the steps shown in Figure 7-11, the receiving router would then decrypt the original packet.

Configuring GRE Tunnels

Configuring GRE tunnels requires only a few commands. The challenge with GRE configuration comes in organizing the configuration parameters. The configuration requires a tunnel interface, with IP addresses from the secured part of the network configured with the **ip address** interface command. It also requires that the two routers declare both their own IP address (source) and the other router's IP address (destination), used in the unsecure part of the network. Figure 7-12 shows the organization of the various configuration parameters.

Addresses from Secured Network

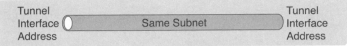

Addresses from Unsecured Network (Usually Internet)

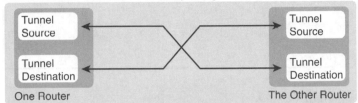

Figure 7-12   *GRE Tunnel Configuration: Relationship of Parameters*

The following list details the configuration steps on each router:

Step 1. Create a tunnel interface using the **interface tunnel** *number* command. The interface numbers have local meaning only and do not have to match between the two routers.

Step 2. Assign an IP address to the tunnel interface with the **ip address** *address mask* command, using a subnet from the secure network's address range. The two routers on the tunnel should use addresses from the same subnet.

Step 3. Configure the tunnel's source IP address in the public part of the network with the **tunnel source** *interface* or the **tunnel source** *ip-address* interface subcommand. If referring to an interface, the local router uses the IP address configured on the listed interface. (This value must match the other router's tunnel destination.)

Step 4. Configure the tunnel's destination IP address in the public part of the network with the **tunnel destination** *ip-address* command. (This value must match the IP address used by the other router as its tunnel source IP address.)

Step 5. Configure the routers to use the tunnel with IP routes, either by enabling a dynamic routing protocol on the tunnel or by configuring static IP routes.

As usual, an example can help quite a bit. The example, as you probably guessed, matches the example used throughout the last several pages. R1 and R2 form a tunnel using public addresses 1.1.1.1 and 2.2.2.2, respectively. The tunnel uses subnet 10.1.3.0/24, with R1 and R2 using IP addresses 10.1.3.1 and 10.1.3.2, respectively. Example 7-1 shows the configuration on R1, and Example 7-2 shows the configuration on R2.

Example 7-1   *Tunnel Configuration on R1*

```
R1# show running-config
! Only the related configuration is listed

interface serial 0/0/0
```

```
 ip address 1.1.1.1 255.255.255.0
!
interface Tunnel0
 ip address 10.1.3.1 255.255.255.0
 tunnel source Serial0/0/0
 tunnel destination 2.2.2.2
!
! The OSPF configuration enables OSPF on the tunnel interface as well.
router ospf 1
 network 10.0.0.0 0.255.255.255 area 0
```

Example 7-2   *Tunnel Configuration on R2*

```
R2# show running-config
! Only the related configuration is listed
interface serial 0/0/1
 ip address 2.2.2.2 255.255.255.0

!
interface Tunnel1
 ip address 10.1.3.2 255.255.255.0
 tunnel source Serial0/0/1
 tunnel destination 1.1.1.1

! The OSPF configuration enables OSPF on the tunnel interface as well.
router ospf 1
 network 10.0.0.0 0.255.255.255 area 0
```

Just to make sure the matching logic is clear, take a look at R2's configuration. R2's S0/0/1 interface has been configured with IP address 2.2.2.2. Then, under interface tunnel 1, the **tunnel source Serial0/0/1** command refers to that same interface, making R2's source IP address for the tunnel 2.2.2.2. Finally, referring back up to R1's configuration, its **tunnel destination 2.2.2.2** command clearly refers to the same IP address used by R2 as its source address. The same trail can be checked for R1's source address of 1.1.1.1 and R2's destination address 1.1.1.1.

Verifying a GRE Tunnel

The ultimate test of the tunnel is whether it can pass end-user traffic. However, some other **show** commands from the router tell us a lot about the status before trying a ping or traceroute from the user's device.

First, because the tunnel acts very much like a serial link, with interfaces on both routers, the usual commands that list interface status, IP addresses, and IP routes all show information about the GRE tunnel. For instance, Example 7-3 shows the familiar **show ip interface brief** command on R1, with R1's tunnel0 interface highlighted.

Example 7-3 *Displaying the Interface State and IP Addresses, Including the Tunnel Interface*

```
R1# show ip interface brief
Interface              IP-Address      OK? Method Status                 Protocol
GigabitEthernet0/0     10.1.1.9        YES manual up                     up
GigabitEthernet0/1     unassigned      YES manual administratively down  down
Serial0/0/0            1.1.1.1         YES manual up                     up
Serial0/0/1            unassigned      YES manual administratively down  down
Tunnel0                10.1.3.1        YES manual up                     up
```

The **show interfaces tunnel** *interface-number* command lists many counters plus the configuration settings, in addition to the interface status. Example 7-4 lists a sample, again for R1's Tunnel0 interface. Note that it lists the local router (R1) configuration of the source (1.1.1.1) and destination (2.2.2.2) IP addresses, and it confirms the use of GRE encapsulation, as highlighted in the example.

Example 7-4 *Tunnel Interface Details*

```
R1# show interfaces tunnel0
Tunnel0 is up, line protocol is up
  Hardware is Tunnel
  Internet address is 10.1.3.1/24
  MTU 17916 bytes, BW 100 Kbit/sec, DLY 50000 usec,
     reliability 255/255, txload 1/255, rxload 1/255
  Encapsulation TUNNEL, loopback not set
  Keepalive not set
  Tunnel source 1.1.1.1 (Serial0/0/0), destination 2.2.2.2
   Tunnel Subblocks:
      src-track:
         Tunnel0 source tracking subblock associated with Serial0/0/0
          Set of tunnels with source Serial0/0/0, 1 member (includes iterators), on
interface <OK>
  Tunnel protocol/transport GRE/IP
! Lines omitted for brevity
```

Although a working tunnel interface is important, the routers will not use the tunnel interface unless routes try to forward packets over the tunnel interface. The configuration in this example shows that OSPF has been enabled on all interfaces in Class A network 10.0.0.0, the secure part of the internetwork. As a result, the routers should exchange OSPF routes and learn the same routes shown in earlier Figure 7-7. Example 7-5 shows proof, with R1 listing an OSPF-learned route to R2's LAN subnet of 10.1.2.0/24.

Example 7-5   *R1 Routes in Network 10.0.0.0*

```
R1# show ip route 10.0.0.0
Routing entry for 10.0.0.0/8, 5 known subnets
  Attached (4 connections)
  Variably subnetted with 2 masks
C        10.1.1.0/24 is directly connected, GigabitEthernet0/0
L        10.1.1.9/32 is directly connected, GigabitEthernet0/0
O        10.1.2.0/24 [110/1001] via 10.1.3.2, 00:07:55, Tunnel0
C        10.1.3.0/24 is directly connected, Tunnel0
L        10.1.3.1/32 is directly connected, Tunnel0
! Lines omitted for brevity
```

NOTE   The **show ip route 10.0.0.0** command lists the known routes inside network 10.0.0.0.

Finally, to prove the tunnel can forward traffic, the user can generate some traffic, or a handy extended ping or traceroute can serve as well. Example 7-6 shows an extended traceroute, sourced from R1's LAN IP address of 10.1.1.9, and sent to server 1's 10.1.2.2 IP address.

Example 7-6   *Extended Traceroute Shows the Tunnel Is Working*

```
R1# traceroute
Protocol [ip]:
Target IP address: 10.1.2.2
Source address: 10.1.1.9
Numeric display [n]:
Timeout in seconds [3]:
Probe count [3]:
Minimum Time to Live [1]:
Maximum Time to Live [30]:
Port Number [33434]:
Loose, Strict, Record, Timestamp, Verbose[none]:
Type escape sequence to abort.
Tracing the route to 10.1.2.2
VRF info: (vrf in name/id, vrf out name/id)
  1 10.1.3.2 0 msec 4 msec 0 msec
  2 10.1.2.2 4 msec 4 msec 0 msec
R1#
```

Example 7-6 shows that the traceroute completes, and it also lists R2's tunnel IP address (10.1.3.2) as the first router in the route. Note that the traceroute does not list any routers in the unsecure part of the network, because the packets created by the traceroute command get encapsulated and sent from R1 to R2, just like any other packet.

Exam Preparation Tasks

Review All the Key Topics

Review the most important topics from this chapter, noted with the Key Topic icon. Table 7-4 lists these key topics and where each is discussed.

Table 7-4   Key Topics for Chapter 7

Key Topic Element	Description	Page Number
List	Desired security features for VPNs	207
Table 7-2	Three types of VPNs and their typical purpose	209
Figure 7-3	Significant parts of the VPN encryption process	210
Table 7-3	Facts about the three IPsec VPN encryption algorithms for encrypting the entire packet	211
Figure 7-7	Routes using a GRE tunnel	214
Figure 7-9	GRE encapsulation over a GRE tunnel	215
Figure 7-12	Details that must match with a GRE tunnel	217
List	GRE configuration checklist	217

Complete the Tables and Lists from Memory

Print a copy of DVD Appendix D, "Memory Tables," or at least the section for this chapter, and complete the tables and lists from memory. DVD Appendix E, "Memory Tables Answer Key," includes completed tables and lists to check your work.

Definitions of Key Terms

After your first reading of the chapter, try to define these key terms, but do not be concerned about getting them all correct at that time. Chapter 22 directs you in how to use these terms for late-stage preparation for the exam.

IPsec, shared key, SSL, VPN, VPN client, generic routing encapsulation (GRE), GRE tunnel

Command Reference to Check Your Memory

Although you should not necessarily memorize the information in the tables in this section, this section does include a reference for the configuration and EXEC commands covered in this chapter. Practically speaking, you should memorize the commands as a side effect of reading the chapter and doing all the activities in this exam preparation section. To check to see how well you have memorized the commands as a side effect of your other studies, cover the left side of the table with a piece of paper, read the descriptions on the right side, and see whether you remember the command.

Table 7-5   Chapter 7 Configuration Command Reference

Command	Description
tunnel source *interface-type interface-number*	Tunnel interface subcommand that defines the source IP address of the tunnel on the local router, but indirectly; the router uses the IP address configured on the listed IP address.
tunnel source *ip-address*	Tunnel interface subcommand that directly defines the source IP address of the tunnel on the local router.
tunnel destination *ip-address*	Tunnel interface subcommand that defines the destination IP address of the tunnel, which exists on the other end of the tunnel.
tunnel mode gre	Tunnel interface subcommand that defines the mode of the tunnel, which must match on both ends of the tunnel. The default is **gre**.

Part II Review

Keep track of your part review progress with the checklist in Table P2-1. Details about each task follow the table.

Table P2-1 Part II Part Review Checklist

Activity	First Date Completed	Second Date Completed
Repeat All DIKTA Questions		
Answer Part Review Questions		
Review Key Topics		
Create IPv4 Root Causes Mind Map		
Create FHRP Commands Mind Map		

Repeat All DIKTA Questions

For this task, answer the "Do I Know This Already?" questions again for the chapters in Part II of this book using the PCPT software. See the section "How to View Only DIKTA Questions by Part" in the Introduction to this book to learn how to make the PCPT software show you DIKTA questions for this part only.

Answer Part Review Questions

For this task, answer the Part Review questions for this part of the book using the PCPT software. See the section "How to View Only DIKTA Questions by Part" in the Introduction to this book to learn how to make the PCPT software show you DIKTA questions for this part only.

Review Key Topics

Browse back through the chapters, and look for the Key Topic icons. If you do not remember some details, take the time to reread those topics.

Create IPv4 Root Causes Mind Map

Chapters 4 and 5 focus on how to troubleshoot problems with IPv4 networks. For this first Part Review mind map, work through all the items you can think of that can fail and cause a problem in an IPv4 network. In other words, think about the root causes. Then organize those into a mind map.

To organize the mind map, once you see several root causes that are related, group those root causes by whatever category comes to mind. These might be the same kinds symptoms you would see when doing problem isolation. For instance, you might note root causes about Dynamic Host Configuration Protocol (DHCP), like a router missing its DHCP Relay configuration (**ip helper-address**), and another cause that no IP connectivity exists to the DHCP server. So, group these DHCP root causes together in one category, something like Host DHCP. Figure P2-1 shows an example.

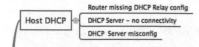

Figure P2-1   *Subset Example of the IPv4 Root Cause Mind Map*

> **NOTE**   For more information about mind mapping, see the section "About Mind Maps" in the Introduction to this book.

Create FHRP Commands Mind Map

This part also introduced the configuration and verification details of three features: Hot Standby Router Protocol (HSRP), Gateway Load Balancing Protocol (GLBP), and generic routing encapsulation (GRE) tunnels. Create a mind map that organizes the commands by each of these three topics, and inside each topic organize the commands as either configuration or verification commands.

DVD Appendix F, "Mind Map Solutions," provides sample mind map answers.

TCP/IP networks need IP routes. Part III collects four chapters focused on the IPv4 routing protocols discussed within the scope of ICND2: OSPF Version 2 (Chapter 8), EIGRP (Chapters 9 and 10), and a chapter focused on how to troubleshoot both OSPFv2 and EIGRP (Chapter 11). Note that Chapter 8 adds to a topic that the ICND1 book has already discussed in some detail, and Chapters 9 and 10 discuss EIGRP, which was not explained in any depth in the ICND1 book.

Part III

IP Version 4 Routing Protocols

This chapter covers the following exam topics:

IP Routing Technologies

Configure and verify OSPF (single area)

neighbor adjacencies

OSPF states

Discuss Multi area

Configure OSPF v2

Router ID

LSA types

Differentiate methods of routing and routing protocols

Administrative distance

metric

next hop

CHAPTER 8

Implementing OSPF for IPv4

Cisco happened to put some Open Shortest Path First Version 2 (OSPFv2) topics into the ICND1 exam and some into the ICND2 exam. So, this chapter takes the three perspectives on OSPFv2 discussed for ICND1—concepts, configuration, and verification—and takes each a step or two further.

In particular, this chapter takes a long look at OSPFv2 concepts. It discusses specific link-state advertisement (LSA) types, how OSPF does path determination by calculating the metric for each route, and more details on the hidden OSPF processes. In the second major section, this chapter examines multi-area configuration and how to influence path determination by changing the OSPF interface costs. Finally, the verification discussion focuses on multi-area details and the new concepts about LSAs.

Depending on your own personal reading and study plan, this chapter may or may not present a big challenge. Those of you headed toward the one-exam path to CCNA, using one reading plan, may have read the ICND1 book's OSPFv2 coverage recently (Chapter 17 of that book). Others of you, particularly those taking the two-exam path toward CCNA Routing and Switching, may have last thought about OSPFv2 a month or two ago.

This chapter does review the most important OSPFv2 concepts and configuration steps from the ICND1 book. However, if it has been a while, it might be worth a few minutes of review of your ICND1 OSPFv2 notes before jumping into this chapter.

"Do I Know This Already?" Quiz

Use the "Do I Know This Already?" quiz to help decide whether you might want to skim this chapter, or a major section, moving more quickly to the Exam Preparation Tasks section near the end of the chapter. You can find the answers at the bottom of the page following the quiz. For thorough explanations, see DVD Appendix C, "Answers to the 'Do I Know This Already?' Quizzes."

Table 8-1 "Do I Know This Already?" Foundation Topics Section-to-Question Mapping

Foundation Topics Section	Questions
OSPF Protocols and Operation	1–3
OSPF Configuration and Verification	4–6

1. Router R1, an internal router in OSPFv2 area 51, has an LSDB that includes some Type 1, some Type 2, and some Type 3 LSAs. Which of these types of LSAs could R1 not possibly have created inside area 51?

   a. Type 1

   b. Type 2

   c. Type 3

   d. R1 would be allowed to create all three types.

2. A company has a network with 15 routers and 40 subnets and uses OSPFv2. Which of the following is considered an advantage of using a single-area design as opposed to a multi-area design?

   a. Reduces the processing overhead on most routers.

   b. Status changes to one link may not require SPF to run on all other routers.

   c. Simpler planning and operations.

   d. Allows for route summarization, reducing the size of IP routing tables.

3. Which of the following OSPF neighbor states is expected when the exchange of topology information is complete between two OSPF neighbors?

   a. 2-way

   b. Full

   c. Up/up

   d. Final

4. Routers R1, R2, and R3 are internal routers in areas 1, 2, and 3, respectively. Router R4 is an ABR connected to the backbone area (0) and to areas 1, 2, and 3. Which of the following answers describes the configuration on router R4, which is different from the other three routers, that makes it an ABR?

   a. The **abr enable** router subcommand.

   b. The **network** router subcommands refer to a single nonbackbone area.

   c. The **network** router subcommands refer to multiple areas, including the backbone.

   d. The router has an interface in area 0, whereas an OSPF neighbor's interface sits in a different area.

5. Which of the following configuration settings on a router does not influence which IPv4 route a router chooses to add to its IPv4 routing table when using OSPFv2?

   a. **auto-cost reference-bandwidth**

   b. **delay**

   c. **bandwidth**

   d. **ip ospf cost**

6. An engineer connects to router R1 and issues a **show ip ospf neighbor** command. The status of neighbor 2.2.2.2 lists Full/BDR. What does the BDR mean?

   a. R1 is an Area Border Router.

   b. R1 is a backup designated router.

   c. Router 2.2.2.2 is an Area Border Router.

   d. Router 2.2.2.2 is a backup designated router.

8

Foundation Topics

OSPF Protocols and Operation

Between the two routing protocols discussed in depth in this book—OSPF and EIGRP—OSPF happens to have more rules, more processes, and more theoretical details. This first of two major sections of the chapter examines many of these details about OSPF concepts. These details help prepare network engineers who take over the problem from the first- and second-level support in a network to work the problem and find the true root cause of any OSPF problem.

This first section of the chapter lays the conceptual groundwork, and the second section then works through some new related configuration. Chapter 11, "Troubleshooting IPv4 Routing Protocols," works through several specific troubleshooting scenarios for OSPF.

OSPF Overview

If you think back to what you already learned about OSPFv2 (OSPF for IPv4 networks) in the ICND1 book, or for the ICND1 exam, you probably remember that the big ideas follow a logical sequence. Figure 8-1 shows that sequence on the left, from top to bottom.

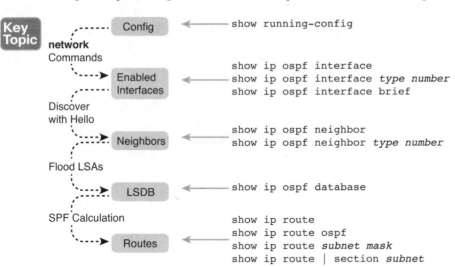

Figure 8-1   *Roadmap of Topics (Left) and Verification Commands (Right)*

Take a moment to consider the steps in the figure. That is, start with the configuration, which enables OSPFv2 on some interfaces by using **network** commands. As a result, the router sends and receives OSPF Hellos on those interfaces, hoping to discover OSPF neighbors. Once a potential neighbor is discovered, the neighbors check each others' parameters, and if

---

they pass, the neighbors flood their known LSAs to each other, completing their link-state databases (LSDB). Finally, the router's shortest path first (SPF) algorithm calculates the best route to each subnet, putting those routes into the IPv4 routing table.

In fact, Figure 8-1 summarizes the big concepts from the ICND1 book's Chapter 17, and summarizes that same chapter's verification commands on the right.

The OSPF router ID (RID), introduced back in the ICND1 book, plays a big role in many of the OSPFv2 internals discussed in this chapter. To review the basics, the RID serves as a router's unique identifier for OSPFv2. Each router then uses RIDs for many purposes, such as the following:

- When routers send a Hello message, they basically state "Hello, my RID is...."
- Neighbors identify each other by their RID, as listed in the output of the **show ip ospf neighbor** command.
- Many LSAs list the RID of one of the routers.

Because OSPFv2 uses RIDs so much, most network engineers choose to control the RID setting with configuration. It is much easier to operate an OSPFv2 network if everyone knows the RID of each router or can easily predict them. Most engineers choose an OSPF RID numbering plan with either a list of routers and their OSPF RIDs, or an easy way to predict each router's RID. For example, R1 could use RID 172.16.1.1, R2 could use 172.16.2.2, R3 could use 172.16.3.3, and so on.

The following list shows the sequential steps that a router completes when choosing its own RID when the router reloads and brings up the OSPF process:

1. Use the value in the **router-id** *rid* OSPF subcommand.
2. If unset per Step 1, among all loopback interfaces that have an IP address configured, and for which the interface has an interface status of up, choose the highest numeric IPv4 address among these loopback interfaces.
3. If unset per Steps 1 and 2, use the same logic as Step 2, but for all nonloopback interfaces.

Finally, one last note on the OSPF RID: Each router chooses its OSPF RID when OSPF is initialized. Initialization happens during the initial load of IOS or with the **clear ip ospf process** command. For instance, if you add a loopback interface and IPv4 address later, after configuring OSPFv2, the OSPFv2 process will not consider (as RID) the IP address of that new loopback interface until the next time the OSPF process starts.

Also note that if the OSPF process simply cannot find a RID to use, the OSPF process cannot work.

Becoming Neighbors and Exchanging the LSDB

The whole point of using OSPFv2 is to learn IPv4 routes. To do that, OSPFv2 routers must become neighbors, and then exchange the LSAs in their link-state databases (LSDB). The next few pages work through some particulars of the OSPFv2 protocols and neighbor states.

NOTE OSPF protocols work slightly differently on point-to-point links (simpler) versus Ethernet links (more complex). To keep the next examples simpler, for easier learning, the examples assume the rules for point-to-point links. Later, in the "Using Designated Routers on Ethernet" section, you'll read about variations in OSPF that happen on other topologies like Ethernet.

Agreeing to Become Neighbors

When a point-to-point link is down, OSPF cannot have any neighbors over that link. When the link comes up, the routers on the ends of the link go through a couple of interim neighbor states while working through important steps, such as discovering the existence of the neighbor, checking parameters to see whether they are allowed to become neighbors, and exchanging their LSAs in a process known as database exchange.

Figure 8-2 shows several of the neighbor states used by the early formation of an OSPF neighbor relationship. The figure shows the Hello messages in the center and the resulting neighbor states on the left and right edges of the figure.

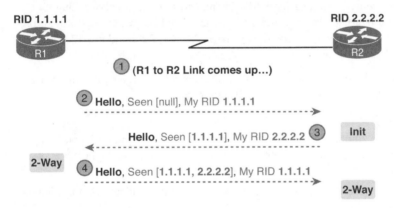

Figure 8-2 *Early Neighbor States*

Following the steps in the figure, the scenario begins with the link down, so the routers have no knowledge of each other as OSPF neighbors. As a result, they have no state (status) information about each other as neighbors, and they would not list each other in the output of the **show ip ospf neighbor** command. At Step 2, R1 sends the first Hello, so R2 learns of the existence of R1 as an OSPF router. At that point, R2 lists R1 as a neighbor, with an interim state of Init.

The process continues at Step 3, with R2 sending back a Hello. This message tells R1 that R2 exists, and it allows R1 to move to a 2-way state. At Step 4, R2 receives the next Hello from R1, and R2 can also move to a 2-way state.

To see more about why the routers move to the next state, rescan the detail in these messages and look for the notes listed as "seen." When a router receives a Hello from a potential neighbor, and that potential neighbor's parameters match with the local router's parameters, the local router believes it has seen a new legitimate neighbor on the link. For example, the message labeled as Step 3 in the figure, from R2 to R1, lists "Seen [1.1.1.1]," meaning R2 received R1's earlier Hello (at Step 2) and that R2 thinks the parameters all match so that the two routers can become neighbors.

Once through these early steps, each router reaches a 2-way state with their neighbor. At that point, the following two major facts are true:

- The router received a Hello from the neighbor, with that router's own RID listed as being seen by the neighbor.

- The router has checked all the parameters in the Hello received from the neighbor, with no problems. The router is willing to become a neighbor.

Fully Exchanging LSAs with Neighbors

The OSPF neighbor state 2-way means that the router is available to exchange its LSDB with the neighbor. In other words, it is ready to begin a 2-way exchange of the LSDB. So, once two routers on a point-to-point link reach the 2-way state, they can immediately move on to the process of database exchange.

The database exchange process can be quite involved, with several OSPF messages and several interim neighbor states. This chapter is more concerned with a few of the messages and the final state when database exchange has completed: the full state.

After two routers decide to exchange databases, they do not simply send the contents of the entire database. First, they tell each other a list of LSAs in their respective databases—not all the details of the LSAs, just a list. (Think of these lists as checklists.) Then, each router can check which LSAs it already has, and then ask the other router for only the LSAs that are not known yet.

For instance, R1 might send R2 a checklist that lists 10 LSAs (using an OSPF Database Description, or DD, packet). R2 then checks its LSDB and finds 6 of those 10 LSAs. So, R2 asks R1 (using a Link-State Request packet) to send the four additional LSAs.

Thankfully, most OSPFv2 work does not require detailed knowledge of these specific protocol steps. However, a few of the terms are used quite a bit and should be remembered. In particular, the OSPF messages that actually send the LSAs between neighbors are called a Link-State Update (LSU) packet. That is, the packet (LSU) holds data structures called LSAs. The link-state advertisements (LSA) are not packets, but rather data structures, which sit inside the LSDB and describe the topology.

Figure 8-3 pulls some of these terms and processes together, with a general example. The story picks up the example shown in Figure 8-2, with Figure 8-3 showing an example of the database exchange process between routers R1 and R2. The center shows the protocol messages, and the outer items show the neighbor states at different points in the process. Focus on two items in particular:

- The routers exchange the LSAs inside LSU packets.

- When finished, the routers reach a full state, meaning they have fully exchanged the contents of their LSDBs.

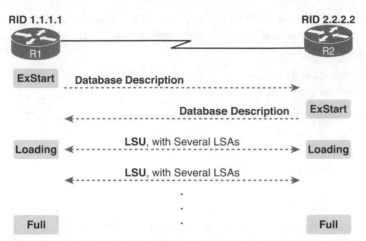

Figure 8-3 *A Database Exchange Example, Ending in a Full State*

Maintaining Neighbors and the LSDB

Once neighbors reach a full state, they have done all the initial work to exchange OSPF information between the two neighbors. However, neighbors still have to do some small ongoing tasks to maintain the neighbor relationship.

First, routers monitor each neighbor relationship using Hello messages and two related timers: The Hello Interval and the Dead Interval. Routers send Hellos every Hello Interval to each neighbor. Each router expects to receive a Hello from each neighbor based on the Hello Interval, so if a neighbor is silent for the length of the Dead Interval (by default 4 times as long as the Hello Interval), the loss of Hellos means that the neighbor has failed.

Next, routers must react when the topology changes as well, and neighbors play a key role in that process. When something changes, one or more routers change one or more LSAs. Then, the routers must flood the changed LSAs to each neighbor so that the neighbor can change its LSDB.

For example, imagine a LAN switch loses power, so a router's G0/0 interface fails from up/up to down/down. That router updates an LSA that shows the router's G0/0 as being down. That router then sends the LSA to its neighbors, and they in turn send it to their neighbors, until all routers again have an identical copy of the LSDB. Each router's LSDB now reflects the fact that the original router's G0/0 interface failed, so each router will then use SPF to recalculate any routes affected by the failed interface.

A third maintenance task done by neighbors is to reflood each LSA occasionally, even when the network is completely stable. By default, each router that creates an LSA also has the responsibility to reflood the LSA every 30 minutes (the default), even if no changes occur. (Note that each LSA has a separate timer, based on when the LSA was created, so there is no single big event where the network is overloaded with flooding LSAs.)

The following list summarizes these three maintenance tasks for easier review:

- Maintain neighbor state by sending Hello messages based on the Hello Interval, and listening for Hellos before the Dead Interval expires

- Flood any changed LSAs to each neighbor

- Reflood unchanged LSAs as their lifetime expires (default 30 minutes)

Using Designated Routers on Ethernet Links

OSPF behaves differently on some types of interfaces, particularly comparing point-to-point and Ethernet links. In particular, on Ethernet links, OSPF elects one of the routers on the same subnet to act as the *designated router* (DR). The DR plays a key role in how the database exchange process works, with different rules than with point-to-point links. To see how, consider the example that begins with Figure 8-4. The figure shows five OSPFv2 routers on the same Ethernet VLAN. These five OSPF routers elect one router to act as the DR, and one router to be backup DR (BDR). The figure shows A and B as DR and BDR, for no other reason than the Ethernet must have one of each.

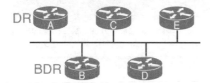

Figure 8-4   *Routers A and B Elected as DR and BDR*

The database exchange process on an Ethernet link does not happen between every pair of routers on the same VLAN/subnet. Instead, it happens between the DR and each of the other routers, with the DR making sure that all the other routers get a copy of each LSA. In other words, the database exchange happens over the flows shown in Figure 8-5.

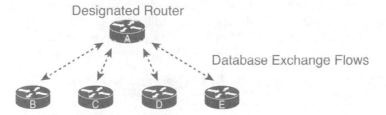

Figure 8-5   *Database Exchange to and from the DR on an Ethernet*

OSPF uses the BDR concept because the DR is so important to the database exchange process. The BDR watches the status of the DR and takes over for the DR if it fails. (When the DR fails, the BDR takes over, and then a new BDR is elected.)

At this point, you might be getting a little tired of some of the theory, but finally, the theory actually shows something that you may see in **show** commands on a router. Because the DR and BDR both do full database exchange with all the other OSPF routers in the LAN, they reach a full state with all neighbors. However, routers that are neither a DR nor a BDR—called *DROthers* by OSPF—never reach a full state because they do not do database exchange with each other. As a result, the **show ip ospf neighbor** command on these routers list some neighbors, permanently, in a state of 2-way, and not in a full state.

For instance, with OSPF working normally on the Ethernet LAN in Figure 8-5, a **show ip ospf neighbor** command on router C (a DROther) would show the following:

■ Two neighbors (A and B, the DR and BDR, respectively) with a full state (called fully adjacent)

■ Two neighbors (D and E) with a 2-way state (called adjacent)

This different behavior on OSPF neighbors on a LAN—where some neighbors reach full state and some do not—calls for the use of two more OSPF terms: *adjacent* and *fully adjacent*. Fully adjacent neighbors reach a full state, after having exchanged their LSDBs directly. Adjacent neighbors are those DROther routers that (correctly) choose to stay in 2-way state but never reach a full state. Table 8-2 summarizes these key concepts and terms related to OSPF states.

Table 8-2   Stable OSPF Neighbor States and Their Meanings

Neighbor State	Adjacency Lingo	Meaning
2-way	Adjacent	The neighbor has sent a Hello that lists the local router's RID in the list of seen routers, also implying that neighbor verification checks all passed. If both neighbors are DROther routers, the neighbors should remain in this state.
Full	Fully adjacent	Both routers know the exact same LSDB details and are fully adjacent, meaning they have completed the exchange of LSDB contents.

Scaling OSPF Using Areas

OSPF can be used in some networks with very little thought about design issues. You just turn on OSPF in all the routers, put all interfaces into the same area (usually area 0), and it works! Figure 8-6 shows one such network example, with 11 routers and all interfaces in area 0.

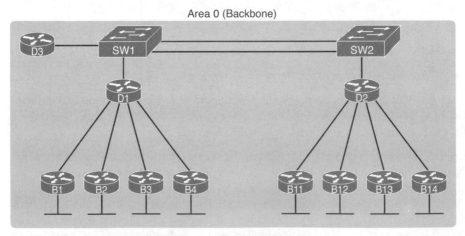

Figure 8-6   *Single-Area OSPF*

Larger OSPFv2 networks suffer with a single-area design. For instance, now imagine an enterprise network with 900 routers, rather than only 11, and several thousand subnets. As it turns out, the CPU time to run the SPF algorithm on all that topology data just takes time. As a result, OSPFv2 convergence time—the time required to react to changes in the network—can be slow. The routers may run low on RAM, as well. Additional problems include the following:

- A larger topology database requires more memory on each router.

- Processing the larger topology database with the SPF algorithm requires processing power that grows exponentially with the size of the topology database.

- A single interface status change, anywhere in the internetwork (up to down, or down to up), forces *every router* to run SPF again!

The solution is to take the one large LSDB and break it into several smaller LSDBs by using OSPF areas. With areas, each link is placed into one area. SPF does its complicated math on the topology inside the area, and that area's topology only. For instance, an internetwork with 1000 routers and 2000 subnets, broken in 100 areas, would average 10 routers and 20 subnets per area. The SPF calculation on a router would have to only process topology about 10 routers and 20 links, rather than 1000 routers and 2000 links.

So, how large does a network have to be before OSPF needs to use areas? Well, there is no set answer, because the behavior of the SPF process depends largely on CPU processing speed, the amount of RAM, the size of the LSDB, and so on. Generally, networks larger than a few dozen routers benefit from areas, and some documents over the years have listed 50 routers as the dividing line at which network really should use areas.

The next few pages look at how OSPF area design works, with more reasons as to why areas helps make larger OSPF networks work better.

OSPF Areas

OSPF area design follows a couple of basic rules. To apply the rules, start with a clean drawing of the internetwork, with routers, and all interfaces. Then, choose the area for each router interface, as follows:

- Put all interfaces connected to the same subnet inside the same area.

- An area should be contiguous.

- Some routers may be internal to an area, with all interfaces assigned to that single area.

- Some routers may be ABRs, because some interfaces connect to the backbone area, and some connect to nonbackbone areas.

- All nonbackbone areas must connect to the backbone area (area 0) by having at least one ABR connected to both the backbone area and the nonbackbone area.

Figure 8-7 shows one example. Some engineer started with a network diagram that showed all 11 routers and their links. On the left, the engineer put four serial links, and the LANs connected to branch routers B1 through B4, into area 1. Similarly, he placed the links to branches B11 through B14, and their LANs, in area 2. Both areas need a connection to the backbone area, area 0, so he put the LAN interfaces of D1 and D2 into area 0, along with D3, creating the backbone area.

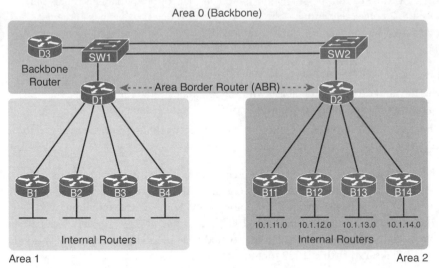

Figure 8-7   *Three-Area OSPF with D1 and D2 as ABRs*

The figure also shows a few important OSPF area design terms. Table 8-3 summarizes the meaning of these terms, plus some other related terms, but pay closest attention to the terms from the figure.

Table 8-3   OSPF Design Terminology

Term	Description
Area Border Router (ABR)	An OSPF router with interfaces connected to the backbone area and to at least one other area
Backbone router	A router in one area (the backbone area)
Internal router	A router in one area (not the backbone area)
Area	A set of routers and links that share the same detailed LSDB information, but not with routers in other areas, for better efficiency
Backbone area	A special OSPF area to which all other areas must connect—area 0
Intra-area route	A route to a subnet inside the same area as the router
Interarea route	A route to a subnet in an area of which the router is not a part

How Areas Reduce SPF Calculation Time

Figure 8-7 shows a sample area design and some terminology related to areas, but it does not show the power and benefit of the areas. To understand how areas reduce the work SPF has to do, you need to understand what changes about the LSDB inside an area, as a result of the area design.

SPF spends most of its processing time working through all the topology details, namely routers and the links that connect routers. Areas reduce SPF's workload because, for a given area, the LSDB lists only routers and links inside that area, as shown on the left side of Figure 8-8.

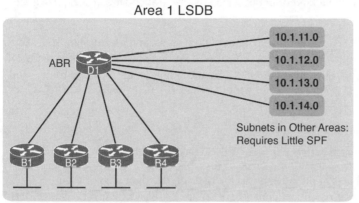

Detailed Topology Data (Routers and Links):
Requires Heavy SPF

Figure 8-8 *The Smaller Area 1 LSDB Concept*

While the LSDB has less topology information, it still has to have information about all subnets in all areas, so that each router can create IPv4 routes for all subnets. So, with an area design, OSPFv2 uses very brief summary information about the subnets in other areas. These LSAs do not include topology information about the other areas, so they do not require much SPF processing at all. Instead, these subnets all appear like subnets connected to the ABR (in this case, ABR D1).

OSPF Area Design Advantages

In summary, using a single-area OSPF design works well for smaller OSPF networks. It avoids the added complexity, making the network slightly easier to operate. It also requires less planning effort because no one has to plan which parts of the network end up in which area.

Using multiple areas improves OSPF operations in many ways for larger networks. The following list summarizes some of the key points arguing for the use of multiple areas in larger OSPF networks:

- The smaller per-area LSDB requires less memory.

- Routers require fewer CPU cycles to process the smaller per-area LSDB with the SPF algorithm, reducing CPU overhead and improving convergence time.

- Changes in the network (for example, links failing and recovering) requires SPF calculations only on routers connected to the area where the link changed state, reducing the number of routers that must rerun SPF.

- Less information must be advertised between areas, reducing the bandwidth required to send LSAs.

Link-State Advertisements

Many people tend to get a little intimidated by OSPF LSAs when first learning about them. The output of the **show ip ospf database** command—a command that lists a summary of the output—is pretty long. Commands that look at specific LSAs list a lot more information. The details appear to be in some kind of code, using lots of numbers. It can seem like a bit of a mess.

However, if you examine LSAs while thinking about OSPF areas, and area design, some of the most common LSA types will make a lot more sense. For instance, think about the LSDB in one area, like the example shown in Figure 8-8. The topology details included routers and the links between the routers. As it turns out, OSPF defines the first two types of LSAs to define those exact details, as follows:

■ One *router LSA* for each router in the area

■ One *network LSA* for each network that has a DR plus one neighbor of the DR

Next, think about the subnets in the other areas, the ones on the right side of Figure 8-8. That brief summary information about subnets in other areas—basically just the subnet IDs and masks—exist as a third type of LSA:

■ One *summary* LSA for each subnet ID that exists in a different area

The next few pages discuss these three LSA types in a little more detail; Table 8-4 lists some information about all three for easier reference and study.

Table 8-4 The Three OSPFv2 LSA Types Seen with a Multi-Area OSPF Design

Name	Number	Primary Purpose	Contents of LSA
Router LSA	1	Describe a router	RID, interfaces, IP address/mask, current interface state (status)
Network	2	Describe a network that has a DR	DR and BDR IP addresses, subnet ID, mask
Summary	3	Describe a subnet in another area	Subnet ID, mask, RID of ABR that advertises the LSA

NOTE In some networks, both OSPF and other routing protocols are used. In that case, one or more routers run both OSPF and the other routing protocol, with those routers acting as an OSPF Autonomous System Border Router, or ASBR, redistributing routing information between OSPF and the other protocol. In such a case, the ASBR creates a Type 4 LSA, which describes the ASBR itself, and Type 5 LSAs for each external route learned from the other routing protocol and then advertised into OSPF.

Router LSAs Build Most of the Intra-Area Topology

OSPF needs very detailed topology information inside each area. The routers inside area X need to know all the details about the topology inside area X. And the mechanism to give routers all these details is for the routers to create and flood router (Type 1) and network (Type 2) LSAs about the routers and links in the area.

Router LSAs, also known as Type 1 LSAs, describe the router in detail. It lists a router's RID, its interfaces, its IPv4 addresses and masks, its interface state, and notes about what neighbors the router knows out its interfaces.

To see a specific instance, first review Figure 8-9. It lists internetwork topology, with subnets listed. As a small internetwork, the engineer chose a single-area design, with all interfaces in backbone area 0.

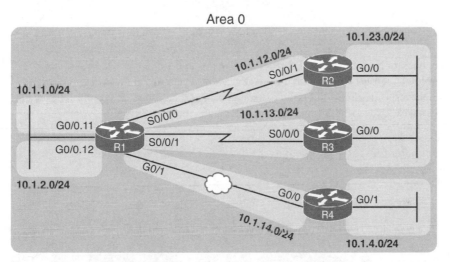

Figure 8-9   *An Enterprise Network with Seven IPv4 Subnets*

With the single-area design planned for this small internetwork, the LSDB will contain four router LSAs. Each router creates a router LSA for itself, with its own RID as the LSA identifier. The LSA lists that router's own interfaces, IP address/mask, with pointers to neighbors.

Once all four routers have copies of all four router LSAs, SPF can mathematically analyze the LSAs to create a model. The model looks a lot like the concept drawing in Figure 8-10. Note that the drawing shows each router with an obvious RID value. Each router has pointers that represent each of its interfaces, and because the LSAs identify neighbors, SPF can figure out which interfaces connect to which other routers.

Network LSAs Complete the Intra-Area Topology

Whereas router LSAs define most of the intra-area topology, network LSAs define the rest. As it turns out, when OSPF elects a DR on some subnet *and* that DR has at least one neighbor, OSPF treats that subnet as another node in its mathematical model of the network. To represent that network, the DR creates and floods a network (Type 2) LSA for that network (subnet).

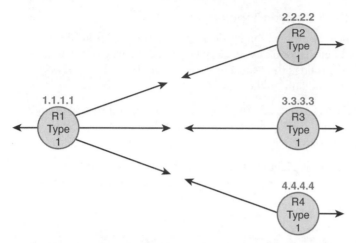

Figure 8-10   *Type 1 LSAs, Assuming a Single-Area Design*

For instance, back in Figure 8-9, one Ethernet LAN and one Ethernet WAN exists. The Ethernet LAN between R2 and R3 will elect a DR, and the two routers will become neighbors; so, whichever router is the DR will create a network LSA. Similarly, R1 and R4 connect with an Ethernet WAN, so the DR on that link will create a network LSA.

Figure 8-11 shows the completed version of the intra-area LSAs in area 0 with this design. Note that the router LSAs actually point to the network LSAs when they exist, which lets the SPF processes connect the pieces together.

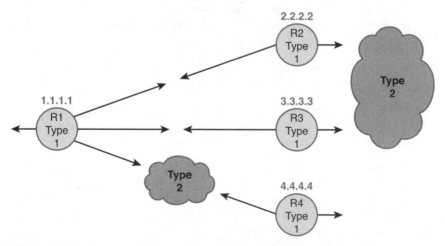

Figure 8-11   *Type 1 and Type 2 LSAs in Area 0, Assuming a Single-Area Design*

NOTE   The drawings in the last two figures work a little like a jigsaw puzzle. The SPF algorithm basically solves the jigsaw puzzle, but by looking at all the numbers inside the different LSAs, to see which LSAs fit next to which other LSAs.

Finally, note that in this single-area design example that no summary (Type 3) LSAs exist at all. These LSA represent subnets in other areas, and there are no other areas. The next example shows some summary LSAs.

LSAs in a Multi-Area Design

Migrating from a single-area design to a multi-area design has a couple of effects on LSAs:

■ Each area has a smaller number of router and network LSAs.

■ The ABRs have a copy of the LSDB for each area to which they connect.

■ The ABRs each have a router LSA in each area's LSDB.

■ Each area has a need for some summary (Type 3) LSAs to describe subnets in other areas.

Before focusing on these summary LSAs, first work through a new example for a moment. Figure 8-12 begins this new example using the same internetwork topology as Figure 8-9, but now with a multi-area design, with router R1 as the only ABR.

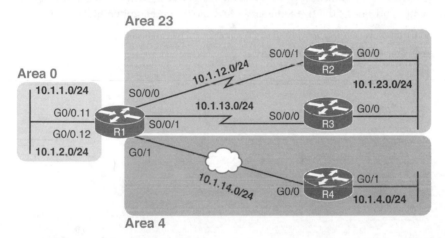

Figure 8-12 *A Multi-Area Design for the Same Internetwork as Figure 8-9*

Next, consider what router and network LSAs should be in the area 4 LSDB. Remember, inside an area, the LSDB should have router LSAs for routers inside the area, and network LSAs for certain networks inside the area (those with a DR that has at least one neighbor). So, the area 4 LSDB will include two router LSAs (for R1 and R4), plus one network LSA, for the network between R1 and R4, as shown in Figure 8-13.

Now focus on the subnets in the entire internetwork for a moment. Breaking it down by area, we have the following:

■ Three subnets in area 23

■ Two subnets in area 4

■ Two subnets in area 0

The routers inside area 4 need to know about the five subnets outside area 4, and to do that, the ABR (R1) advertises summary LSAs into area 4.

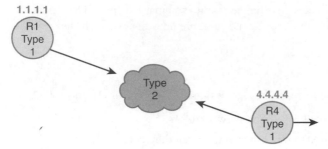

Figure 8-13 *Router and Network LSAs in Area 4 Only, Assuming the Multi-Area Design in Figure 8-12*

Summary (Type 3) LSAs describes a subnet that sits in another area. First, it has to list the subnet ID and mask to identify the specific subnet. The LSA also lists the RID of the ABR that creates and advertises the summary LSA into the area. By identifying the ABR, from a topology perspective, these subnets appear to be connected to the ABR. In this new example, ABR R1 creates and floods the five Summary LSAs shown in the upper left of Figure 8-14.

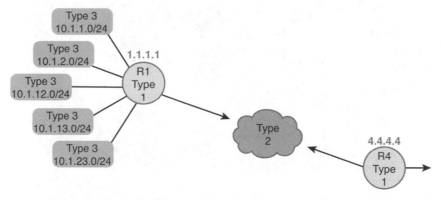

Figure 8-14 *Type 3 LSAs Injected by ABR R1 into the Area 4 LSDB*

> **NOTE** Note that the OSPF summary LSA does not mean that the router is performing route summarization, which is the process of taking multiple routes, for multiple subnets, and advertising them as one route for a larger subnet.

Calculating the Best Routes with SPF

As you can see from these LSAs, they contain useful information, but they do not contain the specific information that a router needs to add to its IPv4 routing table. In other words, a router cannot just copy information from the LSDB into a route in the IPv4 routing table. Instead, the router must do the SPF math, choose the best route, and add a route: a route with a subnet number and mask, an outgoing interface, and a next-hop router IP address.

Although engineers do not need to know the details of how SPF does the math, they do need to know how to predict which routes SPF will choose as the best route. The SPF algorithm calculates all the routes for a subnet—that is, all possible routes from the router to the destination subnet. If more than one route exists, the router compares the metrics, picking the best (lowest) metric route to add to the routing table. Although the SPF math can be complex, engineers with a network diagram, router status information, and simple addition can calculate the metric for each route, predicting what SPF will choose.

Once SPF has identified a route, it calculates the metric for a route as follows:

Key Topic

The sum of the OSPF interface costs for all outgoing interfaces in the route

Figure 8-15 shows an example with three possible routes from R1 to Subnet X (172.16.3.0/24) at the bottom of the figure.

Key Topic

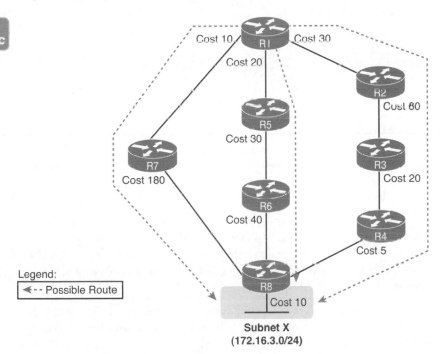

Figure 8-15 *SPF Tree to Find R1's Route to 172.16.3.0/24*

> **NOTE** OSPF considers the costs of the outgoing interfaces (only) in each route. It does not add the cost for incoming interfaces in the route.

Table 8-5 lists the three routes shown in Figure 8-15, with their cumulative costs, showing that R1's best route to 172.16.3.0/24 starts by going through R5.

Table 8-5   Comparing R1's Three Alternatives for the Route to 172.16.3.0/24

Route	Location in Figure 8-15	Cumulative Cost
R1–R7–R8	Left	10 + 180 + 10 = 200
R1–R5–R6–R8	Middle	20 + 30 + 40 + 10 = 100
R1–R2–R3–R4–R8	Right	30 + 60 + 20 + 5 + 10 = 125

As a result of the SPF algorithm's analysis of the LSDB, R1 adds a route to subnet 172.16.3.0/24 to its routing table, with the next-hop router of R5.

In real OSPF networks, an engineer can do the same process by knowing the OSPF cost for each interface. Armed with a network diagram, the engineer can examine all routes, add the costs, and predict the metric for each route.

NOTE   OSPF calculates costs using different processes depending on the area design. The example surrounding Figure 8-15 best matches OSPF's logic when using a single-area design.

Administrative Distance

OSPF can choose the best route for each subnet based on OSPF's metric, as discussed in the previous page or two of this chapter. However, IOS must also be able to choose the best route to reach a subnet when the router knows of routes from different sources. To make such a choice, routers use a concept called administrative distance (AD).

First, think about a common case, in which all the routers use OSPF, and only OSPF, as the one routing protocol for IPv4. A router learns routes with OSPF, but it also learns connected routes. It may also have some **ip route** commands that define static IPv4 routes. It could be that one router knows about a connected, static, and OSPF route for a single subnet. How does a router choose which to use?

Any time a router must choose between competing connected, static, and OSPF routes, the router uses the connected route by default. Why? Although it might appear to be just good common sense, the router actually chooses the connected route because of its lower (better) AD of 0. Static routes have an AD of 1 by default, and OSPF routes have an AD of 110 by default.

Taking the idea a step further, in some cases, a company needs to use multiple routing protocols. For instance, if two companies connect their networks so that they can exchange information, they need to exchange some routing information. If one company uses OSPF, and the other uses EIGRP on at least one router, both OSPF and Enhanced Interior Gateway Routing Protocol (EIGRP) must be used. Then, that router can take routes learned by OSPF and advertise them into EIGRP, and vice versa, through a process called *route redistribution*.

Depending on the network topology, one router might learn a route to a subnet with both OSPF and with EIGRP. In this case, because each routing protocol's metric is based on different information, IOS cannot compare the metrics. In this case, IOS again chooses the best route based on the administrative distance.

The AD values are configured on a single router and are not exchanged with other routers. Table 8-6 lists the various sources of routing information, along with the default ADs.

Table 8-6   Default Administrative Distances

Route Type	Administrative Distance
Connected	0
Static	1
BGP (external routes)	20
EIGRP (internal routes)	90
IGRP	100
OSPF	110
IS-IS	115
RIP	120
EIGRP (external routes)	170
BGP (internal routes)	200
Unusable	255

NOTE   The **show ip route** command lists each route's administrative distance as the first of the two numbers inside the brackets. The second number in brackets is the metric.

The table shows the default administrative distance values, but IOS can be configured to change the AD of a particular routing protocol or even a single route. For instance, the command **distance 80**, from OSPF configuration mode, sets the AD of all OSPF learned routes on that router to an AD value of 80.

OSPF Configuration and Verification

Now that you have a big dose of OSPF theory, this second half of the chapter shows how to make OSPF work, with multi-area designs, and with influencing route selection by changing OSPF interface costs. Then the verification topics show the specifics of these features, plus some of the OSPF and LSA features discussed in the first half of the chapter.

OSPFv2 Configuration Overview

First, for those of you who might not remember the OSPF configuration from the ICND1 book, take a few moments to review the configuration. This checklist lists the commands, with some commentary about the **network** command to follow. Also, note that the upcoming configuration example uses these same commands.

Step 1. Enter OSPF configuration mode for a particular OSPF process using the **router ospf** *process-id* global command.

Step 2. (Optional) Configure the OSPF router ID by

    A. Configuring the **router-id** *id-value* router subcommand

    B. Configuring an IP address on a loopback interface (chooses the highest IP address of all working loopbacks)

    C. Relying on an interface IP address (chooses the highest IP address of all working nonloopbacks)

Step 3. Configure one or more **network** *ip-address wildcard-mask* **area** *area-id* router subcommands, with any matched interfaces being enabled for the OSPF process and being assigned to the listed area.

Step 4. (Optional) Configure any OSPF interfaces as passive if no neighbors can or should be discovered on the interface, using the **passive-interface** *type number* interface subcommand.

Of these commands, the only one that causes much trouble is the OSPF **network** command. The OSPF **network** command compares the first parameter in the command to each interface IP address on the local router, trying to find a match. However, rather than comparing the entire number in the **network** command to the entire IPv4 address on the interface, the router can compare a subset of the octets, based on the access control list (ACL)-style wildcard mask.

For perspective, this list shows several **network** commands, with a description of what IP addresses the command would match:

network 10.1.1.1 0.0.0.0 area 0: Matches an interface with exactly address 10.1.1.1

network 10.1.1.0 0.0.0.255 area 0: Matches any interface whose address begins with 10.1.1

network 10.0.0.0 0.255.255.255 area 0: Matches any interface whose address begins with 10

network 0.0.0.0 255.255.255.255 area 0: Matches any interface that has some IP address configured

Basically, a wildcard mask value of 0 in an octet tells IOS to compare to see whether the numbers match, and a value of 255 tells IOS to ignore that octet when comparing the numbers.

Multi-Area OSPFv2 Configuration Example

Before looking at the multi-area configuration, bear with me for a brief tangent about the exam topics for OSPF. Frankly, the OSPF exam topics (at the time of publication) skirt around the dividing line of whether you need to know how to configure multi-area OSPF (both OSPFv2 and OSPFv3). The configuration-oriented exam topics clearly imply single-area configuration only, while the troubleshooting topics may imply that you need knowledge of multi-area configuration. The good news is this: When you understand multi-area concepts and single-area configuration, adding multi-area configuration is incredibly simple. So, this topic shows the multi-area details, just in case you need them for the exam.

Next, the text shows a configuration example for a multi-area OSPF design, based on the same three-area design shown earlier as Figure 8-12. Figure 8-16 repeats the internetwork topology and subnet IDs, and Figure 8-17 shows the area design. Note that Figure 8-16 lists the last octet of each router's IPv4 address near each interface, rather than the entire IPv4 address, to reduce clutter.

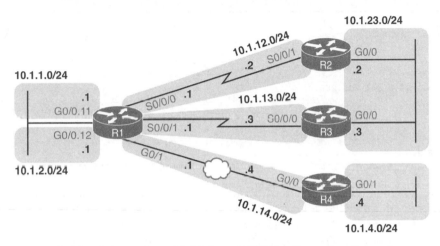

Figure 8-16   *Subnets for a Multi-Area OSPF Configuration Example*

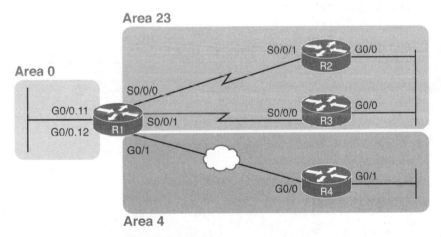

Figure 8-17   *Area Design for an Example Multi-Area OSPF Configuration*

The configurations on the four routers in this example also serve as a review for ICND1-level OSPF configuration. To that end, for no other reason than to show a variety of options, the configurations show several ways to set the OSPF RID and several different wildcard masks on OSPF **network** commands. It also shows the use of passive interfaces where no other OSPF routers should exist off an interface.

Single-Area Configurations

Example 8-1 begins the configuration example by showing the OSPF and IP address configuration on R2. Note that R2 acts as an internal router in area 23, meaning that the configuration will refer to only one area (23). The configuration sets R2's RID to 2.2.2.2 directly with the **router-id** command. And, because R2 should find neighbors on both its two interfaces, neither can reasonably be made passive, so R2's configuration lists no passive interfaces.

Example 8-1 *OSPF Configuration on R2, Placing Two Interfaces into Area 23*

```
interface GigabitEthernet0/0
 ip address 10.1.23.2 255.255.255.0
!
interface serial 0/0/1
 ip address 10.1.12.2 255.255.255.0
!
router ospf 1
 network 10.0.0.0 0.255.255.255 area 23
 router-id 2.2.2.2
```

Example 8-2 continues reviewing commands originally introduced in ICND1, showing the configuration for both R3 and R4. R3 puts both its interfaces into area 23, per its **network** command, sets its RID to 3.3.3.3 by using a loopback interface, and like R2, cannot make either of its interfaces passive. The R4 configuration is somewhat different, with both interfaces placed into area 4, setting its RID based on a nonloopback interface (G0/0, for OSPF RID 10.1.14.4), and making R4's G0/1 interface passive, because no other OSPF routers sit on that link.

Example 8-2 *OSPF Single-Area Configuration on R3 and R4*

```
! First, on R3
interface gigabitEthernet0/0
 ip address 10.1.23.3 255.255.255.0
!
interface serial 0/0/0
 ip address 10.1.13.3 255.255.255.0
!
interface loopback 0
 ip address 3.3.3.3 255.255.255.0
!
router ospf 1
 network 10.0.0.0 0.255.255.255 area 23
! Next, on R4
interface GigabitEthernet0/0
 description R4 will use this interface for its OSPF RID
 ip address 10.1.14.4 255.255.255.0
!
interface GigabitEthernet0/1
```

```
 ip address 10.1.4.4 255.255.255.0
!
router ospf 1
 network 10.0.0.0 0.255.255.255 area 4
 passive-interface gigabitethernet0/1
```

Multi-Area Configuration

So far, the examples have not actually shown a multi-area configuration. Routers R2, R3, and R4 each sit inside a single area, as internal OSPF routers, so their configuration lists only a single area. None of them use a multi-area configuration.

The only router that has a multi-area config is an ABR, by virtue of the configuration referring to more than one area. In this design (as shown in Figure 8-17), only router R1 acts as an ABR, with interfaces in three different areas. Example 8-3 shows R1's OSPF configuration. Note that the configuration does not state anything about R1 being an ABR; instead, it uses multiple **network** commands, some placing interfaces into area 0, some into area 23, and some into area 4.

Example 8-3   *OSPF Multi-Area Configuration on Router R1*

```
interface GigabitEthernet0/0.11
 encapsulation dot1q 11
 ip address 10.1.1.1 255.255.255.0
!
interface GigabitEthernet0/0.12
 encapsulation dot1q 12
 ip address 10.1.2.1 255.255.255.0
!
interface GigabitEthernet0/1
 ip address 10.1.14.1 255.255.255.0
!
interface serial 0/0/0
 ip address 10.1.12.1 255.255.255.0
!
interface serial 0/0/1
 ip address 10.1.13.1 255.255.255.0
!
router ospf 1
 network 10.1.1.1 0.0.0.0 area 0
 network 10.1.2.1 0.0.0.0 area 0
 network 10.1.12.1 0.0.0.0 area 23
 network 10.1.13.1 0.0.0.0 area 23
 network 10.1.14.1 0.0.0.0 area 4
 router-id 1.1.1.1
 passive-interface gigabitethernet0/0.11
 passive-interface gigabitethernet0/0.12
```

8

Focus on the highlighted **network** commands in the example. All five commands happen to use a wildcard mask of 0.0.0.0, so that each command requires a specific match of the listed IP address. If you compare these **network** commands to the various interfaces, you can see that the configuration enables OSPF, for area 0, on subinterfaces G0/0.11 and G0/0.12, area 23 for the two serial interfaces, and area 4 for R1's G0/1 interface.

> **NOTE** Many networks make a habit of using a 0.0.0.0 wildcard mask on OSPF **network** commands, requiring an exact match of each interface IP address, as shown in Example 8-3. This style of configuration makes it more obvious exactly which interfaces match which **network** command.

Finally, note that R1's configuration also sets its RID directly and makes its two LAN subinterfaces passive.

So, what's the big difference between single area and multi-area OSPF configuration? Practically nothing. The only difference is that with multi-area the ABR's **network** commands list different areas.

Verifying the Multi-Area Configuration

The next few pages look at how to verify a few of the new OSPF features introduced in this chapter. For a more thorough verification of OSPF, use all the commands suggested in the review figure (Figure 8-1) at the beginning of this chapter. This section looks at the following new topics:

- Verifying the ABR interfaces are in the correct (multiple) areas
- Finding which router is DR and BDR on multiaccess links
- Confirming the correct number of different types of LSAs exist in each area
- Displaying IPv6 routes

Verifying the Correct Areas on Each Interface on an ABR

The easiest place to make a configuration oversight with a multi-area configuration is to place an interface into the wrong OSPF area. Several commands mention the OSPF area. The **show ip protocols** command basically relists the OSPF **network** configuration commands, which indirectly identify the interfaces and areas. Also, the **show ip ospf interface** and **show ip ospf interface brief** commands directly show the area configured for an interface; Example 8-4 shows an example of the briefer version of these commands.

Example 8-4 *Listing the OSPF-Enabled Interfaces and the Matching OSPF Areas*

```
R1# show ip ospf interface brief
Interface    PID   Area         IP Address/Mask    Cost   State Nbrs F/C
Gi0/0.12     1     0            10.1.2.1/24        1      DR    0/0
Gi0/0.11     1     0            10.1.1.1/24        1      DR    0/0
Gi0/1        1     4            10.1.14.1/24       1      BDR   1/1
Se0/0/1      1     23           10.1.13.1/24       64     P2P   1/1
Se0/0/0      1     23           10.1.12.1/24       64     P2P   1/1
```

In the output, to correlate the areas, just look at the Interface in the first column, and the area in the third column. Also, for this example, double-check this information with Figures 8-16 and 8-17 to confirm that the configuration matches the design.

Verifying Which Router Is DR and BDR

Several **show** commands identify the DR and BDR in some way, as well. In fact, the **show ip ospf interface brief** command output, just listed in Example 8-4, lists the local router's State, showing that R1 is DR on two subinterfaces and BDR on its G0/1 interface.

Example 8-5 shows two other examples that identify the DR and BDR, but with a twist. The **show ip ospf interface** command lists detailed output about OSPF settings, per interface. Those details include the RID and interface address of the DR and BDR. At the same time, the **show ip ospf neighbor** command lists shorthand information about the neighbor's DR or BDR role as well; this command does not say anything about the local router's role. Example 8-5 shows examples of both commands.

Example 8-5   *Discovering the DR and BDR on the R1-R4 Ethernet (from R4)*

```
R4# show ip ospf interface gigabitEthernet 0/0
GigabitEthernet0/0 is up, line protocol is up
  Internet Address 10.1.14.4/24, Area 4, Attached via Network Statement
  Process ID 1, Router ID 10.1.14.4, Network Type BROADCAST, Cost: 1
  Topology-MTID    Cost    Disabled    Shutdown    Topology Name
       0            1         no          no           Base
  Transmit Delay is 1 sec, State DR, Priority 1
  Designated Router (ID) 10.1.14.4, Interface address 10.1.14.4
  Backup Designated router (ID) 1.1.1.1, Interface address 10.1.14.1
!
! Lines omitted for brevity
R4# show ip ospf neighbor

Neighbor ID     Pri    State        Dead Time    Address      Interface
1.1.1.1          1     FULL/BDR     00:00:33     10.1.14.1    GigabitEthernet0/0
```

First, focus on the highlighted lines from the **show ip ospf interface** command output. It lists the DR as RID 10.1.14.4, which happens to be R4. It also lists the BDR as 1.1.1.1, which is R1. (As a reminder, while the earlier conceptual figures showed R4 with an RID of 4.4.4.4, the configuration for R4, in Example 8-2, results in an RID of 10.1.14.4. That configuration did not use the **router-id** configuration command and did not use a loopback interface on R4.)

The end of the example shows the **show ip ospf neighbor** command on R4, listing R4's single neighbor, with Neighbor RID 1.1.1.1 (R1). The command lists R4's concept of its neighbor state with neighbor 1.1.1.1 (R1), with the current state listed as FULL/BDR. The FULL state means that R4 has fully exchanged its LSDB with R1. The BDR means that the neighbor (R1) is acting as the BDR, implying that R4 (the only other router on this link) is acting as the DR.

Verifying the Number and Type of LSAs

Earlier in this chapter, the "Link-State Advertisements" section discussed LSA Types 1, 2, and 3 in some depth. The multi-area configuration example uses the exact same area design as the earlier multi-area LSA examples, so a quick check of the OSPF LSDB should confirm the concepts discussed earlier in the chapter.

Figure 8-14 showed how area 4's LSDB should have two router LSAs, one network LSA, and five summary LSAs. The **show ip ospf database** command in Example 8-6, taken from router R4, shows R4's view of the area 4 LSDB.

Example 8-6 *Verifying the Number and Type of LSAs in Area 4*

```
R4# show ip ospf database

            OSPF Router with ID (10.1.14.4) (Process ID 1)

                Router Link States (Area 4)

Link ID         ADV Router      Age        Seq#       Checksum Link count
1.1.1.1         1.1.1.1         1252       0x80000015 0x00AE30 1
10.1.14.4       10.1.14.4       1453       0x80000015 0x00A2E7 2


                Net Link States (Area 4)

Link ID         ADV Router      Age        Seq#       Checksum
10.1.14.4       10.1.14.4       1453       0x80000014 0x007259


                Summary Net Link States (Area 4)

Link ID         ADV Router      Age        Seq#       Checksum
10.1.1.0        1.1.1.1         1493       0x80000014 0x00B563
10.1.2.0        1.1.1.1         1493       0x80000014 0x00AA6D
10.1.12.0       1.1.1.1         1493       0x80000014 0x00B41A
10.1.13.0       1.1.1.1         1493       0x80000014 0x00A924
10.1.23.0       1.1.1.1         1493       0x80000014 0x00457D
```

Note that the example highlights the three heading lines for the three LSA types, plus in the Router LSA area, the highlights focus on the link IDs for the router LSAs. The Router LSA section highlights the RIDs that identify the two router LSAs: the router LSA for R1 (RID 1.1.1.1) and for R4 (RID 10.1.14.4). If you look inside the Net (Network) LSAs area, you will find a single LSA listed, with ID 10.1.14.4. Finally, the last section lists the five summary LSAs inside area 4.

> **NOTE** The terms *neighbor table*, *topology table*, and *routing table* are sometimes used to refer to three of OSPFv2 key lists. The term neighbor table refers to the list of neighbors, and the term topology table refers to the topology database, as displayed in Example 8-6.

Verifying OSPF Routes

Finally, all this OSPF theory and all the **show** commands do not matter if the routers do not learn IPv4 routes. To verify the routes, Example 8-7 shows R4's IPv4 routing table.

Example 8-7   *Verifying OSPF Routes on Router R1*

```
R4# show ip route
Codes: L - local, C - connected, S - static, R - RIP, M - mobile, B - BGP
       D - EIGRP, EX - EIGRP external, O - OSPF, IA - OSPF inter area
       N1 - OSPF NSSA external type 1, N2 - OSPF NSSA external type 2
       E1 - OSPF external type 1, E2 - OSPF external type 2
       i - IS-IS, su - IS-IS summary, L1 - IS-IS level-1, L2 - IS-IS level-2
       ia - IS-IS inter area, * - candidate default, U - per-user static route
       o - ODR, P - periodic downloaded static route, H - NHRP, l - LISP
       + - replicated route, % - next hop override


      10.0.0.0/8 is variably subnetted, 9 subnets, 2 masks
O IA     10.1.1.0/24 [110/2] via 10.1.14.1, 11:04:43, GigabitEthernet0/0
O IA     10.1.2.0/24 [110/2] via 10.1.14.1, 11:04:43, GigabitEthernet0/0
C        10.1.4.0/24 is directly connected, GigabitEthernet0/1
L        10.1.4.4/32 is directly connected, GigabitEthernet0/1
O IA     10.1.12.0/24 [110/65] via 10.1.14.1, 11:04:43, GigabitEthernet0/0
O IA     10.1.13.0/24 [110/65] via 10.1.14.1, 11:04:43, GigabitEthernet0/0
C        10.1.14.0/24 is directly connected, GigabitEthernet0/0
L        10.1.14.4/32 is directly connected, GigabitEthernet0/0
O IA     10.1.23.0/24 [110/66] via 10.1.14.1, 11:04:43, GigabitEthernet0/0
```

This example shows a couple of new codes that are particularly interesting for OSPF. As usual, a single character on the left identifies the source of the route, with O meaning OSPF. In addition, IOS notes any interarea routes with an IA code as well. (The example does not list any intra-area OSPF routes, but these routes would simply omit the IA code.) Also, note that R4 has routes to all seven subnets in this example: two connected routes and five inter-area OSPF routes.

OSPF Metrics (Cost)

Earlier, the "Calculating the Best Routes with SPF" section discussed how SPF calculates the metric for each route, choosing the route with the best metric for each destination subnet. OSPF routers can influence that choice by changing the OSPF interface cost on any and all interfaces.

Cisco routers allow two different ways to change the OSPF interface cost. The one straight-forward way is to set the cost directly, with an interface subcommand: **ip ospf cost** *x*. The other method is to let IOS choose default costs, based on a formula, but to change the inputs to the formula. This second method requires a little more thought and care and is the focus of this next topic.

8

Setting the Cost Based on Interface Bandwidth

The default OSPF cost values can actually cause a little confusion, for a couple of reasons. So, to get through some of the potential confusion, this section begins with some examples.

First, IOS uses the following formula to choose an interface's OSPF cost. IOS puts the interface's bandwidth in the denominator, and a settable OSPF value called the *reference bandwidth* in the numerator:

Reference_bandwidth / Interface_bandwidth

With this formula, a higher interface bandwidth is better. The higher (faster) the interface bandwidth, the lower the calculated OSPF cost for the interface. The lower the interface cost, the lower the metric for routes using that interface, and the more likely the interface is used in a route chosen by SPF.

Now, for some examples. Assume a default reference bandwidth, set to 100,000 Kbps. Assume defaults for interface bandwidth on serial, Ethernet, and Fast Ethernet interfaces, as shown in the output of the **show interfaces** command, respectively, of 1544 Kbps, 10,000 Kbps (meaning 10 Mbps), and 100,000 Kbps (meaning 100 Mbps). Table 8-7 shows the results of how IOS calculates the OSPF cost for some interface examples.

Table 8-7   OSPF Cost Calculation Examples with Default Bandwidth Settings

Interface	Interface Default Bandwidth (Kbps)	Formula (Kbps)	OSPF Cost
Serial	1544 Kbps	100,000/1544	64
Ethernet	10,000 Kbps	100,000/10,000	10
Fast Ethernet	100,000 Kbps	100,000/100,000	1

To change the OSPF cost on these interfaces, the engineer simply needs to use the **bandwidth** *speed* interface subcommand to set the bandwidth on an interface. The interface bandwidth does not change the Layer 1 transmission speed at all; instead, it is used for other purposes, including routing protocol metric calculations. For instance, if you add the **bandwidth 10000** command to a serial interface, with a default reference bandwidth, the serial interface's OSPF cost could be calculated as 100,000 / 10,000 = 10.

Example 8-8 shows the cost settings on R1's OSPF interfaces, all based on default OSPF (reference bandwidth) and default interface bandwidth settings.

Example 8-8   *Confirming OSPF Interface Costs*

```
R1# show ip ospf interface brief
Interface   PID   Area       IP Address/Mask    Cost   State Nbrs F/C
Gi0/0.12    1     0          10.1.2.1/24        1      DR    0/0
Gi0/0.11    1     0          10.1.1.1/24        1      DR    0/0
Gi0/1       1     4          10.1.14.1/24       1      BDR   1/1
Se0/0/1     1     23         10.1.13.1/24       64     P2P   1/1
Se0/0/0     1     23         10.1.12.1/24       64     P2P   1/1
```

Note that if the calculation of the default metric results in a fraction, OSPF rounds down to the nearest integer. For instance, the example shows the cost for interface S0/0/0 as 64. The calculation used the default serial interface bandwidth of 1.544 Mbps, with reference bandwidth 100 (Mbps), with the 100/1.544 calculation resulting in 64.7668394. OSPF rounds down to 64.

The Need for a Higher Reference Bandwidth

This default calculation works nicely as long as the fastest link in the network runs at 100 Mbps. The default reference bandwidth is set to 100, meaning 100 Mbps, the equivalent of 100,000 Kbps. As a result, with default settings, faster router interfaces end up with the same OSPF cost, as shown in Table 8-8, because the lowest allowed OSPF cost is 1.

Table 8-8   Faster Interfaces with Equal OSPF Costs

Interface	Interface Default Bandwidth (Kbps)	Formula (Kbps)	OSPF Cost
Fast Ethernet	100,000 Kbps	100,000/100,000	1
Gigabit Ethernet	1,000,000 Kbps	100,000/1,000,000	1
10 Gigabit Ethernet	10,000,000 Kbps	100,000/10,000,000	1
100 Gigabit Ethernet	100,000,000 Kbps	100,000/100,000,000	1

To avoid this issue, and change the default cost calculation, you can change the reference bandwidth with the **auto-cost reference-bandwidth** *speed* OSPF mode subcommand. This command sets a value in a unit of megabits per second (Mbps). To avoid the issue shown in Table 8-8, set the reference bandwidth value to match fastest link speed in the network. For instance, **auto-cost reference-bandwidth 10000** accommodates links up to 10 Gbps in speed.

> **NOTE**   Cisco recommends making the OSPF reference bandwidth setting the same on all OSPF routers in an enterprise network.

For convenient study, the following list summarizes the rules for how a router sets its OSPF interface costs:

1. Set the cost explicitly, using the **ip ospf cost** *x* interface subcommand, to a value between 1 and 65,535, inclusive.

2. Change the interface bandwidth with the **bandwidth** *speed* command, with speed being a number in kilobits per second (Kbps).

3. Change the reference bandwidth, using router OSPF subcommand **auto-cost reference-bandwidth** *ref-bw*, with a unit of megabits per second (Mbps).

OSPF Load Balancing

When a router uses SPF to calculate the metric for each of several routes to reach one subnet, one route may have the lowest metric, so OSPF puts that route in the routing table. However, when the metrics tie for multiple routes to the same subnet, the router can put multiple equal-cost routes in the routing table (the default is four different routes) based on the setting of the **maximum-paths** *number* router subcommand. For example, if an internetwork has six possible paths between some parts of the network, and the engineer wants all routes to be used, the routers can be configured with the **maximum-paths 6** subcommand under **router ospf**.

The more challenging concept relates to how the routers use those multiple routes. A router could load balance the packets on a per-packet basis. For example, if the router has three equal-cost OSPF routes for the same subnet in the routing table, the router could send the one packet over the first route, the next packet over the second route, the next packet over the third route, and then start over with the first route for the next packet. Alternatively, the load balancing could be on a per-destination IP address basis.

Exam Preparation Tasks

Review All the Key Topics

Review the most important topics from this chapter, noted with the Key Topic icon. Table 8-9 lists these key topics and where each is discussed.

Table 8-9   Key Topics for Chapter 8

Key Topic Element	Description	Page Number
Figure 8-1	Major OSPF concepts and matching OSPF verification commands	234
List	Rules for setting the router ID	235
Table 8-2	Key OSPF neighbor states	240
List	OSPF area design rules	241
Figure 8-7	Sample OSPF multi-area design with terminology	242
Table 8-3	OSPF design terms and definitions	242
List	Reasons why a multi-area design works better for larger internetworks	243
Table 8-4	Three primary LSA types	244
Item	Definition of how OSPF calculates the cost for a route	249
Figure 8-15	Example of calculating the cost for multiple competing routes	249
Table 8-6	Default administrative distances	251
Step list	Configuration steps for OSPF configuration reviewed from ICND1 book	252
Example 8-3	Example of a multi-area OSPFv2 configuration	255
List	Details of how IOS determines an interface's OSPF cost	261

Complete the Tables and Lists from Memory

Print a copy of DVD Appendix D, "Memory Tables," or at least the section for this chapter, and complete the tables and lists from memory. DVD Appendix E, "Memory Tables Answer Key," includes completed tables and lists to check your work.

Definitions of Key Terms

After your first reading of the chapter, try to define these key terms, but do not be concerned about getting them all correct at that time. Chapter 22 directs you in how to use these terms for late-stage preparation for the exam.

2-way state, full state, Area Border Router (ABR), designated router, backup designated router, fully adjacent, Hello Interval, Dead Interval, link-state advertisement, link-state update, neighbor, router ID (RID), topology database, shortest path first (SPF), internal router, router LSA, network LSA, summary LSA, backbone area

Command Reference to Check Your Memory

Although you should not necessarily memorize the information in the tables in this section, this section does include a reference for the configuration and EXEC commands covered in this chapter. Practically speaking, you should memorize the commands as a side effect of reading the chapter and doing all the activities in this exam preparation section. To see how well you have memorized the commands as a side effect of your other studies, cover the left side of the table, read the descriptions on the right side, and see if you remember the command.

Table 8-10   Chapter 8 Configuration Command Reference

Command	Description
router ospf *process-id*	Enters OSPF configuration mode for the listed process
network *ip-address wildcard-mask* area *area-id*	Router subcommand that enables OSPF on interfaces matching the address/wildcard combination and sets the OSPF area
ip ospf cost *interface-cost*	Interface subcommand that sets the OSPF cost associated with the interface
bandwidth *bandwidth*	Interface subcommand that directly sets the interface bandwidth (Kbps)
auto-cost reference-bandwidth *number*	Router subcommand that tells OSPF the numerator in the *Ref-BW / Int-BW* formula used to calculate the OSPF cost based on the interface bandwidth
router-id *id*	OSPF command that statically sets the router ID
interface loopback *number*	Global command to create a loopback interface and to navigate to interface configuration mode for that interface
maximum-paths *number-of-paths*	Router subcommand that defines the maximum number of equal-cost routes that can be added to the routing table
passive-interface *type number*	Router subcommand that makes the interface passive to OSPF, meaning that the OSPF process will not form neighbor relationships with neighbors reachable on that interface
passive-interface default	OSPF subcommand that changes the OSPF default for interfaces to be passive instead of active (not passive)
no passive-interface *type number*	OSPF subcommand that tells OSPF to be active (not passive) on that interface or subinterface

Table 8-11 Chapter 8 EXEC Command Reference

Command	Description
show ip ospf	Lists information about the OSPF process running on the router, including the OSPF router ID, areas to which the router connects, and the number of interfaces in each area.
show ip ospf interface brief	Lists the interfaces on which the OSPF protocol is enabled (based on the **network** commands), including passive interfaces.
show ip ospf interface *type number*	Lists a long section of settings, status, and counters for OSPF operation on all interfaces, or on the listed interface, including the Hello and Dead Timers.
show ip protocols	Shows routing protocol parameters and current timer values.
show ip ospf neighbor [*type number*]	Lists brief output about neighbors, identified by neighbor router ID, including current state, with one line per neighbor; optionally, limit the output to neighbors on the listed interface.
show ip ospf neighbor *neighbor-ID*	Lists the same output as the **show ip ospf neighbor detail** command, but only for the listed neighbor (by neighbor RID).
show ip ospf database	Lists a summary of the LSAs in the database, with one line of output per LSA. It is organized by LSA type (first type 1, then type 2, and so on).
show ip route	Lists all IPv4 routes.
show ip route ospf	Lists routes in the routing table learned by OSPF.
show ip route *ip-address mask*	Shows a detailed description of the route for the listed subnet/mask.
clear ip ospf process	Resets the OSPF process, resetting all neighbor relationships and also causing the process to make a choice of OSPF RID.

8

This chapter covers the following exam topics:

IP Routing Technologies

Configure and verify EIGRP (single AS)

Feasible Distance / Feasible Successors /Administrative distance

Feasibility condition

Metric composition

Router ID

Auto summary

Path selection

Load balancing

Equal

Unequal

Passive interface

Differentiate methods of routing and routing protocols

split horizon

metric

next hop

CHAPTER 9

Understanding EIGRP Concepts

This chapter takes an in-depth look at a second option for an IPv4 routing protocol: the Enhanced Interior Gateway Routing Protocol, or EIGRP. This Cisco-proprietary routing protocol uses configuration commands much like Open Shortest Path First (OSPF), with the primary difference being that EIGRP configuration does not need to refer to an area. However, EIGRP does not use link-state (LS) logic, instead using some advanced distance vector (DV) logic. So, this chapter discusses quite a bit of detail about how routing protocols work and how EIGRP works before moving on to EIGRP configuration.

This chapter breaks the topics into two major sections. The first looks at the details of how DV routing protocols work, comparing the basic features of RIP with the more advanced features of EIGRP. The second major section looks at the specifics of EIGRP, including EIGRP neighbors, exchanging routing information, and calculating the currently best routes to reach each possible subnet.

"Do I Know This Already?" Quiz

Use the "Do I Know This Already?" quiz to help decide whether you might want to skim this chapter, or a major section, moving more quickly to the Exam Preparation Tasks section near the end of the chapter. You can find the answers at the bottom of the page following the quiz. For thorough explanations, see DVD Appendix C, "Answers to the 'Do I Know This Already?' Quizzes."

Table 9-1 "Do I Know This Already?" Foundation Topics Section-to-Question Mapping

Foundation Topics Section	Questions
Distance Vector Routing Protocol Features	1–3
EIGRP Concepts and Operation	4–6

1. Which of the following distance vector features prevents routing loops by causing the routing protocol to advertise only a subset of known routes, as opposed to the full routing table, under normal stable conditions?

   a. Route poisoning

   b. Poison reverse

   c. DUAL

   d. Split horizon

2. Which of the following distance vector features prevents routing loops by advertising an infinite metric route when a route fails?

  a. Dijkstra SPF

  b. DUAL

  c. Split horizon

  d. Route poisoning

3. Routers A and B use EIGRP. How does router A watch for the status of router B so that router A can react if router B fails?

  a. By using EIGRP Hello messages, with A needing to receive periodic Hello messages to believe B is still working

  b. By using EIGRP update messages, with A needing to receive periodic update messages to believe B is still working

  c. Using a periodic ping of B's IP address based on the EIGRP neighbor timer

  d. None of the above

4. Which of the following affect the calculation of EIGRP metrics when all possible default values are used? (Choose two answers.)

  a. Bandwidth

  b. Delay

  c. Load

  d. Reliability

  e. MTU

  f. Hop count

5. Which of the following is true about the concept of EIGRP feasible distance?

  a. A route's feasible distance is the calculated metric of a feasible successor route.

  b. A route's feasible distance is the calculated metric of the successor route.

  c. The feasible distance is the metric of a route from a neighboring router's perspective.

  d. The feasible distance is the EIGRP metric associated with each possible route to reach a subnet.

6. Which of the following is true about the concept of EIGRP reported distance?

  a. A route's reported distance is the calculated metric of a feasible successor route.

  b. A route's reported distance is the calculated metric of the successor route.

  c. A route's reported distance is the metric of a route from a neighboring router's perspective.

  d. The reported distance is the EIGRP metric associated with each possible route to reach a subnet.

Foundation Topics

EIGRP and Distance Vector Routing Protocols

IPv4's long history has resulted in many competing interior gateway protocols (IGP). Each of those different IPv4 IGPs differs in some ways, including the underlying routing protocol algorithms like link state and distance vector. This first section of the chapter looks at how EIGRP acts like distance vector routing protocols to some degree, while at the same time, EIGRP does not fit easily into any category at all.

In particular, this first section first positions EIGRP against the other common IPv4 routing protocols. Then this section looks at basic DV concepts as implemented with RIP. Using the simpler RIP to learn the basics helps the discussion focus on the DV concepts. This section ends then with a discussion of how EIGRP uses DV features but in a more efficient way than RIP uses them.

Introduction to EIGRP

Historically speaking, the first IPv4 routing protocols used DV logic. RIP Version 1 (RIP-1) was the first popularly used IP routing protocol, with the Cisco-proprietary Interior Gateway Routing Protocol (IGRP) being introduced a little later, as shown in Figure 9-1.

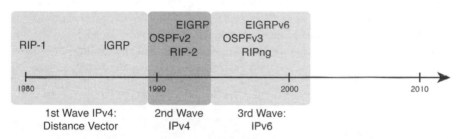

Figure 9-1 *Timeline for IP IGPs*

By the early 1990s, business and technical factors pushed the IPv4 world toward a second wave of better routing protocols. First, RIP-1 and IGRP had some technical limitations, even though they were great options for the technology levels of the 1980s. The bigger motivation for better routing protocols was the huge movement toward TCP/IP in the 1990s. Many enterprises migrated from older vendor-proprietary networks to networks built with routers, LANs, and TCP/IP. These businesses needed better performance from their routing protocols, including better metrics and better convergence. All these factors led to the introduction of a new wave of IPv4 Interior routing protocols: RIP Version 2 (RIP-2), OSPF Version 2 (OSPFv2), and EIGRP.

Answers to the "Do I Know This Already?" quiz:

1 D **2** D **3** A **4** A and B **5** B **6** C

NOTE   As an aside, many documents refer to EIGRP's support for learning IPv4 routes simply as EIGRP, and EIGRP support for IPv6 as EIGRPv6. This book follows that same convention. OSPF RFCs define specific versions, OSPF Version 2 (OSPFv2) learning IPv4 routes, and OSPF Version 3 (OSPFv3) learning IPv6 routes.

Even today, EIGRP and OSPFv2 remain the two primary competitors as the IPv4 routing protocol to use in a modern enterprise IPv4 internetwork. RIP-2 has fallen away as a serious competitor, in part due to its less robust hop-count metric, and in part due to its slower (worse) convergence time. Even today, you can walk in to most corporate networks and find either EIGRP or OSPFv2 as the routing protocol used throughout the network.

So, with so many IPv4 routing protocols, how does a network engineer choose which routing protocol to use? Well, consider two key points about EIGRP that drive engineers toward wanting to use it:

- EIGRP uses a robust metric based on both link bandwidth and link delay, so routers make good choices about the best route to use (see Figure 9-2).
- EIGRP converges quickly, meaning that when something changes in the internetwork, EIGRP quickly finds the currently best loop-free routes to use.

For example, RIP uses a basic metric of hop count, meaning the number of routers between the destination subnet and the local router. These metrics make RIP to choose a short route (fewest router hops away), even shorter routes with slow links, so that route might not be the truly best route. EIGRP's metric calculation uses a math formula that avoids routes with slow links by giving those routes worse (higher) metrics. Figure 9-2 shows an example.

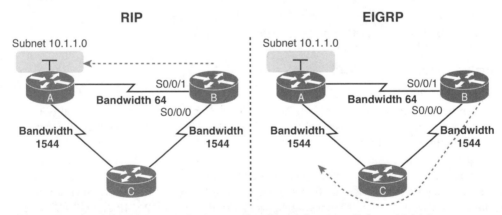

Figure 9-2   *EIGRP Choosing the Longer But Better Route to Subnet 10.1.1.0*

Traditionally, from the introduction of EIGRP in the 1990s until 2013, the one big negative about EIGRP was that Cisco kept the protocol as a Cisco-proprietary protocol. That is, to run Cisco's EIGRP, you had to buy Cisco routers. In an interesting change, Cisco published EIGRP as an informational RFC, meaning that now other vendors can choose to implement EIGRP as well. In the past, many companies chose to use OSPF rather than EIGRP to give themselves options for what router vendor to use for future router hardware purchases. In the future, it might be that you can buy some routers from Cisco, some from other vendors, and still run EIGRP on all routers.

Today, EIGRP and OSPFv2 remain the two best options for IPv4 interior routing protocols. Both converge quickly. Both use a good metric that considers link speeds when choosing the route. EIGRP can be much simpler to implement. Many reasonable network engineers have made these comparisons over the years, with some choosing OSPFv2, and others choosing EIGRP.

For reference and study, Table 9-2 lists several features of OSPFv2 and EIGRP, as well as RIP-2. (Note that the table mentions a topic not yet discussed in this book—autosummarization—as discussed in Chapter 10's section "Auto-summarization and Discontiguous Networks.")

Table 9-2   Interior IP Routing Protocols Compared

Feature	RIP-2	EIGRP	OSPF
Classless/supports VLSM	Yes	Yes	Yes
Distance vector (DV) or link state (LS)	DV	DV[1]	LS
Originally Cisco proprietary	No	Yes	No
Default metrics based at least partially on link bandwidth	No	Yes	Yes
Convergence	Slow	Fast	Fast
Requires the added complexity of areas	No	No	Yes
Supports manual route summarization	Yes	Yes	Yes
Routing updates are sent to a multicast IP address	Yes	Yes	Yes

[1] EIGRP is often described as a balanced hybrid routing protocol, instead of link-state or distance vector. Some documents refer to EIGRP as an advanced distance vector protocol.

Basic Distance Vector Routing Protocol Features

EIGRP does not fit cleanly into the category of DV routing protocols or LS routing protocols. However, it most closely matches DV protocols. The next topic explains the basics of DV routing protocols as originally implemented with RIP, to give a frame of reference of how DV protocols work. In particular, the next examples show routes that use RIP's simple hop-count metric, which, although a poor option in real networks today, is a much simpler option for learning than EIGRP's more complex metric.

The Concept of a Distance and a Vector

The term *distance vector* describes what a router knows about each route. At the end of the process, when a router learns about a route to a subnet, all the router knows is some measurement of distance (the metric) and the next-hop router and outgoing interface to use for that route (a vector, or direction).

9

Figure 9-3 shows a view of both the vector and the distance as learned with RIP. The figure shows the flow of RIP messages that cause R1 to learn some IPv4 routes, specifically three routes to reach subnet X:

■ The four-hop route through R2

■ The three-hop route through R5

■ The two-hop route through R7

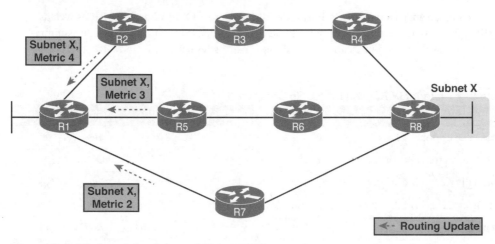

Figure 9-3   *Information Learned Using DV Protocols*

DV protocols learn two pieces of information about a possible route to reach a subnet: the distance (metric), and the vector (the next hop router). In this case, R1 learns three routes to reach subnet X. When only one route for a single subnet exists, the router chooses that one route. However, with the three possible routes in this case, R1 picks the two-hop route through next-hop router R7, because that route has the lowest RIP metric.

While Figure 9-3 shows how R1 learns the routes with RIP Updates, Figure 9-4 gives a better view into R1's distance vector logic. R1 knows three routes, each with:

Distance: The metric for a possible route

Vector: The direction, based on the next-hop router for a possible route

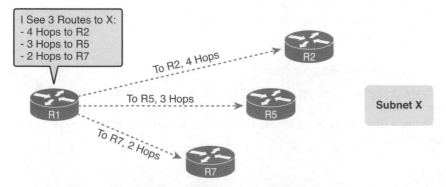

Figure 9-4   *Graphical Representation of the DV Concept*

Note that R1 knows no other topology information about the internetwork. Unlike LS protocols, RIP's DV logic has no idea about the overall topology, instead just knowing about next-hop routers and metrics.

Full Update Messages and Split Horizon

DV routing protocols have a couple of functions that require messages between neighboring routers.

First, routers need to send routing information inside some message, so that the sending router can advertise routing information to neighboring routers. For instance, in Figure 9-3, R1 received RIP messages to learn routes. As discussed in Chapter 8, OSPF calls those messages link-state updates (LSU). RIP and EIGRP both happen to call their messages an update message.

In addition, routers need to monitor whether each neighboring router is still working or not; routers do so by sending and receiving regular messages with each neighbor. By quickly realizing when a neighboring router fails, routers can more quickly converge to use any still-available routes.

All routing protocols use some mechanism to monitor the state of neighboring routers. OSPF uses Hello messages, on a relatively short timer (default 10 seconds on many interfaces). EIGRP happens to use a Hello message and process, as well. However, old basic DV protocols like RIP do not use a separate Hello type of message, instead using the same update message both to advertise routing information and be aware of whether the neighboring router is still alive. In other words, the function of advertising routing information, and the function of monitoring neighbor state, is done with the same update message.

These older basic DV routing protocols like RIP send periodic full routing updates based on a relatively short timer. *Full update* means that a router advertises all its routes, using one or more RIP update messages, no matter whether the route has changed or not. *Periodic* means that the router sends the message based on a timed period (30 seconds with RIP).

Figure 9-5 illustrates this concept in an internetwork with two routers, three LAN subnets, and one WAN subnet. The figure shows both routers' full routing tables, plus listing the periodic full updates sent by each router.

This figure shows a lot of information, so take the time to work through the details. For example, consider what router R1 learns for subnet 172.30.22.0/24, which is the subnet connected to R2's G0/1 interface:

1.   R2 interface G0/1 has an IP address, and is in an up/up state.

2.   R2 adds a connected route for 172.30.22.0/24, off interface G0/1, to R2's routing table.

3.   R2 advertises its route for 172.30.22.0/24 to R1, with metric 1, meaning that R1's metric to reach this subnet will be metric 1 (hop count 1).

4.   R1 adds a route for subnet 172.30.22.0/24, listing it as a RIP learned route with metric 1.

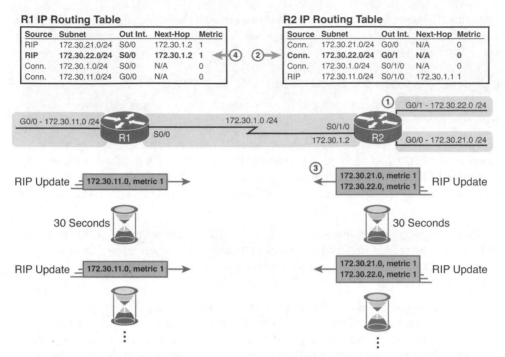

Figure 9-5 *Normal Steady-State RIP Operations: Full Update with Split Horizon*

Also, take a moment to focus more on the route learned at Step 4: The bold route in R1's routing table. This route is for 172.30.22.0/24, as learned from R2. It lists R1's local S0/0 interface as the outgoing interface, because R1 receive the update on that interface. It also lists R2's serial IP address of 172.30.1.2 as next-hop router because that's the IP address from which R1 learned the route.

Next, look at the bottom of the figure, which shows the RIP update message being used to monitor neighbor state. The routers repeat the exact same update message based on 30-second timers. Note that in this internetwork, if nothing changed for a year, with RIP, every 30 seconds, the routers would repeat this same routing information to each other. Why? If a router fails to receive the update messages for a defined time period, the local router knows the silent neighbor has failed.

Finally, the figure shows an example of *split horizon*. Note that both routers list all four subnets in their IP routing tables, yet the RIP update messages do not list four subnets. The reason? Split horizon. Split horizon is a DV feature that tells the routing protocol to not advertise some routes in an update sent out an interface: routes that list that interface as the outgoing interface. Those routes that are not advertised on an interface usually include the routes learned in routing updates received on that interface.

Split horizon is difficult to learn by reading words, and much easier to learn by seeing an example. Figure 9-6 continues the same example as 9-5, but focusing on R1's RIP update sent out R1's S0/0 interface to R2. This figure shows R1's routing table with three light-colored routes, all of which list S0/0 as the outgoing interface. When building the RIP update to send out S0/0, split-horizon rules tell R1 to ignore those light-colored routes. Only the bold route, which does not list S0/0 as an outgoing interface, can be included in the RIP update sent out S0/0.

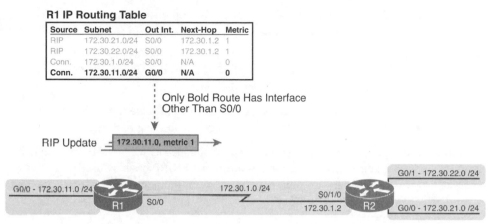

Figure 9-6 *R1 Does Not Advertise Three Routes due to Split Horizon*

Route Poisoning

DV protocols help prevent routing loops by ensuring that every router learns that the route has failed, through every means possible, as quickly as possible. One of these features, *route poisoning*, helps all routers know for sure that a route has failed.

Route poisoning refers to the practice of advertising a failed route, but with a special metric value called *infinity*. Routers consider routes advertised with an infinite metric to have failed.

Route poisoning works a little like in real life, when two people have a conflict. They can ignore the conflict, and just not talk about it. However, it helps if the two people openly talk about the problem, even if the process is a bit uncomfortable, so both people can make a reasonable choice about what to do next. Route poisoning lets two routers talk openly about a particular type of problem: a failed route.

Figure 9-7 shows an example of route poisoning with RIP, with R2's G0/1 interface failing, meaning that R2's route for 172.30.22.0/24 has failed. RIP defines infinity as 16.

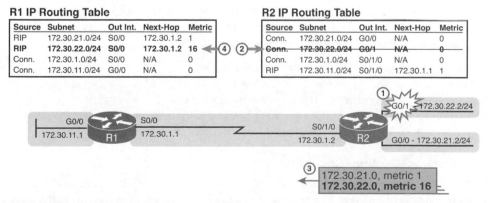

Figure 9-7 *Route Poisoning*

Figure 9-7 shows the following process:

1. R2's G0/1 interface fails.

2. R2 removes its connected route for 172.30.22.0/24 from its routing table.

3. R2 advertises 172.30.22.0 with an infinite metric (which for RIP is 16).

4. Depending on other conditions, R1 either immediately removes the route to 172.30.22.0 from its routing table, or marks the route as unusable (with an infinite metric) for a few minutes before removing the route.

By the end of this process, router R1 knows for sure that its old route for subnet 172.30.22.0/24 has failed, which helps R1 not introduce any looping IP routes.

Each routing protocol has its own definition of an infinite metric. RIP uses 16, as shown in the figure, with 15 being a valid metric for a usable route. EIGRP has long used $2^{32} - 1$ as infinity (a little over 4 billion), with some new IOS versions bumping that value to $2^{56} - 1$ (over 10^{16}). OSPFv2 uses $2^{24} - 1$ as infinity.

EIGRP as an Advanced DV Protocol

EIGRP acts a little like a DV protocol, and a little like no other routing protocol. Frankly, over the years, different Cisco documents and different books (mine included) have characterized EIGRP as either its own category, called a balanced hybrid routing protocol, or as some kind of advanced DV protocol.

Regardless of what label you put on EIGRP, the protocol uses several features that work either like basic DV protocols like RIP, or they work similarly enough. The next few pages walk through a few of the similarities and differences between RIP and EIGRP.

EIGRP Sends Partial Update Messages, As Needed

EIGRP does not use a short periodic update timer, sending a full update with all routes, like RIP does. EIGRP instead sends information about each route once, when the router learns the information. Then, the router sends only partial updates.

EIGRP partial updates are EIGRP update messages that list any new or changed information about a route. For instance, when a router interface fails, some routes will be affected. The router sends an immediate partial update message to any other neighboring EIGRP routers, listing new information. Or, when new routes become available, the router sends a partial update, about only the new routes. These update messages are not full updates, because they only contain changed or new information.

The idea works a little like OSPF's convention of flooding an LSA once inside an area. However, the router that creates an OSPF LSA does reflood that LSA every 30 minutes. EIGRP does not even bother to reflood its routing information. For instance, if the routing information about a route does not change for a year, EIGRP will literally remain silent about that route in its update messages for that whole year after it first advertises the route.

EIGRP Maintains Neighbor Status Using Hello

EIGRP does not send full or partial update messages based on a periodic timer, so EIGRP cannot rely on update messages to monitor the state of EIGRP neighbors. So, using the same basic ideas as OSPF, EIGRP defines a Hello message. The EIGRP Hello message and protocol defines that each router should send a periodic Hello message on each interface, so that all EIGRP routers know that the router is still working. Figure 9-8 shows the idea.

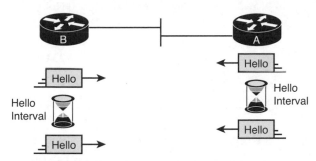

Figure 9-8 *EIGRP Hello Packets*

The routers use their own independent Hello Interval, which defines the time period between each EIGRP Hello. For instance, routers R1 and R2 do not have to send their Hellos at the same time. Routers also must receive a Hello from a neighbor with a time called the Hold Interval, with a default setting of three times the Hello Interval.

For instance, imagine both R1 and R2 use default settings of 5 and 15 for their Hello and Hold Intervals. Under normal conditions, R1 receives Hellos from R2 every 5 seconds, well within R1's Hold Interval (15 seconds) before R1 would consider R2 to have failed. If R2 does fail, R2 no longer sends Hello messages. R1 notices that 15 seconds pass without receiving a Hello from R2, so then R1 can choose new routes that do not use R2 as a next-hop router.

EIGRP does not require two neighboring routers to use the same Hello and hold timers, but it makes good sense to use the same Hello and hold timers on all routers. Unfortunately, the flexibility to use different settings on neighboring routers makes it possible to prevent the neighbors from working properly, just by the poor choice of Hello and hold timers.

Summary of Interior Routing Protocol Features

Table 9-3 summarizes the features discussed in this chapter, for RIP-2, EIGRP, and OSPFv2. Following the table, the second major section of this chapter begins, which moves into depth about the specifics of how EIGRP works.

Table 9-3   Interior IP Routing Protocols Compared

Feature	RIP-2	EIGRP	OSPFv2
Metric is based on the following:	Hop count	Bandwidth and delay	Cost
Sends periodic full updates	Yes	No	No
Sends periodic Hello messages	No	Yes	Yes

Feature	RIP-2	EIGRP	OSPFv2
Uses route poisoning for failed routes	Yes	Yes	Yes
Uses split horizon to limit updates about working routes	Yes	Yes	No
Address to which messages are sent	224.0.0.9	224.0.0.10	224.0.0.5, 224.0.0.6
Metric considered to be infinite	16	$2^{32} - 1$ or $2^{56} - 1$	$2^{24} - 1$

EIGRP Concepts and Operation

EIGRP differs from OSPF in some pretty obvious ways, but in some ways EIGRP acts a lot like OSPF. In fact, EIGRP uses a three-step model similar to OSPF when a router first joins a network. These steps each lead to a list or table: the neighbor table, the topology table, and the routing table. All these processes and tables lead toward building the IPv4 routes in the routing table, as follows:

1. **Neighbor discovery:** EIGRP routers send Hello messages to discover potential neighboring EIGRP routers and perform basic parameter checks to determine which routers should become neighbors. Neighbors that pass all parameter checks are added to the EIGRP neighbor table.

2. **Topology exchange:** Neighbors exchange full topology updates when the neighbor relationship comes up, and then only partial updates as needed based on changes to the network topology. The data learned in these updates is added to the router's EIGRP topology table.

3. **Choosing routes:** Each router analyzes its respective EIGRP topology tables, choosing the lowest-metric route to reach each subnet. EIGRP places the route with the best metric for each destination into the IPv4 routing table.

This second major section of this chapter discusses the particulars of how EIGRP goes about building its routing table, using these three steps. Although the overall three-step process looks similar to OSPF, the details differ greatly, especially those related to how OSPF uses LS logic to process topology data, whereas EIGRP does not. Also, in addition to these three steps, this section explains some unique logic EIGRP uses when converging and reacting to changes in an internetwork—logic that is not seen with the other types of routing protocols.

EIGRP Neighbors

An EIGRP neighbor is another EIGRP-speaking router, connected to a common subnet, with which the router is willing to exchange EIGRP topology information. EIGRP uses EIGRP Hello messages, sent to multicast IP address 224.0.0.10, to dynamically discover potential neighbors. A router learns of potential neighbors by receiving a Hello.

Routers perform some basic checking of each potential neighbor before that router becomes an EIGRP neighbor. A potential neighbor is a router from which an EIGRP Hello has been received. Then the router checks the following settings to determine whether the router should be allowed to be a neighbor:

- It must pass the authentication process if used.
- It must use the same configured autonomous system number (which is a configuration setting).
- The source IP address used by the neighbor's Hello must be in the same subnet as the local router's interface IP address/mask.

> **NOTE**   The router's EIGRP K values must also match, but this topic is beyond the scope of this book.

EIGRP uses relatively straightforward verification checks for neighbors. First, if authentication is configured, the two routers must be using the same type of authentication and the same authentication key (password). Second, EIGRP configuration includes a parameter called an *autonomous system number* (ASN), which must be the same on two neighboring routers. Finally, the IP addresses used to send the EIGRP Hello messages—the routers' respective interface IP addresses—must be in the range of addresses on the other routers' respective connected subnet.

EIGRP makes the neighbor relationship much simpler than OSPF. Whereas OSPF neighbors have several interim states and a few stable states, EIGRP simply moves to a working state as soon as the neighbor passes the basic verification checks. At that point, the two routers can begin exchanging topology information using EIGRP update messages.

Exchanging EIGRP Topology Information

EIGRP uses EIGRP *update messages* to send topology information to neighbors. These update messages can be sent to multicast IP address 224.0.0.10 if the sending router needs to update multiple routers on the same subnet; otherwise, the updates are sent to the unicast IP address of the particular neighbor. (Hello messages are always sent to the 224.0.0.10 multicast address.) The use of multicast packets on LANs allows EIGRP to exchange routing information with all neighbors on the LAN efficiently.

EIGRP sends update messages without UDP or TCP, but it does use a protocol called *Reliable Transport Protocol* (RTP). RTP provides a mechanism to resend any EIGRP messages that are not received by a neighbor. By using RTP, EIGRP can better avoid loops because a router knows for sure that the neighboring router has received any updated routing information. (The use of RTP is just another example of a difference between basic DV protocols like RIP, which have no mechanism to know whether neighbors receive update messages, and the more advanced EIGRP.)

> **NOTE**   The acronym RTP also refers to a different protocol, Real-time Transport Protocol (RTP), which is used to transmit voice and video IP packets.

Neighbors use both full routing updates and partial updates. A full update means that a router sends information about all known routes, whereas a partial update includes only information about recently changed routes. Full updates occur when neighbors first come up. After that, the neighbors send only partial updates in reaction to changes to a route.

Figure 9-9 summarizes many of the details discussed so far in this section, from top to bottom. It first shows neighbor discovery with Hellos, the sending of full updates, the maintenance of the neighbor relationship with ongoing Hellos, and partial updates.

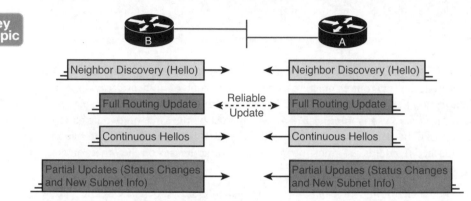

Figure 9-9 *Full and Partial EIGRP Updates*

Note that EIGRP refers to the information exchanged in the updates as topology information. The information is not nearly as detailed as OSPF LS topology data, and it does not attempt to describe every router and link in the network. However, it does describe more than just a distance (metric) and vector (next-hop router) for the local router—a local router also learns the metric as used by the next-hop router. This added information is used to help EIGRP converge quickly, without causing loops, as discussed in the upcoming section "EIGRP Convergence."

Calculating the Best Routes for the Routing Table

EIGRP calculates the metric for routes much differently than any other routing protocol. For instance, with OSPF, anyone with a network diagram and knowledge of the configured OSPF interface costs can calculate the exact OSPF metric (cost) for each route. EIGRP uses a math equation and a composite metric, making the exact metric value hard to predict.

The EIGRP Metric Calculation

The EIGRP composite metric means that EIGRP feeds multiple inputs (called metric components) into the math equation. By default, EIGRP feeds two metric components into the calculation: bandwidth and delay. (EIGRP supports also using the interface load and interface reliability in the metric calculation, although Cisco recommends against using either.) EIGRP also advertises the maximum transmission unit (MTU) associated with the route—that is, the longest IP packet allowed over the route—but does not use the MTU when calculating the metric.

NOTE   Past documents and books often stated that EIGRP, and its predecessor, IGRP, also could use MTU as a part of the metric, but MTU cannot be used and was never considered as part of the calculation.

EIGRP's metric calculation formula actually helps describe some of the key points about the composite metric. (In real life, you seldom if ever need to sit down and calculate what a router will calculate with this formula.) The formula, assuming that the default settings that tell the router to use just bandwidth and delay, is as follows:

$$\text{Metric} = \left(\left(\frac{10^7}{\text{least-bandwidth}} \right) + \text{cumulative-delay} \right) * 256$$

In this formula, the term *least-bandwidth* represents the lowest-bandwidth link in the route, using a unit of kilobits per second. For instance, if the slowest link in a route is a 10-Mbps Ethernet link, the first part of the formula is $10^7 / 10^4$, which equals 1000. You use 10^4 in the formula because 10 Mbps is equal to 10,000 Kbps (10^4 Kbps).

The cumulative-delay value used in the formula is the sum of all the delay values for all outgoing interfaces in the route, with a unit of "tens of microseconds."

Using these two inputs helps EIGRP pick the best route with a little more balance than does OSPF. Using the least bandwidth lets EIGRP avoid routes with the slowest individual links, which are usually the links with the most congestion. At the same time, the delay part of the equation adds the delay for every link, so that routes with a large number of links will be relatively less desirable than a route with fewer links.

You can set both bandwidth and delay for each link, using the cleverly named **bandwidth** and **delay** interface subcommands.

NOTE   Most **show** commands, including **show ip eigrp topology** and **show interfaces**, list delay settings as the number of microseconds of delay. Note that the EIGRP metric formula uses a unit of tens of microseconds.

An Example of Calculated EIGRP Metrics

Now that you have an idea of how the router's EIGRP math works, next consider an example that connects what a router learns in an EIGRP update message, local configuration settings, and the calculation of the metric for a single route.

A local router must consider the information received from the neighboring router and its local interface settings. First, EIGRP update messages list the subnet number and mask, along with all the metric components: the cumulative delay, minimum bandwidth, along with the other usually unused metric components. The local router then considers the bandwidth and delay settings on the interface on which the update was received, and calculates a new metric.

For example, Figure 9-10 shows router R1 learning about subnet 10.1.3.0/24 from router R2. The EIGRP update message from R2 lists a minimum bandwidth of 100,000 Kbps, and a cumulative delay of 100 microseconds. R1's S0/1 interface has an interface bandwidth set to 1544 Kbps—the default bandwidth on a serial link—and a delay of 20,000 microseconds.

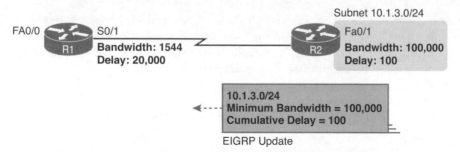

Figure 9-10   *How R1 Calculates Its EIGRP Metric for 10.1.3.0/24*

Next, consider how R1 thinks about the least bandwidth part of the calculation. R1 discovers that its S0/1 interface bandwidth (1544 Kbps, or 1.544 Mbps) is less than the advertised minimum bandwidth of 100,000 Kbps, or 100 Mbps. R1 needs to use this new, slower bandwidth in the metric calculation. (If R1's S0/1 interface had a bandwidth of 100,000 Kbps or more in this case, R1 would instead use the minimum bandwidth listed in the EIGRP Update from R2.)

As for interface delay, the router always adds its interface delay to the delay listed in the EIGRP Update. However, the unit for delay can be a bit of a challenge. The units, and their use, are as follows:

Unit of microseconds: Listed in the output of **show** commands like **show interfaces** and **show ip eigrp topology**, and in the EIGRP update messages.

Unit of tens-of-microseconds: Used by the interface mode configuration command (**delay**), with which to set the delay, and in the EIGRP metric calculation.

Because of this weird difference in units, when looking at the delay, make sure you keep the units straight. In this particular example:

- R1 received an update that lists delay of 100 (microseconds), which R1 converts to the equivalent 10 tens of microseconds before using it in the formula.

- R1 sees its S0/1 interface setting of 2000 tens of microseconds, so for the purposes of the calculation, R1 adds 10 tens of microseconds for a total delay of 2010 tens of microseconds.

This example results in the following metric calculation:

$$\text{Metric} = \left(\left(\frac{10^7}{1544} \right) + (10 + 2000) \right) * 256 = 2,172,416$$

> **NOTE** For those of you who repeat this math at home, IOS rounds down the division in this formula to the nearest integer before performing the rest of the formula. In this case, $10^7 / 1544$ is rounded down to 6476, before adding the 2010 and then multiplying by 256.

If multiple possible routes to subnet 10.1.3.0/24 existed, router R1 also calculates the metric for those routes and chooses the route with the best (lowest) metric to be added to the routing table.

> **NOTE** The examples in this chapter show routers with gigabit interfaces, which default their delay settings to 10 microseconds. However, IOS adjusts the delay based on the actual speed of a LAN interface. In the examples in this chapter and the next, all the LAN interfaces happen to run at 100 Mbps, making the delay be 100 microseconds.

Caveats with Bandwidth on Serial Links

EIGRP's robust metric gives it the ability to choose routes that include more router hops but with faster links. However, to ensure that the right routes are chosen, engineers must take care to configure meaningful bandwidth and delay settings. In particular, serial links default to a bandwidth of 1544 and a delay of 20,000 microseconds, as used in the example shown in Figure 9-10. However, IOS cannot automatically change the bandwidth and delay settings based on the Layer 1 speed of a serial link. So, using default bandwidth and delay settings, particularly the bandwidth setting on serial links, can lead to problems.

Figure 9-11 shows the problem with using default bandwidth settings and how EIGRP uses the better (faster) route when the bandwidth is set correctly. The figure focuses on router B's route to subnet 10.1.1.0/24 in each case. In the left side of the figure, all serial interfaces use defaults, even though the top serial link actually runs at a slow 64 Kbps. The right side of the figure shows the results when the slow serial link's **bandwidth** command is changed to reflect the correct (slow) speed.

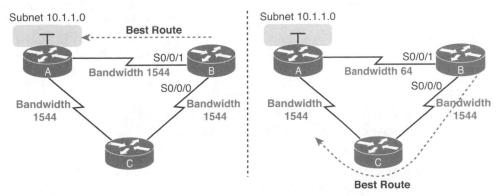

Figure 9-11 *Impact of the Bandwidth on EIGRP's Metric Calculation*

Generally, a good metric strategy for networks that use EIGRP is to set the WAN bandwidth to match the actual Layer 1 speed, use defaults for LAN interfaces, and EIGRP will usually choose the best routes.

EIGRP Convergence

Now that you have seen the details of how EIGRP forms neighbor relationships, exchanges routing information, and calculates the best route, the rest of this section looks at the most interesting part of EIGRP: EIGRP's work to converge to a new loop-free route.

Loop avoidance poses one of the most difficult problems with any dynamic routing protocol. DV protocols overcome this problem with a variety of tools, some of which create a large portion of the minutes-long convergence time after a link failure. LS protocols overcome this problem by having each router keep a full topology of the network, so by running a rather involved mathematical model, a router can avoid any loops.

EIGRP avoids loops by keeping some basic topological information, while keeping much less information as compared to LS protocols like OSPF. EIGRP keeps a record of each possible next-hop router for alternate routes, and some metric details related to those routes, but no information about the topology beyond the next-hop routers. This sparser topology information does not require the sophisticated shortest path first (SPF) algorithm, but it does allow quick convergence to loop-free routes.

Feasible Distance and Reported Distance

First, before getting into how EIGRP converges, you need to know a few additional EIGRP terms. With EIGRP, a local router needs to consider its own calculated metric for each route, but at the same time, the local router considers the next-hop router's calculated metric for that same destination subnet. And EIGRP has special terms for those metrics, as follows:

- **Feasible Distance (FD):** The local router's metric of the best route to reach a subnet, as calculated on the local router
- **Reported Distance (RD):** The next-hop router's best metric for that same subnet

As usual, the definition makes more sense with an example. Using the same advertisement as in earlier Figure 9-10, Figure 9-12 shows the two calculations done by R1. One calculation finds R1's own metric (FD) for its one route for subnet 10.1.3.0/24, as discussed around Figure 9-10. The other uses the metric components in the update received from R2, to calculate what R2 would have calculated for R2's metric to reach this same subnet. R1's second calculation based on R2's information—a slowest bandwidth of 100,000 Kbps and a cumulative delay of 100 microseconds—is R1's RD for this route.

Following the steps in the figure:

1. R2 calculates its own metric (its FD) for R2's route for 10.1.3.0/24, based on a bandwidth of 100,000 Kbps and a delay of 100 microseconds.
2. R2 sends the EIGRP update that lists 10.1.3.0/24, with these same metric components.
3. R1 calculates the RD for this route, using the same math R2 used at Step 1, using the information in the update message from Step 2.
4. R1 calculates its own metric, from R1's perspective, by considering the bandwidth and delay of R1's S0/1 interface, as discussed earlier around Figure 9-10.

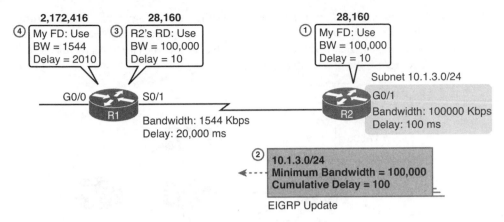

Figure 9-12 *How R1 Calculates RD and FD for 10.1.3.0/24*

In fact, based on the information in Figure 9-12, R2's FD to reach subnet 10.1.3.0/24, which is also R1's RD to reach 10.1.3.0/24, could be easily calculated:

$$\left(\left(\frac{10^7}{100,000}\right) + (10)\right) * 256 = 28,160$$

The EIGRP convergence process uses one of two branches in its logic, based on whether the failed route does or does not have a *feasible successor* route. The decision of whether a router has a feasible successor route depends on the FD and RD values of the competing routes to reach a given subnet. The next topic defines this concept of a feasible successor route and discusses what happens in that case.

EIGRP Successors and Feasible Successors

EIGRP calculates the metric for each route to reach each subnet. For a particular subnet, the route with the best metric is called the successor, with the router filling the IP routing table with this successor route. (This successor route's metric is called the feasible distance, as introduced earlier.)

Of the other routes to reach that same subnet—routes whose metrics were larger than the FD for the successor route—EIGRP needs to determine which alternate route can be used immediately if the currently best route fails, without causing a routing loop. EIGRP runs a simple algorithm to identify which routes could be used, keeping these loop-free backup routes in its topology table and using them if the currently best route fails. These alternative, immediately usable routes are called *feasible successor* routes because they can feasibly be used as the new successor route when the previous successor route fails.

A router determines whether a route is a feasible successor based on the feasibility condition:

If a nonsuccessor route's RD is less than the FD, the route is a feasible successor route.

Although it is technically correct, this definition is much more understandable with an example. Figure 9-13 begins an example in which router E chooses its best route to subnet 1. Router E learns three routes to subnet 1, from Routers B, C, and D. The figure shows the metrics as calculated on router E, as listed in router E's EIGRP topology table. Router E finds that the route through Router D has the lowest metric, making that route E's successor route for subnet 1. Router E adds that route to its routing table, as shown. The FD is the metric calculated for this route, a value of 14,000 in this case.

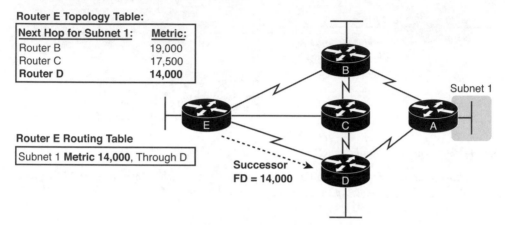

Figure 9-13 *Route Through Router D is the Successor Route to Subnet 1*

At the same time, EIGRP on router E decides whether either of the other two routes to subnet 1 can be used immediately if the route through router D fails for whatever reason. Only a feasible successor route can be used. To meet the feasibility condition, the alternate route's RD must be less than the FD of the successor route. Figure 9-14 shows an updated version of Figure 9-13. Router E uses the following logic to determine that the route through router B is not a feasible successor route, but the route through router C is, as follows:

- Router E compares the FD of 14,000 to the RD of the route through B (15,000). The RD is worse than the FD, so this route is not a feasible successor.

- Router E compares the FD of 14,000 to the RD of the route through C (13,000). The RD is better than the FD, making this route a feasible successor.

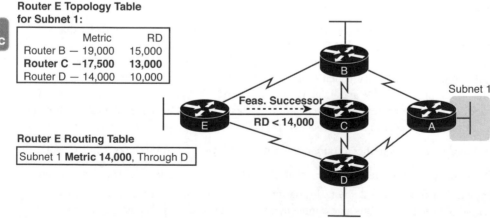

Figure 9-14 *Route Through Router C Is a Feasible Successor*

If the route to subnet 1 through router D fails, Router E can immediately put the route through router C into the routing table without fear of creating a loop. Convergence occurs almost instantly in this case.

The Query and Reply Process

When a route fails, and the route has no feasible successor, EIGRP uses a distributed algorithm called *Diffusing Update Algorithm* (DUAL) to choose a replacement route. DUAL sends queries looking for a loop-free route to the subnet in question. When the new route is found, DUAL adds it to the routing table.

The EIGRP DUAL process simply uses messages to confirm that a route exists, and would not create a loop, before deciding to replace a failed route with an alternative route. For instance, in Figure 9-14, imagine that both Routers C and D fail. Router E does not have any remaining feasible successor route for subnet 1, but there is an obvious physically available path through Router B. To use the route, Router E sends EIGRP *query* messages to its working neighbors (in this case, Router B). Router B's route to subnet 1 is still working fine, so router B replies to Router E with an EIGRP *reply* message, simply stating the details of the working route to subnet 1 and confirming that it is still viable. Router E can then add a new route to subnet 1 to its routing table, without fear of a loop.

Replacing a failed route with a feasible successor takes a very short amount of time, usually less than a second or two. When queries and replies are required, convergence can take slightly longer, but in most networks, convergence can still occur in less than 10 seconds.

9

Exam Preparation Tasks

Review All the Key Topics

Review the most important topics from this chapter, noted with the Key Topic icon. Table 9-4 lists these key topics and where each is discussed.

Table 9-4   Key Topics for Chapter 9

Key Topic Element	Description	Page Number
List	Key comparison points for EIGRP versus other routing protocols	270
Table 9-2	Table comparing IGPs	271
List	Breakdown of the term distance vector	272
Figure 9-6	Example of split horizon	275
Table 9-3	More comparisons of IGPs	277
List	Reasons why EIGRP routers are prevented from becoming neighbors	279
Figure 9-9	Depicts the normal progression through neighbor discovery, full routing updates, ongoing Hellos, and partial updates	280
List	Definitions of feasible distance and reported distance	284
Definition	Feasibility condition	285
Figure 9-14	Example of how routers determine which routes are feasible successors	286

Complete the Tables and Lists from Memory

Print a copy of DVD Appendix D, "Memory Tables," or at least the section for this chapter, and complete the tables and lists from memory. DVD Appendix E, "Memory Tables Answer Key," includes completed tables and lists to check your work.

Definitions of Key Terms

After your first reading of the chapter, try to define these key terms, but do not be concerned about getting them all correct at that time. Chapter 22 directs you in how to use these terms for late-stage preparation for the exam.

convergence, distance vector, interior gateway protocol (IGP), partial update, poison reverse, poisoned route, split horizon, triggered update, feasibility condition, feasible distance, feasible successor, full update, reported distance, successor

This chapter covers the following exam topics:

IP Routing Technologies

Configure and verify EIGRP (single AS)

Feasible distance / feasible successors /administrative distance

Feasibility condition

Metric composition

Router ID

Auto summary

Path selection

Load balancing

Equal

Unequal

Passive interface

Differentiate methods of routing and routing protocols

administrative distance

split horizon

metric

next hop

CHAPTER 10

Implementing EIGRP for IPv4

Whereas the preceding chapter looked solely at Enhanced Interior Gateway Routing Protocol (EIGRP) concepts, this chapter looks at the details of making it work in a Cisco router.

This chapter works through a variety of EIGRP configuration options. It starts with the most fundamental EIGRP configuration options. This chapter also works through a few less-common configuration tasks, such as how to configure unequal-metric load balancing, as well as the autosummary feature, which might sound great, but which today is mostly a potential area for causing problems.

Throughout this chapter, the text moves back and forth between the configuration and the related commands to verify that the configured feature is working. In particular, this chapter takes a careful look at how to look for the feasible distance, reported distance, and find the successor and feasible successor routes.

"Do I Know This Already?" Quiz

Use the "Do I Know This Already?" quiz to help decide whether you might want to skim this chapter, or a major section, moving more quickly to the Exam Preparation Tasks section near the end of the chapter. You can find the answers at the bottom of the page following the quiz. For thorough explanations, see DVD Appendix C, "Answers to the 'Do I Know This Already?' Quizzes."

Table 10-1 "Do I Know This Already?" Foundation Topics Section-to-Question Mapping

Foundation Topics Section	Questions
Core EIGRP Configuration and Verification	1–4
EIGRP Metrics, Successors, and Feasible Successors	5–6
Other EIGRP Configuration Settings	7

1. Which of the following **network** commands, following the command **router eigrp 1**, tells this router to start using EIGRP on interfaces whose IP addresses are 10.1.1.1, 10.1.100.1, and 10.1.120.1? (Choose two answers.)

    a. network 10.0.0.0

    b. network 10.1.1x.0

    c. network 10.0.0.0 0.255.255.255

    d. network 10.0.0.0 255.255.255.0

2. Routers R1 and R2 attach to the same VLAN with IP addresses 10.0.0.1 and 10.0.0.2, respectively. R1 is configured with the commands **router eigrp 99** and **network 10.0.0.0**. Which of the following commands might be part of a working EIGRP configuration on R2 that ensures that the two routers become neighbors and exchange routes? (Choose two answers.)

   a. network 10

   b. network 10.0.0.1 0.0.0.0

   c. network 10.0.0.2 0.0.0.0

   d. network 10.0.0.0

3. In the **show ip route** command, what code designation implies that a route was learned with EIGRP?

   a. E

   b. I

   c. G

   d. D

4. Examine the following excerpt from a **show** command on router R1:

```
EIGRP-IPv4 Neighbors for AS(1)
H    Address             Interface         Hold Uptime    SRTT   RTO  Q   Seq
                                           (sec)          (ms)        Cnt Num
1    10.1.4.3            Se0/0/1           13 00:05:49    2      100  0   29
0    10.1.5.2            Se0/0/0           12 00:05:49    2      100  0   39
```

Which of the following answers is true about this router based on this output?

   a. Address 10.1.4.3 identifies a working neighbor based on that neighbor's current EIGRP router ID.

   b. Address 10.1.5.2 identifies a router that may or may not become an EIGRP neighbor at some point after both routers check all neighbor requirements.

   c. Address 10.1.5.2 identifies a working neighbor based on that neighbor's interface IP address on the link between R1 and that neighbor.

   d. Address 10.1.4.3 identifies R1's own IP address on interface S0/0/1.

5. Examine the following excerpt from a router's CLI:

```
P 10.1.1.0/24, 1 successors, FD is 2172416
          via 10.1.6.3 (2172416/28160), Serial0/1
          via 10.1.4.2 (2684416/2284156), Serial0/0
          via 10.1.5.4 (2684416/2165432), Serial1/0
```

Which of the following identifies a next-hop IP address on a feasible successor route?

   a. 10.1.6.3

   b. 10.1.4.2

   c. 10.1.5.4

   d. It cannot be determined from this command output.

6. Router R1's EIGRP process knows of three possible routes to subnet 1. One route is a successor, and one is a feasible successor. R1 is not using the **variance** command to allow for unequal cost load balancing. Which of the following commands happen to show information about the feasible successor route, including its metric, whether as EIGRP topology information or as an IPv4 route?

    a. show ip eigrp topology

    b. show ip eigrp database

    c. show ip route eigrp

    d. show ip eigrp interfaces

7. Router R1 has four routes to subnet 2. The one successor route has a metric of 100, and the one feasible successor route has a metric of 350. The other routes have metrics of 450 and 550. R1's EIGRP configuration includes the **variance 5** command. Choose the answer that refers to the highest-metric route to subnet 2 that will be visible in the output of the **show ip route eigrp** command on R1.

    a. The successor route (metric 100)

    b. The feasible successor route (metric 350)

    c. The route with metric 450

    d. The route with metric 550

10

Foundation Topics

Core EIGRP Configuration and Verification

This first of three major sections of the chapter starts the discussion of EIGRP by showing the most commonly used parts of EIGRP configuration. As is usual with this book's implementation chapters, this section begins with configuration topics, followed by verification.

EIGRP Configuration

EIGRP configuration closely resembles OSPF configuration. The **router eigrp** command enables EIGRP and puts the user in EIGRP configuration mode, in which one or more **network** commands are configured. For each interface matched by a **network** command, EIGRP tries to discover neighbors on that interface, and EIGRP advertises the subnet connected to the interface.

The following configuration checklist outlines the main configuration tasks covered in this chapter:

Step 1. Enter EIGRP configuration mode and define the EIGRP autonomous system number (ASN) by using the **router eigrp** *as-number* global command.

Step 2. Configure one or more **network** *ip-address* [*wildcard-mask*] router subcommands. This enables EIGRP on any matched interface and causes EIGRP to advertise the connected subnet.

Step 3. (Optional) Set the EIGRP router ID (RID) explicitly with the **eigrp router-id** *value* router subcommand.

Step 4. (Optional) Change the interface Hello and hold timers using the **ip hello-interval eigrp** *asn time* and **ip hold-time eigrp** *asn time* interface subcommands.

Step 5. (Optional) Impact metric calculations by tuning bandwidth and delay using the **bandwidth** *value* and **delay** *value* interface subcommands.

Step 6. (Optional) Configure support for multiple equal-cost routes using the **maximum-paths** *number* and **variance** *multiplier* router subcommands.

Step 7. (Optional) Enable automatic summarization of routes at the boundaries of classful IPv4 networks using the **auto-summary** router subcommand.

Example 10-1 begins the configuration discussion with the simplest possible EIGRP configuration. This configuration uses as many defaults as possible, but it does enable EIGRP on each router on all the interfaces shown in Figure 10-1. All three routers can use the exact same configuration, with only two commands required on each router.

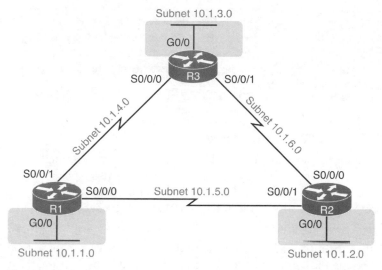

Figure 10-1 *Sample Internetwork Used in Most of the EIGRP Examples*

Example 10-1 *EIGRP Configuration on All Three Routers in Figure 10-1*

```
router eigrp 1
 network 10.0.0.0
```

This simple configuration only uses two parameters that the network engineer must choose: the autonomous system number and the classful network number in the **network** command.

The actual ASN does not matter, but all the routers must use the same ASN in the **router eigrp** command. For instance, they all use **router eigrp 1** in this example. (Routers that use different ASNs will not become EIGRP neighbors.) The range of valid ASNs is 1 through 65,535, which is the same range of valid process IDs with the **router ospf** command.

The EIGRP **network** commands allows two syntax options: one with a wildcard mask at the end and one without, as shown with Example 10-1's **network 10.0.0.0** command. With no wildcard mask listed, this command must list a classful network (a Class A, B, or C network number). Once configured, this command tells the router to do the following:

- Look for that router's own interfaces with addresses in that classful network
- Enable EIGRP on those interfaces

Once enabled, EIGRP starts advertising about the subnet connected to an interface. It also starts sending Hello messages and listening for incoming Hello messages, trying to form neighbor relationships with other EIGRP routers.

> **NOTE** Interestingly, on real routers, you can type an EIGRP **network** *number* command and use a dotted-decimal number that is not a classful network number; in that case, IOS does not issue an error message. However, IOS changes the number you typed to be the classful network number in which that number resides. For example, IOS changes the **network 10.1.1.1** command to **network 10.0.0.0**.

Configuring EIGRP Using a Wildcard Mask

The EIGRP **network** command syntax without the wildcard mask, as shown in Example 10-1, may be exactly what an engineer wants to use, but it also might prove a bit clumsy. For instance, if an engineer wants to enable EIGRP on G0/0, and not on G0/1, and they both have IP addresses in Class A network 10.0.0.0, the **network 10.0.0.0** EIGRP subcommand would match both interfaces, instead of just G0/0.

IOS has a second option for the EIGRP **network** command that uses a wildcard mask so that the engineer can match exactly the correct interface IP addresses intended. In this case, the **network** command does not have to list a classful **network** number. Instead, IOS matches an interface IP address that would be matched if the address and wildcard mask in the **network** command were part of an access control list (ACL). The logic works just like an ACL address and wildcard mask, and just like the address/mask logic in the OSPF **network** commands discussed in Chapter 8, "Implementing OSPF for IPv4."

For example, looking back at Figure 10-1, router R3 has IP addresses in three subnets: 10.1.3.0/24, 10.1.4.0/24, and 10.1.6.0/24. Example 10-2 shows an alternate EIGRP configuration for router R3 that uses a **network** command to match the range of addresses in each subnet for R3's three connected subnets. With a subnet mask of /24, each of the **network** commands uses a wildcard mask of 0.0.0.255, with an address parameter of the subnet ID off one of R3's interfaces.

Example 10-2 *Using Wildcard Masks with EIGRP Configuration*

```
R3(config)# router eigrp 1
R3(config-router)# network 10.1.3.0 0.0.0.255
R3(config-router)# network 10.1.4.0 0.0.0.255
R3(config-router)# network 10.1.6.0 0.0.0.255
```

Alternatively, R3 could have matched each interface with commands that use a wildcard mask of 0.0.0.0, listing the specific IP address of each interface. For instance, the **network 10.1.3.3 0.0.0.0** command would match R3's LAN interface address of 10.1.3.3, enabling EIGRP on that one interface.

Verifying EIGRP Core Features

Like OSPF, EIGRP uses three tables to match its three major blocks of logic: a neighbor table, a topology table, and the IPv4 routing table. But before EIGRP even attempts to build these tables, IOS must connect the configuration logic to its local interfaces. Once enabled on an interface, a router can then start to build its three tables.

The next several pages walk through the verification steps to confirm a working internetwork that uses EIGRP. Figure 10-2 shows the progression of concepts from top to bottom on the left, with a reference for the various **show** commands on the right. The topics to follow use that same sequence.

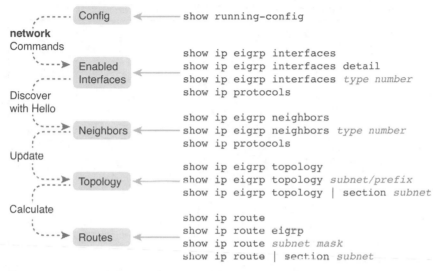

Figure 10-2 *Roadmap of Topics (Left) and Verification Commands (Right)*

NOTE All the upcoming verification examples list output taken from the routers in Figure 10-1. From that figure, routers R1 and R2 use the EIGRP configuration Example 10-1, and router R3 uses the configuration shown in Example 10-2. Also, note that all routers use gigabit LAN interfaces, but run at 100 Mbps due to their connections to the switches; this fact impacts the metrics to a small degree.

Finding the Interfaces on Which EIGRP is Enabled

First, each router must enable EIGRP on the correct interfaces. Example 10-3 begins the verification process by connecting the configuration to the router interfaces on which EIGRP is enabled. IOS gives us three ways to find the list of interfaces:

■ Use **show running-config** to look at the EIGRP and interface configuration, and apply the same logic as EIGRP to find the list of interfaces on which EIGRP should be enabled.

■ Use **show ip protocols** to list a shorthand version of the EIGRP configuration, to again apply the same logic as EIGRP and predict the list of interfaces.

■ Use **show ip eigrp interfaces** to list the interfaces on which the router has actually enabled EIGRP.

Of these three options, only the **show ip eigrp interfaces** command gives us the true list of interfaces as actually chosen by the router. The other two methods give us the configuration, and let us make an educated guess. (Both are important!)

The **show ip eigrp interfaces** command lists EIGRP-enabled interfaces directly, and briefly, with one line per interface. Alternatively, the **show ip eigrp interfaces detail** command lists much more detail per interface, including the Hello and Hold Intervals, as well as noting whether split horizon is enabled. Example 10-3 shows an example of both from router R1.

Example 10-3 *Looking for Interfaces on Which EIGRP Has Been Enabled on R1*

```
R1# show ip eigrp interfaces
EIGRP-IPv4 Interfaces for AS(1)
                    Xmit Queue   PeerQ       Mean Pacing Time  Multicast  Pending
Interface Peers  Un/Reliable Un/Reliable  SRTT Un/Reliable  Flow Timer  Routes
Gi0/0       0        0/0         0/0          0     0/0          0          0
Se0/0/0     1        0/0         0/0          2     0/16         50         0
Se0/0/1     1        0/0         0/0          1     0/15         50         0


R1# show ip eigrp interfaces detail S0/0/0
EIGRP-IPv4 Interfaces for AS(1)
                    Xmit Queue   PeerQ       Mean Pacing Time  Multicast  Pending
Interface Peers  Un/Reliable Un/Reliable  SRTT Un/Reliable  Flow Timer  Routes
Se0/0/0     1        0/0         0/0          2     0/16         50         0
  Hello-interval is 5, Hold-time is 15
  Split-horizon is enabled
! lines omitted for brevity
```

Note that the first command, **show ip eigrp interfaces**, lists all interfaces for which EIGRP is enabled and for which the router is currently sending Hello messages trying to find new EIGRP neighbors. R1, with a single **network 10.0.0.0** EIGRP subcommand, enables EIGRP on all three of its interfaces (per Figure 10-1). The second command lists more detail per interface, including the local router's own Hello interval and hold time and the split-horizon setting.

Note that neither command lists information about interfaces on which EIGRP is not enabled. For instance, had EIGRP not been enabled on S0/0/0, the **show ip eigrp interfaces detail S0/0/0** command would have simply listed no information under the heading lines. The shorter output of the **show ip eigrp interface** command omits interfaces on which EIGRP is not enabled.

Also, note that the **show ip eigrp interfaces...** command does not list information for passive interfaces. Like Open Shortest Path First (OSPF), EIGRP supports the **passive-interface** *type number* subcommand. This command tells EIGRP to not discover and form neighbor relationships on the listed interface. However, EIGRP still advertises about the subnet connected to the interface.

In summary, the **show ip eigrp interfaces** command lists information about interfaces enabled by EIGRP, but it does not list interfaces made passive for EIGRP.

The other two methods to find the EIGRP-enabled interfaces require an examination of the configuration and some thinking about the EIGRP rules. In real life, **show ip eigrp interfaces** is the place to start, but for the exam, you might have just the configuration, or you might not even have that. As an alternative, the **show ip protocols** command lists many details about EIGRP, including a shorthand repeat of the EIGRP **network** configuration commands. Example 10-4 lists these commands as gathered from router R1.

Example 10-4 *Using* show ip protocols *to Derive the List of EIGRP-Enabled Interfaces on R1*

```
R1# show ip protocols
*** IP Routing is NSF aware ***


Routing Protocol is "eigrp 1"
  Outgoing update filter list for all interfaces is not set
  Incoming update filter list for all interfaces is not set
  Default networks flagged in outgoing updates
  Default networks accepted from incoming updates
  EIGRP-IPv4 Protocol for AS(1)
    Metric weight K1=1, K2=0, K3=1, K4=0, K5=0
    NSF-aware route hold timer is 240
    Router-ID: 10.1.5.1
    Topology : 0 (base)
      Active Timer: 3 min
      Distance: internal 90 external 170
      Maximum path: 4
      Maximum hopcount 100
      Maximum metric variance 1

  Automatic Summarization: disabled
  Maximum path: 4
  Routing for Networks:
    10.0.0.0
  Routing Information Sources:
    Gateway         Distance      Last Update
    10.1.4.3              90      00:22:32
    10.1.5.2              90      00:22:32
  Distance: internal 90 external 170
```

To see the shorthand repeat of the EIGRP configuration, look toward the end of the example, for under the heading Routing for Networks. In this case, the next line that lists 10.0.0.0 is a direct reference to the **network 10.0.0.0** configuration command shown in Example 10-1. For configurations that use the wildcard mask option, the format differs a little, as shown in Example 10-5, which shows an excerpt of the **show ip protocols** command from R3. R3 uses the three **network** commands shown earlier in Example 10-2.

10

Example 10-5   *Seeing the Configured network Commands with show ip protocols*

```
R3# show ip protocols
! Lines omitted for brevity


  Automatic Summarization: disabled
  Maximum path: 4
  Routing for Networks:
    10.1.3.0/24
    10.1.4.0/24
    10.1.6.0/24
! Lines omitted for brevity
```

To interpret the meaning of the highlighted portions of this **show ip protocols** command, you have to do a little math. The output lists a number in the format of /x (in this case, /24). It represents a wildcard mask with x binary 0s, or in this case, 0.0.0.255.

Before moving on from the **show ip protocols** command, take a moment to read some of the other details of this command's output from Example 10-4. For instance, it lists the EIGRP router ID (RID), which for R1 is 10.1.5.1. EIGRP allocates its RID just like OSPF, based on the following:

1.   The value configured with the **eigrp router-id** *number* EIGRP subcommand

2.   The numerically highest IP address of an up/up loopback interface at the time the EIGRP process comes up

3.   The numerically highest IP address of a nonloopback interface at the time the EIGRP process comes up

The only difference compared to OSPF is that the EIGRP RID is configured with the **eigrp router-id** *value* router subcommand, whereas OSPF uses the **router-id** *value* subcommand.

Displaying EIGRP Neighbor Status

Once a router has enabled EIGRP on an interface, the router tries to discover neighboring routers by listening for EIGRP Hello messages. If two neighboring routers hear Hellos from each other and the required parameters match correctly, the routers become neighbors.

The best and most obvious command to list EIGRP neighbors is **show ip eigrp neighbors.** This command lists neighbors based on their interface IP address (and not based on their router ID, which is the convention with OSPF). The output also lists the local router's inter-face out which the neighbor is reachable.

For instance, Example 10-6 shows router R1's neighbors, listing a neighbor with IP address 10.1.4.3 (R3). It is reachable from R1's S0/0/1 interface according to the first highlighted line in the example.

Example 10-6   *Displaying EIGRP Neighbors from Router R1*

```
R1# show ip eigrp neighbors
EIGRP-IPv4 Neighbors for AS(1)
H   Address             Interface         Hold Uptime   SRTT   RTO  Q   Seq
                                          (sec)         (ms)       Cnt  Num
1   10.1.4.3            Se0/0/1           13 00:05:49    2    100  0   29
0   10.1.5.2            Se0/0/0           12 00:05:49    2    100  0   39
```

The right side of the output also lists some interesting statistics. The four rightmost columns have to do with RTP, as discussed back in Chapter 9, "Understanding EIGRP Concepts." The uptime lists the elapsed time since the neighbor relationship started. Finally, the hold time should be the current countdown from the Hold Interval (15 seconds in this case) down toward 0. In this case, with a Hello Interval of 5 and a Hold Interval of 15, this counter will vary from 15 down to 10 and then reset to 15 when the next Hello arrives.

Another less-obvious way to list EIGRP neighbors is the **show ip protocols** command. Look back again to Example 10-4, to the end of the **show ip protocols** command output from R1. That output under the heading Routing Information Sources lists the same two neighboring routers' IP addresses, as does the **show ip eigrp neighbors** command in Example 10-6.

Displaying the IPv4 Routing Table

Once EIGRP routers become neighbors, they exchange routing information, store it in their topology tables, and then they calculate their best IPv4 routes. This section skips past the verification steps for the EIGRP topology table, saving that for the second major topic in the chapter, as an end to itself. However, you should find the IP routing table verification steps somewhat familiar at this point. Example 10-7 shows a couple of examples from R1 in Figure 10-1: The first showing the entire IPv4 routing table and with the **show ip route eigrp** command at the end listing only EIGRP-learned routes.

Example 10-7   *IP Routing Table on Router R1 from Figure 10-1*

```
R1# show ip route
Codes: L - local, C - connected, S - static, R - RIP, M - mobile, B - BGP
       D - EIGRP, EX - EIGRP external, O - OSPF, IA - OSPF inter area
       N1 - OSPF NSSA external type 1, N2 - OSPF NSSA external type 2
       E1 - OSPF external type 1, E2 - OSPF external type 2
       i - IS-IS, su - IS-IS summary, L1 - IS-IS level-1, L2 - IS-IS level-2
       ia - IS-IS inter area, * - candidate default, U - per-user static route
       o - ODR, P - periodic downloaded static route, H - NHRP, l - LISP
       + - replicated route, % - next hop override

Gateway of last resort is not set

      10.0.0.0/8 is variably subnetted, 9 subnets, 2 masks
C        10.1.1.0/24 is directly connected, GigabitEthernet0/0
L        10.1.1.1/32 is directly connected, GigabitEthernet0/0
```

10

```
D          10.1.2.0/24 [90/2172416] via 10.1.5.2, 00:06:39, Serial0/0/0
D          10.1.3.0/24 [90/2172416] via 10.1.4.3, 00:00:06, Serial0/0/1
C          10.1.4.0/24 is directly connected, Serial0/0/1
L          10.1.4.1/32 is directly connected, Serial0/0/1
C          10.1.5.0/24 is directly connected, Serial0/0/0
L          10.1.5.1/32 is directly connected, Serial0/0/0
D          10.1.6.0/24 [90/2681856] via 10.1.5.2, 00:12:20, Serial0/0/0
                       [90/2681856] via 10.1.4.3, 00:12:20, Serial0/0/1


R1# show ip route eigrp
! Legend omitted for brevity


      10.0.0.0/8 is variably subnetted, 9 subnets, 2 masks
D          10.1.2.0/24 [90/2172416] via 10.1.5.2, 00:06:43, Serial0/0/0
D          10.1.3.0/24 [90/2172416] via 10.1.4.3, 00:00:10, Serial0/0/1   .
D          10.1.6.0/24 [90/2681856] via 10.1.5.2, 00:12:24, Serial0/0/0
                       [90/2681856] via 10.1.4.3, 00:12:24, Serial0/0/1
```

The **show ip route** and **show ip route eigrp** commands both list the EIGRP-learned routes with a D beside them. Cisco chose to use D to represent EIGRP because when EIGRP was created, the letter E was already being used for a now-extinct Exterior Gateway Protocol (EGP) routing protocol. Cisco chose the next-closest unused letter, D, to denote EIGRP-learned routes.

Next, take a moment to think about the EIGRP routes learned by R1 versus R1's connected routes. Six subnets exist in the design in Figure 10-1: three on the LANs, and three on the WANs. The first command in the example lists three of these subnets as connected routes (10.1.1.0/24, 10.1.4.0/24, and 10.1.5.0/24). The other three subnets appear as EIGRP-learned routes.

Finally, note that the two numbers in brackets for each route list the administrative distance and the composite metric, respectively. IOS uses the administrative distance to choose the better route when IOS learns multiple routes for the same subnet but from two different sources of routing information. Refer back to Chapter 8's "Administrative Distance" section for a review.

EIGRP Metrics, Successors, and Feasible Successors

Both OSPF and EIGRP use similar big ideas: enabling the protocol on the routers interfaces, forming neighbor relationships, building topology tables, and adding IPv4 routes to the routing table. These two routing protocols differ most in the topology data they create and use. As a link-state protocol, OSPF creates and saves a lot of topology data, enough data to model the entire network topology in an area. EIGRP saves different kinds of data, in less detail, and uses a completely different algorithm to analyze the data.

This second major section in this chapter focuses on the details of the EIGRP topology database and specifically on the key ideas stored in the database. To review, as defined in Chapter 9, an EIGRP successor route is a router's best route to reach a subnet. Any of the other possible loop-free routes that can be used if the successor route fails is called a feasible successor (FS) route. And all the information used to determine which route is the successor, FS, or neither, sits inside the EIGRP topology table.

This section demonstrates how to use **show** commands to identify successor routes and FS routes by looking at the EIGRP topology table. To make the discussion more interesting, the examples in this section use an expanded sample network, as shown in Figure 10-3.

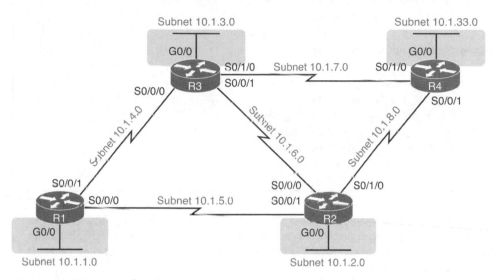

Figure 10-3 *Expanded Sample Internetwork*

Viewing the EIGRP Topology Table

To begin, first consider the EIGRP topology table in router R1, with this expanded network of Figure 10-3. The new network has five WAN and four LAN subnets, with multiple routes to reach each subnet. All the links use default bandwidth and delay settings. (Like the earlier examples, note that all router Gigabit interfaces happen to autonegotiate to use a speed of 100 Mbps, which changes the interface delay setting and therefore the EIGRP metric calculations.)

Example 10-8 begins the discussion with the output of the **show ip eigrp topology** command from R1. This command lists a few lines of information about each known subnet in R1's EIGRP topology table.

Example 10-8 *The EIGRP Topology Table on Router R1*

```
R1# show ip eigrp topology
EIGRP-IPv4 Topology Table for AS(1)/ID(10.1.5.1)
Codes: P - Passive, A - Active, U - Update, Q - Query, R - Reply,
       r - reply Status, s - sia Status


P 10.1.5.0/24, 1 successors, FD is 2169856
       via Connected, Serial0/0/0
```

```
P 10.1.7.0/24, 1 successors, FD is 2681856
        via 10.1.4.3 (2681856/2169856), Serial0/0/1
P 10.1.3.0/24, 1 successors, FD is 2172416
        via 10.1.4.3 (2172416/28160), Serial0/0/1
P 10.1.2.0/24, 1 successors, FD is 2172416
        via 10.1.5.2 (2172416/28160), Serial0/0/0
P 10.1.6.0/24, 2 successors, FD is 2681856
        via 10.1.4.3 (2681856/2169856), Serial0/0/1
        via 10.1.5.2 (2681856/2169856), Serial0/0/0
P 10.1.4.0/24, 1 successors, FD is 2169856
        via Connected, Serial0/0/1
P 10.1.33.0/24, 2 successors, FD is 2684416
        via 10.1.4.3 (2684416/2172416), Serial0/0/1
        via 10.1.5.2 (2684416/2172416), Serial0/0/0
P 10.1.1.0/24, 1 successors, FD is 28160
        via Connected, GigabitEthernet0/0
P 10.1.8.0/24, 1 successors, FD is 2681856
        via 10.1.5.2 (2681856/2169856), Serial0/0/0
```

First, look through all the output, and count the subnets, in the lines that align with the left edge of the example. Note that R1 lists a group of messages for all nine subnets, including the connected subnets off R1. EIGRP keeps its topology information about all the subnets, even the connected subnets.

Next, focus on the first highlighted entry, for subnet 10.1.3.0/24, the subnet off R3's LAN interface. The first line for a given subnet lists the subnet ID and mask. It also lists the number of successor routes, and the feasible distance (FD). (As a reminder, the FD is the metric of the successor route, which is the best route to reach a particular subnet.)

To help make sure the items are clear, Figure 10-4 breaks down these items, using these same details about subnet 10.1.3.0/24 from R1's EIGRP topology table.

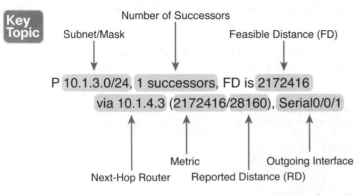

Figure 10-4 *Reference to Fields in the Output from* **show ip eigrp topology**

Continuing to focus on subnet 10.1.3.0/24 for a few more moments, the output lists one line per destination subnet and then one line per route below it, indented, beginning with the word *via*. In Figure 10-4, the main line (as usual) lists the subnet, prefix mask, the number of successor routes, and the FD. The second (indented) line lists information about the route, with the next-hop router (after the word *via*), and the outgoing interface. If the router puts this particular route into the IP routing table, the IP route would use this next-hop IP address and local outgoing interface in that route. Note that if EIGRP can list multiple such lines that begin with via if EIGRP has multiple possible routes for that subnet.

Finally, note that the **show ip eigrp topology** command also lists two calculated EIGRP metrics in parentheses. The first is the metric as calculated by the local router for that route. The second is the reported distance (RD): the metric calculated from the perspective of the next-hop router. In the example shown in Figure 10-4, the RD of 28,160 is R1's RD for that route, which is the metric on next-hop router 10.1.4.3 (R3).

Finding Successor Routes

Unfortunately, the **show ip eigrp topology** command does not make it obvious which routes are successor (in other words, best) routes and which ones are feasible successor (in other words, quickly used loop-free replacement) routes. The next few pages walk through how to look at the data in the output of this command and identify the successor and FS routes.

First, for perspective, note that the output in Example 10-8 happens to list only successor routes, with no feasible successor routes. With all default bandwidth and delay settings, no routes qualify as feasible successor routes in this network. Upcoming Example 10-11 changes some settings, causing some routes to have feasible successors. For now, just note that all routes listed in Example 10-8 are successor routes.

The best way to recognize successor routes is that the successor route has the same metric value as the FD. The first line of topology output for a subnet lists the FD (that is, the best metric among all the routes to reach that destination subnet). The successor route, by definition, has the best metric, so the successor route's metric should equal the FD. As shown in Figure 10-5, just look for the FD on the first line and then for the individual routes that have the same metric in the first number inside parentheses.

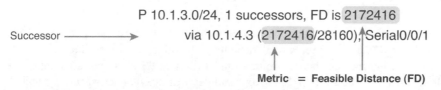

Figure 10-5 *Identifying the Successor: FD (First Line) = Metric (Second Line)*

When EIGRP calculates the metrics for all possible routes, sometimes one clear winner exists, so EIGRP chooses one successor route (as shown in Figure 10-5). However, in other cases, the metrics for competing routes for the same subnet tie. In that case, with default

EIGRP configuration settings, EIGRP supports a feature called *equal-cost load balancing*, which tells EIGRP to treat all the routes that tie as successor routes.

Example 10-9 shows two successor routes. The example shows an excerpt of the R1 EIGRP topology table for R1's route to subnet 10.1.33.0/24. That subnet exists off R4's LAN interface. In this case, R1 lists two routes, out two different interfaces to two different neighboring next-hop routers. Both routes list the same metric, which matches the FD (2,684,416), so both are successor routes.

Example 10-9   *Displaying Two Successor Routes on R1 for Subnet 10.1.33.0/24*

```
R1# show ip eigrp topology | section 10.1.33.0
P 10.1.33.0/24, 2 successors, FD is 2684416
        via 10.1.4.3 (2684416/2172416), Serial0/0/1
        via 10.1.5.2 (2684416/2172416), Serial0/0/0
```

In this case, with default settings, R1 would add both routes to its IP routing table. Later in this chapter, the section "EIGRP Maximum Paths and Variance" discusses some similar logic of how a router deals with somewhat equal-cost routes to the same subnet. That section also gives a little more insight into the equal-cost load-balancing option.

> **NOTE**   The command in Example 10-9 pipes the output of the **show ip eigrp topology** command to the **section** command. This process asks IOS to find a section or group of messages with the listed text (in this case, 10.1.33.0) and display only that group of messages. It is just a way to getting the desired subset of the output without listing the entire command.

Finding Feasible Successor Routes

By convention, the **show ip eigrp topology** lists both successor and feasible successor routes when both exist. The examples so far in this chapter, which used all default bandwidth and delay settings, simply did not happen to result in any FS routes. The next topic changes the configuration, creating a FS route, and then shows how to recognize this route in the topology database.

First, consider Example 10-9's listing of R1's topology data for subnet 10.1.33.0/24, the LAN subnet off R4. From R1's perspective, with all default bandwidth and delay settings, two routes are as identical as they can be. The route from R1 through R3 uses two serial links with default settings for bandwidth of 1544 Kbps and delay of 20,000 microseconds on all the serial links. The route from R1 through R2 also uses two serial links, also with default bandwidth and delay. As a result, R1 has the two equal-cost routes for subnet 10.1.33.0/24, as shown on the left side of Figure 10-6.

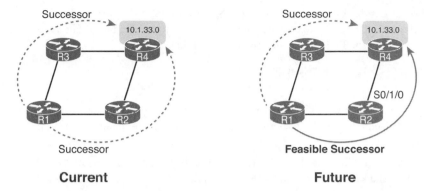

Figure 10-6 *Comparing Two Successor Routes to One Successor and One FS*

The next example makes the route through R2 worse than the route through R3, by simply lowering the bandwidth on R2's serial link connected to R4. Currently, the path R1-R2-R4 has, from R1's perspective, a slowest bandwidth of 1544 Kbps. By lowering the bandwidth to some other number lower than 1544 Kbps, the metrics of the two routes will no longer exactly tie. A slightly lower bandwidth will result in the upper R1-R3-R4 route being the only successor route, with the R1-R2-R4 route being a FS route.

First, to change the configuration to use a worse (slower) slowest bandwidth, Example 10-10 shows R2's S0/1/0 configuration being changed with the **bandwidth 1400** command.

Example 10-10 *Tuning EIGRP Routes by Changing Interface Bandwidth*

```
R2# configure terminal
Enter configuration commands, one per line.  End with CNTL/Z.
R2(config)# interface s0/1/0
R2(config-if)# bandwidth 1400
```

As soon as R2 changes its bandwidth, R2 sends a partial EIGRP update, as discussed back in Chapter 9. The other routers learn some new information, and they recalculate their own metrics, and the RD values, as appropriate. To see the differences, Example 10-11 repeats the **show ip eigrp topology | section 10.1.33.0** command on R1, as last seen in Example 10-9. In Example 10-9, that command showed R1 with two successor routes for this subnet. Now, in Example 10-11, R1 has only 1 successor route, but with the FS actually hidden there in the output, as explained after the example.

Example 10-11 *Viewing a Feasible Successor Route on R1 for 10.1.33.0/24*

```
R1# show ip eigrp topology | section 10.1.33.0
P 10.1.33.0/24, 1 successors, FD is 2684416
        via 10.1.4.3 (2684416/2172416), Serial0/0/1
        via 10.1.5.2 (2854912/2342912), Serial0/0/0
```

10

To see the feasible successor route, and why it is an FS, work through the various numbers in the output in Example 10-11. Or, work through that same output, repeated in Figure 10-7, with notes. In either case, the logic works like the notes in this list:

■ Per the first line, one successor route exists.

■ The FD is 2,684,416.

■ Of the two lines that begin with via—the two possible routes listed—the first route's metric of 2,684,416 equals the FD. As a result, this first line lists the details of the one successor route.

■ The other line that begins with via has a metric (first number in parentheses) of 2,854,912, which differs from the FD value of 2,684,416. As a result, this route is not a successor route.

■ The second line that begins with via has a reported distance (RD, the second number) of 2,342,912, which is less than the FD of 2,684,416. This second route meets the feasibility condition, making it a feasible successor route.

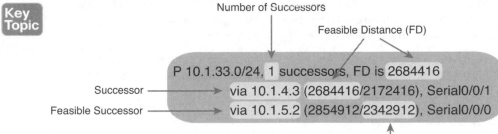

RD < FD: Meets Feasibility Condition!

Figure 10-7 *Identifying the Feasible Successor Route*

NOTE   The **show ip eigrp topology** command lists only successor and FS routes. To see other routes, use the **show ip eigrp topology all-links** command, which lists all routes, even those that are neither successor nor feasible successor routes.

Convergence Using the Feasible Successor Route

One motivation for EIGRP to have a FS concept is to help EIGRP converge very quickly, using a FS route immediately when a successor route fails. The next example shows the convergence process, with R1 losing its current successor route to 10.1.33.0/24, through R3, and replacing it with the FS route through R2, as shown in Figure 10-8.

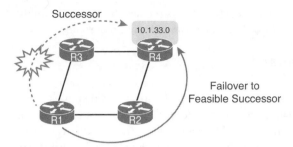

Figure 10-8 *Diagram of the Convergence Event Described in the Next Example*

Example 10-12 shows not only the net results of the failover and convergence, but also the process by using some **debug** messages. Be warned, some of the **debug** messages might not make a lot of sense. However, the example removes some of the less-useful messages, and highlights the more understandable output, to demonstrate what happens with the failover.

For this example, the link between R3 and R4 is disabled (**shutdown**). The **debug** messages on R1 show the effects of EIGRP's logic in changing routes. Pay particular attention to the timestamps on the debug messages, which amazingly all occur within the same millisecond.

Example 10-12 *Debug Messages During Convergence to the FS Route for Subnet 10.1.33.0/24*

```
!!!!!!!!!!!!!!!!!!!!!!!!!!!!!!!!!!!!!!!!!!!!!!!!!!!!!!!!!!!!!!!!!!!!!!!!!!!!!!!!!!!!
! Below, debug eigrp fsm is enabled, and then R3's S0/1/0 link to R4 is disabled,
! but not shown in the example text. SOME DEBUG MESSAGES are omitted to
! improve readability.
R1# debug eigrp fsm
EIGRP FSM Events/Actions debugging is on
R1#
*Nov 13 23:50:41.099: EIGRP-IPv4(1): Find FS for dest 10.1.33.0/24. FD is 2684416, RD
is 2684416 on tid 0
*Nov 13 23:50:41.099: EIGRP-IPv4(1):    10.1.4.3 metric 72057594037927935/72057594037
927936
*Nov 13 23:50:41.099: EIGRP-IPv4(1):    10.1.5.2 metric 2854912/2342912 found Dmin is
2854912
*Nov 13 23:50:41.099: DUAL: AS(1) RT installed 10.1.33.0/24 via 10.1.5.2
!
! Next, R1 lists a new successor route, to 10.1.5.2: R2.
R1# show ip eigrp topology | section 10.1.33.0
P 10.1.33.0/24, 1 successors, FD is 2854912
        via 10.1.5.2 (2854912/2342912), Serial0/0/0
R1# show ip route | section 10.1.33.0
D       10.1.33.0/24 [90/2854912] via 10.1.5.2, 00:16:50, Serial0/0/0
```

Finally, make sure to note the ending state of the convergence, as shown at the end of the example. The example shows R1's updated topology database entries for subnet 10.1.33.0/24, with a new successor, new FD (2,854,912 versus the old 2,684,416 shown in Example 10-10),

10

and a new next-hop router (R2, 10.1.5.2). The last command lists the new IPv4 route, with the new FD listed as the metric in brackets, and R2 (10.1.5.2) as the new next-hop router.

Examining the Metric Components

Most of the discussion about metrics in this chapter so far has centered on the composite EIGRP metric. However, EIGRP advertises different metric components, and then uses some of those components to calculate the composite metric. Before leaving this discussion about choosing successor routes (with the best metric), and FS routes (loop-free backup routes), all based on their composite metrics, this short topic shows how to look at the individual metric components stored by EIGRP.

When using the defaults (which Cisco recommends), EIGRP bases its composite metric on the minimum bandwidth link in a route and the total delay for all links in the route. However, the EIGRP routers still advertise all the metric components, which includes the link reliability and load. Example 10-13 lists the output from the **show ip eigrp topology 10.1.3.0/24** command on router R1, a command that lists the details of the EIGRP topology data for the routes for this subnet. The highlighted lines in the example list the composite metric as well as the individual components of the metric.

Example 10-13 *EIGRP Metric Components as Shown in the EIGRP Topology Database*

```
!!!!!!!!!!!!!!!!!!!!!!!!!!!!!!!!!!!!!!!!!!!!!!!!!!!!!!!!!!!!!!!!!!!!!!!!!!!!!!!!!!!!!
R1# show ip eigrp topology 10.1.3.0/24
EIGRP-IPv4 Topology Entry for AS(1)/ID(10.1.13.1) for 10.1.3.0/24
  State is Passive, Query origin flag is 1, 1 Successor(s), FD is 2172416
  Descriptor Blocks:
  10.1.4.3 (Serial0/0/1), from 10.1.4.3, Send flag is 0x0
      Composite metric is (2172416/28160), route is Internal
      Vector metric:
        Minimum bandwidth is 1544 Kbit
        Total delay is 20100 microseconds
        Reliability is 255/255
        Load is 1/255
        Minimum MTU is 1500
        Hop count is 1
        Originating router is 3.3.3.3
  10.1.5.2 (Serial0/0/0), from 10.1.5.2, Send flag is 0x0
      Composite metric is (2684416/2172416), route is Internal
      Vector metric:
        Minimum bandwidth is 1544 Kbit
        Total delay is 40100 microseconds
        Reliability is 255/255
        Load is 1/255
        Minimum MTU is 1500
        Hop count is 2
```

Other EIGRP Configuration Settings

So far, this chapter has focused on the core functions of EIGRP. The configuration details have been relatively sparse, just due to the nature of EIGRP. However, this chapter has spent a fair amount of time and effort to show the results of enabling EIGRP on the routers in a network, showing EIGRP working on interfaces, creating neighbor relationships, learning topology information, and ultimately adding routes to the IP routing table.

This third and final major section this chapter turns away from these core features. The topics in this section are either completely optional or have default settings that the chapter has not discussed so far. This section now examines this small set of other EIGRP topics, including load balancing, EIGRP metric tuning, and autosummary.

Load Balancing Across Multiple EIGRP Routes

Like OSPF, EIGRP supports the ability to put multiple equal-metric routes in the IPv4 routing table. Like OSPF, EIGRP defaults to support four such routes for each subnet, and it can be configured to other values using the **maximum-paths** *number* EIGRP subcommand. (Note that the maximum number of equal cost paths depends on the IOS version and router platform.)

In fact, Example 10-9, earlier in this chapter, showed just such an example, with router R1's route for subnet 10.1.33.0/24. Example 10-14 revisits that same scenario, this time with both the topology table and the IP routing table displayed. Due to the default EIGRP configuration setting of **maximum-paths 4**, R1 places both successor routes into R1's IP routing table.

Example 10-14   *R1's Routing Table with Multiple Equal-Cost EIGRP Routes*

```
R1# show ip eigrp topology | section 10.1.33.0
P 10.1.33.0/24, 2 successors, FD is 2684416
        via 10.1.4.3 (2684416/2172416), Serial0/0/1
        via 10.1.5.2 (2684416/2172416), Serial0/0/0

R1# show ip route | section 10.1.33.0
D       10.1.33.0/24 [90/2684416] via 10.1.5.2, 00:02:23, Serial0/0/0
                     [90/2684416] via 10.1.4.3, 00:02:23, Serial0/0/1
```

Although the ability to add multiple routes with exactly equal metrics may be useful, EIGRP often calculates similar metric values that do not happen to be exactly equal. EIGRP metrics often range into the millions, making it less likely that metrics would be exactly the same.

IOS also includes the concept *unequal-cost load balancing* using an EIGRP setting called *variance*, to overcome this problem. Variance allows routes whose metrics are relatively close in value to be considered equal, allowing multiple unequal-metric routes to the same subnet to be added to the routing table.

The **variance** *multiplier* EIGRP router subcommand defines an integer between 1 and 128. The router then multiplies the variance times a route's FD—the best metric with which to reach that subnet. Any FS routes whose metric is less than the product of the variance times the FD are considered to be equal routes and may be placed in the routing table, depending on the setting of the **maximum-paths** command.

The previous paragraph does summarize the rules for variance and unequal-cost load balancing, but working through the idea with an example works much better. To keep the numbers more obvious, Table 10-2 lists an example with small metric values. The table lists the metric for three routes to the same subnet, as calculated on router R4. The table also lists the neighboring routers' RD and the decision to add routes to the routing table based on various variance settings.

Table 10-2 Example of Routes Chosen as Equal Because of Variance

Next Hop	Metric	RD	Added to RT at Variance 1?	Added to RT at Variance 2?	Added to RT at Variance 3?
R1	50	30	Yes	Yes	Yes
R2	90	40	No	Yes	Yes
R3	120	60	No	No	No

Before considering the variance, note that in this case the route through R1 is the successor route because it has the lowest metric. This also means that the metric for the route through R1, 50, is the FD. The route through R2 is an FS route because its RD of 40 is less than the FD of 50. The route through R3 is not an FS route because its RD of 60 is more than the FD of 50.

At a default configuration of **variance 1**, the metrics must be exactly equal to be considered equal, so only the successor route is added to the routing table.

With the **variance 2** command configured, the FD (50) is multiplied by the variance (2) for a product of 100. The route through R2, with metric 90, is less than the calculated variance × FD = 100, so R4 adds the route through R2 to the routing table as well. The router can then load balance traffic across these two routes. The third route's metric, 120, is more than the calculated variance × FD = 100, so it is not added to the routing table.

With the **variance 3** command configured, the product of the FD (50) times 3 results in a product of 150, and all three routes' calculated metrics are less than 150. However, the route through R3 is not an FS route, so it cannot be added to the routing table for fear of causing a routing loop.

The following list summarizes the key points about variance:

- The variance is multiplied by the current FD (the metric of the best route to reach the subnet).
- Any FS routes whose calculated metric is less than or equal to the product of variance times the FD are added to the IP routing table, assuming that the **maximum-paths** setting allows more routes.
- Routes that are neither successor nor FS can never be added to the IP routing table, regardless of the variance setting, because doing so may cause packets to loop.

As soon as the routes have been added to the routing table, the router supports a variety of options for how to load balance traffic across the routes. The router can balance the traffic proportionally with the metrics, meaning that lower metric routes send more packets. The router can send all traffic over the lowest-metric route, with the other routes just being in the routing table for faster convergence in case the best route fails. However, the details of the load-balancing process require a much deeper discussion of the internals of the forwarding process in IOS, and this topic is beyond the scope of this book.

Tuning the EIGRP Metric Calculation

By default, EIGRP calculates an integer metric based on interface bandwidth and delay. You can change the settings on any interface using the **bandwidth** *value* and the **delay** *value* interface subcommands, which in turn influences a router's choice of routes.

Cisco recommends setting each interface's bandwidth to an accurate value, rather than setting the bandwidth to some inaccurate value for the purpose of changing EIGRP's metric calculation. Router serial links should be configured with the **bandwidth** *speed* command, with a speed value in kilobits per second (Kbps), matching the interface's actual speed. Router Ethernet interfaces can use default settings; by default, IOS actually changes the router Ethernet interface bandwidth setting to match the actual physical transmission speed.

Because fewer other IOS features rely on the interface delay setting, Cisco recommends that if you want to tune EIGRP metric, change the interface delay settings. To change an interface's delay setting, use the **delay** *value* command, where the *value* is a delay setting with an unusual unit: tens of microseconds. Interestingly, the EIGRP metric formula also uses the unit of tens of microseconds; however, **show** commands list the delay with a unit of microseconds, as shown in Example 10-15 with the following details:

1. The router's Fa0/0 has a default delay setting of 100 microseconds (usec), assuming the interface is actually running at a speed of 100 Mbps.

2. The **delay 123** command is configured on the interface, meaning 123 tens of microseconds.

3. The **show interfaces fa0/0** command now lists a delay of 1230 microseconds.

Example 10-15   *Configuring Interface Delay*

```
Yosemite# show interfaces fa0/0
FastEthernet0/0 is up, line protocol is up
  Hardware is Gt96k FE, address is 0013.197b.5026 (bia 0013.197b.5026)
  Internet address is 10.1.2.252/24
  MTU 1500 bytes, BW 100000 Kbit, DLY 100 usec,
! lines omitted for brevity

Yosemite# configure terminal
Enter configuration commands, one per line.  End with CNTL/Z.
Yosemite(config)# interface fa0/0
Yosemite(config-if)# delay 123
Yosemite(config-if)# ^z
```

```
Yosemite# show interfaces fa0/0
FastEthernet0/0 is up, line protocol is up
  Hardware is Gt96k FE, address is 0013.197b.5026 (bia 0013.197b.5026)
  Internet address is 10.1.2.252/24
  MTU 1500 bytes, BW 100000 Kbit, DLY 1230 usec,
! lines omitted for brevity
```

Autosummarization and Discontiguous Classful Networks

Older routing protocols, namely RIP-1 and IGRP, were classified as *classful routing protocols*. This term comes from the fact that these classful routing protocols had to pay more attention to details about Class A, B, and C networks, in part because of the simplicity of the routing protocol.

These older classful routing protocols also had to use a more careful and cautious subnet design plan to avoid a problem called a discontiguous classful network. These simpler old routing protocols just got confused when a classful network became discontiguous, because of a required feature of classful routing protocols called autosummarization.

Today, most enterprises use OSPF or EIGRP, or in rare cases, RIP-2. All these protocols are classless routing protocols. As a result, these newer routing protocols can be configured so that the old problem with discontiguous classful networks is not a problem at all.

However, while the more recent IOS versions use good default settings so that this problem can be ignored, EIGRP allows the possibility of enabling the autosummary feature, which then requires the network engineer to be aware of this old discontiguous network problem. So, just in case, these next few pages first discuss the autosummary feature, followed by a discussion of the routing problems that can occur as a result.

> NOTE   In real networks, most people simply choose to avoid using autosummary today.

Automatic Summarization at the Boundary of a Classful Network

A routing protocol that uses autosummary automatically creates a summary route under certain conditions. In particular, when a router sits at the boundary between classful networks—that is, with some interfaces in one Class A, B, or C network and other interfaces in another Class A, B, or C network—the router summarizes routes. Routes from one classful network are summarized as one route to the entire Class A, B, or C network. More formally:

Routes related to subnets in network X, when advertised out an interface whose IP address is not in network X, are summarized and advertised as one route. That route is for the entire Class A, B, or C network X.

As usual, an example makes the concept much clearer. Consider Figure 10-9, which shows two networks in use: 10.0.0.0 and 172.16.0.0. R3 has four (connected) routes to subnets of network 10.0.0.0 on the right, and one interface on the left connected to a different classful network, class B network 172.16.0.0. As a result, R3, with autosummary enabled, will summarize a route for all of class A network 10.0.0.0.

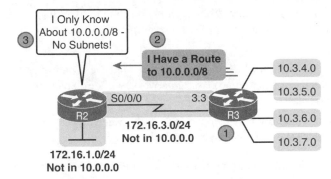

Figure 10-9 *Autosummarization*

Let's follow the steps in the figure:

1. R3 has autosummary enabled, with the EIGRP **auto-summary** router subcommand.

2. R3 advertises a route for all of Class A network 10.0.0.0, instead of advertising routes for each subnet inside network 10.0.0.0 because the link to R2 is a link in another network (172.16.0.0).

3. R2 learns one route in network 10.0.0.0: A route to 10.0.0.0/8, which represents all of network 10.0.0.0, with R3 as the next-hop router.

Example 10-16 shows the output of the **show ip route** command on R2, confirming the effect of the **auto-summary** setting on R3.

Example 10-16 *R2 with a Single Route in Network 10.0.0.0 for the Entire Network*

```
R2# show ip route eigrp
! lines omitted for brevity

D    10.0.0.0/8 [90/2207856] via 172.16.3.3, 00:12:59, Serial0/0/0
```

Note that **auto-summary** by itself causes no problems. In the design shown in Figure 10-9, and in the command output in Example 10-16, no problems exist. R2 can forward packets to all subnets of network 10.0.0.0 using the one highlighted summary route, sending those packets to R3 next.

Discontiguous Classful Networks

Autosummarization does not cause any problems as long as the summarized network is contiguous rather than discontiguous. U.S. residents can appreciate the concept of a discontiguous network based on the common term *contiguous 48*, referring to the 48 U.S. states besides Alaska and Hawaii. To drive to Alaska from the contiguous 48, for example, you must drive through another country (Canada, for the geographically impaired), so Alaska is not contiguous with the 48 states. In other words, it is discontiguous.

To better understand what the terms *contiguous* and *discontiguous* mean in networking, refer to the following two formal definitions when reviewing the example of a discontiguous classful network that follows:

- **Contiguous network:** A classful network in which packets sent between every pair of subnets can pass only through subnets of that same classful network, without having to pass through subnets of any other classful network
- **Discontiguous network:** A classful network in which packets sent between at least one pair of subnets must pass through subnets of a different classful network

Figure 10-10 creates an expanded version of the internetwork shown in Figure 10-9 to create an example of a discontiguous network 10.0.0.0. In this design, some subnets of network 10.0.0.0 sit off R1 on the left, whereas others still connect to R3 on the right. Packets passing between subnets on the left to subnets on the right must pass through subnets of Class B network 172.16.0.0.

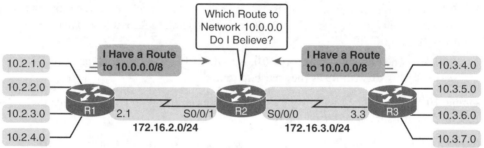

Figure 10-10 *Discontiguous Network 10.0.0.0*

Autosummarization causes problems in that routers like R2 that sit totally outside the discontiguous network become totally confused about how to route packets to the discontiguous network. Figure 10-10 shows the idea, with both R1 and R3 advertising a route for 10.0.0.0/8 to R2 in the middle of the network. Example 10-17 shows the resulting routes on router R2.

Example 10-17 *Albuquerque Routing Table: Autosummarization Causes Routing Problem with Discontiguous Network 10.0.0.0*

```
R2# show ip route | section 10.0.0.0
D      10.0.0.0/8 [90/2297856] via 172.16.3.3, 00:00:15, Serial0/0/0
                  [90/2297856] via 172.16.2.1, 00:00:15, Serial0/0/1
```

As shown in Example 10-17, R2 now has two routes to network 10.0.0.0/8: one pointing left toward R1 and one pointing right toward R3. R2 simply uses its usual load-balancing logic, because as far as R2 can tell, the two routes are simply equal-cost routes to the same destination: the entire network 10.0.0.0. Sometimes R2 happens to forward a packet toward the correct destination, and sometimes not.

This problem has two solutions. The old-fashioned solution is to create IP addressing plans that do not create discontiguous classful networks. The other: Just do not use autosummary, by using EIGRP defaults, or by disabling it with the **no auto-summary** EIGRP subcommand. Example 10-18 shows the resulting routing table in R2 for routes in network 10.0.0.0 with the **no auto-summary** command configured on routers R1 and R3.

Example 10-18   *Classless Routing Protocol with No Autosummarization Allows Discontiguous Network*

```
R2# show ip route 10.0.0.0
Routing entry for 10.0.0.0/24, 8 known subnets
  Redistributing via eigrp 1
D      10.2.1.0 [90/2297856] via 172.16.2.1, 00:00:12, Serial0/0/1
D      10.2.2.0 [90/2297856] via 172.16.2.1, 00:00:12, Serial0/0/1
D      10.2.3.0 [90/2297856] via 172.16.2.1, 00:00:12, Serial0/0/1
D      10.2.4.0 [90/2297856] via 172.16.2.1, 00:00:12, Serial0/0/1
D      10.3.4.0 [90/2297856] via 172.16.3.3, 00:00:06, Serial0/0/0
D      10.3.5.0 [90/2297856] via 172.16.3.3, 00:00:06, Serial0/0/0
D      10.3.6.0 [90/2297856] via 172.16.3.3, 00:00:06, Serial0/0/0
D      10.3.7.0 [90/2297856] via 172.16.3.3, 00:00:06, Serial0/0/0
```

10

Exam Preparation Tasks

Review All the Key Topics

Review the most important topics from this chapter, noted with the Key Topic icon. Table 10-3 lists these key topics and where each is discussed.

Table 10-3   Key Topics for Chapter 10

Key Topic Element	Description	Page Number
List	EIGRP configuration checklist	294
Example 10-5	The **show ip protocols** command and how it reveals the configured **network** commands	300
List	Rules with which EIGRP chooses its router ID	300
Figure 10-4	Breakdown of the output of a successor route in the output of the **show ip eigrp topology** command	304
Figure 10-7	Breakdown of the output of a FS route in the output of the **show ip eigrp topology** command	308
List	Key points about EIGRP variance	312
Text	Definition of autosummary	314
List	Definition of contiguous and discontiguous networks	316
Figure 10-10	An example of the problem caused by autosummary and the use of a discontiguous network	316

Complete the Tables and Lists from Memory

Print a copy of DVD Appendix D, "Memory Tables," or at least the section for this chapter, and complete the tables and lists from memory. DVD Appendix E, "Memory Tables Answer Key," includes completed tables and lists to check your work.

Definitions of Key Terms

After your first reading of the chapter, try to define these key terms, but do not be concerned about getting them all correct at that time. Chapter 22 directs you in how to use these terms for late-stage preparation for the exam.

feasibility condition, feasible distance, feasible successor, reported distance, successor, unequal cost load balancing, variance, autosummary, discontiguous network

Command Reference to Check Your Memory

Although you should not necessarily memorize the information in the tables in this section, this section does include a reference for the configuration and EXEC commands covered in this chapter. Practically speaking, you should memorize the commands as a side effect of reading the chapter and doing all the activities in this exam preparation section. To see how well you have memorized the commands as a side effect of your other studies, cover the left side of the table, read the descriptions on the right side, and see if you remember the command.

Table 10-4   Chapter 10 Configuration Command Reference

Command	Description
router eigrp *autonomous-system*	Global command to move the user into EIGRP configuration mode for the listed ASN
network *network-number* [*wildcard-mask*]	EIGRP router subcommand that matches either all interfaces in a classful network or a subset of interfaces based on the ACL-style wildcard mask, enabling EIGRP on those interfaces
maximum-paths *number-paths*	Router subcommand that defines the maximum number of equal-cost routes that can be added to the routing table
variance *multiplier*	Router subcommand that defines an EIGRP multiplier used to determine whether an FS route's metric is close enough to the successor's metric to be considered equal
bandwidth *bandwidth*	Interface subcommand directly sets the interface bandwidth (Kbps)
delay *delay-value*	Interface subcommand to set the interface delay value with a unit of tens of microseconds
ip hello-interval eigrp *as-number timer-value*	Interface subcommand that sets the EIGRP Hello interval for that EIGRP process
ip hold-time eigrp *as-number timer-value*	Interface subcommand that sets the EIGRP hold time for the interface
maximum-paths *number-of-paths*	Router subcommand that defines the maximum number of equal-cost routes that can be added to the routing table
[no] auto-summary	Router subcommand that disables (with the **no** option) or enables the automatic summarization of routes at the boundary of a classful network
passive-interface *type number*	Router subcommand that makes the interface passive to OSPF, meaning that the OSPF process will not form neighbor relationships with neighbors reachable on that interface
passive-interface default	OSPF subcommand that changes the OSPF default for interfaces to be passive instead of active (not passive)
no passive-interface *type number*	OSPF subcommand that tells OSPF to be active (not passive) on that interface or subinterface

10

Table 10-5   Chapter 10 EXEC Command Reference

Command	Description
show ip eigrp interfaces	Lists one line per interface on which EIGRP has been enabled, but for which it is not made passive with the **passive-interface** configuration command
show ip eigrp interfaces *type number*	Lists statistics interfaces on which EIGRP has been enabled, but for which it is not made passive with the **passive-interface** configuration command
show ip eigrp interfaces detail [*type number*]	Lists detailed configuration and statistics, for all interfaces or for the listed interface, again for enabled interfaces that are not passive
show ip protocols	Shows routing protocol parameters and current timer values
show ip eigrp neighbors	Lists EIGRP neighbors and status
show ip eigrp neighbors *type number*	Lists EIGRP neighbors reachable off the listed interface
show ip eigrp topology	Lists the contents of the EIGRP topology table, including successors and FSs
show ip eigrp topology *subnet/prefix*	Lists detailed topology information about the listed subnet
show ip eigrp topology	section *subnet*	Lists a subset of the **show ip eigrp topology** command (just the section for the listed subnet ID)
show ip route	Lists all IPv4 routes
show ip route eigrp	Lists routes in the IPv4 routing table learned by EIGRP
show ip route *ip-address mask*	Shows a detailed description of the route for the listed subnet/mask
show ip route	section *subnet*	Lists a subset of the **show ip route** command: just the section for the listed subnet ID
debug eigrp fsm	Displays changes to the EIGRP successor and FS routes

This chapter covers the following exam topics:

Troubleshooting

Troubleshoot and Resolve OSPF problems

Neighbor adjacencies

Hello and Dead timers

OSPF area

Interface MTU

Network types

Neighbor states

OSPF topology database

Troubleshoot and Resolve EIGRP problems

Neighbor adjacencies

AS number

Load balancing

Split horizon

CHAPTER 11

Troubleshooting IPv4 Routing Protocols

To begin the problem-isolation process when troubleshooting a possible IPv4 routing protocol problem, first focus on interfaces, and then on neighbors. The routing protocol configuration identifies the interfaces on which the router should use the routing protocol. After identifying those interfaces, a network engineer can look at the neighbors each router finds on each interface, searching for neighbors that should exist but do not.

This chapter focuses on issues related to these two main branches of logic: on which interfaces should a router enable the routing protocol and which neighbor relationships should each router create. This chapter relies on the configuration discussed in the other three chapters in this part of the book (Chapters 8, "Implementing OSPF for IPv4," 9, "Understanding EIGRP Concepts," and 10, "Implementing EIGRP for IPv4"), while emphasizing how to find incorrect configuration problems by using only **show** and **debug** commands.

This chapter first briefly introduces a few broad concepts related to troubleshooting problems with routing protocols. The next major section examines problems related to which interfaces on which a router enables the routing protocol, with the final major section focusing of routing protocol neighbor relationships. Note that the entire chapter moves back and forth between discussing both Enhanced Interior Gateway Routing Protocol (EIGRP) and Open Shortest Path First (OSPF).

"Do I Know This Already?" Quiz

The troubleshooting chapters of this book pull in concepts from many other chapters, including some chapters in *Cisco CCENT/CCNA ICND1 Official Cert Guide*. They also show you how to approach some of the more challenging questions on the CCNA exams. Therefore, it is useful to read these chapters regardless of your current knowledge level. For these reasons, the troubleshooting chapters do not include a "Do I Know This Already?" quiz. However, if you feel particularly confident about troubleshooting OSPF and EIGRP, feel free to move to the "Exam Preparation Tasks" section near the end of this chapter to bypass the majority of the chapter.

Foundation Topics

Perspectives on Troubleshooting Routing Protocol Problems

Because a routing protocol's job is to fill a router's routing table with the currently best routes, it makes sense that troubleshooting potential problems with routing protocols could begin with the IP routing table. Given basic information about an internetwork, including the routers, their IP addresses and masks, and the routing protocol, you could calculate the subnet numbers that should be in the router's routing table and list the likely next-hop routers for each route. For example, Figure 11-1 shows an internetwork with six subnets. Router R1's routing table should list all six subnets, with three connected routes, two routes learned from R2 (172.16.4.0/24 and 172.16.5.0/24), and one route learned from R3 (172.16.6.0/24).

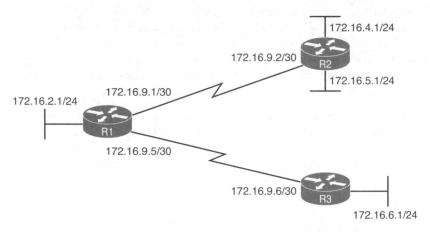

Figure 11-1   *Internetwork with Six Subnets*

So, one possible troubleshooting process is to analyze the internetwork, look at the routing table, and look for missing routes. If one or more expected routes are missing, the next step would be to determine whether that router has learned any routes from the expected next-hop (neighbor) router. The next steps to isolate the problem differ greatly if a router is having problems forming a neighbor relationship with another router, versus having a working neighbor relationship but not being able to learn all routes.

For example, suppose that R1 in Figure 11-1 has learned a route for subnet 172.16.4.0/24 in Figure 11-1 but not for subnet 172.16.5.0/24. In this case, it is clear that R1 has a working neighbor relationship with R2. In these cases, the root cause of this problem might still be related to the routing protocol, or it might be unrelated to the routing protocol. For example, the problem may be that R2's lower LAN interface is down. However, if R1 did not have a route for either 172.16.4.0/24 or 172.16.5.0/24, R1's neighbor relationship with R2 could be the problem.

Troubleshooting routing protocol problems in real internetworks can be very complex— much more complex than even the most difficult CCNA exam questions. Defining a generic troubleshooting process with which to attack both simple and complex routing protocol problems would require a lot of space and be counterproductive for preparing for the CCNA exams. This chapter instead offers a straightforward process for attacking routing protocol problems—specifically, problems similar to the depth and complexity of the CCNA exams.

If an exam question appears to be related to a problem with a routing protocol, you can quickly identify some common configuration errors with the following process—even if the question does not list the configuration. The process has three main tasks:

Step 1.   Examine the internetwork design to determine on which interfaces the routing protocol should be enabled and which routers are expected to become neighbors.

Step 2.   Verify whether the routing protocol is enabled on each interface (as per Step 1). If it isn't, determine the root cause and fix the problem.

Step 3.   Verify that each router has formed all expected neighbor relationships. If it hasn't, find the root cause and fix the problem.

For instance, as noted with asterisks in Figure 11-2, each router should enable the routing protocol on each of the interfaces shown in the figure. Also, routing protocol neighbor relationships should form between R1 and R2, and R1 and R3, but not between R2 and R3.

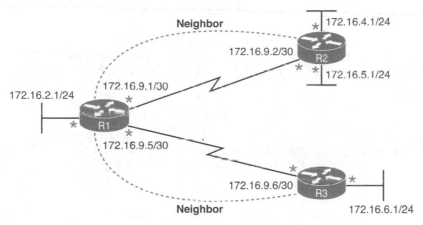

Figure 11-2   *Routing Protocol Interfaces and Neighbor Relationships*

While the concepts outlined in Figure 11-2 should be somewhat obvious by now, this chapter discusses how some of the most common configuration mistakes can impact the interfaces used by a routing protocol and whether a routing protocol creates neighbor relationships.

Interfaces Enabled with a Routing Protocol

This section examines the second major troubleshooting step outlined in the previous section of the chapter: how to verify the interfaces on which the routing protocol has been enabled. Both EIGRP and OSPF configuration enable the routing protocol on an interface by using the **network** router subcommand. For any interfaces matched by the **network** commands, the routing protocol tries the following two actions:

- Attempt to find potential neighbors on the subnet connected to the interface
- Advertise the subnet connected to that interface

At the same time, the **passive-interface** router subcommand can be configured so that the router does not attempt to find neighbors on the interface (the first action just listed), but still advertises the connected subnet (the second action).

Three **show** commands are all that is needed to know exactly which interfaces have been enabled with EIGRP and which interfaces are passive. In particular, the **show ip eigrp interfaces** command lists all EIGRP-enabled interfaces that are not passive interfaces. The **show ip protocols** command essentially lists the contents of the configured **network** commands for each routing protocol and a separate list of the passive interfaces. Comparing these two commands identifies all EIGRP-enabled interfaces and those that are passive.

For OSPF, the command works slightly differently, with the **show ip ospf interface brief** command listing all OSPF-enabled interfaces (including passive interfaces). Using this command, along with the list of passive interfaces listed by the **show ip protocols** command, again identifies all fully enabled OSPF interfaces as well as all passive interfaces.

Table 11-1 summarizes these commands for easier reference.

Table 11-1   Key Commands to Find Routing Protocol-Enabled Interfaces

Command	Key Information	Lists Passive Interfaces?
show ip eigrp interfaces	Lists the interfaces on which the routing protocol is enabled (based on the **network** commands), *excluding* passive interfaces.	No
show ip ospf interface brief	Lists the interfaces on which the OSPF is enabled (based on the **network** commands), *including* passive interfaces.	Yes
show ip protocols	Lists the contents of the **network** configuration commands for each routing process, and lists enabled but passive interfaces.	Yes

NOTE   All the commands in Table 11-1 list the interfaces regardless of interface status, in effect telling you the results of the **network** and **passive-interface** configuration commands.

So, for the major troubleshooting step covered in this section, the task is to use the commands in Table 11-1 and analyze the output. First, an EIGRP example will be shown, followed by an OSPF example.

EIGRP Interface Troubleshooting

This section shows a few examples of the commands in the context of Figure 11-3, which is used in all the examples in this chapter.

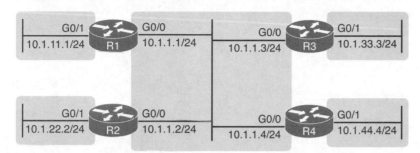

Figure 11-3 *Internetwork for EIGRP/OSPF Troubleshooting Examples*

This example includes four routers, with the following scenario in this case:

- R1 and R2 are configured correctly on both LAN interfaces.
- R3 is mistakenly not enabled with EIGRP on its G0/1 interface.
- R4 meant to use a **passive-interface G0/1** command because no other routers are off R4's G0/1 LAN. However, R4 has instead configured a **passive-interface G0/0** command.

This example begins by showing the working details between routers R1 and R2, and then moves on to discuss the issues related to R3 and R4.

Examining Working EIGRP Interfaces

Examples 11-1 and 11-2 list configuration and **show** commands, for R1 and R2, respectively. Each lists the related configuration, the **show ip eigrp interfaces** and **show ip protocols** command, and the EIGRP-learned routes on each router.

Example 11-1 *EIGRP Interfaces Problem: R1 Commands*

```
R1# show running-config
! only pertinent lines shown
router eigrp 99
 network 10.0.0.0
!
R1# show ip eigrp interfaces
EIGRP-IPv4 Interfaces for AS(99)
                   Xmit Queue   PeerQ        Mean  Pacing Time  Multicast    Pending
Interface   Peers  Un/Reliable  Un/Reliable  SRTT  Un/Reliable  Flow Timer   Routes
Gi0/0          3      0/0          0/0          2     0/0          50           0
Gi0/1          0      0/0          0/0          0     0/0          0            0


R1# show ip protocols
*** IP Routing is NSF aware ***
```

11

```
Routing Protocol is "eigrp 99"
  Outgoing update filter list for all interfaces is not set
  Incoming update filter list for all interfaces is not set
  Default networks flagged in outgoing updates
  Default networks accepted from incoming updates
  EIGRP-IPv4 Protocol for AS(99)
    Metric weight K1=1, K2=0, K3=1, K4=0, K5=0
    NSF-aware route hold timer is 240
    Router-ID: 1.1.1.1
    Topology : 0 (base)
      Active Timer: 3 min
      Distance: internal 90 external 170
      Maximum path: 4
      Maximum hopcount 100
      Maximum metric variance 1

  Automatic Summarization: disabled
  Maximum path: 4
  Routing for Networks:
    10.0.0.0
  Routing Information Sources:
    Gateway         Distance        Last Update
    10.1.1.2              90         09:55:51
    10.1.1.3              90         00:02:00
  Distance: internal 90 external 170


R1# show ip route eigrp
! Legend omitted for brevity


      10.0.0.0/8 is variably subnetted, 5 subnets, 2 masks
D        10.1.22.0/24 [90/30720] via 10.1.1.2, 00:00:40, GigabitEthernet0/0
```

Example 11-2 *EIGRP Interfaces Problem: R2 Commands*

```
R2# show running-config
! only pertinent lines shown
router eigrp 99
 network 10.1.0.0 0.0.255.255


R2# show ip eigrp interfaces
EIGRP-IPv4 Interfaces for AS(99)
                     Xmit Queue    PeerQ        Mean   Pacing Time    Multicast    Pending
Interface    Peers   Un/Reliable   Un/Reliable  SRTT   Un/Reliable    Flow Timer   Routes
Gi0/0            2      0/0           0/0          1       0/1            50           0
Gi0/1            0      0/0           0/0          0       0/0             0           0
```

```
R2# show ip protocols
*** IP Routing is NSF aware ***

Routing Protocol is "eigrp 99"
  Outgoing update filter list for all interfaces is not set
  Incoming update filter list for all interfaces is not set
  Default networks flagged in outgoing updates
  Default networks accepted from incoming updates
  EIGRP-IPv4 Protocol for AS(99)
    Metric weight K1=1, K2=0, K3=1, K4=0, K5=0
    NSF-aware route hold timer is 240
    Router-ID: 2.2.2.2
    Topology : 0 (base)
      Active Timer: 3 min
      Distance: internal 90 external 170
      Maximum path: 4
      Maximum hopcount 100
      Maximum metric variance 1

  Automatic Summarization: disabled
  Maximum path: 4
  Routing for Networks:
    10.1.0.0/16
  Routing Information Sources:
    Gateway         Distance      Last Update
    10.1.1.3              90      00:02:30
    10.1.1.1              90      09:56:20
  Distance: internal 90 external 170

R2# show ip route eigrp
! Legend omitted for brevity
     10.0.0.0/8 is variably subnetted, 5 subnets, 2 masks
D        10.1.11.0/24 [90/30720] via 10.1.1.1, 00:03:25, GigabitEthernet0/0
```

The **show ip eigrp interfaces** command output on both R1 and R2 shows how both R1 and R2 have configured EIGRP using process ID 99, and that EIGRP has been enabled on both G0/0 and G0/1 on both these routers. This command lists only interfaces on which EIGRP has been enabled, excluding passive interfaces.

The highlighted parts of the **show ip protocols** command output on each router are particularly interesting. These sections show the parameters of the configured **network** commands. The **show ip protocols** command lists a separate line under the header "Routing for Networks," one for each configured **network** command. Example 11-1's output suggests R1 has a **network 10.0.0.0** configuration command (as shown at the beginning of the example), and Example R2's "10.1.0.0/16" suggests R2 has a **network 10.1.0.0 0.0.255.255** command.

11

Examining the Problems with EIGRP Interfaces

The next few pages now look at the problems caused by the configuration on routers R3 and R4.

First, Example 11-2 gives brief insight into the current problem caused by R3. The end of R2's **show ip protocols** command (Example 11-2) lists two routing information sources: 10.1.1.1 (R1) and 10.1.1.3 (R3). However, R2 has learned only one EIGRP route (10.1.11.0/24), as shown in the **show ip route eigrp** command output. When working properly, R2 should learn three EIGRP routes—one for each of the other LAN subnets shown in Figure 11-3.

Example 11-3 shows the root cause on R3. First, R3's **show ip eigrp interfaces** command list G0/0, but not G0/1, so a problem might exist with how EIGRP has been configured on G0/1. The configuration at the top of the example lists the root cause: an incorrect **network** command, which does not enable EIGRP on R3's G0/1 interface.

Example 11-3 *EIGRP Problems on R3*

```
R3# show running-config
! lines omitted for brevity
router eigrp 99
 network 10.1.1.3 0.0.0.0
 network 10.1.13.3 0.0.0.0
 auto-summary


R3# show ip eigrp interfaces
EIGRP-IPv4 Interfaces for AS(99)
                    Xmit Queue   PeerQ        Mean  Pacing Time  Multicast    Pending
Interface    Peers  Un/Reliable  Un/Reliable  SRTT  Un/Reliable  Flow Timer   Routes
Gi0/0          2        0/0          0/0        1        0/1         50           0


R3# show ip protocols
*** IP Routing is NSF aware ***

Routing Protocol is "eigrp 99"
  Outgoing update filter list for all interfaces is not set
  Incoming update filter list for all interfaces is not set
  Default networks flagged in outgoing updates
  Default networks accepted from incoming updates
  EIGRP-IPv4 Protocol for AS(99)
    Metric weight K1=1, K2=0, K3=1, K4=0, K5=0
    NSF-aware route hold timer is 240
    Router-ID: 3.3.3.3
    Topology : 0 (base)
      Active Timer: 3 min
      Distance: internal 90 external 170
      Maximum path: 4
      Maximum hopcount 100
      Maximum metric variance 1
```

```
Automatic Summarization: disabled
Maximum path: 4
Routing for Networks:
   10.1.1.3/32
   10.1.13.3/32
Routing Information Sources:
   Gateway         Distance      Last Update
   10.1.1.2              90      00:05:14
   10.1.1.1              90      00:05:14
Distance: internal 90 external 170
```

The root cause of R3's problem is that R3 has a **network 10.1.13.3 0.0.0.0** configuration command, which does not match R3's 10.1.33.3 G0/1 IP address. If the configuration was not available in the exam question, the **show ip protocols** command could be used to essentially see the same configuration details. In this case, the **show ip protocols** command on R3 lists the text "10.1.13.3/32" as a reference to the contents of the incorrect **network** command's parameters, with "/32" translating to a wildcard mask of 32 binary 0s, or decimal 0.0.0.0.

R3's incorrect configuration means that two actions do not happen on R3's G0/1 interface. First, R3 does not try to find neighbors on its G0/1 interface, which is not a big deal in this case. However, R3 also does not advertise subnet 10.1.33.0/24, the connected subnet off R3's G0/1 interface.

Moving on to R4's problem, Example 11-4 shows why R1 and R2 do not learn R4's 10.1.44.0/24 subnet. In this case, on R4, the engineer could have correctly used a **passive-interface Gigabitethernet0/1** router subcommand because no other routers should exist off R4's G0/1 interface. However, the engineer mistakenly made R4's G0/0 interface passive.

Example 11-4 *EIGRP Problems on R4*

```
R4# show running-config
! lines omitted for brevity
router eigrp 99
 passive-interface GigabitEthernet0/0
 network 10.0.0.0
 auto-summary

R4# show ip eigrp interfaces
EIGRP-IPv4 Interfaces for AS(99)
                  Xmit Queue   PeerQ        Mean  Pacing Time  Multicast    Pending
Interface  Peers  Un/Reliable  Un/Reliable  SRTT  Un/Reliable  Flow Timer   Routes
Gi0/1        0       0/0          0/0         0       0/1          0           0

R4# show ip protocols | begin Routing for Networks
  Routing for Networks:
    10.0.0.0
  Passive Interface(s):
    GigabitEthernet0/0
```

11

```
Routing Information Sources:
  Gateway          Distance       Last Update
Distance: internal 90 external 170
```

NOTE The last command on the example, **show ip protocols | begin Routing for Networks**, lists the command output, but starting with the line with the literal case-sensitive string **Routing for Networks**. You can use this feature with any output from a command when you prefer to view only later lines of the command's output.

To find this mistake without the configuration, Example 11-4 lists two useful commands. R4's **show ip eigrp interfaces** command omits the (G0/0) passive interface, which means that R4 will not attempt to find EIGRP neighbors off that interface. Also, the highlighted part of R4's **show ip protocols** command output lists G0/0 as a passive interface, which again means that R4 does not even attempt to become neighbors with others off its G0/0 interface.

OSPF Interface Troubleshooting

OSPF has the same basic requirements as EIGRP for interfaces, with a few exceptions. First, EIGRP routers need to use the same autonomous system number (ASN) as their neighboring routers, as configured in the **router eigrp** *asn* global configuration command. OSPF routers can use any process ID on the **router ospf** *process-id* command, with no need to match their neighbors. Second, OSPF requires that the interfaces connected to the same subnet be assigned to the same OSPF area, whereas EIGRP has no concept of areas.

Example 11-5 shows a mostly working OSPF internetwork, again based on Figure 11-3. The problem in this case relates to the area design, as shown in the revised version of Figure 11-3, as shown here in Figure 11-4. All subnets should be placed into area 0. However, the engineer made a configuration mistake on R2, putting both its interfaces into area 1. As a result, R2's G0/0 interface breaks the OSPF design rule of being in the same subnet as R1, R3, and R4, but not being in the same OSPF area.

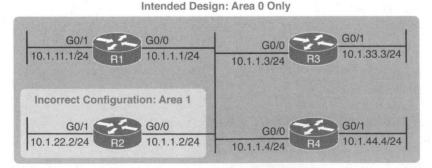

Figure 11-4 *Intended Area Design Using Only Area 0, with R2 Breaking the Design*

Example 11-5 begins to break down the problem by looking at the status of OSPF on the router interfaces of R1 and R2, using the **show ip ospf interface brief** command.

Example 11-5   show ip interface brief *on R1 and R2*

```
R1> show ip ospf interface brief
Interface   PID   Area       IP Address/Mask    Cost   State Nbrs F/C
Gi0/1        1     0         10.1.11.1/24        1     DR    0/0
Gi0/0        1     0         10.1.1.1/24         1     DROTH 2/2
! The following command is from R2
R2> show ip ospf interface brief
Interface   PID   Area       IP Address/Mask    Cost   State Nbrs F/C
Gi0/1        2     1         10.1.22.2/24        1     WAIT  0/0
Gi0/0        2     1         10.1.1.2/24         1     WAIT  0/0
```

From a general perspective, the **show ip ospf interface brief** command lists output similar to the **show ip eigrp interface** command, with one line for each enabled interface. The **show ip ospf interface** command, not shown in the example, lists detailed OSPF information for each interface.

Specific to this problem, the output in Example 11-5 shows that R1 and R2 both have OSPF enabled on both LAN interfaces. However, this command also lists the area number for each interface, with R2 having both LAN interfaces in area 1. Also, these commands repeat the IP address and mask of the interfaces, so together, you can see that R1's 10.1.1.1/24 address is in the same subnet as R2's 10.1.1.2/24 address, putting these two routers in the same subnet but in different OSPF areas.

Example 11-6 shows another way to look at the problem, with the **show ip protocols** commands on both R1 and R2. Because this command lists the OSPF **network** commands in shorthand form, it can point toward a possible configuration error, even if the configuration is not available.

Example 11-6   *Finding OSPF Configuration Errors with* **show ip protocols** *R1 and R2*

```
R1> show ip protocols
*** IP Routing is NSF aware ***

Routing Protocol is "ospf 1"
  Outgoing update filter list for all interfaces is not set
  Incoming update filter list for all interfaces is not set
  Router ID 1.1.1.1
  Number of areas in this router is 1. 1 normal 0 stub 0 nssa
  Maximum path: 4
  Routing for Networks:
    10.0.0.0 0.255.255.255 area 0
  Routing Information Sources:
    Gateway         Distance      Last Update
    2.2.2.2              110      00:14:32
    3.3.3.3              110      00:14:32
    10.1.44.4            110      00:14:42
  Distance: (default is 110)
```

11

```
R1> show ip route ospf
! Legend omitted for brevity

     10.0.0.0/8 is variably subnetted, 6 subnets, 2 masks
O        10.1.33.0/24 [110/2] via 10.1.1.3, 00:15:32, GigabitEthernet0/0
O        10.1.44.0/24 [110/2] via 10.1.1.4, 00:15:42, GigabitEthernet0/0
```

```
! Now moving to router R2


R2> show ip protocols
*** IP Routing is NSF aware ***

Routing Protocol is "ospf 2"
  Outgoing update filter list for all interfaces is not set
  Incoming update filter list for all interfaces is not set
  Router ID 2.2.2.2
  Number of areas in this router is 1. 1 normal 0 stub 0 nssa
  Maximum path: 4
  Routing for Networks:
    10.0.0.0 0.255.255.255 area 1
Routing Protocol is "ospf 2"
Outgoing update filter list for all interfaces is not set
Incoming update filter list for all interfaces is not set
Router ID 2.2.2.2
Number of areas in this router is 1. 1 normal 0 stub 0 nssa
Maximum path: 4
Routing for Networks:
   10.0.0.0 0.255.255.255 area 1
Routing Information Sources:
  Gateway          Distance      Last Update
Distance: (default is 110)


R2>
Nov 15 12:16:39.377: %OSPF-4-ERRRCV: Received invalid packet: mismatched area
ID, from backbone area must be virtual-link but not found from 10.1.1.1,
GigabitEthernet0/0
```

Interestingly, a closer look at R2's **show ip protocols** command output, particularly the highlighted portion, points out the configuration error. As usual, the section with heading "Routing for Networks:" points to a shorthand version of the configuration. In this case, the highlighted phrase "10.0.0.0 0.255.255.255 area 1" is actually the exact syntax of the one **network** command on router R2, minus the word *network*, or **network 10.0.0.0 0.255.255.255 area 1**. Because Figure 11-4 shows the design should put all interfaces in area 0, reconfiguring this command to instead be **network 10.0.0.0 0.255.255.255 area 0** would solve this particular problem.

The end of the example also shows an unsolicited log message generated by router R2, notifying the console user that this router has received a Hello from a router in a different area.

As you check the interfaces, you could also check several other details. It makes sense to go ahead and check the interface IP addresses, masks, and interface status values by using the **show interfaces** and **show ip interface brief** commands. In particular, it is helpful to note which interfaces are up/up because a router will send no packets (including routing protocol packets) out interfaces that are not in an up/up state. These interface verification checks were discussed in detail in Chapter 5, "IPv4 Troubleshooting Part 2," so they are not repeated here.

Neighbor Relationships

This final major section of the chapter examines the large number of facts that each router must check with each potential neighbor before the two routers become neighbors.

At a very basic level, routing protocols can easily create neighbor relationships using a Hello protocol. First, the routing protocol must be enabled on an interface. In addition, interface may not be configured as a passive interface, because that stops the routing protocol from sending the Hello messages.

Beyond this basic process, the routing protocols actually check several other parameters to find out whether the routers should become neighbors. Both OSPF and EIGRP use Hello messages, and these messages each list information used to perform some basic verification checks. For example, as just shown in earlier Example 11-5, an OSPF router should not become neighbors with another router in another area because all routers on a common subnet should be in the same OSPF area by design.

After an EIGRP or OSPF router hears a Hello from a new neighbor, the routing protocol examines the information in the Hello, and compares that information with the local router's own settings. If the settings match, great. If not, the routers do not become neighbors. Because there is no formal term for all these items that a routing protocol considers, this book just calls them *neighbor requirements*.

Table 11-2 lists the neighbor requirements for both EIGRP and OSPF. Following the table, the next few pages examine some of these settings for both EIGRP and OSPF, again using examples based on Figure 11-3.

11

NOTE   Even though it is important to study and remember the items in this table, when reading this chapter the first time, just keep reading. When later reviewing the chapter or part, make sure you remember the details in the table.

Table 11-2   Neighbor Requirements for EIGRP and OSPF

Requirement	EIGRP	OSPF
Interfaces must be in an up/up state.	Yes	Yes
Interfaces must be in the same subnet.	Yes	Yes
Access control lists (ACL) must not filter routing protocol messages.	Yes	Yes
Must pass routing protocol neighbor authentication (if configured).	Yes	Yes
Must use the same ASN/PID on the **router** configuration command.	Yes	No
Hello and hold/dead timers must match.	No	Yes
Router IDs (RID) must be unique.	No[1]	Yes
K-values must match.	Yes	N/A
Must be in the same area.	N/A	Yes

[1] Having duplicate EIGRP RIDs does not prevent routers from becoming neighbors, but it can cause problems when external EIGRP routes are added to the routing table.

Unlike most of the neighbor requirements listed in Table 11-2, the first three requirements have very little to do with the routing protocols themselves. The two routers must be able to send packets to each other over the physical network to which they are both connected. To do that, the router interfaces must be up/up, and they must be in the same subnet. In addition, the routers must not be using an ACL that filters the routing protocol traffic.

For instance, OSPF sends many messages to the well-known multicast IP addresses 224.0.0.5 and 224.0.0.6, whereas EIGRP uses 224.0.0.10. An ACL command like **access-list 101 deny ip any host 224.0.0.10**, in an inbound ACL on a router interface, would filter incoming EIGRP packets. Or, an ACL command like **access-list 102 deny ospf any any** could filter all OSPF traffic. So, take extra care to watch for ACLs, especially when it seems like all the routing protocol configuration looks good.

In practice, before examining the rest of the details of why two routers do not become neighbors, confirm that the two routers can ping each other on the local subnet. If the ping fails, investigate all the Layer 1, 2, and 3 issues that could prevent the ping from working (such as an interface not being up/up), as covered in Chapters 4, "Troubleshooting IPv4 Routing Part I," and 5, "Troubleshooting IPv4 Routing Part II," of this book and in many chapters of this book and in the ICND1 book.

Now, on to the specific discussions about EIGRP and OSPF. Because the details differ slightly between the two routing protocols, this section first examines EIGRP, followed by OSPF.

NOTE   This section assumes that the routing protocol has actually been enabled on each required interface, as covered earlier in this chapter in the "Interfaces Enabled with a Routing Protocol" section.

EIGRP Neighbor Verification Checks

Any two EIGRP routers that connect to the same data link, and whose interfaces have been enabled for EIGRP and are not passive, will at least consider becoming neighbors. To quickly and definitively know which potential neighbors have passed all the neighbor requirements for EIGRP, just look at the output of the **show ip eigrp neighbors** command. This command lists only neighbors that have passed all the neighbor verification checks.

Example 11-7 shows an example of the **show ip eigrp neighbors** command, with the four routers from Figure 11-3 again. In this case, all the routers have been configured correctly, so each has a neighbor relationship with the other three routers on the same LAN subnet.

Example 11-7   *R1* **show ip eigrp neighbors** *Command with All Problems Fixed*

```
R1# show ip eigrp neighbors
EIGRP-IPv4 Neighbors for AS(99)
H   Address                 Interface          Hold Uptime   SRTT   RTO  Q  Seq
                                               (sec)         (ms)       Cnt Num
1   10.1.1.3                Gi0/0              13 00:00:20    1    100  0  31
2   10.1.1.4                Gi0/0              13 00:00:43    80   480  0  10
0   10.1.1.2                Gi0/0              13 00:13:52    1    100  0  20
```

If the **show ip eigrp neighbors** command does not list one or more expected neighbors, the first problem isolation step should be to find out if the two routers can ping each others' IP addresses on the same subnet. If that works, start looking at the list of neighbor verification checks, as relisted for EIGRP here in Table 11-3. Table 11-3 summarizes the EIGRP neighbor requirements, while noting the best commands with which to determine which requirement is the root cause of the problem.

Table 11-3   EIGRP Neighbor Requirements and the Best **show/debug** Commands

Requirement	Best Commands to Isolate the Problem
Must be in the same subnet.	show interfaces, show ip interface
Must use the same ASN on the **router** configuration command.	show ip eigrp interfaces, show ip protocols
Must pass EIGRP neighbor authentication.	debug eigrp packets
K-values must match.	show ip protocols

Of the four rows of requirements listed in Table 11-3, the first two have already been discussed; the last two have not.

For EIGRP authentication, EIGRP supports the capability for routers to trust routers as EIGRP neighbors only if the routers share the same security key (password); if that check fails, the neighbor relationship fails. By default, routers do not attempt EIGRP authentication, which allows the routers to form EIGRP neighbor relationships. If one router uses authentication, and the other does not, they will not become neighbors. If both use authentication, they must use the same authentication key to become neighbors.

11

The last item in the table, EIGRP K-values, refers to the EIGRP metric components and the metric calculation. These K-values are variables that basically enable or disable the use of the different components in the EIGRP composite metric. Cisco recommends leaving these values at their default settings, using only bandwidth and delay in the metric calculation. The K-value settings must match before two routers will become neighbors; you can check the K-values on both routers with the **show ip protocols** command.

EIGRP Neighbor Troubleshooting Example

Example 11-8 shows three problems that can cause EIGRP routers to fail to become neighbors. This example uses the usual design for this chapter, as repeated in Figure 11-5. The figure shows the same routers, and same interfaces, but with the following problems:

■ R2 has been configured with IP address 10.1.2.2/24 in a different subnet than R1, R3, and R4.

■ R3 has been configured to use ASN 199 with the **router eigrp 199** command instead of ASN 99, as used on the other three routers.

■ R4 has been configured to use message digest 5 (MD5) authentication, whereas the other routers use no authentication.

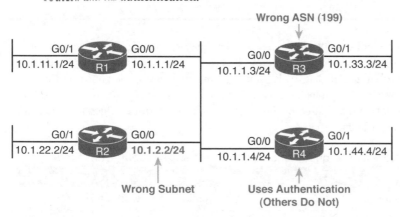

Figure 11-5 *Summary of Problems That Prevent EIGRP Neighbors on the Central LAN*

R1 can actually detect two of the problems using local commands and messages, as shown in Example 11-8. R1 generates an unsolicited log message for the mismatched subnet problem, and a **debug** command on R1 can reveal the authentication failure. The example shows some running commentary inside the example.

Example 11-8 *Common Problems Preventing the Formation of EIGRP Neighbors (R1)*

```
! First, R1 has no neighbor relationships yet. R1 uses ASN (process) 99.
R1# show ip eigrp neighbors
EIGRP-IPv4 Neighbors for AS(99)

R1#
! Next, R1 generates a log message, which shows up at the console, stating
! that the router with IP address 10.1.2.2 is not on the same subnet as R1.
!
```

```
*Nov 15 16:19:14.740: %DUAL-6-NBRINFO: EIGRP-IPv4 99: Neighbor 10.1.2.2
(GigabitEthernet0/0) is blocked: not on common subnet (10.1.1.1/24)


! Next, R1 enables a debug that shows messages for each packet received from R4,
! which uses the wrong password (authentication key string)
!
R1# debug eigrp packets
EIGRP Packets debugging is on
    (UPDATE, REQUEST, QUERY, REPLY, HELLO, IPXSAP, PROBE, ACK, STUB, SIAQUERY,
     SIAREPLY)
R1#


*Nov 15 16:20:30.865: EIGRP: Gi0/0: ignored packet from 10.1.1.4, opcode = 5 (authen-
tication off or key-chain missing)
```

Example 11-8 shows some evidence of the mismatched subnet with R2, and the invalid authentication problem with R4, but it does not show any information about the incorrect ASN configured on R3. Example 11-9 lists excerpts from two **show** commands on R3, both of which identify the ASN configured on that router. By using these same commands on all the routers, you could note that R1, R2, and R4 use ASN 99, whereas R3 uses 199, as shown in Example 11-9.

Example 11-9   *Displaying the Incorrect ASN (199) on R3*

```
R3# show ip protocols
Routing Protocol is "eigrp 199"
!
! The first line of output from show ip eigrp interfaces lists ASN 199
!
R3# show ip eigrp interfaces
EIGRP-IPv4 Interfaces for AS(199)
                         Xmit Queue    Mean   Pacing Time   Multicast    Pending
Interface      Peers    Un/Reliable   SRTT   Un/Reliable   Flow Timer   Routes
Gi0/0            0          0/0         0         0/1           0           0
Gi0/1            0          0/0         0         0/1           0           0
```

OSPF Neighbor Troubleshooting

Similar to EIGRP, a router's **show ip ospf neighbor** command lists all the neighboring routers that have met all the requirements to become an OSPF neighbor as listed in Table 11-2. So, the first step in troubleshooting OSPF neighbors is to look at the list of neighbors.

Example 11-10 lists the output of a **show ip ospf neighbor** command on router R2, from Figure 11-4. All four routers sit on the same LAN subnet, in area 0, with correct configurations, so all four routers form a valid OSPF neighbor relationship.

11

Example 11-10   *Normal Working* **show ip ospf neighbors** *Command on Router R2*

```
R2# show ip ospf neighbor

Neighbor ID     Pri   State          Dead Time   Address     Interface
1.1.1.1           1   FULL/BDR       00:00:37    10.1.1.1    GigabitEthernet0/0
3.3.3.3           1   2WAY/DROTHER   00:00:37    10.1.1.3    GigabitEthernet0/0
4.4.4.4           1   FULL/DR        00:00:31    10.1.1.4    GigabitEthernet0/0
```

First, note that the neighbor IDs, listed in the first column, identify neighbors by their router ID (RID). For this example network, all four routers use an easily guessed RID. Further to the right, the Address column lists the interface IP address used by that neighbor on the common subnet.

A brief review of OSPF neighbor states (as explained in Chapter 8) can help you understand a few of the subtleties of the output in the example. A router's listed status for each of its OSPF neighbors—the neighbor's state—should settle into either a 2-way or full state under normal operation. For neighbors that do not need to directly exchange their databases, typically two non-designated router (DR) routers on a LAN, the routers should settle into a 2-way neighbor state. In most cases, two neighboring routers need to directly exchange their full link-state databases (LSDB) with each other. As soon as that process has been completed, the two routers settle into a full neighbor state.

In Example 11-10, router R4 is the DR, and R1 is the backup DR (BDR), so R2 and R3 (as non-DRs) do not need to directly exchange routes. Therefore, R2's neighbor state for R3 (RID 3.3.3.3) in Example 11-10 is listed as 2-way.

> **NOTE**   Notably, OSPF neighbors do not have to use the same process ID on the **router ospf** *process-id* command to become neighbors. In Example 11-10, all four routers use different PIDs.

If the **show ip ospf neighbor** command does not list one or more expected neighbors, you should confirm, even before moving on to look at OSPF neighbor requirements, that the two routers can ping each other on the local subnet. But if the two neighboring routers can ping each other, and the two routers still do not become OSPF neighbors, the next step is to examine each of the OSPF neighbor requirements. Table 11-4 summarizes the requirements, listing the most useful commands with which to find the answers.

Table 11-4   OSPF Neighbor Requirements and the Best **show/debug** Commands

Requirement	Best Commands to Isolate the Problem
Must be in the same subnet.	show interfaces, debug ip ospf hello
Must pass any neighbor authentication.	show ip ospf interface, debug ip ospf adj
Hello and dead timers must match.	show ip ospf interface, debug ip ospf hello
Must be in the same area.	show ip ospf interface brief, debug ip ospf adj
RIDs must be unique.	show ip ospf

This topic looks at a couple of OSPF neighbor problems using the usual four-router network from Figure 11-4 is used, with all interfaces in area 0. However, the following problems have been introduced into the design:

■ R2 has been configured with both LAN interfaces in area 1, whereas the other three routers' G0/0 interfaces are assigned to area 0.

■ R3 is using the same RID (1.1.1.1) as R1.

■ R4 has been configured with a Hello/Dead timer of 5/20 on its G0/0 interface, instead of the 10/40 used (by default) on R1, R2, and R3.

Figure 11-6 shows these same problems for reference.

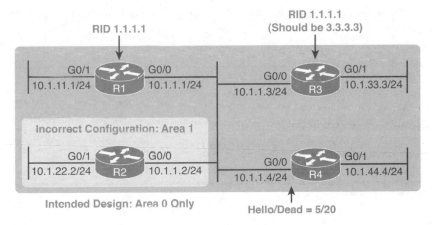

Figure 11-6 *Summary of Problems That Prevent OSPF Neighbors on the Central LAN*

Finding Area Mismatches

Earlier in this chapter, the "OSPF Interface Troubleshooting" section showed how to use the **show ip ospf interface** command to list the area numbers and find OSPF area mismatches. This next topic shows how to see that same issue using the **debug ip ospf adj** command, as shown in Example 11-11. This command lists messages related to OSPF neighbor adjacency events, and shows messages that identify the area mismatch (with R2).

Example 11-11 *Finding Mismatched Area Problem with R1 debug*

```
R1# debug ip ospf adj
OSPF adjacency events debugging is on
R1#
*Nov 15 13:42:02.288: OSPF-1 ADJ    Gi0/0: Rcv pkt from 10.1.1.2, area 0.0.0.0, mis-
matched area 0.0.0.1 in the header
R1#
R1# undebug all
All possible debugging has been turned off
```

As noted in Table 11-4, the **debug ip ospf adj** command helps troubleshoot mismatched OSPF area problems and authentication problems. The first highlighted messages in the example lists shorthand about a received packet ("Rcv pkt") from 10.1.1.2, which is R2's IP address. The rest of the message mentions R1's area (0.0.0.0), and the area claimed by the other router (0.0.0.1). (Note that these messages list the 32-bit area number as a dotted-decimal number.)

Finding Duplicate OSPF Router IDs

Next, Example 11-12 shows R1 and R3 both trying to use RID 1.1.1.1. Interestingly, both routers automatically generate a log message for the duplicate OSPF RID problem between R1 and R3; the end of Example 11-12 shows one such message. For the exams, just use the **show ip ospf** commands on both R3 and R1 to easily list the RID on each router, noting that they both use the same value.

Example 11-12 *Comparing OSPF Router IDs on R1 and R3*

```
! Next, on R3: ! R3 lists the RID of 1.1.1.1
!
R3# show ip ospf
Routing Process "ospf 3" with ID 1.1.1.1
Start time: 00:00:37.136, Time elapsed: 02:20:37.200
! lines omitted for brevity
```

```
! Back to R1: R1 also uses RID 1.1.1.1

R1# show ip ospf
Routing Process "ospf 1" with ID 1.1.1.1
Start time: 00:01:51.864, Time elapsed: 12:13:50.904
Supports only single TOS(TOS0) routes
Supports opaque LSA
Supports Link-local Signaling (LLS)
Supports area transit capability
Supports NSSA (compatible with RFC 3101)
Event-log enabled, Maximum number of events: 1000, Mode: cyclic
Router is not originating router-LSAs with maximum metric
Initial SPF schedule delay 5000 msecs
Minimum hold time between two consecutive SPFs 10000 msecs
Maximum wait time between two consecutive SPFs 10000 msecs
Incremental-SPF disabled
Minimum LSA interval 5 secs
Minimum LSA arrival 1000 msecs
LSA group pacing timer 240 secs
Interface flood pacing timer 33 msecs
Retransmission pacing timer 66 msecs
Number of external LSA 0. Checksum Sum 0x000000
Number of opaque AS LSA 0. Checksum Sum 0x000000
```

```
Number of DCbitless external and opaque AS LSA 0
Number of DoNotAge external and opaque AS LSA 0
Number of areas in this router is 1. 1 normal 0 stub 0 nssa
Number of areas transit capable is 0
External flood list length 0
IETF NSF helper support enabled
Cisco NSF helper support enabled
Reference bandwidth unit is 100 mbps
    Area BACKBONE(0) (Inactive)
        Number of interfaces in this area is 3
        Area has no authentication
        SPF algorithm last executed 00:52:42.956 ago
        SPF algorithm executed 9 times
        Area ranges are
        Number of LSA 1. Checksum Sum 0x00C728
        Number of opaque link LSA 0. Checksum Sum 0x000000
        Number of DCbitless LSA 0
        Number of indication LSA 0
        Number of DoNotAge LSA 0
        Flood list length 0
```

```
*May 29 00:01:25.679: %OSPF-4-DUP_RTRID_NBR: OSPF detected duplicate router-id
1.1.1.1 from 10.1.1.3 on interface GigabitEthernet0/0
```

First, focus on the problem: the duplicate RIDs. The first line of the **show ip ospf** command on the two routers quickly shows the duplicate use of 1.1.1.1. To solve the problem, assuming R1 should use 1.1.1.1 and R3 should use another RID (maybe 3.3.3.3), change the RID on R3, and restart the OSPF process. To do so, use the **router-id 3.3.3.3** OSPF subcommand and use the EXEC mode command **clear ip ospf process**.

Also, take a moment to read over the log message generated on each router when a duplicate RID exists.

Finally, note that the **show ip ospf** commands in Example 11-12 also show a common false positive for a root cause of OSPF neighbor problems. OSPF PIDs—the number of the **router ospf** command—do not have to match. Note that in Example 11-12 that same first line of output shows that R3 uses the **router ospf 3** command, per the phrase "Process ospf 3," whereas R1 uses the **router ospf 1** command, as noted with the phrase "Process ospf 1." These mismatched numbers are not a problem.

Finding OSPF Hello and Dead Timer Mismatches

Finally, consider the problem created on R4, with the configuration of a different Hello and dead timer as compared with the default settings on R1, R2, and R3. Whereas EIGRP allows neighbors to use a different Hello timer, OSPF does not, so this mismatch prevents R4 from becoming neighbors with any of the other three OSPF routers.

11

Example 11-13 shows the easiest way to find the mismatch, using the **show ip ospf interface** command on both R1 and R4. This command lists the Hello and dead timer for each inter-face, as highlighted in the example. Note that R1 uses 10 and 40 (Hello and dead), whereas R4 uses 5 and 20.

Example 11-13 *Finding Mismatched Hello/Dead Timers*

```
R1# show ip ospf interface G0/0
GigabitEthernet0/0 is up, line protocol is up
  Internet Address 10.1.1.1/24, Area 0, Attached via Network Statement
  Process ID 1, Router ID 1.1.1.1, Network Type BROADCAST, Cost: 1
  Topology-MTID    Cost    Disabled    Shutdown    Topology Name
       0            1         no          no          Base
  Transmit Delay is 1 sec, State DR, Priority 1
  Designated Router (ID) 1.1.1.1, Interface address 10.1.1.1
  No backup designated router on this network
  Timer intervals configured, Hello 10, Dead 40, Wait 40, Retransmit 5
! lines omitted for brevity
```
```
! Moving on to R4 next
!
R4# show ip ospf interface Gi0/0
GigabitEthernet0/0 is up, line protocol is up
  Internet Address 10.1.1.4/24, Area 0, Attached via Network Statement
  Process ID 4, Router ID 10.1.44.4, Network Type BROADCAST, Cost: 1
  Topology-MTID    Cost    Disabled    Shutdown    Topology Name
       0            1         no          no          Base
  Transmit Delay is 1 sec, State DR, Priority 1
  Designated Router (ID) 10.1.44.4, Interface address 10.1.1.4
  No backup designated router on this network
  Timer intervals configured, Hello 5, Dead 20, Wait 20, Retransmit 5
! lines omitted for brevity
```

The **debug ip ospf hello** command can also uncover this problem because it lists a message for each Hello that reveals the Hello/dead timer mismatch, as shown in Example 11-14.

Example 11-14 *Finding Mismatched Hello/Dead Timers*

```
R1# debug ip ospf hello
OSPF hello events debugging is on
R1#
*Nov 15 14:05:10.616: OSPF-1 HELLO Gi0/0: Rcv hello from 10.1.44.4 area 0 10.1.1.4
*Nov 15 14:05:10.616: OSPF-1 HELLO Gi0/0: Mismatched hello parameters from 10.1.1.4
*Nov 15 14:05:10.616: OSPF-1 HELLO Gi0/0: Dead R 20 C 40, Hello R 5 C 10 Mask R
255.255.255.0 C 255.255.255.0
```

Although debug messages can be a little difficult to understand, a few comments make the meaning of these messages much clearer. The highlighted message uses a *C* to mean "configured value"—in other words, the value on the local router, or R1 in this case. The *R* in the message means "received value," or the value listed in the received Hello. In this case

■ "Dead R 20 C 40" means that R1 received a Hello with a dead timer set to 20, while R1's configured value is set to 40.

■ "Hello R 5 C 10" means that R1 received a Hello with the Hello timer set to 5, while R1's configured value is set to 10.

Note that any IP subnet mismatch problems could also be found with this same debug, based on the received and configured subnet masks.

Other OSPF Issues

OSPFv2 can have a few other problems, two of which Cisco included in the OSPF troubleshooting exam topics. This last short discussion in this chapter looks at these two additional topics: the OSPF network type and the interface maximum transmission unit (MTU) size.

Mismatched OSPF Network Types

OSPF defines a concept for each interface called a network type. The OSPF *network type* tells OSPF some ideas about the data link to which the interface connects. In particular, the network type tells a router:

■ Whether the router can dynamically discover neighbors on the attached link (or not)

■ Whether to elect a DR and BDR (or not)

So far in this book, only two OSPF network types have been used based on default settings. Serial interfaces that use some point-to-point data link protocol, like HDLC or PPP, default to use an OSPF network type of *point-to-point*. Ethernet interfaces default to use an OSPF network type of *broadcast*. Both types allow the routers to dynamically discover the neighboring OSPF routers, but only the broadcast network type causes the router to use a DR/BDR.

The **show ip ospf interface** command lists an interface's current OSPF network type. Example 11-15 shows router R1, from the earlier examples, with a network type of "broadcast" on its G0/0 interface.

Example 11-15 *Displaying the OSPF Network Type on an Interface*

```
R1# show ip ospf interface g0/0
GigabitEthernet0/0 is up, line protocol is up
  Internet Address 10.1.1.1/24, Area 0, Attached via Network Statement
  Process ID 1, Router ID 1.1.1.1, Network Type BROADCAST, Cost: 1
! Lines omitted for brevity
```

It is possible to change the OSPF network type on an interface and, by making poor choices about the settings on neighboring routers, to prevent the routers from becoming OSPF neighbors. Normally, engineers either leave this setting at its default value, or they change

11

the setting for all routers on the same link. However, by choosing poorly, and using different network types on different neighboring routers, problems can occur.

For instance, if routers R1 and R2 from the sample internetwork used in this chapter still connect to the same VLAN, both using their G0/0 interfaces, they both by default use OSPF network type broadcast. These routers work best on their Ethernet interfaces with an OSPF network type of broadcast. As a result, both dynamically learn about each other as an OSPF router, and they both try to use a DR/BDR. However, if R1 was changed to use network type point-to-point on its G0/0 interface instead, problems occur. The result? The routers actually still become neighbors, but fail to exchange their LSDBs, as shown by R1 no longer having any OSPF-learned routes in Example 11-16

Example 11-16   *Mismatched OSPF Network Types Causing a Failure to Exchange LSDBs*

```
R1# configure terminal
Enter configuration commands, one per line.  End with CNTL/Z.
R1(config)# interface gigabitethernet0/0
R1(config-if)# ip ospf network point-to-point
R1(config-if)# ^z
R1#
R1# show ip route ospf
Codes: L - local, C - connected, S - static, R - RIP, M - mobile, B - BGP
       D - EIGRP, EX - EIGRP external, O - OSPF, IA - OSPF inter area
       N1 - OSPF NSSA external type 1, N2 - OSPF NSSA external type 2
       E1 - OSPF external type 1, E2 - OSPF external type 2
       i - IS-IS, su - IS-IS summary, L1 - IS-IS level-1, L2 - IS-IS level-2
       ia - IS-IS inter area, * - candidate default, U - per-user static route
       o - ODR, P - periodic downloaded static route, H - NHRP, l - LISP
       + - replicated route, % - next hop override


Gateway of last resort is not set


R1#
! Lines omitted for brevity
```

Note that in production networks you want to use the default OSPF network types unless you have a reason to override the values. Chapter 14, "Implementing Frame Relay," shows the one common case of configuring a nondefault value when using one particular style of Frame Relay configuration.

Mismatched MTU Settings

The MTU size defines a per-interface setting used by the router for its Layer 3 forwarding logic, defining the largest network layer packet that the router will forward out each interface. For instance, the IPv4 MTU size of an interface defines the maximum size IPv4 packet that the router can forward out an interface.

Routers often use a default mtu size of 1500 bytes, with the ability to set the value as well. The **ip mtu** *size* interface subcommand defines the IPv4 mtu setting, and the **ipv6 mtu** *size* command sets the equivalent for IPv6 packets.

In an odd twist, two OSPFv2 routers can actually become OSPF neighbors, and reach 2-way state, even if they happen to use different IPv4 mtu settings on their interfaces. However, they fail to exchange their LSDBs. Eventually, after trying and failing to exchange their LSDBs, the neighbor relationship also fails.

The concepts behind what happens with an MTU mismatch work the same with both OSPFv2 and OSPFv3. In Chapter 17, "Implementing OSPF for IPv6," the "Troubleshooting OSPFv3 LSAs" section shows an example of this particular problem with OSPFv3. Read that section for a little more detail about this issue.

11

Exam Preparation Tasks

Review All the Key Topics

Review the most important topics from this chapter, noted with the Key Topic icon. Table 11-5 lists these key topics and where each is discussed.

Table 11-5   Key Topics for Chapter 11

Key Topic Element	Description	Page Number
List	Two things that happen when EIGRP or OSPF is enabled on a router's interface	326
Table 11-1	Three commands that enable you to determine on which interfaces EIGRP or OSPF has been enabled	326
Table 11-2	Neighbor requirements for both EIGRP and OSPF	336
Table 11-3	EIGRP neighbor requirements and useful commands to isolate that requirement as the root cause of a neighbor problem	337
Table 11-4	The same information as Table 11-3, but for OSPF	340

Complete the Tables and Lists from Memory

Print a copy of DVD Appendix D, "Memory Tables," or at least the section for this chapter, and complete the tables and lists from memory. DVD Appendix E, "Memory Tables Answer Key," includes completed tables and lists to check your work.

Command Reference to Check Your Memory

Although you should not necessarily memorize the information in the tables in this section, does include a reference for the configuration and EXEC commands covered in this chapter. Practically speaking, you should memorize the commands as a side effect of reading the chapter and doing all the activities in this exam preparation section. To see how well you have memorized the commands as a side effect of your other studies, cover the left side of the table, read the descriptions on the right side, and see if you remember the command.

Table 11-6   Chapter 11 Configuration Command Reference

Command	Description
ip hello-interval eigrp *as-number timer-value*	Interface subcommand that sets the EIGRP Hello interval for that EIGRP process
ip hold-time eigrp *as-number seconds*	Interface subcommand that sets the EIGRP hold time for the interface

Command	Description
ip ospf hello-interval *seconds*	Interface subcommand that sets the interval for periodic Hellos
ip ospf dead-interval *number*	Interface subcommand that sets the OSPF dead timer
passive-interface *type number*	Router subcommand, for both OSPF and EIGRP that tells the routing protocol to stop sending Hellos and stop trying to discover neighbors on that interface

Table 11-7   Chapter 11 **show** Command Reference

Command	Description
show ip protocols	Shows routing protocol parameters and current timer values, including an effective copy of the routing protocols' **network** commands and a list of passive interfaces
show ip eigrp interfaces	Lists the interfaces on which EIGRP has been enabled for each EIGRP process, except passive interfaces
show ip route eigrp	Lists only EIGRP-learned routes from the routing table
show ip eigrp neighbors	Lists EIGRP neighbors and status
show ip ospf interface brief	Lists the interfaces on which the OSPF protocol is enabled (based on the **network** commands), including passive interfaces
show ip ospf interface [*type number*]	Lists detailed OSPF settings for all interfaces, or the listed interface, including Hello and Dead timers and OSPF area
show ip route ospf	Lists routes in the routing table learned by OSPF
show ip ospf neighbor	Lists neighbors and current status with neighbors, per interface
show ip ospf	Lists a group of messages about the OSPF process itself, listing the OSPF Router ID in the first line
show interfaces	Lists a long set of messages, per interface, that lists configuration, state, and counter information
show interfaces description	Lists one line of output per interface with brief status information

11

Table 11-8   Chapter 11 **debug** Command Reference

Command	Description
debug eigrp packets	Lists log messages for EIGRP packets that flow in and out of the router
debug ip ospf adj	Issues log messages for adjacency events, meaning events related to routers becoming neighbors
debug ip ospf events	Issues log messages for each action taken by OSPF, including the receipt of messages
debug ip ospf packet	Issues log messages describing the contents of all OSPF packets
debug ip ospf hello	Issues log messages describing Hellos and Hello failures
undebug all	EXEC command used to disable all current debugs

Part III Review

Keep track of your part review progress with the checklist in Table P3-1. Details about each task follow the table.

Table P3-1   Part III Part Review Checklist

Activity	First Date Completed	Second Date Completed
Repeat All DIKTA Questions		
Answer Part Review Questions		
Review Key Topics		
Create OSPF and EIGRP Root Causes Mind Map		
Create OSPF and EIGRP Commands Mind Map		

Repeat All DIKTA Questions

For this task, answer the "Do I Know This Already?" questions again for the chapters in Part I of this book using the PCPT software. See the section "How to View Only DIKTA Questions by Part" in the Introduction to this book to learn how to make the PCPT software show you DIKTA questions for this part only.

Answer Part Review Questions

For this task, answer the Part Review questions for this part of the book using the PCPT software. See the section "How to View Only DIKTA Questions by Part" in the Introduction to this book to learn how to make the PCPT software show you DIKTA questions for this part only.

Review Key Topics

Browse back through the chapters and look for the Key Topic icons. If you do not remember some details, take the time to reread those topics.

Create OSPF and EIGRP Root Causes Mind Map

Chapter 11, "Troubleshooting IPv4 Routing Protocols," focuses on how to troubleshoot problems with both Open Shortest Path First (OSPF) and Enhanced Interior Gateway Routing Protocol (EIGRP), specifically related to interfaces and to neighbor relationships. For this first Part Review mind map, work through all the items you can think of that can fail and cause a problem that prevents a routing protocol from working in IPv4 internetworks like those discussed in this part of the book. In other words, think about the root causes. Then organize those into a mind map.

To organize the mind map, start by just listing whatever comes to mind. Then, once you see several root causes that are related, group those root causes by whatever category comes to mind. There is no right or wrong organization to the root causes.

For instance, you might note root causes, like a shutdown LAN interface on a router or mismatched IP addresses (not in the same subnet). Then you might categorize those as "IP Connectivity on Same Subnet" or "Pingable Same Subnet," as shown in Figure P3-1.

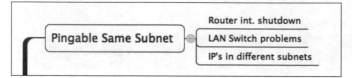

Figure P3-1   *Subset Example of the IPv4 Routing Protocol Root Cause Mind Map*

NOTE   For more information about mind mapping, see the section "About Mind Maps" in the Introduction to this book.

Create OSPF and EIGRP Commands Mind Map

This part also discussed both OSPF and EIGRP configuration and verification. Create a command mind map, like in many other part reviews. The first level of organization should be for OSPF versus EIGRP, then for configuration versus verification. Inside the verification area, further organize the commands similar to the organization in Chapter 10, "Implementing EIGRP for IPv4," with commands related to interfaces, neighbors, topology, and routes.

DVD Appendix F, "Mind Map Solutions," lists sample mind map answers, but as usual, your mind maps can and will look different.

The world of networking offers a large variety of WAN options. Part IV of this book looks at two traditional options in enough depth to help you comfortably implement the features in Cisco routers: point-to-point WANs (Chapter 12) and Frame Relay (Chapters 13 and 14). Chapter 15 then takes a broad look at a large variety of other WAN options, to enough depth so that you can recognize the main features of each of the technologies.

Part IV

Wide-Area Networks

This chapter covers the following exam topics:

IP Routing Technologies

Configure and verify operation status of a serial interface

WAN Technologies

Configure and verify a basic WAN serial connection

Configure and verify a PPP connection between Cisco routers

Identify Different WAN Technologies

T1 / E1

Troubleshooting

Troubleshoot and Resolve WAN implementation issues

Serial Interfaces

PPP

CHAPTER 12

Implementing Point-to-Point WANs

Leased-line WANs—also known as serial links—require much less thought than many other topics, at least to the depth required for the CCENT and CCNA exams. That simplicity allows the Cisco exams to discuss leased lines briefly for the ICND1 exam, while using leased lines as part of larger discussions of IP routing.

This chapter finally takes the discussion of leased-line WANs deeper than has been discussed so far. This chapter briefly repeats the leased line concepts from the ICND1 book, to lay a foundation to discuss other concepts. More important, this chapter looks at the configuration, verification, and troubleshooting steps for leased lines that use the familiar High-level Data Link Control (HDLC) data-link protocol and the Point-to-Point Protocol (PPP).

This chapter breaks the material down into three major sections. The first looks at leased line WANs that use HDLC, by reviewing and adding details about the physical links themselves, along with HDLC (and related) configuration. The second major section discusses PPP, an alternate data-link protocol that you can use instead of HDLC, with a focus on concepts and configuration. The final major section then discusses typical root causes of serial link problems and how to find those problems.

"Do I Know This Already?" Quiz

Use the "Do I Know This Already?" quiz to help decide whether you might want to skim this chapter, or a major section, moving more quickly to the "Exam Preparation Tasks" section near the end of the chapter. You can find the answers at the bottom of the page following the quiz. For thorough explanations, see DVD Appendix C, "Answers to the 'Do I Know This Already?' Quizzes."

Table 12-1   "Do I Know This Already?" Foundation Topics Section-to-Question Mapping

Foundation Topics Section	Questions
Leased Line WANs with HDLC	1–3
Leased Line WANs with PPP	4–6
Troubleshooting Serial Links	7

1. In the cabling for a leased line, which of the following usually connects to a four-wire line provided by a telco?

   a. Router serial interface without internal CSU/DSU
   b. CSU/DSU
   c. Router serial interface with internal transceiver
   d. Switch serial interface

2. Which of the following fields in the HDLC header used by Cisco routers does Cisco add beyond the ISO standard HDLC?

    a. Flag

    b. Type

    c. Address

    d. FCS

3. Two routers connect with a serial link, each using their S0/0/0 interface. The link is currently working using PPP. The network engineer wants to migrate to use the Cisco proprietary HDLC that includes a protocol type field. Which of the following commands can be used to migrate to HDLC successfully? (Choose two answers.)

    a. encapsulation hdlc

    b. encapsulation cisco-hdlc

    c. no encapsulation ppp

    d. encapsulation-type auto

4. Which of the following PPP authentication protocols authenticates a device on the other end of a link without sending any password information in clear text?

    a. MD5

    b. PAP

    c. CHAP

    d. DES

5. Two routers have no initial configuration whatsoever. They are connected in a lab using a DTE cable connected to R1 and a DCE cable connected to R2, with the DTE and DCE cables then connected to each other. The engineer wants to create a working PPP link by configuring both routers. Which of the following commands are required in the R1 configuration for the link to reach a state in which R1 can ping R2's serial IP address, assuming that the physical back-to-back link physically works? (Choose two answers.)

    a. encapsulation ppp

    b. no encapsulation hdlc

    c. clock rate

    d. ip address

6. Consider the following excerpt from the output of a **show** command:

```
Serial0/0/1 is up, line protocol is up
  Hardware is GT96K Serial
  Internet address is 192.168.2.1/24
  MTU 1500 bytes, BW 1544 Kbit, DLY 20000 usec,
     reliability 255/255, txload 1/255, rxload 1/255
  Encapsulation PPP, LCP Open
  Open: CDPCP, IPCP, loopback not set
```

Which of the following are true about this router's S0/0/1 interface? (Choose two answers.)

a. The interface is using HDLC.

b. The interface is using PPP.

c. The interface currently cannot pass IPv4 traffic.

d. The link should be able to pass PPP frames at the present time.

7. Consider the following excerpt from the output of a **show interfaces** command on an interface configured to use PPP:

```
Serial0/0/1 is up, line protocol is down
  Hardware is GT96K Serial
  Internet address is 192.168.2.1/24
```

A ping of the IP address on the other end of the link fails. Which of the following are reasons for the failure, assuming that the problem listed in the answer is the only problem with the link? (Choose two answers.)

a. The CSU/DSU connected to the other router is not powered on.

b. The IP address on the router at the other end of the link is not in subnet 192.168.2.0/24.

c. CHAP authentication failed.

d. The router on the other end of the link has been configured to use HDLC.

e. None of the above.

12

Foundation Topics

Leased Line WANs with HDLC

A physical leased line WAN works a lot like with an Ethernet crossover cable connecting two routers, but with no distance limitations. As shown in Figure 12-1, each router can send at any time (full duplex). The speed is also symmetric, meaning that both routers send bits at the same speed.

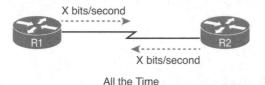

Figure 12-1   *Leased Line: Same Speed, Both Directions, Always On*

Although the leased line provides a physical layer bit transmission facility, routers also need to use a data link protocol on the WAN link to send bits over the link. The story should be familiar by now: routers receive frames in LAN interfaces, and then the router deencapsulates the network layer packet. Before forwarding the packet, the router encapsulates the packet inside a WAN data link protocol like High-level Data Link Control (HDLC), as shown at Step 2 of Figure 12-2. (Note that the figure does not bother to show the data link trailers in each frame, but each frame does indeed have both a data link header and trailer.)

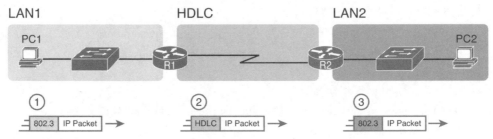

Figure 12-2   *Routers and Their Use of HDLC to Encapsulate Packets*

These first two figures review some of the Layer 1 and Layer 2 details, respectively, of leased-line WANs. This first major section of this chapter begins by discussion these links again, first with the Layer 1 details, followed by the Layer 2 details. This section ends with an explanation of HDLC configuration details.

Answers to the "Do I Know This Already?" quiz:

1 B   **2** B   **3** A and C   **4** C   **5** A and D   **6** B and D   **7** C and D

> **NOTE**   The topics from here up to the "HDLC Configuration" section repeat some concepts from the ICND1 book and the ICND1 exam. For those of you who remember the details of leased lines well, as discussed in Chapter 3 of the ICND1 book, you might want to skim the topics of this chapter up to the heading "HDLC Configuration."

Layer 1 Leased Lines

Leased lines have been around a long time, roughly 20 years longer than LANs. However, they still exist today as a WAN service.

As a result of their long history in the market, the networking world has used a large number of different terms. First, the term *leased line* refers to the fact that the company using the leased line does not own the line, but instead pays a monthly lease fee to use it. Often, you lease the service from a telephone company, or *telco*. However, many people today use the generic term *service provider* to refer to a company that provides any form of WAN connectivity, including Internet services. Table 12-2 lists some of those names so that you can understand the different terms you will encounter in a real networking job.

Table 12-2   Different Names for a Leased Line

Name	Meaning or Reference
Leased circuit, circuit	The words *line* and *circuit* are often used as synonyms in telco terminology; circuit makes reference to the electrical circuit between the two endpoints.
Serial link, serial line	The words *link* and *line* are also often used as synonyms. *Serial* in this case refers to the fact that the bits flow serially and that routers use serial interfaces.
point-to-point link, point-to-point line	Refers to the fact that the topology stretches between two points, and 2 points only. (Some older leased lines allowed more than 2 devices.)
T1	A specific type of leased line that transmits data at 1.544 megabits per second (1.544 Mbps).
WAN link, Link	Both these terms are very general, with no reference to any specific technology.

The Physical Components of a Leased Line

To create a leased line, the telco must create some physical transmission path between the two routers on the ends of the link. The physical cabling must leave the buildings where each router sits. Then the telco must create the equivalent of a two-pair circuit from end to end, with one circuit to send data in each direction (full duplex). Figure 12-3 shows one such example, in which the telco uses a couple of traditional central office (CO) switches to create a short leased line between two routers.

12

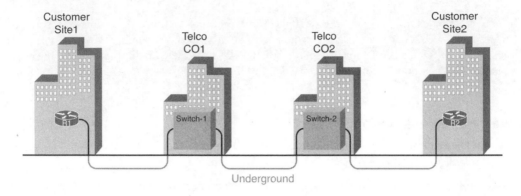

ICND1 - 3-3

Figure 12-3   *Possible Cabling Inside a Telco for a Short Leased Line*

The details in the center of Figure 12-3 probably show more than you ever need to know about leased-line WANs, at least from the enterprise customer perspective. More commonly, most network engineers think more about a leased line from the perspective of Figure 12-4, which shows a few key components and terms for the equipment on the ends of a leased line, as follows:

Customer premise equipment (CPE): This telco term refers to the gear that sits at their customer's sites on the ends on the link.

Channel service unit/data service unit (CSU/DSU): This device provides a function called *clocking*, in which it physically controls the speed and timing at which the router serial interface sends and receives each bit over the serial cable.

Serial cable: This is a short cable that connects the CSU and the router serial interface.

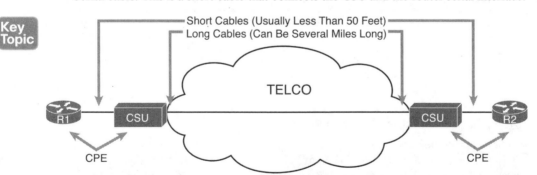

Figure 12-4   *Point-to-Point Leased Line: Components and Terminology*

The CPE includes several separately orderable parts. With an external CSU/DSU, a serial cable must be used to connect to the CSU to the router serial interface. Many routers today use serial interfaces. These serial interfaces usually exist as part of a removable card on the router, called WAN interface cards (WIC). The WIC has one style (size/shape) physical connector, whereas the CSU has one of several other types of connectors. So, when installing the leased line, the engineer must choose the correct cable type, with connectors to match the WIC on one end and the CSU/DSU on the other.

Figure 12-5 shows drawings of three types of serial cables. All have a smart serial connector on the top end, which is a commonly used connector on many Cisco serial interface cards. The other end in each cable uses one of the common physical serial connector standards found in CSU/DSU products.

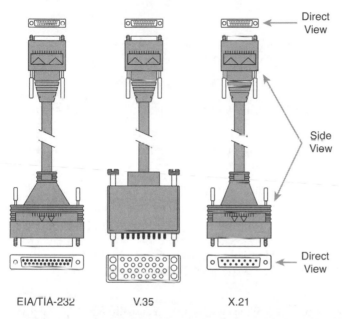

Figure 12-5 *Serial Cables Used Between a CSU and a Router*

Today, many leased lines make use of Cisco WICs with an integrated CSU/DSU. That is, the WIC hardware includes the same functions as a CSU/DSU, so an external CSU/DSU is not needed. Compared to Figure 12-4, the external CSU/DSU and serial cable on each end are not needed, with the cable from the telco connecting directly to the WIC.

Figure 12-6 shows a photo of a router with four WIC slots. Each slot currently shows a faceplate with no WIC cards installed. The foreground of the figure shows a WIC-4T1/E1, a card that supports four serial links with integrated CSU/DSU. The WIC shows four RJ-48 ports on the front of the card; these connectors have the same size and shape as the familiar RJ-45.

Leased Lines and the T-Carrier System

Telcos offer a wide variety of speeds for leased lines. However, a telco customer cannot pick just any speed. Instead, the speeds follow the standards of an age-old technology called the T-carrier system.

12

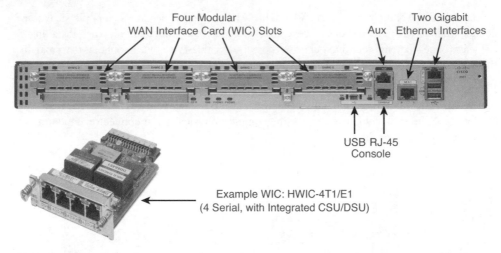

Figure 12-6   *Photo of Router with Serial WIC with Integrated CSU/DSU and RJ-48 Ports*

Back in the 1950s and 1960s, the U.S.-based Bell companies developed and deployed digital voice and the T-carrier system. As part of that work, they standardized different transmission speeds, including 64 Kbps, 1.544 Mbps, and 44.736 Mbps.

Those same Bell companies developed time-division multiplexing (TDM) technology that let them combine multiple of these base speeds onto a single line. For instance, one popular standard, a Digital Signal level 1 (DS1), or T1, combines 24 DS0s (at 64 Kbps) plus 8 Kbps of overhead into one physical line that runs at 1.544 Mbps. However, to allow flexibility of speeds offered to customers, the telco could install a T1 line to many sites, but run some at slower speeds and some and faster speeds—as long as those speeds were multiples of 64 Kbps.

Now back to the idea of the speed of a leased line. What can you actually buy? Basically, at slower speeds, you get any multiple of 64 Kbps, up to T1 speed. At faster speeds, you can get multiples of T1 speed, up to T3 speed. Table 12-3 summarizes the speeds.

Table 12-3   WAN Speed Summary

Names of Line	Bit Rate
DS0	64 Kbps
Fractional T1	Multiples of 64 Kbps, up to 24X
DS1 (T1)	1.544 Mbps (24 DS0s, for 1.536 Mbps, plus 8 Kbps overhead)
Fractional T3	Multiples of 1.536 Mbps, up to 28X
DS3 (T3)	44.736 Mbps (28 DS1s, plus management overhead)

The Role of the CSU/DSU

For our last bit of discussion about WAN links in a working enterprise internetwork, next consider the role of the CSU/DSU (called CSU for short). For the sake of discussion, the next few paragraphs, leading up to Figure 12-7, assume a leased line with external CSU/DSUs, like earlier in Figure 12-4.

> **NOTE** Many people refer to a CSU/DSU as simply a CSU.

The CSU sits between the telco leased line and the router; it understands both worlds and their conventions at Layer 1. On the telco side, that means the CSU connects to the line from the telco, so it must understand all these details about the T-carrier system, TDM, and the speed used by the telco. The CSU must be configured to match the telco's settings to run at the same speed. For instance, a CSU connected to a 256-Kbps fractional T1 requires different configuration from one connected to a full T1 (1.544 Mbps).

On the router side of the equation, the CSU connects to the router, with roles called the DCE and DTE, respectively. The CSU, acting as DCE (data circuit-terminating equipment), controls the speed of the router. The router, acting as DTE (data terminal equipment), is controlled by the clocking signals from CSU (DCE). That is, the CSU tells the router when to send and receive bits; the router attempts to send and receive bits only when the DCE creates the correct electrical impulses (called clocking) on the cable.

The DCE and DTE concept works a little like an overanxious child who is ready to throw balls to the parent as fast as possible. But the child must wait until each time his parent shouts "Now!" The parent sits there and shouts "Now! Now! Now! Now!" at a regular pace: the pace at which the parent is willing to catch the balls. Similarly, the CSU/DSU has configuration that tells it the speed at which to clock the router, with the CSU shouting "Now!" by changing the electrical current on some wires (clock signals) in the serial cable.

Figure 12-7 shows a diagram of those main concepts of the role of the CSU/DSU.

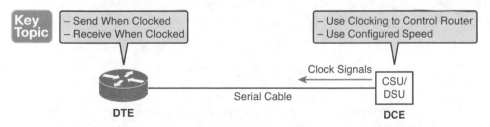

Figure 12-7 *DCE and DTE Roles for a CSU/DSU and a Router Serial Interface*

Building a WAN Link in a Lab

On a practical note, to prepare for the CCENT and CCNA exams, you might choose to buy some used router and switch hardware for hands-on practice. If you do, you can create the equivalent of a leased line, without a real leased line from a telco and without CSU/DSUs, just using a cabling trick. This short discussion tells you enough information to create a WAN link in your home lab.

First, when building a real WAN link with a real telco facility between sites, the serial cables normally used between a router and an external CSU/DSU are called *DTE cables*. For example, the conceptual drawing in earlier Figure 12-4 would use a DTE serial cable between each router and the CSU.

You can create an equivalent WAN link just by connecting two routers' serial interfaces using one DTE cable and a slightly different DCE cable, with no CSUs and with no leased line from the telco. The DCE cable has a female connector, and the DTE cable has a male connector, which allows the two cables can be attached directly. That completes the physical connection, providing a path for the data. The DCE cable also does the equivalent of an Ethernet crossover cable by swapping the transmit and receive wire pairs, as shown in Figure 12-8.

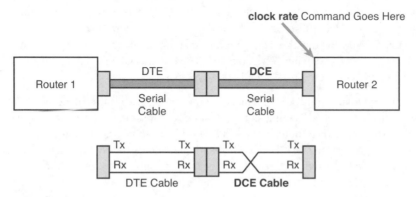

Figure 12-8 *Serial Cabling Uses a DTE Cable and a DCE Cable*

The figure shows the cable details at the top, with the wiring details at the bottom. In particular, at the bottom of the figure, note that the DTE serial cable acts as a straight-through cable and does not swap the transmit and receive pair, whereas the DCE cable does swap the pairs.

NOTE Many vendors, for convenience, sell a single cable that combines the two cables shown in Figure 12-8 into a single cable. Search online for "Cisco serial crossover" to find examples.

Finally, to make the link work, the router with the DCE cable installed must provide clocking. A router serial interface can provide clocking, but it can do so only if a DCE cable is connected to the interface and by the configuration of the **clock rate** command. (Note that the more recent versions of IOS, when the router notices a DCE cable connected to a serial interface, but with no **clock rate** command configured, the router automatically adds a **clock rate** command so that the link can work.)

Layer 2 Leased Lines with HDLC

A leased line provides a Layer 1 service. In other words, it promises to deliver bits between the devices connected to the leased line. However, the leased line itself does not define a data link layer protocol to be used on the leased line. HDLC provides one option for a data link protocol for a leased line.

HDLC has only a few big functions to perform with the simple point-to-point topology of a point-to-point leased line. First, the frame header lets the receiving router know that a new frame is coming. Plus, like all the other data link protocols, the HDLC trailer has a Frame Check Sequence (FCS) field that the receiving router can use to decide whether the frame had errors in transit, and if so, discard the frame.

Cisco adds another function to the ISO standard HDLC protocol by adding an extra field (a Type field) to the HDLC header, creating a Cisco-specific version of HDLC, as shown in Figure 12-9. The Type field allows Cisco routers to support multiple types of network layer packets to cross the HDLC link. (The original HDLC standard, which predated routers by many years, did not have a Type field.) For example, an HDLC link between two Cisco routers can forward both IPv4 and IPv6 packets because the Type field can identify which type of packet is encapsulated inside each HDLC frame.

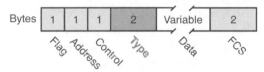

Figure 12-9 *Cisco HDLC Framing*

Today, the HDLC address and control fields have little work to do. For instance, with only two routers on a link, when a router sends a frame, it is clear that the frame is sent to the only other router on the link. Both the Address and Control fields had important purposes in years past, but today they are unimportant.

NOTE In case you wonder why HDLC has an Address field at all, in years past the telcos offered multidrop circuits. These circuits included more than two devices, so there was more than one possible destination, requiring an Address field to identify the correct destination.

Routers often use HDLC as the data link protocol on a leased line, as shown in Figure 12-10. Routers use HDLC just like any other data link protocol used by routers: to move packets to the next router. Figure 12-10 shows three familiar routing steps, with the role of HDLC sitting at Step 2. (Note that the figure does not show the data link trailer with each frame.)

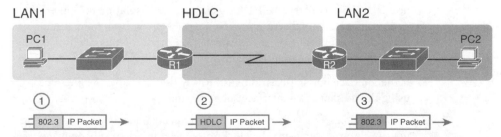

Figure 12-10 *General Concept of Routers Deencapsulating and Reencapsulating IP Packets*

Here is a walkthrough of the steps in the figure:

1. To send the IP packet to router R1, PC1 encapsulates the IP packet in an Ethernet frame.

2. Router R1 deencapsulates (removes) the IP packet, encapsulates the packet into a HDLC frame using an HDLC header and trailer, and forwards the HDLC frame to router R2.

3. Router R2 deencapsulates (removes) the IP packet, encapsulates the packet into an Ethernet frame, and forwards the Ethernet frame to PC2.

In summary, a leased line with HDLC creates a WAN link between two routers so that they can forward packets for the devices on the attached LANs. The leased line itself provides the physical means to transmit the bits, in both directions. The HDLC frames provide the means to encapsulate the network layer packet correctly so it crosses the link between routers.

Configuring HDLC

Think back to router LAN interfaces for a moment. Routers require no configuration related to Layers 1 and 2 for the interface to be up and working, forwarding IP traffic. The Layer 1 details occur by default once the cabling has been installed correctly. Router Ethernet interfaces of course use Ethernet as the data link protocol by default. The router only needs to configure an IP address on the interface, and possibly enable the interface with the **no shutdown** command if the interface is in an "administratively down" state.

Similarly, serial interfaces on Cisco routers need no specific Layer 1 or 2 configuration commands. For Layer 1, the cabling needs to be completed, of course, but the router attempts to use the serial interface once the **no shutdown** command is configured. For Layer 2, IOS defaults to use HDLC on serial interfaces. As on Ethernet interfaces, router serial interfaces usually only need an **ip address** command, and possibly the **no shutdown** command.

However, many optional commands exist for serial links. The following list outlines some configuration steps, listing the conditions for which some commands are needed, plus commands that are purely optional:

Step 1. Configure the interface IP address using the **ip address** interface subcommand.

Step 2. The following tasks are required only when the specifically listed conditions are true:

    A. If an **encapsulation** *protocol* interface subcommand already exists, for a non-HDLC protocol, enable HDLC using the **encapsulation hdlc** interface subcommand. Alternatively, make the interface revert back to its default encapsulation by using the **no encapsulation** *protocol* interface subcommand to disable the currently enabled protocol.

    B. If the interface line status is administratively down, enable the interface using the **no shutdown** interface subcommand.

    C. If the serial link is a back-to-back serial link in a lab (or a simulator), configure the clocking rate using the **clock rate** *speed* interface subcommand, but only on the one router with the DCE cable (per the **show controllers serial** *number* command).

Step 3. The following steps are always optional and have no impact on whether the link works and passes IP traffic:

    A. Configure the link's speed using the **bandwidth** *speed-in-kbps* interface subcommand to match the actual speed of the link.

    B. For documentation purposes, configure a description of the purpose of the interface using the **description** *text* interface subcommand.

In practice, when you configure a Cisco router with no preexisting interface configuration and install a normal production serial link with CSU/DSUs, the **ip address** and **no shutdown** commands are likely the one configuration commands you would need.

Figure 12-11 shows a sample internetwork, and Example 12-1 shows the matching HDLC configuration. In this case, the serial link was created with a back-to-back serial link in a lab, requiring Steps 1 (**ip address**) and 2C (**clock rate**) from the preceding list. It also shows optional Step 3B (**description**).

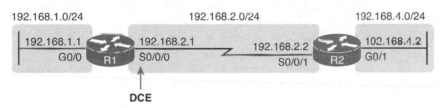

Figure 12-11 *Typical Serial Link Between Two Routers*

Example 12-1 *HDLC Configuration*

```
R1# show running-config
! Note - only the related lines are shown
interface GigabitEthernet0/0
 ip address 192.168.1.1 255.255.255.0
!
interface Serial0/0/0
 ip address 192.168.2.1 255.255.255.0
 description link to R2
 clock rate 2000000
!
router eigrp 1
 network 192.168.1.0
 network 192.168.2.0
```

The configuration on R1 is relatively simple. The matching configuration on R2's S0/0/1 interface simply needs an **ip address** command plus the default settings of **encapsulation hdlc** and **no shutdown**. The **clock rate** command would not be needed on R2 because R1 has the DCE cable, so R2 must be connected to a DTE cable.

Example 12-2 lists two commands that confirm the configuration on R1 and some other default settings. First, it lists the output from the **show controllers** command for S0/0/0, which confirms that R1 indeed has a DCE cable installed and that the clock rate has been set to 2000000 bps. The **show interfaces S0/0/0** command lists the various configuration settings near the top, including the default encapsulation value (HDLC) and default bandwidth setting on a serial interface (1544, meaning 1544 Kbps or 1.544 Mbps). It also lists the IP address, prefix-style mask (/24), and description, as configured in Example 12-1.

Example 12-2   *Verifying the Configuration Settings on R1*

```
R1# show controllers serial 0/0/0
Interface Serial0/0/0
Hardware is SCC
DCE V.35, clock rate 2000000
! lines omitted for brevity


R1# show interfaces s0/0/0
Serial0/0/0 is up, line protocol is up
  Hardware is WIC MBRD Serial
  Description: link to R2
  Internet address is 192.168.2.1/24
  MTU 1500 bytes, BW 1544 Kbit/sec, DLY 20000 usec,
     reliability 255/255, txload 1/255, rxload 1/255
  Encapsulation HDLC, loopback not set
  Keepalive set (10 sec)
  Last input 00:00:01, output 00:00:00, output hang never
  Last clearing of "show interface" counters never
  Input queue: 0/75/0/0 (size/max/drops/flushes); Total output drops: 0
  Queueing strategy: fifo
  Output queue: 0/40 (size/max)
  5 minute input rate 0 bits/sec, 0 packets/sec
  5 minute output rate 0 bits/sec, 0 packets/sec
     276 packets input, 19885 bytes, 0 no buffer
     Received 96 broadcasts (0 IP multicasts)
     0 runts, 0 giants, 0 throttles
     0 input errors, 0 CRC, 0 frame, 0 overrun, 0 ignored, 0 abort
     284 packets output, 19290 bytes, 0 underruns
     0 output errors, 0 collisions, 5 interface resets
     0 unknown protocol drops
     0 output buffer failures, 0 output buffers swapped out
     7 carrier transitions
     DCD=up  DSR=up  DTR=up  RTS=up  CTS=up
```

Finally, the router uses the serial interface only if it reaches an up/up interfaces status, as shown in the first line of the output of the **show interfaces S0/0/0** command in Example 12-2. Generally speaking, the first status word refers to Layer 1 status, and the second refers to Layer 2 status. For a quicker look at the interface status, instead use either the **show ip interface brief** and **show interfaces description** commands, as listed in Example 12-3.

Example 12-3 *Brief Lists of Interfaces and Interface Status*

```
R1# show ip interface brief
Interface               IP-Address      OK? Method Status                Protocol
GigabitEthernet0/0      192.168.1.1     YES manual up                    up
GigabitEthernet0/1      unassigned      YES manual administratively down down
Serial0/0/0             192.168.2.1     YES manual up                    up
Serial0/0/1             unassigned      YES NVRAM  administratively down down
Serial0/1/0             unassigned      YES NVRAM  administratively down down
Serial0/1/1             unassigned      YES NVRAM  administratively down down

R1# show interfaces description
Interface               Status          Protocol Description
Gi0/0                   up              up       LAN at Site 1
Gi0/1                   admin down      down
Se0/0/0                 up              up       link to R2
Se0/0/1                 admin down      down
Se0/1/0                 admin down      down
Se0/1/1                 admin down      down
```

Leased-Line WANs with PPP

Point-to-Point Protocol (PPP) plays the same role as HDLC: a data link protocol for use on serial links. However, HDLC was created for a world without routers. In contrast, PPP, defined in the 1990s, was designed with routers, TCP/IP, and other network layer protocols in mind, with many more advanced features.

This second major section of this chapter first discusses PPP concepts, including one example of a more advanced PPP feature (authentication). This section ends with some configuration examples using PPP.

PPP Concepts

PPP provides several basic but important functions that are useful on a leased line that connects two devices:

- Definition of a header and trailer that allows delivery of a data frame over the link
- Support for both synchronous and asynchronous links
- A protocol Type field in the header, allowing multiple Layer 3 protocols to pass over the same link
- Built-in authentication tools: Password Authentication Protocol (PAP) and Challenge Handshake Authentication Protocol (CHAP)
- Control protocols for each higher-layer protocol that rides over PPP, allowing easier integration and support of those protocols

The next several pages take a closer look at the protocol field, authentication, and the control protocols.

12

PPP Framing

Unlike the standard version of HDLC, the PPP standard defines a protocol field. The protocol field identifies the type of packet inside the frame. When PPP was created, this field allowed packets from the many different Layer 3 protocols to pass over a single link. Today, the protocol Type field still provides the same function, usually supporting packets for the two different versions of IP (IPv4 and IPv6). Figure 12-12 shows the PPP framing, which happens to mirror the Cisco proprietary HDLC framing that includes a protocol Type field (as shown earlier in Figure 12-9).

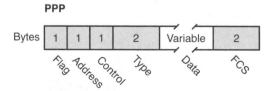

Figure 12-12 *PPP Framing*

PPP Control Protocols

In addition to HDLC-like framing, PPP defines a set of Layer 2 control protocols that perform various link control functions. The idea of these extra protocols works a little like how Ethernet includes additional protocols like Spanning Tree Protocol (STP). Ethernet has headers and trailers to deliver frames, plus it defines overhead protocols like STP to help make the frame forwarding process work better. Likewise, PPP defines the frame format in Figure 12-12, plus it defines other protocols to help manage and control the serial link.

PPP separates these control protocols into two main categories:

■ **Link Control Protocol (LCP):** This one protocol has several different individual functions, each focused on the data link itself, ignoring the Layer 3 protocol sent across the link.

■ **Network Control Protocols (NCP):** This is a category of protocols, one per network layer protocol. Each protocol does functions specific to its related Layer 3 protocol.

The PPP LCP implements the control functions that work the same regardless of the Layer 3 protocol. For features related to any higher-layer protocols, usually Layer 3 protocols, PPP uses a series of PPP *control protocols* (CP), such as IP Control Protocol (IPCP). PPP uses one instance of LCP per link and one NCP for each Layer 3 protocol defined on the link. For example, on a PPP link using IPv4, IPv6, and Cisco Discovery Protocol (CDP), the link uses one instance of LCP plus IPCP (for IPv4), IPv6CP (for IPv6), and CDPCP (for CDP).

Table 12-4 summarizes the functions of LCP, gives the LCP feature names, and describes the features briefly. Following the table, the text explains one of the features, PPP authentication, in more detail.

Table 12-4   PPP LCP Features

Function	LCP Feature	Description
Looped link detection	Magic number	Detects whether the link is looped, and disables the interface, allowing rerouting over a working route
Error detection	Link-quality monitoring (LQM)	Disables an interface that exceeds an error percentage threshold, allowing rerouting over better routes
Multilink support	Multilink PPP	Load balances traffic over multiple parallel links
Authentication	PAP and CHAP	Exchanges names and passwords so that each device can verify the identity of the device on the other end of the link

PPP Authentication

In networking, *authentication* gives one device a way to confirm that another device is truly the correct and approved device with which communications should occur. In other words, authentication confirms that the other party is the authentic other party, and not some imposter.

For instance, with PPP, if R1 and R2 are supposed to be communicating over a serial link, R1 might want R2 to somehow prove that the device claiming to be R2 really is R2. In that scenario, R1 wants to authenticate R2, with the authentication process providing a way for R2 to prove its identity.

WAN authentication is most often needed when dial lines are used. However, the configuration of the authentication features remains the same whether a leased line or dial line is used.

PPP defines two authentication protocols: PAP and CHAP. Both protocols require the exchange of messages between devices, but with different details. With PAP, the process works with the to-be-authenticated device starting the messages, claiming to be legitimate by listing a secret password in clear text, as shown in Figure 12-13.

Figure 12-13   *PAP Authentication Process*

In the figure, when the link comes up, authentication takes two steps. At Step 1, Barney sends the shared password in clear text. Fred, who wants to authenticate Barney—that is, confirm that Barney is the real Barney—sees the password, confirms that it is the correct password, and sends back an acknowledgment that Barney has passed the authentication process.

12

CHAP, a much more secure option, uses different messages, and it hides the password. With CHAP, the device doing the authentication (Fred) begins with a message called a *challenge*, which asks the other device to reply. The big difference is that the second message in the flow (as shown in Figure 12-14) hides the authentication password by instead sending a hashed version of the password. If Fred confirms that the hashed password is indeed the correct password, Fred sends back a third message to confirm the successful authentication of Barney.

Figure 12-14 *CHAP Authentication Process*

Both Figure 12-13 and 12-14 show authentication flows when authentication works. When it fails (for instance, if the passwords do not match), a different final message flows. Also, if the authentication fails, PPP leaves the interface in an up/down state, and the router cannot forward and receive frames on the interface.

PAP flows are much less secure than CHAP because PAP sends the hostname and password in clear text in the message. These can be read easily if someone places a tracing tool in the circuit. CHAP instead uses a one-way hash algorithm, called message digest 5 (MD5), with input to the algorithm being a password that never crosses the link plus a shared random number.

The CHAP process also uses a hash value only one time so that an attacker cannot just make a copy of the hashed value and send it at a later date. To make that work, the CHAP challenge (the first CHAP message) states a random number. The challenged router runs the hash algorithm using the just-learned random number and the secret password, and sends the results back to the router that sent the challenge. The router that sent the challenge runs the same algorithm using the random number (sent across the link) and the password (as stored locally); if the results match, the passwords must match. Later, the next time the authentication process work occurs, the authenticating router generates and uses a different random number.

PAP and CHAP are a few examples of the work done by PPP's LCP. The next topic looks at how to configure and verify PPP.

Configuring PPP

Configuring PPP, as compared to HDLC, requires only one change: using the **encapsulation ppp** command on both ends of the link. As with HDLC, other items can be optionally configured, such as the interface **bandwidth**, and a **description** of the interface. And of course, the interface must be enabled (**no shutdown**). But the configuration to migrate from HDLC to PPP just requires the **encapsulation ppp** command on both routers' serial interfaces.

Example 12-4 shows a simple configuration using the two routers shown in Figure 12-11, the same internetwork used for the HDLC example. The example includes the IP address configuration, but the IP addresses do not have to be configured for PPP to work.

Example 12-4   *Basic PPP Configuration*

```
! The example starts with router R1
interface Serial0/0/0
 ip address 192.168.2.1 255.255.255.0
 encapsulation ppp
 clockrate 2000000

! Next, the configuration on router R2
interface Serial0/0/1
 ip address 192.168.2.2 255.255.255.0
 encapsulation ppp
```

The one **show** command that lists PPP details is the **show interfaces** command, with an example from R1 listed in Example 12-5. The output looks just like it does for HDLC up until the first highlighted line in the example. The two highlighted lines confirm the configuration ("Encapsulation PPP"). These lines also confirm that LCP has completed its work successfully, as noted with the "LCP Open" phrase. Finally, the output lists the fact that two CPs, CDPCP and IPCP, have also successfully been enabled—all good indications that PPP is working properly.

Example 12-5   *Finding PPP, LCP, and NCP Status with* **show interfaces**

```
R1# show interfaces serial 0/0/0
Serial0/0/0 is up, line protocol is up
  Hardware is WIC MBRD Serial
  Description: link to R2
  Internet address is 192.168.2.1/24
  MTU 1500 bytes, BW 1544 Kbit/sec, DLY 20000 usec,
     reliability 255/255, txload 1/255, rxload 1/255
  Encapsulation PPP, LCP Open
  Open: IPCP, CDPCP, loopback not set
! Lines omitted for brevity
```

CHAP Configuration and Verification

The simplest version of CHAP configuration requires only a few commands. The configuration uses a password configured on each router. (As an alternative, the password could be configured on an external authentication, authorization, and accounting [AAA] server outside the router.)

12

To migrate from a configuration that only uses PPP, to a configuration that adds CHAP authentication, follow these steps:

Step 1.   Configure the routers' hostnames using the **hostname** *name* global configuration command.

Step 2.   Configure the username for the other router, and the shared secret password, using the **username** *name* **password** *password* global configuration command or the **username** *name* secret password command.

Step 3.   Enable CHAP on the interface on each router using the **ppp authentication chap** interface subcommand.

Figure 12-15 shows the configuration on both R1 and R2 to both enable PPP and add CHAP to the link. The figure shows how the name in the **hostname** command on one router must match the **username** command on the other router. It also shows that the password defined in each **username** command must be the same (mypass in this case).

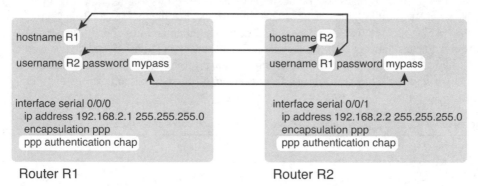

Figure 12-15   *CHAP Configuration*

Because CHAP is a function of LCP, if the authentication process fails, LCP does not complete and the interface falls to an up and down interface state.

Troubleshooting Serial Links

This final major section discusses how to isolate and find the root cause of problems related to topics covered earlier in this chapter. Also, this section does not attempt to repeat the IP troubleshooting coverage in Parts II and III of this book, but it does point out some of the possible symptoms on a serial link when a Layer 3 subnet mismatch occurs on opposite ends of a serial link, which prevents the routers from routing packets over the serial link.

A simple **ping** command can determine whether a serial link can or cannot forward IP packets. A ping of the other router's serial IP address—for example, a working **ping 192.168.2.2** command on R1 in Figure 12-11, the figure used for both the HDLC and PPP configuration examples—proves that the link either works or does not.

If the **ping** does not work, the problem could be related to functions at Layers 1, 2, or 3. The best way to isolate which layer is the most likely cause is to examine the interface status codes described in Table 12-5.

Table 12-5   Interface Status Codes and Typical Meanings When a Ping Does Not Work

Line Status	Protocol Status	Likely General Reason/Layer
Administratively down	Down	Interface shutdown
Down	Down	Layer 1
Up	Down	Layer 2
Up	Up	Layer 3

The serial link verification and troubleshooting process should begin with a simple three-step process:

Step 1.   From one router, ping the other router's serial IP address.

Step 2.   If the ping fails, examine the interface status on both routers and investigate problems related to the likely problem areas listed in Table 12-5.

Step 3.   If the ping works, also verify that any routing protocols are exchanging routes over the link, as discussed in Chapter 11, "Troubleshooting IPv4 Routing Protocols."

NOTE   The interface status codes can be found using the **show interfaces, show ip interface brief,** and **show interfaces description** commands.

The rest of this section explores the specific items to be examined when the ping fails, based on the combinations of interface status codes listed in Table 12-5.

Troubleshooting Layer 1 Problems

The interface status codes, or interface state, play a key role in isolating the root cause of problems on serial links. In fact, the status on both ends of the link may differ, so it is important to examine the status on both ends of the link to help determine the problem.

For example, a serial link fails when just one of the two routers has administratively disabled its serial interface with the **shutdown** interface subcommand. When one router shuts down its serial interface, the other router sits in a down/down state (line status down, line protocol status down), assuming the second router is not also shutdown. The solution is to just configure a **no shutdown** interface configuration command on the interface.

A serial interface with a *down* line status on both ends of the serial link—that is, both ends in a down/down state—usually points to some Layer 1 problem. Figure 12-16 summarizes the most common causes of this state. In the figure, R2's serial interface has no problems at all; the center and left side of the figure show common root causes that then result in R2's serial interface being in a down/down state.

12

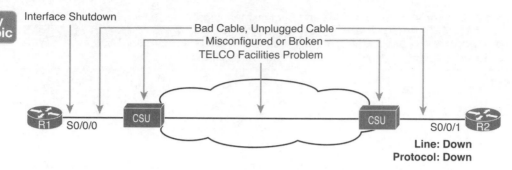

Figure 12-16 *Problems That Result in a Down/Down State on Router R2*

Troubleshooting Layer 2 Problems

Data link layer problems on serial links usually result in at least one of the routers having a serial interface status of up/down. In other words, the line status (the first status code) is up, while the second status (the line protocol status) is down. Table 12-6 summarizes these types of problems.

Table 12-6 Likely Reasons for Data Link Problems on Serial Links

Line Status	Protocol Status	Likely Reason
Up	Down on both ends[1]	Mismatched **encapsulation** commands
Up	Down on one end, up on the other	Keepalive disabled on the end in an up state when using HDLC
Up	Down on both ends	PAP/CHAP authentication failure

[1] In this case, the state may flap from up/up, to up/down, to up/up, and so on, while the router keeps trying to make the encapsulation work.

> **NOTE** As with the other troubleshooting topics in this book, Table 12-6 lists some of the more common types of failures but not all.

The first of these problems—a mismatch between the configured data link protocols—is easy to identify and fix. The **show interfaces** command lists the encapsulation type on about the seventh line of the output, so using this command on both routers can quickly identify the problem. Alternatively, a quick look at the configuration, plus remembering that HDLC is the default serial encapsulation, can confirm whether the encapsulations are mismatched. The solution is simple: Reconfigure one of the two routers to match the other router's **encapsulation** command.

The other two root causes require a little more discussion to understand the issue and determine if they are the real root cause. The next two headings take a closer look at each.

Keepalive Failure

The router *keepalive* feature helps a router notice when a link is no longer functioning. Once a router believes the link no longer works, the router can bring down the interface, allowing the routing protocol to converge to use other routes it they exist.

The keepalive function causes routers to send keepalive messages to each other every 10 seconds (the default setting). The keepalive message for HDLC is a Cisco proprietary message, whereas PPP defines a keepalive message as part of LCP. Both protocols use a keepalive interval, a timer that defines the time period between keepalives.

Regular keepalives keeps the link up, whereas a lack of keepalives makes the link fail. In particular, if a router does not receive any keepalive messages from the other router for a number of keepalive intervals (three or five intervals by default, depending on the IOS version), the router brings down the interface, thinking that the interface of the other router is no longer working.

As long as both routers use keepalives, or both routers disable keepalives, the link works. However, a mistake can be made in which one end leaves keepalives enabled and one end disables keepalives. This mistake only breaks HDLC links; the PPP keepalive feature prevents the problem. Figure 12-17 shows one such example with HDLC and with R1 mistakenly disabling keepalives.

interface serial 0/0/0
  encapsulation hdlc
  no keepalive

interface serial 0/0/1
  encapsulation hdlc

192.168.2.1
S0/0/1
R1

192.168.2.2
S0/0/1
R2

Line: Up
Protocol: Up

Line: Up
Protocol: Down

Figure 12-17 *Problems That Result in a Down/Down State on Router R2*

In the scenario shown in Figure 12-17, R2's interface fails because

- R1 does not send keepalive messages, because keepalives are disabled.

- R2 still expects to receive keepalive messages, because keepalives are enabled.

After not hearing the keepalive messages for a number of keepalive intervals, R2 would fail the link to an up/down state. Over time, R2 might bring the link to an up/up state, and then after three more keepalive intervals fail it back to up/down state.

Example 12-6 shows how to find evidence of this keepalive mismatch. First, it lists enough of the output of the **show interfaces S0/0/0** command on R1 to show the line that confirms R1's **no keepalive** configuration setting. It shows the same command on R2, confirming the keepalive is enabled, and the interface state of up/down.

Example 12-6 *Line Problems Because of Keepalive Only on R2*

```
! R1 disables keepalives, and remains in an up/up state.
R1# show interfaces s0/0/0
Serial0/0/0 is up, line protocol is up
  Hardware is WIC MBRD Serial
  Description: link to R2
  Internet address is 192.168.2.1/24
  MTU 1500 bytes, BW 1544 Kbit/sec, DLY 20000 usec,
     reliability 255/255, txload 1/255, rxload 1/255
  Encapsulation HDLC, loopback not set
  Keepalive not set
! lines omitted for brevity
```

```
! Below, R2 still has keepalives enabled (default)
R2# show interfaces S0/0/1
Serial0/0/1 is up, line protocol is down
  Hardware is WIC MBRD Serial
  Internet address is 192.168.2.2/24
  MTU 1500 bytes, BW 1544 Kbit/sec, DLY 20000 usec,
     reliability 255/255, txload 1/255, rxload 1/255
  Encapsulation HDLC, loopback not set
  Keepalive set (10 sec)
! lines omitted for brevity
```

PAP and CHAP Authentication Failure

As mentioned earlier, a failure in the PAP/CHAP authentication process results in both routers falling to an up and down state. To discover whether a PAP/CHAP failure is really the root cause, you can use the **debug ppp authentication** command. For perspective, Example 12-7 shows the output of this command when CHAP has been configured as in earlier Example 12-5, with CHAP working correctly in this case.

Example 12-7 *Debug Messages Confirming the Correct Operation of CHAP*

```
R1# debug ppp authentication
PPP authentication debugging is on
R1#
*Nov 18 23:34:30.060: %LINK-3-UPDOWN: Interface Serial0/0/0, changed state to up
*Nov 18 23:34:30.060: Se0/0/0 PPP: Using default call direction
*Nov 18 23:34:30.060: Se0/0/0 PPP: Treating connection as a dedicated line
*Nov 18 23:34:30.060: Se0/0/0 PPP: Session handle[58000009] Session id[7]
*Nov 18 23:34:30.064: Se0/0/0 CHAP: O CHALLENGE id 1 len 23 from "R1"
*Nov 18 23:34:30.084: Se0/0/0 CHAP: I CHALLENGE id 1 len 23 from "R2"
*Nov 18 23:34:30.084: Se0/0/0 PPP: Sent CHAP SENDAUTH Request
*Nov 18 23:34:30.084: Se0/0/0 CHAP: I RESPONSE id 1 len 23 from "R2"
*Nov 18 23:34:30.084: Se0/0/0 PPP: Received SENDAUTH Response PASS
*Nov 18 23:34:30.084: Se0/0/0 CHAP: Using hostname from configured hostname
```

```
*Nov 18 23:34:30.084: Se0/0/0 CHAP: Using password from AAA
*Nov 18 23:34:30.084: Se0/0/0 CHAP: O RESPONSE id 1 len 23 from "R1"
*Nov 18 23:34:30.084: Se0/0/0 PPP: Sent CHAP LOGIN Request
*Nov 18 23:34:30.084: Se0/0/0 PPP: Received LOGIN Response PASS
*Nov 18 23:34:30.088: Se0/0/0 CHAP: O SUCCESS id 1 len 4
*Nov 18 23:34:30.088: Se0/0/0 CHAP: I SUCCESS id 1 len 4
```

CHAP uses a three-message exchange, as shown back in Figure 12-14, with a set of messages flowing for authentication in each direction by default. The three highlighted lines show the authentication process by which R1 authenticates R2, as follows:

1. This line refers to a CHAP Challenge message, sent out of router R1, per the O, meaning "output." The end of the line confirms it was sent from the router with hostname R1.

2. This line refers to a CHAP Response message, sent from router R2, with an I for "input," meaning the messages comes into R1.

3. This line refers to a CHAP Success message, sent out (O) by R1, stating that the authentication was successful.

You can see the same three messages for R2's authentication of R1 in the output, as well, but those messages are not highlighted in the example.

When CHAP authentication fails, the **debug** output shows a couple of fairly obvious messages. Example 12-8 shows the results using the same two-router internetwork shown in Figure 12-15, which was used for the CHAP configuration example. However, this time, the passwords are misconfigured, so CHAP fails.

Example 12-8 *Debug Messages Confirming the Failure of CHAP*

```
R1# debug ppp authentication
PPP authentication debugging is on
! Lines omitted for brevity
*Nov 18 23:45:48.820: Se0/0/0 CHAP: O CHALLENGE id 1 len 23 from "R1"
*Nov 18 23:45:48.820: Se0/0/0 CHAP: I RESPONSE id 1 len 23 from "R2"
*Nov 18 23:45:48.820: Se0/0/0 CHAP: O FAILURE id 1 len 25 msg is "Authentication failed"
```

Troubleshooting Layer 3 Problems

This chapter suggests that the best starting place to troubleshoot serial links is to ping the IP address of the router on the other end of the link—specifically, the IP address on the serial link. Interestingly, the serial link can be in an up and up state but the ping can still fail because of Layer 3 misconfiguration. In some cases, the ping may work but the routing protocols might not be able to exchange routes. This short section examines the symptoms, which differ slightly depending on whether HDLC or PPP is used and the root cause.

First, consider an HDLC link on which the physical and data link details are working fine. In this case, both routers' interfaces are in an up and up state. However, if the IP addresses configured on the serial interfaces on the two routers are in different subnets, a ping to the IP address on the other end of the link will fail because the routers do not have a matching route. For example, in Figure 12-17, if R1's serial IP address remained 192.168.2.1, and R2's was changed to 192.168.3.2 (instead of 192.168.2.2), still with a mask of /24, the two routers would have connected routes to different subnets. They would not have a route matching the opposite router's serial IP address.

Finding and fixing a mismatched subnet problem with HDLC links is relatively simple. You can find the problem by doing the usual first step of pinging the IP address on the other end of the link and failing. If both interfaces have a status of up/up, the problem is likely this mismatched IP subnet.

For PPP links with the same IP address/mask misconfiguration, the ping to the other router's IP address actually works. However, the IP subnet mismatch still prevents EIGRP and OSPF neighbor relationships from forming, so it is still a good idea to follow the rules and put both serial interface IP addresses in the same subnet.

PPP makes the ping work with the mismatched subnet by adding a host route, with a /32 prefix length, for the IP address of the other router. This happens as part of the IP Control Protocol work. Example 12-9 shows this exact scenario.

> **NOTE** A route with a /32 prefix, representing a single host, is called a *host route*.

Example 12-9 *PPP Allowing a Ping over a Serial Link, Even with Mismatched Subnets*

```
R1# show ip route
! Legend omitted for brevity
      192.168.1.0/24 is variably subnetted, 2 subnets, 2 masks
C        192.168.1.0/24 is directly connected, GigabitEthernet0/0
L        192.168.1.1/32 is directly connected, GigabitEthernet0/0
      192.168.2.0/24 is variably subnetted, 2 subnets, 2 masks
C        192.168.2.0/24 is directly connected, Serial0/0/0
L        192.168.2.1/32 is directly connected, Serial0/0/0
      192.168.3.0/32 is subnetted, 1 subnets
C        192.168.3.2 is directly connected, Serial0/0/0


R1# ping 192.168.3.2


Type escape sequence to abort.
Sending 5, 100-byte ICMP Echos to 192.168.3.2, timeout is 2 seconds:
!!!!!
Success rate is 100 percent (5/5), round-trip min/avg/max = 1/2/4 ms
```

The first highlighted line in the example shows the normal connected route on the serial link, for network 192.168.2.0/24. R1 thinks this subnet is the subnet connected to S0/0/0 because of R1's configured IP address (192.168.2.1/24). The second highlighted line shows the host route created by PPP, specifically for R2's new serial IP address (192.168.3.2). (R2 will have a similar route for 192.168.2.1/32, R1's serial IP address.) So, both routers have a route to allow them to forward packets to the IP address on the other end of the link, even though the other router's address is in a different subnet. This extra host route allows the ping to the other side of the serial link to work in spite of the addresses on each end being in different subnets.

Table 12-7 summarizes the behavior on HDLC and PPP links when the IP addresses on each end do not reside in the same subnet but no other problems exist.

Table 12-7   Summary of Symptoms for Mismatched Subnets on Serial Links

Symptoms When IP Addresses on a Serial Link Are in Different Subnets	HDLC	PPP
Does a ping of the other router's serial IP address work?	No	Yes
Can routing protocols exchange routes over the link?	No	No

12

Exam Preparation Tasks

Review All the Key Topics

Review the most important topics from this chapter, noted with the Key Topic icon. Table 12-8 lists these key topics and where each is discussed.

Table 12-8   Key Topics for Chapter 12

Key Topic Element	Description	Page Number
Figure 12-4	Components of a leased line	364
Table 12-3	Speeds for WAN links per the T-carrier system	366
Figure 12-7	Role of the CSU/DSU and the router as DCE and DTE	367
Step list	HDLC configuration checklist	370
List	PPP features	373
List	Comparison of PPP LCP and NCP	374
Figure 12-14	Example of messages sent by CHAP	376
Step list	Configuration checklist for CHAP	378
Figure 12-16	Common reasons for Layer 1 serial link problems	380
Table 12-6	Common symptoms and reasons for common Layer 2 problems on serial links	380

Complete the Tables and Lists from Memory

Print a copy of DVD Appendix D, "Memory Tables," or at least the section for this chapter, and complete the tables and lists from memory. DVD Appendix E, "Memory Tables Answer Key," includes completed tables and lists to check your work.

Definitions of Key Terms

After your first reading of the chapter, try to define these key terms, but do not be concerned about getting them all correct at that time. Chapter 22 directs you in how to use these terms for late-stage preparation for the exam.

leased line, telco, serial link, WAN link, T1, DS0, DS1, T3, customer premise equipment, CSU/DSU, serial cable, DCE, DTE, HDLC, PPP, CHAP, IP control protocol, keepalive, Link Control Protocol

Command Reference to Check Your Memory

Although you should not necessarily memorize the information in the tables in this section, this section does include a reference for the configuration and EXEC commands covered in this chapter. Practically speaking, you should memorize the commands as a side effect of reading the chapter and doing all the activities in this exam preparation section. To see how well you have memorized the commands as a side effect of your other studies, cover the left side of the table, read the descriptions on the right side, and see if you remember the command.

Table 12-9   Chapter 12 Configuration Command Reference

Command	Description
encapsulation {hdlc	ppp}	Interface subcommand that defines the serial data-link protocol.
[no] shutdown	Administratively disables (**shutdown**) or enables **no shutdown**) the interface in whose mode the command is issued.
clock rate *speed*	Serial interface subcommand that, when used on an interface with a DCE cable, sets the clock speed in bps.
bandwidth *speed-kbps*	Interface subcommand that sets the router's opinion of the link speed, in kilobits per second, but has no effect on the actual speed.
description *text*	Interface subcommand that can set a text description of the interface.
ppp authentication {pap	chap	pap chap	chap pap}	Interface subcommand that enables only PAP, only CHAP, or both (order dependent).
username *name* password *secret*	Global command that sets the password that this router expects to use when authenticating the router with the listed hostname.

Table 12-10   Chapter 12 EXEC Command Reference

Command	Description
show interfaces [*type number*]	Lists statistics and details of interface configuration, including the encapsulation type.
show interfaces [*type number*] description	Lists a single line per interface (or if the interface is included, just one line of output total) that lists the interface status and description.
show ip interface brief	Lists one line of output per interface, with IP address and interface status.
show controllers serial *number*	Lists whether a cable is connected to the interface, and if so, whether it is a DTE or DCE cable.
debug ppp authentication	Generates messages for each step in the PAP or CHAP authentication process.
debug ppp negotiation	Generates **debug** messages for the LCP and NCP negotiation messages sent between the devices.

12

This chapter covers the following exam topics:

WAN Technologies

Identify Different WAN Technologies

Frame Relay

Understanding Frame Relay Concepts

Frame Relay was at one time the most popular WAN technology used in computer networks. Today, Frame Relay has become less popular, being replaced by several other WAN options. These include the virtual private network (VPN) technology, as discussed back in Chapter 7, "Virtual Private Networks," and Ethernet WANs, as introduced in the ICND1 book. In addition, many enterprises use Multiprotocol Label Switching (MPLS) VPNs, which follow the same basic service model as Frame Relay, usually offered by the same Frame Relay providers but with significant technical advantages.

Although many companies choose other WAN options today, Frame Relay still has uses. Some companies still use it as a core WAN technology. It can also be used to connect to MPLS and Internet VPNs. So, Frame Relay will be an important networking topic for some time.

This chapter describes Frame Relay protocol details, with Chapter 14, "Implementing Frame Relay," discussing how to configure Frame Relay. The first section of this chapter focuses on the basics of Frame Relay, including a lot of new terminology. The second section examines Frame Relay data link addressing. This topic requires some attention because Frame Relay addresses are needed for both router configuration and troubleshooting. The last major section of this chapter examines some network layer concerns when using Frame Relay.

"Do I Know This Already?" Quiz

Use the "Do I Know This Already?" quiz to help decide whether you might want to skim this chapter, or a major section, moving more quickly to the Exam Preparation Tasks section near the end of the chapter. You can find the answers at the bottom of the page following the quiz. For thorough explanations, see DVD Appendix C, "Answers to the 'Do I Know This Already?' Quizzes."

Table 13-1 "Do I Know This Already?" Foundation Topics Section-to-Question Mapping

Foundation Topics Section	Questions
Frame Relay Overview	1–2
Frame Relay Addressing	3–4
Network Layer Concerns with Frame Relay	5–6

1. Which of the following is a protocol used between the Frame Relay DTE and the Frame Relay switch?

   a. VC

   b. CIR

   c. LMI

   d. Q.921

   e. DLCI

2. Which of the following statements about Frame Relay are true? (Choose two answers.)

   a. The DTE usually sits at the customer site.

   b. Routers send LMI messages to each other to signal the status of a VC.

   c. A frame's source DLCI must remain unchanged, but the frame's destination DLCI is allowed to change, as the frame traverses the Frame Relay cloud.

   d. The Frame Relay encapsulation type on the sending router should match the encapsulation type on the receiving router for the receiving router to be able to understand the frame's contents.

3. What does DLCI stand for?

   a. Data link connection identifier

   b. Data link connection indicator

   c. Data link circuit identifier

   d. Data link circuit indicator

4. Router R1 receives a frame from router R2 with DLCI value 222 in it. Which of the following statements about this network is the most accurate?

   a. 222 represents Router R1.

   b. 222 represents Router R2.

   c. 222 is the local DLCI on R1 that represents the VC between R1 and R2.

   d. 222 is the local DLCI on R2 that represents the VC between R1 and R2.

5. FredsCo has five sites, with routers connected to the same Frame Relay network. Virtual circuits (VC) have been defined between each pair of routers. What is the fewest subnets that FredsCo could use on the Frame Relay network?

   a. 1

   b. 2

   c. 3

   d. 4

   e. 5

   f. 10

6. BarneyCo has one central site, with ten remote sites, and Frame Relay PVCs connecting the central site to each remote site. Barney, the company president, will fire anyone who configures Frame Relay without using point-to-point subinterfaces. What is the fewest number of subnets that BarneyCo could use on the Frame Relay network?

   a.   1

   b.   4

   c.   8

   d.   10

   e.   12

   f.   15

13

Foundation Topics

Frame Relay Overview

Frame Relay networks provide more features and benefits than simple point-to-point WAN links, but to do that, Frame Relay protocols are more detailed. For example, Frame Relay networks are multiaccess networks, which means that more than two devices can attach to the network, similar to LANs. Unlike with LANs, you cannot send a data link layer broadcast over Frame Relay. Therefore, Frame Relay networks are called nonbroadcast multiaccess (NBMA) networks. Also, because Frame Relay is multiaccess, it requires the use of an address that identifies to which remote router each frame is addressed.

Figure 13-1 outlines the basic physical topology and related terminology in a Frame Relay network.

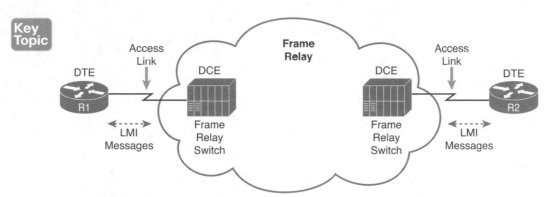

Figure 13-1   *Frame Relay Components*

Figure 13-1 shows the most basic components of a Frame Relay network. A leased line is installed between the router and a nearby Frame Relay switch; this link is called the *access link*. To ensure that the link is working, the device outside the Frame Relay network, called the data terminal equipment (DTE), exchanges regular messages with the Frame Relay switch. These keepalive messages, along with other messages, are defined by the Frame Relay Local Management Interface (LMI) protocol. The routers are considered DTE, and the Frame Relay switches are data communications equipment (DCE).

> **NOTE**   The terms *DCE* and *DTE* have different meanings in different contexts. Here, with a Frame Relay service, the roles are as described in the previous paragraph. On a physical leased line, the DCE provides Layer 1 clocking, and the DTE receives and reacts to the DCE's clock signal. These are two different (and accepted) uses of the same two terms.

Answers to the "Do I Know This Already?" quiz:

1 C   **2** A and D   **3** A   **4** C   **5** A   **6** D

Figure 13-1 shows the physical connectivity at each connection to the Frame Relay network, and Figure 13-2 shows the logical, or virtual, end-to-end connectivity associated with a virtual circuit (VC).

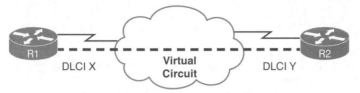

Figure 13-2 *Frame Relay PVC Concepts*

The logical communications path between each pair of DTEs is a VC. The dashed line in the figure represents a single VC; this book uses a thick dashed line style to make sure that you notice the line easily. The service provider usually preconfigures all the required details of a VC; predefined VCs are called permanent virtual circuits (PVC).

Routers use the data link connection identifier (DLCI) as the Frame Relay address; it identifies the VC over which the frame should travel. So, in Figure 13-2, when R1 needs to forward a packet to R2, R1 encapsulates the Layer 3 packet into a Frame Relay header and trailer and then sends the frame. The Frame Relay header includes the correct DLCI, identifying the PVC connecting R1 to R2, so that the provider's Frame Relay switches correctly forward the frame to R2.

Table 13-2 lists the components shown in Figures 13-1 and 13-2 and some associated terms. After the table, the most important features of Frame Relay are described in further detail.

Table 13-2   Frame Relay Terms and Concepts

Term	Description
Virtual circuit (VC)	A logical concept that represents the path that frames travel between DTEs. VCs are particularly useful when you compare Frame Relay to leased physical circuits.
Permanent virtual circuit (PVC)	A predefined VC. A PVC can be equated to a leased line in concept.
Switched virtual circuit (SVC)	A VC that is set up dynamically when needed. An SVC can be equated to a dial connection in concept.
Data terminal equipment (DTE)	DTEs are connected to a Frame Relay service from a telecommunications company. They usually reside at sites used by the company buying the Frame Relay service.
Data communications equipment (DCE)	Frame Relay switches are DCE devices. DCEs are also known as data circuit-terminating equipment. DCEs are usually in the service provider's network.
Access link	The leased line between the DTE and DCE.
Access rate (AR)	The speed at which the access link is clocked. This choice affects the connection's price.

13

Term	Description
Committed information rate (CIR)	The speed at which bits can be sent over a VC, according to the business contract between the customer and provider.
Data link connection identifier (DLCI)	A Frame Relay address used in Frame Relay headers to identify the VC.
Nonbroadcast multiaccess (NBMA)	A network in which broadcasts are not supported but more than two devices can be connected.
Local Management Interface (LMI)	The protocol used between a DCE and DTE to manage the connection. Signaling messages for SVCs, PVC status messages, and keepalives are all LMI messages.

The definitions for Frame Relay are contained in documents from the International Telecommunications Union (ITU) and the American National Standards Institute (ANSI). Originally, back in the 1990s, the Frame Relay Forum, a vendor consortium, defined many of the original specifications. Over time, the ITU and ANSI picked up many of the forum's standards.

Now that you have heard some of the big ideas and key terms from Frame Relay, the next few topics go into more depth about the core functions within Frame Relay: virtual circuits, the LMI protocol, framing, and Frame Relay addressing.

Virtual Circuits

Frame Relay provides significant advantages over simply using point-to-point leased lines. The primary advantage has to do with VCs. Consider Figure 13-3, which shows a typical Frame Relay network with three sites.

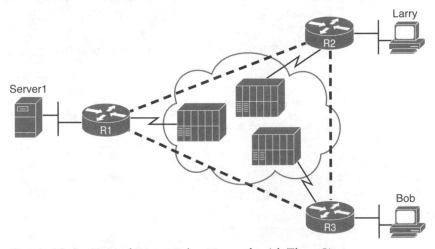

Figure 13-3   *Typical Frame Relay Network with Three Sites*

A VC defines a logical path between two Frame Relay DTEs. The term *virtual circuit* describes the concept well. It acts like a point-to-point circuit, enabling the sending of data between two endpoints over a WAN. There is no physical circuit directly between the two endpoints, so it is virtual. For example, R1 terminates two VCs—one whose other endpoint is R2, and one whose other endpoint is R3. R1 can send traffic directly to either of the other two routers by sending it over the appropriate VC.

VCs share the access link and the Frame Relay network. For example, both VCs terminating at R1 use the same access link. R1 can send one Frame Relay frame to R2, and then another frame to R3, sending both over the same physical access link.

Not only does a single customer router share its access link among many VCs, many customers share the same Frame Relay network. Originally, people with leased-line networks were reluctant to migrate to Frame Relay because they would be competing with other Frame Relay customers for the provider's capacity inside the cloud. To address these fears, Frame Relay uses a concept of a committed information rate (CIR). Each VC has a CIR, which is a guarantee by the provider that a particular VC gets at least that much bandwidth. So, you can migrate from a leased line to Frame Relay, getting a CIR of at least as much bandwidth as you previously had with your leased line.

One big advantage of Frame Relay over leased lines is that Frame Relay provides connectivity to each site, with only a single access link between each router and the Frame Relay provider. Interestingly, even with a three-site network, it's probably less expensive to use Frame Relay than to use point-to-point links because the access links tend to be relatively short, to some nearby Frame Relay provider point of presence (PoP).

Frame Relay and other multiaccess WAN technologies have an even bigger cost advantage with larger enterprise WANs. For instance, imagine an organization with 100 sites, with one router at each site. To connect each pair of routers with a leased line, that company would need 4950 leased lines! And besides that, each router would need 99 serial interfaces. With Frame Relay, each router could use one serial interface and one access link into the Frame Relay cloud, for a total of 100 access links. Then, the Frame Relay provider could create a PVC between each pair of routers (a total of 4950 VCs). The Frame Relay solution requires a lot fewer actual physical links, and you would need only one serial interface on each router.

Service providers can build their Frame Relay networks more cost-effectively than for leased lines. As you would expect, that makes it less expensive for the Frame Relay customer as well. For connecting many WAN sites, Frame Relay is simply more cost-effective than leased lines.

When the Frame Relay network is engineered, the design might not include a VC between each pair of sites. Figure 13-3 includes PVCs between each pair of sites; this is called a *full-mesh* Frame Relay network. When not all pairs have a direct PVC, it is called a *partial-mesh network*. Figure 13-4 shows the same network as Figure 13-3, but this time with a partial mesh and only two PVCs. This is typical when R1 is at the main site and R2 and R3 are at remote offices that rarely need to communicate directly.

13

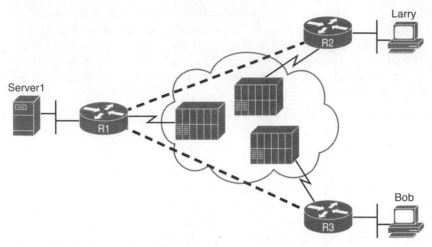

Figure 13-4   *Typical Partial-Mesh Frame Relay Network*

The partial mesh has some advantages and disadvantages compared to a full mesh. Partial-mesh designs save money compared to full-mesh designs because the provider charges per VC. The downside is that traffic from R2's site to R3's site must go to R1 first and then be forwarded. If that is a small amount of traffic, it is a small price to pay. If it is a lot of traffic, a full mesh is probably worth the extra money because traffic going between two remote sites would have to cross R1's access link twice.

LMI and Encapsulation Types

While the PVC gives two customer routers a logical means to send frames to one another, Frame Relay has many physical and logical components that have to work together to make those PVCs work. Physically, each router needs a physical access link from the router to some Frame Relay switch. The provider has to create some kind of physical network between those switches, as well. In addition, the provider has to do some work so that the frames sent over one PVC arrive at the correct destination.

Frame Relay uses the Local Management Interface (LMI) protocol to manage each physical access link and the PVCs that use that link. These LMI messages flow between the DTE (for example, a router) and the DCE (for example, the Frame Relay switch owned by the service provider).

The most important LMI message relating to topics on the exam is the LMI status inquiry message. LMI status messages perform two key functions:

- They perform a keepalive function between the DTE and DCE. If the access link has a problem, the absence of keepalive messages implies that the link is down.
- They signal whether a PVC is active or inactive. Even though each PVC is predefined, its status can change. An access link might be up, but one or more VCs could be down. The router needs to know which VCs are up and which are down. It learns that information from the switch using LMI status messages.

Interestingly, due to historical reasons, Cisco routers have three options for different variations of LMI protocols: Cisco, ITU, and ANSI. Each LMI option differs slightly and therefore is incompatible with the other two. As long as both the DTE and DCE on each end of an access link use the same LMI standard, LMI works fine.

Configuring the LMI type is easy. Today's most popular option is to use the default LMI setting. This setting uses the LMI autosense feature, in which the router simply figures out which LMI type the switch is using. So, you can simply let the router autosense the LMI and never bother coding the LMI type. If you choose to configure the LMI type, the router disables the autosense feature. Table 13-3 outlines the three LMI types, their origin, and the keyword used in the Cisco IOS software **frame-relay lmi-type** interface subcommand.

Table 13-3   Frame Relay LMI Types

Name	Document	IOS LMI-Type Parameter
Cisco	Proprietary	cisco
ANSI	T1.617 Annex D	ansi
ITU	Q.933 Annex A	q933a

Frame Relay Encapsulation and Framing

A Frame Relay-connected router encapsulates each Layer 3 packet inside a Frame Relay header and trailer before it is sent out an access link. The header and trailer are defined by Frame Relay (or more specifically, the Link Access Procedure Frame Bearer Services [LAPF] specification, ITU Q.922-A). The sparse LAPF framing provides error detection with an FCS in the trailer, a DLCI field (discussed in detail later in this chapter), plus a few other header fields. Figure 13-5 diagrams the frame.

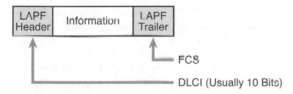

Figure 13-5   *LAPF Framing*

However, routers actually use a longer header than just the standard LAPF header because the standard header does not provide all the fields usually needed by routers. In particular, Figure 13-5 does not show a Protocol Type field. Each data link header needs a field to define the type of packet that follows the data link header. If Frame Relay is using only the LAPF header, DTEs (including routers) cannot support multiprotocol traffic because there is no way to identify the type of protocol in the Information field.

Two solutions were created to compensate for the lack of a Protocol Type field in the standard Frame Relay header:

- Cisco and three other companies created an additional header, which comes between the LAPF header and the Layer 3 packet shown in Figure 13-5. It includes a 2-byte Protocol Type field, with values matching the same field Cisco uses for HDLC.

13

■ RFC 1490 (and later 2427), *Multiprotocol Interconnect over Frame Relay*, defined the second solution. RFC 1490 was written to ensure multivendor interoperability between Frame Relay DTEs. This RFC defines a similar header, also placed between the LAPF header and Layer 3 packet, and includes a Protocol Type field as well as many other options.

Figure 13-6 outlines these two alternatives.

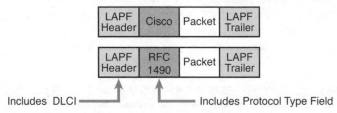

Figure 13-6   *Cisco and RFC 1490/2427 Encapsulation*

Routers should agree on the encapsulation used; the switches do not care. However, each VC can use a different encapsulation. In the configuration, the encapsulation created by Cisco is called **cisco**, and the other one is called **ietf**.

Now that you have a broad understanding of Frame Relay concepts and terminology, the next section takes a much closer look at Frame Relay DLCIs.

Frame Relay Addressing

At a basic conceptual level, Frame Relay addresses, called data link connection identifiers (DLCI), have some similarity with the more familiar MAC and IP addresses. All these addresses exist as binary values, but they all have some more convenient format: hex for MAC addresses, dotted decimal for IP, and decimal for DLCIs. Frame Relay defines the DLCI as a 10-bit value, written in decimal, with the low- and high-end values usually reserved. (The specific range does not matter much because the service provider assigns the values, but they usually range from around 17 to a little less than 1000.)

When you dig deeper, particularly into how DLCIs impact the forwarding of Frame Relay frames, the similarities to MAC and IP addressing fades, and stark differences appear. This section focuses on that forwarding logic, first discussing the idea that Frame Relay addresses actually identify one end of a PVC. Following that, the discussion turns to the forwarding logic used inside the Frame Relay cloud.

Frame Relay Local Addressing

The service provider assigns each PVC two local DLCI values: one on one end of the PVC, and one for the other end. The term *local DLCI* has several different origins, but you can think of the word *local* as emphasizing the fact that from a router's perspective, the local DLCI is the DLCI used on the local end of the PVC where the router sits. Figure 13-7 shows the idea.

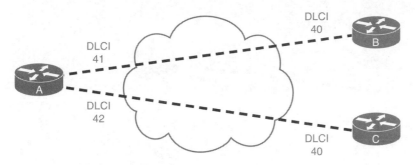

Figure 13-7 *Two PVCs, with One DLCI per End of Each PVC*

In this example, the PVC between routers A and B has two DLCIs assigned by the provider. Router A's end uses local DLCI 41 to identify the PVC, and router B's end uses DLCI 40 to identify the same PVC. Similarly, the PVC between routers A and C, as usual, has two local DLCIs assigned, one on each end. In this case, router A's end uses 42, and router C's end uses 40.

The service provider could have used any DLCI values within the range of legal values, with one exception:

> The local DLCIs on a single access link must be unique among all PVCs that use one physical Frame Relay access link, because Frame Relay DLCIs are locally significant.

Because the provider chooses the DLCIs, the enterprise network engineer does not need to worry about avoiding making the wrong choice for DLCI value. For the sake of understanding the technology, know that on each physical access link from one router to the Frame Relay network, the DLCI values must be unique. In Figure 13-7, the provider has defined two PVCs that cross R1's one Frame Relay access link: one with local DLCI 41, and one with local DLCI 42. If another PVC were added, connected to router A, the provider just could not use 41 or 42 as the local DLCI on R1's access link.

The local router only sees or knows the local DLCI. When you configure a router, you configure only the local DLCI value, not the DLCI on the other end of the PVC. Likewise, **show** commands list only local DLCI values.

Frame Forwarding with One DLCI Field

The most significant difference between the two other popular addresses in CCNA Routing and Switching (MAC and IP) versus DLCIs relates to the whole forwarding process. The Ethernet header includes both a source and destination MAC address, and the IP header includes a source and destination IP address. However, the Frame Relay header lists only one DLCI field, and it does not identify a source or a destination, but the PVC.

To get an idea of how the provider forwards a Frame Relay frame, consider the fact that the provider knows the local DLCI used on both ends of the PVC, plus the access links that connect to those routers. For instance, in Figure 13-8, the provider knows that a PVC exists between router A and router B. They know it uses local DLCI 41 on the router A side. And they know it uses DLCI 40 on the router B side. Keeping that in mind, take a look at Figure 13-8, which shows what happens when router A sends a frame to router B.

13

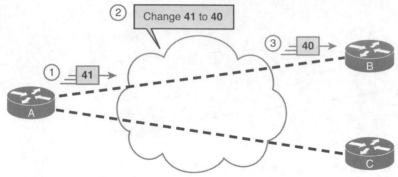

Figure 13-8   *Frame Relay Forwarding: Router A to Router B*

The figure shows three major steps. First, router A decides to send a frame over the PVC connected to router B. From router A's perspective, A knows that PVC only as the PVC with local DLCI 41, so A sends a frame with DLCI 41 in the header. At Step 2, the service provider does a lot. They look at the information they know about this PVC, forward the frame over toward router B, *and they change the DLCI to 40*. At Step 3, when the frame arrives at router B, it has a DLCI value of 40. Router B correctly thinks that the frame arrived over the PVC from router A, because router B's only knowledge of that PVC is that it is the PVC whose local DLCI (on router B's end) is 40.

Note that when A sent the frame, A used its local DLCI value (41), and when B received the frame, B saw its local DLCI (40).

To complete the process, think about a packet sent by router B back toward router A. Again, the routers only know local DLCI values, so as shown in Figure 13-9, B sends the frame with DLCI 40, which identifies the A-to-B PVC; the cloud changes the DLCI to 41; and router A receives the frame with DLCI 41 in it.

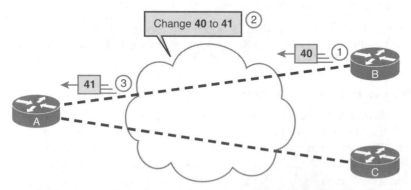

Figure 13-9   *Frame Relay Forwarding: Router B to Router A*

The same idea happens on each and every PVC. Earlier, Figure 13-7 introduced two PVCs, including an A-to-C PVC, with local DLCIs 42 (A side) and 40 (C side). Figure 13-10 shows the local DLCIs in two different frame flows: first from A to C, and then from C back to A.

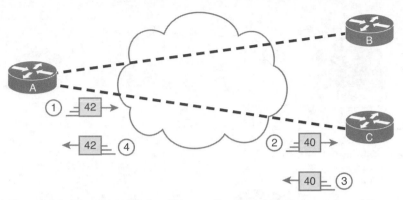

Figure 13-10 *Frame Relay Forwarding Between Routers A and C*

This figure does not point out the cloud's action of swapping the DLCI values, but the action still takes place. At Step 1, router A forward a frame, DLCI 42. At Step 2, when it exits the cloud toward router C, it has been changed to use DLCI 40, router C's local DLCI for this PVC. Similarly, at Step 3, router C sends a frame, with local DLCI 40. The cloud changes the DLCI to 40, so that when it exits the cloud toward router A at Step 4, the frame lists router A's local DLCI, which is 42.

Network Layer Addressing with Frame Relay

Frame Relay networks have both similarities and differences as compared to LAN and point-to-point WAN links. These differences introduce some additional considerations for passing Layer 3 packets across a Frame Relay network. In particular, Frame Relay gives us three different options for assigning subnets and IP addresses on Frame Relay interfaces:

- One subnet containing all Frame Relay DTEs
- One subnet per VC
- A hybrid of the first two options

This section examines the three main options for IP addressing over Frame Relay.

Frame Relay Layer 3 Addressing: One Subnet Containing All Frame Relay DTEs

Figure 13-11 shows the first alternative, which is to use a single subnet for the Frame Relay network. This figure shows a fully meshed Frame Relay network because the single-subnet option is usually used when a full mesh of VCs exists. In a full mesh, each router has a VC to every other router, meaning that each router can send frames directly to every other router. This more closely resembles how a LAN works. So, a single subnet can be used for all the routers' Frame Relay interfaces, as configured on the routers' serial interfaces. Table 13-4 summarizes the addresses used in Figure 13-11.

13

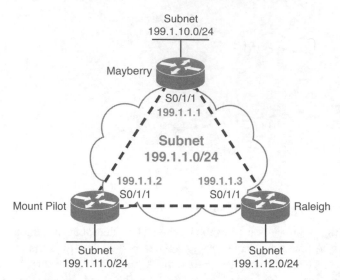

Figure 13-11 *Full Mesh with IP Addresses*

Table 13-4 IP Addresses with No Subinterfaces

Router	IP Address of Frame Relay Interface
Mayberry	199.1.1.1
Mount Pilot	199.1.1.2
Raleigh	199.1.1.3

The single-subnet alternative is straightforward, and it conserves your IP address space. It also looks like what you are used to with LANs, which makes it easier to conceptualize. Unfortunately, most companies build partial-mesh Frame Relay networks, and the single-subnet option has some deficiencies when the network is a partial mesh.

Frame Relay Layer 3 Addressing: One Subnet Per VC

The second IP addressing alternative, having a single subnet for each VC, works better with a partially meshed Frame Relay network, as shown in Figure 13-12. Boston cannot forward frames directly to Charlotte because no VC is defined between the two. This is a more typical Frame Relay network because most organizations with many sites tend to group applications on servers at a few centralized locations and most of the traffic is between each remote site and those servers.

The single-subnet-per-VC subnetting design uses the same logic as a set of point-to-point links. Using multiple subnets instead of one larger subnet does waste some IP addresses. However, using a single subnet in the partial-mesh design of Figure 13-12 introduces several problems with routing protocols because not all routers in the subnet can send messages directly to each other. Partial-mesh designs work better with a single-subnet-per-VC approach.

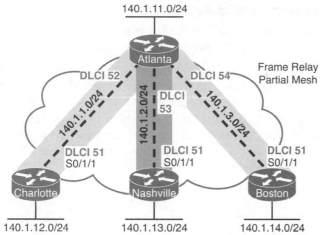

Figure 13-12   *Partial Mesh with IP Addresses*

Table 13-5 shows the IP addresses for the partially meshed Frame Relay network shown in Figure 13-12.

Table 13-5   IP Addresses with Point-to-Point Subinterfaces

Router	Subnet	IP Address
Atlanta	140.1.1.0	140.1.1.1
Charlotte	140.1.1.0	140.1.1.2
Atlanta	140.1.2.0	140.1.2.1
Nashville	140.1.2.0	140.1.2.3
Atlanta	140.1.3.0	140.1.3.1
Boston	140.1.3.0	140.1.3.4

Cisco IOS software has a configuration feature called *subinterfaces* that creates a logical subdivision of a physical interface. Subinterfaces allow the Atlanta router to have three IP addresses associated with its serial 0/1/1 physical interface by configuring three separate subinterfaces. A router can treat each subinterface, and the VC associated with it, as if it were a point-to-point serial link. Each of the three subinterfaces of serial 0/1/1 on Atlanta would be assigned a different IP address from Table 13-5 (Example 14-8 in Chapter 14 shows Atlanta's configuration to match the address in Table 13-5, including the subinterfaces of S0/1/1.)

NOTE   The example uses IP address prefixes of /24 to keep the math simple. In production networks, point-to-point subinterfaces usually use a prefix of /30 (mask 255.255.255.252) because that allows for only two valid IP addresses—the exact number needed on a point-to-point subinterface. Of course, using different masks in the same network means that your routing protocol must also support VLSM.

13

Frame Relay Layer 3 Addressing: Hybrid Approach

The third alternative for Layer 3 addressing is a hybrid of the first two alternatives. Consider Figure 13-13, which shows a trio of routers with VCs between each of them, and two other VCs to remote sites.

Two options exist for Layer 3 addressing in this case. The first is to treat each VC as a separate Layer 3 group. In this case, five subnets are needed for the Frame Relay network. However, Routers A, B, and C create a smaller full mesh between each other. This allows Routers A, B, and C to use one subnet. The other two VCs—one between Routers A and D and one between Routers A and E—are treated as two separate Layer 3 groups. The result is a total of three subnets.

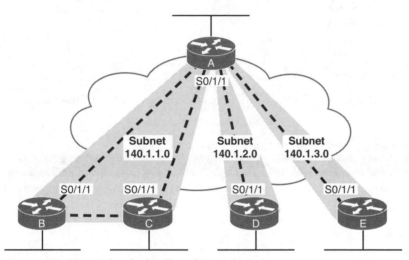

Figure 13-13 *Hybrid of Full and Partial Mesh*

To accomplish either style of Layer 3 addressing in this third and final case, subinterfaces are used. Point-to-point subinterfaces are used when a single VC is considered to be all that is in the group—for instance, between routers A and D and between routers A and E. Multipoint subinterfaces are used when more than two routers are considered to be in the same group—for instance, with routers A, B, and C.

Multipoint subinterfaces logically terminate more than one VC. In fact, the name *multipoint* implies the function, because more than one remote site can be reached via a VC associated with a multipoint subinterface.

Table 13-6 summarizes the addresses and subinterfaces that are used in Figure 13-13.

Table 13-6 IP Addresses with Point-to-Point and Multipoint Subinterfaces

Router	Subnet	IP Address	Subinterface Type
A	140.1.1.0/24	140.1.1.1	Multipoint
B	140.1.1.0/24	140.1.1.2	Multipoint
C	140.1.1.0/24	140.1.1.3	Multipoint
A	140.1.2.0/24	140.1.2.1	Point-to-point
D	140.1.2.0/24	140.1.2.4	Point-to-point
A	140.1.3.0/24	140.1.3.1	Point-to-point
E	140.1.3.0/24	140.1.3.5	Point-to-point

What will you see in a real network? Most of the time, point-to-point subinterfaces are used with a single subnet per PVC. However, you should understand all options for the CCNA exams.

NOTE Chapter 14 provides full configurations for all three cases illustrated in Figures 13-11, 13-12, and 13-13.

13

Exam Preparation Tasks

Review All the Key Topics

Review the most important topics from this chapter, noted with the Key Topic icon. Table 13-7 lists these key topics and where each is discussed.

Table 13-7   Key Topics for Chapter 13

Key Topic Element	Description	Page Number
Figure 13-1	Several terms related to a Frame Relay topology	392
Table 13-2	Key Frame Relay terms and definitions	393
List	Two important functions of the Frame Relay LMI	396
Table 13-3	Frame Relay LMI types and LMI type configuration keywords	397
Figure 13-6	Headers and positions for the Cisco and IETF additional Frame Relay headers	398
Definition	Requirement for using unique local DLCIs on any single Frame Relay access link	399
Figure 13-8	Details of how DLCI values change during the frame forwarding process	400
List	Three options of subnets used on a Frame Relay network	401
Figure 13-12	Example of using one subnet per PVC	403

Definitions of Key Terms

After your first reading of the chapter, try to define these key terms, but do not be concerned about getting them all correct at that time. Chapter 22 directs you in how to use these terms for late-stage preparation for the exam.

access link, access rate, committed information rate (CIR), data link connection identifier (DLCI), Frame Relay DCE, Frame Relay DTE, Local Management Interface (LMI), nonbroadcast multiaccess (NBMA), permanent virtual circuit (PVC), virtual circuit (VC)

This chapter covers the following exam topics:

WAN Technologies

Configure and verify Frame Relay on Cisco routers

Troubleshooting

Troubleshoot and Resolve WAN implementation issues

Frame relay

CHAPTER 14

Implementing Frame Relay

Chapter 13, "Understanding Frame Relay Concepts," introduced and explained the main concepts behind Frame Relay. This chapter shows you how to configure the features on Cisco routers, how to verify that each feature works, and how to troubleshoot problems with forwarding packets over a Frame Relay network.

"Do I Know This Already?" Quiz

Use the "Do I Know This Already?" quiz to help decide whether you might want to skim this chapter, or a major section, moving more quickly to the Exam Preparation Tasks section near the end of the chapter. You can find the answers at the bottom of the page following the quiz. For thorough explanations, see DVD Appendix C, "Answers to the 'Do I Know This Already?' Quizzes."

Table 14-1 "Do I Know This Already?" Foundation Topics Section-to-Question Mapping

Foundation Topics Section	Questions
Frame Relay Configuration and Verification	1–5
Frame Relay Troubleshooting	6–8

1. Imagine two Cisco routers, R1 and R2, using a Frame Relay service. R1 connects to a switch that uses LMI type ANSI T1.617, and R2 connects to a switch that uses ITU Q.933a. What keywords could be used in the R1 and R2 configuration so that the LMIs work correctly?

   a. ansi and itu

   b. T1617 and q933a

   c. ansi and q933a

   d. T1617 and itu

   e. Not possible with two different types

2. A company has five sites with routers connected to the same Frame Relay network. VCs have been defined between each pair of routers. Betty, the company president, will fire anyone who configures anything that could just as easily be left as a default. Which of the following configuration commands, configured for the Frame Relay network, would get the engineer fired? (Choose three answers.)

    a. ip address

    b. encapsulation

    c. lmi-type

    d. frame-relay map

    e. frame-relay inverse-arp

3. A company has some routers connected to a Frame Relay network. R1 is a router at a remote site with a single VC back to the company's headquarters. The R1 configuration currently looks like this:

```
interface serial 0/0
  ip address 10.1.1.1 255.255.255.0
  encapsulation frame-relay
```

Wilma, the company president, has heard that point-to-point subinterfaces are cool, and she wants you to change the configuration to use a point-to-point subinterface. Which of the following commands do you need to use to migrate the configuration? (Choose two answers.)

    a. no ip address

    b. interface-dlci

    c. no encapsulation

    d. encapsulation frame-relay

    e. frame-relay interface-dlci

4. A company has a Frame Relay network, with a main site router that has ten VCs connecting to the ten remote sites. Wilma (the company president) now thinks that multipoint subinterfaces are even cooler than point-to-point. The current main site router's configuration looks like this:

```
interface serial 0/0
  ip address 172.16.1.1 255.255.255.0
  encapsulation frame-relay
```

Wilma wants you to change the configuration to use a multipoint subinterface. Which of the following do you need to use to migrate the configuration? (Note: DLCIs 101 through 110 are used for the ten VCs.)

    a. interface-dlci 101 110

    b. interface dlci 101-110

    c. Ten different **interface-dlci** commands

    d. frame-relay interface-dlci 101 110

    e. frame-relay interface dlci 101-110

    f. Ten different **frame-relay interface-dlci** commands

5. Which of the following commands lists the information learned by Inverse ARP?

    a. show ip arp

    b. show arp

    c. show inverse arp

    d. show frame-relay inverse-arp

    e. show map

    f. show frame-relay map

6. Which of the following are Frame Relay PVC status codes that mean that the router can send frames for the associated PVC?

    a. Up

    b. Down

    c. Active

    d. Inactive

    e. Deleted

7. Central site router RC has a VC connecting to ten remote routers (R1 through R10), with RC's local DLCIs being 101 through 110, respectively. RC has grouped DLCIs 107, 108, and 109 into a single multipoint subinterface S0/0.789, whose current status is "up and up." Which of the following are true? (Choose two answers.)

    a. Serial 0/0 could be in an up/down state.

    b. The PVC with DLCI 108 could be in an inactive state.

    c. The show frame-relay map command lists mapping information for all three VCs.

    d. At least one of the three PVCs is in an active or static state.

8. Frame Relay router R1 uses interface S0/0 to connect to a Frame Relay access link. The physical interface is in an up/down state. Which of the following could cause this problem? (Choose two answers.)

    a. The access link has a physical problem and cannot pass bits between the router and switch.

    b. The switch and router are using different LMI types.

    c. The router configuration is missing the encapsulation frame-relay command on interface S0/0.

    d. The router received a valid LMI status message that listed some of the DLCIs as inactive.

Foundation Topics

Frame Relay Configuration and Verification

Frame Relay configuration can be very basic or somewhat detailed, depending on how many default settings can be used. By default, Cisco IOS automatically senses the Local Management Interface (LMI) type and automatically discovers the mapping between DLCI and next-hop IP addresses (using Inverse Address Resolution Protocol [ARP]). If you use all Cisco routers, the default to use Cisco encapsulation works without any additional configuration. If you also design the Frame Relay network to use a single subnet, you can configure the routers to use their physical interfaces without any subinterfaces—making the configuration shorter still. In fact, using as many default settings as possible, the only new configuration command for Frame Relay, as compared to point-to-point WANs, is the **encapsulation frame-relay** command.

Frame Relay questions on CCNA exams can prove difficult for a couple of reasons. First, Frame Relay includes a variety of optional settings that you can configure. Second, for network engineers who already have some experience with Frame Relay, that experience may be with one of the three main options for Frame Relay configuration (physical, multipoint, or point-to-point), but the exams cover all options. So, it is important for the exams that you take the time to look at samples of all the options, which are covered here.

Planning a Frame Relay Configuration

Engineers must do a fair amount of planning before knowing where to start with the configuration. When planning for new sites, you must consider the following items and communicate them to the Frame Relay provider, which in turn has some impact on the routers' Frame Relay configurations:

- Define which physical sites need a Frame Relay access link installed, and define the clock rate (access rate) used on each link.
- Define each VC by identifying the endpoints and setting the committed information rate (CIR).
- Agree to an LMI type (usually dictated by the provider).

The network engineer who plans the Frame Relay configuration must also choose the following setting, independent of any settings of the Frame Relay provider:

- Choose the IP subnetting scheme: one subnet for all virtual circuits (VC), one subnet for each VC, or a subnet for each fully meshed subset.
- Pick whether to assign the IP addresses to physical, multipoint, or point-to-point subinterfaces.

Answers to the "Do I Know This Already?" quiz:

1 C   **2** C, D, and E   **3** A and E   **4** F   **5** F   **6** C   **7** B and D   **8** B and C

- Choose which VCs need to use IETF encapsulation instead of the default value of cisco. (IETF encapsulation is usually used when one router is not a Cisco router.)

After the planning has been completed, the configuration steps flow directly from the choices made when planning the network. The following list summarizes the configuration steps, mainly as a study tool. (You do not need to memorize the steps; the list is just a tool to help organize your thinking about the configuration.)

Step 1. Configure the physical interface to use Frame Relay encapsulation (**encapsulation frame-relay** interface subcommand).

Step 2. Configure an IP address on the interface or subinterface (**ip address** subcommand).

Step 3. (Optional) Manually set the LMI type on each physical serial interface (**frame-relay lmi-type** interface subcommand).

Step 4. (Optional) Change from the default encapsulation of **cisco**, to **ietf**, by doing the following:

    A. For all VCs on the interface, add the **ietf** keyword to the **encapsulation frame-relay** interface subcommand.

    B. For a single VC, add the **ietf** keyword to the **frame-relay interface-dlci** interface subcommand (point-to-point subinterfaces only) or to the **frame-relay map** command.

Step 5. (Optional) If you aren't using the (default) Inverse ARP to map the DLCI to the next-hop router's IP address, define static mapping using the **frame-relay map ip** *ip-address dlci* **broadcast** subinterface subcommand.

Step 6. On subinterfaces, associate one DLCI (point-to-point) or multiple DLCIs (multipoint) with the subinterface in one of two ways:

    A. Using the **frame-relay interface-dlci** *dlci* subinterface subcommand

    B. As a side effect of static mapping, using the **frame-relay map ip** *ip-address dlci* **broadcast** subinterface subcommand (multipoint only)

The rest of this section shows examples of all these configuration steps, along with some discussion about how to verify that the Frame Relay network is working correctly.

Configuring Using Physical Interfaces and One IP Subnet

The first example shows the briefest possible Frame Relay configuration, one that uses just the first two steps of the configuration checklist in this chapter. The design for the first example includes the following choices:

- Install an access link into three routers.
- Create a full mesh of PVCs.
- Use a single subnet (Class C network 199.1.1.0 in this example) in the Frame Relay network.

■ Configure the routers using their physical interfaces.

■ Take the default settings for LMI, Inverse ARP, and encapsulation.

Examples 14-1, 14-2, and 14-3 show the configuration for the network shown in Figure 14-1.

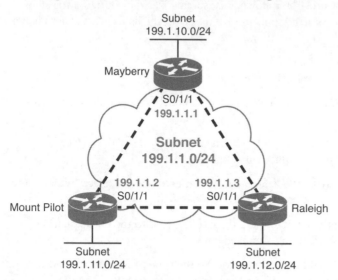

Figure 14-1 *Full Mesh with IP Addresses*

Example 14-1 *Mayberry Configuration*

```
interface serial0/1/1
 encapsulation frame-relay
 ip address  199.1.1.1  255.255.255.0
!
interface gigabitethernet 0/0
 ip address  199.1.10.1  255.255.255.0
!
router eigrp 1
 network 199.1.1.0
 network 199.1.10.0
```

Example 14-2 *Mount Pilot Configuration*

```
interface serial0/1/1
 encapsulation frame-relay
 ip address  199.1.1.2  255.255.255.0
!
interface gigabitethernet 0/0
 ip address  199.1.11.2  255.255.255.0
!
router eigrp 1
 network 199.1.1.0
 network 199.1.11.0
```

Example 14-3 *Raleigh Configuration*

```
interface serial0/1/1
 encapsulation frame-relay
 ip address   199.1.1.3   255.255.255.0
!
interface gigabitethernet 0/0
 ip address   199.1.12.3    255.255.255.0
!
router eigrp 1
 network 199.1.1.0
 network 199.1.12.0
```

The configuration is simple in comparison with the protocol concepts. The **encapsulation frame-relay** command tells the routers to use Frame Relay data link protocols instead of the default, which is High-Level Data Link Control (HDLC). Note that the IP addresses on the three routers' serial interfaces are all in the same Class C network. Also, this simple configuration takes advantage of the following IOS default settings:

- The LMI type is automatically sensed.
- The (default) encapsulation is Cisco.
- PVC DLCIs are learned via LMI status messages.
- Inverse ARP is enabled (by default) and is triggered when a router receives an LMI status message declaring that the VCs are up is received.

Configuring the Encapsulation and LMI

In many cases, using the defaults as listed with the first example works just fine. However, for the purpose of showing an alternative configuration, suppose that the following requirements were added to the requirements surrounding the design in Figure 14-1:

- The Raleigh router requires IETF encapsulation on both VCs.
- Mayberry's LMI type should be ANSI, and LMI autosense should not be used.

To change these defaults, the steps outlined as optional configuration Steps 3 and 4 in the configuration checklist should be used. Examples 14-4 and 14-5 show the changes that would be made to Mayberry and Raleigh.

Example 14-4 *Mayberry Configuration with New Requirements*

```
interface serial0/1/1
 encapsulation frame-relay
 frame-relay lmi-type ansi
 frame-relay map ip 199.1.1.3 53 ietf
 ip address 199.1.1.1  255.255.255.0
! rest of configuration unchanged from Example 14-1.
```

Example 14-5   *Raleigh Configuration with New Requirements*

```
interface serial0/1/1
 encapsulation frame-relay ietf
 ip address  199.1.1.3  255.255.255.0

! rest of configuration unchanged from Example 14-3.
```

These configurations differ from the previous ones (in Examples 14-1 and 14-3) in two ways. First, Raleigh changed its encapsulation for both its PVCs with the **ietf** keyword on the **encapsulation** command. This keyword applies to all VCs on the interface. However, Mayberry cannot change its encapsulation in the same way, because only one of the two VCs terminating in Mayberry needs to use IETF encapsulation, and the other needs to use Cisco encapsulation. So, Mayberry is forced to code the **frame-relay map** command, referencing the DLCI for the VC to Raleigh, with the **ietf** keyword. With that command, you can change the encapsulation setting per VC, as opposed to the configuration on Raleigh, which changes the encapsulation for all VCs.

The second major change is the LMI configuration. The LMI configuration in Mayberry would be fine without any changes because the default use of LMI autosense would recognize ANSI as the LMI type. However, by coding the **frame-relay lmi-type ansi** interface subcommand, Mayberry must use ANSI, because this command not only sets the LMI type, but it also disables autosensing of the LMI type.

> **NOTE**   The LMI setting is a per-physical-interface setting, even if subinterfaces are used, so the **frame-relay lmi-type** command is always a subcommand under the physical interface.

Mount Pilot needs to configure a **frame-relay map** command with the **ietf** keyword for its VC to Raleigh, just like Mayberry. This change is not shown in the examples.

Frame Relay Address Mapping

Figure 14-1 does not even bother listing the DLCIs used for the VCs. The earlier configurations work as stated, and frankly, if you never knew the DLCIs, this network would work! However, for the exams, and for real networking jobs, engineers need to know the DLCIs, and the process of Frame Relay mapping.

Frame Relay mapping matches a next-hop IP address that sits on the Frame Relay network with the right DLCI used to send frames to that next-hop device, with the same goal as ARP on a LAN. Figure 14-2 shows the same network, this time with local DLCI values shown.

Frame Relay "mapping" creates a correlation between a Layer 3 address and its corresponding Layer 2 address. The concept is similar to the ARP cache for LAN interfaces. For example, the IP Address Resolution Protocol (ARP) cache used on LANs is an example of Layer 3-to-Layer 2 address mapping. With IP ARP, you know the IP address of another device on the same LAN, but not the MAC address; when the ARP completes, you know another device's LAN (Layer 2) address. Similarly, routers that use Frame Relay need a mapping between a router's Layer 3 address and the DLCI used to reach that other router.

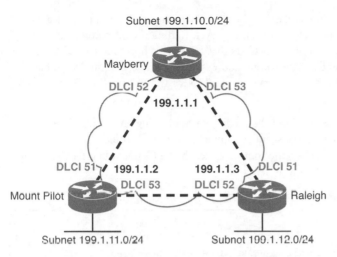

Figure 14-2   *Full Mesh with Local DLCIs Shown*

This section discusses the basics of why mapping is needed for LAN connections and Frame Relay, with a focus on Frame Relay. Here's a more general definition of mapping:

> The information that correlates to the next-hop router's Layer 3 address and the Layer 2 address used to reach it is called mapping. Mapping is needed on multiaccess networks.

Thinking about routing helps make the need for mapping more apparent. For example, consider a packet that enters Mayberry's LAN interface destined for network 199.1.11.0/24, the Class C network off Mount Pilot's LAN interface. As shown in Figure 14-3, the router goes through normal routing steps, removing the packet from between the Ethernet header and trailer, choosing to route the packet out Mayberry's S0/1/1 interface to Mount Pilot next, and so on. But what DLCI should Mayberry put into the new Frame Relay header?

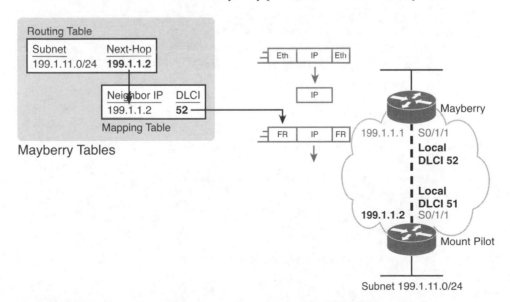

Figure 14-3   *Logic on Mayberry to Choose the Correct DLCI*

The left side of the figure shows the tables Mayberry uses to choose the right DLCI. First, Mayberry looks at the route it uses to forward the packet, finding the next-hop router IP address. Then, the Frame Relay Mapping table lists that same next-hop router IP address, along with the DLCI used to send frames to that address (the equivalent of an ARP table). Mayberry then puts that DLCI (52, Mayberry's local DLCI for the PVC connected to Mount Pilot) into the Frame Relay header.

Interestingly, just like ARP happens behind the scenes, without being enabled, Frame Relay creates the address mappings behind the scene. Example 14-6 puts the pieces together, matching Figure 14-3. The example lists the routing table, the PVCs (including DLCIs), and the Frame Relay mapping table, all on Mayberry.

Example 14-6 show *Commands on Mayberry, Showing the Need for Mapping*

```
Mayberry# show ip route
Codes: L - local, C - connected, S - static, R - RIP, M - mobile, B - BGP
       D - EIGRP, EX - EIGRP external, O - OSPF, IA - OSPF inter area
       N1 - OSPF NSSA external type 1, N2 - OSPF NSSA external type 2
       E1 - OSPF external type 1, E2 - OSPF external type 2
       i - IS-IS, su - IS-IS summary, L1 - IS-IS level-1, L2 - IS-IS level-2
       ia - IS-IS inter area, * - candidate default, U - per-user static route
       o - ODR, P - periodic downloaded static route, H - NHRP, l - LISP
       + - replicated route, % - next hop override


Gateway of last resort is not set


      199.1.1.0/24 is variably subnetted, 2 subnets, 2 masks
C        199.1.1.0/24 is directly connected, Serial0/1/1
L        199.1.1.1/32 is directly connected, Serial0/1/1
      199.1.10.0/24 is variably subnetted, 2 subnets, 2 masks
C        199.1.10.0/24 is directly connected, GigabitEthernet0/0
L        199.1.10.1/32 is directly connected, GigabitEthernet0/0
D     199.1.11.0/24 [90/2172416] via 199.1.1.2, 00:00:03, Serial0/1/1
D       199.1.12.0/24 [90/2172416] via 199.1.1.3, 00:19:14, Serial0/1/1


Mayberry# show frame-relay pvc


PVC Statistics for interface Serial0/1/1 (Frame Relay DTE)


            Active      Inactive      Deleted       Static
  Local       2            0             0            0
  Switched    0            0             0            0
  Unused      0            0             0            0


DLCI = 52, DLCI USAGE = LOCAL, PVC STATUS = ACTIVE, INTERFACE = Serial0/1/1


  input pkts 37          output pkts 39        in bytes 2542
  out bytes 2752         dropped pkts 0        in pkts dropped 0
  out pkts dropped 0         out bytes dropped 0
```

```
    in FECN pkts 0          in BECN pkts 0          out FECN pkts 0
    out BECN pkts 0         in DE pkts 0            out DE pkts 0
    out bcast pkts 26       out bcast bytes 1664
    5 minute input rate 0 bits/sec, 0 packets/sec
    5 minute output rate 0 bits/sec, 0 packets/sec
    pvc create time 00:20:02, last time pvc status changed 00:20:02


DLCI = 53, DLCI USAGE = LOCAL, PVC STATUS = ACTIVE, INTERFACE = Serial0/1/1


    input pkts 37           output pkts 37          in bytes 2618
    out bytes 2746          dropped pkts 0          in pkts dropped 0
    out pkts dropped 0           out bytes dropped 0
    in FECN pkts 0          in BECN pkts 0          out FECN pkts 0
    out BECN pkts 0         in DE pkts 0            out DE pkts 0
    out bcast pkts 25       out bcast bytes 1630
    5 minute input rate 0 bits/sec, 0 packets/sec
    5 minute output rate 0 bits/sec, 0 packets/sec
    pvc create time 00:20:02, last time pvc status changed 00:20:02


Mayberry# show frame-relay map
Serial0/1/1 (up): ip 199.1.1.2 dlci 52(0x34,0xC40), dynamic,
           broadcast,, status defined, active
Serial0/1/1 (up): ip 199.1.1.3 dlci 53(0x35,0xC50), dynamic,
           broadcast,, status defined, active
```

The example highlights all the related information on Mayberry for sending packets to network 199.1.11.0/24 off Mount Pilot. Mayberry's route to 199.1.11.0 refers to outgoing interface serial 0/1/1 and to 199.1.1.2 as the next-hop address. The **show frame-relay pvc** command lists two DLCIs, 52 and 53, and both are active. How does Mayberry know the DLCIs? Well, the LMI status messages tell Mayberry about the VCs, the associated DLCIs, and the status (active).

Which DLCI should Mayberry use to forward the packet? The **show frame-relay map** command output holds the answer. Notice the highlighted phrase "ip 199.1.1.2 dlci 52" in the output. Somehow, Mayberry has mapped 199.1.1.2, which is the next-hop address in the route, to the correct local DLCI, which is 52. So, Mayberry knows to use local DLCI 52 to reach next-hop IP address 199.1.1.2.

Mayberry can use two methods to build the mapping shown in Example 14-6. One uses a statically configured mapping, and the other uses a dynamic process called *Inverse ARP*. The next two small sections explain the details of each of these options.

Inverse ARP

Inverse ARP dynamically creates a mapping between the Layer 3 address (for example, the IP address) and the Layer 2 address (the local DLCI). The end result of Inverse ARP is the same as IP ARP on a LAN: The router builds a mapping between a neighboring Layer 3 address and the corresponding Layer 2 address. However, the process used by Inverse ARP differs for ARP on a LAN. After the VC is up, each router announces its network layer address by sending an Inverse ARP message over that VC. Figure 14-4 shows how this works.

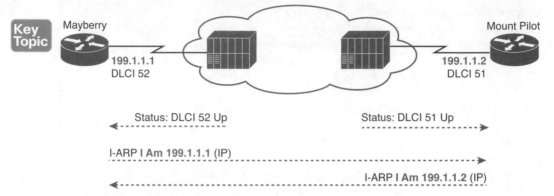

Figure 14-4 *Inverse ARP Process*

As shown in Figure 14-4, Inverse ARP announces its Layer 3 addresses as soon as the LMI signals that the PVCs are up. Inverse ARP starts by learning the DLCI data link layer address (via LMI messages), and then it announces its own Layer 3 addresses that use that VC. Inverse ARP is enabled by default.

In Example 14-6, Mayberry shows two different entries in the **show frame-relay map** command output. Mayberry uses Inverse ARP to learn that DLCI 52 is mapped to next-hop IP address 199.1.1.2, and that DLCI 53 is mapped to next-hop IP address 199.1.1.3. Interestingly, Mayberry learns this information by receiving an Inverse ARP from Mount Pilot and Raleigh, respectively.

The Inverse ARP process has a few subtle turns of how it works. First, Inverse ARP messages announce a router's IP address, with the frame flowing over a PVC. The receiving router learns the IP address in the message, and it notes the DLCI of the InARP frame. For example, based on Figure 14-4:

■ Mayberry sends an InARP with 199.1.1.1; Mount Pilot receives the InARP with DLCI 51 in the header, so Mount Pilot's mapping lists 199.1.1.1 and DLCI 51.

■ Mount Pilot sends an InARP with 199.1.1.2; Mayberry receive the InARP with DLCI 52 in the header, so Mayberry's mapping lists 199.1.1.2 and DLCI 52.

Static Frame Relay Mapping

You can statically configure the same mapping information instead of using Inverse ARP. In a production network, you probably would just go ahead and use Inverse ARP. For the exams, you need to know how to configure the static **map** command statements. Example 14-7 lists the static Frame Relay map for the three routers shown in Figure 14-2, along with the configuration used to disable Inverse ARP.

Example 14-7   frame-relay map *Commands*

```
Mayberry
interface serial 0/0/0
 no frame-relay inverse-arp
 frame-relay map ip 199.1.1.2 52 broadcast
 frame-relay map ip 199.1.1.3 53 broadcast
Mount Pilot
interface serial 0/0/0
 no frame-relay inverse-arp
 frame-relay map ip 199.1.1.1 51 broadcast
 frame-relay map ip 199.1.1.3 53 broadcast
Raleigh
interface serial 0/0/0
 no frame-relay inverse-arp
 frame-relay map ip 199.1.1.1 51 broadcast
 frame-relay map ip 199.1.1.2 52 broadcast
```

As an example to better understand the meaning of the **frame-relay map** command, consider the command on Mayberry referencing 199.1.1.2. The command sits on Mayberry, so it adds a mapping entry in Mayberry. The command tells Mayberry that when Mayberry sends a packet to 199.1.1.2 (Mount Pilot), Mayberry must use DLCI 52. Mayberry's **frame-relay map** statement correlates Mount Pilot's IP address, 199.1.1.2, to the local DLCI used to reach Mount Pilot—namely, DLCI 52.

As another example, consider Mount Pilot's **frame-relay map ip 199.1.1.1 51 broadcast** command. This command creates a mapping entry for Mount Pilot, so when it sends a packet to 199.1.1.1 (Mayberry), Mount Pilot uses DLCI 51.

Mapping is needed for each next-hop Layer 3 address for each Layer 3 protocol being routed. Even with a network this small, the configuration process can be laborious.

> **NOTE**   The **broadcast** keyword on the **frame-relay map** command is required when the router needs to send broadcasts or multicasts to the neighboring router—for example, to support routing protocol messages such as Hellos.

Configuring Point-to-Point Subinterfaces

The second sample network, based on the environment shown in Figure 14-5, uses point-to-point subinterfaces. Point-to-point subinterfaces work well when the subnetting design calls for one subnet for each PVC. Examples 14-8 through 14-11 show the configuration for this sample network, with all four routers using only point-to-point subinterfaces. Pay close attention to the command prompts Example 14-8, because they change when you configure subinterfaces.

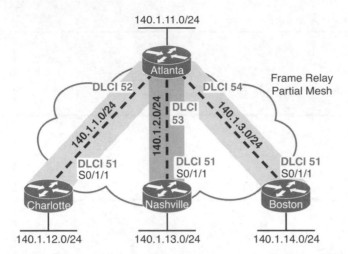

140.1.11.0/24

Figure 14-5   *Partial Mesh with Subnets and Local DLCIs*

Example 14-8   *Atlanta Configuration*

```
Atlanta(config)# interface serial0/1/1
Atlanta(config-if)# encapsulation frame-relay

Atlanta(config-if)# interface serial 0/1/1.1 point-to-point
Atlanta(config-subif)# ip address 140.1.1.1  255.255.255.0
Atlanta(config-subif)# frame-relay interface-dlci 52

Atlanta(config-fr-dlci)# interface serial 0/1/1.2 point-to-point
Atlanta(config-subif)# ip address 140.1.2.1 255.255.255.0
Atlanta(config-subif)# frame-relay interface-dlci 53

Atlanta(config-fr-dlci)# interface serial 0/1/1.3 point-to-point
Atlanta(config-subif)# ip address 140.1.3.1 255.255.255.0
Atlanta(config-subif)# frame-relay interface-dlci 54

Atlanta(config-fr-dlci)# interface gigabitethernet 0/0
Atlanta(config-if)# ip address 140.1.11.1 255.255.255.0
```

Example 14-9   *Charlotte Configuration*

```
interface serial0/1/1
 encapsulation frame-relay
!
interface serial 0/1/1.1 point-to-point
 ip address 140.1.1.2  255.255.255.0
 frame-relay interface-dlci 51
```

```
!
interface gigabitethernet 0/0
 ip address 140.1.12.2 255.255.255.0
```

Example 14-10 *Nashville Configuration*

```
interface serial0/1/1
 encapsulation frame-relay
!
interface serial 0/1/1.2 point-to-point
 ip address 140.1.2.3 255.255.255.0
 frame-relay interface-dlci 51
!
interface gigabitethernet 0/0
 ip address 140.1.13.3 255.255.255.0
```

Example 14-11 *Boston Configuration*

```
interface serial0/1/1
 encapsulation frame-relay
!
interface serial 0/1/1.3 point-to-point
 ip address 140.1.3.4 255.255.255.0
 frame-relay interface-dlci 51
!
interface gigabitethernet 0/0
 ip address 140.1.14.4  255.255.255.0
```

Again, defaults abound in this configuration, but some defaults are different than when you're configuring on the physical interface. The LMI type is autosensed, and Cisco encapsulation is used, which is just like the fully meshed examples. Inverse ARP is not really needed on point-to-point subinterfaces, but it is enabled by default in case the router on the other end of the VC needs to use Inverse ARP, as explained later in this section.

Two new commands create the configuration required with point-to-point subinterfaces. First, the **interface serial 0/1/1.1 point-to-point** command creates logical subinterface number 1 under physical interface serial 0/1/1. This command also defines the subinterface as a point-to-point subinterface instead of point-to-multipoint. Then, the configuration must associate one PVC with the subinterface; the **frame-relay interface-dlci** subinterface subcommand tells the router which single local DLCI is associated with that subinterface.

An example of how the **frame-relay interface-dlci** command works can help. Consider router Atlanta in Figure 14-5. Atlanta receives LMI messages on serial 0/01/1 stating that three PVCs, with local DLCIs 52, 53, and 54, are up. Which PVC goes with which subinterface? Cisco IOS software needs to associate the correct PVC with the correct subinterface. This is accomplished with the **frame-relay interface-dlci** command.

Take a moment to work through all the subinterface configuration and **frame-relay interface-dlci** configuration in Example 14-8 through 14-11, and compare it to the DLCIs and IP subnets listed in Figure 14-5. Note that in each case the local DLCI configured on the **frame-relay interface-dlci** command corresponds to the subnet (based on the **ip address** command).

Before leaving the point-to-point configuration, note that the subinterface numbers do not have to match on the router on the other end of the PVC. In this example, I just numbered the subinterfaces to be easier to remember. In real life, it is useful to encode some information about your network numbering scheme into the subinterface number.

For example, a company might encode part of the carrier's circuit ID in the subinterface number so that the operations staff could find the correct information to tell the telco when troubleshooting the link. Many sites use the DLCI as the subinterface number. Of course, useful troubleshooting information, such as the DLCI, the name of the router on the other end of the VC, and so on, could be configured as text with the **description** command as well. In any case, there are no requirements for matching subinterface numbers. This example just matches the subinterface number to the third octet of the IP address.

Verifying Point-to-Point Frame Relay

Example 14-12 shows the output from the most popular Cisco IOS software Frame Relay EXEC commands for monitoring Frame Relay as issued on router Atlanta.

Example 14-12   *Output from EXEC Commands on Atlanta*

```
Atlanta# show frame-relay pvc


PVC Statistics for interface Serial0/1/1 (Frame Relay DTE)


              Active    Inactive    Deleted      Static
  Local         2          0           0           0
  Switched      0          0           0           0
  Unused        1          0           0           0


DLCI = 52, DLCI USAGE = LOCAL, PVC STATUS = ACTIVE, INTERFACE = Serial0/1/1


  input pkts 80          output pkts 76        in bytes 5940
  out bytes 5594         dropped pkts 0        in pkts dropped 0
  out pkts dropped 0            out bytes dropped 0
  in FECN pkts 0         in BECN pkts 0        out FECN pkts 0
  out BECN pkts 0        in DE pkts 0          out DE pkts 0
  out bcast pkts 45      out bcast bytes 3030
  5 minute input rate 0 bits/sec, 0 packets/sec
  5 minute output rate 0 bits/sec, 0 packets/sec
  pvc create time 00:39:49, last time pvc status changed 00:27:29


DLCI = 53, DLCI USAGE = LOCAL, PVC STATUS = ACTIVE, INTERFACE = Serial0/1/1
```

```
   input pkts 64            output pkts 82           in bytes 4206
   out bytes 6612           dropped pkts 0           in pkts dropped 0
   out pkts dropped 0              out bytes dropped 0
   in FECN pkts 0           in BECN pkts 0           out FECN pkts 0
   out BECN pkts 0          in DE pkts 0             out DE pkts 0
   out bcast pkts 38        out bcast bytes 2532
   5 minute input rate 0 bits/sec, 0 packets/sec
   5 minute output rate 0 bits/sec, 0 packets/sec
   pvc create time 00:33:49, last time pvc status changed 00:27:19


DLCI = 54, DLCI USAGE = UNUSED, PVC STATUS = ACTIVE, INTERFACE = Serial0/1/1

   input pkts 0             output pkts 0            in bytes 0
   out bytes 0              dropped pkts 0           in pkts dropped 0
   out pkts dropped 0              out bytes dropped 0
   in FECN pkts 0           in BECN pkts 0           out FECN pkts 0
   out BECN pkts 0          in DE pkts 0             out DE pkts 0
   out bcast pkts 0         out bcast bytes 0            5 minute input rate 0 bits/sec,
0 packets/sec
   5 minute output rate 0 bits/sec, 0 packets/sec
   pvc create time 00:00:59, last time pvc status changed 00:00:59


Atlanta# show frame-relay map
Serial0/0/0.3 (up): point-to-point dlci, dlci 54(0x36,0xC60), broadcast
        status defined, active
Serial0/0/0.2 (up): point-to-point dlci, dlci 53(0x35,0xC50), broadcast
        status defined, active
Serial0/0/0.1 (up): point-to-point dlci, dlci 52(0x34,0xC40), broadcast
        status defined, active


Atlanta# debug frame-relay lmi
Frame Relay LMI debugging is on
Displaying all Frame Relay LMI data

Serial0/0/0(out): StEnq, myseq 163, yourseen 161, DTE up
datagramstart = 0x45AED8, datagramsize = 13
FR encap = 0xFCF10309
00 75 01 01 01 03 02 A3 A1

Serial0/0/0(in): Status, myseq 163
RT IE 1, length 1, type 1
KA IE 3, length 2, yourseq 162, myseq 163
```

The **show frame-relay pvc** command lists useful management information. In particular, the output includes a variety of counters and rates for packets going over each permanent virtual circuit (PVC). Also, the PVC status is a great place to start when troubleshooting.

The **show frame-relay map** command lists mapping information. With the earlier example of a fully meshed network, in which the configuration did not use any subinterfaces, a Layer 3 address was listed with each DLCI. In this example, a DLCI is listed in each entry, but no mention of corresponding Layer 3 addresses is made. The whole point of mapping is to correlate a Layer 3 address to a Layer 2 address, but there is no Layer 3 address in the **show frame-relay map** command output! The reason is that with point-to-point subinterfaces routers can find the correct mapping information just from the local configuration, as follows:

■ A router matches a route that forwards packet out a point-to-point subinterface.

■ The router looks for the one (and only) **frame-relay interface-dlci** configuration command on that subinterface and uses that DLCI when encapsulating the packet.

Finally, the **debug frame-relay lmi** output lists information for the sending and receiving LMI inquiries. The switch sends the status message, and the data terminal equipment (DTE) (router) sends the status inquiry. The default setting with Cisco IOS software is to send, and to expect to receive, these status messages. The Cisco IOS software **no keepalive** command is used to disable the use of LMI status messages. Unlike other interfaces, Cisco keepalive messages do not flow from router to router over Frame Relay. Instead, they are simply used to detect whether the router has connectivity to its local Frame Relay switch.

Configuring with Multipoint Subinterfaces

You can also choose to use multipoint subinterfaces for a Frame Relay configuration. This last sample network, based on the network shown in Figure 14-6, uses both multipoint and point-to-point subinterfaces. Examples 14-13 through 14-17 show the configuration for this network. Table 14-2 summarizes the addresses and subinterfaces used.

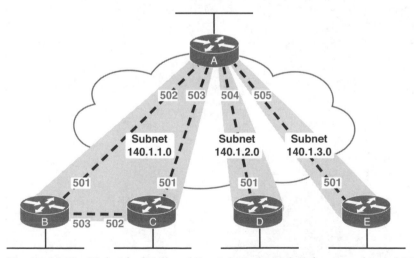

Figure 14-6 *Hybrid of Full and Partial Mesh, with Subnets and Local DLCIs*

Example 14-13 *Router A Configuration*

```
interface serial0/1/1
 encapsulation frame-relay
!
interface serial 0/1/1.1 multipoint
 ip address 140.1.1.1  255.255.255.0
 frame-relay interface-dlci 502
 frame-relay interface-dlci 503
!
interface serial 0/1/1.2 point-to-point
 ip address 140.1.2.1 255.255.255.0
 frame-relay interface-dlci 504
!
interface serial 0/1/1.3 point-to-point
 ip address 140.1.3.1 255.255.255.0
 frame-relay interface-dlci 505
```

Example 14-14 *Router B Configuration*

```
interface serial0/1/1
 encapsulation frame-relay
!
interface serial 0/1/1.1 multipoint
 ip address 140.1.1.2  255.255.255.0
 frame relay interface-dlci 501
 frame-relay interface-dlci 503
```

Example 14-15 *Router C Configuration*

```
interface serial0/1/1
 encapsulation frame-relay
!
interface serial 0/1/1.1 multipoint
 ip address 140.1.1.3  255.255.255.0
 frame-relay interface-dlci 501
 frame-relay interface-dlci 502
```

Example 14-16 *Router D Configuration*

```
interface serial0/0/0
encapsulation frame-relay
!
interface serial 0/1/1.1 point-to-point
 ip address 140.1.2.4  255.255.255.0
 frame-relay interface-dlci 501
```

Example 14-17   *Router E Configuration*

```
interface serial0/0/0
 encapsulation frame-relay
!
interface serial 0/1/1.1 point-to-point
 ip address 140.1.3.5 255.255.255.0
 frame-relay interface-dlci 501
```

Table 14-2   IP Addresses with Point-to-Point and Multipoint Subinterfaces

Router	Subnet	IP Address	Subinterface Type
A	140.1.1.0/24	140.1.1.1	Multipoint
B	140.1.1.0/24	140.1.1.2	Multipoint
C	140.1.1.0/24	140.1.1.3	Multipoint
A	140.1.2.0/24	140.1.2.1	Point-to-point
D	140.1.2.0/24	140.1.2.4	Point-to-point
A	140.1.3.0/24	140.1.3.1	Point-to-point
E	140.1.3.0/24	140.1.3.5	Point-to-point

Multipoint subinterfaces work best when you have a full mesh between a set of routers. On Routers A, B, and C, a multipoint subinterface is used for the configuration referencing the other two routers, because you can think of these three routers as forming a fully meshed subset of the network.

The term *multipoint* simply means that there is more than one VC, so you can send and receive to and from more than one VC on the subinterface. Like point-to-point subinterfaces, multipoint subinterfaces use the **frame-relay interface-dlci** command. Notice that there are two commands for each multipoint subinterface in this case, because each of the two PVCs associated with this subinterface must be identified as being used with that subinterface.

Router A is the only router using both multipoint and point-to-point subinterfaces. On Router A's multipoint serial 0/1/1.1 interface, DLCIs for Router B and Router C are listed. On Router A's other two subinterfaces, which are point-to-point, only a single DLCI needs to be listed. In fact, only one **frame-relay interface-dlci** command is allowed on a point-to-point subinterface because only one VC is allowed. Otherwise, the configurations between the two types are similar.

No mapping statements are required for the configurations shown in Examples 14-13 through 14-17 because Inverse ARP is enabled on the multipoint subinterfaces by default. No mapping is ever needed for the point-to-point subinterface because the only DLCI associated with the interface is statically configured with the **frame-relay interface-dlci** command.

Example 14-18 lists another **show frame-relay map** command, showing the mapping information learned by Inverse ARP for the multipoint subinterface. Notice that the output now includes the Layer 3 addresses, whereas the same command when using point-to-point sub-interfaces (in Example 14-12) did not. The router needs mapping information on multipoint subinterfaces so that when the router routes packets out that subinterface, the router can choose the correct DLCI to use when encapsulating the packet.

Example 14-18 *Frame Relay Maps and Inverse ARP on Router C*

```
RouterC# show frame-relay map
Serial0/1/1.1 (up): ip 140.1.1.1 dlci 501(0x1F5,0x7C50), dynamic,
              broadcast,, status defined, active
Serial0/1/1.1 (up): ip 140.1.1.2 dlci 502(0x1F6,0x7C60), dynamic,
              broadcast,, status defined, active
```

OSPF Issues on Frame Relay Multipoint and Physical Interfaces

In many enterprise networks that use Frame Relay, the engineers choose to use only point-to-point subinterfaces for Frame Relay. Many Frame Relay WANs connect remote sites to a central site, so the point-to-point model works well. Also, Open Shortest Path First (OSPF) and Enhanced Interior Gateway Routing Protocol (EIGRP) both work well with default settings over point-to-point Frame Relay subinterfaces.

As it turns out, OSPF requires a little more configuration attention when using Frame Relay configurations with multipoint or physical interfaces. This brief section summarizes the issues.

Routers using OSPF do not become neighbors over a Frame Relay physical interface or a multipoint subinterface if using only the OSPF configuration discussed in Chapter 8, "Implementing OSPF for IPv4." The issue? Frame Relay physical and multipoint subinterfaces, by default, use an OSPF network type of nonbroadcast. This OSPF network type means that the router will not attempt to dynamically discover any OSPF neighbors on that interface.

The OSPF problem has multiple solutions, but the simplest is to just change OSPF to use a different OSPF network type on the Frame Relay interfaces. (Chapter 8 introduced the idea of OSPF network types for interfaces, but you needed knowledge about Frame Relay before learning about this one small issue and its solution.) The specific solution: Change the OSPF network type to point-to-multipoint, which lets the routers dynamically discover each other over the physical or multipoint subinterface.

For instance, the previous examples (Examples 14-13, 14-14, and 14-15) showed routers A, B, and C all using a multipoint subinterface and sharing the same subnet. If using OSPF, all three routers should become OSPF neighbors. To make OSPF work between those routers, besides the expected OSPF configuration to enable OSPF on the multipoint subinterface of each route, use the **ip ospf network point-to-multipoint** command on all three router's multipoint subinterface. This command changes the OSPF network type to point-to-multipoint, which tells each router to dynamically discover neighbors (and to not use a designated router/backup designated router [DR/BDR]).

> **NOTE**   Study tip: When reading this chapter for the first time, take a break before moving into this troubleshooting section. Take some time to practice Frame Relay configuration using whatever lab choice you made (real gear, simulator, and so on).

Frame Relay Troubleshooting

Frame Relay has many features and options that you can configure. For both real life and the exams, troubleshooting Frame Relay problems often means that you need to look at all the routers' configurations and make sure that the configurations meet the requirements. The LMI types must match or be autosensed, the Layer 3 mapping information must be learned or statically mapped, the right DLCI values must be associated with each subinterface, and so on. So, to be well prepared for the CCNA exams, you should review and memorize the many Frame Relay configuration options and what each option means.

However, the exams may have Frame Relay questions that require you to determine a problem without looking at the configuration. This second major section of the chapter examines Frame Relay troubleshooting, with an emphasis on how to use **show** commands, along with the symptoms of a problem to isolate the root cause of the problem.

A Suggested Frame Relay Troubleshooting Process

To isolate a Frame Relay problem, the process should start with some pings. Optimally, pings from an end-user host on a LAN to another host on a remote LAN can quickly determine whether the network currently can meet the true end goal of delivering packets between computers. If that ping fails, a ping from one router to the other router's Frame Relay IP address is the next step. If that ping works, but the end user's ping failed, the problem probably has something to do with Layer 3 issues (troubleshooting those issues was well covered in Chapters 4, "Troubleshooting IPv4 Routing Part I," 5, "Troubleshooting IPv4 Routing Part II," and 11, "Troubleshooting IPv4 Routing Protocols"). However, if a ping from one router to another router's Frame Relay IP address fails, the problem is most likely related to the Frame Relay network.

This section focuses on troubleshooting problems when a Frame Relay router cannot ping another router's Frame Relay IP address. At that point, the engineer should ping the Frame Relay IP addresses of all the other routers on the other end of each VC to determine the following:

> Do the pings fail for all remote routers' Frame Relay IP addresses or do some pings fail and some pings work?

For example, Figure 14-7 shows a sample Frame Relay network that will be used with the remaining examples in this chapter. If R1 tried to ping R2's Frame Relay IP address (10.1.2.2 in this case) and failed, the next question is whether R1's pings to R3 (10.1.34.3) and R4 (10.1.34.4) work.

This chapter organizes its explanations of how to troubleshoot Frame Relay based on this first problem isolation step. The following list summarizes the major actions, with each step in the following list being examined in order following the list.

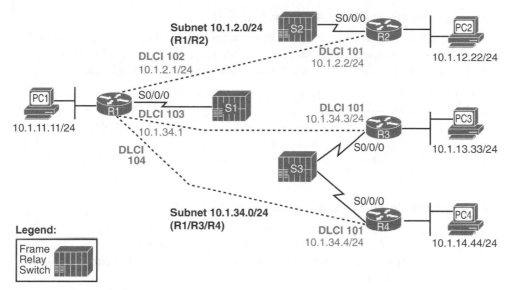

Figure 14-7   *Sample Frame Relay Network for the Troubleshooting Examples*

If a Frame Relay router's pings fail for all remote routers whose VCs share a single access link, do the following:

Step 1.   Check for Layer 1 problems on the access link between the router and the local Frame Relay switch (all routers).

Step 2.   Check for Layer 2 problems on the access link, particularly encapsulation and LMI.

After resolving any problems in the first two steps, or if the original ping tests showed that the Frame Relay router can ping some, but not all, of the other Frame Relay routers whose VCs share a single access link, follow these steps:

Step 3.   Check for PVC problems based on the PVC status and subinterface status.

Step 4.   Check for Layer 2 or 3 problems with both static and dynamic (Inverse ARP) mapping.

Step 5.   Check for Layer 2 or 3 problems related to a mismatch of end-to-end encapsulation (cisco or ietf).

Step 6.   Check for other Layer 3 issues, including mismatched subnets.

The rest of this chapter explains some of the details of each step of this suggested troubleshooting process.

Layer 1 Issues on the Access Link (Step 1)

If a router's physical interface used for the Frame Relay access link is not in an "up and up" state, the router cannot send any frames over the link. If the interface has a line status (the first interface status code) of down, the interface most likely has a Layer 1 issue.

From a Layer 1 perspective, a Frame Relay access link is merely a leased line between a router and a Frame Relay switch. As such, the exact same Layer 1 issues exist for this link as for a point-to-point leased line. Because the possible root causes and suggested troubleshooting steps mirror what should be done on a leased line, refer to the section "Troubleshooting Layer 1 Problems" in Chapter 12, "Implementing Point-to-Point WANs," for more information about this step.

Layer 2 Issues on the Access Link (Step 2)

If a router's physical interface line status is up, but the line protocol status (second status code) is down, the link usually has a Layer 2 problem between the router and the local Frame Relay switch. With Frame Relay interfaces, the problem is often related to either the **encapsulation** command or the Frame Relay LMI.

The potential problem related to the **encapsulation** command is simple to check. If a router's serial interface configuration omits the **encapsulation frame-relay** interface subcommand but the physical access link is working, the physical interface settles into an up/down state. If the configuration is unavailable, the **show interfaces** command can be used to see the configured encapsulation type, which is listed in the first few lines of command output.

The other potential problem relates to the LMI. LMI status messages flow in both directions between a router (data terminating equipment [DTE]) and Frame Relay switch (data circuit-terminating equipment [DCE]) for two main purposes:

- For the DCE to inform the DTE about each VC's DLCI and its status
- To provide a keepalive function so that the DTE and DCE can easily tell when the access link can no longer pass traffic

A router places the physical link in an up/down state when the link physically works, but the router ceases to hear LMI messages from the switch. With the interface not in an up/up state, the router does not attempt to send any IP packets out the interface, so all pings should fail at this point.

A router might cease to receive LMI messages from the switch because of both legitimate reasons and mistakes. The normal legitimate purpose for the LMI keepalive function is that if the link really is having problems, and cannot pass any data, the router can notice the loss of keepalive messages and bring the link down. This allows the router to use an alternative route, assuming that an alternative route exists. However, a router might cease to receive LMI messages and bring down the interface because of the following mistakes:

- Disabling LMI on the switch, but leaving it enabled on the router
- Configuring different LMI types on the router (with the **frame-relay lmi-type** *type* physical interface subcommand) and the switch, so that the router and Frame Relay switch do not understand each other's LMI messages

14

You can easily check for both encapsulation and LMI using the **show frame-relay lmi** command. This command lists output for interfaces only if the interface has the **encapsulation frame-relay** command configured, so you can quickly confirm whether the **encapsulation frame-relay** command is configured on the correct serial interfaces. This command also lists the LMI type used by the router, and it shows counters for the number of LMI messages sent and received. Example 14-19 shows an example from router R1 in Figure 14-6.

Example 14-19   show frame-relay lmi *Command on R1*

```
R1# show frame-relay lmi


LMI Statistics for interface Serial0/0/0 (Frame Relay DTE) LMI TYPE = ANSI
  Invalid Unnumbered info 0          Invalid Prot Disc 0
  Invalid dummy Call Ref 0           Invalid Msg Type 0
  Invalid Status Message 0           Invalid Lock Shift 0
  Invalid Information ID 0           Invalid Report IE Len 0
  Invalid Report Request 0           Invalid Keep IE Len 0
  Num Status Enq. Sent 122           Num Status msgs Rcvd 34
  Num Update Status Rcvd 0           Num Status Timeouts 88
  Last Full Status Req 00:00:04      Last Full Status Rcvd 00:13:24
```

For this example, router R1 was statically configured with the **frame-relay lmi-type ansi** interface subcommand, with switch S1 still using LMI type cisco. At the point in time that the configuration was changed, the statistics for the number of sent and received status messages were both at 34. (When working, these numbers will grow at the same rate.) From that point forward, R1 has now sent 88 ANSI status messages, for a total of 122 status messages sent. The number of status messages received still sits at 34, because R1 no longer understands the Cisco LMI messages sent by the switch. Also, R1 has been expecting an ANSI status message for the last 88 LMI status time intervals, as noted in the status timeouts counter.

If repeated use of the **show frame-relay lmi** command shows that the number of status messages received remains the same, the likely cause, other than a truly nonworking link, is that the LMI types do not match. The best solution is to allow for LMI autosense by configuring the **no frame-relay lmi-type** physical interface subcommand. Alternatively, configure the same LMI type that is used by the switch.

If you troubleshoot and fix any problems found in Steps 1 and 2 on all Frame Relay connected routers, all the routers' access link physical interfaces should be in an up/up state. The last four steps examine issues that apply to individual PVCs and neighbors.

PVC Problems and Status (Step 3)

The goal at this step in the troubleshooting process is to discover the DLCI of the PVC used to reach a particular neighbor, and then find out if the PVC is working.

To determine the correct PVC, particularly if little or no configuration or documentation is available, you have to start with the failed **ping** command for the neighboring router's IP address on the Frame Relay network. From there, you can follow this chain of logic:

Step 3a.   Discover the IP address and mask of each Frame Relay interface/subinterface (**show interfaces, show ip interface brief**) and calculate the connected subnets.

Step 3b.   Compare the IP address of the neighbor (from the failed **ping** command) and pick the local interface/subinterface whose connected subnet is the same subnet.

Step 3c.   Discover the PVCs assigned to that interface or subinterface (**show frame-relay pvc**).

Step 3d.   If more than one PVC is assigned to the interface or subinterface, determine which PVC is used to reach a particular neighbor (**show frame-relay map**).

> **NOTE**   As a reminder, lists like this one are meant for convenient reference when you read the chapter. It is easy to find the list when you study and want to remember a particular part of how to attack a given problem. You do not need to memorize the list or practice it until you internalize the information.

Steps 3a, 3b, 3c, and 3d discover the correct PVC to examine. After it is discovered, Step 3 in the suggested troubleshooting process interprets the status of that PVC, and the associated interface or subinterface, to determine the cause of any problems.

This section takes a closer look at an example in which R1 cannot ping R2's 10.1.2.2 Frame Relay IP address from Figure 14-7. Before focusing on the process to determine which VC is used, it is helpful to see the final answer, so Figure 14-8 lists some of the details. For this example, R1's **ping 10.1.2.2** command fails in this case.

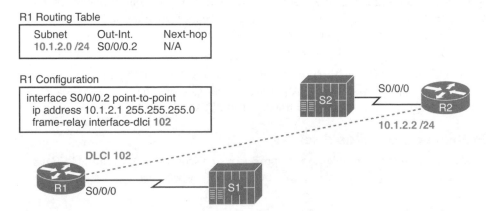

Figure 14-8   *Configuration Facts Related to R1's Failed* **ping 10.1.2.2** *Command*

Find the Connected Subnet and Outgoing Interface (Steps 3a and 3b)

The first two substeps to find R1's PVC (DLCI) connecting to R2 (Substeps 3a and 3b) should be relatively easy assuming that you have already finished Parts II and III of this book. Any time you ping the Frame Relay IP address of a neighboring router, that IP address should be in one of the subnets also connected to the local router. To find the interface used on a local router when forwarding packets to the remote router, you just have to find that common connected subnet.

In this example, with R1 pinging 10.1.2.2, Example 14-20 shows a few commands that confirm that R1's S0/0/0.2 subinterface is connected to subnet 10.1.2.0/24, which includes R2's 10.1.2.2 IP address.

Example 14-20   *Finding Subnet 10.1.2.0/24 and Subinterface S0/0/0.2*

```
R1> show ip interface brief
Interface              IP-Address      OK? Method Status                  Protocol
FastEthernet0/0        10.1.11.1       YES NVRAM  up                       up
FastEthernet0/1        unassigned      YES NVRAM  administratively down down
Serial0/0/0            unassigned      YES NVRAM  up                       up
Serial0/0/0.2          10.1.2.1        YES NVRAM  down                     down
Serial0/0/0.5          10.1.5.1        YES manual down                     down
Serial0/0/0.34         10.1.34.1       YES NVRAM  up                       up


R1# show interfaces s 0/0/0.2
Serial0/0/0.2 is down, line protocol is down
  Hardware is GT96K Serial
  Internet address is 10.1.2.1/24
  MTU 1500 bytes, BW 1544 Kbit, DLY 20000 usec,
     reliability 255/255, txload 1/255, rxload 1/255
  Encapsulation FRAME-RELAY
  Last clearing of "show interface" counters never
! Lines omitted for brevity
```

Find the PVCs Assigned to That Interface (Step 3c)

The **show frame-relay pvc** command directly answers the question of which PVCs have been assigned to which interfaces and subinterfaces. If the command is issued with no parameters, the command lists about ten lines of output for each VC, with the end of the first line listing the associated interface or subinterface. Example 14-21 lists the beginning of the command output.

Example 14-21 *Correlating Subinterface S0/0/0.2 to the PVC with DLCI 102*

```
R1> show frame-relay pvc

PVC Statistics for interface Serial0/0/0 (Frame Relay DTE)

                Active      Inactive     Deleted      Static
  Local           1            2            0            0
  Switched        0            0            0            0
  Unused          0            0            0            0


DLCI = 102, DLCI USAGE = LOCAL, PVC STATUS = INACTIVE, INTERFACE = Serial0/0/0.2

    input pkts 33            output pkts 338         in bytes 1952
    out bytes 29018          dropped pkts 0          in pkts dropped 0
    out pkts dropped 0            out bytes dropped 0
    in FECN pkts 0           in BECN pkts 0          out FECN pkts 0
    out BECN pkts 0          in DE pkts 0            out DE pkts 0
    out bcast pkts 332       out bcast bytes 28614
    5 minute input rate 0 bits/sec, 0 packets/sec
    5 minute output rate 0 bits/sec, 0 packets/sec
    pvc create time 00:30:05, last time pvc status changed 00:04:14

DLCI = 103, DLCI USAGE = LOCAL, PVC STATUS = INACTIVE, INTERFACE = Serial0/0/0.34

    input pkts 17            output pkts 24          in bytes 1106
    out bytes 2086           dropped pkts 0          in pkts dropped 0
    out pkts dropped 0            out bytes dropped 0
    in FECN pkts 0           in BECN pkts 0          out FECN pkts 0
    out BECN pkts 0          in DE pkts 0            out DE pkts 0
    out bcast pkts 11        out bcast bytes 674
    5 minute input rate 0 bits/sec, 0 packets/sec
    5 minute output rate 0 bits/sec, 0 packets/sec
    pvc create time 00:30:07, last time pvc status changed 00:02:57

DLCI = 104, DLCI USAGE = LOCAL, PVC STATUS = ACTIVE, INTERFACE = Serial0/0/0.34

    input pkts 41            output pkts 42          in bytes 2466
    out bytes 3017           dropped pkts 0          in pkts dropped 0
    out pkts dropped 0            out bytes dropped 0
    in FECN pkts 0           in BECN pkts 0          out FECN pkts 0
    out BECN pkts 0          in DE pkts 0            out DE pkts 0
    out bcast pkts 30        out bcast bytes 1929
    5 minute input rate 0 bits/sec, 0 packets/sec
    5 minute output rate 0 bits/sec, 0 packets/sec
    pvc create time 00:30:07, last time pvc status changed 00:26:17
```

To find all the PVCs associated with an interface or subinterface, just scan the highlighted parts of the output in Example 14-21. In this case, S0/0/0.2 is listed with only one PVC, the one with DLCI 102, so only one PVC is associated with S0/0/0.2 in this case.

Determine Which PVC Is Used to Reach a Particular Neighbor (Step 3d)

If the router's configuration associates more than one PVC with one interface or subinterface, the next step is to figure out which of the PVCs is used to send traffic to a particular neighbor. For instance, Example 14-21 shows R1 uses a multipoint subinterface S0/0/0.34 with DLCIs 103 and 104. So, if you were troubleshooting a problem in which the **ping 10.1.34.3** command failed on R1, the next step would be to determine which of the two DLCIs (103 or 104) identifies the VC connecting R1 to R3.

Unfortunately, you cannot always find the answer without looking at other documentation. The only **show** command that can help is **show frame-relay map**, which can correlate the next-hop IP address and DLCI. Unfortunately, if the local router relies on Inverse ARP, the local router cannot learn the mapping information right now either, so the mapping table might not have any useful information in it. However, if static mapping is used, the correct PVC/DLCI can be identified.

In the example of R1 failing when pinging 10.1.2.2 (R2), only one PVC is associated with the correct interface (S0/0/0.2). As a result, this example ignores this step and moves on to look at PVC status.

PVC Status

At this point in major troubleshooting Step 3, the correct outgoing interface/subinterface and correct PVC/DLCI have been identified. Finally, the PVC status can be examined to see if it means that the PVC has a problem.

Routers use four different PVC status codes. A router learns about two of the possible status values, *active* and *inactive*, via LMI messages from the Frame Relay switch. The switch's LMI message lists all DLCIs for all configured PVCs on the access link and whether the PVC is currently usable (active) or not (inactive). An LMI message that lists these states means:

> **Active:** The Frame Relay network knows about the PVC with the listed DLCI, and the PVC is working right now.

> **Inactive:** The Frame Relay network knows about the PVC with the listed DLCI, and the PVC is not working right now.

Routers have two other PVC states that require a little more thought to understand. First, the static state means that the router has configured a DLCI for some PVC but the LMI is down. Because the LMI is down, the router does not know whether the PVC will work, because the router receives no LMI status messages. However, the router can at least send frames using those DLCIs and hope that the Frame Relay network can deliver them.

The other PVC state, *deleted*, means that the router configuration refers to the DLCI, but the LMI is working and lists no information about that DLCI value. The LMI status messages list status for all the PVCs defined over the access link, so this state means that the Frame Relay network does not have a definition for the PVC. Basically, this state means that the router has configured the DLCI but the switch has not.

Table 14-3 summarizes the four Frame Relay PVC status codes.

Table 14-3   PVC Status Values

Status	Active	Inactive	Deleted	Static
The PVC is defined to the Frame Relay network.	Yes	Yes	No	Unknown
The router will attempt to send frames on a VC in this state.	Yes	No	No	Yes

As noted in the last row of the table, routers only send data over PVCs in an active or static state. Also even if the PVC is in a static state, there is no guarantee that the Frame Relay network can actually send frames over that PVC, because the static state implies that LMI is turned off and that the router has not learned any status information.

The next step in the troubleshooting process is to find the status of the PVC used to reach a particular neighbor. Continuing with the problem of R1 failing when pinging R2 (10.1.2.2), Example 14-22 shows the status of the PVC with DLCI 102, as identified earlier.

Example 14-22   show frame-relay pvc *Command on R1*

```
R1> show frame-relay pvc 102


PVC Statistics for interface Serial0/0/0 (Frame Relay DTE)


DLCI = 102, DLCI USAGE = LOCAL, PVC STATUS = INACTIVE, INTERFACE = Serial0/0/0.2


   input pkts 22            output pkts 193          in bytes 1256
   out bytes 16436          dropped pkts 0           in pkts dropped 0
   out pkts dropped 0           out bytes dropped 0
   in FECN pkts 0           in BECN pkts 0           out FECN pkts 0
   out BECN pkts 0          in DE pkts 0             out DE pkts 0
   out bcast pkts 187       out bcast bytes 16032
   5 minute input rate 0 bits/sec, 0 packets/sec
   5 minute output rate 0 bits/sec, 0 packets/sec
   pvc create time 01:12:56, last time pvc status changed 00:22:45
```

In this case, R1 cannot ping R2 because the PVC with DLCI 102 is in an inactive state.

To further isolate the problem and find the root cause, you need to look deeper into the reasons why a PVC can be in an inactive state. First, as always, repeat the same troubleshooting steps on the other router (in this case, R2). If no problems are found on R2, other than an inactive PVC, the problem may be a genuine problem in the Frame Relay provider's network, so a call to the provider may be the next step. However, you may find some other problem on the remote router. For example, to create the failure and **show** commands in this section, R2's access link was shut down, so a quick examination of troubleshooting Step 1 on router R2 would have identified the problem. However, if further troubleshooting shows that both routers list their ends of the PVC in an inactive state, the root cause (in this case) lies within the Frame Relay provider's network.

Finding the root cause of a problem related to a PVC in a deleted state is relatively easy. The deleted status means that the Frame Relay switch's configuration and the router's configuration do not match, with the router configuring a DLCI that is not also configured on the switch. Either the provider said it would configure a PVC with a particular DLCI and did not, or the router engineer configured the wrong DLCI value.

Subinterface Status

Subinterfaces have a line status and protocol status code, just like physical interfaces. However, because subinterfaces are virtual, the status codes and their meanings differ a bit from physical interfaces. This section briefly examines how Frame Relay subinterfaces work and how IOS decides whether a Frame Relay subinterface should be in an up/up state or a down/down state.

Frame Relay configuration associates one or more DLCIs with a subinterface using two commands: **frame-relay interface-dlci** and **frame-relay map**. Of all the DLCIs associated with a subinterface, IOS uses the following rules to determine the status of a subinterface:

- **Down/down:** All the DLCIs associated with the subinterface are inactive or deleted, or the underlying physical interface is not in an up/up state.

- **Up/up:** At least one of the DLCIs associated with the subinterface is active or static.

For example, to cause the problems shown in Example 14-22, R2 and R3 simply shut down their Frame Relay access links. Figure 14-9 shows the next LMI status message that switch S1 sends to R1.

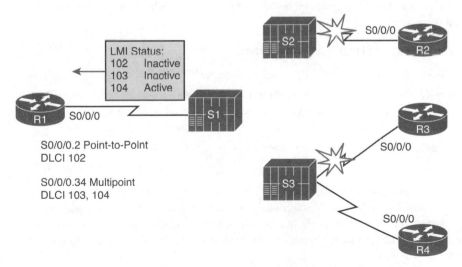

Figure 14-9 *Results of Shutting Down R2 and R3 Access Links*

As shown in the figure, R1 uses a point-to-point subinterface (S0/0/0.2) for the VC connecting to R2 and a multipoint subinterface (S0/0/0.34) associated with the VCs to R3 and R4

(103 and 104, respectively). Earlier, the beginning of Example 14-20 shows that S0/0/0.2 is in a down/down state; the reason is that the only DLCI associated with the subinterface (102) is inactive. However, S0/0/0.34 has two DLCIs, one of which is active, so IOS leaves S0/0/0.34 in an up/up state.

It is useful to look at subinterface status when troubleshooting, but keep in mind that just because a subinterface is up, if it is a multipoint subinterface the up/up state does not necessarily mean that all DLCIs associated with the subinterface are working.

Frame Relay Mapping Issues (Step 4)

If you follow the first three steps of the troubleshooting process suggested in this chapter and resolve the problems at each step, at this point each router's access link interfaces should be in an up/up state, and the PVC between the two routers should be in an active (or static) state. If the routers still cannot ping each other's Frame Relay IP addresses, the next thing to check is the Frame Relay address mapping information, which maps DLCIs to next-hop IP addresses.

This section does not repeat the detailed coverage of address mapping that appears in this chapter. However, for perspective, the following list points out some tips and hints as reminders when you perform this troubleshooting step:

On point-to-point subinterfaces:

- These subinterfaces do not need Inverse ARP or static mapping.
- IOS automatically maps any other IP addresses in the same subnet as a point-to-point subinterface as being reachable via the only DLCI on the subinterface.
- The **show frame-relay map** command output does list point-to-point subinterfaces, but with no next-hop IP address and no "dynamic" notation (which would imply InARP learned the mapping).

On physical interfaces and multipoint subinterfaces

- They need to use either Inverse ARP or static mapping.
- The **show frame-relay map** command should list the remote router's Frame Relay IP address and the local router's local DLCI for each PVC associated with the interface or subinterface. The "dynamic" notation means the mapping was learned with InARP.
- If you're using static mapping, the **broadcast** keyword is needed to support a routing protocol.

For completeness, Example 14-23 shows the output of the **show frame-relay map** command on router R1 from Figure 14-7 with no problems with the mapping. (The earlier problems that were introduced have been fixed.) In this case, interface S0/0/0.2 is a point-to-point subinterface, and S0/0/0.34 is a multipoint with one Inverse ARP-learned mapping and one statically configured mapping.

Example 14-23   show frame-relay map *Command on R1*

```
R1# show frame-relay map
Serial0/0/0.34 (up): ip 10.1.34.4 dlci 104(0x68,0x1880), static,
          broadcast,
          CISCO, status defined, active
Serial0/0/0.34 (up): ip 10.1.34.3 dlci 103(0x67,0x1870), dynamic,
          broadcast,, status defined, active
Serial0/0/0.2 (up): point-to-point dlci, dlci 102(0x66,0x1860), broadcast
        status defined, active
```

End-to-End Encapsulation (Step 5)

The end-to-end encapsulation on a PVC refers to the headers that follow the Frame Relay header, with two options: the Cisco-proprietary header and an IETF standard header. The configuration details were covered earlier in this chapter, in the section "Configuring the Encapsulation and LMI."

As it turns out, a mismatched encapsulation setting on the routers on opposite ends of the link might cause a problem in one particular case. If one router is a Cisco router using Cisco encapsulation and the other router is a non-Cisco router using IETF encapsulation, pings might fail because of the encapsulation mismatch. However, two Cisco routers can understand both types of encapsulation, so it should not be an issue in networks with only Cisco routers.

Mismatched Subnet Numbers (Step 6)

At this point, if the problems found in the first five of the six troubleshooting steps have been resolved, all the Frame Relay problems should be resolved. However, if the two routers on either end of the PVC have mistakenly configured IP addresses in different subnets, the routers will not be able to ping one another, and the routing protocols will not become adjacent. So, as a last step, you should confirm the IP addresses on each router and the masks and ensure that they connect to the same subnet. To do so, just use the **show ip interface brief** and **show interfaces** commands on the two routers.

Exam Preparation Tasks

Review All the Key Topics

Review the most important topics from this chapter, noted with the Key Topic icon. Table 14-4 lists these key topics and where each is discussed.

Table 14-4   Key Topics for Chapter 14

Key Topic Element	Description	Page Number
List	Frame Relay configuration checklist	413
Definition	Frame Relay address mapping concept and definition	417
Figure 14-4	Frame Relay Inverse ARP process	420
List	Six-step Frame Relay troubleshooting checklist	431
List	Summary of the two main functions of LMI	432
Table 14-3	List of PVC status values and their meanings	438
List	Reasons for subinterfaces to be up/up or down/down	439
List	Summary of mapping information seen on point-to-point subinterfaces	440
List	Summary of mapping information seen on multipoint subinterfaces	440

Complete the Tables and Lists from Memory

Print a copy of DVD Appendix D, "Memory Tables," or at least the section for this chapter, and complete the tables and lists from memory. DVD Appendix E, "Memory Tables Answer Key," includes completed tables and lists to check your work.

Command Reference to Check Your Memory

Although you should not necessarily memorize the information in the tables in this section, this section does include a reference for the configuration and EXEC commands covered in this chapter. Practically speaking, you should memorize the commands as a side effect of reading the chapter and doing all the activities in this exam preparation section. To see how well you have memorized the commands as a side effect of your other studies, cover the left side of the table, read the descriptions on the right side, and see if you remember the command.

Table 14-5 Chapter 14 Configuration Command Reference

Command	Description
encapsulation frame-relay [ietf]	Interface configuration mode command that defines the Frame Relay encapsulation that is used rather than HDLC, PPP, and so on
frame-relay lmi-type {ansi | q933a | cisco}	Interface configuration mode command that defines the type of LMI messages sent to the switch
no frame-relay lmi-type	Interface configuration mode command that reverts back to the default LMI setting of autosensing the LMI type
bandwidth *num*	Interface subcommand that sets the router's perceived interface speed
frame-relay map {*protocol protocol-address dlci*} [broadcast] [ietf | cisco]	Interface configuration mode command that statically defines a mapping between a network layer address and a DLCI
frame-relay interface-dlci *dlci* [ietf | cisco]	Subinterface configuration mode command that links or correlates a DLCI to the subinterface
keepalive *sec*	Interface configuration mode command that defines whether and how often LMI status inquiry messages are sent and expected
interface serial *number.sub* [point-to-point | point-to-multipoint]	Global configuration mode command that creates a subinterface or references a previously created subinterface
[no] frame-relay inverse-arp	Physical and multipoint subcommand to disable Frame Relay Inverse ARP (no inverse-arp) or enable it

Table 14-6 Chapter 14 EXEC Command Reference

Command	Description
show frame-relay pvc [interface *interface*][*dlci*]	Lists information about the PVC status
show frame-relay lmi [*type number*]	Lists LMI status information
show frame-relay map [*type number*]	Lists Frame Relay mapping information matching next-hop IP addresses to local DLCIs
show interfaces [*type number*]	Lists statistics and details of interface configuration, including the encapsulation type
show ip interface brief	Lists one line of output per interface with IP address and interface status
debug frame-relay lmi	Displays the contents of LMI messages

This chapter covers the following exam topics:

WAN Technologies

Identify Different WAN Technologies

Metro Ethernet

VSAT

Cellular 3G / 4G

MPLS

T1 / E1

ISDN

DSL

Cable

Implement and troubleshoot PPPoE

CHAPTER 15

Identifying Other Types of WANs

Many of the chapters in this book introduce a topic, and then go deeper, because the related exam requires that deeper knowledge. Unlike most other chapters in this book, this chapter introduces each topic briefly, and then moves on to the next topic. The point of this chapter is to introduce you to the general ideas behind a handful of other WAN protocols.

Just to give the technologies some context, this chapter breaks down the technologies into two major sections. The first looks at WAN technologies used to create private WAN services, usually for businesses. The second section looks at WAN technologies used to access the Internet, whether for businesses or consumers.

"Do I Know This Already?" Quiz

Use the "Do I Know This Already?" quiz to help decide whether you might want to skim this chapter, or a major section, moving more quickly to the Exam Preparation Tasks section near the end of the chapter. You can find the answers at the bottom of the page following the quiz. For thorough explanations, see DVD Appendix C, "Answers to the 'Do I Know This Already?' Quizzes."

Table 15-1   "Do I Know This Already?" Foundation Topics Section-to-Question Mapping

Foundation Topics Section	Questions
Private WANs to Connect Enterprises	1–4
Public WANs and Internet Access	5

1. Which of the following private WAN services operates primarily as a Layer 3 service, delivering IP packets between two customer sites?

   a. Leased line

   b. MPLS

   c. Ethernet WAN

   d. Frame Relay

2. Which of the following private WAN services supports 100-Mbps Ethernet as an access link? (Choose two answers.)

   a. Leased line

   b. MPLS

   c. Ethernet WAN

   d. Frame Relay

3. Which of the following private WAN services would use a serial interface on the customer router? (Choose two answers.)

   a. Leased line

   b. VSAT

   c. Ethernet WAN

   d. Frame Relay

4. Which of the following Internet access technology is considered to be an "always on" service, not requiring the user to do something before sending packets into the Internet? (Choose two answers.)

   a. DSL

   b. Analog dial-up

   c. Cable Internet

   d. ISDN

5. Which of the following Internet access technologies is considered to use symmetric speeds, with the same speed downstream, toward the customer, as upstream, toward the ISP?

   a. DSL

   b. ISDN

   c. Cable Internet

   d. None of the above

6. The sample PPPoE configuration for a customer router shows four commands with a parameter of 2. Which two commands must have the same value for the configuration to work correctly? (Choose two answers.)

```
interface dialer 2
  dialer pool 2
  encapsulation ppp
  ppp chap hostname Fred
  ppp chap password 2
  ip address negotiated
  mtu 1492

interface gigabitethernet 0/1
  pppoe-client dial-pool-number 2
```

   a. interface dialer 2

   b. dialer pool 2

   c. ppp chap password 2

   d. pppoe-client dial-pool-number 2

Foundation Topics

Private WANs to Connect Enterprises

WAN services usually create either a private WAN service or a public WAN service. With a private service, one customer connects to the WAN service provider with connections from many sites. The provider promises to forward data between those sites. Later, when a second customer connects to that same WAN service, the WAN service keeps the two customer's data traffic private. While the data may flow through the same devices inside the provider's network, the provider never forwards data sent by customer 1 to customer 2, and vice versa, making the network private from the customer perspective.

In contrast, a connection to the Internet relies on the fact that each Internet service provider's (ISP) customer can and will allow packets from other customers. Adding a connection to the Internet through an ISP announces a willingness to send and receive packets over that connection. To protect that connection, people then must pay attention to security, allowing only the right kinds of traffic over their Internet access links.

You can use most of the WAN technology mentioned in this chapter to build both private WANs and the public Internet. However, some technologies make a better fit in one or the other, so this chapter discusses each WAN technology in a likely place where the technology would be used.

This first section of the chapter looks at WAN technologies in private WAN services, with these WAN technologies:

- Leased lines
- Frame Relay
- Ethernet WANs
- MPLS
- VSAT

Leased Lines

Of all the WAN topics mentioned in this book, leased lines and Frame Relay obviously get the most attention. Chapter 12, "Implementing Point-to-Point WANs," already discussed leased lines, and the data link protocols most often used with them, in some depth. Why mention more about them here in this chapter? To set the stage to make comparisons to the other WAN technologies introduced in this chapter.

One of the ICND2 (and CCNA) exam topics states that you need to be ready to identify various WAN technologies. So, in what ways can you identify leased lines when you see them on the exam? To review a few items, consider this list:

Answers to the "Do I Know This Already?" quiz:

1 B **2** B and C **3** A and D **4** A and C **5** B **6** B and D

- First, leased lines go by many names, so review the names in Table 12-2, back in Chapter 12, at some point.

- In figures, the generic version shows the generic crooked line that looks like a lightning bolt. Other figures look more like Figure 15-1, which shows the channel service unit/ data service unit (CSU/DSU) that is needed for each router; note that the figure shows an external CSU/DSU.

- As for other words, the technology used to create the line includes terms like T-carrier and time-division multiplexing (TDM), as well as the names for the common line speeds: DS1, T1, E1, T3, and E3.

- As for protocols, leased lines provide a Layer 1 service, in that the provider promises to deliver bits to the other end of the line. The service provider lets the customer use any data link and higher-layer protocols that the customer wants to use.

Figure 15-1 shows a sample figure of a leased line, when the figure focuses on the cabling to an external CSU/DSU.

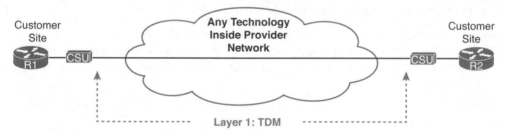

Figure 15-1 *Point-to-Point Leased Line*

Finally, one goal for this chapter is to help you identify WAN technologies by noticing their differences. To that end, Table 15-2 notes a few key facts about leased lines, with other upcoming tables adding new technologies to similar tables to make some comparisons.

Table 15-2 Key Identifiers for Leased Lines

	Leased Line
Typical physical access links	TDM (T1, E1, and so on)
Router interface	Serial
Protocols	HDLC, PPP[1]
WAN service promise	Deliver bits to other end of line

[1] The leased line service does not require or use a data link protocol. However, routers usually use High-Level Data-Link Control (HDLC) or Point-to-Point Protocol (PPP).

Frame Relay

Frame Relay concepts and terminology should be pretty fresh in your mind after just finishing Chapters 13, "Understanding Frame Relay Concepts," and 14, "Implementing Frame Relay." What items should you watch for to notice Frame Relay WANs in the exam as opposed to other WAN technology? This list gives a few items:

- The access links—the link from the customer router to the Frame Relay network—typically use a leased line.

- The customer routers (called data terminal equipment [DTE] in Frame Relay) use Frame Relay data link protocols.

- The Frame Relay service provider makes this promise: to deliver Frame Relay frames to the correct other customer router (based on its permanent virtual circuit [PVC] data-link connection identifier [DLCI]).

- The service is private, in that frames sent by customer A will not be sent to routers owned by customer B.

- The Frame Relay provider can use any technology they want to use inside their network, so figures will likely show a cloud in the middle.

Figure 15-2 reinforces a few of these key comparison points.

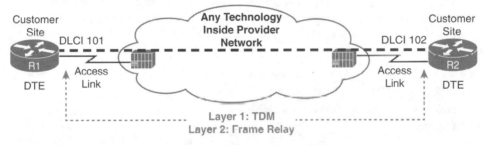

Figure 15-2 *Common Items Used to Identify Frame Relay WANs*

Ethernet WANs

As a technology, Ethernet began life as a LAN technology only, mainly because Ethernet distance limitations made it impractical for creating the longer links in WAN services. Over time, fiber-based Ethernet Layer 1 standards kept improving, both in speed and in distance. The result: WAN services providers can and do use Ethernet links to offer WAN services, both on the edge with customer access links, and in the core of the provider's network.

One particular Ethernet-based private WAN service uses has a similar model as Frame Relay. The access links use Ethernet standards instead of leased lines, and the routers use Ethernet data link protocols rather than Frame Relay. The routers can send Ethernet frames to each other over the WAN. However, this Ethernet WAN service does not define a concept like PVCs. Figure 15-3 shows the general idea.

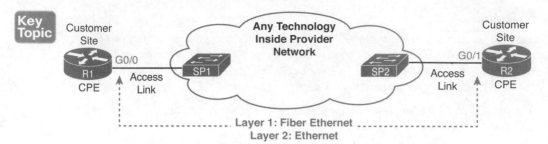

Figure 15-3   *Ethernet WAN Service in a Direct Comparison to Frame Relay*

The Ethernet WAN service shown in Figure 15-3 can go by many names. This book tends to use the same names mentioned in the associated Cisco courses, namely Ethernet over MPLS (EoMPLS) and the more generic term Ethernet WAN. Other terms for the different kinds of Ethernet WAN services include Metropolitan Ethernet (MetroE) and Virtual Private LAN Service (VPLS). Finally, the term *Ethernet emulation* emphasizes the fact that the provider emulates (acts like) a big Ethernet network but that the provider can use any technology to create the service.

The figure shows one way to think about Ethernet WAN services, with an emphasis on how it is similar to Frame Relay. Certainly, Ethernet WAN services support much faster speeds, with Frame Relay usually using no faster than the 44 Mbps or so of a T3 link, whereas Ethernet WAN services support 100-Mbps or 1-Gbps Ethernet. The following list summarizes some of the key similarities and differences between an Ethernet WAN service and Frame Relay:

- The access links use any *Ethernet* physical layer standard, but usually some fiber-optic standard to take advantage of the longer cable lengths.

- The customer routers (or LAN switches) will use some kind of Ethernet interface, not a serial interface.

- The customer routers (or LAN switches) use *Ethernet data link* protocols.

- The figure will not show DLCIs, but may show MAC addresses on the WAN.

- The figure may show Ethernet switches inside the Provider's cloud.

- Private, for the same reasons as leased lines and Frame Relay.

- The Ethernet WAN provider can use any technology they want to use inside their network, so figures will likely show a cloud in the middle.

Table 15-3 summarizes the key comparison points between the three WAN technologies discussed so far in this chapter.

Table 15-3 Key Comparison Points for Ethernet WAN, Frame Relay, and Leased Lines

	Leased Line	**Frame Relay**	**Ethernet WAN**
Typical physical access links	TDM (T1, E1, and so on)	TDM (T1, E1, and so on)	Ethernet (fiber)
Router interface	Serial	Serial	Ethernet
Protocols	HDLC, PPP[1]	Frame Relay	Ethernet
WAN service promise	Deliver bits to other end of line	Deliver FR frames to other end of each PVC	Deliver Ethernet frames to specific endpoints

[1] The leased line service does not require or use a data link protocol. However, routers typically use HDLC or PPP.

MPLS

Multiprotocol Label Switching (MPLS) follows some ideas similar to both Frame Relay and Ethernet WANs. However, like Ethernet WANs, many types of MPLS WAN services exist, so to nail one down, just to get the general idea, this section talks about one specific use of MPLS, called MPLS VPNs.

MPLS VPN services follow a familiar private WAN model, with a customer connecting sites to an MPLS cloud, and the cloud forwarding data to all that customer's sites connected to the cloud. To keep the data private, as usual, for two unrelated customers A and B, MPLS promises not to forward A's data to B's routers and vice versa.

Many facts make MPLS VPNs different from other WAN services, but the biggest difference is that the service promises to deliver the customer's IP packets between sites, instead of delivering bits (leased lines) or delivering data link frames (Frame Relay and Ethernet WAN). Basically, to the customer, the MPLS network acts much like an IP network, routing the customers IP packets between sites.

Figure 15-4 shows the idea. Customer B connects four routers, B1 through B4, to an MPLS service. Router B3 forwards an IP packet into the MPLS service (Step 1). The MPLS service somehow (details not listed here) forwards that IP packet to the other side of the MPLS service. The service then forwards the IP packet out the access link to the correct customer router, B4 in this case (Step 3).

MPLS has much more flexibility than some other WAN services as a side effect of forwarding IP packets. MPLS can support pretty much any kind of access link that supports IP packets, like the links shown in Figure 15-4. In fact, while Frame Relay has grown less popular in this century, you can still find it in many networks in use as an access link into an MPLS service, as shown in Figure 15-4.

Of the WAN services discussed so far in this chapter, MPLS has the most similarities with Frame Relay and Ethernet WANs. Table 15-4 compares these three options, focusing on the key differences.

15

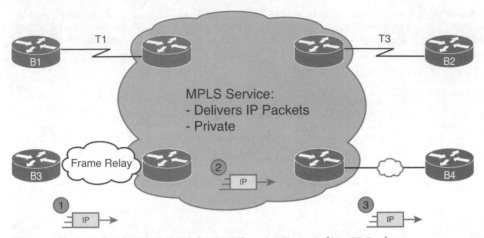

Figure 15-4   *MPLS WAN (MPLS VPN) Service Forwarding IP Packets*

Key Topic

Table 15-4   Key Comparison Points for Ethernet WAN, Frame Relay, and MPLS

	MPLS	Frame Relay	Ethernet WAN
Physical access links	Any that support IP	TDM (T1, E1, and so on)	Ethernet (fiber)
Router interface	Any that support IP	Serial	Ethernet
Protocols	Any that support IP	Frame Relay	Ethernet
WAN service promise	Deliver IP packets	Deliver FR frames	Deliver Ethernet frames

VSAT

Finally, note that all the private WAN services discussed so far in this chapter happen to use some kind of cabling. However, in some cases, the locations that need a WAN connection are in places where no service provider offers a WAN service. Maybe the sites are in very remote geographies, on islands where the population is too small to justify expensive underwater cabling, or maybe the terrain just does not allow for cables to be run.

In these cases, a company can create a private WAN using satellite communications and VSAT terminals. VSAT, or very small aperture terminal, refers to a type of satellite dish like the ones you see used for satellite TV from the home, usually about 1 meter in width. The VSAT dish sits outside, pointed at a specific satellite, and is cabled to a special router interface, with the router inside the building. Figure 15-5 shows an example, with the VSAT dishes on the roofs of the buildings.

Using VSATs creates a private WAN somewhat like using leased lines while meeting an important need: connectivity to locations where connectivity is difficult.

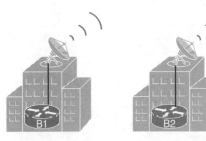

Figure 15-5   *VSAT*

Public WANs and Internet Access

To build the Internet, an Internet service provider (ISP) needs links to other ISPs and links to the ISP's customers. The Internet core connects ISPs using a variety of high-speed technologies. Internet access links connect an ISP to each customer, again with a wide variety of technologies. For these customer access links, the technologies need to be inexpensive so that a typical consumer can afford to pay for the service.

Some WAN technologies happen to work particularly well as Internet access technologies. In fact, several use the same telephone line installed into most homes by the phone company so that the ISPs do not have to install additional cabling. Others use the cable TV cabling, whereas others use wireless.

This section briefly touches on several WAN technologies and how they are used to access the Internet. This section ends with a slight tangent to discuss the configuration of one related protocol, called PPP over Ethernet (PPPoE).

Internet Access (WAN) Links

Each WAN technology may be used to build both public and private WANs; some are just a more natural fit for one or the other. However, just to be complete, note that all the WAN technologies discussed in the first half of the chapter happen to work just fine as Internet access technologies, particularly for businesses. Businesses often use TDM serial links, Frame Relay, Ethernet WAN services, or even an MPLS service to access the Internet. Figure 15-6 shows a few of these, just as a visual reminder of these options.

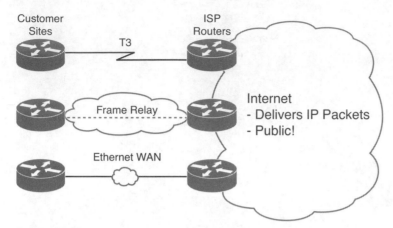

Figure 15-6   *Three Examples of Internet Access Links for Companies*

Dial Access with Modems and ISDN

The next two Internet access technologies require us to think back to the early days of the Internet for some perspective. The Internet had many booming growth periods over time, but one such period took off in the very early 1990s, when commercial traffic was beginning to drive huge growth in the Internet.

Back in those early days of the Internet, for consumers, most people accessed the Internet using dial-up. That is, they used their analog phone line and an analog modem and basically placed a phone call to an ISP.

As a brief bit of background, when using a home telephone line, a phone call creates an electrical circuit that uses analog signals. Computers use digital signals; so to use an analog circuit, something had to convert from digital to analog. The solution: an analog modem.

Analog modems would sit at each end of the call—one at the customer site, and one at the ISP. To send the digital data from the customer's PC or router, the modem would modulate, or convert, the digital signal to an analog signal. The sending modem then transmits the analog signals to the receiving modem, which would then demodulate the analog back into the original digits. (The term *modem* comes from the squashing of those two terms together: modulate and demodulate.)

Figure 15-7 shows the general idea, with two examples. One shows a PC with an external modem, meaning that the PC connects to the modem with a cable. The other shows an internal modem. The ISP would then have a matching set of modems, called a modem bank. A phone call to the ISP's phone number would ring to any available modem, allowing a customer to connect to any one of the ISP modems and be connected to the Internet.

Today, most ISPs refer to this option as *dial access* or simply *dial*. And even though ISPs have used it for decades, most ISPs still offer dial services. Dial can be an inexpensive in some markets and a workable service for people in remote areas where faster Internet access options are not available.

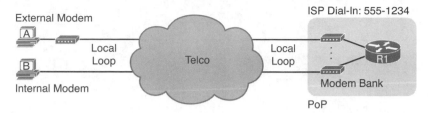

Figure 15-7 *Internet Access Using External and Internal Modems*

> **NOTE** Telcos refer to the telephone cable that runs into a customer's home or business the *local loop*.

Dial access happens to have several cost advantages compared to other consumer Internet access options. The ISP purposefully puts a point of presence (PoP) in most local calling areas, so the phone call to connect to the Internet is free, rather than having a long-distance charge. Also the equipment cost fell pretty quickly over time, so the price to get started is relatively low. And in many markets, almost every home has a home phone line already, so there is no need to spend more for the physical access link. As a result, the only added cost is the fee to the ISP to allow access into the Internet.

Of course, there are negatives, too. You can either surf the Internet or make a voice phone call, but not both. To use the Internet, you had to make a phone call first, so the Internet was not "on" all the time. But the speed is the biggest issue, with a fast modem having a bit rate over the line of only 56 Kbps, an incredibly slow speed by today's standards.

Over time, the telcos of the world set out to improve over the analog modem option. One early improvement used an entirely new technology called Integrated Services Digital Network (ISDN). ISDN allowed some of the same cost advantages as analog modems, but with faster speeds. For instance:

- ISDN used the same local loop (local phone line), which most people already had.

- ISDN required the equivalent of a phone call to the ISP, just like with analog modems.

- ISPs already had a PoP in each local calling areas to support analog modems, so these ISDN calls would not require any long-distance charges.

The big advantage of ISDN was speed. ISDN uses digital signals over the local loop, instead of analog. In addition, it supports two calls at the same time, each at 64 Kbps, over that one local loop phone line. Both calls (channels) could be dialed to the ISP, for a 128-Kbps Internet service. Or, the user could make one voice phone call and have one 64-Kbps Internet connection at the same time. ISDN did cost a little more—you had to pay the telco for the upgraded ISDN service—but you got concurrent Internet and voice, plus better speed than analog modems.

Figure 15-8 shows some particulars of ISDN. The consumer side of an ISDN used a line called a Basic Rate Interface (BRI), which has the two 64-Kbps channels for user traffic. Physically, the connection used some type of ISDN-aware device, often referred to as an ISDN modem, taking the place of an analog modem.

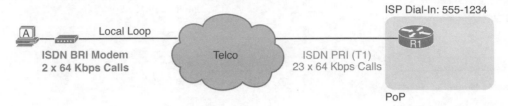

Figure 15-8 *Typical ISDN Connection*

The ISP side of the connection could use many different technologies, as well, including an ISDN technology called a Primary Rate Interface (PRI). This technology turned a T1 physical line into 23 ISDN channels ready to accept those ISDN calls, as shown on the right.

Both analog modems and ISDN filled big needs for Internet access in the early days of the Internet. Using existing phone lines that people already paid for anyway was a great business model. However, their relatively slow speeds led to innovation to faster Internet access—both from the telcos of the world and their emerging competitors of the time, the cable TV companies. Table 15-5 summarizes a few of the key comparison points so far.

Table 15-5   Comparison of Internet Access Technologies

	Analog Modem	**ISDN**
Physical access link	Phone line (local loop)	Phone line (local loop)
Internet is always on?	No	No
Data service promise	Send bits to any called party	Send bits to any called party
Speed (general)	56 Kbps	128 Kbps
Asymmetric?	No	No

Digital Subscriber Line

In the consumer Internet access space, the big speed breakthrough happened with the introduction of the digital subscriber line (DSL). It represented a big technological breakthrough in terms of raw speed. These faster speeds also changed how people could use the Internet because many of today's common applications would be unusable at analog modem and ISDN speeds.

As with ISDN, telcos greatly influenced the creation of DSL. As a technology, DSL gave telcos a way to offer much faster Internet access speeds. As a business, DSL gave telcos a way to offer a valuable high-speed Internet service to many of their existing telephone customers, which created a great way for telcos to make money.

As a technology, DSL works much differently than both analog modems and ISDN. To see how, first focus on the home side of the DSL connection, as shown on the left side of Figure 15-9. The phone can do what it has always done: plug into a phone jack and send analog. For the data, a DSL modem connects to a spare phone outlet. The DSL modem sends and receives the data, as digital signals, at higher frequencies, over the same local loop, even at the same time as a telephone call.

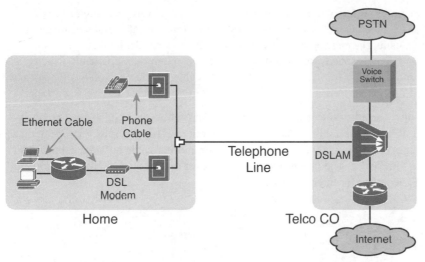

Figure 15-9   *Wiring and Devices for a Home DSL Link*

Because DSL uses analog (voice) and digital (data) signals on the line, the telco has to somehow split those signals on the telco side of the connection. To do so, the local loop must be connected to a DSL access multiplexer (DSLAM) located in the nearby telco central office (CO). The DSLAM splits out the digital data over to the router on the lower right, which completes the connection to the Internet. The DSLAM also splits out the analog voice signals over to the voice switch on the upper right.

DSL has many advantages, particularly compared to the analog and ISDN dial options. For instance, asymmetric DSL (ADSL), in which many of the consumer DSL offerings is based, routinely supports speeds in the 5-Mbps range, and up to 24 Mbps in ideal conditions. Also, ADSL supports asymmetric speeds, which better matches most consumer traffic models. Asymmetric speeds means that the transmission speed toward the home (downstream) is much faster than the transmissions toward the ISP (upstream). Asymmetric speeds work better for consumer Internet access from the home because clicking a web page sends only a few hundred bytes upstream into the Internet but may trigger many megabytes of data to be delivered downstream to the home.

Of course, every option, including DSL, has some negatives. DSL may cost more than dial—probably worth the money to most people, but it does usually cost more. Also, as a technology, DSL has limitations. DSL works only at certain distances from the CO to the home, and the speeds degrade within the longer of the working cabling distances. So, the quality of the service, or availability of the service at all, may be impacted simply by the distance between the home and the CO.

Cable Internet

Analog modems, ISDN, and DSL all use the local link (telephone line) from the local telco. This next option instead uses the cabling from what has become the primary competitor to the telco in most markets: the cable company.

Cable Internet creates an Internet access service which, when viewed generally rather than specifically, has many similarities to DSL. Like DSL, cable Internet takes full advantage of existing cabling, using the existing cable TV (CATV) cable to send data. Like DSL, cable Internet uses asymmetric speeds, sending data faster downstream than upstream, which works well for most consumer locations. And like DSL, cable Internet still allows the normal service on the cable (cable TV), at the same time as the Internet access service is working.

Cable Internet also uses the same general idea for in-home cabling as DSL, just using CATV cabling instead of telephone cabling. The left side of Figure 15-10 shows a TV connected to the CATV cabling, just as it would normally connect. At another cable outlet, a cable modem connects to the same cable. The Internet service flows over one frequency, like yet another TV channel, just reserved for Internet service.

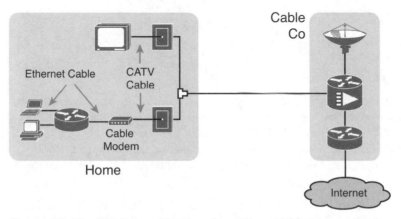

Figure 15-10   *Wiring and Devices for a Home Cable Internet Link*

Similar to DSL, on the CATV company side of the connection (on the right side of the figure), the CATV company must split out the data and video traffic. Data flows to the lower right, through a router, to the Internet. The video comes in from video dishes for distribution out to the TVs in people's homes.

Cable Internet service and DSL directly compete in both the consumer and business markets. Generally speaking, while both offer high speeds, cable Internet usually runs at faster speeds than DSL, with DSL providers often keeping their prices a little lower to compete. Both support asymmetric speeds, and both provide an "always on" service, in that you can communicate with the Internet without the need to first take some action to start the Internet connection.

Table 15-6 summarizes some of the key comparison points again.

Table 15-6   Comparison of Internet Access Technologies

	Analog Modem	ISDN	DSL	Cable
Physical access link	Phone line (local loop)	Phone line (local loop)	Phone line (local loop)	CATV cable
Internet is always on?	No	No	Yes	Yes
Data service promise	Send bits to any called party	Send bits to any called party	Send all data to the ISP	Send data to the ISP
Speed (general)	56 Kbps	128 Kbps	10s of Mbps	10s of Mbps
Asymmetric?	No	No	Yes	Yes

Mobile Phone Access with 3G/4G

Many of you reading this book have a mobile phone that has Internet access. That is, you can check your email, surf the web, download apps, and watch videos. Most social media addicts rely on their mobile phones, and the Internet access built in to that phone, for most of their tweets and the like. This section touches on the big concepts behind the Internet access technology behind those mobile phones.

Mobile phones use radio waves to communicate through a nearby mobile phone tower. The phone has a small radio antenna, and the provider has a much larger antenna sitting at the top of a tower somewhere within miles of you and your phone. Phones, tablet computers, laptops, and even routers (with the correct interface cards) can communicate through to the Internet using this technology, as represented in Figure 15-11.

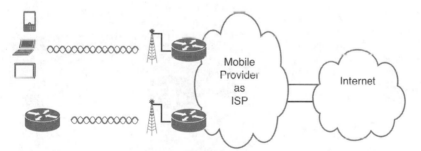

Figure 15-11   *Wireless Internet Access Using 3G/4G Technology*

The mobile phone radio towers also have cabling and equipment, including routers. The mobile provider builds their own IP network, much like an ISP builds out an IP network. The customer IP packets pass through the IP router at the tower into the mobile provider's IP network and then out to the Internet.

The market for mobile phones and wireless Internet access for other devices is both large and competitive. As a result, the mobile providers spend a lot of money advertising their services, with lots of names for one service or the other. Frankly, it can be difficult to tell what all the marketing jargon means, but a few terms tend to be used throughout the industry:

Wireless Internet: A general term for Internet services from a mobile phone or from any device that uses the same technology.

3G/4G Wireless: Short for third generation and fourth generation, these terms refer to the major changes over time to the mobile phone companies' wireless networks.

LTE: Long-Term Evolution, which is a newer and faster technology considered to be part of fourth generation (4G) technology.

The takeaway from all this jargon is this: When you hear about wireless Internet services with a mobile phone tower in the picture—whether the device is phone, tablet, or PC—it is probably a 3G, 4G, or LTE wireless Internet connection.

PPP over Ethernet

To finish off this chapter, this final topic takes a brief departure away from listing WAN technologies, instead discussing one technology overlaid on top of some DSL connections: PPP over Ethernet (PPPoE).

PPP over Ethernet Concepts

First, think back to Chapter 12's discussion of PPP and CHAP for a moment. PPP is one of those frankly boring data link protocols used on point-to-point links, whereas Challenge Handshake Authentication Protocol (CHAP) is that part of PPP that allows authentication. PPP can be used on serial links, which includes those links created with dial-up analog and ISDN modems. For instance, the link from a dial user to an ISP, using analog modems, likely uses PPP today. Figure 15-12 shows a basic representation of that analog dial connection with PPP.

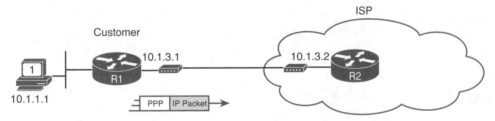

Figure 15-12 *PPP Frames Between Routers over a Dial Connection to an ISP*

ISPs used PPP as the data link protocol for a couple of reasons. First, PPP supports a way to assign IP addresses to the other end of the PPP link. ISPs can use PPP to assign each customer one public IPv4 address to use. But more important for this discussion is that PPP supports CHAP, and ISPs may want to use CHAP to authenticate customers. Then, when using CHAP to authenticate, ISPs could check accounting records to determine whether the customer's bill was paid before letting the customer connect to the Internet.

Now, think back a bit to the history of some of these Internet access technologies. The following technologies came to market in the following order, with varying support for PPP:

1. Analog modems for dial-up, which could use PPP and CHAP

2. ISDN for dial-up, which could use PPP and CHAP

3. DSL, which did not create a point-to-point link and could not support PPP and CHAP

So, telcos and ISPs liked DSL, but some ISPs still wanted their PPP! However, the customer often used an Ethernet link between the customer PC or router and the DSL modem (see earlier Figure 15-9). That Ethernet link only supported Ethernet data link protocols, and not PPP.

What ISPs needed was a way to create the equivalent of a PPP connection between the customer router and the ISP router over the various technologies used on the various DSL connections. As you might guess, several new protocols were created, including one that allowed the sending of PPP frames encapsulated inside Ethernet frames: the PPP over Ethernet (PPPoE) protocol.

PPPoE basically creates a tunnel through the DSL connection for the purpose of sending PPP frames between customer router and the ISP router, as shown in Figure 15-13. DSL does not create a single point-to-point link between these routers. With PPPoE (and related protocols), the routers logically create such a tunnel. From one perspective, the routers create and send PPP frames, as if the link were a dial link between the routers. But before sending the frames over any physical link, the routers encapsulate the frames inside various headers, shown generically in the figure as a tunnel header.

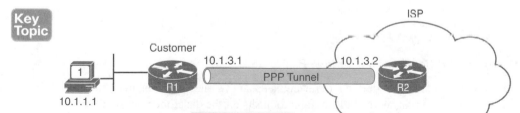

Figure 15-13 *Tunneling Concept to Create a PPP Link over Ethernet*

> **NOTE** For the purposes of this chapter, the specifics of the tunnel header do not matter. However, literally, the PPPoE tunnel header in this case has a typical Ethernet header, a short header defined for PPPoE's use, and then the PPP frame (which includes the IP packet).

PPP over Ethernet Configuration

With the ability to send and receive PPP frames between the routers, the ISP could continue to use the same authentication model as they did with analog and ISDN dial. To make it all work, the client and ISP routers need some new configuration, including PPP configuration. The remainder of this topic looks at the big picture of the client side configuration.

For this configuration, take a slightly different approach. Imagine that you will see a sample configuration like the sample shown in Figure 15-14. Then you have to decide which parameters need to match. (Do not worry about building these configurations from scratch.) To begin understanding the configuration, keep the following facts in mind:

- The configuration uses a dialer interface, which is the virtual interface used to create the PPP tunnel. The PPP configuration goes on the dialer interface.

- The physical Ethernet interface that connects to the DSL modem will have a command that both enables PPPoE and links the interface to the dialer interface.

- The PPP CHAP configuration usually defines one-way authentication; that is, the ISP authenticates the customer, as shown in the upcoming example. (The examples in Chapter 12 show two-way authentication.)

- The client can configure a static IP address, but will more likely ask to be assigned a public IP address by the ISP (as shown here).

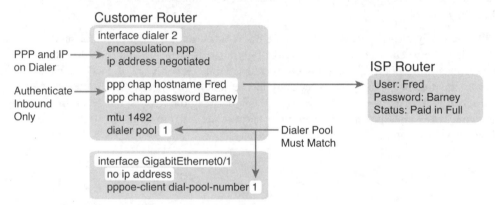

Figure 15-14   *Client Configuration for PPPoE*

So, if faced with a sample configuration to review, keep an eye out for the big items in the configuration. For instance, the PPP configuration sits on the dialer interface, not the Ethernet interface. Check the CHAP username and password, which must match the settings on the ISP. Make sure that the **dialer interface** is linked to the Ethernet interface with the **dialer pool** and **pppoe-client** commands, with the same number as noted in the figure. (The dialer interface number itself does not have to match.) And the maximum transmission unit (MTU) should be set down to 1492 (versus the default of 1500) to accommodate the PPPoE headers.

Exam Preparation Tasks

Review All the Key Topics

Review the most important topics from this chapter, noted with the Key Topic icon. Table 15-7 lists these key topics and where each is discussed.

Table 15-7 Key Topics for Chapter 15

Key Topic Element	Description	Page Number
Figure 15-3	Ethernet WAN key concepts	450
List	Key comparison points for Ethernet WANs versus Frame Relay	450
Table 15-3	Comparisons of leased lines, Frame Relay, and Ethernet WANs	451
Table 15-4	Comparisons of MPLS, Frame Relay, and Ethernet WAN	452
Table 15-6	Comparison of consumer Internet access technologies	459
List	Names for wireless Internet service	460
Figure 15-13	PPP over Ethernet tunneling concept	461

Complete the Tables and Lists from Memory

Print a copy of DVD Appendix D, "Memory Tables," or at least the section for this chapter, and complete the tables and lists from memory. DVD Appendix E, "Memory Tables Answer Key," includes completed tables and lists to check your work.

Definitions of Key Terms

After your first reading of the chapter, try to define these key terms, but do not be concerned about getting them all correct at that time. Chapter 22 directs you in how to use these terms for late-stage preparation for the exam.

MPLS, Ethernet WAN, VSAT, analog modem, ISDN, dial access, DSL, cable Internet, 3G/4G Internet, PPP over Ethernet

Part IV Review

Keep track of your part review progress with the checklist in Table P4-1. Details about each task follow the table.

Table P4-1   Part IV Part Review Checklist

Activity	First Date Completed	Second Date Completed
Repeat All DIKTA Questions		
Answer Part Review Questions		
Review Key Topics		
Create Problem Isolation and Root Cause Mind Map		
Create Frame Relay Configuration Mind Map		

Repeat All DIKTA Questions

For this task, answer the "Do I Know This Already?" questions again for the chapters in Part I of this book using the PCPT software. See the section "How to View Only DIKTA Questions by Part" in the Introduction to this book to learn how to make the PCPT software show you DIKTA questions for this part only.

Answer Part Review Questions

For this task, answer the Part Review questions for this part of the book using the PCPT software. See the section "How to View Only DIKTA Questions by Part" in the Introduction to this book to learn how to make the PCPT software show you DIKTA questions for this part only.

Review Key Topics

Browse back through the chapters and look for the Key Topic icons. If you do not remember some details, take the time to reread those topics.

Create Problem Isolation and Root Cause Mind Map

For this first Part Review mind map, think about troubleshooting serial links and Frame Relay. Think about all the symptoms, whether they are the root cause or whether they help you isolate a problem to get closer to the root cause. Then put them together in a mind map. Basically, if R1 and R2 connect with the same serial link, or the same Frame Relay permanent virtual circuit (PVC), what can prevent them from successfully pinging each other's IP address? Then organize those into a mind map.

To organize the mind map, start by just listing whatever comes to mind. Then, group the symptoms and root causes. One of the main points is to organize these ideas into your frame of reference, so the organizing of the information is just as important as the individual facts. However, do group the serial link causes into one set and Frame Relay causes in another.

NOTE   For more information about mind mapping, see the section "About Mind Maps" in the Introduction to this book.

Create Frame Relay Configuration Mind Map

Frame Relay has two big challenges related to the configuration. First, it has three main styles of configuration: using the physical interface, multipoint subinterfaces, and point-to-point subinterfaces. Second, it has many useful default settings.

For this mind map, treat Frame Relay configuration as three topics. For the first, assume the IP addresses and data link connection identifiers (DLCI) will be used on the physical interface. Then list all configuration commands, and list their default values as well. Use a different color for commands whose default value can be used for this branch.

Then, do the same thing for a second branch: multipoint subinterface configurations. Finally, repeat the exercise again for a point-to-point subinterface branch. Include the commands to create the subinterfaces.

At the end, your mind map will repeat most commands three times. However, it should also help you see the differences in the commands used in each style of configuration.

DVD Appendix F, "Mind Map Solutions," lists sample mind map answers, but as usual, your mind maps can and will look different.

As with IPv4, Cisco has organized the IP Version 6 (IPv6) topics for the exams by spreading the topics between the ICND1 and ICND2 exams. For ICND1, Cisco included the basics: addressing, subnetting, routing, router address and static route configuration, as well as basic OSPF configuration. ICND2 then takes the routing protocol topics a little deeper, with more OSPF, adding EIGRP, and with troubleshooting for the routing (forwarding) process and for the routing protocols.

Part V of this book follows the same general approach for IPv6 as the chapters in Parts II and III did for IPv4. Chapter 16 first reviews IPv6 addressing and routing, to the depth of the ICND1 exam, while discussing troubleshooting of those same topics. Chapter 17 takes OSPF Version 3 (OSPFv3) a little deeper, while giving troubleshooting tips as well. Finally, Chapter 18 details a second IPv6 routing protocol, EIGRP for IPv6 (EIGRPv6).

Part V

IP Version 6

This chapter covers the following exam topics:

Troubleshooting

Identify and correct common network problems

Troubleshoot and resolve routing issues

Routing is enabled

Routing table is correct

Correct path selection

CHAPTER 16

Troubleshooting IPv6 Routing

The first step in troubleshooting any networking technology is to understand what should happen under normal conditions. Then, the troubleshooting process can compare the current network behavior with what should be happening, looking for differences, until the root cause of those differences can be found.

This chapter begins with a review of the ICND1 book's discussion about how IPv6 works normally. Thankfully, IPv6 has many similarities to IPv4, other than the obvious differences in addressing. This section builds on those similarities and summarizes the core features of IPv6 to set the stage for a discussion of troubleshooting IPv6.

The second major section of the chapter examines a variety of problems that can occur in an IPv6 network. All these problems take a part of IPv6 that should work normally and show some issues that prevent that function from working.

"Do I Know This Already?" Quiz

This chapter does not have a "Do I Know This Already Quiz" because the chapter focuses on troubleshooting. The troubleshooting chapters include several hints and tips that show how to solve particular problems; so even if you know the topics well, a quick reading of the chapter should be useful. For these reasons, the troubleshooting chapters do not include a "Do I Know This Already?" quiz. However, if you feel particularly confident about the IPv6 features covered in this book and in the *Cisco CCENT/CCNA ICND1 100 101 Official Cert Guide*, feel free to move to the "Exam Preparation Tasks" section near the end of this chapter to bypass the majority of the chapter.

Foundation Topics

Normal IPv6 Operation

To be ready to troubleshoot an IPv6 problem, you have to remember many facts about how IPv6 works. Thankfully, many IPv6 concepts work much like IPv4, but there are enough differences to make it worth the time to review IPv6 as an end to itself. This first section of the chapter reviews the details of IPv6, condensing five chapters of the ICND1 book into one concise review section.

This first section, from this page up to the heading "IPv6 Troubleshooting," repeats concepts discussed in the ICND1 book. If you are using both books, you might need to go back and review, or you might be ready to skip this section, as suggested here:

> **Skip to "IPv6 Troubleshooting":** If you know IPv6 well, right now, skip ahead. For instance, maybe you are following a reading plan under which you just finished reading the ICND1 book's IPv6 chapters and the material is fresh in your mind. Just know that this first section introduces no new concepts as compared to the ICND1 book's IPv6 chapters.

> **Read this section:** If you remember some of your IPv6 knowledge, but not all, this section is built for you. Keep reading!

> **Go back and review the ICND1 book:** If you have not thought about IPv6 for quite a while, and you really do not remember much at all about it, you might be better off reviewing the IPv6 chapters in the ICND1 book first.

So, what is in this section? It hits the highlights of IPv6. Of course, it reviews IPv6 unicast addressing and subnetting. This section also discusses host IPv6 configuration, including stateless address autoconfiguration (SLAAC) and stateful Dynamic Host Configuration Protocol (DHCP). It reviews basic protocols, like Neighbor Discovery Protocol (NDP), and commands, like **ping** and **traceroute**. This section also reviews router configuration for addressing and static routes (leaving OSPFv3 configuration review for Chapter 17, "Implementing OSPF for IPv6").

Unicast IPv6 Addresses and IPv6 Subnetting

IPv6 defines two major types of unicast IPv6 addresses. *Global unicast* addresses work like public IPv4 addresses in that the enterprise obtains a unique prefix with all addresses inside the enterprise beginning with that prefix. With all companies using unique prefixes, all addresses in the IPv6 Internet should be unique.

Unique local unicast addresses work more like private addresses. A company can randomly create a prefix and assign addresses that begin with that prefix. Unique local addresses let companies avoid having to register a prefix while still having a good statistical chance of not using the same address range as other companies.

To create subnets with global unicast addresses, a company starts with the global routing prefix—the prefix assigned to the enterprise—and then breaking the address structure into three parts. In almost all cases, including most cases in this book and the ICND1 book, the combined global routing prefix and subnet part of the address make up the first half (64 bits) of the address structure. The subnet part gives the enterprise network engineer a place to number each subnet with a different value, uniquely identifying each subnet. Then, the remainder of the structure leaving room for a 64-bit interface ID (or host field). Figure 16-1 summarizes these rules.

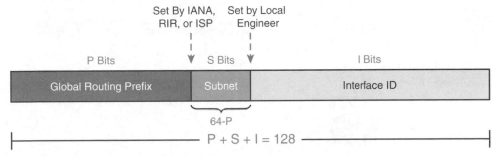

Figure 16-1 *Structure of Subnetted IPv6 Global Unicast Addresses*

For example, a company might receive a global routing prefix of 2001:DB8:1111::/48. That is, all addresses must begin with those 12 hex digits. The subnet part of the addresses exists in the entire fourth quartet. Those subnet numbers can be (hex) 0000, 0001, 0002, and so on, up through FFFF, for 65,536 possible subnets in this example. As a result, the company might end up with a subnet design as shown in Figure 16-2.

NOTE IPv6 formally uses the term *prefix* rather than *subnet*, but many people use either term when discussing IPv6 addressing.

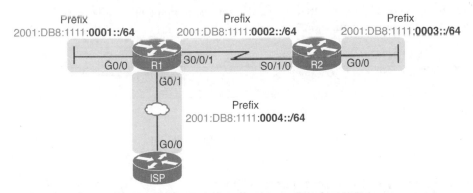

Figure 16-2 *Subnet Design with Global Routing Prefix of 2001:0DB8:1111*

Although Figure 16-2 is helpful for subnet planning, it does not list the specific IPv6 addresses. Like IPv4, IPv6 follows the same general rules. For example, hosts and routers connected to the same Ethernet VLAN needing to be in the same IPv6 subnet. Figure 16-3 shows an example with the IPv6 addresses in the appropriate subnets to match Figure 16-2.

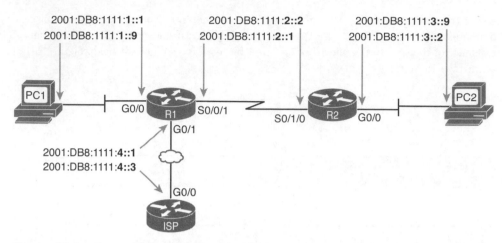

Figure 16-3 *Example Static IPv6 Addresses Based on the Subnet Design of Figure 16-2*

Hosts can use global unicast and unique local unicast addresses to send and receive IPv6 packets with other hosts, but IPv6 defines a special type of unicast address used for packets that stay on a single link: the *link-local* address. Many protocols need to send IPv6 packets that flow only in the local subnet, with no need for routers to forward the packets to any other subnets. IPv6 uses link-local addresses for these protocols. Note that hosts can create their own link-local address even before the host has a valid global unicast or unique local address.

IPv6 hosts and routers create their own link-local address for each interface using some basic rules. First, all link-local addresses start with the same 16-digit prefix (FE80:0000:0000:0000), as shown on the left side of Figure 16-4. The router or host then forms the final 16 hex digits using EUI-64 rules, as discussed in the upcoming section "Stateless Address Autoconfiguration."

64 Bits	64 Bits
FE80 : 0000 : 0000 : 0000	Interface ID: EUI-64

Figure 16-4 *Link-local Address Format*

Table 16-1 summarizes a few bits of reference information about global unicast and unique local unicasts for reference.

Table 16-1 Summary of IPv6 Unicast Address Types

Type	First Digits	Similar to IPv4 Public or Private?
Global unicast	2 or 3[1]	Public
Unique local unicast	FD	Private
Link-local	FE80	Neither

[1] IANA actually defines the global unicast address range as any address not otherwise reserved for some other purpose. However, actual address assignments normally happen from 2000::/3 because that was the original range used for these addresses. Many IPv6 references simply quote 2000::/3 as the prefix, which means the first hex digit is either a 2 or 3.

Assigning Addresses to Hosts

Once all the addressing details have been discussed, registered, and documented, the addresses must be configured on the various hosts and routers. This next topic examines how to add IPv6 configuration (including addressing) to IPv6 hosts.

From a learning perspective, IPv6 host configuration is a little more complex than IPv4. IPv6 adds another protocol to the mix—Neighbor Discovery Protocol (NDP)—and has two options through which hosts can learn their IPv6 settings. Learning how IPv6 hosts dynamically learn their IPv6 settings just takes a little more effort than with IPv4.

IPv6 hosts have three basic options to set their IPv6 options: static configuration, stateful DHCP, and SLAAC. With static configuration, someone just types the options into the right part of the user interface, so this section does not discuss the static configuration option further. The next two topics look at the two dynamic options.

Stateful DHCPv6

Stateful DHCPv6 follows the same general process as DHCP for IPv4 (DHCPv4):

1. A DHCP server or servers exist somewhere in the internetwork.

2. User hosts use DHCP messages to ask for a lease of an IP address and information about other settings.

3. The server replies, assigning an address to the host and informing the host of the other settings.

The one noticeable difference between DHCPv4 and stateful DHCPv6 is that the stateful DHCPv6 server does not supply the default router information. Instead, a built-in protocol, NDP, lets the host ask the local routers to identify themselves. Otherwise, hosts use the same general process as with DHCPv4. Figure 16-5 shows a comparison of what is learned by a host using DHCPv4 and stateful DHCPv6.

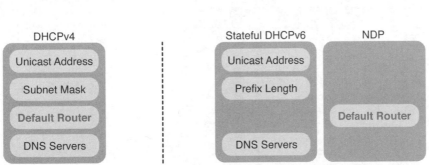

Figure 16-5 *Sources of Specific IPv6 Settings When Using Stateful DHCP*

If the stateful DHCPv6 server sits on a different subnet than the host, DHCPv6 relies on the DHCPv6 *relay agent* function, as shown in Figure 16-6. For instance, on the left, host A begins its attempt to learn an address to use by sending a DHCPv6 Solicit message. This message goes to an IPv6 multicast destination address of FF02::1:2, and routers, like R1, would not normally forward a packet sent to this local scope multicast address. However, with the DHCPv6 relay agent configuration added to R1's G0/0 interface, as shown in the figure, R1 forwards host A's DHCPv6 message to the DHCP server.

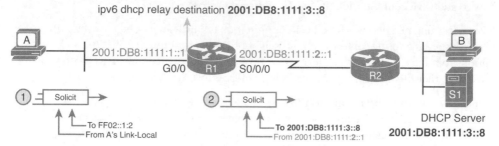

Figure 16-6 *DHCPv6 Relay Agent and DHCP IPv6 Addresses*

Stateless Address Autoconfiguration

IPv6's stateless address autoconfiguration (SLAAC) provides an alternative method for dynamic IPv6 address assignment—without needing a stateful server. In other words, SLAAC does not require a server to lease the IPv6 address and record (keep state information) about which host has which IPv6 address, as is the case with the stateful DHCPv6 service.

SLAAC defines an overall process that also uses NDP and DHCPv6 with a stateless service; the server keeps no state information. First, the process takes advantage of NDP, through which the host can learn the following from any router on the link: the IPv6 prefix (subnet ID), the prefix length (mask equivalent), and the default router IPv6 address. The host uses SLAAC rules to build the rest of its address. Finally, the host uses stateless DHCPv6 to learn the DNS server IPv6 addresses. Figure 16-7 summarizes these details for easy study and reference.

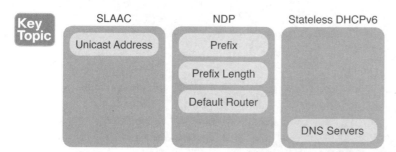

Figure 16-7 *Sources of Specific IPv6 Settings When Using SLAAC*

With SLAAC, a host learns values for three settings (prefix length, router address, and DNS servers), but the host builds the value to use as its address. To build the address, a host uses these steps:

1. Learn the IPv6 prefix used on the link, from any router, using NDP Router Solicitation (RS) and Router Advertisement (RA) messages.

2. Choose an interface ID value to follow the just-learned IPv6 prefix, either by randomly choosing a number, or by using the host's MAC address and using EUI-64 rules

If the host uses the EUI-64 option, the address built by the host can be predicted. The prefix part of the address is the prefix as defined on the local IPv6 router. Then, the host's MAC address feeds into a few EUI-64 rules to change the 48-bit MAC address into a 64-bit interface ID, as follows:

1. Split the 6-byte (12 hex digits) MAC address in two halves (6 hex digits each).

2. Insert FFFE in between the two, making the interface ID now have a total of 16 hex digits (64 bits)

3. Invert the seventh bit of the first byte.

Figure 16-8 shows the major pieces of how the address is formed.

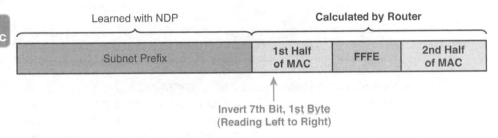

Figure 16-8 *IPv6 Address Format with Interface ID and EUI-64*

Router Address and Static Route Configuration

At this point in this section, you have reviewed IPv6 addresses, IPv6 subnetting, and how to assign addresses to hosts. The next topic looks at how to assign addresses to routers, enable IPv6 routing, and configure static IPv6 routes.

Configuring IPv6 Routing and Addresses on Routers

To enable IPv6 on a router, you have two basic tasks:

Step 1. Enable IPv6 routing using the **ipv6 unicast-routing** global command.

Step 2. Enable IPv6 on each desired interface, and set the interface IPv6 address and prefix length, using the **ipv6 address** *address/length* subcommand in interface configuration mode.

In many cases inside enterprises, the IPv6 implementation plan uses a *dual-stack* strategy, at least on the routers and possibly on hosts. That is, the routers still route IPv4 packets and still have IPv4 addresses on their interfaces. The configuration then adds IPv6 routing as a second Layer 3 protocol routed by the routers, leading to the name dual stack.

Example 16-1 shows a configuration example for adding IPv6 configuration to router R1, based on what you saw in Figure 16-3. In that figure, R1 uses three interfaces, with the entire address shown in each case. As a result, Example 16-1 statically configures the entire address. Note also that the prefix length, /64 in this case, sits immediately after the address, without a space. (The IPv4 configuration, not shown, usually already exists with a dual-stack approach.)

Example 16-1   *IPv6 Addressing Configuration on Router R1 from Figure 16-3*

```
ipv6 unicast-routing
!
interface serial0/0/1
  ipv6 address 2001:db8:1111:2::1/64
!
interface gigabitethernet0/0
  ipv6 address 2001:db8:1111:1::1/64
!
interface gigabitethernet0/1
  ipv6 address 2001:db8:1111:4::1/64
```

Alternatively, routers can also use addresses formed using EUI-64 rules. To configure a router for this option, the **ipv6 address** command has two changes. First, the command lists only the prefix, and not the entire address, because the router creates the interface ID part of the address. The command also lists an **eui-64** keyword at the end. For instance, to instead use EUI-64 on R1's G0/0 interface, you use the command **ipv6 address 2001:db8:1111:1::/64 eui-64**.

IPv6 Static Routes on Routers

As for IPv6 routes, most enterprises use a dynamic IPv6 routing protocol, such as Open Shortest Path Version 3 (OSPFv3, Chapter 17) or Enhanced Interior Gateway Routing Protocol Version 6 (EIGRPv6; Chapter 18, "Implementing EIGRP for IPv6"). However, routers also support static routes, of course.

Routers support three basic options for IPv6 static routes about how to tell a router where to send packets next. Figure 16-9 shows all three options, as follows:

1. Direct the packets out an interface on the local router.

2. Direct the packets to the unicast address of a neighboring router.

3. Direct the packets to the link-local address of a neighboring router (requires the outgoing interface, as well).

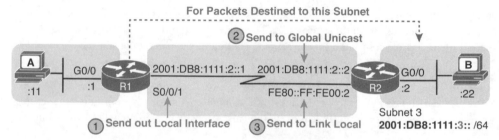

Figure 16-9   *Three Options for IPv6 Static Route Configuration*

Example 16-2 shows a static route to match the figure in each of the three styles. A single router would not use three static routes for the same destination IPv6 prefix; the example just shows all three as a review of the syntax of each command.

Example 16-2 *Static IPv6 Routes: Three Options*

```
! The next command uses R1's S0/0/1 as the outgoing interface
ipv6 route 2001:db8:1111:3::/64 S0/0/1


! The next command uses R2's address as the next-hop router unicast address
ipv6 route 2001:db8:1111:3::/64 2001:DB8:1111:2::2


! The next command uses R1's S0/0/1 as the outgoing interface, and
! R2's link-local address as the next-hop router address
ipv6 route 2001:db8:1111:3::/64 S0/0/1 FE80::FF:FE00:2
```

Verifying IPv6 Connectivity

Most troubleshooting tasks, both on the job and for the exam, begin with a partially working network. To find the existing problems, the engineer needs to try various commands to test the network to verify what works properly and what does not. This next topic reviews a few commands useful for verifying IPv6 connectivity both on hosts and on routers.

Verifying Connectivity from IPv6 Hosts

The first item to check with on any IPv6 host should be the four key IPv6 settings on a host, as shown on the left side of Figure 16-10. This verification step should not only look at the host itself but also compare the host's settings to the other devices in the network. For instance, the host's default router (default gateway) setting should match the address configured on a local router.

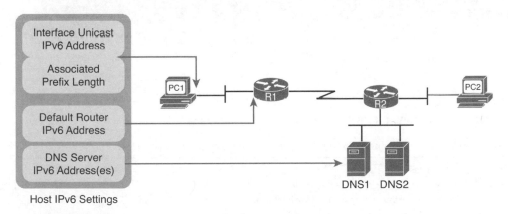

Figure 16-10 *IPv6 Settings Needed on Hosts*

Hosts usually support some way to see IPv6 settings from the graphical user interface (GUI) and use commands. For the main four IPv6 settings, the **ipconfig** (Windows operating systems) and **ifconfig** (Linux and Mac OS) usually show some of the settings. Example 16-3 shows an **ifconfig** command from a Linux host with the address and prefix length highlighted for the global unicast and link-local addresses.

Example 16-3   ifconfig *Command Using Linux*

```
WOair$ ifconfig en0
eth0: Link encap:Ethernet  Hwaddr 02:00:11:11:11:11
      inet addr:10.1.1.99  Bcast:10.1.1.255  Mask:255.255.255.0
      inet6 addr: fe80::11ff:fe11:1111/64 Scope:Link
      inet6 2001:db8:1111:1::11/64 Scope:Global
      UP BROADCAST RUNNING MULTICAST  MTU:1500  Metric:1
      RX packets: 45 errors:0 droppped:0 overruns:0 frame:0
      TX packets: 804 errors:0 droppped:0 overruns:0 carrier:0
      collisions:0 txqueuelen:1000
      RX bytes:5110 (5.1 KB)  TX bytes:140120 (140.1 KB)
```

Of course, the best two commands for testing connectivity are the **ping** and **traceroute** commands. Some hosts use the same exact **ping** and **traceroute** commands for both IPv4 and IPv6, whereas others (notably Mac OS and Linux) use a different command for IPv6 (for instance, the **ping6** and **traceroute6** commands).

When using **ping6** for troubleshooting, pinging the nearest IPv6 address and then pinging router addresses further and further away until one of the pings fails can help you isolate the problem. For instance, in Figure 16-11, from PC1 the user could first ping the nearer interface on R1, then the serial interface IPv6 address on R1, then R2s IPv6 address on S0/1/0, and so on.

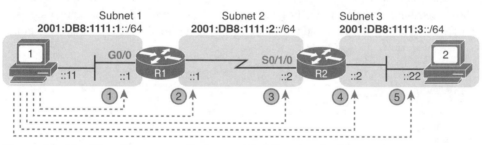

Figure 16-11   *Ping Sequence to Isolate an IPv6 Routing Problem*

Example 16-4 shows the pings from Steps 1 and 5 from Figure 16-11.

Example 16-4   *The* **ping6** *Command from PC, for R1's Nearer Interface and for PC2*

```
Master@PC1:~$ ping6 2001:db8:1111:1::1
PING 2001:db8:1111:1::1 (2001:db8:1111:1::1) 56 data bytes
64 bytes from 2001:db8:1111:1::11: icmp_seq=1 ttl=64 time=1.26 ms
64 bytes from 2001:db8:1111:1::11: icmp_seq=2 ttl=64 time=1.15 ms
^C
--- 2001:db8:1111:1::1 ping statistics ---
2 packets transmitted, 2 received, 0% packet loss, time 1001 ms
rtt min/avg/max/mdev = 1.156/1.210/1.263/0.062 ms
```

```
Master@PC1:~$ ping6 2001:db8:1111:3::22
PING 2001:db8:1111:3::22 ( 2001:db8:1111:3::22) 56 data bytes
64 bytes from 2001:db8:1111:3::22: icmp_seq=1 ttl=64 time=2.33 ms
64 bytes from 2001:db8:1111:3::22: icmp_seq=2 ttl=64 time=2.59 ms
64 bytes from 2001:db8:1111:3::22: icmp_seq=3 ttl=64 time=2.03 ms
^C
--- 2001:db8:1111:3::22 ping statistics ---
3 packets transmitted, 3 received, 0% packet loss, time 2003 ms
rtt min/avg/max/mdev = 2.039/2.321/2.591/0.225 ms
```

16

Verifying IPv6 from Routers

Cisco routers support IPv6 with the **ping** and **traceroute** commands. Both commands accept either an IPv4 or an IPv6 address or hostname, and both work as either as a standard or an extended command.

The extended **ping** and **traceroute** commands give you a lot of power to sit at a router CLI and test the reverse route used by the hosts on the connected LANs. Chapter 4, "Troubleshooting IPv4 Routing Part I," in the "Using Extended Ping to Test the Reverse Route" section, discusses the details for IPv4, and the same concepts apply for IPv6. For a brief review here, the extended IPv6 options on the router **ping** and **traceroute** commands let you test routes back to the correct source subnet. For instance, in Figure 16-12, an extended ping from R1 to PC2's IPv6 address tests the forward route to PC2. However, if the extended ping uses R1's G0/0 interface as the source, this command also tests the reverse route back to PC1's IPv6 subnet.

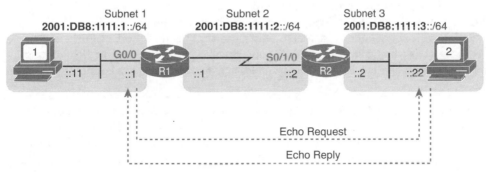

Figure 16-12 *Destination and Source Address of Extended Ping in Example 16-5*

Example 16-5 shows the extended IPv6 ping from R1 to PC2 using R1's G0/0 interface as the source of the packets. The second command shows a standard IPv6 **traceroute** from R1 to PC2.

Example 16-5 *Extended Ping and Standard Traceroute for IPv6 from Router R1*

```
R1# ping
Protocol [ip]: ipv6
Target IPv6 address: 2001:db8:1111:3::22
Repeat count [5]:
```

```
Datagram size [100]:
Timeout in seconds [2]:
Extended commands? [no]: yes
Source address or interface: GigabitEthernet0/0
UDP protocol? [no]:
Verbose? [no]:
Precedence [0]:
DSCP [0]:
Include hop by hop option? [no]:
Include destination option? [no]:
Sweep range of sizes? [no]:
Type escape sequence to abort.
Sending 5, 100-byte ICMP Echos to 2001:DB8:1111:3::22, timeout is 2 seconds:
Packet sent with a source address of 2001:DB8:1111:1::1
!!!!!
Success rate is 100 percent (5/5), round-trip min/avg/max = 0/1/4 ms


R1# traceroute 2001:db8:1111:3::22
Type escape sequence to abort.
Tracing the route to 2001:DB8:1111:3::22

  1 2001:DB8:1111:2::2 4 msec 0 msec 0 msec
  2 2001:DB8:1111:3::22 0 msec 4 msec 0 msec
```

When an IPv6 **ping** or **traceroute** points to some kind of routing problem, several more steps can help isolate the problem to find the root cause. However, this chapter leaves most of the IPv6 routing troubleshooting discussions until Chapters 17 and 18. Both chapters discuss specific reasons why OSPFv3 and EIGRPv6 might fail to put a route into the IPv6 routing table. For now, keep the following two examples in mind when troubleshooting IPv6 problems.

To display the specific IPv6 route a router would use to send packets to a specific destination address, just use the **show ipv6 route** *address* command. The command lists several lines that detail the route the router will use. If the router has no matching route, the router lists a message of "Route not found." Example 16-6 shows an example in which the matched route is a static route that forwards packets out interface S0/0/1. It also shows an example where no route was found.

Example 16-6 *Displaying the Router R1 Uses to Forward to 2001:DB8:1111:3::22*

```
R1# show ipv6 route 2001:db8:1111:3::22
Routing entry for 2001:DB8:1111:3::/64
  Known via "static", distance 1, metric 0
  Route count is 1/1, share count 0
  Routing paths:
    directly connected via Serial0/0/1
```

```
       Last updated 00:01:29 ago

R1# show ipv6 route 2001:1:1:1::1
% Route not found
```

In addition, the **show ipv6 neighbors** command lists the IPv6 replacement for the IPv4 Address Resolution Protocol (ARP) table. If a ping fails, and an expected entry is missing from this table, that fact might point to an issue that is preventing NDP from discovering the neighbor's MAC address. Example 16-7 shows this command on router R2 from Figure 16-12, listing PC2's IPv6 and matching MAC address.

Example 16-7 *The* **show ipv6 neighbors** *Command on Router R2*

```
R2# show ipv6 neighbors
IPv6 Address                         Age Link-layer Addr State Interface
FE80::11FF:FE11:1111                   0 0200.1111.1111  STALE Gi0/0
FE80::22FF:FE22:2222                   1 0200.2222.2222  STALE Gi0/0
2001:DB8:1111:3::22                    0 0200.2222.2222  REACH Gi0/0
FE80::D68C:B5FF:FE7D:8200              1 d48c.b57d.8200  DELAY Gi0/0
2001:DB8:1111:3::33                    0 0200.1111.1111  REACH Gi0/0
2001:DB8:1111:3::3                     0 d48c.b57d.8200  REACH Gi0/0
```

Troubleshooting IPv6

Imagine that you work with a medium-sized enterprise network that uses IPv6. It works well, you go home on time every day, and life is good. Then one day you go to work and get a text about a problem with the network. So, what do you do? You try some commands, try to isolate the problem, and eventually, find the root cause of the problem. For example, maybe a user had a problem and a co-worker "helped" and configured that user's PC with static IPv6 settings and made a typo in the default router IPv6 address.

The rest of this chapter presents seven different IPv6 troubleshooting scenarios, as if an engineer had just started working a problem. Each problem assumes that the engineer has determined that the problem exists in a particular part of the network or for a particular set of reasons.

Each scenario then gives us a place to talk about potential root causes that happen to show up with a particular set of symptoms and to review the whys and wherefores behind those symptoms.

Before getting into the specific scenarios, the following three lists break down some important facts that should be true about a working IPv6 network. Many of the root causes of problems in this section of the chapter happen because one of these rules was broken.

Host-Focused Issues

1. Hosts should be in the same IPv6 subnet as their default router.
2. Hosts should use the same prefix length as their default router.

3. Hosts should have a default router setting that points to a real router's address.

4. Hosts should have correct Domain Name Service (DNS) server addresses.

Router-Focused Issues

1. Router interfaces in use should be in an up/up state.

2. Two routers that connect to the same data link should have addresses in the same IPv6 subnet.

3. Routers should have IPv6 routes to all IPv6 subnets as per the IPv6 subnet design.

Filtering Issues

1. Watch for MAC address filtering on the LAN switches.

2. Watch for missing VLANs in switches.

3. Watch for IPv6 access control lists (ACL) in routers.

Before diving into the scenarios, if you stop and think about these lists, all the items apply in concept to both IPv4 and IPv6. So, the IPv6 troubleshooting process and concepts should mirror IPv4 to some degree. Of course, the specifics do differ, and these scenarios bring out those differences as well.

Now on to a variety of IPv6 problem symptoms!

Pings from the Host Work Only in Some Cases

Our network engineer has responded to a new problem request by calling the user. The engineer asks the user to do some IPv6 **ping** commands from the user's PC. Some pings actually work, but some do not. What should he try next?

Frankly, at this point, if you ask that same question to ten experienced network engineers, you would probably get five or six different suggested next steps. But one highly productive next step when a host gets some pings to work and some do not work is to check the host's IPv6 settings.

The static IPv6 settings on a host can be one of the most common places to find a mistake, and some of those mistakes results in the "some pings work, some do not" symptom. First, the numbers are long and easy to mis-type. Second, you have to make sure that you understand what has to match on the router and DNS server, as well. Finally, for exams, the people writing the exam questions have a lot of small settings to change to make new questions, so it is easy to create a new question by just editing a drawing and changing one number. So, just as with IPv4, you need to be ready to check IPv6 host settings.

Figure 16-13 collects all the pieces that should match. The concepts mirror the same concepts in IPv4.

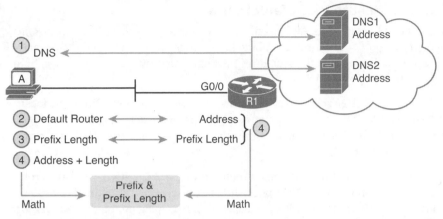

Figure 16-13 *Host IPv6 Settings Compared to What the Settings Should Match*

Next, think about the symptoms of the ping tests, assuming one, but only one, of these settings is wrong. (If more than one setting is wrong, it makes the symptoms harder to describe here.) Here is a walkthrough of the settings numbered in the figure:

1. With the DNS setting as the one incorrect setting, pings that refer to a hostname will fail, but pings to an IPv6 address should work (again assuming no other problems exist).

2. With the default router setting as the only incorrect setting, pings based on IPv6 address in the local LAN should work. However, pings to addresses outside the subnet (that therefore use the default router) fail. Also, because name resolution would fail, all pings that use names would also fail.

3. If the prefix lengths do not match, the host and router disagree about the subnet on the LAN (see the next step).

4. If the host and router disagree about what IPv6 subnet exists on the VLAN, the routers might not be able to route packets back to the host. As a result, the same ping symptoms as Step 2 occur.

From an exam-taking perspective, you want to work through these symptoms as fast as possible. So, if the question gives you the host settings, check them against the router interface address and prefix length and the DNS server address info, because doing so should take only a little time.

From the perspective of troubleshooting for your job, these symptoms reduce to basically two sets of symptoms:

■ Pings that use names happen to fail

■ Pings that require off-subnet packets happen to fail

For these two sets of symptoms, the first case points to some DNS problem, and the second points to either a default router issue or a mismatched subnet issue.

Pings Fail from a Host to Its Default Router

Now, on to a second scenario. The engineer has checked out a problem with commands on the host and on that host's default router. All the IPv6 settings on the host and the default router look good. However, when the user at the host pings faraway servers, the pings, both by name and by IPv6 address, fail.

As a next step, the network engineer tries to narrow down the scope a bit with some local pings. The engineer asks the user to just ping from the host to the default router IPv6 address. This ping fails, as well. The engineer tries the reverse—a ping from the default router to the host—and it fails as well.

To summarize, the host cannot ping its default router or vice versa. With these initial problem symptoms, the question is this: What possible root causes would result in these symptoms? For instance, in Figure 16-14, what prevents host B from pinging router R3, particular after you rule out the host and router IPv6 settings?

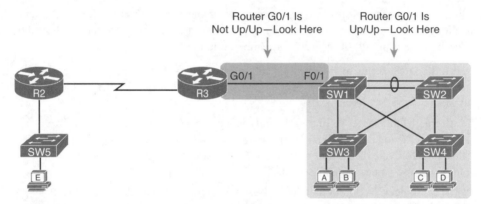

Figure 16-14 *Where to Look for Problems Based on Router LAN Interface Status*

To find the problem, the engineer needs to start thinking outside the IPv6 world and start thinking about the LAN between the host and the router. In particular, the probable root causes can be broken down into these categories:

1. The router or host LAN interface is administratively disabled.

2. The LAN has some problem that prevents the flow of Ethernet frames.

3. The LAN has filtering (for example, port security) that filters the Ethernet frames.

First, the router and host can be told to stop using an interface. Routers, of course, use the **shutdown** interface subcommand; if R3's G0/1 were shut down at this point, the engineer would have seen the **ping** results described for this scenario. Hosts also have ways to disable and enable their interfaces, which again would result in this same set of ping symptoms. The solution? Use a **no shutdown** command on the router or enable the interface on the host.

As for in the second problem in the list, Part I of this book has already discussed LAN problems at length. However, as a troubleshooting tip, note that if R3's G0/1 interface is in a down/down state, a LAN problem would likely exist on the Ethernet link directly connected to R3's G0/1 interface. However, if R3's G0/1 is in an up/up state, any LAN problem probably exists elsewhere in the LAN itself. If the ping still does not work, review the information covered in Chapter 3, "Troubleshooting LAN Switching."

As for the third problem in the list, it could be that some filtering mechanism, like port security, is purposefully filter the frames sent by the host (B) or the router (R3 G0/1). Also, router R3 could have an inbound IPv6 ACL on its G0/1 interface, one that unfortunately filtered inbound ICMPv6 packets, which would discard the incoming packets generated by the **ping** commands.

Problems Using Any Function That Requires DNS

Moving on to the third unique troubleshooting scenario, our engineer is troubleshooting a problem for host C. A ping from host C to a Server1 by hostname fails, but a ping to Server1's IPv6 address succeeds. The engineer tries another similar testing, pinging another server (Server2), with the same results: The ping to the hostname fails, and the ping to the IPv6 address works.

These symptoms pretty clearly point to "some kind of name resolution problem." However, that does not define the specific root cause that the engineer can go fix to get the user working again. In this case, the root causes could fall into these categories:

1. An incorrect host DNS server setting, as statically defined on the host
2. An incorrect host DNS server setting, as learned with (stateless or stateful) DHCPv6
3. An IPv6 connectivity problem between the user's host and the DNS server

As for the first root cause listed here, if the host's DNS server setting is wrong, the host sends the DNS requests to the wrong destination address. As a result, the host gets no DNS response and does not learn the IPv6 address of the destination host. The root cause? Someone typed the wrong information into the host IPv6 configuration settings.

The second root cause in the list is similar to the first, but different enough to be worth having a second category. The user's computer has an incorrect DNS server setting, but that IPv6 learned the setting using DHCPv6. Basically, you have the same problem symptoms but a different root cause. As a reminder, both with stateful DHCPv6 and with SLAAC, the host learns the DNS addresses using DHCPv6.

The third root cause requires a little more discussion and an example. The example shows host C in Figure 16-15, with the two-step process that happens the first time the host tests Server1 with a **ping Server1** command. First, IPv6 packets must flow from C to the DNS server and back for the purpose of name resolution. At Step 2 in the figure, IPv6 packets can flow to Server1's IPv6 address.

Depending on the topology in the cloud, a connectivity problem may exist between host C and the DNS server, whereas no such problem exists between C and Server1. So, when the problem symptoms point to a "name resolution is not working" set of symptoms, but the host appears to point to the right DNS server addresses, start looking at basic IPv6 connectivity from the host to the DNS server.

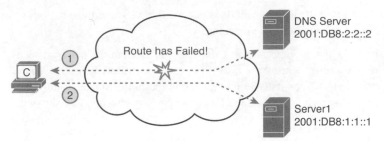

Figure 16-15   *DNS Name Resolution Before Forwarding the Packet to the Server*

Host Is Missing IPv6 Settings: Stateful DHCP Issues

Turning the page to yet another new scenario, our network engineer is now working a problem for a user of a host D. The engineer has called and asked the user to issue a few commands, and the engineer has determined that the host is trying to dynamically learn its IPv6 settings and that the host does not have an IPv6 unicast address yet.

For the sake of discussion, assume that this network uses a strategy of assigning IPv6 addresses using DHCPv6 to assign IPv6 addresses. The engineer knows this strategy, so the engineer is already wondering why the process failed. This scenario walks through some potential root causes of straightforward mistakes.

NOTE   This book leaves out some details of what happens in the process of how a host is told whether to use SLAAC or stateful DHCPv6. To keep the discussion clean and in scope of the topics in this book, assume that for this discussion only stateful DHCP is in use.

Stateful DHCP troubleshooting follows the same basic logic as for IPv4 DHCP, as discussed in Chapter 5, "Troubleshooting IPv4 Routing Part II," in the "DHCP Relay Issues" section. So, repeating rules like those introduced in Chapter 5, the following must be true for an IPv6 host to successfully use either stateful or stateless DHCPv6 to learn information from a DHCPv6 server:

1. The server must be in the same subnet as the client.

   Or

2. The server may be in a different subnet, with

   A. The router that sits on the same subnet as the client host correctly implementing DHCP relay

   B. IPv6 connectivity working between that local router (the router near the client host) and the DHCPv6 server

The two most likely root causes of a host failing to dynamically learn its IPv6 settings with stateful DHCPv6 are root causes 2A and 2B. For 2A, the solution requires a configuration command on the correct interface on each LAN that is remote from the DHCPv6 server. For instance, in Figure 16-16, host D sits on a LAN subnet on the left, with R1's G0/0 interface connected to the same subnet. R1 should have the command listed at the bottom of the figure to enable the IPv6 DHCP relay function pointing to the DHCPv6 server on the right.

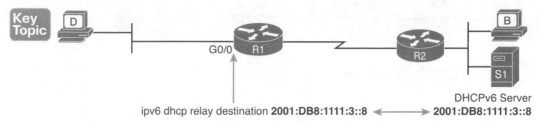

Figure 16-16 *IPv6 DHCP Relay*

If R1 is missing the **ipv6 dhcp relay** command or points to the wrong IPv6 address, host D's attempt to use DHCPv6 will fail.

The item listed as 2B is not actually a root cause. Instead, it is just another problem symptom that needs further investigation. Connectivity must exist between R1 and the DHCPv6 server, and back to the address R1 uses to source the DHCPv6 message. (R1 sources the DHCPv6 request from the outgoing interface of the sent message, not necessarily the same interface where the **ipv6 dhcp relay** command is configured; in this case, R1 would use its serial interface IPv6 address.) A good test of this problem is to ping the DHCPv6 server's IPv6 address from R1.

Host Is Missing IPv6 Settings: SLAAC Issues

For the fifth troubleshooting scenario, take the previous scenario but assume the enterprise uses SLAAC rather than stateful DHCPv6 for IPv6 address assignment. To review, the engineer has discovered that host D has not learned its IPv6 address. So, what could cause SLAAC to fail? This next topic explores the potential root causes.

To understand some of the root causes for such a problem, first review the three steps a host takes when using SLAAC to learn and build its IPv6 settings:

1. Use NDP to learn the prefix, prefix length, and default router address from a router on the same subnet.

2. Use SLAAC rules, locally on the host (no network messages required), to build the host's own IPv6 address.

3. Use stateless DHCPv6 to learn the addresses of the DNS servers from a DHCPv6 server.

The first of these steps uses the NDP Router Solicitation (RS) message, with the router sending back an NDP Router Advertisement (RA) message, as shown in Figure 16-17. The RS message, sent to the all IPv6 routers multicast address FF02::2, should go to all IPv6 routers on the same VLAN as host D in the figure. In this case, R1 replies, listing R1's IPv6 address (to be used as D's default router) and the prefix/length host D should use.

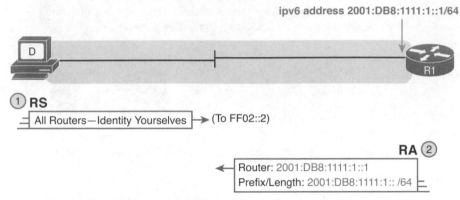

Figure 16-17 *NDP RS and RA Process*

Hosts that use SLAAC rely on the information in the RA message. So, when a host fails to learn and build these three settings when using SLAAC, including the IPv6 address, the next question really should be this: What could cause the NDP RS/RA process to fail? The following list details these potential root causes:

1. No LAN connectivity between the host and any router in the subnet.

2. The router is missing an **ipv6 address** interface subcommand.

3. The router is missing an **ipv6 unicast-routing** global configuration command.

Of these reasons, the first is somewhat obvious. If the LAN cannot forward Ethernet frames from the host to the router, or vice versa, the NDP RS and RA messages cannot be delivered.

As for the second reason, to respond to an RS message, a router must have an **ipv6 address** command. This command enables IPv6 on the interface, but it also defines the information that the router will list in the RA message. For instance, in Figure 16-17, R1 has been configured with the **ipv6 address 2001:db8:1111:1::1/64** command. This command directly lists two of the pieces of information R1 supplies in the RA message, and R1 uses the address and prefix length to calculate the IPv6 prefix as well.

The third root cause in the list may be the most surprising: The router must enable IPv6 routing with the **ipv6 unicast-routing** global command. Why? Without this command, Cisco routers do not try to route IPv6 packets. If omitted, the router does not consider itself an IPv6 router and does not reply to the NDP RS message with an RA.

Traceroute Shows Some Hops, But Fails

This chapter's sixth different troubleshooting scenario now moves away from the host and toward the routers, leading toward IPv6 routing issues.

In this case, the engineer hears that a host cannot connect to a server. Clearly, a ping from the host to the server fails, so the engineer does several of the steps discussed already in this chapter:

- The host IPv6 settings look good.

- The host IPv6 settings match the default router and DNS server as they should.

- The host can ping its default router.

To continue troubleshooting, the engineer next calls the user and asks him to try a **traceroute** command with a destination of the server's IPv6 address. The **traceroute** shows a couple of routers in the output, but then the command never completes until interrupted by the user. What could the root causes be? Usually, but not always, these symptoms point to some kind of an IPv6 routing problem. For the next page or two, this discussion examines some potential root causes for these routing problems.

Routing problems happen for many reasons. Some routing problems happen because routes are missing from a router (perhaps because of many specific root causes). Some routing problems happen because a router has an incorrect route. The following list gives just some of the reasons why a router might be missing a needed route or might have an incorrect route:

- Links between routers are down.
- Routing protocol neighbor problems exist.
- Routing protocol route filtering prevents the route from being added to the IPv6 routing table.
- Incorrect static routes send packets to the wrong next router.
- Poor subnet design duplicates subnets in different locations in the network, falsely advertising a subnet.

For example, take a look at Figure 16-18. Host A fails when attempting to ping host C, which sits in subnet 33 (2001:DB8:1:33::/64). A traceroute of host C from host A lists R1's and R2's IPv6 addresses, but then it never finishes.

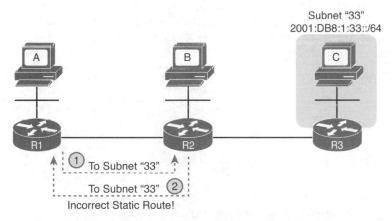

Figure 16-18 *Incorrect Static Route Creates Routing Loop*

As you can see from the notes in the figure, the routing problem exists because of an incorrect static route on R2. Host A can forward IPv6 packets to R1, its default router. R1 can correctly forward packets sent to host C to router R2. However, R2 has an incorrect static route for subnet 33 pointing back to R1.

As for other root causes of routing problems, take the list and look for those issues as well. Check the interfaces on routers that should be up to make sure the interfaces still work. Do troubleshooting for your routing protocol. (Chapters 17 and 18 discuss how to troubleshoot OSPFv3 and EIGRPv6, respectively.) And even look for the possibility that someone misconfigured a router interface, so that the routing protocols advertise about the same subnet number as existing in two places, which breaks design rules on paper and confuses the routing of packets to hosts in that IPv6 subnet.

Routing Looks Good, But Traceroute Still Fails

To finish this set of scenarios, this last scenario focuses on one particular root cause: IPv6 access control lists (ACL).

You have already learned how **ping** and **traceroute** commands can imply that a routing problem may exist. When ping and traceroute show that the host can forward a packet at least as far as the default router but not all the way to the destination, the problem probably sits in one of these two categories:

- A routing problem exists.
- Routing works, but some filter, like an IPv6 ACL, is discarding the packets.

Although neither this book nor the ICND1 book discusses IPv6 ACLs, the ICND1 book discussed IPv4 ACLs quite a bit. IPv6 ACLs work very much the same, but of course, they filter IPv6 packets rather than IPv4 packets. IPv6 ACL configuration defines a list of statements, with each statement matching source and destination IPv6 address ranges, port numbers, and so on. You can enable the ACL to filter IPv6 packets as they flow in or out of an interface.

For instance, Figure 16-19 shows a single line IPv6 ACL (with correct syntax). IPv6 ACLs define the source and destination address ranges as an address/prefix pair, just like in the **ipv6 address** interface subcommand. To filter Telnet traffic going from subnet 1 to subnet 3 in this network, you could add the ACL in one of the four locations noted with the arrowed lines in the figure. (Note that the ACL would also need some other statements to permit other traffic.)

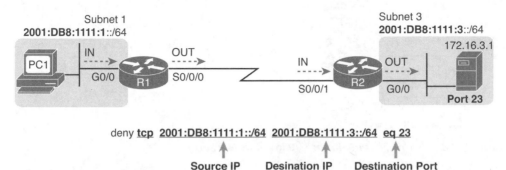

Figure 16-19 *Filtering IPv6 Packets Based on Destination Port*

Before reading more about troubleshooting, take a closer look at the one-line ACL example. The address ranges are based on the IPv6 prefix (subnet) as calculated based on the address and prefix length. As a result, this ACL defines a source address range of all addresses in subnet 1 (2001:DB8:1111:1::/64) and a destination address range of all addresses in subnet 3

(2001:DB8:1111:3::/64). It also lists a destination port of 23 (Telnet). So, with a deny action, this ACL command would discard IPv6 Telnet traffic.

Now back to troubleshooting. In short, when you see symptoms that look like a routing problem, check to see whether any IPv6 ACLs have been enabled. On IPv4 routers, the command to check for any enabled ACLs is **show ip interface**. So, with IPv6, you use the command **show ipv6 interface**. Example 16-8 shows this command applied to a router, with the highlighted line noting the enabled IPv6 ACL.

Example 16-8   *The* show ipv6 interface *Command on Router R2*

```
R2# show ipv6 interface
Serial0/0/0 is up, line protocol is up
  IPv6 is enabled, link-local address is FE80::FF:FE00:1
  No Virtual link-local address(es):
  Global unicast address(es):
    2001:DB8:1:12::1, subnet is 2001:DB8:1:12::/64
  Joined group address(es):
    FF02::1
    FF02::2
    FF02::5
    FF02::1:FF00:1
  MTU is 1500 bytes
  ICMP error messages limited to one every 100 milliseconds
  ICMP redirects are enabled
  ICMP unreachables are sent
  Output features: Access List
  Outgoing access list book
! Lines omitted for brevity
```

Exam Preparation Tasks

Review All the Key Topics

Review the most important topics from this chapter, noted with the Key Topic icon. Table 16-2 lists these key topics and where each is discussed.

Table 16-2   Key Topics for Chapter 16

Key Topic Element	Description	Page Number
Table 16-1	IPv6 address types	474
Figure 16-5	Comparisons of IPv4 DHCP versus IPv6 stateful DHCP	475
Figure 16-7	Details of source of host IPv6 settings when using SLAAC	476
List	Steps to build an address using SLAAC and EUI-64	477
Figure 16-8	Concepts behind using SLAAC and EUI-64	477
List	IPv6 addressing and routing configuration steps	477
List	Working with hosts in IPv6 networks	483
List	Working with routers in IPv6 networks	484
List	Working with filtering in IPv6 networks	484
Figure 16-13	Specific host settings to compare to other devices when troubleshooting	485
List	Categories of issues that prevent an IPv6 host from pinging its default router	486
List	Categories of issues that prevent IPv6 hosts from using DNS server functions	487
List	Requirements for DHCPv6 to work correctly	488
Figure 16-16	DHCPv6 relay agent configuration in a router	489
List	Reasons why the NDP RS/RA process would fail between a host and router	490
List	Possible reasons for IPv6 routing problems	491

Complete the Tables and Lists from Memory

Print a copy of DVD Appendix D, "Memory Tables," or at least the section for this chapter, and complete the tables and lists from memory. DVD Appendix E, "Memory Tables Answer Key," includes completed tables and lists to check your work.

Definitions of Key Terms

After your first reading of the chapter, try to define these key terms, but do not be concerned about getting them all correct at that time. Chapter 22 directs you in how to use these terms for late-stage preparation for the exam.

Neighbor Discovery Protocol (NDP) Router Solicitation (RS), Router Advertisement (RA), Neighbor Solicitation (NS), Neighbor Advertisement (NA), stateless address autoconfiguration (SLAAC), stateful DHCPv6, stateless DHCPv6, global unicast address, unique local unicast address, link-local address, EUI-64, dual stack

16

Command Reference to Check Your Memory

Although you should not necessarily memorize the information in the tables in this section, this section does include a reference for the configuration and EXEC commands covered in this chapter. Practically speaking, you should memorize the commands as a side effect of reading the chapter and doing all the activities in this exam preparation section. To check to see how well you have memorized the commands as a side effect of your other studies, cover the left side of the table with a piece of paper, read the descriptions on the right side, and see whether you remember the command.

Table 16-3   Chapter 16 Configuration Command Reference

Command	Description
ipv6 unicast-routing	Global command that enables IPv6 routing on the router
ipv6 address {*ipv6-address/prefix-length* | *prefix-name sub-bits/ prefix-length*} [eui-64]	Interface subcommand that manually configures either the entire interface IP address, or a /64 prefix with the router building the EUI-64 format interface ID automatically
ipv6 dhcp relay destination *server-address*	Interface subcommand that enables the IPv6 DHCP relay agent
ipv6 router ospf *process-id*	Enters OSPFv3 configuration mode for the listed process
router-id *id*	OSPF subcommand that statically sets the router ID.
ipv6 ospf *process-id* area *area-number*	Interface subcommand that enables OSPFv3 on the interface, for a particular process, and defines the OSPFv3 area

Table 16-4   Chapter 16 EXEC Command Reference

Command	Description
show ipv6 route [ospf | connected | static]	Lists routes in the routing table learned by OSPFv3
show ipv6 ospf	Shows routing protocol parameters and current timer values for OSPFv3 and the OSPFv3 router ID

Command	Description
show ipv6 ospf interface brief	Lists one line of output per OSPFv3-enabled interface, with basic settings listed, like OSPFv3 process, area number, and interface cost
show ipv6 interface [*type number*]	Lists IPv6 settings on an interface, including link-local and other unicast IP addresses
show ipv6 ospf neighbor [*neighbor-RID*]	Lists neighbors and current status with neighbors, per interface, and optionally lists details for the router ID listed in the command
show ipv6 ospf database	Lists a summary of the LSAs in the local router's LSDB, listing one line for each LSA
show ipv6 ospf	Lists a variety of facts about the local router's OSPF process, notably with the first line listing the router's router ID
show ipv6 protocols	Lists briefer information than the IPv4 **show ip protocols** command, primarily listing all means through which a router can learn or build IPv6 routes and interfaces on which a routing protocol is enabled
ping {*host-name* | *ipv6-address*}	Tests IPv6 routes by sending an ICMP packet to the destination host
traceroute {*host-name* | *ipv6-address*}	Tests IPv6 routes by discovering the IP addresses of the routes between a router and the listed destination
show ipv6 neighbors	Lists the router's IPv6 neighbor table
show ipv6 routers	Lists any neighboring routers that advertised themselves through an NDP RA message

Table 16-5   Chapter 16 Host Command Reference

Command (Microsoft, Apple, Linux)	Description
ipconfig/ifconfig/ifconfig	Lists interface settings, including IPv4 and IPv6 addresses
ping/ping6/ping6	Tests IP routes by sending an ICMPv6 packet to the destination host
tracert/traceroute6/traceroute6	Tests IP routes by discovering the IPv6 addresses of the routes between a router and the listed destination
netsh interface ipv6 show neighbors / ndp -an / ip -6 neighbor show	Lists a host's IPv6 neighbor table

This chapter covers the following exam topics:

IP Routing Technologies

Configure and verify OSPF (single area)

neighbor adjacencies

OSPF states

Discuss Multi area

Configure OSPF v3

Router ID

LSA types

Differentiate methods of routing and routing protocols

metric

next hop

Troubleshooting

Troubleshoot and Resolve OSPF problems

Neighbor adjacencies

Hello and Dead timers

OSPF area

Interface MTU

Network types

Neighbor states

OSPF topology database

CHAPTER 17

Implementing OSPF for IPv6

By this point in your reading, you should know a lot about OSPF Version 3 (OSPFv3), but for a couple of different reasons. First, the ICND1 book and the CCENT exam include the basics of OSPFv3 concepts, configuration, and verification. Beyond that, OSPFv3 works much like OSPFv2 in many ways, and this book's Chapters 8, "Implementing OSPF for IPv4," and 11, "Troubleshooting IPv4 Routing Protocols," took the discussion of OSPFv2 to a deeper level.

This chapter pulls all the OSPFv3 puzzle pieces together by taking advantage of all the other material on both OSPFv2 and OSPFv3. Because you have already read about almost every bit of the conceptual knowledge required for this chapter's OSPFv3 discussion, this chapter moves immediately to the configuration in the first major section. This initial section both reviews the ICND1 OSPFv3 configuration topics and examines them more closely. It also introduces all the new configuration topics for this chapter.

The second major section pulls many OSPF concepts together by using verification commands. This section discusses and reminds you of both OSPFv2 and OSPFv3 topics, using the verification commands to demonstrate how the routers implement those concepts. At the same time, the discussion includes a list of common root causes of OSPFv3 problems and explains how to recognize those problems.

"Do I Know This Already?" Quiz

Use the "Do I Know This Already?" quiz to help decide whether you might want to skim this chapter, or a major section, moving more quickly to the "Exam Preparation Tasks" section near the end of the chapter. You can find the answers at the bottom of the page following the quiz. For thorough explanations, see DVD Appendix C, "Answers to the 'Do I Know This Already?' Quizzes."

Table 17-1 "Do I Know This Already?" Foundation Topics Section-to-Question Mapping

Foundation Topics Section	Questions
OSPFv3 Configuration	1–3
OSPFv3 Concepts, Verification, and Troubleshooting	4–6

1. An engineer wants to set the OSPFv3 router ID for router R1. Which of the following answers could affect R1's choice of OSPFv3 router ID?

   a. The **ipv6 address** command on interface Gigabit0/0

   b. The **ip address** command on interface Serial0/0/1

   c. The **ospf router-id** command in OSPFv3 configuration mode

   d. The **ipv6 address** command on interface loopback2

2. Router R1 has a Serial0/0/0 interface with address 2001:1:1:1::1/64, and a G0/0 interface with address 2001:2:2:2::1/64. The OSPFv3 process uses process ID 1. Which of the following OSPFv3 configuration commands enable OSPFv3 on R1's G0/0 interface and places it into area 0?

   a. A **network 2001:1:1:1::/64 1 area 0** command in router configuration mode

   b. An **ipv6 ospf 1 area 0** command in G0/0 interface configuration mode

   c. A **network 2001:1:1:1::/64 1 area 0** command in router configuration mode

   d. An **ospf 1 area 0** command in G0/0 interface configuration mode

3. An enterprise uses a dual-stack model of deployment for IPv4 and IPv6, using OSPF as the routing protocol for both. Router R1 has IPv4 and IPv6 addresses on its G0/0 and S0/0/0 interfaces only, with OSPFv2 and OSPFv3 enabled on both interfaces for area 0 and the router ID explicitly set for both protocols. Comparing the OSPFv2 and OSPFv3 configuration, which of the following statements is true?

   a. The OSPFv3 configuration, but not OSPFv2, uses the **router-id** *router-id* router subcommand.

   b. Both protocols use the **router-id** *router-id* router subcommand.

   c. Both protocols use the **network** *network-number wildcard* **area** *area-id* router subcommand.

   d. The both protocols use the **ipv6 ospf** *process-id* **area** *area-id* interface subcommand.

4. R1 and R2 are routers that connect to the same VLAN. Which of the answers lists an item that can prevent the two routers from becoming OSPFv3 neighbors? (Choose three answers.)

   a. Mismatched Hello timers

   b. Mismatched process IDs

   c. IPv6 addresses in different subnets

   d. Equal router IDs

   e. One passive router interface (used on this link)

5. The example shows an excerpt from the **show ipv6 route ospf** command on a router (R1). Which of the answers are correct about the interpretation of the meaning of the output of this command? (Choose two answers.)

```
R1# show ipv6 route ospf
OI  2001:DB8:1:4::/64 [110/129]
     via FE80::FF:FE00:1, Serial0/0/1
```

  a. 110 is the metric for the route.

  b. S0/0/1 is an interface on R1.

  c. FE80::FF:FE00:1 is a link-local address on R1.

  d. OI means that the route is an interarea OSPF route.

6. Router R1 has been configured as a dual-stack IPv4/IPv6 router, using interfaces S0/0/0, S0/0/1, and GigabitEthernet0/1. As a new engineer hired at the company, you do not know whether any of the interfaces are passive. Which of the following commands lets you find whether G0/1 is passive, either by the command listing that fact or by that command leaving passive interfaces out of its list of interfaces?

  a. show ipv6 ospf interface brief

  b. show ipv6 protocols

  c. show ipv6 ospf interface G0/1

  d. show ipv6 ospf interface passive

17

Foundation Topics

OSPFv3 Configuration

Cisco expects you to know some OSPFv3 details for the ICND1 exam, but for the ICND2 exam, you should both remember all the ICND1 OSPFv3 topics plus add some new knowledge and skills. This first of two major sections in the chapter looks at OSPFv3 configuration, reviewing ICND1 configuration topics and adding some for ICND2. The new topics include multi-area OSPFv3 configuration, setting OSPF costs, load balancing, and injecting default routes.

OSPFv3 ICND1 Configuration Review

As a first step, review the OSPFv3 configuration that was part of your study for the ICND1 exam topics. The following list summarizes the configuration steps for the OSPFv3 configuration included in ICND1:

Step 1.   Create an OSPFv3 process number and enter OSPF configuration mode for that process using the **ipv6 router ospf** *process-id* global command.

Step 2.   Ensure that the router has an OSPF router ID, through either:

   A. Configuring the **router-id** *id-value* router subcommand

   B. Configuring an IP address on a loopback interface (chooses the highest IP address of all working loopbacks)

   C. Relying on an interface IP address (chooses the highest IP address of all working nonloopbacks)

Step 3.   Configure the **ipv6 ospf** *process-id* **area** *area-number* command on each interface on which OSPFv3 should be enabled, to both enable OSPFv3 on the interface and set the area number for the interface.

Step 4.   (Optional) Configure any OSPFv3 interfaces as passive if no neighbors can or should be discovered on the interface, using the **passive-interface** *type number* interface subcommand.

Before looking at the multi-area configuration, bear with me on a brief tangent about the exam topics for OSPF. Frankly, the OSPF exam topics (at the time of this writing) skirt around the dividing line of whether you need to know how to configure multi-area OSPF (both OSPFv2 and OSPFv3). The configuration-oriented exam topics clearly imply single-area configuration only, although the troubleshooting topics may imply that you need knowledge of multi-area configuration. The good news is this: Once you understand multi-area concepts and single-area configuration, adding multi-area configuration is incredibly simple. So, this topic shows the multi-area details, just in case you need them for the exam.

Example Multi-Area OSPFv3 Configuration

Many OSPFv3 facts listed in this chapter work like the same idea in OSPFv2. So, to make those similarities pop even more, this configuration section uses a multi-area configuration example with the exact same internetwork topology as the multi-area example shown in the OSPFv2 chapter (Chapter 8, "Implementing OSPF for IPv4").

Figure 17-1 begins to describe the design, before getting into the configuration, showing the IPv6 subnets. The figure does not show the individual router IPv6 addresses, to reduce clutter, but to make the addresses easier to recognize, the addresses all end with the same number as the router. For example, all five of router R1's interface addresses end with 1.

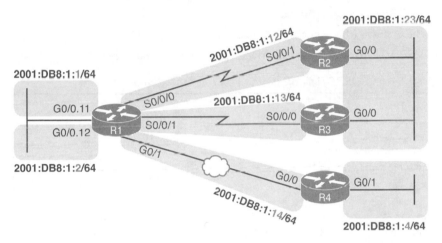

Figure 17-1 *The Internetwork for an Example Multi-Area OSPFv3 Configuration*

Figure 17-2 next shows the OSPFv3 area design. For those of you with an excellent memory, the design is literally identical to Chapter 8's Figure 8-12, which defined the area design for that chapter's multi-area design example. The design makes R2 and R3 internal routers inside area 23, R4 an internal router inside area 4, and R1 an Area Border Router (ABR) connected to all three areas.

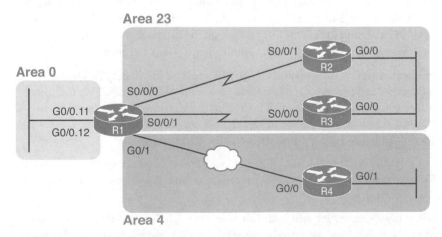

Figure 17-2 *Area Design for the Multi-Area OSPFv3 Example*

Single Area Configuration on the Three Internal Routers

The configurations on the three internal routers in this example review ICND1-level single-area OSPF configuration. In a multi-area OSPF design, the configuration on any internal routers—routers for which all interfaces connect to a single area—looks like a single-area configuration because all the interfaces are placed into one area.

Example 17-1 begins the example with R2's complete IPv6 configuration, including OSPFv3. In other words, all the commands needed on R2 to add IPv6 support are in the example. Note that for OSPFv3 in particular, the example shows the following actions, as highlighted in the example:

1. Creates an OSPFv3 process with process ID 2
2. Defines the OSPFv3 RID explicitly as 2.2.2.2
3. Enables OSPFv3 process 2 on two interfaces, putting both in area 23

Example 17-1 *IPv6 and OSPFv3 Configuration on Internal Router R2*

```
ipv6 unicast-routing
!
interface GigabitEthernet0/0
 mac-address 0200.0000.0002
 ipv6 address 2001:db8:1:23::2/64
 ipv6 ospf 2 area 23
!
interface serial 0/0/1
 ipv6 address 2001:db8:1:12::2/64
 ipv6 ospf 2 area 23
!
ipv6 router ospf 2
 router-id 2.2.2.2
```

First, focus on the two commands that should be in every OSPFv3 configuration: the **ipv6 router ospf** *process-id* global command and the **ipv6 ospf** *process-id* **area** *area-id* interface subcommand. The first command creates the OSPFv3 process by number. The second command, one per interface, enables that OSPFv3 process on the interface and assigns the area number. In this case, R2 has a process ID of 2, with both interfaces assigned to area 23.

Next, consider one completely optional feature: OSPFv3 passive interfaces. This feature uses the same concepts and literally the exact same command syntax as OSPFv2. If a router should not form neighbor relationships on an interface, that interface may be made passive. In this case, R2 should find at least one OSPFv3 neighbor on each of its two interfaces, so the configuration does not include the **passive-interface** command at all.

Finally, OSPFv3 follows the same rules as OSPFv2 when setting the OSPFv3 router ID (RID). In this case, R2 sets its RID using the OSPFv3 **router-id** command, but you should be ready to understand all three ways.

Now on to the configuration on R3, which should have a very similar OSPFv3 configuration compared to router R2. Both are internal routers in area 23, and both have at least one neighbor off their two interfaces, respectively, so both cannot make either of their interfaces passive. Also, just to make the point that OSPFv3 neighbors may use different process ID values, R3 uses OSPFv3 process ID 3, while R2 uses 2. Example 17-2 shows the resulting configuration.

Example 17-2 *IPv6 and OSPFv3 Configuration on R3*

```
ipv6 unicast-routing
!
interface GigabitEthernet0/0
 mac-address 0200.0000.0003
 ipv6 address 2001:db8:1:23::3/64
 ipv6 ospf 3 area 23
!
interface serial 0/0/0
 ipv6 address 2001:db8:1:13::3/64
 ipv6 ospf 3 area 23
!
ipv6 router ospf 3
 router-id 3.3.3.3
```

Moving on to R4, in Example 17-3, the configuration differs slightly from the previous two routers. First, R4 can make its G0/1 interface passive because R4 expects to create no OSPFv3 neighbor relationships off that LAN interface. R4 also uses a different OSPFv3 process ID.

NOTE Although these examples use different OSPFv3 process IDs, to show that such a choice causes no problems, most enterprises would use the same process ID value on all routers for consistency.

Example 17-3 *IPv6 and OSPFv3 Configuration on R4*

```
ipv6 unicast-routing
!
interface GigabitEthernet0/0
 mac-address 0200.0000.0004
 ipv6 address 2001:db8:1:14::4/64
 ipv6 ospf 4 area 4
!
interface GigabitEthernet0/1
 ipv6 address 2001:db8:1:4::4/64
 ipv6 ospf 4 area 4
!
ipv6 router ospf 4
 router-id 4.4.4.4
 passive-interface gigabitethernet0/1
```

Adding Multi-Area Configuration on the Area Border Router

The configuration for multi-area OSPF is just as anticlimactic for OSPFv3 as it was for OSPFv2. Multi-area OSPF may lead to some interesting design discussions when deciding which links to put in which areas. Once decided, the configuration is just a matter of reading the documentation correctly and typing the correct area number into the **ipv6 ospf** *process-id* **area** *area-id* interface subcommand.

In this example, ABR R1 has an OSPFv3 process (process ID 1), with OSPFv3 enabled on five interfaces, as follows, to match earlier Figure 17-2:

> **Area 0:** G0/0.11 and G0/0.12
>
> **Area 23:** S0/0/0 and S0/0/1
>
> **Area 4:** G0/1

To be clear, nothing in R1's configuration mentions multi-area or ABR—R1 simply acts as an ABR because its configuration puts some interfaces in area 0 and others in other nonbackbone areas. Example 17-4 shows the configuration.

Example 17-4   *IPv6 and OSPFv3 Configuration on ABR R1*

```
ipv6 unicast-routing
!
interface GigabitEthernet0/0
 mac-address 0200.0000.0001
!
interface GigabitEthernet0/0.11
 encapsulation dot1q 11
 ipv6 address 2001:db8:1:1::1/64
 ipv6 ospf 1 area 0
!
interface GigabitEthernet0/0.12
 encapsulation dot1q 12
 ipv6 address 2001:db8:1:2::1/64
 ipv6 ospf 1 area 0
!
interface GigabitEthernet0/1
 ipv6 address 2001:db8:1:14::1/64
 ipv6 ospf 1 area 4
!
interface serial 0/0/0
 ipv6 address 2001:db8:1:12::1/64
 ipv6 ospf 1 area 23
!
interface serial 0/0/1
 ipv6 address 2001:db8:1:13::1/64
 ipv6 ospf 1 area 23
!
ipv6 router ospf 1
 router-id 1.1.1.1
```

Other OSPFv3 Configuration Settings

The example completes all the review of ICND1 OSPFv3 configuration, while adding that small bit of information about multi-area configuration. The next few short configuration topics take some other OSPF features discussed for OSPFv2 back in Chapter 8 and discusses how to configure those for OSPFv3. And as usual, the details are nearly identical.

Setting OSPFv3 Interface Cost to Influence Route Selection

OSPFv3 works much like OSPFv2 in how it calculates the metric for a route, with some slight differences with the concepts, configuration commands, and verification commands.

To review the concepts, as discussed back in the OSPFv2 chapter (Chapter 8), shortest path first (SPF) on a router finds all possible routes for a subnet. Then, it adds the OSPF interface cost for all outgoing interfaces in a route.

For instance, Figure 17-3 repeats a figure from Chapter 8, changed slightly to now show an IPv6 subnet. The figures shows a single-area design in which R1 finds three possible routes to reach subnet 33 (2001:DB8:1:33::/64), the middle route having the lowest cost.

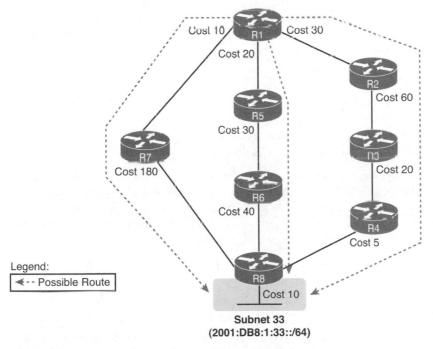

Figure 17-3 *SPF Tree to Find R1's Route to 2001:DB8:1:33::/64*

To influence the metric for the route, OSPFv3 gives us a few ways to change an interface's OSPFv3 cost, with the same basic rules as OSPFv2, as summarized in this list:

1. Set the cost explicitly using the **ipv6 ospf cost** *x* interface subcommand to a value between 1 and 65,535, inclusive.

2. Change the interface bandwidth with the **bandwidth** *speed* command, with speed being a number in kilobits per second (Kbps), and let the router calculate the value based on the OSPFv3 **reference-bandwidth / interface-bandwidth**.

3. Change the reference bandwidth router OSPFv3 subcommand **auto-cost reference-bandwidth** *ref-bw*, with a unit of megabits per second (Mbps).

OSPF Load Balancing

OSPFv3 and OSPFv2 follow the same concept, with the exact same configuration command, to effect equal-cost load balancing.

When OSPFv3 on a router calculates multiple equal-metric routes to reach one subnet, the router can put multiple equal-cost routes in the routing table. The OSPFv3 **maximum-paths** *number* router subcommand defines just how many such routes OSPFv3 will add to the IPv6 routing table. For example, if an internetwork has six possible routes for some subnet, and all have the exact same metric, and the engineer wants all routes to be used, he could configure the router with the **maximum-paths 6** subcommand under the **ipv6 router ospf** command.

Injecting Default Routes

Finally, with yet another OSPFv3 feature that works very much like OSPFv2, OSPFv3 supports a router's capability to advertise a default route with OSPFv3. This function allows one router to have a default route and then basically tell all other routers, "Hey, if you need a default route, send packets to me, and I'll send them with my good default route."

One classic case for using a routing protocol to advertise a default route has to do with an enterprise's connection to the Internet. If a company has one IPv6-enabled Internet connection, that one router can use a default IPv6 route to route all IPv6 Internet traffic out that one link. But the rest of the enterprise's routers need to send their Internet traffic to this one router, so the enterprise engineer uses these design goals:

■ All routers learn specific routes for subnets inside the company, so a default route is not needed for destinations inside the company.

■ The one router that connects to the Internet has a static default IPv6 route that points all IPv6 traffic (that does not match any other IPv6 route) into the Internet.

■ All routers learn (by using OSPFv3) a default route from the Internet-facing router so that all IPv6 packets going to the Internet first go to this one router.

Figure 17-4 shows the ideas of how the routing information is propagated from the Internet-facing router (R1) to the other routers in the company. In this case, a company connects to an ISP with their router R1. Router R1 uses the OSPFv3 **default-information originate** command in OSPFv3 configuration mode; this command is literally the same command used for OSPFv2 (Step 1). As a result, R1 advertises a default route to the other OSPFv3 routers

(Step 2). (The prefix for the default route with IPv6 is ::/0, with a prefix length 0, somewhat like the 0.0.0.0/0 used with IPv4.)

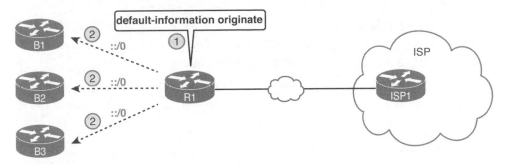

Figure 17-4   *Using OSPFv3 to Advertise a Default Route*

Once the process in Figure 17-4 completes, the three routers on the left each have a default route. Their default routes point to R1 as the next-hop router so that all traffic destined for the Internet first goes to R1 and then out to the ISP.

That completes the discussion of new configuration for OSPFv3. The next section covers various OSPFv3 concepts, including verification and troubleshooting.

OSPF Concepts, Verification, and Troubleshooting

To the depth discussed for CCNA Routing and Switching, OSPFv3 and OSPFv2 behave very much like each other. So far, between this book and your reading for the ICND1 exam, you should have already read about all the equivalent OSPFv2 concepts, seen the OSPFv2 verification commands, and seen many OSPFv2 troubleshooting issues. This second major section of the chapter just needs to show where OSPFv3 uses the same concepts and show where, in those rare cases, OSPFv3 differs from OSPFv2.

For instance, to the depth discussed in these books, OSPFv3 works much like OSPFv2 with regard to:

- Area design and the related terms.
- The configuration idea of enabling the routing process, per interface, for an area.
- The neighbor discovery process with Hello messages.
- Transitioning through neighbor states and the topology exchange process.
- The use of full and 2-way as the normal stable state for working neighbor relationships, with other states being either temporary or pointing to some problem with the neighbor.
- The general ideas behinds LSA Types 1, 2, and 3 and the link-state database (LSDB).
- SPF and how it uses interface cost to calculate metrics.
- Messages are sent to reserved multicast addresses (FF02::5 for all OSPF routers, FF02::6 for all DR and BDR routers), similar to OSPFv2's use of 224.0.0.5 and 224.0.0.6.

So, what is different between the two? The next list mentions a few differences. However, note that many of the differences happen to be outside the scope of the coverage of topics in this book:

- The name of the Type 3 LSA.

- That OSPFv3 neighbors do not have to have IPv6 addresses in the same IPv6 subnet, whereas OSPFv2 neighbors must be in the same IPv4 subnet.

- New LSA types used by OSPFv3 but not by OSPFv2 (also beyond scope).

- The details defined inside LSA types 1, 2, and 3 differ (details beyond the scope of this book).

As you can see, the list of differences is relatively short.

Because of the many similarities between OSPFv3 and OSPFv2, Cisco keeps the verification commands similar too. Figure 17-5 summarizes the OSPFv3 verification commands relative to the kinds of information they show. Note that all the commands that list **ipv6** can be changed to **ip** to create the exact syntax of the matching OSPFv2 **show** command.

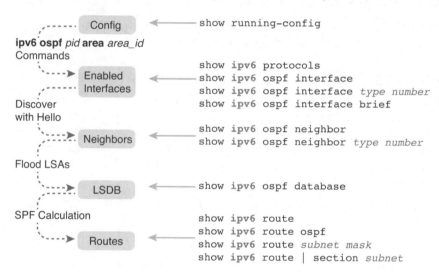

Figure 17-5 *Reference of OSPFv3 Verification Commands*

When a router first brings up the OSPFv3 process, IOS reads the OSPFv3 configuration and enables OSPFv3 on interfaces. So, this section begins by discussing OSPFv3 interface verification and troubleshooting. Following that, the discussion moves on to OSPFv3 neighbors, then to the OSPFv3 topology database, and finally to OSPFv3 routes added to the IPv6 routing table.

NOTE All the troubleshooting examples in the rest of this chapter use routers R1, R2, R3, and R4 from the multi-area configuration example earlier in this chapter. Look back to Figures 17-1 and 17-2 for a reference to the topology and area diagrams for this network.

OSPFv3 Interfaces

The style of OSPFv3 configuration clearly identifies on which interfaces the OSPFv3 process should be working. The **ip ospf** *process-id* **area** *area-id* interface subcommand basically means "run OSPFv3 on this interface." A quick scan of the interface in the output of the **show running-config** command can identify the interfaces and the area number for each.

The next few pages first takes a look at a few other methods of verifying OSPFv3 interfaces, and then the discussion turns to some OSPFv3 interface troubleshooting tips.

Verifying OSPFv3 Interfaces

Suppose that, from studying you have both seen and practiced OSPFv3 configuration and you feel confident about the configuration. Then, on the exam, you happen to get a simlet question on OSPFv3. Unfortunately, like many simlet questions, the question does not let you into enable mode, so you cannot see the configuration! A **show running-config** command plus your good configuration skills would let you answer any question, but you cannot see the config. How can you find out, for example, on which interfaces the OSPFv3 process has been enabled?

Three commands tell you something about interfaces enabled for OSPFv3: **show ipv6 protocols, show ipv6 ospf interface brief**, and **show ipv6 ospf interface**. All three commands list the interfaces on which OSPFv3 has been enabled. The first two commands list the information briefly, and the third command lists many, many lines of output per interface. (If you want a quick answer, use either of the first two commands.)

Note that all three of these commands list both passive and nonpassive OSPFv3 interfaces—a handy fact to know when troubleshooting neighbor issues. To see the effect, look at Example 17-5. But first, note that before gathering the output in the example, the command **passive-interface gigabitethernet0/0.11** was added to R1's OSPFv3 process.

Example 17-5 *Verifying OSPFv3 Interfaces and Related Parameters*

```
R1# show ipv6 protocols
IPv6 Routing Protocol is "connected"
IPv6 Routing Protocol is "ND"
IPv6 Routing Protocol is "ospf 1"
  Interfaces (Area 0):
    GigabitEthernet0/0.12
    GigabitEthernet0/0.11
  Interfaces (Area 4):
    GigabitEthernet0/1
  Interfaces (Area 23):
    Serial0/0/1
    Serial0/0/0
  Redistribution:
    None
```

As you can see in the example, the output of the **show ipv6 protocols** command lists all five OSPFv3 interfaces on router R1, including passive interface G0/0.11.

Troubleshooting OSPFv3 Interfaces

Most troubleshooting discussions with OSPFv3 revolve around the problems that can occur between two OSPFv3 neighbors. However, mistakes with interface subcommands can actually cause many of these OSPF neighbor problems. To get the discussions started, just consider the problems that can occur with the interface subcommands mentioned so far in this chapter:

■ Configuring the wrong area with the **ip ospf** *process-id* **area** *area-id* interface subcommand prevents neighbor relationships off that interface.

■ Making an interface passive to the OSPFv3 process prevents the local router from forming neighbor relationships off that interface.

For the first item in the list, note that all OSPFv3 routers on the same data link need to be assigned to the same area. On the exam, you need to check any information about the intended area design. To find out which interfaces have been assigned to which area, use the **show ipv6 ospf interface** and **show ipv6 ospf interface brief** commands.

As for the issue in making an interface passive to OSPFv3, when a neighbor relationship needs to be made out that interface, the router should not make that interface passive to OSPFv3. Note that only the **show ipv6 ospf interface** command mentions which OSPFv3 interfaces happen to be passive.

Example 17-6 lists two commands that can be helpful for finding both of these problems. Both list area information, but only the second makes mention of an interface being passive.

Example 17-6   *Finding OSPFv3 Passive Interfaces on R1*

```
R1# show ipv6 ospf interface brief
Interface     PID   Area          Intf ID   Cost   State Nbrs F/C
Gi0/0.12      1     0             16        1      DR    0/0
Gi0/0.11      1     0             17        1      DR    0/0
Gi0/1         1     4             4         1      DR    1/1
Se0/0/1       1     23            7         64     P2P   1/1
Se0/0/0       1     23            6         64     P2P   1/1


R1# show ipv6 ospf interface G0/0.11
GigabitEthernet0/0.11 is up, line protocol is up
  Link Local Address FE80::FF:FE00:1, Interface ID 17
  Area 0, Process ID 1, Instance ID 0, Router ID 1.1.1.1
  Network Type BROADCAST, Cost: 1
  Transmit Delay is 1 sec, State DR, Priority 1
  Designated Router (ID) 1.1.1.1, local address FE80::FF:FE00:1
  No backup designated router on this network
  Timer intervals configured, Hello 10, Dead 40, Wait 40, Retransmit 5
    No Hellos (Passive interface)
! remaining lines omitted for brevity
```

Finally, to see an example of one of the problems, take another look at the configuration for router R4. For the correct configuration in Example 17-3, the engineer made LAN interface G0/1 passive because no other routers existed on that LAN. However, note that R4 uses one Ethernet interface as its WAN interface (G0/0) and one as its LAN interface (G0/1). Suppose that the engineer made the simple mistake of making R4's G0/0 passive instead of G0/1. To show what happens, Example 17-7 changes R4's G0/0 interface to be passive to OSPFv3; note that R4's neighbor relationship to R4 fails almost immediately after the **passive-interface** command is issued.

Example 17-7   *Failure of R4's Neighbor Relationship with R1 Due to Passivity*

```
R4# configure terminal
Enter configuration commands, one per line.  End with CNTL/Z.
R4(config)# ipv6 router ospf 4
R4(config-rtr)# passive-interface gigabitEthernet 0/0
R4(config-rtr)# ^Z
R4#
Jan 17 23:49:56.379: %OSPFv3-5-ADJCHG: Process 4, Nbr 1.1.1.1 on GigabitEthernet0/0
from FULL to DOWN, Neighbor Down: Interface down or detached
```

OSPFv3 Neighbors

As usual, OSPFv3 follows OSPFv2's conventions for how neighbors do their work as well. OSPFv3 uses many of the same protocol message names, neighbor states, and concepts from the processes to form neighbor relationships and exchange the link-state database (LSDB). This next topic looks at some samples of the process, and more important, looks at the number one place to look for OSPF problems: issues that prevent routers from becoming neighbors.

Verifying OSPFv3 Neighbors

Next, Example 17-8 shows some similarities between OSPFv3 and OSPFv2 message names and neighbor states. When reading through the debug output in the example, do not worry about all the detail; instead, focus on the highlighted portions. The highlights list some familiar neighbor states from OSPFv2, like 2-way, exstart, exchange, loading, and full, which is the final desired state in this case.

The example first shows the output from the **debug ipv6 ospf adj** command, which lists messages for OSPFv3 "adjacency" events—that is, what happens when neighbors work through their neighbor states. The end of the example shows R2's **show ipv6 ospf neighbor** command output, which confirms that R2's neighbor state with R3 is the final full state, as mentioned in the debug message. (Note that some debug messages were deleted for the sake of readability.)

Example 17-8   *From R2, Watching Changes to Its Neighbor State for R3*

```
R2# debug ipv6 ospf adj
R2#
Jan 15 14:50:58.098: OSPFv3-2-IPv6 ADJ   Gi0/0: Added 3.3.3.3 to nbr list
Jan 15 14:50:58.098: OSPFv3-2-IPv6 ADJ   Gi0/0: 2 Way Communication to 3.3.3.3, state
2WAY
Jan 15 14:50:58.098: OSPFv3-2-IPv6 ADJ   Gi0/0: DR: 3.3.3.3 (Id)   BDR: 2.2.2.2 (Id)
Jan 15 14:50:58.098: OSPFv3-2-IPv6 ADJ   Gi0/0: Nbr 3.3.3.3: Prepare dbase exchange
Jan 15 14:50:58.098: OSPFv3-2-IPv6 ADJ   Gi0/0: Send DBD to 3.3.3.3 seq 0x2AC5B307 opt
0x0013 flag 0x7 len 28
Jan 15 14:50:58.102: OSPFv3-2-IPv6 ADJ   Gi0/0: Rcv DBD from 3.3.3.3 seq 0xBD091ED opt
0x0013 flag 0x7 len 28  mtu 1500 state EXSTART
Jan 15 14:50:58.102: OSPFv3-2-IPv6 ADJ   Gi0/0: NBR Negotiation Done. We are the SLAVE
Jan 15 14:50:58.102: OSPFv3-2-IPv6 ADJ   Gi0/0: Nbr 3.3.3.3: Summary list built, size
14
Jan 15 14:50:58.106: OSPFv3-2-IPv6 ADJ   Gi0/0: Rcv DBD from 3.3.3.3 seq 0xBD091EE opt
0x0013 flag 0x1 len 308  mtu 1500 state EXCHANGE
Jan 15 14:50:58.106: OSPFv3-2-IPv6 ADJ   Gi0/0: Exchange Done with 3.3.3.3
Jan 15 14:50:58.106: OSPFv3-2-IPv6 ADJ   Gi0/0: Synchronized with 3.3.3.3, state FULL
Jan 15 14:50:58.106: %OSPFv3-5-ADJCHG: Process 2, Nbr 3.3.3.3 on GigabitEthernet0/0
from LOADING to FULL, Loading Done

R2# show ipv6 ospf neighbors

Neighbor ID    Pri   State        Dead Time    Interface ID    Interface
1.1.1.1          0   FULL/  -     00:00:38     6               Serial0/0/1
3.3.3.3          1   FULL/DR      00:00:37     3               GigabitEthernet0/0
```

Just like with OSPFv2, working OSPFv3 neighbors will stabilize either in a full state or a 2-way state. Most neighbors reach a full state, meaning that they fully exchanged their LSDBs directly to/from each other. However, for any OSPF network type that uses a designated router (DR), only the neighbor relationships with the DR and backup DR (BDR) reach a full state. Neighbor relationships between routers that are neither DR nor BDR—DROther routers—will stabilize to a 2-way state.

Troubleshooting OSPFv3 Neighbors

Any time it appears that OSPFv3 fails to learn routes that it should be learning, look at the expected OSPFv3 neighbor relationships. Then, if you find a relationship that does not exist, or exists but does not reach the expected state (full or 2-way), you can focus on the various reasons why a neighbor relationship would not work.

NOTE   As with OSPFv2, a neighbor in a full state is said to be *fully adjacent*, whereas two DROther neighbors that stabilize to a 2-way state are said to simply be *adjacent*.

Troubleshooting OSPF neighbor relationships requires that you remember many details about items that could prevent two routers from becoming neighbors at all. Thankfully, OSPFv3 uses the same list as OSPFv2, with one noticeable difference: OSPFv3 does not require the neighbors to be in the same subnet. Table 17-2 lists the items to consider when troubleshooting OSPF neighbor relationships.

Table 17-2   Neighbor Requirements for OSPFv2 and OSPFv3

Requirement	OSPFv2	OSPFv3
Interfaces must be in an up/up state.	Yes	Yes
Interfaces must be in the same subnet.	Yes	No
ACLs must not filter routing protocol messages.	Yes	Yes
Must pass routing protocol neighbor authentication (if configured).	Yes	Yes
Hello and dead timers must match.	Yes	Yes
Router IDs must be unique.	Yes	Yes
Must use the same process ID on the **router** configuration command.	No	No

When troubleshooting a problem, use the commands listed in Table 17-3 to quickly find the right piece of information to determine if that particular setting is preventing two routers from becoming neighbors.

Table 17-3   OSPF Neighbor Requirements and the Best **show/debug** Commands

Requirement	Best Commands to Isolate the Problem
Must pass any neighbor authentication.	show ipv6 ospf interface
Hello and dead timers must match.	show ipv6 ospf interface
Must be in the same area.	show ipv6 ospf interface brief, show ipv6 protocols
Router IDs must be unique.	show ipv6 ospf
Interfaces must not be passive.	show ipv6 ospf interface

This section shows a couple of examples of problems that can exist between OSPFv3 neighbors. First, Example 17-9 shows a configuration in which a router (R4) purposefully sets its RID to the same number as a neighbor (R1, RID 1.1.1.1). Reading down in the example's highlighted portions, the following happens:

1. R4 changes its RID to 1.1.1.1.

2. R4 clears its OSPFv3 process, so that it starts using the new 1.1.1.1 RID.

3. R4 lists a syslog message stating the neighbor relationship went down (due to the **clear** command).

4. R4 lists a syslog message stating why R4 will not now become neighbors with R1 (1.1.1.1).

Example 17-9   *Results from R4 Changing Its RID to the Same 1.1.1.1 Value as R1*

```
R4# configure terminal
Enter configuration commands, one per line.  End with CNTL/Z.
R4(config)# ipv6 router ospf 4
R4(config-rtr)# router-id 1.1.1.1
% OSPFv3: Reload or use "clear ipv6 ospf process" command, for this to take effect
R4(config-rtr)# ^Z

R4# clear ipv6 ospf process
Reset ALL OSPF processes? [no]: yes
R4#
Jan 17 23:22:03.211: %OSPFv3-5-ADJCHG: Process 4, Nbr 1.1.1.1 on GigabitEthernet0/0
from FULL to DOWN, Neighbor Down: Interface down or detached
R4#
Jan 17 23:22:05.635: %OSPFv3-4-DUP_RTRID_NBR: OSPF detected duplicate router-id
1.1.1.1 from FE80::604:5FF:FE05:707 on interface GigabitEthernet0/0
R4#
R4# show ipv6 ospf neighbor
R4#
```

At the end of the example, the **show ipv6 ospf neighbor** command confirms that R4 now
has no OSPFv3 neighbors. (Note that these examples still use the same network design
shown in Figures 17-1 and 17-2, with the router normally having one neighbor, namely R1.)
The duplicate RID now prevents R4 and R1 from becoming neighbors, so R4's **show ipv6
ospf neighbor** command lists no lines of output at all.

The next example (Example 17-10) mimics the OSPFv2 Hello and dead timer mismatch
issue shown back in Chapter 11, "Troubleshooting IPv4 Routing Protocols," in the section "Finding OSPF Hello and Dead Timer Mismatches." Again based on Figures 17-1 and
17-2, R3's Hello and dead timers are 10 and 40, respectively, which are the default values on
Ethernet interfaces. Before gathering this output, R2's configuration of the **ipv6 ospf
hello-interval 5** interface subcommand on R2's G0/0 interface changed R2's Hello and dead
timers to 5 and 20, respectively. (This command sets the Hello timer, and IOS then sets the
dead timer to four times the Hello timer.)

Example 17-10   *R3 Missing from R2's OSPFv3 Neighbor Table*

```
R2# show ipv6 ospf neighbor

Neighbor ID     Pri   State         Dead Time   Interface ID   Interface
1.1.1.1           0   FULL/  -      00:00:35    6              Serial0/0/1

R2# show ipv6 ospf interface g0/0
GigabitEthernet0/0 is up, line protocol is up
  Link Local Address FE80::FF:FE00:2, Interface ID 3
  Area 23, Process ID 2, Instance ID 0, Router ID 2.2.2.2
  Network Type BROADCAST, Cost: 1
```

```
Transmit Delay is 1 sec, State DR, Priority 1
Designated Router (ID) 2.2.2.2, local address FE80::FF:FE00:2
No backup designated router on this network
Timer intervals configured, Hello 5, Dead 20, Wait 20, Retransmit 5
```

The two commands listed in Example 17-10 confirm that R2 and R3 are not longer neighbors over the LAN. However, just as with the similar OSPFv2 example back in Chapter 11, the router does not issue a syslog message telling us the root cause of the problem. With **show** commands, the only way to find this particular mismatch is to look at both routers with the **show ipv6 ospf interface** command; Example 17-10 shows an example from R2, listing its new values of 5 and 20 for the Hello and dead timers.

OSPFv3 LSDB and LSAs

Once OSPFv3 routers become neighbors, they proceed to exchange their LSDBs over that subnet. In most cases, the two routers exchange their LSDBs directly, and when finished, each router lists its neighbor as having reached a full state. Once in a full state, the two routers should have the same link-state advertisements (LSA) for that area.

This section takes a brief look at the LSDB and the LSAs in an area, which once again look similar to the LSDB and LSAs used for OSPFv2. Then this section looks at one rare configuration issue that allows two routers to become OSPFv3 neighbors for a short time, while causing the topology exchange process to fail.

Verifying OSPFv3 LSAs

OSPFv3 uses similar concepts, with slightly different naming for the equivalent of OSPFv2's Type 1, 2, and 3 LSAs. As explained back in Chapter 8, OSPFv2 uses the Type 1 router LSA and Type 2 network LSA to define the topology inside an area. The Type 3 summary LSA then describes for one area a subnet that exists in some other area—an interarea subnet, if you will.

For the configuration options shown for OSPFv2 in this book, only these three types of LSAs are needed in the OSPFv2 LSDB.

OSPFv3 keeps those same three LSA concepts, renaming the summary LSA. The following list summarizes these three key OSPFv3 LSA types and the reasons why OSPFv3 routers create each:

- One router LSA (Type 1 LSA) for each router in the area (including ABRs attached to the area)
- One network LSA (Type 2 LSA) for each network that has a DR plus one neighbor of the DR
- One interarea prefix (Type 3 LSA) LSA for each IPv6 prefix (subnet) that exists in a different area

For example, in area 4 in the sample network used throughout this chapter, two routers exist: internal router R4 and ABR R1. So, the area 4 LSDB will have a router LSA for each router. One network exists in this area for which a DR will be used (the Ethernet WAN between R1 and R4). R1 and R4 will become neighbors, as well, so one network LSA will be created for that network. Finally, ABR R1 will know about five different IPv6 prefixes that exist outside area 4, so ABR R1 should create and flood five interarea prefix LSAs into area 4. Figure 17-6 shows the conceptual model of these LSAs for area 4.

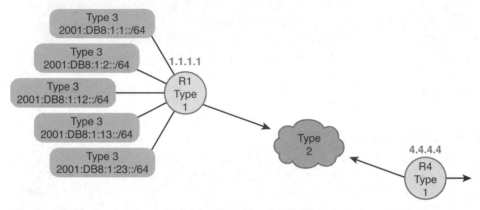

Figure 17-6 *Type 1, 2, and 3 LSAs That Should Exist in Area 4*

Beyond this basic LSA structure, OSPFv3 does make several changes to LSAs compared to OSPFv2. The details inside these LSAs change, and OSPFv3 adds several new LSA types not seen in OSPFv2. However, these details are beyond the scope of this book.

NOTE For perspective, at the time this book was published in 2013, the then-current *CCNP ROUTE Official Cert Guide* did not cover the differences in LSAs between OSPFv2 and OSPFv3 either.

To see the LSAs of Figure 17-6 in an actual router, Example 17-11 lists the beginning of the area 4 LSDB as it exists in router R4. The example highlights the headings and the IPv6 prefixes of the interarea prefix LSAs. Note that the output indeed shows two router LSAs, one line for the single network LSA and five lines with the interarea prefixes.

Example 17-11 *LSDB Content in Area 4, as Viewed from R4*

```
R4# show ipv6 ospf database

            OSPFv3 Router with ID (4.4.4.4) (Process ID 4)

            Router Link States (Area 4)

ADV Router        Age          Seq#         Fragment ID  Link count  Bits
1.1.1.1           258          0x80000072   0            1           B
4.4.4.4           257          0x80000003   0            1           None


            Net Link States (Area 4)
```

```
ADV Router        Age         Seq#          Link ID    Rtr count
   4.4.4.4        257         0x80000001    4          2


               Inter Area Prefix Link States (Area 4)


ADV Router        Age         Seq#          Prefix
   1.1.1.1        878         0x80000069    2001:DB8:1:1::/64
   1.1.1.1        878         0x80000068    2001:DB8:1:2::/64
   1.1.1.1        364         0x8000000A    2001:DB8:1:13::/64
   1.1.1.1        364         0x8000000A    2001:DB8:1:23::/64
   1.1.1.1        364         0x8000000A    2001:DB8:1:12::/64


! Lines omitted for brevity
```

Troubleshooting OSPFv3 LSAs

Database exchange normally works correctly if two routers indeed become neighbors. That is, most of the problems for both OSPFv2 and OSPFv3 show up before the topology database exchange process happens. By way of review, two routers must first pass all the neighbor compatibility checks and reach 2-way state before attempting to exchange the topology databases. So, the configuration problems that prevent routers from becoming neighbors have been passed before the database exchange is attempted.

One misconfiguration problem actually allows two routers to become neighbors, attempt to do database exchange, and then fail after trying for a few minutes. The problem: mismatched IPv4 or IPv6 maximum transmission unit (MTU) sizes.

First, consider the idea of the MTU size, ignoring OSPF for a moment. The MTU size is a setting for a Layer 3 protocol, both IPv4 and IPv6. For now, consider only IPv6. The IPv6 MTU size of an interface defines the maximum size IPv6 packet that the router can forward out an interface. The same idea works for IPv4, with the IPv4 MTU.

NOTE In IPv4, routers can fragment IPv4 packets into smaller packets if a packet exceeds an interface MTU. In IPv6, hosts can detect the smallest MTU over an entire end-to-end route and avoid sending packets that exceed any MTU.

Most router interfaces default to an IPv4 and IPv6 MTU of 1500 bytes. You can change these values with the **ip mtu** *size* and **ipv6 mtu** *size* interface subcommands for IPv4 and IPv6, respectively.

Now think back to OSPFv3 and the fact that two routers can become neighbors and then fail to exchange their LSDBs because of unequal MTU settings. Specifically, the neighbors learn of each other with Hellos, reach a 2-way state, and reach exstart state at the beginning of the database exchange process. However, database exchange fails because of the MTU mismatch, and the neighbor relationship fails to a down state.

Example 17-12 shows an example of that specific failure on R4. The example first changes R4's G0/0 IPv6 MTU to 1400, and then resets the OSPFv3 process.

Example 17-12   *Failure to Exchange the LSDB Because of a Mismatched IPv6 MTU*

```
R4# configure terminal
Enter configuration commands, one per line.  End with CNTL/Z.
R4(config)# interface gigabitethernet0/0
R4(config-if)# ipv6 mtu 1400
R4(config-if)# ^Z
R4#
R4# clear ipv6 ospf 4 process
Reset OSPF process? [no]: yes
R4#
Jan 17 23:53:24.439: %OSPFv3-5-ADJCHG: Process 4, Nbr 1.1.1.1 on GigabitEthernet0/0
from FULL to DOWN, Neighbor Down: Interface down or detached

R4# show ipv6 ospf neighbor


Neighbor ID    Pri   State          Dead Time    Interface ID   Interface
1.1.1.1          1   EXSTART/DR     00:00:37     4              GigabitEthernet0/0


Jan 17 23:55:29.063: %OSPFv3-5-ADJCHG: Process 4, Nbr 1.1.1.1 on GigabitEthernet0/0
from EXSTART to DOWN, Neighbor Down: Too many retransmits
R4# show ipv6 ospf neighbor


Neighbor ID    Pri   State          Dead Time    Interface ID   Interface
1.1.1.1          1   DOWN/DROTHER   -            4              GigabitEthernet0/0
```

The last command in the example may be the key to noticing this particular problem on the exam. The two routers (R1 and R4) know of each other because the OSPF Hello messages have no problems at all. So, the **show ipv6 ospf neighbor** command on each router still lists the other router, as shown in R4's output that mentions neighbor R1 (1.1.1.1). However, after a while, the neighbor relationship fails to a down state. So, when you see a neighbor in what looks like a permanent down state, check the IPv6 MTU on both sides (with the **show ipv6 interface** command).

OSPFv3 Metrics and IPv6 Routes

At the end of all this noise about LSAs, database exchange, matching parameters for neighbors, and so on, the routers need to choose the best IPv6 routes to use. This final topic of the chapter reviews a few verification steps for how OSPFv3 calculates the metrics, and then looks at some more troubleshooting tips—this time about what to do with missing or suboptimal IPv6 routes.

Verifying OSPFv3 Interface Cost and Metrics

The SPF algorithm looks for all possible routes, or paths, from the local router to each and every subnet. When redundant paths exist between the local router and some remote subnet, the SPF algorithm has to pick the better route, based on the lower metric of the end-to-end route, as shown in the example shown earlier in Figure 17-3.

When OSPFv3 adds a route to the IPv6 routing table, the metric for the route is the second of the two numbers in brackets for the route. (The first number in brackets is the administrative distance (AD); the IPv6 routing protocols use the same default AD values as their IPv4 counterparts.)

For example, first focus on the two metric 65 routes R1 learns for subnet 2001:DB8:1:23::/64, as shown in Figure 17-7. For the route through R2, R1 adds its S0/0/0 cost of 64 to R2's G0/0 cost of 1, for a total cost of 65. R1 calculates a metric 65 route through R3, as well. With a default setting of **maximum-paths 4**, R1 placed both routes into the routing table. (One route uses R2 as the next hop, and one uses R3.)

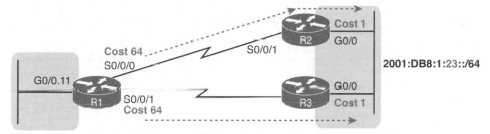

Figure 17-7   *Two Equal-Metric Routes from R1 to 2001:DB8:1:23::/64*

Example 17-13 shows these two routes for subnet 2001:DB8:1:23::/64, as highlighted in the output of the **show ipv6 route ospf** command on router R1. As usual, the OSPF-learned routes list a next-hop link-local address. To see which route refers to R2, and which refers to R3, check the outgoing interfaces and compare them to Figure 17-7.

Example 17-13   *OSPFv3 Routes on R1*

```
R1# show ipv6 route ospf
! Legend omitted for brevity

O    2001:DB8:1:4::/64 [110/1]
     via GigabitEthernet0/1, directly connected
O    2001:DB8:1:23::/64 [110/65]
     via FE80::FF:FE00:3, Serial0/0/1
     via FE80::FF:FE00:2, Serial0/0/0
```

To see an example of what happens when a router has multiple routes but chooses one route because it has a better metric, next look at R2's OSPF-learned IPv6 routes in Example 17-14, focusing on the router to the subnet to the left side of router R1 (subnet 2001:DB8:1:1::/64):

- R2 has two possible routes (per the topology diagram 17-1) to reach subnet 2001:DB8:1:1::/64: one through R1, out R2's S0/0/1 interface; and one through R3, out R2's G0/0 interface.

- R2 only placed one of these two routes into the IPv6 routing table: a route with metric 65, out R2's S0/0/1 interface. This cost is based on R2's default S0/0/1 cost of 64, plus R1's G0/0.11 cost of 1.

■ R2 decided the route through R3 was worse because the cost was the sum of R2's G0/0 cost (1), R3's S0/0/0 cost (64), and R1's G0/0.11 cost (1), for a total of 66.

Figure 17-8 shows the interface costs for these two competing routes. Note that the drawing omits parts of the network as shown earlier in Figure 17-1.

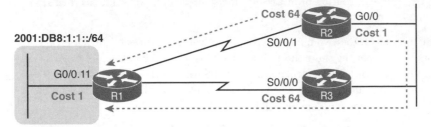

Figure 17-8   *R2's Competing Routes to Reach Subnet 1*

Example 17-14   *OSPFv3 Routes on R1*

```
R2# show ipv6 route ospf
! Legend omitted for brevity
OI  2001:DB8:1:1::/64 [110/65]
     via FE80::FF:FE00:1, Serial0/0/1
OI  2001:DB8:1:2::/64 [110/65]
     via FE80::FF:FE00:1, Serial0/0/1
OI  2001:DB8:1:4::/64 [110/65]
     via FE80::FF:FE00:1, Serial0/0/1
O   2001:DB8:1:13::/64 [110/65]
     via FE80::FF:FE00:3, GigabitEthernet0/0
OI  2001:DB8:1:14::/64 [110/65]
     via FE80::FF:FE00:1, Serial0/0/1
```

Also, note that the code letters on the left of most of these routes on R2 are *OI*. The O identifies the route as being learned by OSPF, and the *I* identifies the route as an interarea route. For instance, the highlighted entry lists prefix/subnet 1 (2001:DB8:1:1::/64), which sits in area 0, and R2 is in area 23. So, R2's route to this subnet is an interarea route. (Earlier, Example 17-13 showed several intra-area OSPF routes, each with code letter O instead of *OI*.)

OSPFv3 displays the settings for OSPFv3 interface cost with commands similar to OSPFv2. For the default calculations, the **show ipv6 ospf** command lists the reference bandwidth, and the **show interfaces** command lists the interface bandwidth. Example 17-15 shows the current OSPFv3 interface costs on R1 with the **show ipv6 ospf interface brief** command.

Example 17-15   *Finding a Router's OSPFv3 Interface Costs*

```
R1# show ipv6 ospf interface brief
Interface     PID   Area      Intf ID   Cost   State  Nbrs F/C
Gi0/0.12      1     0         16        1      DR     0/0
```

Gi0/0.11	1	0	17	1	DR	0/0
Gi0/1	1	4	4	1	BDR	1/1
Se0/0/0	1	23	6	64	P2P	1/1
Se0/0/1	1	23	7	64	P2P	1/1

Troubleshooting IPv6 Routes Added by OSPFv3

If a problem appears to be related to IPv6 routing, the problems can be put into two broad categories. First, a router may be missing a route for some prefix, so the router discards the packet, and pings fail. Second, a router may have a working route, but it appears to take a suboptimal route to the destination. (Chapter 16, "Troubleshooting IPv6 Routing," in the "Traceroute Shows Some Hops, But Fails" section, discusses yet a third category in which a routing loop occurs.)

For example, in Figure 17-9, router R1 has two possible routes to reach subnet 33, an IPv6 subnet off router R3. The top route appears to be the better route, at least in terms of the number of routers between R1 and subnet 33. If R1 has no routes at all to subnet 33, you might look for one type of root cause; but if R1 uses the lower route through five routers, you might look for a different root cause.

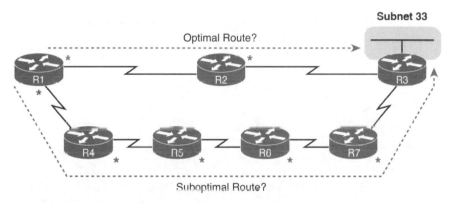

Figure 17-9   *Competing Long and Short Routes from R1 to Subnet 33*

When a router simply has no route to a given subnet—for instance, if R1 has no route at all for subnet 33—do the following:

Step 1.   Check the routers with interfaces directly connected to that IPv6 prefix. A router must have OSPFv3 enabled on that interface before OSPFv3 will advertise about the subnet.

Step 2.   Check OSPFv3 neighbor relationships for all routers between the local router and the routers with an interface connected to IPv6 prefix X.

For instance, in Figure 17-9, if router R3 did not have an **ipv6 ospf** *process-id* **area** *area-id* command on its LAN interface, all seven routers could have working neighbor relationships, but R3 still would not advertise about subnet 33.

If a router has a route, but it appears to be the wrong (suboptimal) route, take these steps:

Step 1. Check for broken neighbor relationships over what should be the optimal path from the local router and prefix Y.

Step 2. Check the OSPFv3 cost settings on the interfaces in the optimal path.

For instance, in Figure 17-9, suppose that R1 indeed has one route for subnet 33, pointing over the lower route, with R4 as the next-hop router. The root cause of that choice could be the following:

- The R2-R3 neighbor relationship is not working.
- The sum of the costs for the top route is larger (worse) than the sum of the costs for the lower route. (Note that the figure shows an asterisk beside each interface whose cost is part of the calculation.)

Exam Preparation Tasks

Review All the Key Topics

Review the most important topics from this chapter, noted with the Key Topic icon. Table 17-4 lists these key topics and where each is discussed.

Table 17-4   Key Topics for Chapter 17

Key Topic Element	Description	Page Number
List	OSPFv3 configuration steps	502
Example 17-4	Multi-area OSPFv3 configuration	506
List	Ways to impact the calculation of the metric for an OSPFv3 route	508
List	Similarities between OSPFv3 and OSPFv2	509
List	Differences between OSPFv3 and OSPFv2	510
List	Common OSPFv3 issues on interfaces	512
Table 17-2	Reasons why OSPF routers fail to become neighbors	515
Table 17-3	Commands to verify OSPFv3 neighbor requirements	515
List	Three common OSPFv3 LSA types in a multi-area design	517
List	Common OSPFv3 issues for missing IPv6 routes	523
List	Common OSPFv3 issues for having a suboptimal OSPFv3 route	524

Complete the Tables and Lists from Memory

Print a copy of DVD Appendix D, "Memory Tables," or at least the section for this chapter, and complete the tables and lists from memory. DVD Appendix E, "Memory Tables Answer Key," includes completed tables and lists to check your work.

Definitions of Key Terms

After your first reading of the chapter, try to define these key terms, but do not be concerned about getting them all correct at that time. Chapter 22 directs you in how to use these terms for late-stage preparation for the exam.

multi-area, area border router, internal router, backbone area, router ID, full, 2-way, router LSA, network LSA, interarea prefix LSA, maximum transmission unit (MTU)

Command Reference to Check Your Memory

Although you should not necessarily memorize the information in the tables in this section, this section does include a reference for the configuration and EXEC commands covered in this chapter. Practically speaking, you should memorize the commands as a side effect of reading the chapter and doing all the activities in this exam preparation section. To see how well you have memorized the commands as a side effect of your other studies, cover the left side of the table, read the descriptions on the right side, and see if you remember the command.

Table 17-5   Chapter 17 Configuration Command Reference

Command	Description
ipv6 router ospf *process-id*	Enters OSPF configuration mode for the listed process
ipv6 ospf *process-id* area *area-number*	Interface subcommand that enables OSPFv3 on the interface, for a particular process, and defines the OSPFv3 area
ipv6 ospf cost *interface-cost*	Interface subcommand that sets the OSPF cost associated with the interface
bandwidth *bandwidth*	Interface subcommand that directly sets the interface bandwidth (Kbps)
auto-cost reference-bandwidth *number*	Router subcommand that tells OSPF the numerator in the *Ref-BW/Int-BW* formula used to calculate the OSPF cost based on the interface bandwidth
router-id *id*	OSPF command that statically sets the router ID
maximum-paths *number-of-paths*	Router subcommand that defines the maximum number of equal-cost routes that can be added to the routing table

Table 17-6   Chapter 17 **show** Command Reference

Command	Description
show ipv6 ospf	Lists information about the OSPF process running on the router, including the OSPF router ID, areas to which the router connects and the number of interfaces in each area.
show ipv6 ospf interface brief	Lists the interfaces on which the OSPF protocol is enabled (based on the **network** commands), including passive interfaces.
show ipv6 ospf interface *type number*	Lists a long section of settings, status, and counters for OSPF operation on all interfaces, or on the listed interface, including the Hello and dead timers.
show ipv6 protocols	Lists all means through which a router can learn or build IPv6 routes, including the interfaces on which each routing protocol is enabled.

Command	Description
show ipv6 ospf neighbor [*type number*]	Lists brief output about neighbors, identified by neighbor router ID, including current state, with one line per neighbor; optionally, limit the output to neighbors on the listed interface.
show ipv6 ospf neighbor *neighbor-ID*	Lists the same output as the **show ip ospf neighbor detail** command, but only for the listed neighbor (by neighbor router ID).
show ipv6 ospf database	Lists a summary of the LSAs in the database, with one line of output per LSA. It is organized by LSA type (first Type 1, then Type 2, and so on).
show ipv6 route	Lists all IPv4 routes.
show ipv6 route ospf	Lists routes in the routing table learned by OSPF.
show ipv6 route *prefix/length*	Shows a detailed description of the route for the listed subnet/mask.

17

This chapter covers the following exam topics:

IP Routing Technologies

Configure and verify EIGRP (single AS)

Feasible distance / feasible successors /administrative distance

Feasibility condition

Metric composition

Router ID

Path selection

Load balancing

Equal

Unequal

Passive interface

Differentiate methods of routing and routing protocols

metric

next hop

Troubleshooting

Troubleshoot and Resolve EIGRP problems

Neighbor adjacencies

AS number

Load balancing

Split horizon

CHAPTER 18

Implementing EIGRP for IPv6

When creating Enhanced Interior Gateway Routing Protocol (EIGRP) for IPv6 (EIGRPv6), Cisco made the new EIGRPv6 as much like EIGRP for IPv4 (EIGRPv4) as possible. How close are they? Incredibly close, even closer than the IPv4 and IPv6 versions of the Open Shortest Path First (OSPF) Protocol. With EIGRP, the only noticeable difference is the configuration, which enables EIGRPv6 directly on the interfaces and, of course, the use of IPv6 addresses and prefixes. However, the old and new EIGRP protocols are practically twins when it comes to the concepts, **show** commands, and troubleshooting steps.

This chapter follows the same sequence as the preceding chapter. The first major section shows the EIGRPv6 configuration options, comparing those steps with EIGRPv4. The second major section shows how to verify EIGRPv6 while giving some troubleshooting tips.

"Do I Know This Already?" Quiz

Use the "Do I Know This Already?" quiz to help decide whether you might want to skim this chapter, or a major section, moving more quickly to the "Exam Preparation Tasks" section near the end of the chapter. You can find the answers at the bottom of the page following the quiz. For thorough explanations, see DVD Appendix C, "Answers to the 'Do I Know This Already?' Quizzes."

Table 18-1   "Do I Know This Already?" Foundation Topics Section-to-Question Mapping

Foundation Topics Section	Questions
EIGRPv6 Configuration	1–3
EIGRPv6 Concepts, Verification, and Troubleshooting	4–6

1. An enterprise uses a dual-stack model of deployment for IPv4 and IPv6, using EIGRP as the routing protocol for both. Router R1 has IPv4 and IPv6 addresses on its G0/0 and S0/0/0 interfaces only, with EIGRPv4 and EIGRPv6 enabled on both interfaces. Which of the following answers is a valid way to configure R1 so that it enables EIGRPv6 on the exact same interfaces as EIGRPv4 in this case?

    a. Adding the **dual-stack all-interfaces** router subcommand for EIGRPv6

    b. Adding the **dual-stack** interface subcommand to interfaces G0/0 and S0/0/0

    c. Adding the **ipv6 eigrp** *asn* interface subcommand to interfaces G0/0 and S0/0/0

    d. Adding the **dual-stack all-interfaces** router subcommand for EIGRPv4

2. Which of the following configuration settings do not have a separate IPv4/EIGRPv4 and IPv6/EIGRPv6 setting, instead using one setting that both EIGRPv4 and EIGRPv6 both use?

    a. Interface bandwidth

    b. Hello timer

    c. Variance

    d. Maximum paths

3. An enterprise uses a dual-stack model of deployment for IPv4 and IPv6, using EIGRP as the routing protocol for both. Router R1 has IPv4 and IPv6 addresses on its G0/0 and S0/0/0 interfaces only, with EIGRPv4 and EIGRPv6 enabled on both interfaces and the router ID explicitly set for both protocols. Comparing the EIGRPv4 and EIGRPv6 configuration, which of the following statements are true?

    a. The EIGRPv6 configuration uses the **router eigrp** *asn* global command

    b. Both protocols use the **router-id** *router-id* router subcommand

    c. Both protocols use the **network** *network-number* router subcommand

    d. The EIGRPv6 configuration uses the **ipv6 eigrp** *asn* interface subcommand

4. Three redundant IPv6 routes exist on R1 to reach IPv6 subnet 9 (2009:9:9:9::/64), a subnet connected to router R9's G0/0 interface. R1's current successor route uses R2 as the next hop, with feasible successor routes through routers R3 and R4. Then, another engineer makes changes to the configuration in the network, resulting in R1 having no routes to reach subnet 9. Which of the answers lists one configuration that would result in R1 having no routes at all to subnet 9?

    a. Make R9's G0/0 interface passive.

    b. Change R2's EIGRP ASN to some other number, but otherwise keep the same configuration.

    c. Change the Hello timers on all of R1's interfaces from 5 to 4.

    d. Change R1's EIGRP ASN to some other number, but otherwise keep the same configuration.

5. R1 and R2 are routers that connect to the same VLAN. Which of the answers lists an item that can prevent the two routers from becoming EIGRPv6 neighbors? (Choose two answers.)

    a. Mismatched Hello timers

    b. Mismatched ASNs

    c. IPv6 addresses in different subnets

    d. Using the same router ID

    e. One passive router interface (used on this link)

6. The output of the **show ipv6 eigrp neighbors** command from R2 lists one neighbor. Which of the following answers is correct about the meaning of the output of the command in this example?

```
R2# show ipv6 eigrp neighbors
EIGRP-IPv6 Neighbors for AS(1)
H   Address              Interface     Hold Uptime   SRTT   RTO  Q  Seq
                                       (sec)         (ms)        Cnt Num
0   Link-local address:  Gi0/0         11 06:46:11    1     100  0  30
    FE80::FF:FE22.2222
```

   a. The neighbor's link-local address on their common link must be FE80::FF:FE22:2222.

   b. The neighbor's EIGRPv6 router ID must be FE80::FF:FE22:2222.

   c. R2's link-local address on their common link must be FE80::FF:FE22:2222.

   d. R2's EIGRPv6 router ID must be FE80::FF:FE22:2222.

18

Foundation Topics

EIGRPv6 Configuration

EIGRPv6 behaves much like its IPv4 counterpart, EIGRP. Once enabled on all routers in an internetwork, the routers exchange EIGRP messages. Those messages allow the routers to discover neighbors, form neighbor relationships, advertise subnets along with their metric components, and calculate metrics for competing routes using the same old calculation. EIGRPv6 also uses the same successor and feasible successor (FS) logic, and DUAL processing when no FS exists.

Differences do exist, of course, with the most obvious being that EIGRPv6 advertises IPv6 prefixes, not IPv4 subnets. The messages flow in IPv6 packets, many going to IPv6 multicast address FF02::A. But most of the big ideas mirror EIGRP for IPv4.

EIGRPv6 configuration requires the usual steps for all routing protocols. The EIGRPv6 routing protocol process must be created, and then the protocol must then be enabled on various interfaces. The rest of the EIGRPv6 configuration is optional, to change some default setting, with changes to what happens between neighbors, what metric is calculated, and so on.

This first section first works through both the most common EIGRPv6 configuration commands, followed by a look at the various other commands used to change some small feature.

EIGRPv6 Configuration Basics

EIGRPv6 configuration works much like OSPFv3. That is, the commands create the EIGRPv6 process in one part of the configuration, with interface subcommands enabling the routing protocol on the interface. Figure 18-1 shows the fundamentals of this core configuration for IPv6.

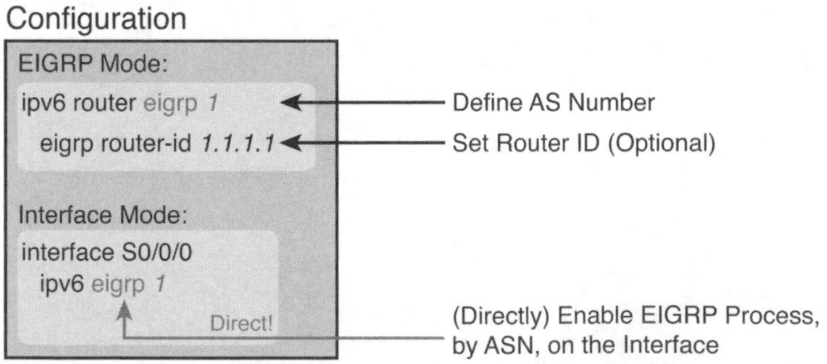

Configuration

Figure 18-1 *Fundamentals of EIGRPv6 Configuration*

If you remember EIGRPv4 configuration, you will quickly see one key difference between the configuration in Figure 18-1 and what you know about EIGRPv4. The example in the figure does not use any EIGRP **network** commands at all because EIGRPv6 does not even support the **network** command. Instead, it uses the **ipv6 eigrp asn** interface subcommand. This process works like the OSPFv3 configuration from the preceding chapter, just with a slightly different command for EIGRPv6.

The rest of the EIGRPv6 configuration commands work either exactly like the EIGRPv4 commands or very similarly to them. To show the similarities, Table 18-2 lists the EIGRPv4 configuration options introduced in Chapter 10, "Implementing EIGRP for IPv4," making comparisons to the similar configuration options in EIGRPv6.

Table 18-2   Comparison of EIGRPv4 and EIGRPv6 Configuration Commands

Function	EIGRPv4	EIGRPv6
Create process, define ASN	**router eigrp** *as-number*	**ipv6 router eigrp** *as-number*
Define router ID explicitly (router mode)	**eigrp router-id** *number*	Identical
Change number of concurrent routes (router mode)	**maximum-paths** *number*	Identical
Set the variance multiplier (router mode)	**variance** *multiplier*	Identical
Influence metric calculation (interface mode)	**bandwidth** *value* **delay** *value*	Identical
Change Hello and hold timers (interface mode)	**ip hello-interval eigrp** *asn time* **ip hold-time eigrp** *asn time*	Change **ip** to **ipv6**
Enable EIGRP on an interface	**network** *ip-address* [*wildcard mask*]	**ipv6 eigrp** *as-number* (interface subcommand)
Disable and enable automatic summarization (router mode)	[**no**] **auto-summary**	Not needed for EIGRPv6

EIGRPv6 Configuration Example

To show EIGRPv6 configuration in context, the next several pages show an example using the internetwork from Figure 18-2. The figure shows the IPv6 subnets. It also shows the last quartet of each router's interface IPv6 address as ::X, where X is the router number, to make it more obvious as to which router uses which address.

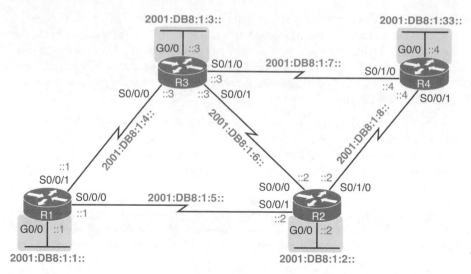

Figure 18-2 *The Internetwork for an Example Multi-Area EIGRPv6 Configuration*

Note that Figure 18-2 mimics Figure 10-3, used in several EIGRPv4 examples in Chapter 10. Figure 18-2 uses the exact same interface types and numbers and router names. In fact, it uses a similar subnet numbering pattern. For instance, think of the four LAN-based IPv6 subnets as subnets 1, 2, 3, and 33, based on the last quartet values. Those same subnets in the examples in Chapter 10, based on the third octet of the IPv4 subnet numbers, are also 1, 2, 3, and 33, respectively.

Why does it matter that the internetwork used for this chapter mirrors the one used in Chapter 10? Not only are the EIGRP configuration commands similar but also the **show** command output. The **show** commands in this chapter, by using the exact same network topology, list almost the exact same output for EIGRPv6 as they did for EIGRPv4.

For this specific example, Example 18-1 begins by listing the additional IPv6 configuration required on R1 to make it a dual-stack router, including EIGRPv6 configuration. The highlighted lines are the EIGRPv6-specific configuration commands, while the rest of the configuration adds IPv6 routing and addressing.

Example 18-1 *IPv6 and EIGRPv6 Configuration on Router R1*

```
ipv6 unicast-routing
!
ipv6 router eigrp 1
 eigrp router-id 1.1.1.1
!
interface GigabitEthernet0/0
 ipv6 address 2001:db8:1:1::1/64
 ipv6 eigrp 1
!
interface serial 0/0/0
 description link to R2
```

```
  ipv6 address 2001:db8:1:5::1/64
  ipv6 eigrp 1
 !
interface serial 0/0/1
 description link to R3
 ipv6 address 2001:db8:1:4::1/64
 ipv6 eigrp 1
```

With this first example, take a few moments to review the configuration thoroughly. All the routers need to use the same EIGRPv6 autonomous system number (ASN), as configured on the **ipv6 router eigrp** *asn* global command. Just after this command, the R1 explicitly sets its EIGRP router ID (RID) using the **eigrp router-id** command. Note that EIGRPv6 also uses a 32-bit RID, as does OSPFv3, with the same exact rules for how a router picks the value.

The rest of the configuration simply enables EIGRPv6 on each interface by referring to the correct EIGRPv6 process, by ASN, using the **ipv6 eigrp** *asn* interface subcommand.

Example 18-2 shows the configuration on a second router (R2). Note that it also uses ASN 1 because it must match the ASN used by router R1. Otherwise, these two routers will not become neighbors. Also, note that R2 sets its RID to 2.2.2.2.

Example 18-2   *EIGRPv6 Configuration on R2*

```
ipv6 unicast-routing
!
ipv6 router eigrp 1
 eigrp router-id 2.2.2.2
!
interface GigabitEthernet0/0
 ipv6 address 2001:db8:1:2::2/64
 ipv6 eigrp 1
!
interface serial 0/0/0
 description link to R3
 ipv6 address 2001:db8:1:6::2/64
 ipv6 eigrp 1
!
interface serial 0/0/1
 description link to R1
 ipv6 address 2001:db8:1:5::2/64
 ipv6 eigrp 1
!
interface serial 0/1/0
 description link to R4
 ipv6 address 2001:db8:1:8::2/64
 ipv6 eigrp 1
```

18

> **NOTE**   IOS allows the EIGRPv6 routing process to be disabled, and then reenabled, using the **shutdown** and **no shutdown** commands in EIGRP configuration mode. Examples 18-1 and 18-2 do not include the **no shutdown** command because the IOS version used on the routers for this book (15.2(M)) defaults to an enabled (**no shutdown**) state. However, note that earlier IOS versions defaulted to a disabled state, requiring the configuration of a **no shutdown** command in EIGRP configuration mode before EIGRPv6 would work.

Other EIGRPv6 Configuration Settings

The example shows the basics for EIGRPv6 configuration. The next few pages discuss a few configuration options in comparison to EIGRPv4.

Setting Bandwidth and Delay to Influence EIGRPv6 Route Selection

By default, EIGRPv6 uses the exact same settings as EIGRPv4 when calculating the metrics for each route. And to be extra clear, the settings are not similar or simply using the same command syntax. EIGRPv6 uses the exact same settings as EIGRPv4, specifically the interface bandwidth and delay settings, as configured with the **bandwidth** and **delay** interface subcommands. A change to these values impacts both EIGRPv4's calculation of metrics as well as EIGRPv6's calculation.

EIGRPv6 also uses the exact same formula as EIGRPv4 to calculate the metric for a route. As a result, in some conditions, the EIGRPv4 metric for a route to an IPv4 subnet will be the same metric as the EIGRPv6 route from the same router to IPv6 subnet in the same location.

For instance, in Figure 18-3, all the routers are dual-stack routers, with EIGRPv4 and EIGRPv6 enabled on all the interfaces in the design. Subnet 10.1.33.0/24 has been noted in the upper right, in the same location as IPv6 subnet 33 (2001:DB8:1:33::/64). R1's EIGRPv4 and EIGRPv6 processes will calculate the same exact metric for these routes based on the same collection of interface bandwidth and delay settings.

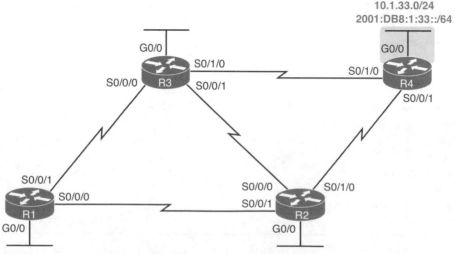

Figure 18-3   *Same Location off R4 for IPv4 Subnet 33 and IPv6 Subnet 33*

Example 18-3 shows the IPv4 and IPv6 routes on R1 for the subnets shown in Figure 18-3. Note the highlighted metrics in all cases are 2,684,416.

Example 18-3   *Identical Metrics for IPv4 and IPv6 Routes with EIGRPv4 and EIGRPv6*

```
R1# show ip route | section 10.1.33.0
D        10.1.33.0/24 [90/2684416] via 10.1.5.2, 00:02:23, Serial0/0/0
                      [90/2684416] via 10.1.4.3, 00:02:23, Serial0/0/1


R1# show ipv6 route | section 2001:DB8:1:33::/64
D   2001:DB8:1:33::/64 [90/2684416]
      via FE80::FF:FE00:3, Serial0/0/1
      via FE80::FF:FE00:2, Serial0/0/0
```

Note that both commands list two equal-cost routes on R1, for subnet 33, but the format of the output differs a little. The format of the **show ip route** command puts the destination subnet on the same first line as the first route's forwarding instructions. The **show ipv6 route** command lists the destination prefix on the first line, with each route's forwarding instructions on the second and third lines, respectively.

EIGRP Load Balancing

EIGRPv6 and EIGRPv4 use the exact same concepts, with the exact same configuration command syntax, for equal-cost and unequal-cost load balancing. However, EIGRPv6 has its own configuration settings, made with the **maximum-paths** and **variance** commands inside EIGRPv6 configuration mode. EIGRPv4 has separate settings, using these same two commands, in EIGRPv4 configuration mode.

For example, imagine that in a dual-stack network, the routers use EIGRPv4 and EIGRPv6. The network engineer would probably choose the same **variance** and **maximum-paths** settings for both routing protocols. However, for the sake of pointing out the differences, imagine the engineer chose different settings, like these:

- **EIGRPv4:** At most 2 routes, with variance 3 for unequal cost routes
- **EIGRPv6:** At most 5 routes, with variance 4 for unequal cost routes

Example 18-4 shows how to make these different settings for these two different routing processes. However, note that the commands happen to use the exact same syntax.

Example 18-4   *Setting Load-Balancing Parameters per Routing Process*

```
R1# configure terminal
Enter configuration commands, one per line.  End with CNTL/Z.
! First, configure the settings for IPv4
R1(config)# router eigrp 10
R1(config-router)# maximum-paths 2
R1(config-router)# variance 3
! Next, configure the similar settings for IPv6
R1(config-router)# ipv6 router eigrp 11
```

18

```
R1(config-rtr)# maximum-paths 5
R1(config-rtr)# variance 4
R1(config-rtr)# ^Z
R1#
```

EIGRP Timers

EIGRPv6 and EIGRPv4 use the exact same concepts for the Hello and hold timers as does EIGRPv4. To allow these values to be set differently for each routing process, IOS gives us slightly different syntax on the EIGRPv6 and EIGRPv4 commands, with the EIGRPv6 commands using the keyword **ipv6** rather than **ip**. Otherwise, the EIGRPv6 syntax mirrors the EIGRPv4 version of the commands.

Example 18-5 shows a sample that changes both the EIGRPv4 and EIGRPv6 Hello timer, just to show the different commands side by side. For EIGRPv4, the Hello timer is set to 6 seconds, and for EIGRPv6, it is set to 7 seconds.

Example 18-5   *Setting the EIGRPv4 and EIGRPv6 Hello Timers*

```
R1# configure terminal
Enter configuration commands, one per line.  End with CNTL/Z.
R1(config)# interface gigabitethernet0/1
R1(config-if)# ip hello-interval eigrp 10 6
R1(config-if)# ipv6 hello-interval eigrp 11 7
R1(config-rtr)# ^Z
R1#
```

The choices for the timer values are arbitrary, just to make it clear which command is for each routing protocol. In real networks, these settings will likely have the same values for both EIGRPv4 and EIGRPv6.

EIGRPv6 Concepts, Verification, and Troubleshooting

To the depth discussed in this book, EIGRPv4 and EIGRPv6 behave almost identically. Earlier, Table 18-2 listed the configuration commands, side by side, to show the similarities. This second major section of the chapter now looks at EIGRPv6 verification and troubleshooting, with even more similarities between EIGRPv6 as its older cousin EIGRPv4.

So many similarities exist between EIGRPv6 and EIGRPv4 that you should just assume that they work the same, except for a few differences, as noted in the following list:

- EIGRPv6 advertises IPv6 prefixes, whereas EIGRPv4 advertises IPv4 subnets.

- EIGRPv6 **show** commands use a keyword of **ipv6**, in the sample position where EIGRP **show** commands use a keyword of **ip**.

- EIGRPv6 uses the same checklist for choosing whether to become neighbors, except EIGRPv6 routers may become neighbors if they have IPv6 addresses in difference subnets. (EIGRPv4 neighbors must be in the same IPv4 subnet.)

- EIGRPv6 does not have an autosummary concept (while EIGRPv4 does).

As you can see, the list of differences mentioned here is short. The similarities will become clearer through the many examples of **show** command output in the remainder of this chapter. To begin, Figure 18-4 reviews the EIGRPv6 **show** commands discussed in this chapter. Note that all the commands in the figure use the same syntax as the EIGRPv4 equivalent but with **ip** changed to **ipv6**.

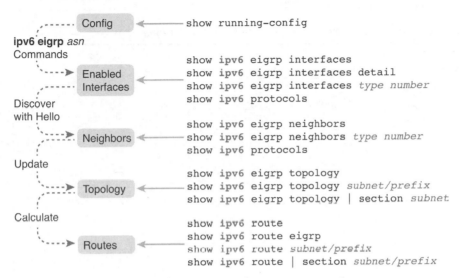

Figure 18-4 *Reference of EIGRPv6 Verification Commands*

Similar to the preceding chapter's flow, this chapter's second major section breaks the discussion down in the same general sequence as EIGRPv6 does when bringing up the EIGRPv6 process. This section first examines EIGRPv6 interfaces, then neighbors, topology, and finally, IPv6 routes.

> **NOTE** All the troubleshooting examples in the rest of this chapter use the example configuration from routers R1, R2, R3, and R4, as shown in Figure 18-2.

EIGRPv6 Interfaces

By enabling EIGRPv6 on an interface, the router attempts to do two things:

1. Discover EIGRPv6 neighbors off that interface
2. Advertise about the prefix connected to that interface

To make sure that EIGRPv6 works correctly, an engineer should verify that EIGRPv6 is enabled on the right interfaces. Or, from a troubleshooting perspective, some of the most common problems with EIGRPv6 may be because a router did not enable EIGRPv6 on an interface.

As was the case for EIGRPv4, with EIGRPv6, some commands list all interfaces on which EIGRP is enabled (including passive), some list all EIGRP interfaces but note which are passive, and some simply do not list the passive interfaces. Example 18-6 shows a sample that points out these differences, by first making R1's G0/0 interface passive. It then lists output from the **show ipv6 eigrp interfaces** command, which omits G0/0, and then **show ipv6 protocols** command, which includes G0/0, but noted as a passive interface.

Example 18-6   *Verifying OSPFv3 Interfaces and Related Parameters*

```
R1# configure terminal
Enter configuration commands, one per line.  End with CNTL/Z.
R1(config)# ipv6 router eigrp 1
R1(config-rtr)# passive-interface g0/0
R1(config-rtr)# ^Z
R1#

R1# show ipv6 eigrp interfaces
EIGRP-IPv6 Interfaces for AS(1)
                        Xmit Queue    Mean   Pacing Time   Multicast    Pending
Interface      Peers    Un/Reliable   SRTT   Un/Reliable   Flow Timer   Routes
Se0/0/0          1        0/0          1       0/15          50           0
Se0/0/1          1        0/0          1       0/15          50           0


R1# show ipv6 protocols
IPv6 Routing Protocol is "connected"
IPv6 Routing Protocol is "eigrp 1"
EIGRP-IPv6 Protocol for AS(1)
  Metric weight K1=1, K2=0, K3=1, K4=0, K5=0
  NSF-aware route hold timer is 240
  Router-ID: 1.1.1.1
  Topology : 0 (base)
    Active Timer: 3 min
    Distance: internal 90 external 170
    Maximum path: 16
    Maximum hopcount 100
    Maximum metric variance 1

  Interfaces:
    Serial0/0/0
    Serial0/0/1
    GigabitEthernet0/0 (passive)
  Redistribution:
    None
IPv6 Routing Protocol is "ND"
```

Note that the **show ipv6 eigrp interfaces** command lists many lines of output per interface. Also, like the **show ipv6 protocols** command, it lists all EIGRP-enabled interfaces, including passive interfaces.

Next, focus for a moment on troubleshooting related to EIGRPv6 interfaces. As with OSPF, most troubleshooting revolves around the neighbor relationships. However, this short list describes two problems that can happen related to the interfaces:

- The omission of an **ipv6 eigrp** *asn* interface subcommand on an interface that has no possible neighbors may go overlooked. This omission does not impact EIGRPv6 neighbors. However, this omission means that EIGRPv6 is not enabled on that interface, and therefore the router will not advertise about that connected subnet. This problem shows up as a missing route.

- Making an interface passive to the EIGRPv6 process, when a potential EIGRPv6 neighbor is connected to that link, prevents the two routers from becoming neighbors. Note that the neighbor relationship fails with just one of the two routers having a passive interface.

For example, consider router R4 in this chapter's sample network. Its G0/0 interface connects to a LAN, with no other routers. Currently, R4's configuration includes the **ipv6 eigrp 1** interface subcommand on R4's G0/0 interface. If instead that command were mistakenly missing (or if it were just removed as an experiment in lab), R4 would not advertise a route for the connected subnet (subnet 33, or 2001:DB8:1:33::/64).

Example 18-7 shows that specific example. To re-create the problem, though, before gathering the output in Example 18-7 on R4, the **no ipv6 eigrp 1** command was issued on R4's G0/0 interface, disabling EIGRP from that interface. Example 18-7 then shows R1 does not have a route to subnet 33 or EIGRP topology data.

Example 18-7   *Missing Route to Subnet 33 on R1*

```
R1# show ipv6 route 2001:DB8:1:33::
% Route not found


R1# show ipv6 eigrp topology | include 2001:DB8:1:33
R1#
```

EIGRPv6 Neighbors

From one perspective, EIGRP neighbor relationships are simple. When two EIGRPv6 routers sit on the same data link, they discover each other with EIGRPv6 Hello messages. Those Hello messages list some parameters, and the neighbors check the Hello to determine whether the routers should be come neighbors:

- If the parameters match, each router adds the other router to their EIGRPv6 neighbor table, as listed with the **show ipv6 eigrp neighbors** command.

- If the parameters do not match, the routers do not become neighbors, do not add each other to their neighbor tables, and do not list each other in the output of the **show ipv6 eigrp neighbors** command.

From another perspective, troubleshooting EIGRP neighbor relationships means that you have to remember a lot of small details. The neighbors check lists of parameters that must match. At the same time, other problems can prevent the routers from becoming neighbors as well. Thankfully, EIGRPv6 uses the same list as EIGRPv4, with one noticeable difference: EIGRPv6 does not require the neighbors to be in the same subnet.

Table 18-3 lists the items to consider when troubleshooting EIGRP neighbor relationships.

Table 18-3   Neighbor Requirements for EIGRPv4 and EIGRPv6

Requirement	EIGRPv4	EIGRPv6
Interfaces must be in an up/up state.	Yes	Yes
Interfaces must be in the same subnet.	Yes	No
Access control lists (ACL) must not filter routing protocol messages.	Yes	Yes
Must pass routing protocol neighbor authentication (if configured).	Yes	Yes
Must use the same ASN on the **router** configuration command.	Yes	Yes
K-values must match.	Yes[1]	Yes[1]
Hello and hold timers must match.	No	No
Router IDs must be unique.	No[2]	No[2]

[1] K values define the EIGRP metric calculation algorithm. This book does not discuss how to change these settings, and Cisco recommends that the settings be left as is.

[2] Having duplicate EIGRP RIDs does not prevent routers from becoming neighbors, but it can cause problems when external EIGRP routes are added to the routing table.

For instance, in the configuration example in this chapter, all four routers used EIGRPv6 ASN 1. However, suppose that router R2's configuration had mistakenly used ASN 2, while the other three routers correctly used ASN 1. What would happen? R2 would have failed to form a neighbor relationship with any of the other routers.

Many EIGRPv6 **show** commands mention the EIGRPv6 ASN, but the **show ipv6 protocols** command shows the value in a couple of obvious places. Example 18-6, earlier, shows this.

As a troubleshooting strategy for the exam, note that every pair of EIGRPv6 routers on the same link should become neighbors. So, when an exam question appears to point to some IPv6 routing problem, check the routers, count the EIGRP neighbor relationships and make sure all the neighbor relationships exist. If any are missing, start troubleshooting EIGRPv6 neighbor relationships based on Table 18-3.

To examine the neighbors, use the **show ipv6 eigrp neighbors** command. Because of the length of IPv6 addresses, this command lists two lines per neighbor rather than one line (as is the case with the EIGRPv4 version of this command). The output in Example 18-8 shows this command's output from router R2, with highlights in two lines for a single neighbor (R3).

Example 18-8   *R2's EIGRPv6 Neighbors*

```
R2# show ipv6 eigrp neighbors
EIGRP-IPv6 Neighbors for AS(1)
H    Address                 Interface          Hold Uptime   SRTT   RTO  Q   Seq
                                                (sec)         (ms)        Cnt Num
```

```
2    Link-local address:    Se0/1/0                    10 06:37:34 104   624  0  13
     FE80::D68C:B5FF:FE6B:DB48
1    Link-local address:    Se0/0/0                    11 06:37:54   1   100  0  38
     FE80::FF:FE00:3
0    Link-local address:    Se0/0/1                    11 06:46:11   1   100  0  30
     FE80::FF:FE00:1
```

Take a moment to focus on the IPv6 address and interface listed in the highlighted two lines. The output, taken from router R2, lists R3's link-local address that sits on the other end of R2's S0/0/0 interface. The listed S0/0/0 interface is R2's interface. In summary, the details list the local router's interface and the neighbor's link-local address. So, to identify the EIGRPv6 neighbor, you have to use that neighbor's link-local address (and not their EIGRPv6 RID).

EIGRPv6 Topology Database

If you keep the discussions to topics within the scope of this book, once EIGRPv6 routers become neighbors, they should exchange all appropriate topology data. Outside the scope of this book, other router features can filter the topology data sent between routers. But for now, if the neighbor comes up, you can assume they exchange the topology data.

However, you should be ready to interpret the meaning of some of the topology data described by EIGRPv6. Thankfully, the EIGRPv6 topology data works just like it does for EIGRPv4, other than one obvious difference: It lists IPv6 prefixes. The following list points out the concepts that remain identical between the two:

■ The metric components (bandwidth, delay, reliability, load).

■ The metric calculation uses the same math.

■ The idea of a successor route (the best route).

■ The idea of FS routes.

■ The feasibility condition, in which the reported distance (the composite metric reported by the neighbor) is lower (better) than the local router's metric.

For example, Figure 18-5 shows an excerpt from the output of the **show ipv6 eigrp topology** command. This output shows R1's topology data for subnet 3 (2001:DB8:1:3::/64), the subnet off R3's G0/0 LAN interface. The left side shows the two details particular to IPv6: the IPv6 prefix/length and the next-hop router's link-local address.

Note that while the left side shows the IPv6 prefix and IPv6 next-hop router address, the right side shows the exact same ideas as used with EIGRPv4. In fact, this example mirrors an example back in Chapter 10, shown there as Figure 10-4. That chapter also showed topology data from R1's database for the subnet off R3's G0/0 LAN interface. However, that example was for EIGRPv4 and for subnet 10.1.3.0/24. If you take the time to flip back to Figure 10-4, you will see the exact same information for all the data on the right based on the EIGRPv4 topology database, but IPv4 information about the subnet, mask, and next-hop address on the left.

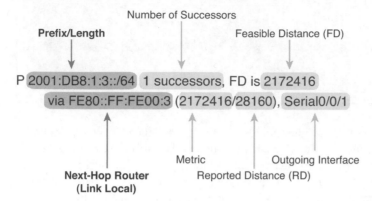

Figure 18-5 *Comparing IPv6 Details Versus Common Parts of EIGRP Topology Data*

In short, study Chapter 10's details about the metric components, the metric computed as a formula, the successor and FS, and so on. If you master those details for EIGRPv4, you have mastered the equivalent for EIGRPv6.

Example 18-9 shows the EIGRP topology table for one last insight into the internals of EIGRPv6. The output shows R1's detailed topology data for subnet 3 (2001:DB8:1:3::/64). Note that the first highlighted line lists the next-hop address and outgoing interface. It lists the composite metric—that is, the metric as calculated from the input of the various metric components—on the second highlighted line. The next two highlighted lines show the two metric components that impact the calculation (by default): bandwidth and delay. Finally, note that it mentions that EIGRP uses the minimum bandwidth (1544 Kbps) and the total delay (20,100).

Example 18-9 *R2's EIGRPv6 Neighbors*

```
R1# show ipv6 eigrp topology 2001:DB8:1:3::/64
EIGRP-IPv6 Topology Entry for AS(1)/ID(1.1.1.1) for 2001:DB8:1:3::/64
  State is Passive, Query origin flag is 1, 1 Successor(s), FD is 2172416
  Descriptor Blocks:
  FE80::FF:FE00:3 (Serial0/0/1), from FE80::FF:FE00:3, Send flag is 0x0
      Composite metric is (2172416/28160), route is Internal
      Vector metric:
        Minimum bandwidth is 1544 Kbit
        Total delay is 20100 microseconds
        Reliability is 255/255
        Load is 1/255
        Minimum MTU is 1500
        Hop count is 1
        Originating router is 3.3.3.3
  FE80::FF:FE00:2 (Serial0/0/0), from FE80::FF:FE00:2, Send flag is 0x0
      Composite metric is (2684416/2172416), route is Internal
      Vector metric:
        Minimum bandwidth is 1544 Kbit
        Total delay is 40100 microseconds
```

```
      Reliability is 255/255
      Load is 1/255
      Minimum MTU is 1500
      Hop count is 2
```

EIGRPv6 IPv6 Routes

Verifying EIGRPv6-learned routes is relatively easy as long as you realize that the code for EIGRP is D and not E. Example 18-10 shows R1's entire IPv6 routing table, with six EIGRP-learned IPv6 routes.

Example 18-10 *EIGRPv6 Routes on R1*

```
R1# show ipv6 route
IPv6 Routing Table - default - 13 entries
Codes: C - Connected, L - Local, S - Static, U - Per-user Static route
       B - BGP, R - RIP, I1 - ISIS L1, I2 - ISIS L2
       IA - ISIS interarea, IS - ISIS summary, D - EIGRP, EX - EIGRP external
       ND - Neighbor Discovery, l - LISP
       O   OSPF Intra, OI - OSPF Inter, OE1 - OSPF ext 1, OE2 - OSPF ext 2
       ON1 - OSPF NSSA ext 1, ON2 - OSPF NSSA ext 2
C   2001:DB8:1:1::/64 [0/0]
     via GigabitEthernet0/0, directly connected
L   2001:DB8:1:1::1/128 [0/0]
     via GigabitEthernet0/0, receive
D   2001:DB8:1:2::/64 [90/2172416]
     via FE80::FF:FE00:2, Serial0/0/0
D   2001:DB8:1:3::/64 [90/2172416]
     via FE80::FF:FE00:3, Serial0/0/1
C   2001:DB8:1:4::/64 [0/0]
     via Serial0/0/1, directly connected
L   2001:DB8:1:4::1/128 [0/0]
     via Serial0/0/1, receive
C   2001:DB8:1:5::/64 [0/0]
     via Serial0/0/0, directly connected
L   2001:DB8:1:5::1/128 [0/0]
     via Serial0/0/0, receive
D   2001:DB8:1:6::/64 [90/2681856]
     via FE80::FF:FE00:3, Serial0/0/1
     via FE80::FF:FE00:2, Serial0/0/0
D   2001:DB8:1:7::/64 [90/2681856]
     via FE80::FF:FE00:3, Serial0/0/1
D   2001:DB8:1:8::/64 [90/2681856]
     via FE80::FF:FE00:2, Serial0/0/0
```

```
D    2001:DB8:1:33::/64 [90/2684416]
        via FE80::FF:FE00:3, Serial0/0/1
        via FE80::FF:FE00:2, Serial0/0/0
L    FF00::/8 [0/0]
        via Null0, receive
```

The pair of highlighted lines about halfway through the example describes the one route to IPv6 subnet 3 (2001:DB8:1:3::/64). Each route lists at least two lines, with the first line listing the prefix/length and, in brackets, the administrative distance and the metric (feasible distance). The second line lists the forwarding instructions for a route.

When a router has multiple routes to reach one IPv6 prefix, the output shows one line with the prefix and then one line for each route. The line for each route lists the forwarding instructions (neighbor's link-local address and local router's outgoing interface). The highlighted lines at the end of the example, for subnet 33, show one such example, with two routes, each with a different next-hop address and different outgoing interface.

As for troubleshooting IPv6 routes, again, most of the troubleshooting for routes begins with questions about neighbors. Thinking through a potential EIGRPv6 problem actually follows the same logic as working through an OSPFv3 problem. Repeating some of the logic from the preceding chapter, when a router simply has no route to a given subnet—for instance, if R1 had no route at all for subnet 33—then do the following:

Step 1.   Check the routers with interfaces directly connected to that IPv6 prefix. A router must have EIGRPv6 enabled on that interface before EIGRPv6 will advertise about the subnet.

Step 2.   Check EIGRPv6 neighbor relationships for all routers between the local router and the routers with an interface connected to IPv6 prefix X.

For instance, in Figure 18-2, if router R4 did not have an **ipv6 eigrp 1** command under its G0/0 interface, all the routers would have their correct EIGRPv6 neighbor relationships, but R4 would not advertise about subnet 33.

If a router has a route, but it appears to be the wrong (suboptimal) route, take these steps:

Step 1.   Check for broken neighbor relationships over what should be the optimal path from the local router and prefix Y.

Step 2.   Check the interface bandwidth and delay settings. Pay particular attention to the lowest bandwidth in the end-to-end route, because EIGRP ignores the faster bandwidths, using only the lowest (slowest) bandwidth in its metric calculation.

Exam Preparation Tasks

Review All the Key Topics

Review the most important topics from this chapter, noted with the Key Topic icon. Table 18-4 lists these key topics and where each is discussed.

Table 18-4   Key Topics for Chapter 18

Key Topic Element	Description	Page Number
Table 18-2	Comparison of EIGRPv4 and EIGRPv6 configuration commands	533
List	Differences in EIGRPv4 and EIGRPv6 concepts	538
List	Possible issues with EIGRPv6 related to interfaces	541
Table 18-3	Items that may prevent EIGRPv4 and EIGRPv6 routers from becoming neighbors	542
List	Items to consider when using EIGRPv6 and a route is missing	546
List	Items to consider when using EIGRPv6 and a suboptimal route is used	546

Complete the Tables and Lists from Memory

Print a copy of DVD Appendix D, "Memory Tables," or at least the section for this chapter, and complete the tables and lists from memory. DVD Appendix E, "Memory Tables Answer Key," includes completed tables and lists to check your work.

Definitions of Key Terms

After your first reading of the chapter, try to define these key terms, but do not be concerned about getting them all correct at that time. Chapter 22 directs you in how to use these terms for late-stage preparation for the exam.

autonomous system number (ASN), EIGRP for IPv6 (EIGRPv6), successor, feasible successor

Command Reference to Check Your Memory

Although you should not necessarily memorize the information in the tables in this section, this section does include a reference for the configuration and EXEC commands covered in this chapter. Practically speaking, you should memorize the commands as a side effect of reading the chapter and doing all the activities in this exam preparation section. To see how well you have memorized the commands as a side effect of your other studies, cover the left side of the table, read the descriptions on the right side, and see if you remember the command.

Table 18-5 Chapter 18 Configuration Command Reference

Command	Description
ipv6 router eigrp *autonomous-system*	Global command to move the user into EIGRP configuration mode for the listed ASN
ipv6 eigrp *asn*	Interface subcommand to enable EIGRPv6 on the interface
maximum-paths *number-paths*	Router subcommand that defines the maximum number of equal-cost routes that can be added to the routing table
variance *multiplier*	Router subcommand that defines an EIGRP multiplier used to determine whether a FS route's metric is close enough to the successor's metric to be considered equal
bandwidth *bandwidth*	Interface subcommand directly sets the interface bandwidth (kbps)
delay *delay-value*	Interface subcommand to set the interface delay value with a unit of tens of microseconds
ipv6 hello-interval eigrp *as-number timer-value*	Interface subcommand that sets the EIGRP Hello Interval for that EIGRP process
ipv6 hold-time eigrp *as-number timer-value*	Interface subcommand that sets the EIGRP hold time for the interface
eigrp router-id *router-id*	Router subcommand to define the EIGRPv6 router ID
[no] shutdown	Router subcommand to disable (**shutdown**) or enable (**no shutdown**) the EIGRPv6 process

Table 18-6 Chapter 18 **show** Command Reference

Command	Description
show ipv6 eigrp interfaces	Lists one line per interface on which EIGRP has been enabled, but for which it is not made passive with the **passive-interface** configuration command
show ipv6 eigrp interfaces *type number*	Lists statistics interfaces on which EIGRP has been enabled, but for which it is not made passive with the **passive-interface** configuration command
show ipv6 eigrp interfaces detail [*type number*]	Lists detailed configuration and statistics, for all interfaces, or for the listed interface, again for enabled interfaces that are not passive
show ipv6 protocols	Shows brief information about each source of routing information, including listing interfaces enabled for EIGRPv6 and noting which interfaces are passive
show ipv6 eigrp neighbors	Lists EIGRP neighbors and status

Command	Description
show ipv6 eigrp neighbors *type number*	Lists EIGRP neighbors reachable off the listed interface
show ipv6 eigrp topology	Lists the contents of the EIGRP topology table, including successors and feasible successors
show ipv6 eigrp topology *prefix/length*	Lists detailed topology information about the listed prefix
**show ipv6 eigrp topology	section** *prefix/length*	Lists a subset of the **show ipv6 eigrp topology** command: just the section for the listed prefix/length
show ipv6 route	Lists all IPv6 routes
show ipv6 route eigrp	Lists routes in the IPv6 routing table learned by EIGRPv6
show ipv6 route *prefix/length*	Shows a detailed description of the route for the listed prefix/length
**show ipv6 route	section** *prefix*	Lists a subset of the **show ip route** command (just the section for the listed prefix)

18

Part V Review

Keep track of your part review progress with the checklist in Table P5-1. Details about each task follow the table.

Table P5-1 Part V Part Review Checklist

Activity	First Date Completed	Second Date Completed
Repeat All DIKTA Questions		
Answer Part Review Questions		
Review Key Topics		
Create Troubleshooting Root Causes Mind Map		
Create OSPFv3 and EIGRPv6 Commands Mind Map		

Repeat DIKTA Questions

For this task, answer the "Do I Know This Already?" questions again for the chapters in Part I of this book using the PCPT software. See the section "How to View Only DIKTA Questions by Part" in the Introduction to this book to learn how to make the PCPT software show you DIKTA questions for this part only.

Answer Part Review Questions

For this task, answer the Part Review questions for this part of the book using the PCPT software. See the section "How to View Only DIKTA Questions by Part" in the Introduction to this book to learn how to make the PCPT software show you DIKTA questions for this part only.

Review Key Topics

Browse back through the chapters, and look for the Key Topic icons. If you do not remember some details, take the time to reread those topics.

Create Troubleshooting Root Causes Mind Map

Chapter 16, "Troubleshooting IPv6 Routing," focuses on how to troubleshoot IPv6 routing problems while ignoring Open Shortest Path First Version 3 (OSPFv3) and Enhanced Interior Gateway Routing Protocol Version 6 (EIGRPv6). Then, Chapters 17, "Implementing OSPF for IPv6," and 18, "Implementing EIGRP for IPv6," fold in the troubleshooting discussion for these two routing protocols.

For this first Part Review mind map, try to collect all root causes of problems in an IPv6 network and organize those into a mind map. As usual, use short reminders, rather than long descriptions, with just enough information for you to remember the meaning. Also, organize the concepts in a way that makes sense to you. And avoid looking at the chapters when first building these; as usual, the point is to help you organize the ideas in your own head, rather than to read lists from the book again.

If you want a little guidance, you can organize the topics based on the chapters. To match the chapters, put EIGRPv6 troubleshooting in one part of the mind map, OSPFv3 in another, and IPv6 routing in a third.

> **NOTE**   For more information about mind mapping, see the section "About Mind Maps" in the Introduction to this book.

Create OSPFv3 and EIGRPv6 Commands Mind Map

This part also discussed both OSPFv3 and EIGRPv6 configuration and verification. Create a command mind map, like in many other part reviews. The first level of organization should be for OSPFv3 versus EIGRPv6, then for configuration versus verification. Inside the verification area, further organize the commands related to interfaces, neighbors, topology, and routes. (Note that you made similar mind maps for Part III review, for the IPv4 versions of these routing protocols.)

DVD Appendix F, "Mind Map Solutions," lists sample mind map answers, but as usual, your mind maps can and will look different.

Part VI of this book examines a wide variety of small topics, all related in some way to managing the network and the devices in the network. The topics include network management with SNMP, managing network traffic with NetFlow, managing informational messages with syslog, manipulating IOS images on routers, and managing software features and licenses.

Part VI

Network Management

Chapter 19: Managing Network Devices

Chapter 20: Managing IOS Files

Chapter 21: Managing IOS Licensing

Part VI Review

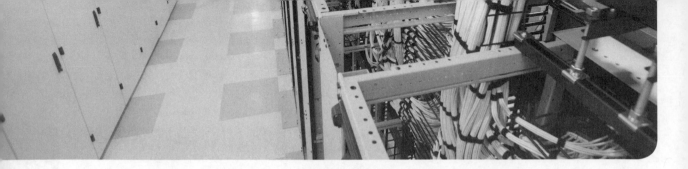

This chapter covers the following exam topics:

IP Services

   Configure and verify Syslog

    Utilize Syslog Output

   Describe SNMP v2 & v3

Troubleshooting

   Utilize netflow data

   Monitor NetFlow statistics

CHAPTER 19

Managing Network Devices

The modern network is called upon to do so much. No longer is it adequate to simply transmit the data (spreadsheets, transactions, documents) that a company needs to carry out its operations. Often, networks must also carry the voice and video traffic of an organization. These networks must be faster and more reliable than ever. They must be highly available and must scale at the snap of a manager's fingers. Although this might seem daunting, the excellent news is that a wide range of mature and highly useful network management protocols and techniques can aid an administrator of even the most complex networks.

This chapter explores three predominate tools in the field of network management for Cisco devices. A proper implementation of Simple Network Management (SNMP), system message logging (syslog), and NetFlow can ease a Cisco administrator's workload and overall stress levels (and even help save his or her job). Protocols and best practices in these areas can help the admin be *proactive* rather than *reactive*. Proactive network management will indeed be a major theme of this chapter that should serve the reader very well.

"Do I Know This Already?" Quiz

Use the "Do I Know This Already?" quiz to help decide whether you might want to skim this chapter, or a major section, moving more quickly to the "Exam Preparation Tasks" section near the end of the chapter. You can find the answers at the bottom of the page following the quiz. For thorough explanations, see DVD Appendix C, "Answers to the 'Do I Know This Already?' Quizzes."

Table 19-1 "Do I Know This Already?" Foundation Topics Section-to-Question Mapping

Foundation Topics Section	Questions
Simple Network Management Protocol	1–4
Syslog	5–6
NetFlow	7–8

1. What is the name of the database that runs on network devices and can be accessed with an SNMP agent?

   a. The NetFlow Repository

   b. The Management Store

   c. The Management Variable Store

   d. The Management Information Base

2. Which software package is an example of an NMS that can rely on SNMP?

   a. Cisco Monitor

   b. Cisco Insight

   c. Cisco Prime

   d. Cisco View

3. Which command configures a device to be monitored, but not configured, by version 2c of SNMP using a community string of CiscoSanFran?

   a. snmp-server secret CiscoSanFran ro

   b. snmp-server community CiscoSanFran ro

   c. snmp-server 2c community CiscoSanFran read-only

   d. snmp-server 2c community CiscoSanFran monitor-only

4. Which SNMP Version 3 mode relies on a username for authentication and does not feature encryption?

   a. noAuthPriv

   b. AuthPriv

   c. noAuthNoPriv

   d. AuthOnly

5. What level of logging to the console is the default for a Cisco device?

   a. Informational

   b. Errors

   c. Warnings

   d. Debugging

6. What command limits the messages sent to a syslog server to levels 4 through 0?

   a. logging trap 0-4

   b. logging trap 1,2,3,4

   c. logging trap 4

   d. logging trap through 4

7. Which item is not used by NetFlow to identify a flow?

   a. Destination port number

   b. Type of Service (ToS) marking

   c. Layer 3 protocol type

   d. Output logical interface

8. Which command ensures that NetFlow captures egress traffic statistics under an interface?

    a. ip netflow egress

    b. ip flow out

    c. ip flow egress

    d. ip netflow egress

Foundation Topics

Simple Network Management Protocol

The year was 1988 and RFC 1065 was published: *Structure and Identification of Management Information for TCP/IP-based Internets.* The superb idea behind this document was the fact that devices on a TCP/IP-based network could be broken down into a database of variables and that these variables could be monitored to manage the overall IP-based network. After all, the elements of any IP-based machines would have commonalities. For example, a PC, a network printer, and a router would all have commonalities such as interfaces, IP addresses, and buffers. Why not create a standardized database of these variables and a simple system for monitoring and managing them? This idea was brilliant, caught on, and became three different versions of the Simple Network Management Protocol (SNMP).

Describing SNMP

Simple Network Management Protocol is an application layer protocol that provides a message format for communication between what are termed managers and agents. An SNMP manager is a network management application running on a PC, and the agent is software running on the device that is to be managed. The agent's job is to retrieve (or optionally write) to the variables stored in the database of variables that make up the parameters of the device. This database is called the Management Information Base (MIB). Cisco Prime is a classic example of an SNMP manager. A Cisco router might run the SNMP agent, and a MIB variable might be the load on the router's interface. Figure 19-1 shows these elements of an SNMP environment.

The MIB

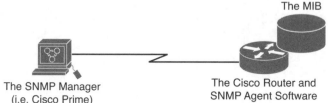

The SNMP Manager
(i.e. Cisco Prime)

The Cisco Router and
SNMP Agent Software

Figure 19-1   *Elements of Simple Network Management Protocol*

Through the process of periodically querying or polling the SNMP agent on a device, you can gather and analyze statistics about the managed device. You can even reconfigure the device through these SNMP variables in the MIB if you permit this level of control. The messages that poll information from the SNMP agent software are termed GET messages, and the messages that write variables are termed SET messages.

SNMP permits much flexibility in how you monitor variables in the MIB. Most commonly, a network administrator gathers and stores statistics over time using Network Management Station (NMS) software like Cisco Prime. Important to these administrators is to analyze various statistical facts such as averages, minimums, and maximums. To be proactive, administrators can set thresholds for certain key variables. They can then be dynamically notified by the NMS when a value is nearing unacceptable values. Figure 19-2 demonstrates the use of SNMP for proactive network management.

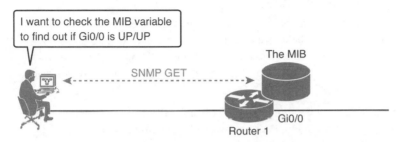

Figure 19-2   *SNMP in Use for Monitoring the Network*

An excellent example of this style of network management is monitoring the CPU utilization on a Cisco router. Thanks to SNMP, the NMS can sample this value periodically and present this information in a graph for the network administrator. This information creates a baseline for administrators so that they can easily see when CPU utilization is driving away from normal values for the network.

In addition to consistently polling an SNMP managed device for its MIB variable information, using the GET SNMP command, the device itself can independently notify the NMS when a problem occurs using SNMP *traps*. Traps are SNMP messages that are sent from the network device that also list the state of a MIB variable, but because the device decides to send the information without being asked, the NMS can react differently.

For instance, suppose that router 1's G0/0 interface fails, as shown at Step 1 of Figure 19-3. With traps configured, the router would send an SNMP trap message to the NMS, with that trap message noting the down state of the G0/0 interface. Then the NMS software can send a text message to the network support staff, pop a window on the NMS screen, turn the correct router icon red on the graphical interface, and so on.

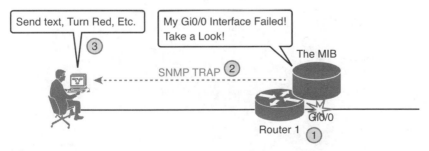

Figure 19-3   *SNMP in Use for Monitoring the Network*

SNMP provides two options to send these unsolicited messages from a managed device to the NMS. Figure 19-3 shows the trap message. Devices send trap messages with no acknowledgment that the NMS received the message; using protocol terminology, these messages are considered unreliable. A later version of the SNMP protocols (Version 3) supports an alternative process with inform messages, which use an acknowledgment process, so they are called reliable.

The Management Information Base

As mentioned in the earlier discussion, the Management Information Base (MIB) defines variables, and those variables enable the management software to monitor/control the network device. Formally, the MIB defines each variable as an object ID (OID). The MIB then organizes the OIDs based on RFC standards into a hierarchy of OIDs, usually shown as a tree.

The MIB for any given device includes some branches of the MIB tree with variables common to many networking devices and branches with variables specific to that device. RFCs define some common public variables, and most all devices implement these MIB variables. In addition, networking equipment vendors like Cisco can define their own private branches of the tree to accommodate new variables specific to their own devices.

Figure 19-4 shows portions of the MIB structure defined by Cisco Systems. Note how the OID can be described in words or numbers to locate a particular variable in the tree.

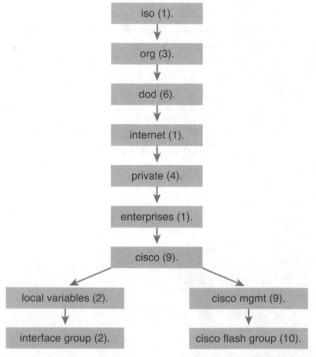

Figure 19-4   *The Management Information Base (MIB)*

As another example of a tool you can try in your home lab, the freeware SNMPGET utility allows quick retrieval of information from the MIB. In Example 19-1, the SNMPGET utility is used on a PC to obtain the 5-minute exponential moving average of the CPU busy percentage from a router.

Example 19-1   *Obtaining a MIB Value with SNMPGET*

```
[13:22][cisco@NMS~ ]$ snmpget -v2c -c community 10.250.250.14
1.3.6.1.4.1.9.2.1.58.0
SNMPv2-SMI::enterprises.9.2.1.58.0 = INTEGER: 11
```

The bold text shows a rather long command with several parameters, as follows:

-v2c: The version on SNMP in use

-c community: The SNMP password, called a community string

10.250.250.14: The IP address of the monitored device

1.3.6.1.4.1.9.2.1.58.0: The numeric object identifier (OID) of the MIB variable

The last line shows the response. The output shows a shortened version of the MIB variable. It then lists the actual value in the MIB location—in this case, the 5-minute exponential moving average of the CPU busy percentage (11 percent).

The utility shown in Example 19-1 gives some insight into the basic mechanics of how SNMP works. However, working with long MIB variable names like 1.3.6.1.4.1.9.2.1.58.0 could be a real problem for the average user. More commonly, the network operations staff uses a network management product like Cisco Prime, with its easy-to-use graphical interface, with all the MIB data variable naming hidden from the typical user.

Configuring SNMP Version 2c

The three main versions of SNMP used throughout the years are Versions 1, 2c, and 3. Because Version 1 is extremely legacy, and not often encountered in networks today, this text focuses on Versions 2c and 3.

SNMP Version 2c had several enhancements over the first version. Many of these were improvements in the messaging system to make obtaining large amounts of statistics from the device more efficient. Unfortunately, not much was done in the area of security.

Both SNMP Version 1 and SNMP Version 2c rely on what are termed SNMP *community strings* to authenticate access to MIB objects. These community strings are really just clear-text passwords. These days, clear-text passwords are really not even considered a security mechanism because they are so vulnerable to a man-in-the-middle attack in which they are compromised through the capture of packets.

There are two types of community strings in SNMP Version 2c:

Read-only (RO): Provides access to the MIB variables, but does not allow these variables to changed, only read. Because security is so weak in Version 2c, many organizations only use SNMP in this read-only mode.

Read-write (RW): Provides read and write access to all objects in the MIB.

> **NOTE** SNMP security is not truly provided until Version 3. This version is described later in the chapter.

Configuring SNMP Version 2c on a Cisco router or switch requires only one configuration command: the **snmp-server community** global command. However, most SNMP configurations include a couple of optional settings, as well. The following configuration checklist identifies the common steps:

Step 1.   (Required) Configure the community string and access level (read-only or read-write) with the **snmp-server community** *string* **RO|RW** global command.

Step 2.   (Optional) Document the location of the device using the **snmp-server location** *text-describing-location* global configuration command.

Step 3.   (Optional) Document the location of the device using the **snmp-server contact** *contact-name* global configuration command.

Step 4.   (Optional) Restrict SNMP access to NMS hosts that are permitted by an access control list (ACL) by defining an ACL and referencing the ACL on the **snmp-server community** *string acl-name-or-number* global configuration command.

Example 19-2 uses the one required command plus the other optional commands from the list. It uses a difficult-to-guess community string, allows access from only the NMS at address 10.10.10.101, and defines the location and contact name for this device (router R1).

Example 19-2   *Configuring SNMP Version 2c for Read-Only Access*

```
R1(config)# ip access-list standard ACL_PROTECTSNMP
R1(config-std-nacl)# permit host 10.10.10.101
R1(config-std-nacl)# exit
R1(config)# snmp-server community V011eyB@11!!! RO ACL_PROTECTSNMP
R1(config)# snmp-server location Tampa
R1(config)# snmp-server contact Anthony Sequeira
R1(config)# end
R1#
```

Example 19-3 adds a similar configuration to router R2, located in New York. The example allows a different NMS (also in New York) to manage the router, and in this case, it allows read/write (RW) access.

Example 19-3   *Configuring SNMP Version 2c for Read and Write Access*

```
R2(config)# ip access-list standard ACL_PROTECTSNMP
R2(config-std-nacl)# permit host 10.20.20.201
R2(config-std-nacl)# exit
R2(config)# snmp-server community T3nn1sB@11 RW ACL_PROTECTSNMP
```

```
R2(config)# snmp-server location New York
R2(config)# snmp-server contact John Sequeira
R2(config)# end
R2#
```

The choice of read-only SNMP access on router R1, and read-write access on router R2, has a much bigger impact on operation of the network than you might guess from just one small difference in the configuration. Routers and switches that allow read-write access allow the NMS to change the configuration of the router or switch. For instance, with read-write access, the NMS can shut down an interface or bring it up again, whereas read-only access does not allow changes to the configuration.

SNMP Version 3

SNMP Version 3 arrived with much celebration among network administrators. Finally, security arrived with the powerful network management protocol. The security features provided in SNMPv3 are as follows:

- **Message integrity:** This helps ensure that a packet has not been tampered with in transit.
- **Authentication:** This helps ensure that the packet came from a known and trusted source.
- **Encryption:** This helps to ensure that information cannot be read if the data is captured in transit.

This list defines what the SNMPv3 protocol can do as a whole, but devices can choose to implement only some of these features, based on the configuration. However, even the least secure SNMPv3 option improves security compared to SNMPv2c, with the managed device requiring a username to identify the user (the NMS). As shown in Table 19-2, each SNMPv3 security level offers a different combination of security features, including protecting the authentication with a hash and encrypting the data that is sent between the device and the NMS.

Table 19-2   Possible Security Modes of SNMP Version

Level Name	Keyword in snmp-server Command	Authentication Method	Encryption
noAuthNoPriv	noauth	Username	None
authNoPriv	auth	Message Digest 5 (MD5) or Secure Hash Algorithm (SHA)	None
authPriv	priv	Message Digest 5 (MD5) or Secure Hash Algorithm (SHA)	DES or DES-56

NOTE   Even the noAuthNoPriv level is an improvement over SNMP Version 2c because activity can be tracked to a certain user account.

System Message Logging (Syslog)

It is amazing just how helpful Cisco devices try to be to their administrators. When major (and even not-so-major) events take place, these Cisco devices attempt to notify administrators with detailed system messages. As you learn in this section, these messages vary from the very mundane to those that are incredibly important. Thankfully, administrators have a large variety of options for storing these messages and being alerted to those that could have the largest impact on the network infrastructure.

An Overview of System Message Logging

The most common method of taking advantage of this wealth of system messages that Cisco devices provide is to use a protocol called syslog. Syslog permits your various Cisco devices (and some other non-Cisco devices) to send their system messages across the network to syslog servers. You should note that you can even build a special out-of-band (OOB) network for this purpose. There are many different Syslog server software packages for Windows and UNIX. Many of them are even freeware.

Internally, Cisco network devices send system messages and debug output to a local logging process inside the device. You can then dictate (using configuration) what this logging process does with these messages. For example, you might want them sent across the network to a syslog server, as described earlier. Or perhaps you would like them sent to an internal buffer so that you can view them at your convenience at a later time right through the device CLI. You can even specify that only certain types of system messages are sent to various destinations. For example, perhaps you do not want debug-level messages sent to the external syslog server because you always plan to observe those messages at the CLI.

Popular destinations for syslog messages include the following:

- The logging buffer (RAM inside the router or switch)
- The console line
- The terminal lines
- A syslog server

Figure 19-5 shows various Cisco devices sending system messages to a syslog server.

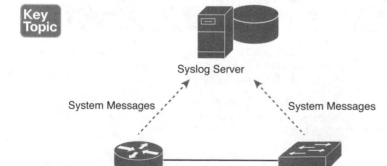

Figure 19-5 *Syslogging in the Network*

System Message Format

Let's examine one of the messages from our Cisco router to examine the default message format:

```
*Dec 18 17:10:15.079: %LINEPROTO-5-UPDOWN: Line protocol on Interface FastEthernet0/0,
changed state to down
```

Notice that by default on this particular device, we see the following:

- **A timestamp:** *Dec 18 17:10:15.079
- **The facility on the router that generated the message:** %LINEPROTO
- **The severity level:** 5
- **A mnemonic for the message:** UPDOWN
- **The description of the message:** Line protocol on Interface FastEthernet0/0, changed state to down

You have now seen the default system message format on a particular Cisco router, but you should know that you can control the format of your messages. For example, we can turn off timestamps and turn on sequence numbers, as shown in Example 19-4.

Example 19-4 *Modifying System Messages*

```
R1(config)# no service timestamps
R1(config)# service sequence-numbers
R1(config)# end
R1#
000011: %SYS-5-CONFIG_I: Configured from console by console
```

As usual, when a user exits configuration mode, the router issues yet another system message, as shown at the end of the example. Comparing this message to the previous example, it now no longer lists the time of day, but does list a sequence number. The message format now features the following:

- **Sequence number:** 000011
- **Facility:** %SYS
- **Severity level:** 5
- **Mnemonic:** Config_I
- **Description:** Configured from console by console

System Message Severity Levels

By far, one of the most important ingredients in the system message on a Cisco device is the severity level. This is because we can use severity levels to easily control which messages are sent to which logging destinations. Table 19-3 details the various system message severity levels that are possible on a Cisco device.

Table 19-3   System Message Severity Levels

Level	Level Name	Explanation
0	Emergency	The system may be unusable.
1	Alert	Immediate action may be required.
2	Critical	A critical event took place.
3	Error	The router experienced an error.
4	Warning	A condition might warrant attention.
5	Notification	A normal but significant condition occurred.
6	Informational	A normal event occurred.
7	Debugging	The output is a result of a **debug** command.

Notice that levels 0 through 4 are for events that could seriously impact the device, whereas levels 5 through 7 are for less-important events. Obviously, an administrator can consider this when deciding how to handle messages. For instance, the administrator could choose to send only warning level (4) messages and lower (more severe) to the syslog server, instead of cluttering the syslog server with messages for all eight levels.

Configuring and Verifying Syslog

By default, Cisco routers and switches send log messages for all severity levels to the console. On some IOS versions, the device also buffers those log messages by default. To enable these two settings, the configuration would use the **logging console** and **logging buffered** global configuration commands, respectively. To disable either of these logging services, just use the **no** version of either command: **no logging console** or **no logging buffered**.

The **show logging** command lets us examine the logging service settings on a Cisco router, as shown in Example 19-5. The first lines of output list information about the logging process, with the end of the output listing log messages.

Example 19-5   *Viewing the Default Logging Service Settings on a Cisco Router*

```
R1# show logging
Syslog logging: enabled (0 messages dropped, 2 messages rate-limited,0 flushes, 0
overruns, xml disabled, filtering disabled)
No Active Message Discriminator.
No Inactive Message Discriminator.
Console logging: level debugging, 10 messages logged, xml disabled, filtering disabled
Monitor logging: level debugging, 0 messages logged, xml disabled, filtering disabled
Buffer logging:  level debugging, 10 messages logged, xml disabled,filtering disabled
Logging Exception size (8192 bytes)
Count and timestamp logging messages: disabled
Persistent logging: disabled
No active filter modules.
ESM: 0 messages dropped
Trap logging: level informational, 13 message lines logged
```

```
Log Buffer (8192 bytes):
*Dec 18 17:10:14.079: %LINK-3-UPDOWN: Interface FastEthernet0/0, changed state to down
*Dec 18 17:10:15.079: %LINEPROTO-5-UPDOWN: Line protocol on Interface FastEthernet0/0,
changed state to down
...
```

Focus on the first two highlighted lines, which tell us something about the logging service. The first line states that this router logs to the console and will include debug messages, actually meaning debug level messages and all lower levels; see Table 19-3 for the list of levels. The output also notes that ten such messages have been logged. The second highlighted line states that this router logs to an internal buffer.

Because this router has enabled logging to an internal buffer, the **show logging** command also lists the messages in that buffer. You can see some of the system messages that have been logged at the end of the example.

Configuring the router to send system messages to a syslog server where they can be stored, filtered, and analyzed is a simple task:

Step 1.   First, configure the destination hostname or IP address of the syslog server:

```
R1(config)# logging 192.168.1.101
```

Step 2.   Next, you can control which messages are sent there. For example, to limit the messages for levels 4 and lower (0 through 4), use the following command:

```
R1(config)# logging trap 4
```

> **NOTE**   Notice that by specifying the highest level (least severe), this includes the levels below (more severe). Also, this command can also accept the name of the level, so you could use **logging trap warning**.

Using a Syslog Server

Logging to the device's internal buffer is the most efficient method of handling system messages, but the most popular is to log messages to syslog server software.

Syslog servers log the messages and usually provide an easy means to display and sort the messages for easier troubleshooting.

Thanks to syslog servers, administrators can easily use the wealth of information presented in system messages. They can search for messages with certain keywords or severity levels. They can easily script email of text alerts based on the receipt of a certain message/severity.

Of course, administrators can also use syslog server software to delete all of those system messages from the database that are not important. Once again, a key aspect of using the output of system messages is wading through all of the messages that do not provide useful information.

NetFlow

Even with such powerful network management tools like Simple Network Management Protocol (SNMP), it quickly became apparent to Cisco engineers that networking professionals would need a simple and efficient method for tracking TCP/IP flows in the network. This information could be used to easily identify potential network bottlenecks, guide network improvements and redesigns, and could even assist in billing consumers of the network. Because of these needs, Cisco invented NetFlow. This powerful network protocol quickly became a standard, and it is now supported by other networking giants.

An Overview of NetFlow

Whereas network protocols such as SNMP attempt to provide a very wide range of network management features and options, NetFlow is simple and specific in its mission: to as efficiently as possible provide statistics on IP packets flowing through network devices.

For instance, in Figure 19-6, host A connects to host B using some application (for instance, HTTP). NetFlow can monitor that application connection (counting packets, bytes, and so on) for that individual application flow. It can then push the statistics over to an external server called a NetFlow collector.

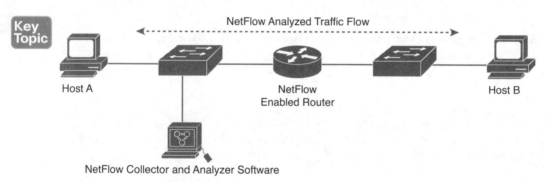

Figure 19-6 *NetFlow in the Typical Network*

While the potential uses of the statistics that NetFlow provides is quite vast, most organizations use NetFlow for some or all of the following key purposes:

■ General network traffic accounting for baseline analysis
■ Usage-based network billing for consumers of network services
■ Network design, including redesigns to include new network devices and applications to meet the needs of growing infrastructures
■ General network security design
■ Denial of service (DoS) and distributed DoS (DDoS) detection and prevention data
■ Ongoing network monitoring

While you can think of a network management protocol like SNMP as remote-control software for an unmanned vehicle, an excellent and often-used analogy for NetFlow is a simple, yet detailed phone bill. These phone records provide call-by-call and aggregated statistics that enable the administrator (the person paying the bill) to track long calls, frequent calls, or even calls that should not have been made at all.

> **NOTE**   It is important not to confuse NetFlow with the purpose and results for packet-capture hardware and software. Whereas packet captures record all possible information exiting or entering a network device for later analysis, NetFlow targets specific statistical information.

When Cisco sought out to create NetFlow, they recognized two key criteria in its creation:

- NetFlow should be completely transparent to the applications and devices in the network.
- NetFlow should not have to be supported and running on all devices in the network to function.

Achieving these design criteria ensured that NetFlow is very easy to implement in the most complex of existing networks.

> **NOTE**   Although NetFlow is simple to implement and transparent to the network, it does consume additional memory on the Cisco router. This is because NetFlow stores record information in "cache" on the device. The default size of this cache varies based on the platform, and the administrator can adjust this value.

Network Flows

A key to NetFlow, as its name implies, is the fact that it breaks down TCP/IP communications for statistical record keeping using the concept of a flow. What is a flow according to the NetFlow application? A flow is a unidirectional stream of packets between a specific source system and a specific destination system. For NetFlow, obviously built around TCP/IP, the source and destination are defined by their network layer IP addresses and their transport layer source and destination port numbers.

NetFlow technology has seen several generations that provide more sophistication in defining traffic flows, but "classic" NetFlow distinguished flows using a combination of seven key fields. Should one of these fields vary in value from another packet, the packets could be safely determined to be of different flows:

- Source IP address
- Destination IP address
- Source port number
- Destination port number
- Layer 3 protocol type
- Type of Service (ToS) marking
- Input logical interface

The first four of the fields NetFlow uses to identify a flow should be familiar. The source and destination IP addresses, plus the source and destination ports, identify the connection between source and destination application. The Layer 3 protocol type identifies the Layer 3 protocol header after the IP header. Also, the ToS byte in the IPv4 header holds information about how devices should apply quality of service (QoS) rules to the packets in that flow.

Configuring NetFlow

Configuring NetFlow on a router requires two separate configuration tasks:

1. Configuring the capture of data about flows, using the **ip flow** interface subcommand

2. Configuring details of how to send that data to the NetFlow collector, using the **ip flow-export** global command

First, to capture the flow data, the engineer needs to add **ip flow ingress** or **ip flow egress** commands to one or more interfaces. Both commands tell the router to capture NetFlow data for flows on the interface. The **ingress** option tells the router to monitor incoming packets on the interface, and the **egress** option tells the router to monitor outgoing packets on the interface. (A NetFlow flow is unidirectional, so one user connection to an application would exist as two NetFlow flows, one for each direction.)

To configure the collector, the router has several items to configure:

1. The NetFlow collector's IP address and UDP port number, on the **ip flow-export destination** *address port* global command

2. The version of NetFlow to follow when formatting the NetFlow records sent to the collector, with the **ip flow-export version** *version* global command

3. The source interface to use as the source of the packets sent to the collector, using the **ip flow-export source** *type number* global command

Example 19-6 shows a configuration based on the network shown in Figure 19-7. R1 collects data about flows on interface F0/0, both for ingress and egress packets. It then refers to the NetFlow collector at IP address 10.1.10.100, using UDP port 99. The configuration also defines the use of NetFlow Version 9 records and the use of a loopback interface for the source IP address of packets sent to the collector.

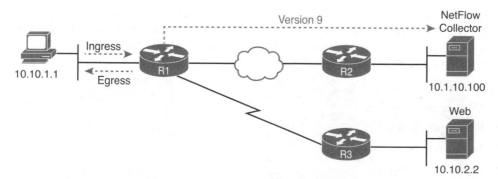

Figure 19-7 *Network Used for NetFlow Configuration Example*

Example 19-6   *Configuring NetFlow on a Cisco Router*

```
R1(config)# interface fastethernet0/0
R1(config-if)# ip flow ingress
R1(config-if)# ip flow egress
R1(config-if)# exit
R1(config)# ip flow-export destination 10.1.10.100 99
R1(config)# ip flow-export version 9
R1(config)# ip flow-export source loopback 0
R1(config)# end
R1#
```

NOTE   As mentioned earlier, NetFlow has been released in many different versions. Five formats are currently available, numbered 1, 5, 7, 8, and 9. The latest, Version, 9, is also known as Flexible NetFlow and is named so for the variety that is permitted when defining flows and record keeping for various parameters. Unfortunately, this version is not backward compatible with all versions of NetFlow.

19

Verifying and Using NetFlow

Once configured, you should verify NetFlow works, and then you can start using the collected data. The ultimate verification of NetFlow is to examine the information stored on the NetFlow collector itself, but you can also check the local NetFlow cache on a router directly, proving that the router is at least collecting the data. You do so with the **show ip cache flow** command shown in Example 19-7.

Example 19-7   *Examining the NetFlow Cache*

```
R1# show ip cache flow
IP packet size distribution (255 total packets):
   1-32   64    96   128   160   192   224   256   288   320   352   384   416   448   480
  .000  .000  .000  1.00  .000  .000  .000  .000  .000  .000  .000  .000  .000  .000  .000


   512   544   576  1024  1536  2048  2560  3072  3584  4096  4608
  .000  .000  .000  .000  .000  .000  .000  .000  .000  .000  .000


IP Flow Switching Cache, 4456704 bytes
  1 active, 65535 inactive, 1 added
  32 ager polls, 0 flow alloc failures
  Active flows timeout in 30 minutes
  Inactive flows timeout in 15 seconds
IP Sub Flow Cache, 533256 bytes
  1 active, 16383 inactive, 1 added, 1 added to flow
  0 alloc failures, 0 force free
  1 chunk, 1 chunk added
```

```
 last clearing of statistics never
Protocol        Total    Flows  Packets Bytes  Packets Active(Sec) Idle(Sec)
--------        Flows    /Sec   /Flow  /Pkt   /Sec   /Flow     /Flow

SrcIf           SrcIPaddress   DstIf        DstIPaddress    Pr SrcP DstP  Pkts
Fa0/0           10.10.1.1      S0/0/0       10.10.2.2       01 0200 0050   255
```

The output at the top of the command confirms that the router is indeed collecting data in the lab. The first highlighted entry lists a count of 255 packets monitored by NetFlow.

The bottom of the output shows statistics about the one flow created for this particular example. The example shows the results of PC1 connecting to a web server in Figure 19-7. The highlighted line shows the source IP address of 10.10.1.1, destination IP address of 10.10.2.2, and the total packets in this flow (255). It also shows the source port (SrcP) and destination port (DstP) in hexadecimal, which better identifies the flow; note that hex 50 is equal to decimal 80, the well-known TCP port for web services.

Although the data in Example 19-7 confirms that the router is collecting data, to ensure that you have NetFlow configured on the correct interfaces in the correct directions, you can use the command **show ip flow interface**, as shown in Example 19-8. Then, to check the configuration of your export parameters, you can use the command **show ip flow export**, also in the example. Note that the highlighted lines in the example track directly back to the configuration shown in Example 19-6.

Example 19-8   *Confirming NetFlow Interface Configurations*

```
R1# show ip flow interface
FastEthernet0/0
  ip flow ingress
  ip flow egress

R1# show ip flow export
Flow export v9 is enabled for main cache
  Export source and destination details :
  VRF ID : Default
    Source(1)       1.1.1.1 (Loopback0)
    Destination(1)  10.1.10.100 (99)
  Version 9 flow records
  0 flows exported in 0 udp datagrams
  0 flows failed due to lack of export packet
  0 export packets were sent up to process level
  0 export packets were dropped due to no fib
  0 export packets were dropped due to adjacency issues
  0 export packets were dropped due to fragmentation failures
  0 export packets were dropped due to encapsulation fixup failures
R1#
```

The NetFlow Collector

As described earlier, the NetFlow collector is a system running application software that is specialized for handling the raw NetFlow data. This system might be configured to receive the NetFlow information from many different systems in the infrastructure. Although viewing all of this raw data might make no sense to the human eye, the NetFlow collector software can aggregate and organize the information in a variety of ways to make perfect sense to network administrators. Custom reports serve to present the information in a variety of ways to different interested parties.

There are many different freeware and paid applications available for NetFlow collectors, but there are also reports that are typical across all applications. These reports often center on identifying the following:

- "Top talkers" in the network
- "Top listeners" in the network
- Most frequently visited websites
- Most frequently downloaded content
- Systems with the least available bandwidth

The amount of information that can be analyzed will vary based on the NetFlow version used. This is because the different versions define different NetFlow records. A NetFlow record contains the specific information about the actual traffic that makes up a NetFlow flow. For example, NetFlow Version 5 includes the following information in its records:

- Input interface index used by SNMP
- Output interface index
- Timestamps for flow start and finish
- Number of bytes and packets in flow
- Layer 3 headers
- TCP flags
- Layer 3 routing information including next hop

NetFlow Version 9 includes these fields and more, including Multiprotocol Label Switching (MPLS) labels and IPv6 addresses and ports.

19

Exam Preparation Tasks

Review All the Key Topics

Review the most important topics from this chapter, noted with the Key Topic icon. Table 19-4 lists these key topics and where each is discussed.

Table 19-4   Key Topics for Chapter 19

Key Topic Element	Description	Page Number
Figure 19-1	Drawing of the components of SNMP	560
List	Configuration steps for SNMPv2c	564
Example 19-2	The configuration of SNMP2c	564
List	Security features of SNMPv3	565
Table 19-2	The security modes of SNMP3	565
Figure 19-5	A drawing of devices sending system messages to a syslog server	566
Table 19-3	System message severity levels	568
Figure 19-6	Comparing a flow to the location of the NetFlow collector	570
Example 19-6	Configuring NetFlow on a Cisco router	573

Complete the Tables and Lists from Memory

Print a copy of DVD Appendix D, "Memory Tables," or at least the section for this chapter, and complete the tables and lists from memory. DVD Appendix E, "Memory Tables Answer Key," includes completed tables and lists to check your work.

Definitions of Key Terms

After your first reading of the chapter, try to define these key terms, but do not be concerned about getting them all correct at that time. Chapter 22 directs you in how to use these terms for late-stage preparation for the exam.

SNMP, MIB, SNMP agent, NMS, Cisco Prime, GET message, SET message, trap, inform, OID, integrity, authentication, encryption, syslog, out-of-band, NetFlow

This chapter covers the following exam topics:

IP Routing Technologies

Describe the boot process of Cisco IOS routers

POST

Router bootup process

Manage Cisco IOS Files

Boot preferences

Cisco IOS image(s)

CHAPTER 20

Managing IOS Files

Network engineers also play a key role in managing the Cisco IOS devices themselves. That work includes managing the configuration files on the devices, keeping backup copies, and backing up and upgrading IOS software images.

This chapter explores three topics related to this vast subject of managing the boot process and image and configuration files of Cisco IOS devices. Although it is not exhaustive in its coverage, it does provide you with an excellent foundation to comprehend file management for many of Cisco's IOS-based routing and switching devices.

"Do I Know This Already?" Quiz

Use the "Do I Know This Already?" quiz to help decide whether you might want to skim this chapter, or a major section, moving more quickly to the "Exam Preparation Tasks" section near the end of the chapter. You can find the answers at the bottom of the page following the quiz. For thorough explanations, see DVD Appendix C, "Answers to the 'Do I Know This Already?' Quizzes."

Table 20-1   "Do I Know This Already?" Foundation Topics Section-to-Question Mapping

Foundation Topics Section	Questions
Managing Cisco IOS Files	1–4
Password Recovery	5
Managing Configuration Files	6–7

1.   What of these steps happens first during the router boot process?

   a.   The router locates the configuration file.

   b.   The POST.

   c.   The router locates the Cisco IOS image.

   d.   The router initiates the bootstrap code from ROM.

2.   What is the first step a typical Cisco router takes, during the boot process, when attempting to locate an operating system to load?

   a.   The router looks for an image on a TFTP server.

   b.   The router checks its configuration register boot field.

   c.   The router boots to ROMMON.

   d.   The router looks in flash memory for an Cisco IOS image file.

3. After your Cisco router boots, what is a simple way to verify the Cisco IOS image that was loaded and the location from which it was copied into RAM?

   a. show running-config

   b. show boot

   c. show cisco ios

   d. show version

4. Which value in the configuration register controls how the router boots?

   a. The third hexadecimal character

   b. The second hexadecimal character

   c. The first hexadecimal character

   d. The last hexadecimal character

5. You have forgotten your privileged mode password and cannot access global configuration mode. During the password recovery process, how can you change the configuration register if you cannot remember enough passwords to get into configuration mode of the router?

   a. Using ROMMON mode

   b. Using the Setup Utility

   c. Using the GUI for configuring the device

   d. Using password reset mode

6. What type of router memory is used to store the configuration used by the router when it is up and working?

   a. RAM

   b. ROM

   c. Flash

   d. NVRAM

7. When a Cisco router boots using the image file located in flash, and this router does not have a startup-config file to load, how does the router respond?

   a. The router enters ROMMON mode.

   b. The router asks users if they want to start the Setup Utility.

   c. The router does not load IOS.

   d. The router prompts the user for the URL of the initial configuration file.

Foundation Topics

Managing Cisco IOS Files

Cisco routers use Cisco IOS software as the operating system (OS) for the router. For the most part, this book and the ICND1 book ignore some of the details about working with the IOS as an end to itself. Instead, the books have discussed the networking functions of IOS a great deal. Now we turn our attention to basic device management issues, such as how to upgrade the IOS and how a router loads the IOS at power-on.

Unlike many other OSs you might have used, Cisco IOS exists as a single file called an IOS image. The software upgrade process includes steps such as copying a newer IOS image into flash memory, configuring the router to tell it which IOS image to use, and deleting the old IOS image when you are confident that the new release works well. The boot process on the router must be ready to pick the correct IOS image to use when the router powers on and, if that process fails for any reason, to have a way to overcome and fix the problem.

This first section of the chapter begins with a discussion of how to upgrade the Cisco IOS software on a router, followed by a discussion of the router boot process.

> **NOTE** This chapter focuses specifically on routers, not switches. However, many of the concepts apply to switches as well.

Upgrading a Cisco IOS Software Image into Flash Memory

Cisco routers do not usually have a disk drive. Instead, they use other types of memory for different purposes, as shown in Figure 20-1.

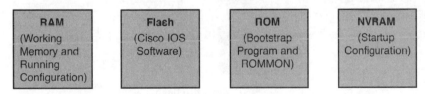

RAM	Flash	ROM	NVRAM
(Working Memory and Running Configuration)	(Cisco IOS Software)	(Bootstrap Program and ROMMON)	(Startup Configuration)

Figure 20-1 *Types of Router Memory and Their Different Purposes*

Routers usually store IOS images in flash memory. Flash memory is rewriteable, permanent storage, which is ideal for storing files that need to be retained when the router loses power. Cisco purposefully uses flash memory rather than disk drives in its products because there are no moving parts in flash memory, so there is a smaller chance of failure as compared with disk drives. Some models of routers use internal flash memory chips, whereas other use external flash memory slots that support flash memory cards commonly seen in consumer electronics. New routers also often support USB flash drives attached to an external USB port on the side of the router.

In addition, Cisco routers can store their IOS images on an external server, reachable over the network, usually using either TFTP or FTP protocols. However, using an external server typically is done for testing or for recovering from a problem with the IOS file in flash. In production, practically every Cisco router loads an IOS image stored in the only type of large permanent memory in a Cisco router: flash memory.

One of the first steps to upgrade a router's IOS to a new version is to obtain the new IOS image and put it in the right location, usually into flash memory on the router. Figure 20-2 illustrates the process to upgrade an IOS image into flash memory, using the steps in the following list:

Step 1. Obtain the IOS image from Cisco, usually by downloading the IOS image from Cisco.com using HTTP or FTP.

Step 2. Place the IOS image someplace that is reachable by the router. Locations include TFTP or FTP servers in the network or on a USB flash drive that is then inserted into the router.

Step 3. Issue the **copy** command from the router, copying the file into the flash memory that usually remains with the router on a permanent basis. (Routers usually cannot boot from the IOS image in a USB flash drive.)

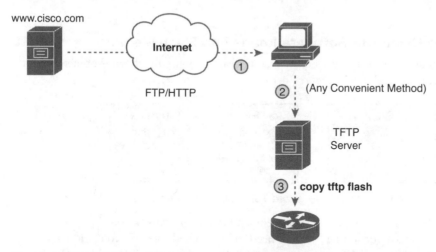

Figure 20-2 *Copying IOS Image as Part of the Cisco IOS Software Upgrade Process*

Example 20-1 provides an example of Step 3 from the figure, copying the IOS image into flash memory. In this case, router R2, a 2901, copies an IOS image from a TFTP server at IP address 2.2.2.1.

Example 20-1   copy tftp flash *Command Copies the IOS Image to Flash Memory*

```
R2# copy tftp flash
Address or name of remote host []? 2.2.2.1
Source filename []? c2900-universalk9-mz.SPA.152-4.M1.bin
Destination filename [c2900-universalk9-mz.SPA.152-4.M1.bin]?
Accessing tftp://2.2.2.1/c2900-universalk9-mz.SPA.152-4.M1.bin...
Loading c2900-universalk9-mz.SPA.152-4.M1.bin from 2.2.2.1 (via GigabitEthernet0/1):
!!!!!!!!!!!!!!!!!!!!!!!!!!!!!!!!!!!!!!!!!!!!!!!!!!!!!!!!!!!!!!!!!!!!!!!!!!!!!!!!!!!
!!!!!!!!!!!!!!!!!!!!!!!!!!!!!!!!!!!!!!!!!!!!!!!!!!!!!!!!!!!!!!!!!!!!!!!!!!!!!!!!!!!
!!!!!!!!!!!!!!!!!!!!!!!!!!!!!!!!!!!!!!!!!!!!!!!!!!!!!!!!!!!!!!!!!!!!!!!!!!!!!!!!!!!
!!!!!!!!!!!!!!!!!!!!!!!!!!!!!!!!!!!!!!
[OK - 74503236 bytes]

74503236 bytes copied in 187.876 secs (396555 bytes/sec)
R2#
```

The **copy** command does a simple task—copy a file—but the command also has several small items to check. It needs a few pieces of information from the user, so the command prompts the user for that information, as shown in the bold items in the example. It then has to check to make sure the copy will work. The command works through these kinds of questions:

1. What is the IP address or host name of the TFTP server?
2. What is the name of the file?
3. Ask the server to learn the size of the file, and then check the local router's flash to ask whether enough space is available for this file in flash memory.
4. Does the server actually have a file by that name?
5. Do you want the router to erase any old files in flash?

The router prompts you for answers to some of these questions, as necessary. For each question, you should either type an answer or press **Enter** if the default answer (shown in square brackets at the end of the question) is acceptable. Afterward, the router erases flash memory if directed, copies the file, and then verifies that the checksum for the file shows that no errors occurred in transmission.

Once finished, you can then use the **show flash** command to verify the contents of flash memory, as demonstrated in Example 20-2. (The **show flash** output can vary among router families.)

Example 20-2   *Verifying Flash Memory Contents with the* **show flash** *Command*

```
R2# show flash
-#- --length-- -----date/time------ path
1    74503236 Feb 12 2013 19:06:54 +00:00 c2900-universalk9-mz.SPA.151-4.M4.bin
2    97794040 Sep 21 2012 14:02:50 +00:00 c2900-universalk9-mz.SPA.152-4.M1.bin

78909440 bytes available (172297280 bytes used)
```

Once the new IOS has been copied into flash, the router must be reloaded to use the new IOS image. For instance, in the output shown in Example 20-2, router R2 now has two IOS images in flash memory: the original Version 15.1(4) image and the newly copied Version 15.2(4) image. The next section, which covers the IOS boot sequence, explains the details of how to configure a router so that it loads the right IOS image, including how to tell the router to start using the new IOS image.

> **NOTE** The IOS image is usually a compressed file so that it consumes less space in flash memory. The router decompresses the IOS image as it is loaded into RAM.

The Cisco IOS Software Boot Sequence

Cisco routers perform the same types of tasks that a typical computer performs when you power it on or reboot (reload) it. However, most end-user computers have a single instance of the OS installed, so the computer does not have to choose which OS to load. In contrast, a router can have multiple IOS images available both in flash memory and on external TFTP servers, so the router needs a process by which to pick which IOS image to load into RAM and use. This section examines the entire boot process, with extra emphasis on the options that impact a router's choice of what IOS image to load.

> **NOTE** The boot sequence details in this section, particularly those regarding the configuration register and the ROMMON OS, differ from Cisco LAN switches, but they do apply to most every model of Cisco router. This book does not cover the equivalent options in Cisco switches.

When a router first powers on, it follows these four steps:

1. The router performs a power-on self-test (POST) process to discover the hardware components and verify that all components work properly.

2. The router copies a bootstrap program from ROM into RAM and runs the bootstrap program.

3. The bootstrap program decides which IOS image (or other OS) to load into RAM, and then the bootstrap program loads the OS. After loading the other OS image, the bootstrap program hands over control of the router hardware to the newly loaded OS.

4. If the bootstrap program loaded IOS (instead of some other OS), IOS finds the configuration file (usually the startup-config file in NVRAM) and loads it into RAM as the running-config.

All routers attempt all four steps each time that the router is powered on or reloaded. The first two steps do not have any options to choose; these steps either work or the router initialization fails and you usually need to call the Cisco Technical Assistance Center (TAC) for support. However, Steps 3 and 4 have several configurable options that tell the router what to do next. Figure 20-3 depicts those options, referencing Steps 2 through 4 shown in the earlier boot process.

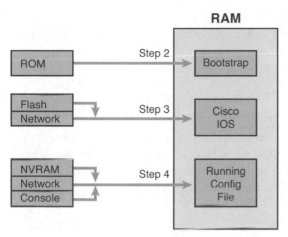

Figure 20-3 *Loading the Bootstrap, IOS, and Initial Configuration*

As you can see, the router has options at both Steps 3 and 4 in the figure. However, at Step 4, routers almost always load the configuration from NVRAM (the startup-config file), when it exists. There is no real advantage to storing the initial configuration anywhere else except NVRAM, so this chapter does not look further into the options of Step 4. But there are reasonable motivations for keeping IOS images in flash and on servers in the network, so the rest of this section examines Step 3 in more detail.

The next few pages discuss the router boot process and how a router chooses which IOS to load. But first you need to know a little more about some other OS options besides IOS and something about a tool used during the boot process: the configuration register.

The Three Router Operating Systems

A router usually loads and uses a Cisco IOS image. However, Cisco routers can use a different OS to perform some troubleshooting, to recover router passwords, and to copy new IOS files into flash when flash has been inadvertently erased or corrupted. Table 20-2 lists the other two router operating systems besides IOS and a few details about each.

Table 20-2 Comparing ROMMON and RxBoot Operating Systems

Operating Environment	Common Name	Stored In	Used In
ROM Monitor	ROMMON	ROM	Old and new routers
Boot ROM	RxBoot, boot helper	ROM	Only in older routers

Note that of these two other OSs besides IOS, the last few generations of Cisco routers have only used ROMMON and do not need nor support RxBoot. For that reason, this book ignores RxBoot, other than the brief mention in Table 20-2. However, ROMMON plays a key role in the password recovery process and some other actions when the router itself does not work correctly.

The Configuration Register

Next, you need some basic understanding of the idea of a Cisco router configuration register before discussing the boot process as well.

Routers use a configuration register to find some configuration settings at boot time, before the router has loaded IOS and read the startup-config file. The 16 bits (4 hex digits) in the configuration register set a variety of different parameters. For example, the console runs at a speed of 9600 bps by default, but that console speed is based on the default settings of a couple of bits in the configuration register. By changing specific bits in the configuration register, the next time the router boots, you can change the speed of the console line.

You can set the configuration register value with the **config-register** global configuration command. Engineers set the configuration register to different values for many reasons, but the most common are to help tell the router what IOS image to load, as explained in the next few pages, and in the password recovery process. For example, the command **config-register 0x2100** sets the value to hexadecimal 2100, which causes the router to load the ROMMON OS rather than IOS next time the router is reloaded.

Interestingly, Cisco routers automatically save the new configuration register value when you press **Enter** at the end of the **config-register** command; you do not need to use the **copy running-config startup-config** command after changing the configuration register. However, the configuration register's new value has no effect until the next time the router is reloaded.

NOTE On most Cisco routers, the default configuration register setting is hexadecimal 2102, which leaves the console speed at 9600 bps, and tells the router to load an IOS image.

How a Router Chooses Which OS to Load

A router chooses the OS to load based on two factors:

- The last hex digit in the configuration register (called the boot field)
- Any **boot system** global configuration commands in the startup-config file

The boot field, the fourth hex digit in the configuration register, tells the router the initial instructions about what OS to try and load. The router looks at the boot field's value when the router is powered on or when reloaded. The boot field's value then tells the router how to proceed with choosing which OS to load.

NOTE Cisco represents hexadecimal values by preceding the hex digits with 0x; for example, 0xA would mean a single hex digit A.

The process to choose which OS to load on more modern routers that do not have an RxBoot OS happens as follows:

1. If boot field = 0, use the ROMMON OS.

2. If boot field = 1, load the first IOS file found in flash memory.

3. If boot field = 2-F:

  A. Try each **boot system** command in the startup-config file, in order, until one works.

  B. If none of the **boot system** commands work, load the first IOS file found in flash memory.

> **NOTE**   The actual step numbers are not important—the list is just numbered for easier reference.

The first two steps are pretty straightforward, but Step 3 then tells the router to look to the second major method to tell the router which IOS to load: the **boot system** global configuration command. This command can be configured multiple times on one router, with each new **boot system** command being added to the end of a list of **boot system** commands. Each command can point to different files in flash memory, and filenames and IP addresses of servers, telling the router where to look for an IOS image to load. The router tries to load the IOS images in the order of the configured **boot system** commands.

Both Step 2 and Step 3B refer to a concept of the "first" IOS file, a concept that needs a little more explanation. Routers number the files stored in flash memory, with each new file usually getting a higher and higher number. When a router tries Step 2 or Step 3B from the preceding list, the router looks in flash memory, starting with file number 1, and then file number 2, and so on, until it finds the lowest numbered file that happens to be an IOS image. The router then loads that file.

Interestingly, most routers end up using Step 3B to find their IOS image. From the factory, Cisco routers do not have any **boot system** commands configured; in fact, they do not have any configuration in the startup-config file at all. Cisco loads flash memory with a single IOS when it builds and tests the router, and the configuration register value is set to 0x2102, meaning a boot field of 0x2. With all these settings, the process tries Step 3 (because boot = 2), finds no **boot system** commands (because the startup-config is empty), and then looks for the first file in flash memory at Step 3B.

Figure 20-4 summarizes the key concepts behind how a router chooses the OS to load.

The **boot system** commands need to refer to the exact file that the router should load. Table 20-3 shows several examples of the commands.

20

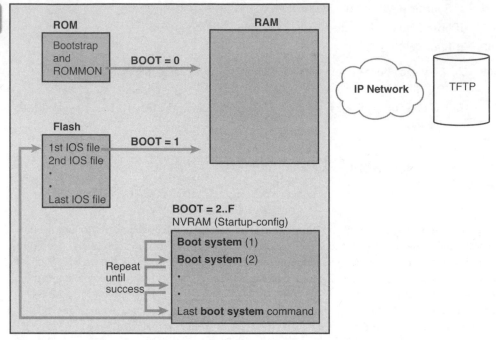

Figure 20-4 *Choices for Choosing the OS at Boot Time: Modern Cisco Router*

Table 20-3 Sample **boot system** Commands

Boot System Command	Result
boot system flash	The first file from system flash memory is loaded.
boot system flash *filename*	IOS with the name *filename* is loaded from system flash memory.
boot system tftp *filename* **10.1.1.1**	IOS with the name *filename* is loaded from the TFTP server at address 10.1.1.1.

Finally, remember the process of upgrading the IOS? Once a new IOS has been copied into flash memory on the router, the upgrade process has a few more steps. Add a **boot system** command to refer to the correct new file, save the configuration, and reload the router. The router will not go through the boot sequence discussed in this section, load the new IOS image, and the IOS upgrade is complete. For instance, Example 20-1 showed a router copying an IOS image into flash; that router would then also need a **boot system flash:c2900-universalk9-mz.SPA.152-4.M1.bin** command saved into the startup-config.

Recovering If the IOS Does Not Load

In some cases, a router fails to load IOS. For example, someone might accidentally erase all the contents of flash, including the IOS image. So, routers need more options to help recover from these unexpected but possible scenarios.

If an OS is not found by the end of Step 3, the router sends broadcasts looking for a TFTP server, guesses at a filename for the IOS image, and loads an IOS image (assuming that a TFTP server is found). In practice, this process is highly unlikely to work. As a final attempt, the router loads ROMMON, which is the first step in the process to recover from these unexpected types of problems. For example, ROMMON provides enough function to copy a new IOS file into flash from a TFTP server to recover if someone has mistakenly erased the IOS image from flash memory.

Verifying the IOS Image Using the **show version** Command

The **show version** command supplies a wide variety of information about a router. In relation to IOS images, it not only lists the version of software, it lists the source from which the router found the IOS image, and the time since it loaded the IOS. As a result, the **show version** command actually identifies some key facts about the results of the previous boot process.

The **show version** command lists many other facts as well, as shown in Example 20-3. The example lists the **show version** command from router R2, the same router shown in Examples 20-1 and 20-2, in which a new IOS image was copied into flash. Since that time, R2 has added the **boot system flash:c2900-universalk9-mz.SPA.152-4.M1.bin** command and been reloaded, migrating to use the new Version 15.2(4) IOS.

To help point out some of the many important facts in this command, the example shows many highlighted items. The following list describes each of the items in the output in the same order as they are shown in the example, top to bottom:

1. The IOS version
2. The uptime (the length of time that has passed since the last reload)
3. The reason for the last reload of IOS (**reload** command, power off/on, software failure)
4. The time of the last loading of IOS (if the router's clock has been set)
5. The source from which the router loaded the current IOS
6. The amount of RAM memory
7. The number and types of interfaces
8. The amount of NVRAM memory
9. The amount of flash memory
10. The configuration register's current and future setting (if different)

Example 20-3   show version *Command Output*

```
R2# show version
Cisco IOS Software, C2900 Software (C2900-UNIVERSALK9-M), Version 15.2(4)M1, RELEASE
SOFTWARE (fc1)
Technical Support: http://www.cisco.com/techsupport
Copyright  1986-2012 by Cisco Systems, Inc.
Compiled Thu 26-Jul-12 20:54 by prod_rel_team
```

```
ROM: System Bootstrap, Version 15.0(1r)M15, RELEASE SOFTWARE (fc1)


R2 uptime is 44 minutes
System returned to ROM by reload at 19:44:01 UTC Tue Feb 12 2013
System restarted at 19:45:53 UTC Tue Feb 12 2013
System image file is "flash:c2900-universalk9-mz.SPA.152-4.M1.bin"
Last reload type: Normal Reload
Last reload reason: Reload Command


This product contains cryptographic features and is subject to United
States and local country laws governing import, export, transfer and
use. Delivery of Cisco cryptographic products does not imply
third-party authority to import, export, distribute or use encryption.
Importers, exporters, distributors and users are responsible for
compliance with U.S. and local country laws. By using this product you
agree to comply with applicable laws and regulations. If you are unable
to comply with U.S. and local laws, return this product immediately.

A summary of U.S. laws governing Cisco cryptographic products may be found at:
http://www.cisco.com/wwl/export/crypto/tool/stqrg.html

If you require further assistance please contact us by sending email to
export@cisco.com.

Cisco CISCO2901/K9 (revision 1.0) with 483328K/40960K bytes of memory.
Processor board ID FTX1628837T
2 Gigabit Ethernet interfaces
4 Serial(sync/async) interfaces
1 terminal line
DRAM configuration is 64 bits wide with parity enabled.
255K bytes of non-volatile configuration memory.
3425968K bytes of USB Flash usbflash1 (Read/Write)
250880K bytes of ATA System CompactFlash 0 (Read/Write)


License Info:

License UDI:

-------------------------------------------------
Device#   PID                   SN
-------------------------------------------------
```

```
*0         CISCO2901/K9         FTX1628837T




Technology Package License Information for Module:'c2900'


----------------------------------------------------------------
Technology    Technology-package          Technology-package
              Current     Type            Next reboot
----------------------------------------------------------------
ipbase        ipbasek9    Permanent       ipbasek9
security      None        None            None
uc            None        None            None
data          None        None            None


Configuration register is 0x2102
```

Password Recovery

Suppose that you are sitting at your desk and you try to Secure Shell (SSH) or telnet to a router. However, you cannot log in. Or, you can get into user mode but not into enable mode because you forgot the enable secret password. You want to recover, or at least reset the passwords, so you can get into the router and change the configuration. What can you do?

Cisco gives us a way to reset the passwords on a router when sitting beside the router. With access to the router console, and the ability to power the router off and back on, anyone can reset all the passwords on the router to new values.

The details differ from router model to router model. However, if you go to www.cisco.com and search for "password recovery," within the first few hits you should see a master password recovery page. This page lists instructions on how to perform password recovery (actually password reset) for almost any model of Cisco product.

> **NOTE**   Cisco generally refers to the topic in this section as password recovery, but you do not actually recover and learn the password that you forgot. Instead, you change the password to a new value.

The General Ideas Behind Cisco Password Recovery/Reset

Although the details differ from model to model, all the password recovery procedures follow the same general principals. First, the end goal of the process is to make the router boot IOS while ignoring the startup-config file. Of course, this startup configuration holds all the passwords. Once the router boots while ignoring the initial configuration, you can log in at the console with no password restrictions and reconfigure all the passwords.

Cisco defines a specific configuration register bit that when set to binary 1 tells the router to ignore the startup-config file next time the router is loaded. To set that value, the default configuration register value of 0x2102 can be changed to 0x2142.

Unfortunately, you need to remember the enable password to reach the mode to configure the configuration register's value. When you need to do password recovery, you clearly do not know the passwords, so how can you change the configuration register? The solution is to use ROMMON mode.

ROMMON lets you issue commands, including a command to set the configuration register. ROMMON contains a small and different set of CLI commands as compared to IOS. These commands even vary from router model to router model. However, each router's ROMMON software supports some command, usually the **confreg** command, that lets you set the configuration register. For instance, the ROMMON command **confreg 0x2142** would set the correct bit to tell the router to ignore the startup-config file at reload.

So, how do you get the router to boot in ROMMON mode? Older routers support a traditional option, using a break key on the console, whereas newer routers may just require that the flash memory be removed, as follows:

- **Older routers:** Sit at the console and use a terminal emulator to type commands at the CLI. You turn the router off, and then power on again. Then, within the first 30 seconds, you press the "break" key on the keyboard. That tells the router to break the normal boot sequence and load ROMMON.

- **Newer routers (with all flash external):** Remove all flash memory cards. Turn off the router, and then power on again. The router fails to load an IOS, and instead loads ROMMON. (Put the flash back in once ROMMON loads.)

In summary, the big ideas behind password recovery are as follows:

Step 1.   Boot ROMMON, either by breaking into the boot process from the console or by first removing all the flash memory.

Step 2.   Set the configuration register to ignore the startup-config file (for example, confreg 0x2142).

Step 3.   Boot the router with an IOS, and now you can reach enable mode from the console without needing any passwords.

A Specific Password Reset Example

Example 20-4 shows an example password recovery/reset process on a 2901 router. The example begins with router R1 powered on and the user connected at the console. 2901 routers have compact flash slots, as well as USB slots that support flash drives, so for this example, I removed the flash memory to make the router boot into ROMMON mode. R1 is powered-on to begin. Here are the steps in the example:

Step 1.   Turn the router power switch off.

Step 2.   Carefully remove compact flash from the router.

Step 3.   Turn the router power switch on.

Step 4.   Watch initialization messages, waiting for the ROMMON> prompt.

Step 5.   Once the router is in ROMMON mode, with a ROMMON> prompt, carefully reinsert the compact flash.

Step 6.   Set configuration register to 0x2142 using the ROMMON **confreg 0x2142** command.

Step 7.   Issue ROMMON **reset** command, which makes the router work through its normal reload process (including using the new configuration register value).

Step 8.   Watch for IOS to ask you to enter setup mode, because IOS should load, but with no initial configuration.

Step 9.   Log in from the console (no passwords required) and move into enable mode. This gets past all password checks, but with no passwords required.

Step 10.   Issue the **copy startup-config running-config** command to put all configuration back to its normal state so that the router begins doing its job again.

Step 11.   Get into configuration mode and reset any forgotten passwords to new values.

Step 12.   Issue the **copy running-config startup-config** command to save all the configuration, including changes to the passwords.

Step 13.   Configure the configuration register back to its normal stable setting, usually 0x2102, so that the next time it reloads, the router does not load ROMMON again.

Example 20-4   *An Example of Password Recovery/Reset*

```
R1#! 1) User walks to the router and powers off the router


! 2) User removes all flash memory


! 3) User turns router back on again



System Bootstrap, Version 15.0(1r)M15, RELEASE SOFTWARE (fc1)
Technical Support: http://www.cisco.com/techsupport
Copyright  2011 by cisco Systems, Inc.


Total memory size = 512 MB - On-board = 512 MB, DIMM0 = 0 MB
CISCO2901/K9 platform with 524288 Kbytes of main memory
Main memory is configured to 72/-1(On-board/DIMM0) bit mode with ECC enabled


! 4) Several lines of messages omitted: ROMMON initializing


Readonly ROMMON initialized
```

20

```
rommon 1 > confreg 0x2142

You must reset or power cycle for new config to take effect
rommon 2 >
! 6) User walks to the router and plugs the flash back in.


rommon 3 > reset

System Bootstrap, Version 15.0(1r)M15, RELEASE SOFTWARE (fc1)
Technical Support: http://www.cisco.com/techsupport
Copyright  2011 by cisco Systems, Inc.


Total memory size = 512 MB - On-board = 512 MB, DIMM0 = 0 MB
CISCO2901/K9 platform with 524288 Kbytes of main memory
Main memory is configured to 72/-1(On-board/DIMM0) bit mode with ECC enabled


! Lots of IOS initialization messages omitted



        --- System Configuration Dialog ---

Would you like to enter the initial configuration dialog? [yes/no]: no




Press RETURN to get started!

! 9) User logs in at the console and needs no passwords to move to enable mode.

Router>
Router>enable


! 10) User copies the starting config to make the router do its normal job
Router# copy startup-config running-config
Destination filename [running-config]?
3297 bytes copied in 0.492 secs (6701 bytes/sec)


! 11) User changes the forgotten enable secret password
R1# configure terminal
Enter configuration commands, one per line.  End with CNTL/Z.
R1(config)# enable secret cisco
R1(config)# ^Z
R1#


! 12) User saves his changes to the password
R1# copy running-config startup-config
```

```
Destination filename [startup-config]?
3297 bytes copied in 0.492 secs (6701 bytes/sec)


! 13) User changes the config register back to its normal 0x2102
R1# configure terminal
Enter configuration commands, one per line.  End with CNTL/Z.
R1(config)# config-reg 0x2102
R1(config)# ^Z
R1#
```

Note that those last few steps are pretty important. Remember, this process makes the router boot with no initial configuration, so it is clearly disruptive to the normal working state of the router, even beyond the time required to work through the process. The **copy startup-config running-config** command makes up for the fact that the router ignored the startup-config file when it booted IOS. Also, to be ready for the next time the router reloads, put the configuration register value back to its normal permanent value, usually hex 2102.

NOTE When using this process, at the end, take the time to check the interface state of the router interfaces. The **copy running-config startup-config** command could result in some of the interfaces remaining in a shutdown state, depending on the current state of the cabling and the state of the connected devices. So, make sure to check and enable any interfaces with the **no shutdown** interface subcommand.

20

Managing Configuration Files

Cisco routers and switches happen to use two different configuration files: a startup-config file to save the configuration to use each time the device boots, and the running-config file that holds the currently used configuration for current use inside RAM.

This last of three major sections of the chapter reviews some key facts about these two configuration files. It also discusses the **copy** command and how you can use it to copy the contents of the configuration files. This section ends with a brief reminder of the setup process by which the router can build an initial configuration file.

Configuration File Basics

Cisco IOS stores the collection of configuration commands in a *configuration file*. In fact, routers use multiple configuration files: one file for the initial configuration used when powering on; and another configuration file for the active, currently used running configuration as stored in RAM. Table 20-4 lists the names of these two files, their purpose, and their storage location.

Table 20-4   Names and Purposes of the Two Main Cisco IOS Configuration Files

Configuration Filename	Purpose	Where It Is Stored
Startup-config	Stores the initial configuration used any time the switch reloads Cisco IOS.	NVRAM
Running-config	Stores the currently used configuration commands. This file changes dynamically when someone enters commands in configuration mode.	RAM

Essentially, when you use configuration mode, you change only the running-config file. If you want to keep that configuration, you have to issue the **copy running-config startup-config** command, overwriting the old startup-config file.

Example 20-5 demonstrates that commands used in configuration mode change only the running configuration in RAM. The example shows the following concepts and steps:

Step 1. The original **hostname** command on the router, with the startup-config file matching the running-config file.

Step 2. The **hostname** command changes the hostname, but only in the running-config file.

Step 3. The **show running-config** and **show startup-config** commands are shown, with only the **hostname** commands displayed for brevity, to make the point that the two configuration files are now different.

Example 20-5   *Changing the Running-config File, But Not the Startup-config File*

```
! Step 1 next (two commands)
!
hannah# show running-config
! (lines omitted)
hostname hannah
! (rest of lines omitted)


hannah# show startup-config
! (lines omitted)
hostname hannah
! (rest of lines omitted)


! Step 2 next. Notice that the command prompt changes immediately after
! the hostname command.
!
hannah# configure terminal
hannah(config)# hostname kris
kris(config)# exit
```

```
! Step 3 next (two commands)
!
kris# show running-config
! (lines omitted)
hostname kris
! (rest of lines omitted - notice that the running configuration reflects the
!  changed hostname)

kris# show startup-config
! (lines omitted)
hostname hannah
! (rest of lines omitted - notice that the changed configuration is not
! shown in the startup config)
```

Copying and Erasing Configuration Files

If you reload the router at the end of Example 20-5, the hostname reverts to hannah because the running-config file has not been copied into the startup-config file. However, if you want to keep the new hostname of kris, you use the command **copy running-config startup-config**, which overwrites the current startup-config file with what is currently in the running configuration file.

You can use the IOS **copy** command to copy files in a router. The files can be any files at all, but most often the files are either IOS images or configuration files.

Other than copying the running-config to the startup-config to save changes, the most common use of the **copy** command for configuration files is to make a backup copy of the configuration. You can copy either the startup-config or running-config to a server or from the server back into the router, as shown in Figure 20-5.

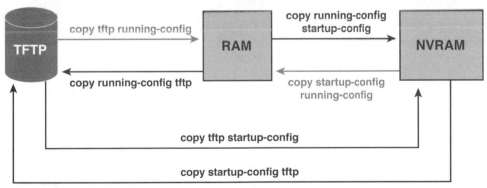

Figure 20-5   *Locations for Copying and Results from Copy Operations*

The commands for copying Cisco IOS configurations in the figure can be summarized as follows:

```
copy {tftp | running-config | startup-config} {tftp | running-config |
  startup-config}
```

The first set of parameters enclosed in braces ({}) is the "from" location; the next set of parameters is the "to" location.

The **copy** command always replaces the existing file when the file is copied into NVRAM or into a TFTP server. In other words, it acts as if the destination file was erased and the new file completely replaced the old one. However, when the **copy** command copies a configuration file into the running-config file in RAM, the configuration file in RAM is not replaced, but is merged instead. Effectively, any **copy** into RAM works just as if you entered the commands in the "from" configuration file in the order listed in the config file.

Who cares? Well, we do. If you change the running config and then decide that you want to revert to what's in the startup-config file, the result of the **copy startup-config running-config** command might not cause the two files to actually match. The only way to guarantee that the two configuration files match is to issue the **reload** command, which reloads, or reboots, the router, which erases RAM and then copies the startup-config into RAM as part of the reload process.

> **NOTE** All of the Cisco IOS image and file management tasks, including the **copy** command, also support the IPv6. Therefore, if you have established IPv6 TFTP servers on your IPv6 network, these **copy** commands work perfectly with that new protocol suite.

When working with nearby routers in a lab, you might find it more convenient to copy files to and from removable flash memory in the router. The USB slots on most recent models of Cisco router allow you to insert and remove the USB flash drives with IOS running. For instance, a Cisco 2901 router has two USB flash drive slots (USBFlash0: and USBflash1:). As demonstrated in Example 20-6, an engineer could easily copy the running-config file to flash.

Example 20-6 *Copying a File to USB Flash*

```
R1# copy running-config usbflash1:temp-copy-of-config
Destination filename [temp-copy-of-config]?
3159 bytes copied in 0.944 secs (3346 bytes/sec)


R1# dir usbflash1:
Directory of usbflash1:/


    1  -rw-        4096  Feb 11 2013 17:17:00 +00:00  ._.Trashes
    2  drw-           0  Feb 11 2013 17:17:00 +00:00  .Trashes
    7  drw-           0  Feb 11 2013 17:17:00 +00:00  .Spotlight-V100
   73  -rw-    97794040  Feb 12 2013 21:49:36 +00:00  c2900-universalk9-mz.SPA.152-4.
M1.bin
   74  -rw-        3159  Feb 12 2013 22:17:00 +00:00  temp-copy-of-config


7783804928 bytes total (7685111808 bytes free)
R1#
```

Besides copying files, you can also delete some files. For instance, IOS supports three different commands to erase the startup-config file in NVRAM. The **write erase** and **erase startup-config** commands are older, whereas the **erase nvram:** command is the more recent, and recommended, command.

Note that Cisco IOS does not have a command that erases the contents of the running-config file. To clear out the running-config file, simply erase the startup-config file, and then **reload** the router.

> **NOTE** Making a copy of all current router configurations should be part of any network's overall backup and security strategy. Keeping copies of the configuration lets you recover from mistakes or attacks that change the configuration.

Note one final thing about the names of the config files: Whereas most people use the common names *startup-config* and *running-config*, Cisco IOS defines a few other more formalized names for these files. These more formalized filenames use a format defined by the *Cisco IOS File System* (IFS), which is the name of the file system created by Cisco IOS to manage files. For example, the copy command can refer to the startup-config file as nvram:startup-config. Table 20-5 lists the alternative names for these two configuration files.

Table 20-5   IFS Filenames for the Startup and Running Config Files

Config File Common Name	Alternative Names
startup-config	nvram:startup-config
running-config	system:running-config

Initial Configuration (Setup Mode)

Cisco IOS software supports two primary methods of giving a switch an initial basic configuration: configuration mode and setup mode. Setup mode leads a switch administrator through a basic router configuration by using questions that prompt the administrator for basic configuration parameters. Because configuration mode is required for most configuration tasks, most networking personnel quickly get comfortable with configuration mode and do not use setup at all. However, new users sometimes like to use setup mode, particularly until they become more familiar with the CLI configuration mode.

Just so you know how to get to setup mode, an engineer can get into setup mode in two ways. Figure 20-6 shows one of the methods that occurs during the boot process: If the router boots, with no initial configuration, the router asks if the user wants to enter the "initial configuration dialogue," also known simply as setup mode. You can also enter setup mode by using the **setup** command from privileged mode.

20

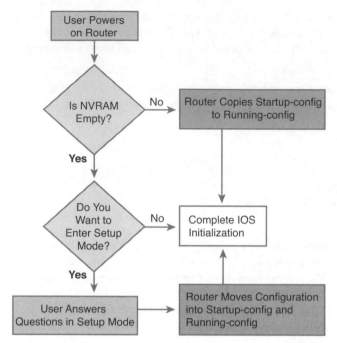

Figure 20-6   *Logic and Decisions for Entering Setup Mode After Reload*

NOTE   Example 20-3, earlier in this chapter, showed the password recovery process. That process caused a router to boot while ignoring the initial configuration, causing the router to ask the user the question shown in Figure 20-6.

Exam Preparation Tasks

Review All the Key Topics

Review the most important topics from this chapter, noted with the Key Topic icon. Table 20-6 lists these key topics and where each is discussed.

Table 20-6 Key Topics for Chapter 20

Key Topic Element	Description	Page Number
List	The boot process of a Cisco router	584
List	Steps with which a router chooses from where to load its OS	587
Figure 20-4	Locating the Cisco IOS file	588
List	Items listed in the **show version** command	589
List	Three key concepts behind the router password recovery process	592
Table 20-4	Summary of the startup-config and running-config files	596

Definitions of Key Terms

After your first reading of the chapter, try to define these key terms, but do not be concerned about getting them all correct at that time. Chapter 22 directs you in how to use these terms for late-stage preparation for the exam.

boot field, configuration register, IOS image, ROMMON, startup-config file, running-config file, setup mode, Internetwork Operating System (IOS), ROM, flash memory, NVRAM

Command References

Table 20-7 lists and briefly describes the configuration commands used in this chapter.

Table 20-7 Chapter 20 Configuration Commands

Command	Mode and Purpose
config-register *value*	Global command that sets the hexadecimal value of the configuration register
boot system {*file-url* | *filename*}	Global command that identifies an externally located IOS image using a URL
boot system flash [*flash-fs*:] [*filename*]	Global command that identifies the location of an IOS image in flash memory
boot system rom	Global command that tells the router to load the RxBoot OS found in ROM, if one exists
boot system {**rcp** | **tftp** | **ftp**} *filename* [*ip-address*]	Global command that identifies an external server, protocol, and filename to use to load an IOS from an external server

20

Table 20-8 lists and briefly describes the EXEC commands used in this chapter.

Table 20-8   Chapter 20 EXEC Command Reference

Command	Purpose
reload	Enable mode EXEC command that reboots the switch or router.
copy *from-location to-location*	Enable mode EXEC command that copies files from one file location to another. Locations include the startup-config and running-config files, files on TFTP and RPC servers, and flash memory.
copy running-config startup-config	Enable mode EXEC command that saves the active config, replacing the startup-config file used when the switch initializes.
copy startup-config running-config	Enable mode EXEC command that merges the startup-config file with the currently active config file in RAM.
show running-config	Lists the contents of the running-config file.
write erase erase startup-config erase nvram:	All three enable mode EXEC commands erase the startup-config file.
setup	Enable mode EXEC command that places the user in setup mode, in which Cisco IOS asks the user for input on simple switch configurations.
show flash	Lists the names and size of the files in flash memory, as well as noting the amount of flash memory consumed and available.

This chapter covers the following exam topics:

IP Routing Technologies

Manage Cisco IOS Files

Licensing

Show license

Change license

CHAPTER 21

Managing IOS Licensing

There have been major important changes in the way that Cisco creates software for its Cisco routers, and also major changes in how this software is licensed to individuals and organizations. In this chapter, we explore the past methods and detail the changes that have occurred.

This important chapter also guides you through the actual process of verifying your current licensing, installing a new license, activating license code, and even backing up and uninstalling licensing from a device.

"Do I Know This Already?" Quiz

Use the "Do I Know This Already?" quiz to help decide whether you might want to skim this chapter, or a major section, moving more quickly to the Exam Preparation Tasks section near the end of the chapter. You can find the answers at the bottom of the page following the quiz. For thorough explanations, see DVD Appendix C, "Answers to the 'Do I Know This Already?' Quizzes."

Table 21-1 "Do I Know This Already?" Foundation Topics Section-to-Question Mapping

Foundation Topics Section	Questions
IOS Packaging	1
IOS Software Activation with Universal Images	2, 6

1. Imagine a Cisco router model X. Cisco produced IOS software for this model of router such that their customer could pay for baseline features, additional data features, additional voice features, and additional security features. With this traditional method of software production from Cisco, for a single IOS version, how many IOS images would be available for this one router model X?

    a. 1

    b. 2

    c. 3

    d. >3

2. What is the name of the new Cisco IOS image file that provides access to all major IOS features?

    a. Universal

    b. Full

    c. Complete

    d. Enhanced

3. What is the name of the license should you want to enable security features on your Cisco router?

   a. Security

   b. VPN

   c. Securityk9

   d. Encrypted

4. What command enables you to show the UDI of your Cisco router?

   a. show udi

   b. show license udi

   c. show base udi

   d. show udi base

5. Which of the following answers lists a CLI command on a router that is useful when installing a paid-for technology package license onto a 2901 router that uses Cisco IOS licensing and an IOS universal image?

   a. license boot module c2900 technology-package *technology-package*

   b. license boot module technology-package *technology-package* install

   c. license install *url technology-package*

   d. license install *url*

6. Which of the following answers lists a CLI command on a router that is useful when installing a right-to-use license onto a 2901 router that uses Cisco IOS licensing and an IOS universal image?

   a. license boot module c2900 technology-package *technology-package*

   b. license boot module technology-package *technology-package* install

   c. license install *url technology-package*

   d. license install *url*

Foundation Topics

IOS Packaging

Cisco builds the Cisco Internetwork Operating System (IOS) software as a single file. Using a single file makes installation of a new IOS simple: You download the one file from Cisco, copy it to flash memory on the router, and then take steps to make sure the router boots the next time using the new IOS image. You learned the details of this process in Chapter 20, "Managing IOS Files."

Cisco continues to build the IOS as a single file today, but they have changed what they include in the IOS image files. This section looks at both the old and new methodologies for constructing images. This chapter also covers the new IOS licensing features that enable a router to use different parts of the IOS.

IOS Images per Model, Series, and per Software Version/Release

Since the early days of Cisco, back in the 1980s, through about the first 10 years of this century, Cisco created each IOS image for a particular router model, version and release, and feature set.

First, Cisco needed different IOS images for different router models, or at least for different router families, because of hardware differences. A low-end router with limited physical interfaces needed different software to support its interfaces than a high-end router that supported many different types of interface cards. Also, different router models often used different processors, so Cisco compiled different IOS images for use on those different processors.

Second, Cisco needed different IOS images for each new version or release of Cisco IOS software. Cisco identifies major revisions to Cisco IOS software using the term *version*, with smaller changes to IOS being called a *release*. However, Cisco did not use a model in which you install the IOS as one file, and then add bug fixes as separate files. Instead, to add a bug fix, to move to a new release, or to a new version, you had to get a whole new IOS file from Cisco, and then install and use the file on your routers. While this process is not necessarily difficult (as you learned in Chapter 20), it does provide administrative overhead as it needs to be planned for carefully.

Figure 21-1 shows a conceptual view of how Cisco ended up with many IOS images for each router. Routers had different IOS images for each router model or model series and, within each model series, different IOS files for each version of the software. For instance, the Cisco 2800 series had one set of IOS images for the 2801 router and another set for the other three routers in that series. For the 2801, for each new release, Cisco created and made available a whole new IOS file, posted for download at Cisco.com.

Answers to the "Do I Know This Already?" quiz:

1 D   **2** A   **3** C   **4** B   **5** D   **6** A

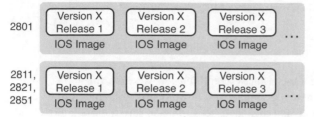

Figure 21-1   *IOS Images per Model or Model Series, per Version/Release*

Original Packaging: One IOS Image per Feature Set Combination

In addition, Cisco also created one image for each combination of IOS feature sets that was allowed on a router. A feature set is a group of related IOS features. For instance, voice features in a router would be in one feature set, while security features, like an intrusion prevention system (IPS), would be in a security feature set.

The feature set concept has a very basic business motivation: pricing. Customers who want fewer features want to pay less. Cisco desired more flexible pricing depending on the needs of a customer.

Using feature sets means that Cisco has to build even more IOS images. Not only did Cisco need one IOS image per model (or model series), per IOS version and even for each release, Cisco needed a different image per combination of feature sets.

To understand the point, Figure 21-2 shows a conceptual view of seven IOS images. Each is for the same model of router for the same software version/release. All the images have the same basic IP functions. Some have additional feature sets as well. And although the figure shows seven options to make the point, the number of combinations in the figure is far smaller than the real number of feature set combinations for a typical router model.

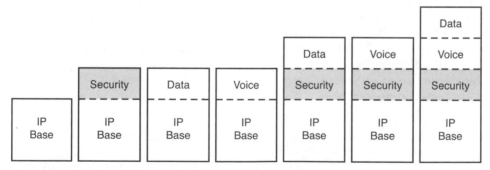

Figure 21-2   *Old IOS Image Packaging: Different Images with Different Feature Sets*

For example, suppose want to use a particular security feature that requires the Security feature set. You could choose to purchase any of the four IOS images with the highlighted Security feature set. If you did not want any advanced IP features, or voice features, you could avoid the IOS images on the right, which would be a little more expensive because of the number of feature sets included.

New IOS Packaging: One Universal Image with All Feature Sets

Cisco has begun using an IOS packaging model with a universal image. The term *universal image* means "all feature sets." Basically, instead of the old model of one image per feature set combination, as in Figure 21-2, Cisco builds one universal image with all feature sets. There would still be a different universal image per router model or model series, per version/release, just not a different image for different feature sets.

For example, if a router supported the IP Base features, plus Voice, Security, and an advanced IP feature set, Cisco would produce one universal image with all those features for each router model/series and for each version/release. Figure 21-3 shows an example of one image containing the IP Base, Security, Voice, Data, and Video features.

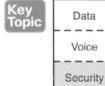

Figure 21-3   *Universal Image: One Image Holds All Features*

IOS Software Activation with Universal Images

Previously, Cisco permitted anyone to download any IOS image for any Cisco router. This download process required you to click that you agree with their terms of use. However, anyone could get the IOS images, and the images worked on real Cisco gear.

Cisco policies worked well for trustworthy customers, but as you would probably guess, it opened up the possibility of people misusing Cisco IOS software. For instance, companies could buy used Cisco hardware, download the latest Cisco IOS software, and use it—in spite of that usage breaking the Cisco terms of use and in spite of not having paid Cisco anything for the use of the software. Or, customers could choose avoid paying for the rights to download new versions of Cisco IOS versions, through a Cisco service agreement (often called SMARTnet), because the older system allowed most anyone to download newer software.

Around the time Cisco introduced the 1900, 2900, and 3900 series of Cisco routers—called Integrated Services Routers Generation 2, or ISR G2—Cisco made a couple of major changes to their software support process to help prevent theft. First, the software download area of the Cisco.com website now checks the user's credentials. The user's profile lists a company, and if that company has paid for a current service agreement that allows software downloads for a particular model of device, the user can indeed download the software. Otherwise, the Cisco download site rejects the attempt to download the software.

In addition, these newer routers, like ISR G2s, use universal IOS images with a software activation process. This idea is simple: To use the feature sets embedded in the universal image, you must unlock the feature set using a software activation process defined by Cisco. The universal image already has all the feature sets in it. The software activation process achieves two major goals:

Enable: It enables or activates the feature on the router. Without software activation, the feature does not work, and the related commands are not recognized by the CLI.

Verifies legal rights: It checks and confirms that the Cisco customer has paid for the right to use that feature set on that router.

For instance, a customer could buy a 2901 router, an ISR G2 router model that uses a universal image and the Cisco software activation process. All such routers come with the most basic feature set (IP Base) enabled already, with a license key for that feature already installed on the router. Later, the customer could choose to use software activation to enable the Security feature set—a process that requires the installation of a license key for the Security feature set, as shown in Figure 21-4.

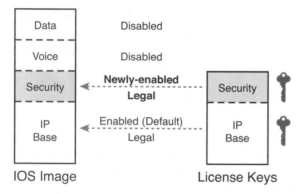

Figure 21-4   *License Keys Inside a Router That Enable IOS Features*

Cisco has a variety of different types of features and licenses that can be enabled. Cisco calls the feature sets with the most significant set of features technology packages. Table 21-2 provides the technology package licenses that are available on the Cisco ISR G2 platforms of the 1900, 2900, and 3900 series routers.

Table 21-2   Some Technology Package Licenses

Technology Package License	Features
ipbasek9 (IP Base)	Entry-level IOS functionality
datak9 (Data)	MPLS, ATM, multiprotocols, IBM support
uck9 (Unified Communications)	VoIP, IP Telephony
securityk9 (Security)	IOS firewall, IPS, IPsec, 3DES, VPN

NOTE   The IP Base license is a prerequisite for installing the Security, Data, and Unified Communications licenses.

Managing Software Activation with Cisco License Manager

Cisco customers can purchase the features when ordering the router or add them later. If purchased when ordering the router, Cisco adds the licenses to the router at the factory, and the customer has no additional work to add licenses. Alternatively, the customer can later purchase a license for a feature set and then follow the software activation process to enable that feature set on the router.

Most larger companies will likely manage Cisco licenses using an application called the Cisco License Manager (CLM). This free software package can be installed on many Windows client and server operating systems, as well as on Sun Solaris and Red Hat Linux. The CLM:

- Communicates with Cisco's Product License Registration Portal over the Internet
- Takes as input information about feature licenses purchased from any Cisco reseller
- Communicates with the company's routers and switches to install license keys, enabling features on the correct devices

Figure 21-5 shows the central location of CLM in the Cisco licensing process.

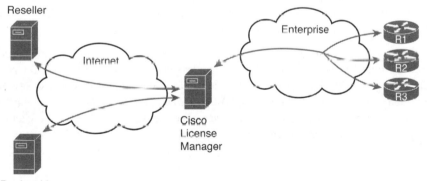

Figure 21-5   *Location of Cisco License Manager in Software Activation*

If you use CLM, you only need to know the big ideas of what needs to be done with licensing, while ignoring many details of how licensing happens. Instead, CLM tracks the information. You can purchase the licenses from any Cisco reseller. The application lets you see what you have purchased and see the licenses that have already been assigned for use on specific devices. You can also choose specific devices to receive new rights to use new feature sets and enable those features through an easy-to-use graphical user interface.

Manually Activating Software Using Licenses

CLM gives you an easier way to manage the entire Cisco software activation process, but you can also use a completely manual process. The manual process requires you to web browse to the Cisco Product License Registration Portal (a part of the Cisco.com website) and do some CLI commands on your router. Plus, you must follow a multistep process to put all the pieces together. Basically, you do all the work that CLM does for you. This next topic looks at the cleanest version of the process, without going into any of the options.

First, each of the same router model that supports software licensing has a unique identifying number named the *unique device identifier* (UDI). The UDI has two main components: the product ID (PID) and the serial number (SN). The following example shows the output from the **show license udi** command. In Example 21-1, you can clearly see the product ID, serial number, and UDI of the router.

Example 21-1   *Examining the UDI on a Cisco Router*

```
R1# show license udi
Device#     PID                SN            UDI
----------------------------------------------------------------------------
*0          CISCO2901/K9       FTX162883H0   CISCO2901/K9:FTX162883H0
```

Next, the process requires proof that you paid for a license to use a particular feature on a particular model of router. The real world uses paper receipts to show that you bought something at a store; for software feature sets, the receipt is called a product authorization key, or PAK. The PAK acts as a receipt, plus it has another unique number on it, which Cisco can find in a database to confirm what feature set license you actually bought.

The next step connects the license, which you can use on any router of that same model, to a specific router. To do so, you walk through a process that marries the PAK (the generic rights to a license) to the UDI (that identifies a specific router) to create a license key. To do so, you open a web browser and copy the PAK and UDI numbers onto a web page at the Cisco Product License Registration Portal. Cisco checks out the details: that the UDI is for a real router, that the PAK is real, that you have not already used that one PAK to enable this feature on another router, and any other checks to prevent fraud. If it all checks out, Cisco emails you with the license key file attached (also available for download).

Figure 21-6 summarizes these first three steps, with Figure 21-7 showing the later steps:

Step 1.   At the Cisco Product License Registration Portal (reachable from www.cisco.com/go/license), input the UDI of the router, as gathered using the **show license udi** command.

Step 2.   At that same portal, type in the PAK for the license you purchased, as learned from your reseller or directly from Cisco.

Step 3.   Copy the license key file (download or email) when prompted at Cisco's Product License Registration Portal website.

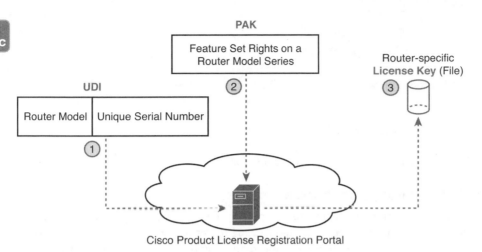

Figure 21-6 *PAK and UDI Needed to Get Unique License Key File from Cisco.com*

> **NOTE** As of the time of this writing, the landing page for the Cisco Product License Registration Portal (www.cisco.com/go/license) included videos about how to do the steps in Figure 21-6 plus the rest of the process of how to work with Cisco licenses. The videos call the process in Steps 1 and 2 "fulfilling a PAK."

After the three steps shown in Figure 21-6, the router still does not have the feature set enabled. At this point, the license key exists as a file after Step 3. That license key unlocks that one feature set on one router: the router whose UDI was used to create the key. The rest of the process enables the license on that one router, by moving the license key file into that one router and reloading the router.

The next step can use any supported method to make the license key file available to the router, with a couple of commands to follow. In a lab, the simplest way is to just copy the file to a USB flash drive and move the flash drive to the router's USB slot. For remote routers, just copy the file to a known TFTP, FTP, or HTTP server. The steps, picking up with Step 4 as a continuation of the previous list, are as follows:

Step 4.   Make the file available to the router via USB or some network server.

Step 5.   From the router CLI, issue the **license install** *url* command to install the license key file into the router. (The URL points to the file.)

Step 6.   Reload the router to pick up the changes.

Figure 21-7 shows these next three steps.

Figure 21-7   *Copying and Installing the License on a Router*

Example of Manually Activating a License

To bring the concept from the general to the specific, the next few pages show an example of the installation of a Data license on a model 2901 router. The example begins by showing the current state of the licenses in a sample router, and then shows how to change the licenses.

Showing the Current License Status

The example begins with Router R1, with only the IP Base feature enabled. No other licenses have been enabled on this router. Example 21-2 shows the status of the available features, with the enabled IP Base highlighted and the three technology package licenses highlighted, as well: Security, Voice, and Data.

Example 21-2   *Initial License Status on Router R1*

```
R1# show license
Index 1 Feature: ipbasek9
        Period left: Life time
        License Type: Permanent
        License State: Active, In Use
        License Count: Non-Counted
        License Priority: Medium
Index 2 Feature: securityk9
        Period left: Not Activated
        Period Used: 0  minute  0  second
        License Type: EvalRightToUse
        License State: Not in Use, EULA not accepted
        License Count: Non-Counted
        License Priority: None
Index 3 Feature: uck9
        Period left: Not Activated
        Period Used: 0  minute  0  second
        License Type: EvalRightToUse
        License State: Not in Use, EULA not accepted
        License Count: Non-Counted
        License Priority: None
```

```
Index 4 Feature: datak9
        Period left: Not Activated
        Period Used: 0  minute  0  second
        License Type: Permanent
        License State: Active, Not in Use
        License Count: Non-Counted
        License Priority: Medium
! Lines omitted for brevity; 8 more feature licenses available
```

The highlighted lines spell out the current state. The first highlight refers to the IP Base feature set, with an unlimited lifetime. (Note that Cisco enables the IP Base feature set on all routers, with the other feature sets being optional upgrades.) The next three highlighted sections list the Security, Voice (Unified Communications, or UC), and Data licenses, respectively, all listed as Not Activated. Also, note that the output of the **show license** command on a 2901 includes several additional feature licenses omitted from the example for the sake of space.

The **show license** command shows several lines of status information per feature, but as shown in Example 21-3, the **show version** and **show license feature** commands list shorter status information. The **show license feature** command lists one line of output, with the Enabled column on the right showing the current status. The **show version** command lists license information for the main technology feature packages at the end of the output.

Example 21-3 *Initial License Status on Router R1*

```
R1# show license feature

Feature name       Enforcement   Evaluation   Subscription   Enabled   RightToUse
ipbasek9           no            no           no             yes       no
securityk9         yes           yes          no             no        yes
uck9               yes           yes          no             no        yes
datak9             yes           yes          no             no        yes
gatekeeper         yes           yes          no             no        yes
SSL_VPN            yes           yes          no             no        yes
ios-ips-update     yes           yes          yes            no        yes
SNASw              yes           yes          no             no        yes
hseck9             yes           no           no             no        no
cme-srst           yes           yes          no             no        yes
WAAS_Express       yes           yes          no             no        yes
UCVideo            yes           yes          no             no        yes


R1# show version
Cisco IOS Software, C2900 Software (C2900-UNIVERSALK9-M), Version 15.1(4)M4, RELEASE
SOFTWARE (fc1)

! Lines omitted for brevity
```

```
License UDI:
-----------------------------------------------

Device#     PID                  SN
-----------------------------------------------
*0          CISCO2901/K9         FTX1628838P


Technology Package License Information for Module:'c2900'


--------------------------------------------------------------
Tecnology    Technology-package         Technology-package
             Current     Type           Next reboot
--------------------------------------------------------------
ipbase       ipbasek9    Permanent      ipbasek9
security     None        None           None
uc           None        None           None
data         None        None           None

Configuration register is 0x2102
```

Adding a Permanent Technology Package License

Next, Example 21-4 shows the engineer installing the license on router R1 for the Data feature set. The engineer has already followed the steps to get the license file from the Cisco Product License Registration Portal, with the file placed onto a USB drive and plugged into R1. That is, from Figures 21-6 and 21-7, the engineer has completed Steps 1 through 4.

Example 21-4 shows the final steps to install the license file on router R1. The example shows the contents of the USB flash drive, with the license file highlighted. It then shows the command to change the licensing on the router.

Example 21-4 *Installing a License on the Cisco Router*

```
R1# dir usbflash1:
Directory of usbflash1:/
    1  -rw-         4096  Feb 11 2013 17:17:00  FTX1628838P_201302111432454180.lic

7783804928 bytes total (7782912000 bytes free)

R1# license install usbflash1:FTX1628838P_201302111432454180.lic

Installing...Feature:datak9...Successful:Supported
1/1 licenses were successfully installed
0/1 licenses were existing licenses
0/1 licenses were failed to install
```

```
R1#
Feb 11 22:35:20.786: %LICENSE-6-INSTALL: Feature datak9 1.0 was installed in this
device. UDI=CISCO2901/K9:FTX1628838P; StoreIndex=1:Primary License Storage

Feb 11 22:35:21.038: %IOS_LICENSE_IMAGE_APPLICATION-6-LICENSE_LEVEL: Module name =
c2900 Next reboot level = datak9 and License = datak9
```

After a **reload** (not shown), the router now supports the features in the Data feature set. Example 21-5 confirms the change in the licensing status, with the Data license now mirroring the status for the IP Base feature set.

Example 21-5 *Verifying the Installed License on a Router*

```
R1# show license
Index 1 Feature: ipbasek9
        Period left: Life time
        License Type: Permanent
        License State: Active, In Use
        License Count: Non-Counted
        License Priority: Medium
Index 2 Feature: securityk9
        Period left: Not Activated
        Period Used: 0  minute  0  second
        License Type: EvalRightToUse
        License State: Not in Use, EULA not accepted
        License Count: Non-Counted
        License Priority: None
Index 3 Feature: uck9
        Period left: Not Activated
        Period Used: 0  minute  0  second
        License Type: EvalRightToUse
        License State: Not in Use, EULA not accepted
        License Count: Non-Counted
        License Priority: None
Index 4 Feature: datak9
        Period left: Life time
        License Type: Permanent
        License State: Active, In Use
        License Count: Non-Counted
        License Priority: Medium
! Lines omitted for brevity
```

You can also verify the installed license using the **show version** command, as shown in Example 21-6.

21

Example 21-6 *Using* show version *to Verify Licensing Information*

```
R1# show version | begin Technology Package
Technology Package License Information for Module:'c2900'


----------------------------------------------------------------
Technology    Technology-package          Technology-package
              Current      Type           Next reboot
----------------------------------------------------------------
ipbase        ipbasek9     Permanent      ipbasek9
security      securityk9   None           None
uc            None         None           None
data          datak9       Permanent      datak9


Configuration register is 0x2102
```

Right-to-Use Licenses

Although a software licensing model may work well in some cases for legitimate Cisco customers, it might not work well in other cases. For instance, when a legitimate Cisco customer wants to test a router feature before they decide to purchase licenses for all their routers, Cisco does not want the mechanics of licensing to get in the way of making that sale. So, Cisco makes the licensing flexible enough to allow use of the licensing without purchasing a PAK.

Cisco has made a few changes over these last few years about how they allow customers to use features without paying for a license. Today, the customer can simply enable most features, without paying for a PAK, for a 60-day evaluation period. After that? The feature stays enabled, with no time limit. The software licensing works on an honor system, asking people to not take advantage.

NOTE Cisco may well change their software licensing strategy more over time. Cisco just wants to strike the right balance.

Cisco allows the use of these features today, without a PAK, using a *right-to-use* license. To enable a feature license as a right-to-use license, the engineer needs to use the **license boot module** command, with a reload to allow the router to start using the feature. For instance, Example 21-7 shows how to add the Security feature set to router R1 as a right-to-use evaluation license.

Example 21-7 *Activating an Evaluation Right-to-Use License*

```
R1(config)# license boot module c2900 technology-package securityk9

PLEASE  READ THE  FOLLOWING TERMS  CAREFULLY. INSTALLING THE LICENSE OR
LICENSE KEY  PROVIDED FOR  ANY CISCO  PRODUCT  FEATURE  OR  USING SUCH
```

```
PRODUCT  FEATURE  CONSTITUTES  YOUR  FULL ACCEPTANCE  OF  THE FOLLOWING
TERMS. YOU MUST NOT PROCEED FURTHER IF YOU ARE NOT WILLING TO  BE BOUND
BY ALL THE TERMS SET FORTH HEREIN.

! The rest of the EULA is omitted…

Activation  of the  software command line interface will be evidence of
your acceptance of this agreement.


ACCEPT? [yes/no]: yes
% use 'write' command to make license boot config take effect on next boot

Feb 12 01:35:45.060: %IOS_LICENSE_IMAGE_APPLICATION-6-LICENSE_LEVEL: Module name =
c2900 Next reboot level = securityk9 and License = securityk9
Feb 12 01:35:45.524: %LICENSE-6-EULA_ACCEPTED: EULA for feature securityk9 1.0 has
been accepted. UDI=CISCO2901/K9:FTX1628838P; StoreIndex=0:Built-In License Storage
R1(config)# ^Z
```

Once the router is reloaded, the feature set is available, and works just as well as if you had
purchased a PAK and downloaded a license file from Cisco.com. Example 21-8 lists the output of the **show license** command again, to show the differences in how the command lists
the results of the installation of a right-to-use license.

Example 21-8   *Activating an Evaluation Right-to-Use License*

```
R1# show license
Index 1 Feature: ipbasek9
        Period left: Life time
        License Type: Permanent
        License State: Active, In Use
        License Count: Non-Counted
        License Priority: Medium
Index 2 Feature: securityk9
        Period left: 8  weeks 4  days
        Period Used: 0  minute  0  second
        License Type: EvalRightToUse
        License State: Active, In Use
        License Count: Non-Counted
        License Priority: Low
Index 3 Feature: uck9
        Period left: Not Activated
        Period Used: 0  minute  0  second
        License Type: EvalRightToUse
        License State: Not in Use, EULA not accepted
        License Count: Non-Counted
        License Priority: None
```

21

```
Index 4 Feature: datak9
        Period left: Life time
        License Type: Permanent
        License State: Active, In Use
        License Count: Non-Counted
        License Priority: Medium
! Lines omitted for brevity
```

In this example, the IP Base and Data licenses are permanent, but the right-to-use license appears to have only 60 days left (8 weeks, 4 days). The first 60 days is considered an evaluation period. The output continues over time to count downward toward 0 days left, at which point, with the current rules as the time of publication of this book, it converts to a lifetime time period.

Exam Preparation Tasks

Review All the Key Topics

Review the most important topics from this chapter, noted with the Key Topic icon. Table 21-3 lists these key topics and where each is discussed.

Table 21-3   Key Topics for Chapter 21

Key Topic Element	Description	Page Number
Figure 21-3	The new Cisco universal image	609
Table 21-2	Some Cisco technology package licenses	610
Figure 21-6	Three steps to manually add software licenses to a Cisco router	613

Complete the Tables and Lists from Memory

Print a copy of DVD Appendix D, "Memory Tables," or at least the section for this chapter, and complete the tables and lists from memory. DVD Appendix E, "Memory Tables Answer Key," includes completed tables and lists to check your work.

Definitions of Key Terms

After your first reading of the chapter, try to define these key terms, but do not be concerned about getting them all correct at that time. Chapter 22 directs you in how to use these terms for late-stage preparation for the exam.

IOS feature set, universal image, product activation key (PAK), universal device identifier (UDI)

Command Reference to Check Your Memory

Although you should not necessarily memorize the information in the tables in this section, this section does include a reference for the configuration and EXEC commands covered in this chapter. Practically speaking, you should memorize the commands as a side effect of reading the chapter and doing all the activities in this exam preparation section. To check to see how well you have memorized the commands as a side effect of your other studies, cover the left side of the table with a piece of paper, read the descriptions on the right side, and see whether you remember the command.

21

Table 21-4   Chapter 21 Configuration Command Reference

Command	Description
license boot module c2900 technology-package *package-name*	Global command used to add a right-to-use license to a router

Table 21-5   Chapter 21 EXEC Command Reference

Command	Description
show license feature	Displays a group of lines for each feature in the currently running IOS image, along with several status variables related to software activation and licensing, whether or not it is in use or activated.
show license feature	Displays one line for each feature in the currently running IOS image, along with several status variables related to software activation and licensing, whether or not it is in use or activated.
show license udi	Displays the UDI of the router.
dir *filesystem*	Displays the files inside the listed file system. For instance, **dir usbflash1:** lists the files in one of the USB slots on a 2901 router.
show version	Displays various information about the current IOS version, including the licensing details at the end of the command's output.
license install *url*	Installs a license key file into a router.

Part VI Review

Keep track of your part review progress with the checklist in Table P6-1. Details about each task follow the table.

Table P6-1 Part VI Part Review Checklist

Activity	First Date Completed	Second Date Completed
Repeat All DIKTA Questions		
Answer Part Review Questions		
Review Key Topics		

Repeat All DIKTA Questions

For this task, answer the "Do I Know This Already?" questions again for the chapters in Part I of this book using the PCPT software. See the section "How to View Only DIKTA Questions by Part" in the Introduction to this book to learn how to make the PCPT software show you DIKTA questions for this part only.

Answer Part Review Questions

For this task, answer the Part Review questions for this part of the book using the PCPT software. See the section "How to View Only DIKTA Questions by Part" in the Introduction to this book to learn how to make the PCPT software show you DIKTA questions for this part only.

Review Key Topics

Browse back through the chapters, and look for the Key Topic icons. If you do not remember some details, take the time to reread those topics.

Part VII

Final Review

Chapter 22: Final Review

Final Review

Congratulations! You made it through the book, and now it's time to finish getting ready for the exam. This chapter helps you get ready to take and pass the exam in three ways.

This chapter begins by talking about the exam itself. You know the content and topics. Now you need to think about what happens during the exam and what you need to do in these last few weeks before taking the exam. At this point, everything you do should focus on getting you ready to pass so that you can finish up this hefty task.

The second section of this chapter gives you some exam review tasks as your final preparation for your ICND1, ICND2, or CCNA exam.

Advice About the Exam Event

Now that you have finished the bulk of this book, you could just register for your Cisco ICND1, ICND2, or CCNA exam, show up, and take the exam. However, if you spend a little time thinking about the exam event itself, learning more about the user interface of the real Cisco exams, and the environment at the Vue testing centers, you will be better prepared, particularly if this is your first Cisco exam. This first of three major sections in this chapter gives some advice about the Cisco exams and the exam event itself.

Learn the Question Types Using the Cisco Certification Exam Tutorial

In the weeks leading up to your exam, think more about the different types of exam questions and have a plan for how to approach those questions. One of the best ways to learn about the exam questions is to use the Cisco Exam Tutorial.

To find the Cisco Certification Exam Tutorial, go to www.cisco.com and search for "exam tutorial." The tutorial sits inside a web page with a flash presentation of the exam user interface. The tutorial even lets you take control as if you were taking the exam. When using the tutorial, make sure you take control and try the following:

- Try to click **Next** on the multiple choice single-answer question without clicking an answer and see that the testing software tells you that you have too few answers.

- On the multiple choice multi-answer questions, select too few answers and click **Next**, to again see how the user interface responds.

- In the drag-and-drop question, drag the answers to the obvious answer locations, but them drag them back to the original location. (You might do this on the real exam if you change your mind when answering the question.)

- On the simulation questions, first just make sure you can get to the command-line interface (CLI) on one of the routers. To do so, you have to click the PC icon for a PC connected to the router console; the console cable appears as a dashed line, and network cables are solid lines.

- Still on the sim questions, look at the scroll areas at the top, side, and in the terminal emulator window.

- Still on the sim question, make sure that you can toggle between the topology window and the terminal emulator window by clicking **Show Topology** and **Hide Topology**.

- On the testlet questions, answer one multiple choice question, move to the second and answer it, and then move back to the first question, confirming that inside a testlet, you can move around between questions.

- Again on the testlet questions, click the **Next** button to see the pop-up window that Cisco uses as a prompt to ask if you want to move on. Testlets may actually allow you to give too few answers and still move on. Once you click to move past the testlet, you cannot go back to change your answer for any of these questions.

Think About Your Time Budget Versus Numbers of Questions

On exam day, you need to keep an eye on your speed. Going too slowly hurts you because you might not have time to answer all the questions. Going too fast might be hurtful if your fast speed is because you are rushing and not taking the time to fully understand the questions. So, you need to be able to somehow know if you are moving quickly enough to answer all the questions while not rushing.

The exam user interface shows some useful information, namely a countdown timer and a question counter. The question counter shows a question number for the question you are answering, and it shows the total number of questions on your exam.

Unfortunately, treating each question as equal does not give you an accurate time estimate. For instance, if your exam allows 90 minutes, and your exam has 45 questions, you have 2 minutes per question. After answering 20 questions, if you have taken 40 minutes, you are right on time. However, several factors make that kind of estimate difficult.

First, Cisco does not tell us beforehand the exact number of questions for each exam. For instance, the Cisco website might list the CCNA exam as having from 45 to 55 questions. (The ICND1 and ICND2 exams have similar ranges.) But you do not know how many questions are on your exam until it begins, when you go through the screens that lead up to the point where you click Start Exam.

Next, some questions (call them *time burners*) clearly take a lot more time to answer:

Normal time questions: Multiple choice and drag-and-drop, approximately 1 minute

Time burners: Sims, simlets, and testlets, approximately 6 to 8 minutes

Finally, in the count of 45 to 55 questions on a single exam, even though testlet and simlet questions contain several multiple choice questions, the exam software counts each testlet and simlet question as one question in the question counter. For instance, if a testlet question has four embedded multiple choice questions, in the exam software's question counter that counts as one question.

NOTE   Cisco does not tell us why you might get 45 questions while someone else taking the same exam might get 55 questions, but it seems reasonable to think that the person with 45 questions might have a few more of the time burners, making the two exams equivalent.

You need a plan for how you will check your time, a plan that does not distract you from the exam. It might worth taking a bit of a guess, to keep things simple, like this:

If you have 50 questions and 90 minutes, you have a little less than 2 minutes per question. Just guess a little based on how many time burner questions you have seen so far.

No matter how you plan to check your time, think about it before exam day. You can even use the method listed under the next heading.

A Suggested Time-Check Method

You can use the following math to do your time check in a way that weights the time based on those time burner questions. You do not have to use this method at all. But, to keep it simple, this math uses only addition of whole numbers. It gives you a pretty close time estimate, in my opinion.

The concept is simple. Just do a simple calculation that estimates the time you should have used so far. Here's the math:

(Number of questions answered so far) + (7 per time burner)

Then, you check the timer to figure out how much time you have spent:

- You have used exactly that much time, or a little more: your timing is perfect.
- You have used less time: you are ahead of schedule.
- You have used noticeably more time: you are behind schedule.

For instance, if you have already finished 17 questions, 2 of which were time burners, your time estimate is 17 + 7 + 7 = 31 minutes. If your actual time is also 31 minutes, or maybe 32 or 33 minutes, you are right on schedule. If you have spent less than 31 minutes, you are ahead of schedule.

So, the math is pretty easy: Questions answered plus 7 per time burner is the guesstimate of how long you should take if you are right on time.

NOTE   This math is an estimate; we make no guarantees that the math will be an accurate predictor on every exam.

Miscellaneous Pre-Exam Suggestions

Here are just a few more suggestions for things to think about before exam day arrives:

- Get some earplugs. Testing centers often have some, but if you do not want to chance it, come prepared. The testing center is usually a room inside the space of a company that does something else as well (often a training center). So, there are people talking in nearby rooms and other office noises. Earplugs can help. (Headphones, as electronic devices, would not be allowed.)

■ Some people like to spend the first minute of the exam writing down some notes for reference. For instance, maybe you want to write down the table of magic numbers for finding IPv4 subnet IDs. If you plan to do that, practice making those notes. Before each practice exam, transcribe those lists, just like you expect to do at the real exam.

■ Plan your travel to the testing center with enough time so that you will not be rushing to make it just in time.

■ If you tend to be nervous before exams, practice your favorite relaxation techniques for a few minutes before each practice exam, just to be ready to use them.

Exam-Day Advice

I hope the exam goes well for you. Certainly, the better prepared you are, the better chances you have on the exam. But these small tips can help you do your best on exam day:

■ Rest the night before the exam rather than stay up late to study. Clarity of thought is more important than one extra fact, especially because the exam requires so much analysis and thinking rather than just remembering facts.

■ If you did not bring earplugs, ask the testing center for some, even if you cannot imagine using them. You never know whether it might help.

■ You may bring personal effects into the building and testing company's space but not into the actual room in which you take the exam. So, take as little extra stuff with you as possible. If you have a safe place to leave briefcases, purses, electronics, and so on, leave them there. However, the testing center should have a place to store your things as well. Simply put, the less you bring, the less to worry about storing. (For example, I have even been asked to remove my analog wristwatch on more than one occasion.)

■ The exam center gives you a laminated sheet (and pen), as a place to take notes. (They usually do not let you bring paper and pen into the room, even if supplied by the testing center.)

■ Leave for the testing center with extra time so that you do not have to rush.

■ Try to find a restroom before going into the testing center. If you cannot find one, you can use the one in the testing center, of course, and they will direct you and give you time before your exam starts.

■ Do not drink a 64-ounce drink on the way to the testing center; once the exam starts, the exam timer will not stop while you go to the restroom.

■ On exam day, use any relaxation techniques that you have practiced to help get your mind focused while you wait for the exam.

Exam Review

This Exam Review completes the study plan materials as suggested by this book. At this point, you have read the other chapters of the book, and you have done the Chapter Review exam preparation tasks and Part Review tasks. Now you need to do the final study and review activities before taking the exam, as detailed in this section.

This section suggests some new activities and reminds you of some you probably already know. Whether you find these new or old, though, the activities all focus on filling in your knowledge gaps, finishing off your skills, and completing the study process. While repeating some tasks you did at Chapter Review and Part Review can help, you need to be ready to take an exam, so the Exam Review asks you to spend a lot of time answering exam questions.

The Exam Review walks through suggestions for several types of tasks and gives you some tracking tables for each activity. The main categories are as follows:

- Practicing for speed
- Taking practice exams
- Finding what you do not know well yet (knowledge gaps)
- Configuring and verifying functions from the CLI
- Repeating the Chapter Review and Part Review tasks

Practice Subnetting and Other Math-Related Skills

Like it or not, some of the questions on the Cisco ICND1, ICND2, and CCNA exams require you to do some math. To pass, you have to be good at the math. You also need to know when to use each process.

Interestingly, both the ICND1 and ICND2 exams require this math, but Cisco put the core learning for these math skills in the ICND1 exam topics. As a result, all these math skills are considered prerequisites for the ICND2 exam, but you still have to be good at the math. In particular, ICND2 has many troubleshooting topics, and all these require that you be pretty comfortable with all the subnetting math.

No matter how you learned subnetting before picking up this book, you should review the concepts and math before taking the ICND2 or CCNA exam. Table 22-1 lists the topics that require speed, and Table 22-2 lists items for which the speed is probably less important. By this point in your study, you should already be confident at finding the right answer to these kinds of problems. Now is the time to finish off your skills at getting the right answers, plus getting faster so you reduce your time pressure on the exams.

22

> **NOTE**   The time goals in the table are goals chosen by the author to give you an idea of a good time. If you happen to be a little slower on a few tasks, that does not mean you cannot do well on the test. But if you take several times as much time, for almost every task, know that the math-related work may cause you some time problems.

Table 22-1   Math-Related Activities That Benefit from Speed Practice

Activity	Book's Excellent Speed Goal (Seconds)	Self Check: Date / Time	Self Check: Date / Time
From a unicast IPv4 address, find key facts about its classful network.	10		
From one mask in any format, convert to the other two mask formats.	10		
Given an IPv4 address and mask, find the number of network, subnet, and host bits, plus the number of hosts/subnet and number of subnets.	15		
Given an IPv4 address and mask, find the resident subnet, subnet broadcast address, and range of usable addresses.	20-30		
Given a set of mask requirements, choose the best subnet mask.	15		
Given a classful network and one mask, find all subnet IDs.	45		

Table 22-2   Math-Related Activities That May Be Less Time Sensitive

ICND1 Book Chapter	Activity	Self Check: Date / Time	Self Check: Date / Time
20	Find VLSM overlaps, with problems that contain 5 or 6 subnets.		
20	Add VLSM subnets, with problems that contain 5 or 6 subnets.		
21	Find the best summary route, with problems that list 4 routes.		
22	Build an ACL command to match a subnet's addresses.		
22	List the addresses matched by one existing ACL command.		
25	Find the best abbreviation for one IPv6 address		
27	Find the IPv6 address of one router interface when using EUI-64.		

Take Practice Exams

One day soon, you need to pass a real Cisco exam at a Vue testing center. So, it is time to practice the real event as much as possible.

A practice exam using the Pearson IT Certification Practice Test (PCPT) exam software lets you experience many of the same issues as when taking a real Cisco exam. The software gives you a number of questions, with a countdown timer shown in the window. Once you answer a question, you cannot go back to it (yes, that's true on Cisco exams). If you run out of time, the questions you did not answer count as incorrect.

The process of taking the timed practice exams helps you prepare in three key ways:

- To practice the exam event itself, including time pressure, the need to read carefully, with a need to concentrate for long periods

- To build your analysis and critical thinking skills when examining the network scenario built in to many questions

- To discover the gaps in your networking knowledge so that you can study those topics before the real exam

As much as possible, treat the practice exam events as if you were taking the real Cisco exam at a Vue testing center. The following list gives some advice on how to make your practice exam more meaningful, rather than as just one more thing to do before exam day rolls around:

- Set aside 2 hours for taking the 90-minute timed practice exam.

- Make a list of what you expect to do for the 10 minutes before the real exam event. Then visualize yourself doing those things. Before taking each practice exam, practice those final 10 minutes before your exam timer starts. (The earlier section titled "Exam Day Advice" lists some suggestions about what to do in those last 10 minutes.)

- You may not bring anything with you into the Vue exam room, so remove all notes and helps from your work area before taking a practice exam. You may use blank paper, pen, and your brain only. Do not use calculators, notes, web browsers, or any other app on your computer.

- Real life may get in the way, but if at all possible, ask anyone around you to leave you alone for the time you will practice. If you must do your practice exam in a distracting environment, wear headphones or earplugs to reduce distractions.

- Do not guess, hoping to improve your score. Answer only when you have confidence in the answer. Then, if you get the question wrong, you can go back and think more about the question in a later study session.

Practicing Taking the ICND2 Exam

Because you are reading this chapter in the *Cisco CCNA Routing and Switching ICND2 200-101 Official Cert Guide*, you should be preparing for either the ICND2 exam or the CCNA exam. The PCPT exam software, and the exams you get with this ICND2 book, let you take practice exams for both the ICND2 and CCNA exams.

To take an ICND2 practice exam, you need to select one or both of the ICND2 exams from PCPT. If you followed the study plan in this book, you will not have seen any of the questions in these two exam databases before now. Once you select one of these two exams, you just need to choose the **Practice Exam** option in the upper right and start the exam.

You should plan to take between one and three ICND2 practice exams with these exam databases. Even people who are already well prepared should do at least one practice exam, just to experience the time pressure and the need for prolonged concentration. For those who want more practice exams, these two exam databases have enough questions for more than two exams. As a result, if you took a fourth practice exam with these exam databases, you will have seen almost all the questions before, making the practice exam a little too easy. If you are interested in purchasing more practice exams, check out the *Cisco CCNA Routing and Switching ICND2 200-101 Official Cert Guide Premium Edition eBook and Practice Test* product at www.ciscopress.com/title/9780133367713 and be sure to use the 70 percent discount coupon included in the DVD sleeve of this book.

Table 22-3 gives you a checklist to record your different practice exam events. Note that recording both the date and the score is helpful for some other work you will do, so note both. Also, in the Time Notes section, if you finish on time, note how much extra time you had; if you run out of time, note how many questions you did not have time to answer.

Table 22-3   ICND2 Practice Exam Checklist

Exam	Date	Score	Time Notes
ICND2			
ICND2			
ICND2			
ICND2			

Practicing Taking the CCNA Exam

If you plan on using the one-exam path to CCNA Routing and Switching, and taking the CCNA exam, you should plan on taking CCNA practice exams, and avoid the ICND1 and ICND2 practice exams. The CCNA practice exams use the same mix of questions as do the ICND1 and ICND2 practice exams, and it is best to save those questions for your CCNA practice exams.

Both the ICND1 book and the ICND2 book give you the rights to two CCNA exam question banks. If you own only one of those two books, simply use the two exams with "CCNA Full Exam" in the title. If you own both books, you have two sets of two CCNA exam banks, for a total of four unique CCNA exams. Figure 22-1 shows the ideas and the names of the exam in the PCPT software.

To take a CCNA exam, select one of the CCNA exam databases from the PCPT window. Then choose the mode option of **Practice Exam**, and start the exam.

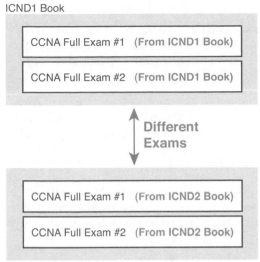

ICND1 Book

CCNA Full Exam #1   (From ICND1 Book)

CCNA Full Exam #2   (From ICND1 Book)

Different
Exams

CCNA Full Exam #1   (From ICND2 Book)

CCNA Full Exam #2   (From ICND2 Book)

ICND2 Book

Figure 22-1   *CCNA Exam Banks in the ICND1 and ICND2 Books*

For CCNA practice exam, plan to take at least one practice exam, but you could take up to four practice exams using these exam databases. Table 22-4 gives you a checklist to record your different practice exam events. Note that recording both the date and the score is helpful for some other work you will do, so note both. Also, in the Time Notes section, if you finish on time, note how much extra time you had; if you run out of time, note how many questions you did not have time to answer.

Table 22-4   CCNA Practice Exam Checklist

Exam Database Name	Date	Score	Time Notes
CCNA Exam 1 (From ICND1 Book)			
CCNA Exam 2 (From ICND1 Book)			
CCNA Exam 1 (From ICND2 Book)			
CCNA Exam 2 (From ICND2 Book)			

22

NOTE   The PCPT software lists, for the ICND2 book, two exam databases with the name ICND2 and two with the name CCNA. The questions in these two pair of exam databases overlap, so it makes sense to either take ICND2 practice exams or CCNA practice exams, depending on what test you are preparing for, but not both.

Advice on How to Answer Exam Questions

Open a web browser. Yes, take a break, and open a web browser, on any device. Do a quick search on a fun topic. Then, before you click a link, get ready to think where your eyes go for the first 5 to 10 seconds after you click the link. Now, click a link, and look at the page. Where did your eyes go?

Interestingly, web browsers, and the content in those web pages, have trained us all to scan. Web page designers actually design content with the expectation that people will scan with different patterns. Regardless of the pattern, when reading a web page, almost no one reads sequentially, and no one reads entire sentences. They scan for the interesting graphics, the big words, and then scan the space around those noticeable items.

Other parts of our electronic culture have also changed how the average person reads. For instance, many of you grew up using texting and social media, sifting through hundreds or thousands of messages, but each messages barely fills an entire sentence. (In fact, that previous sentence would not fit in a tweet, being longer than 140 characters.)

Those every day habits have changed how we all read and think in front of a screen. Unfortunately, those same habits often hurt our scores when taking computer-based exams.

If you scan exam questions like you read web pages, texts, and tweets, you will probably make some mistakes because you missed a key fact in the question, answer, or exhibits. It helps to start at the beginning, and read all the words—a process that is amazingly unnatural for many people today.

NOTE   I have heard from many college professors, in multiple disciplines, and Cisco Networking Academy instructors, and they consistently tell me that the number one test taking issue today is that people do not read the question well enough to understand the details.

For when you are taking the practice exams, and answering individual questions, let me make two suggestions. First, before the practice exam, think about your own personal strategy for how you will read a question. Make your approach to multiple choice questions in particular be a conscious decision on your part. Second, if you want some suggestions on how to read an exam question, use the following strategy:

Step 1.   Read the question itself, thoroughly, from start to finish.

Step 2.   Scan any exhibit (usually command output) or figure.

Step 3.   Scan the answers to look for the types of information. (Numeric? Terms? Single words? Phrases?)

Step 4.   Reread the question, thoroughly, from start to finish, to make sure you understand it.

Step 5. Read each answer thoroughly, while referring to the figure/exhibit as needed. After reading each answer, before reading the next answer, do the following:

    A. If correct, select as correct.

    B. If for sure incorrect, mentally rule it out.

    C. If unsure, mentally note it as a possible correct answer.

NOTE Cisco exams will tell you the number of correct answers. The exam software also helps you finish the question with the right number of answers noted. For instance, the software prevents you from selecting too many answers. Also, if you try to move on to the next question but have too few answers noted, the exam software asks if you truly want to move on.

Use the practice exams as a place to practice your approach to reading. Every time you click to the next question, try to read the question following your approach. If you are feeling time pressure, that is the perfect time to keep practicing your approach, to reduce and eliminate questions you miss because of scanning the question instead of reading thoroughly.

Taking Other Practice Exams

Many people add other practice exams and questions other than the questions that come with this book. Frankly, using other practice exams in addition to the questions that come with this book can be a good idea, for many reasons. The other exam questions may use different terms in different ways, emphasize different topics, and show different scenarios that make you rethink some topics.

No matter where you get additional exam questions, if you use the exam questions for a timed practice exam, it helps to take a few notes about the results. Table 22-5 gives you a place to take those notes. Also, take a guess at the percent of questions you have seen before taking the exam, and note if you think the questions are less, more, or the same challenge level as the questions that come with this book. And as usual, note whether you ran out of time or had extra time left over at the end.

Table 22-5   Checklist for Practice Exams from Other Sources

Exam Source	Other Exam Notes	% Questions Repeated (Estimate)	Challenging?	Date	Score	Time Notes

22

Note that the publisher does sell products that include additional test questions. The *Cisco CCNA Routing and Switching ICND2 Premium Edition eBook and Practice Test* product is basically the publisher's eBook version of this book. It includes a softcopy of the book, in formats you can read on your computer or on the most common book readers and tablets. The product includes all the content you would normally get with the DVD that comes with the print book, including all the question databases mentioned in this chapter. In addition, this product includes two more ICND2 exam database, plus two more CCNA exam databases, for extra exams.

NOTE In addition to getting the extra questions, the Premium Editions have links to every test question, including those in the print book, to the specific section of the book for further reference. This is a great learning tool if you need more detail than what you find in the question explanations. You can purchase the eBooks and additional practice exams at 70 percent off the list price using the coupon on the back of the activation code card in the DVD sleeve, making the Premium Editions the best and most cost-efficient way to get more practice questions.

Find Knowledge Gaps Through Question Review

You just took a number of practice exams. You probably learned a lot, gained some exam taking skills, and improved your networking knowledge and skills. But if you go back and look at all the questions you missed, you might be able to find a few small gaps in your knowledge.

One of the hardest things to find when doing your final exam preparation is to discover gaps in your knowledge and skills. In other words, what topics and skills do you need to know that you do not know? Or what topics do you think you know, but you misunderstand about some important fact? Finding gaps in your knowledge at this late stage requires more than just your gut feel about your strengths and weaknesses.

This next task uses a feature of PCPT to help you find those gaps. The PCPT software tracks each practice exam you take, remembering your answer for every question, and whether you got it wrong. You can view the results, and move back and forth between seeing the question and seeing the results page. To find gaps in your knowledge, follow these steps:

Step 1.   Pick and review one of your practice exams.

Step 2.   Review each incorrect question until you are happy you understand the question.

Step 3.   When finished with your review for a question, mark the question.

Step 4.   Review all incorrect questions from your exam until all are marked.

Step 5.   Move on to the next practice exam.

Figure 22-2 shows a sample Question Review page, in which all the questions were answered incorrectly. The results list a Correct column, with no check mark meaning that the answer was incorrect.

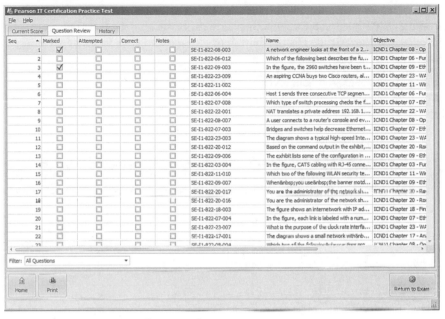

Figure 22-2   *PCPT Grading Results Page*

To perform the process of reviewing questions and marking them as complete, you can move between this Question Review page and the individual questions. Just double-click a question to move back to that question. From the question, click **Grade Exam** to move back to the grading results, and to the Question Review page shown in Figure 22-2. The question window also shows the place to mark the question, in the upper left, as shown in Figure 22-3.

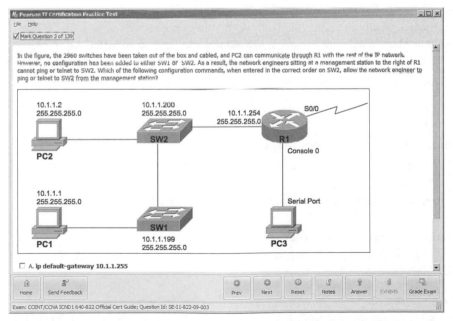

Figure 22-3   *Reviewing a Question, with the Mark Feature in the Upper Left*

If you want to come back later, to look through the questions you missed from an earlier exam, start at the PCPT home screen. From there, instead of clicking the Start button to start a new exam, click the **View Grade History** button to see your earlier exam attempts and work through any missed questions.

Track your progress through your gap review in Table 22-6. PCPT lists your previous practice exams by date and score, so it helps to note those values in the table for comparison to the PCPT menu.

Table 22-6   Tracking Checklist for Gap Review of Practice Exams

Exam (ICND1, ICND2, or CCNA)	Original Practice Exam Date	Original Exam Score	Date Gap Review Was Completed

Practice Hands-On CLI Skills

To do well on sim and simlet questions, you need to be comfortable with many Cisco router and switch commands, and how to use them from a Cisco command-line interface (CLI). As described in the Introduction to this book, sim questions require you to decide which configuration commands you need to configure to fix a problem or to complete a working configuration. Simlet questions require you to answer multiple choice questions by first using the CLI to issue **show** commands to look at the status of routers and switches in a small network.

To be ready for the exam, you need to know the following kinds of information:

CLI navigation: Basic CLI mechanics of moving into and out of user, enable, and configuration modes

Individual configuration: The meaning of the parameters of each configuration command

Feature configuration: The set of configuration commands, both required and optional, for each feature

Verification of configuration: The **show** commands that directly identify the configuration settings

Verification of status: The **show** commands that list current status values

To help remember and review all this knowledge and skill, you can do the tasks listed in the next several pages.

Review Mind Maps from Part Review

During Part Review, you created different mind maps with both configuration and verification commands. To remember the specific mind maps, flip back to each part's Part Review section.

Do Labs

Whatever method you chose for building hands-on CLI skills, take some time to review and do some labs to practice the commands. At this point, you should have thought about configuration quite a bit, whether in a simulator, real gear, or even just as paper exercises. Although it might be impractical to repeat every lab, make it a point to practice any commands and features for which you feel a little unsure about the topics from your review of the mind maps. Make sure to review lab exercises on the major topics in Table 22-7.

Table 22-7 Lab Checklist

Topic	Chapter	Date You Finished Lab Review
STP	2	
VLANs	3	
HSRP and GLBP	6	
OSPFv2 (for IPv4)	8	
EIGRP (for IPv4)	10	
HDLC and PPP	12	
Frame Relay	14	
OSPFv3 (for IPv6)	16	
EIGRPv6 (for IPv6)	17	
SNMP, syslog, and NetFlow	19	
Licensing	21	

One great way to practice is to use the Pearson Network Simulator (the Sim) at http://pearsonitcertification.com/networksimulator.

As a free alternative, you can do some short 5- to 10-minute paper configuration labs listed on the author's blogs. Just browse the Config Museum labs in those blogs (one blog for ICND1 and one for ICND2) and choose the labs you want to use. You can try these on paper or on your own lab gear. To find the blogs, start at www.certskills.com/blogs.

Other Study Tasks

If you get to this point and still feel the need to prepare some more, this last topic gives you three suggestions.

First, the Chapter Review exam preparation tasks and Part Review sections give you some useful study tasks.

Second, take more exam questions from other sources. You can always get more questions in the Cisco Press Premium Edition eBook and Practice Test products, which include an eBook copy of this book plus additional questions in additional PCPT exam banks. However, you can search the Internet for questions from many sources and review those questions as well.

NOTE   Some vendors claim to sell practice exams that contain the literal exam questions from the exam. These exams, called *brain dumps*, are against Cisco's testing policies. Cisco strongly discourages using any such tools for study.

Finally, join in the discussions on the Cisco Learning Network. Try to answer questions asked by other learners; the process of answering makes you think much harder about the topic. When someone posts an answer with which you disagree, think about why, and talk about it online. This is a great way to both learn more and build confidence.

Final Thoughts

You have studied quite a bit, worked hard, and sacrificed time and money to be ready for the exam. I hope your exam goes well, that you pass, and that you pass because you really know your stuff and will do well in your IT and networking career.

I encourage you to celebrate when you pass and to ask advice when you do not. The Cisco Learning Network is a great place to make posts to celebrate and to ask advice for the next time around. I personally would love to hear about your progress through Twitter (@wendellodom) or my Facebook fan page (http://facebook.com/wendellodom). I wish you well, and congratulations for working through the entire book!

Part VIII

Appendixes

Appendix A: Numeric Reference Tables

Appendix B: ICND2 Exam Updates

Glossary

Numeric Reference Tables

This appendix provides several useful reference tables that list numbers used throughout this book. Specifically:

Table A-1: A decimal-binary cross reference, useful when converting from decimal to binary and vice versa.

Table A-1   Decimal-Binary Cross Reference, Decimal Values 0–255

Decimal Value	Binary Value	Decimal Value	Binary Value	Decimal Value	Binary Value	Decimal Value	Binary Value
0	00000000	32	00100000	64	01000000	96	01100000
1	00000001	33	00100001	65	01000001	97	01100001
2	00000010	34	00100010	66	01000010	98	01100010
3	00000011	35	00100011	67	01000011	99	01100011
4	00000100	36	00100100	68	01000100	100	01100100
5	00000101	37	00100101	69	01000101	101	01100101
6	00000110	38	00100110	70	01000110	102	01100110
7	00000111	39	00100111	71	01000111	103	01100111
8	00001000	40	00101000	72	01001000	104	01101000
9	00001001	41	00101001	73	01001001	105	01101001
10	00001010	42	00101010	74	01001010	106	01101010
11	00001011	43	00101011	75	01001011	107	01101011
12	00001100	44	00101100	76	01001100	108	01101100
13	00001101	45	00101101	77	01001101	109	01101101
14	00001110	46	00101110	78	01001110	110	01101110
15	00001111	47	00101111	79	01001111	111	01101111
16	00010000	48	00110000	80	01010000	112	01110000
17	00010001	49	00110001	81	01010001	113	01110001
18	00010010	50	00110010	82	01010010	114	01110010
19	00010011	51	00110011	83	01010011	115	01110011
20	00010100	52	00110100	84	01010100	116	01110100
21	00010101	53	00110101	85	01010101	117	01110101
22	00010110	54	00110110	86	01010110	118	01110110
23	00010111	55	00110111	87	01010111	119	01110111
24	00011000	56	00111000	88	01011000	120	01111000
25	00011001	57	00111001	89	01011001	121	01111001
26	00011010	58	00111010	90	01011010	122	01111010
27	00011011	59	00111011	91	01011011	123	01111011
28	00011100	60	00111100	92	01011100	124	01111100
29	00011101	61	00111101	93	01011101	125	01111101
30	00011110	62	00111110	94	01011110	126	01111110
31	00011111	63	00111111	95	01011111	127	01111111

Decimal Value	Binary Value	Decimal Value	Binary Value	Decimal Value	Binary Value	Decimal Value	Binary Value
128	10000000	160	10100000	192	11000000	224	11100000
129	10000001	161	10100001	193	11000001	225	11100001
130	10000010	162	10100010	194	11000010	226	11100010
131	10000011	163	10100011	195	11000011	227	11100011
132	10000100	164	10100100	196	11000100	228	11100100
133	10000101	165	10100101	197	11000101	229	11100101
134	10000110	166	10100110	198	11000110	230	11100110
135	10000111	167	10100111	199	11000111	231	11100111
136	10001000	168	10101000	200	11001000	232	11101000
137	10001001	169	10101001	201	11001001	233	11101001
138	10001010	170	10101010	202	11001010	234	11101010
139	10001011	171	10101011	203	11001011	235	11101011
140	10001100	172	10101100	204	11001100	236	11101100
141	10001101	173	10101101	205	11001101	237	11101101
142	10001110	174	10101110	206	11001110	238	11101110
143	10001111	175	10101111	207	11001111	239	11101111
144	10010000	176	10110000	208	11010000	240	11110000
145	10010001	177	10110001	209	11010001	241	11110001
146	10010010	178	10110010	210	11010010	242	11110010
147	10010011	179	10110011	211	11010011	243	11110011
148	10010100	180	10110100	212	11010100	244	11110100
149	10010101	181	10110101	213	11010101	245	11110101
150	10010110	182	10110110	214	11010110	246	11110110
151	10010111	183	10110111	215	11010111	247	11110111
152	10011000	184	10111000	216	11011000	248	11111000
153	10011001	185	10111001	217	11011001	249	11111001
154	10011010	186	10111010	218	11011010	250	11111010
155	10011011	187	10111011	219	11011011	251	11111011
156	10011100	188	10111100	220	11011100	252	11111100
157	10011101	189	10111101	221	11011101	253	11111101
158	10011110	190	10111110	222	11011110	254	11111110
159	10011111	191	10111111	223	11011111	255	11111111

A

Table A-2: A hexadecimal-binary cross reference, useful when converting from hex to binary and vice versa.

Table A-2 Hex-Binary Cross Reference

Hex	4-Bit Binary
0	0000
1	0001
2	0010
3	0011
4	0100
5	0101
6	0110
7	0111
8	1000
9	1001
A	1010
B	1011
C	1100
D	1101
E	1110
F	1111

Table A-3: Powers of 2, from 2^1 through 2^{32}.

Table A-3   Powers of 2

X	2^x	X	2^x
1	2	17	131,072
2	4	18	262,144
3	8	19	524,288
4	16	20	1,048,576
5	32	21	2,097,152
6	64	22	4,194,304
7	128	23	8,388,608
8	256	24	16,777,216
9	512	25	33,554,432
10	1024	26	67,108,864
11	2048	27	134,217,728
12	4096	28	268,435,456
13	8192	29	536,870,912
14	16,384	30	1,073,741,824
15	32,768	31	2,147,483,648
16	65,536	32	4,294,967,296

A

Table A-4: Table of all 33 possible subnet masks, in all three formats.

Table A-4   All Subnet Masks

Decimal	Prefix	Binary
0.0.0.0	/0	00000000 00000000 00000000 00000000
128.0.0.0	/1	10000000 00000000 00000000 00000000
192.0.0.0	/2	11000000 00000000 00000000 00000000
224.0.0.0	/3	11100000 00000000 00000000 00000000
240.0.0.0	/4	11110000 00000000 00000000 00000000
248.0.0.0	/5	11111000 00000000 00000000 00000000
252.0.0.0	/6	11111100 00000000 00000000 00000000
254.0.0.0	/7	11111110 00000000 00000000 00000000
255.0.0.0	/8	11111111 00000000 00000000 00000000
255.128.0.0	/9	11111111 10000000 00000000 00000000
255.192.0.0	/10	11111111 11000000 00000000 00000000
255.224.0.0	/11	11111111 11100000 00000000 00000000
255.240.0.0	/12	11111111 11110000 00000000 00000000
255.248.0.0	/13	11111111 11111000 00000000 00000000
255.252.0.0	/14	11111111 11111100 00000000 00000000
255.254.0.0	/15	11111111 11111110 00000000 00000000
255.255.0.0	/16	11111111 11111111 00000000 00000000
255.255.128.0	/17	11111111 11111111 10000000 00000000
255.255.192.0	/18	11111111 11111111 11000000 00000000
255.255.224.0	/19	11111111 11111111 11100000 00000000
255.255.240.0	/20	11111111 11111111 11110000 00000000
255.255.248.0	/21	11111111 11111111 11111000 00000000
255.255.252.0	/22	11111111 11111111 11111100 00000000
255.255.254.0	/23	11111111 11111111 11111110 00000000
255.255.255.0	/24	11111111 11111111 11111111 00000000
255.255.255.128	/25	11111111 11111111 11111111 10000000
255.255.255.192	/26	11111111 11111111 11111111 11000000
255.255.255.224	/27	11111111 11111111 11111111 11100000
255.255.255.240	/28	11111111 11111111 11111111 11110000
255.255.255.248	/29	11111111 11111111 11111111 11111000
255.255.255.252	/30	11111111 11111111 11111111 11111100
255.255.255.254	/31	11111111 11111111 11111111 11111110
255.255.255.255	/32	11111111 11111111 11111111 11111111

ICND2 Exam Updates

Over time, reader feedback allows Cisco Press to gauge which topics give our readers the most problems when taking the exams. In addition, Cisco may make small changes in the breadth of exam topics or in emphasis of certain topics. To assist readers with those topics, the author creates new materials clarifying and expanding on those troublesome exam topics.

The document you are viewing is Version 1.0 of this appendix, and there are no updates. You can check for an updated version at http://www.ciscopress.com/title/9781587143731.

2-way state   In OSPF, a neighbor state that implies that the router has exchanged Hellos with the neighbor and that all required parameters match.

3G/4G Internet   An Internet access technology that uses wireless radio signals to communicate through mobile phone towers, most often used by mobile phones, tablets, and some other mobile devices.

A

ABR   Area Border Router. A router using OSPF in which the router has interfaces in multiple OSPF areas.

access link   In Frame Relay, the physical serial link that connects a Frame Relay DTE, usually a router, to a Frame Relay switch. The access link uses the same physical layer standards as do point-to-point leased lines.

access rate   In Frame Relay, the speed at which bits are sent over an access link.

ACL   Access control list. A list configured on a router to control packet flow through the router, such as to prevent packets with a certain IP address from leaving a particular interface on the router.

Active Virtual Gateway (AVG)   With Gateway Load Balancing Protocol (GLBP), the function by which a router answers ARP requests for the virtual IP address, replying with different virtual MAC addresses for the purpose of load balancing user traffic on a per-host basis.

administrative distance   In Cisco routers, a means for one router to choose between multiple routes to reach the same subnet when those routes are learned by different routing protocols. The lower the administrative distance, the more preferred the source of the routing information.

administrative mode   *See* trunking administrative mode.

ADSL   Asymmetric digital subscriber line. One of many DSL technologies, ADSL is designed to deliver more bandwidth downstream (from the central office to the customer site) than upstream.

analog modem   *See* modem.

AR   *See* access rate.

Area Border Router   *See* ABR.

ARP   Address Resolution Protocol. An Internet protocol used to map an IP address to a MAC address. Defined in RFC 826.

ASBR   Autonomous System Border Router. A router using OSPF in which the router learns routes via another source, usually another routing protocol, exchanging routes that are external to OSPF with the OSPF domain.

authentication   Authentication is the ability to verify the identity of a user or a computer system on a computer network.

Autonomous System Border Router   *See* ASBR.

autonomous system number (ASN)   A number used by BGP to identify a routing domain, often a single enterprise or organization. Within the context of this book, as used with EIGRP, a number that identifies the routing processes on routers that are willing to exchange EIGRP routing information with each other.

autosummarization   A routing protocol feature in which a router that connects to more than one classful network advertises summarized routes for each entire classful network when sending updates out interfaces connected to other classful networks.

autosummary   *See* autosummarization.

B

backbone area   In OSPFv2 and OSPFv3, the special area in a multi-area design, with all nonbackbone areas needing to connect to the backbone area. area 0.

backup designated router   An OSPF router connected to a multiaccess network that monitors the work of the designated router (DR) and takes over the work of the DR if the DR fails.

balanced hybrid   A term referencing the combination of distance vector and link state features as implemented by EIGRP.

blocking state   In 802.1D STP, a port state in which no received frames are processed and the switch forwards no frames out the interface, with the exception of STP messages.

boot field   The low-order 4 bits of the configuration register in a Cisco router. The value in the boot field in part tells the router where to look for a Cisco IOS image to load.

BPDU   Bridge protocol data unit. The generic name for Spanning Tree Protocol messages.

BPDU Guard   A Cisco switch feature that listens for incoming STP BPDU messages, disabling the interface if any are received. The goal is to prevent loops when a switch connects to a port expected to only have a host connected to it.

BRI   Basic Rate Interface. An ISDN interface composed of two bearer channels and one data (D) channel for circuit-switched communication of voice, video, and data.

bridge ID (BID)   An 8-byte identifier for bridges and switches used by STP and RSTP. It is composed of a 2-byte priority field followed by a 6-byte System ID field that is usually filled with a MAC address.

bridge protocol data unit   *See* BPDU.

broadcast address   *See* subnet broadcast address.

broadcast domain   A set of all devices that receive broadcast frames originating from any device in the set. Devices in the same VLAN are in the same broadcast domain.

broadcast subnet   When subnetting a Class A, B, or C network, the one subnet in each classful network for which all subnet bits have a value of binary 1. The subnet broadcast address in this subnet has the same numeric value as the classful network's networkwide broadcast address.

C

cable Internet   An Internet access technology that uses a cable TV (CATV) cable, normally used for video, to send and receive data.

CHAP   Challenge Handshake Authentication Protocol. A security feature defined by PPP that allows either or both endpoints on a link to authenticate the other device as a particular authorized device.

CIDR   Classless interdomain routing. An RFC-standard tool for global IP address range assignment. CIDR reduces the size of Internet routers' IP routing tables, helping deal with the rapid growth of the Internet. The term *classless* refers to the fact that the summarized groups of networks represent a group of addresses that do not confirm to IPv4 classful (Class A, B, and C) grouping rules.

CIDR notation   *See* prefix notation.

circuit switching   The switching system in which a dedicated physical circuit path must exist between the sender and the receiver for the duration of the "call." Used heavily in the telephone company network.

Cisco Prime   Cisco Prime is graphical user interface (GUI) software that utilizes SNMP and can be used to manage your Cisco network devices. The term *Cisco Prime* is an "umbrella" term that encompasses many different individual software products.

classful addressing   A concept in IPv4 addressing that defines a subnetted IP address as having three parts: network, subnet, and host.

classful network   An IPv4 Class A, B, or C network. It is called a classful network because these networks are defined by the class rules for IPv4 addressing.

classful routing protocol   An inherent characteristic of a routing protocol. Specifically, the routing protocol does not send subnet masks in its routing updates. This requires the protocol to make assumptions about classful networks and makes it unable to support VLSM and manual route summarization.

classless addressing   A concept in IPv4 addressing that defines a subnetted IP address as having two parts: a prefix (or subnet) and a host.

classless interdomain routing (CIDR)   *See* CIDR.

classless routing   A variation of the IPv4 forwarding (routing) process that defines the particulars of how the default route is used. The default route is always used for packets whose destination IP address does not match any other routes.

classless routing protocol   An inherent characteristic of a routing protocol. Specifically, the routing protocol sends subnet masks in its routing updates, thereby removing any need to make assumptions about the addresses in a particular subnet or network. This allows the protocol to support VLSM and manual route summarization.

composite metric   A term in EIGRP for the result of the calculation of the EIGRP metric for a route.

configuration register   In Cisco routers, a 16-bit user-configurable value that determines how the router functions during initialization. In software, the bit position is set by specifying a hexadecimal value using configuration commands.

contiguous network   In IPv4, a internetwork design in which packets being forwarded between any two subnets of a single classful network only pass through the subnets of that classful network.

console port   A physical socket on a router or switch to which a cable can be connected between a computer and the router/switch, for the purpose of allowing the computer to use a terminal emulator and use the CLI to configure, verify, and troubleshoot the router/switch.

convergence   The time required for routing protocols to react to changes in the network, removing bad routes and adding new, better routes so that the current best routes are in all the routers' routing tables.

CSU/DSU   Channel service unit/data service unit. A device that connects a physical circuit installed by the telco to some CPE device, adapting between the voltages, current, framing, and connectors used on the circuit to the physical interface supported by the DTE.

customer premise equipment (CPE)   A telco term that refers to equipment on-site at the telco customer site (the enterprise's site) that connects to the WAN service provided by the telco.

D

Database Description   An OSPF packet type that lists brief descriptions of the LSAs in the OSPF LSDB.

data link connection identifier (DLCI)   *See* DLCI.

DCE   Data circuit-terminating equipment. Also refers to data communications equipment. From a physical layer perspective, the device providing the clocking on a WAN link, usually a CSU/DSU, is the DCE. From a packet-switching perspective, the service provider's switch, to which a router might connect, is considered the DCE.

Dead Interval   In OSPF, a timer used for each neighbor. A router considers the neighbor to have failed if no Hellos are received from that neighbor in the time defined by the timer.

deencapsulation   On a computer that receives data over a network, the process in which the device interprets the lower-layer headers and, when finished with each header, removes the header, revealing the next-higher-layer PDU.

default gateway/default router   On an IP host, the IP address of some router to which the host sends packets when the packet's destination address is on a subnet other than the local subnet.

deny   An action taken with an ACL that implies that the packet is discarded.

designated port   In both STP and RSTP, a port role used to determine which of multiple interfaces on multiple switches, each connected to the same segment or collision domain, should forward frames to the segment. The switch advertising the lowest-cost Hello BPDU onto the segment becomes the DP.

designated router   In OSPF, on a multi-access network, the router that wins an election and is therefore responsible for managing a streamlined process for exchanging OSPF

topology information between all routers attached to that network.

dial access   A general term referring to any kind of switched WAN service that uses the telco network in which the device must signal (the equivalent of tapping digits on a phone) to establish a connection before sending data.

Diffusing Update Algorithm (DUAL)   A convergence algorithm used in EIGRP when a route fails and a router does not have a feasible successor route. DUAL causes the routers to send EIGRP Query and Reply messages to discover alternate loop-free routes.

Dijkstra Shortest Path First (SPF) algorithm   The name of the algorithm used by link-state routing protocols to analyze the LSDB and find the least-cost routes from that router to each subnet.

directed broadcast address   The same as a subnet broadcast address.

disabled port   In STP, a port role for non-working interfaces—in other words, interfaces that are not in a connect or up/up interface state.

discarding state   An RSTP interface state in which no received frames are processed and the switch forwards no frames out the interface, with the exception of RSTP messages.

discontiguous network   In IPv4, a internetwork design in which packets being forwarded between two subnets of a single classful network must pass through the subnets of another classful network.

distance vector   The logic behind the behavior of some interior routing protocols, such as RIP and IGRP. Distance vector routing algorithms call for each router to send its entire routing table in each update, but only to its neighbors. Distance vector routing algorithms can be prone to routing loops but are computationally simpler than link-state routing algorithms. Also called Bellman-Ford routing algorithm.

DLCI   Data link connection identifier. The Frame Relay address that identifies a VC on a particular access link.

DNS   Domain Name System. An application layer protocol used throughout the Internet for translating hostnames into their associated IP addresses.

DS0   Digital signal level 0. A 64-Kbps line or channel of a faster line inside a telco whose origins are to support a single voice call using the original voice (PCM) codecs.

DS1   Digital signal level 1. A 1.544-Mbps line from the telco, with 24 DS0 channels of 64 Kbps each, plus an 8-Kbps management and framing channel. Also called a T1.

DS3   Digital signal level 3. A 44.736-Mbps line from the telco, with 28 DS1 channels plus overhead. Also called a T3.

DSL   Digital subscriber line. Public network technology that delivers high bandwidth over conventional telco local-loop copper wiring at limited distances. Usually used as an Internet access technology connecting a user to an ISP.

DSL modem   A device that connects to a telephone line and uses DSL standards to transmit and receive data to/from a telco using DSL.

DTE   Data terminal equipment. From a Layer 1 perspective, the DTE synchronizes its clock based on the clock sent by the DCE. From a packet-switching perspective, the DTE is the device outside the service provider's network, usually a router.

DUAL   *See* Diffusing Update Algorithm.

dual stacks   In IPv6, a mode of operation in which a host or router runs both IPv4 and IPv6.

E

EIGRP   Enhanced Interior Gateway Routing Protocol. An advanced version of IGRP developed by Cisco. Provides superior convergence properties and operating efficiency and combines the advantages of link-state protocols with those of distance vector protocols.

EIGRPv6   EIGRP for IPv6. A version of EIGRP that supports advertising routes for IPv6 prefixes instead of IPv4 subnets.

enable mode   A part of the Cisco IOS CLI in which the user can use potentially disruptive commands on a router or switch, including the ability to then reach configuration mode and reconfigure the router.

encapsulation   The placement of data from a higher-layer protocol behind the header (and in some cases, between a header and trailer) of the next-lower-layer protocol. For example, an IP packet could be encapsulated in an Ethernet header and trailer before being sent over an Ethernet.

encoding   The conventions for how a device varies the electrical or optical signals sent over a cable to imply a particular binary code. For instance, a modem might encode a binary 1 or 0 by using one frequency to mean 1 and another to mean 0.

encryption   Encryption is the ability to take data and send the data in a form that is not readable by someone that intercepts this data.

EtherChannel   A feature in which up to eight parallel Ethernet segments between the same two devices, each using the same speed, can be combined to act as a single link for forwarding and Spanning Tree Protocol logic.

Ethernet WAN   Any WAN service that happens to use any type of Ethernet link as the access link between the customer and the WAN service.

EUI-64 Literally, a standard for an extended unique identifier that is 64 bits long. Specifically for IPv6, a set of rules for forming a 64-bit identifier, used as the interface ID in IPv6 addresses, by starting with a 48-bit MAC address, inserting FFFE (hex) in the middle, and inverting the seventh bit.

extended access list A list of IOS **access-list** global configuration commands that can match multiple parts of an IP packet, including the source and destination IP address and TCP/UDP ports, for the purpose of deciding which packets to discard and which to allow through the router.

extended ping An IOS command in which the **ping** command accepts many other options besides just the destination IP address.

F

feasibility condition In EIGRP, when a router has learned of multiple routes to reach one subnet, if the best route's metric is X, the feasibility condition is another route whose reported distance is < X.

feasible distance In EIGRP, the metric of the best route to reach a subnet.

feasible successor In EIGRP, a route that is not the best route (successor route) but that can be used immediately if the best route fails, without causing a loop. Such a route meets the feasibility condition.

FTP File Transfer Protocol. An application protocol, part of the TCP/IP protocol stack, used to transfer files between network nodes. FTP is defined in RFC 959.

filter Generally, a process or a device that screens network traffic for certain characteristics, such as source address, destination address, or protocol. This process determines whether to forward or discard that traffic based on the established criteria.

First Hop Redundancy Protocol (FHRP) A class of protocols that includes HSRP, VRRP, and GLBP, which allows multiple redundant routers on the same subnet to act as a single default router (first-hop router).

flash memory A type of read/write permanent memory that retains its contents even with no power applied to the memory and that uses no moving parts, making the memory less likely to fail over time.

forward To send a frame toward its ultimate destination by way of an internetworking device.

forward delay An STP timer, defaulting to 15 seconds, used to dictate how long an interface stays in the listening state, and the time spent in learning state. Also called the forward delay timer.

forwarding state An STP and RSTP port state in which an interface operates unrestricted by STP.

forward route From one host's perspective, the route over which a packet travels from that host to some other host.

Frame Relay An international standard data link protocol that defines the capabilities to create a frame-switched (packet-switched) service, allowing DTE devices (usually routers) to send data to many other devices using a single physical connection to the Frame Relay service.

Frame Relay DCE The Frame Relay switch.

Frame Relay DTE The customer device connected to a Frame Relay access link, usually a router.

Frame Relay mapping The information that correlates, or maps, a Frame Relay DLCI to the Layer 3 address of the DTE on the other end of the VC identified by the local DLCI.

framing   The conventions for how Layer 2 interprets the bits sent according to OSI Layer 1. For example, after an electrical signal has been received and converted to binary, framing identifies the information fields inside the data.

full duplex   Generically, any communication in which two communicating devices can concurrently send and receive data. Specifically for Ethernet LANs, the ability of both devices to send and receive at the same time. This is allowed when there are only two stations in a collision domain. Full duplex is enabled by turning off the CSMA/CD collision detection logic.

full state   In OSPF, a neighbor state that implies that the two routers have exchanged the complete (full) contents of their respective LSDBs.

full update   With IP routing protocols, the general concept that a routing protocol update lists all known routes. *See also* partial update.

fully adjacent   In OSPF, a characterization of the state of a neighbor in which the two neighbors have reached the full state

G

Gateway Load Balancing Protocol (GLBP)   A Cisco proprietary protocol that allows two (or more) routers to share the duties of being the default router on a subnet, with an active/active model, with all routers actively forwarding off-subnet traffic for some hosts in the subnet.

generic routing encapsulation (GRE)   A protocol, defined RFC 2784, that defines the headers used when creating a site-to-site VPN tunnel. The protocol defines the use of a normal IP header, called the Delivery Header, and a GRE header that the endpoints use to create and manage traffic over the GRE tunnel.

GET message   GET messages are used by SNMP to read from variable in the MIB.

GLBP active   A Gateway Load Balancing Protocol (GLBP) state in which the router serves as the Active Virtual Gateway (AVG), or, for a GLBP forwarder, a router that actively supports the forwarding of off-subnet packets for hosts in that subnet.

GLBP listen   A Gateway Load Balancing Protocol (GLBP) state for a forwarder in which the router does not currently support the forwarding of off-subnet packets for hosts in that subnet for a given virtual MAC address, instead waiting to take over that role for the currently-active forwarder.

GLBP standby   A Gateway Load Balancing Protocol (GLBP) state in which the router does not serve as the Active Virtual Gateway (AVG), but instead monitors the current AVG, and takes over for that AVG if it fails.

global routing prefix   An IPv6 prefix, which defines an IPv6 address block made up of global unicast addresses, assigned to one organization, so that that organization has a block of globally unique IPv6 addresses to use in their network.

global unicast address   A type of unicast IPv6 address that has been allocated from a range of public globally unique IP addresses as registered through IANA/ICANN, its member agencies, and other registries or ISPs.

GRE tunnel   A site-to-site VPN idea, in which the endpoints act as if a point-to-point link (the tunnel) exists between the sites, while actually encapsulating packets using GRE standards.

H

HDLC   High-Level Data Link Control. A bit-oriented synchronous data link layer protocol developed by the International Organization for Standardization (ISO). Derived from synchronous data link control (SDLC), HDLC specifies a data encapsulation method on synchronous serial links using frame characters and checksums.

Hello   (Multiple definitions) 1) A protocol used by OSPF routers to discover, establish, and maintain neighbor relationships. 2) A protocol used by EIGRP routers to discover, establish, and maintain neighbor relationships. 3) In STP, refers to the name of the periodic message sourced by the root bridge in a spanning tree.

hello BPDU   The STP and RSTP message used for the majority of STP communications, listing the root's bridge ID, the sending device's bridge ID, and the sending device's cost with which to reach the root.

Hello Interval   With OSPF and EIGRP, an interface timer that dictates how often the router should send Hello messages.

hello timer   In STP, the time interval at which the root switch should send hello BPDUs.

Hot Standby Router Protocol (HSRP)   A Cisco proprietary protocol that allows two (or more) routers to share the duties of being the default router on a subnet, with an active/standby model, with one router acting as the default router and the other sitting by waiting to take over that role if the first router fails.

HSRP active   A Hot Standby Router Protocol (HSRP) state in which the router actively supports the forwarding of off-subnet packets for hosts in that subnet.

HSRP standby   A Hot Standby Router Protocol (HSRP) state in which the router does not currently support the forwarding of off-subnet packets for hosts in that subnet, instead waiting for the currently active router to fail before taking over that role.

I

ICMP Echo Request   One type of ICMP message, created specifically to be used as the message sent by the **ping** command to test connectivity in a network. The **ping** command sends these messages to other hosts, expecting the other host to reply with an ICMP Echo Reply message.

ICMP Echo Reply   One type of ICMP message, created specifically to be used as the message sent by the **ping** command to test connectivity in a network. The **ping** command expects to receive these messages from other hosts, after the **ping** command first sends an ICMP Echo Request message to the host.

IEEE 802.11   The IEEE base standard for wireless LANs.

IEEE 802.1AD   The IEEE standard for the functional equivalent of the Cisco proprietary EtherChannel.

IEEE 802.1D   The IEEE standard for the original Spanning Tree Protocol.

IEEE 802.1Q   The IEEE-standard VLAN trunking protocol. 802.1Q includes the concept of a native VLAN, for which no VLAN header is added, and a 4-byte VLAN header is inserted after the original frame's type/length field.

IEEE 802.1W   The IEEE standard for Multiple Instances of Spanning Tree (MIST), which allows for load balancing of traffic among different VLANs.

IEEE 802.1W   The IEEE standard for an enhanced version of STP, called Rapid STP, which speeds convergence.

IEEE 802.3   The IEEE base standard for Ethernet-like LANs.

IGRP   Interior Gateway Routing Protocol. An old, no-longer-supported Interior Gateway Protocol (IGP) developed by Cisco.

inferior hello   When STP compares two or more received hello BPDUs, an inferior hello is a hello that lists a numerically larger root bridge ID than another hello or a hello that lists the same root Bridge ID but with a larger cost.

infinity   In the context of IP routing protocols, a finite metric value defined by the routing protocol that is used to represent an unusable route in a routing protocol update.

inform   The inform message is like a trap message in SNMP. This message is proactively generated by the managed device. This message is based on thresholds configured by a network administrator. The difference between an Inform and a trap is that an inform must be acknowledged by the network management station.

integrity   Integrity in data transfers means that the network administrator can determine that the information has not been tampered with in transit.

inter-area prefix LSA   In OSPFv6, a type of LSA similar to the Type 3 summary LSA in OSPFv2, created by an Area Border Router (ABR), to describe an IPv6 prefix one area in the database of another area.

interior gateway protocol (IGP)   A routing protocol designed to be used to exchange routing information inside a single autonomous system.

Inter-Switch Link (ISL)   The Cisco proprietary VLAN trunking protocol that predated 802.1Q by many years. ISL defines a 26-byte header that encapsulates the original Ethernet frame.

Internal router   In OSPF, a router with all interfaces in the same non-backbone area.

Internetwork Operating System (IOS)   *See* IOS.

Inverse ARP   A Frame Relay protocol with which a router announces its Layer 3 address over a VC, thereby informing the neighbor of useful Layer 3-to-Layer 2 mapping information.

IOS   Cisco operating system software that provides the majority of a router's or switch's features, with the hardware providing the remaining features.

IOS feature set   A set of related features that can be enabled on a router to enable certain functionality. For example, the Security feature set would enable the ability to have the router act as a firewall in the network.

IOS image   A file that contains the IOS.

IP Control Protocol (IPCP)   A control protocol defined as part of PPP for the purpose of initializing and controlling the sending of IPv4 packets over a PPP link.

IPsec   The term referring to the IP Security protocols, which is an architecture for providing encryption and authentication services, usually when creating VPN services through an IP network.

ISDN   Integrated Services Digital Network. A communication protocol offered by telephone companies that permits telephone networks to carry data, voice, and video.

ISL   *See* Inter-Switch Link.

ISP prefix   In IPv6, the prefix that describes an address block that has been assigned to an ISP by some Internet registry.

K

keepalive   A feature of many data link protocols in which the router sends messages periodically to let the neighboring router know that the first router is still alive and well.

L

LAPF   Link Access Procedure Frame Bearer Services. Defines the basic Frame Relay header and trailer. The header includes DLCI, FECN, BECN, and DE bits.

learn   Switches learn MAC addresses by examining the source MAC addresses of frames they receive. They add each new MAC address, along with the port number of the port on which it learned of the MAC address, to an address table.

learning state   In STP, a temporary port state in which the interface does not forward frames, but it can begin to learn MAC addresses from frames received on the interface.

leased line   A transmission line reserved by a communications carrier for a customer's private use. A leased line is a type of dedicated line.

Link Control Protocol   A control protocol defined as part of PPP for the purpose of initializing and maintaining a PPP link.

link-local address   A type of unicast IPv6 address that represents an interface on a single data link. Packets sent to a link-local address cross only that particular link and are never forwarded to other subnets by a router. Used for communications that do not need to leave the local link, such as neighbor discovery.

link state   A classification of the underlying algorithm used in some routing protocols. Link-state protocols build a detailed database that lists links (subnets) and their state (up, down), from which the best routes can then be calculated.

link-state advertisement (LSA)   In OSPF, the name of the data structure that resides inside the LSDB and describes in detail the various components in a network, including routers and links (subnets).

link-state database (LSDB)   In OSPF, the data structure in RAM of a router that holds the various LSAs, with the collective LSAs representing the entire topology of the network.

link-state request   An OSPF packet used to ask a neighboring router to send a particular LSA.

link-state update   An OSPF packet used to send an LSA to a neighboring router.

listening state   A temporary STP port state that occurs immediately when a blocking interface must be moved to a forwarding state. The switch times out MAC table entries during this state. It also ignores frames received on the interface and doesn't forward any frames out the interface.

Local Management Interface (LMI)   A Frame Relay protocol used between a DTE (router) and DCE (Frame Relay switch). LMI acts as a keepalive mechanism. The absence of LMI messages means that the other device has failed. It also tells the DTE about the existence of each VC and DLCI, along with its status.

local username   A username (with matching password), configured on a router or switch. It is considered local because it exists on the router or switch, and not on a remote server.

LSA   *See* link-state advertisement.

M

MaxAge   In STP, a timer that states how long a switch should wait when it no longer receives hellos from the root switch before acting to reconverge the STP topology. Also called the MaxAge timer.

metric A numeric measurement used by a routing protocol to determine how good a route is as compared to other alternate routes to reach the same subnet.

MIB The Management Information Base is used in SNMP. This standard database structure exists on the managed device and contains the variables that can be read from and optionally written to in order to manage the device.

modem Modulator-demodulator. A device that converts between digital and analog signals so that a computer may send data to another computer using analog telephone lines. At the source, a modem converts digital signals to a form suitable for transmission over analog communication facilities. At the destination, the analog signals are returned to their digital form.

MPLS Multiprotocol Label Switching. Method of forwarding packets based on labels, instead of IP headers. Can be combined with other service provider features to provide WAN services to customers.

MTU Maximum transmission unit. The maximum packet size, in bytes, that a particular interface can handle.

multi-area In OSPFv2 and OSPFv3, a design that uses multiple areas.

N

NBMA *See* nonbroadcast multiaccess.

neighbor In routing protocols, another router with which a router decides to exchange routing information.

Neighbor Advertisement (NA) A message defined by the IPv6 Neighbor Discovery Protocol (NDP) and used to declare to other neighbors a host's MAC address. Sometimes sent in response to a previously-received NDP Neighbor Solicitation (NS) message.

Neighbor Discovery Protocol (NDP) A protocol that is part of the IPv6 protocol suite and is used to discover and exchange information about devices on the same subnet (neighbors). In particular, it replaces IPv4 ARP.

Neighbor Solicitation (NS) A message defined by the IPv6 Neighbor Discovery Protocol (NDP) and used to ask a neighbor to reply back with a Neighbor Advertisement, which lists the neighbor's MAC address.

neighbor table For OSPF and EIGRP, a list of routers that have reached neighbor status.

NetFlow NetFlow permits the monitoring of IP traffic in your network. You can use this information for accounting, billing, capacity planning, security, and overall network monitoring.

Network LSA In OSPF, a type of LSA that a designated router (DR) creates for the network (subnet) for which the DR is helping to distribute LSAs.

NMS The Network Management Station is the device that runs network management software to manage network devices. SNMP is often the network management protocol used between the NMS and the managed device.

nonbroadcast multiaccess (NBMA) A characterization of a type of Layer 2 network in which more than two devices connect to the network, but the network does not allow broadcast frames to be sent to all devices on the network.

NVRAM Nonvolatile RAM. A type of random-access memory (RAM) that retains its contents when a unit is powered off.

O

OID   The object identifier is used to uniquely describe a MIB variable in the SNMP database. This is a numeric string that identifies the variable uniquely and also describes where the variable exists in the MIB tree structure.

OSPF   Open Shortest Path First. A popular link-state IGP that uses a link-state database and the Shortest Path First (SPF) algorithm to calculate the best routes to reach each known subnet.

out-of-band   Network management traffic is often sent out-of-band (OOB). This means the traffic does not share the same network paths with user data traffic.

overlapping subnets   An (incorrect) IP subnet design condition in which one subnet's range of addresses includes addresses in the range of another subnet.

P

packet switching   A WAN service in which each DTE device connects to a telco using a single physical line, with the possibility of being able to forward traffic to all other sites connected to the same service. The telco switch makes the forwarding decision based on an address in the packet header.

PAP   Password Authentication Protocol. A PPP authentication protocol that allows PPP peers to authenticate one another.

partial mesh   A network topology in which more than two devices could physically communicate, but by choice, only a subset of the pairs of devices connected to the network are allowed to communicate directly.

partial update   With IP routing protocols, the general concept that a routing protocol update lists a subset of all known routes. *See also* full update.

periodic update   With routing protocols, the concept that the routing protocol advertises routes in a routing update on a regular periodic basis. This is typical of distance vector routing protocols.

permanent virtual circuit (PVC)   A preconfigured communications path between two Frame Relay DTEs, identified by a local DLCI on each Frame Relay access link, that provides the functional equivalent of a leased circuit but without a physical leased line for each VC.

permit   An action taken with an ACL that implies that the packet is allowed to proceed through the router and be forwarded.

ping   Packet Internet groper. An Internet Control Message Protocol (ICMP) echo message and its reply; ping often is used in IP networks to test the reachability of a network device.

port   (Multiple definitions) 1) In TCP and UDP, a number that is used to uniquely identify the application process that either sent (source port) or should receive (destination port) data. 2) In LAN switching, another term for switch interface.

PortFast   A switch STP feature in which a port is placed in an STP forwarding state as soon as the interface comes up, bypassing the listening and learning states. This feature is meant for ports connected to end-user devices.

PPP   Point-to-Point Protocol. A data link protocol that provides router-to-router and host-to-network connections over synchronous and asynchronous circuits.

PPP over Ethernet (PPPoE)   A specific protocol designed to encapsulate PPP frames inside Ethernet frames, for the purpose of delivering the PPP frames between two devices, effectively creating a point-to-point tunnel between the two devices.

prefix notation   A shorter way to write a subnet mask in which the number of binary 1s in the mask is simply written in decimal. For instance, /24 denotes the subnet mask with 24 binary 1 bits in the subnet mask. The number of bits of value binary 1 in the mask is considered to be the prefix.

PRI   Primary Rate Interface. An ISDN interface to primary rate access. Primary rate access consists of a single 64-Kbps D channel plus 23 (T1) or 30 (E1) B channels for voice or data.

private address   Several Class A, B, and C networks that are set aside for use inside private organizations. These addresses, as defined in RFC 1918, are not routable through the Internet.

private IP network   One of several classful IPv4 network numbers that will never be assigned for use in the Internet, meant for use inside a single enterprise.

private key   A secret value used in public/private key encryption systems. Either encrypts a value that can then be decrypted using the matching public key, or decrypts a value that was previously encrypted with the matching public key.

problem isolation   The part of the troubleshooting process in which the engineer attempts to rule out possible causes of the problem, narrowing the possible causes until the root cause of the problem can be identified.

product activation key (PAK)   The number assigned by Cisco, during the IOS licensing process, that gives a Cisco customer the right to enable an IOS feature set on one of that customer's routers of a particular model series (chosen at the time the PAK was purchased).

protocol type   A field in the IP header that identifies the type of header that follows the IP header, usually a Layer 4 header, such as TCP or UDP. ACLs can examine the protocol type to match packets with a particular value in this header field.

public key   A publicly available value used in public/private key encryption systems. Either encrypts a value that can then be decrypted using the matching private key, or decrypts a value that was previously encrypted with the matching private key.

PVC   *See* permanent virtual circuit.

R

RAM   Random-access memory. A type of volatile memory that can be read and written by a microprocessor.

Rapid Spanning Tree Protocol (RSTP)   Defined in IEEE 802.1w. Defines an improved version of STP that converges much more quickly and consistently than STP (802.1d).

Regional Internet Registry (RIR)   The generic term for one of five current organizations that are responsible for assigning the public, globally unique IPv4 and IPv6 address space.

registry prefix   In IPv6, the prefix that describes a block of public, globally unique IPv6 addresses assigned to a Regional Internet Registry by ICANN.

reported distance   From one EIGRP router's perspective, the metric for a subnet as calculated on a neighboring router and reported in a routing update to the first router.

reverse route   From one host's perspective, for packets sent back to the host from another host, the route over which the packet travels.

RIP   Routing Information Protocol. An interior gateway protocol (IGP) that uses distance vector logic and router hop count as the metric. RIP Version 1 (RIP-1) has become unpopular. RIP Version 2 (RIP-2) provides more features, including support for VLSM.

ROM   Read-only memory. A type of nonvolatile memory that can be read but not written by the microprocessor.

ROMMON   A shorter name for ROM Monitor, which is a low-level operating system that can be loaded into Cisco routers for several seldom needed maintenance tasks, including password recovery and loading a new IOS when flash memory has been corrupted.

root bridge   *See* root switch.

root cost   The STP cost from a nonroot switch to reach the root switch, as the sum of all STP costs for all ports out which a frame would exit to reach the root.

root port   In STP, the one port on a nonroot switch in which the least-cost Hello is received. Switches put root ports in a forwarding state.

root switch   In STP, the switch that wins the election by virtue of having the lowest bridge ID, and, as a result, sends periodic hello BPDUs (default, 2 seconds).

routable protocol   *See* routed protocol.

routed protocol   A Layer 3 protocol that defines a packet that can be routed, such as IPv4 and IPv6.

router ID (RID)   In EIGRP and OSPF, a 32-bit number, written in dotted decimal, that uniquely identifies each router.

Router Advertisement (RA)   A message defined by the IPv6 Neighbor Discovery Protocol (NDP) and used by routers to announce their willingness to act as an IPv6 router on a link. These may be sent in response to a previously received NDP Router Solicitation (RS) message.

Router Solicitation (RS)   A message defined by the IPv6 Neighbor Discovery Protocol (NDP) and used to ask any routers on the link to reply, identifying the router, plus other configuration settings (prefixes and prefix lengths).

router LSA   In OSPF, a type of LSA that a router creates to describe itself.

route summarization   The process of combining multiple routes into a single advertised route, for the purpose of reducing the number of entries in routers' IP routing tables.

routing protocol   A set of messages and processes with which routers can exchange information about routes to reach subnets in a particular network. Examples of routing protocols include Enhanced Interior Gateway Routing Protocol (EIGRP), Open Shortest Path First (OSPF), and Routing Information Protocol (RIP).

RSTP   *See* Rapid Spanning Tree Protocol.

running-config file   In Cisco IOS switches and routers, the name of the file that resides in RAM memory and holds the device's currently used configuration.

S

secondary IP address   The second (or more) IP address configured on a router interface, using the **secondary** keyword on the **ip address** command.

Secure Sockets Layer (SSL)   A security protocol that is integrated into commonly used web browsers that provides encryption and authentication services between the browser and a website.

segment   (Multiple definitions) 1) In TCP, a term used to describe a TCP header and its encapsulated data (also called an L4PDU). 2) Also in TCP, the set of bytes formed when TCP breaks a large chunk of data given to it by the application layer into smaller pieces that fit into TCP segments. 3) In Ethernet, either a single Ethernet cable or a single collision domain (no matter how many cables are used).

serial cable   A type of cable with many different styles of connectors used to connect a router to an external CSU/DSU on a leased-line installation.

serial link   Another term for leased line.

SET message   SET messages are used in SNMP to set the value in variables of the MIB. These messages are the key to an administrator configuring the managed device using SNMP.

setup mode   An option on Cisco IOS switches and routers that prompts the user for basic configuration information, resulting in new running-config and startup-config files.

shared key   A reference to a security key whose value is known by both the sender and receiver.

shortest path first   The algorithm used by OSPF to find all possible routes, and then choose the route with the lowest metric for each subnet.

single point of failure   In a network, a single device or link for which, if it fails, causes an outage for a given population of users.

site prefix   In IPv6, the prefix that describes a public globally unique IPv6 address block that has been assigned to an end-user organization (for example, an Enterprise or government agency). The assignment usually is made by an ISP or Internet registry.

SLSM   Static-length subnet mask. The usage of the same subnet mask for all subnets of a single Class A, B, or C network.

SNMP   Simple Network Management Protocol is an Internet-standard protocol for managing devices on IP networks. Devices that usually support SNMP include routers, switches, and servers. It is used mostly in network management systems to monitor network-attached devices for conditions that warrant administrative attention. SNMP is a component of the Internet Protocol Suite as defined by the Internet Engineering Task Force (IETF). It consists of a set of standards for network management, including an application layer protocol, a database schema, and a set of data objects.

SNMP agent   The Simple Network Management Protocol agent resides on the managed device. This software processes the SNMP messages sent by the Network Management Station (NMS).

Spanning Tree Protocol (STP)   A protocol defined by IEEE standard 802.1D. Allows switches and bridges to create a redundant LAN, with the protocol dynamically causing some ports to block traffic, so that the bridge/switch forwarding logic will not cause frames to loop indefinitely around the LAN.

split horizon   A distant vector routing technique in which information about routes is prevented from exiting the router interface through which that information was received. Split-horizon updates are useful in preventing routing loops.

SSL   *See* Secure Sockets Layer.

standard access list   A list of IOS global configuration commands that can match only a packet's source IP address for the purpose of deciding which packets to discard and which to allow through the router.

startup-config file   In Cisco IOS switches and routers, the name of the file that resides in NVRAM memory and holds the device's configuration that will be loaded into RAM as the running-config file when the device is next reloaded or powered on.

stateful DHCP   A term used in IPv6 to contrast with stateless DHCP. Stateful DHCP keeps track of which clients have been assigned which IPv6 addresses (state information).

stateless address autoconfiguration (SLAAC) A feature of IPv6 in which a host or router can be assigned an IPv6 unicast address without the need for a stateful DHCP server.

stateless DHCP A term used in IPv6 to contrast with stateful DHCP. Stateless DHCP servers do not lease IPv6 addresses to clients. Instead, they supply other useful information, such as DNS server IP addresses, but with no need to track information about the clients (state information).

subinterface One of the virtual interfaces on a single physical interface.

subnet A subdivision of a Class A, B, or C network, as configured by a network administrator. Subnets allow a single Class A, B, or C network to be used and still allow for a large number of groups of IP addresses, as is required for efficient IP routing.

subnet broadcast address A special address in each subnet—specifically, the largest numeric address in the subnet—designed so that packets sent to this address should be delivered to all hosts in that subnet.

subnet mask A 32-bit number that describes the format of an IP address. It represents the combined network and subnet bits in the address with mask bit values of 1 and represents the host bits in the address with mask bit values of 0.

subnet prefix In IPv6, a term for the prefix that is assigned to each data link, acting like a subnet in IPv4.

successor In EIGRP, the route to reach a subnet that has the best metric and should be placed in the IP routing table.

summary LSA In OSPFv2, a type of LSA, created by an Area Border Router (ABR), to describe a subnet in one area in the database of another area.

summary route A route created via configuration commands to represent routes to one or more subnets with a single route, thereby reducing the size of the routing table.

switch A network device that filters, forwards, and floods frames based on each frame's destination address. The switch operates at the data link layer of the Open System Interconnection (OSI) reference model.

synchronous The imposition of time ordering on a bit stream. Practically, a device tries to use the same speed as another device on the other end of a serial link. However, by examining transitions between voltage states on the link, the device can notice slight variations in the speed on each end and can adjust its speed accordingly.

syslog A syslog server takes system messages from network devices and stores these messages in a database. The syslog server also provides reporting capabilities on these system messages. Some can even respond to select system messages with certain actions such as emailing and paging.

T

T1 A line from the telco that allows transmission of data at 1.544 Mbps, with the capability to treat the line as 24 different 64-Kbps DS0 channels (plus 8 Kbps of overhead).

T3 A line from the telco that allows transmission of data at 44.736 Mbps, with the capability to treat the line as 28 different 1.544 Mbps DS1 (T1) channels, plus overhead.

telco A common abbreviation for telephone company.

TFTP Trivial File Transfer Protocol. An application protocol that allows files to be transferred from one computer to another over a network, but with only a few features, making the software require little storage space.

topology database   The structured data that describes the network topology to a routing protocol. Link-state and balanced hybrid routing protocols use topology tables, from which they build the entries in the routing table.

traceroute   A program available on many systems that traces the path that a packet takes to a destination. It is used mostly to debug routing problems between hosts.

trap   The trap is a message type in SNMP. This message is proactively generated by the managed device. This message is based on thresholds configured by a network administrator.

triggered update   A routing protocol feature in which the routing protocol does not wait for the next periodic update when something changes in the network, instead immediately sending a routing update.

trunk   In campus LANs, an Ethernet segment over which the devices add a VLAN header that identifies the VLAN in which the frame exists.

trunking   Also called VLAN trunking. A method (using either the Cisco ISL protocol or the IEEE 802.1Q protocol) to support multiple VLANs that have members on more than one switch.

trunking administrative mode   The configured trunking setting on a Cisco switch interface, as configured with the **switchport mode** command.

trunking operational mode   The current behavior of a Cisco switch interface for VLAN trunking.

U

unequal-cost load balancing   A concept in EIGRP by which a router adds multiple unequal cost (unequal metric) routes to the routing table, at the same time, allowing equal-metric routes to be used.

unique local address   A type of IPv6 unicast address meant as a replacement for IPv4 private addresses.

universal device identifier (UDI)   A number Cisco assigns to each router, for the purpose of uniquely identifying the router's type and unique serial number, for the purpose of allowing the IOS software licensing process to work.

universal image   The Cisco IOS universal image contains all feature sets for the specific device for which it was made. The administrator just needs to license and enable the specific features he or she desires.

update timer   The time interval that regulates how often a routing protocol sends its next periodic routing updates. Distance vector routing protocols send full routing updates every update interval.

V

variable-length subnet mask(ing)   *See* VLSM.

variance   IGRP and EIGRP compute their metrics, so the metrics for different routes to the same subnet seldom have the exact same value. The variance value is multiplied with the lower metric when multiple routes to the same subnet exist. If the product is larger than the metrics for other routes, the routes are considered to have "equal" metric, allowing multiple routes to be added to the routing table.

VC   Virtual circuit. A logical concept that represents the path that frames travel between DTEs. VCs are particularly useful when comparing Frame Relay to leased physical circuits.

virtual LAN (VLAN)   A group of devices connected to one or more switches that are grouped into a single broadcast domain through configuration. VLANs allow switch administrators to place the devices connected to the switches in separate VLANs without requiring separate physical switches. This creates design advantages of separating the traffic without the expense of buying additional hardware.

virtual private network (VPN)   A set of security protocols that, when implemented by two devices on either side of an unsecure network such as the Internet, can allow the devices to send data securely. VPNs provide privacy, device authentication, anti-replay services, and data integrity services.

Virtual Router Redundancy Protocol (VRRP)   A TCP/IP RFC protocol that allows two (or more) routers to share the duties of being the default router on a subnet, with an active/standby model, with one router acting as the default router and the other sitting by waiting to take over that role if the first router fails.

virtual IP address   For any FHRP protocol, an IP address that the FHRP shares between multiple routers so that these multiple routers appear as a single default router to hosts on that subnet.

virtual MAC address   For any FHRP protocol, a MAC address that the FHRP uses to receive frames from hosts.

VLAN   *See* virtual LAN.

VLAN Trunking Protocol (VTP)   A Cisco proprietary messaging protocol used between Cisco switches to communicate configuration information about the existence of VLANs, including the VLAN ID and VLAN name.

VLSM   Variable-length subnet mask(ing). The ability to specify a different subnet mask for the same Class A, B, or C network number on different subnets. VLSM can help optimize available address space.

VoIP   Voice over IP. The transport of voice traffic inside IP packets over an IP network.

VPN   *See* virtual private network.

VPN client   Software that resides on a PC, often a laptop, so that the host can implement the protocols required to be an endpoint of a VPN.

VSAT   A term referring to both a type of WAN that uses satellites, and the type of small dish antenna (very small aperture terminal) used to send and receive data through the satellite.

W

WAN link   Another term for leased line.

wildcard mask   The mask used in Cisco IOS ACL commands and OSPF and EIGRP **network** commands.

Z

zero subnet   For every classful IPv4 network that is subnetted, the one subnet whose subnet number has all binary 0s in the subnet part of the number. In decimal, the 0 subnet can be easily identified because it is the same number as the classful network number.

Index

E

K-L

O

Q

R

S

U

W-X-Y-Z

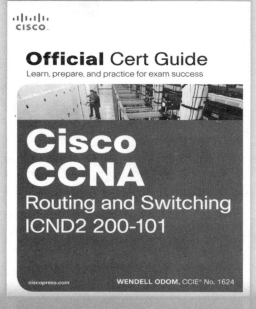

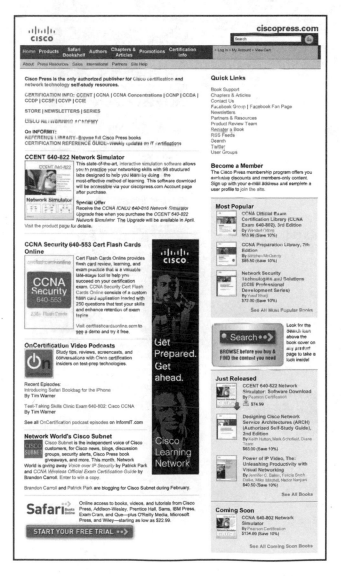

Official Cert Guide
Learn, prepare, and practice for exam success

Cisco CCNA
Routing and Switching
ICND2 200-101

ciscopress.com
WENDELL ODOM, CCIE® No. 1624

FREE
Online Edition

Your purchase of *Cisco CCNA Routing and Switching ICND2 200-101 Official Cert Guide* includes access to a free online edition for 45 days through the **Safari Books Online** subscription service. Nearly every Cisco book is available online through **Safari Books Online**, along with thousands of books and videos from publishers such as Addison-Wesley Professional, Press, Exam Cram, IBM Press, O'Reilly Media, Prentice Hall, Que, Sams, and VMware Press.

Safari Books Online is a digital library providing searchable, on-demand access to thousands of technology, digital media, and professional development books and videos from leading publishers. With one monthly or yearly subscription price, you get unlimited access to learning tools and information on topics including mobile app and software development, tips and tricks on using your favorite gadgets, networking, project management, graphic design, and much more.